lonely planet

Berlin

"All you've got to do is decide to go and the hardest part is over.

So go!"

TONY WHEELER, COFOUNDER – LONELY PLANET

ANDREA SCHULTE-PEEVERS

Contents

Plan Your Trip 4

Explore Berlin 80

Understand Berlin 253

Survival Guide 295

Berlin Maps 322

Alexanderplatz p119
Shopping hub and home to the iconic Fernsehturm

COVID-19

We have re-checked every business in this book before publication to ensure that it is still open after 2020's COVID-19 outbreak. However, the economic and social impacts of COVID-19 will continue to be felt long after the outbreak has been contained, and many businesses, services and events referenced in this guide may experience ongoing restrictions. Some businesses may be temporarily closed, have changed their opening hours and services, or require bookings; some unfortunately could have closed permanently. We suggest you check with venues before visiting for the latest information.

Haus Schwarzenberg p137
Street art and offbeat venues

Right: Berliner Dom (p120) and the Spree River

WELCOME TO Berlin

Berlin is a bon vivant, passionately feasting on the smorgasbord of life, never taking things – or itself – too seriously. To me, this city is nothing short of addictive. It embraces me, inspires me, accepts me and makes me feel good about myself, the world and other people. I enjoy its iconic sights, its vast swathes of green, its sky bars and chic restaurants, but I love its gritty sides more. There's nothing static about Berlin: it's unpredictable, unpretentious and irresistible. And it loves you back – if you let it in.

By Andrea Schulte-Peevers, Writer
For more about our writers, see p352

Berlin's Top Experiences

1 HISTORICAL IMMERSIONS

Berlin's 800-year journey from medieval trading post to German capital has been quite a rollercoaster. It's impossible to escape Berlin's history, especially when it comes to the two key periods that shaped the 20th century: the Third Reich and the Cold War. The city does a fantastic job at documenting both through dozens of free museums and memorials.

Above: Bode-Museum (p114), Museumsinsel

Political Landmark

Moody and majestic, the Reichstag has been set on fire, bombed and wrapped in fabric before becoming the power base of the Bundestag, Germany's parliament. Hop on the free lift for camera-friendly views from the rooftop and a saunter up the glittering glass dome. p86

Right: Reichstag dome

Triumphal Arch

Follow in the footsteps of Prussian kings, Napoleon and Hitler as you strut through the arches of the photogenic Brandenburger Tor. Trapped behind the Berlin Wall during the Cold War, the columned beauty morphed from symbol of division to symbol of a united Germany after reunification. p88

Above: Brandenburger Tor

Berlin Wall Demystified

To truly grasp the barrier's inhumane layout and impact on people's lives, swing by the outdoor Gedenkstätte Berliner Mauer along a one-mile stretch of its former course. Ponder the past while passing an original Wall segment, a guard tower, escape tunnels and border installation remnants. p142

Above: Section of the Berlin Wall at Gedenkstätte Berliner Mauer

ZBIGNIEW GUZOWSKI/SHUTTERSTOCK ©

2 ROYAL ENCOUNTERS

Berlin's youthful and dynamic spirit easily lets one forget that the city was, for five centuries until 1918, the power base of Prussian kings and emperors. Channel your inner prince or princess as you stride around made-to-impress pads, idyllic island retreats or frilly pleasure palaces in Berlin and beyond.

THANAKORN.P/SHUTTERSTOCK ©

MATYAS REHAK/SHUTTERSTOCK ©

Berlin's Mini-Versailles

The most impressive of Berlin's palaces, Schloss Charlottenburg best reflects the splendour and power of the Hohenzollern clan. Poke around the lavishly decorated private quarters, then follow up with a spin around the idyllic park. p216

Above: Schloss Charlottenburg

Dead Royals

Pay your respects to dearly departed Hohenzollern bluebloods resting in elaborate marble sarcophagi in the crypt of the Berliner Dom. Both façade and interior of this former royal court church dazzle while the gallery delivers fine city views. p120

Top: Berliner Dom

Palace 'Without Cares'

Hitch a swift train ride to nearby Potsdam for a tour of Schloss Sanssouci, the petite and giddily rococo summer pad of Prussian king Frederick the Great, and a spin around the blissful park littered with other palaces and buildings. p228

Above: Orangerieschloss (p229)

3 CULTURAL CRAVINGS

A great way to connect with a city is through its cultural offerings, which open a window into its peoples' soul. Luckily, Berliners take culture very seriously. Let the German capital seduce you with a cultural kaleidoscope featuring more museums than rainy days (170), three opera houses, 150 theatres, 10 orchestras and uncountable off- and fringe venues. From improvisational to world-class events and spaces, you'll find them in Berlin.

Historical Treasure Chest

Plunge into 6000 years of art and cultural history on Unesco-listed Museumsinsel, whose five repositories represent the pinnacle of Berlin's museum landscape. Feast your eyes on monumental antiquities, meet eternally gorgeous Egyptian queen Nefertiti, ogle 19th-century European canvasses and marvel at medieval sculptures. p108

Below: Detail from the Pergamonmuseum (p109), Museumsinsel

CLAUDIO DIVIZIA/SHUTTERSTOCK ©

POSZTOS/SHUTTERSTOCK ©

CLAUDIO DIVIZIA/SHUTTERSTOCK ©

Forum of Art & Music

Built in the 1950s as West Berlin's answer to Museumsinsel, the Kulturforum is another sublime cluster of cultural venues. Feast your eyes on paintings and sculpture by masters old and modern along with arts and crafts, etchings and musical instruments.
p164

Above left: Neue Nationalgalerie (p165), designed by Mies Van Der Rohe

Sweet Sounds

Beethoven, Bach and Mozart did not live or work in Berlin, but hearing their music performed by the Berliner Philharmoniker, one of the world's finest classical orchestras, is a transporting experience, aided by the supreme acoustics in the Philharmonie concert hall (above), itself a modernist masterpiece. (p165)

4 ARCHITECTURAL ICONS

It was German 19th-century literary lion Johann Wolfgang von Goethe who first coined the phrase 'architecture is frozen music'. Even though wartime bombing and division during the Cold War left their scars on Berlin's architectural heritage, you can still revel in a symphony of gems from many centuries. But it's the often daring postmodern buildings constructed after the fall of the Wall that are likely to make the biggest impression.

Post-Wall Postmodern

Drift around the Potsdamer Platz city quarter built in the 1990s on wasteland once bisected by the Berlin Wall and compare the styles and talents of the top-flight architects that masterminded it. p157

Below: the Sony Center, designed by Helmut Jahn, on Potsdamer Platz.

ANYAIVANOVA/SHUTTERSTOCK ©

Neoclassical Splendour

Gendarmenmarkt is Berlin's most beautiful and serene square, flanked by chic cafes and anchored by two domed churches and a famous concert hall. p91

Above: Gendarmenmarkt

Mesmerising Metaphor

Connect with Germany's darkest chapter at Daniel Libeskind's zinc-skinned Jewish Museum (right), designed as a powerful symbol for the atrocities during the Nazi years. p180

5 STREET ART CAPITAL

Channel your inner Banksy while keeping an eye out for striking street art that's been part of Berlin's creative DNA since the rebellious 1970s. In some areas it seems that nary a lamp post nor a façade have escaped the guerrilla-style expressions. It's Berlin's unbridled climate of openness and tolerance that has fostered such keen experimentation, DIY ethos and thriving subculture. Kreuzberg, Mitte and Friedrichshain are the main laboratories of creativity.

World's Longest Gallery

Snap a selfie with your favourite murals created by an international cast of aerosol artists for the East Side Gallery, the longest surviving stretch of the Berlin Wall. p204

Above: East Side Gallery

Home for Urban Art

Get a primer on urban contemporary art at Urban Nation, a boundary-pushing museum that showcases all forms of street art and uses its own and adjacent façades as canvasses. p172

Street Art Tour & Workshop

Tap deeper into the scene by joining a combination tour/graffiti workshop. Tours are run by practicing artists with insider knowledge about styles, key works and the latest gossip and trends. p300

6 EPIC EPICUREAN

Gourmet vegan, zero waste cuisine, artisanal breads, organic ice cream – the days when Berlin was a white patch on the foodie map have long been coloured over. The German capital now basks in culinary accolades and not only dishes up a United Nations of cuisines but also a veritable galaxy of Michelin stars. Picking up tasty street food or sitting down to a six-course dinner, the culinary adventures are endless.

JJFARQ/SHUTTERSTOCK ©

MATYAS REHAK/SHUTTERSTOCK ©

Foodie Haven

Keep tabs on Berlin's latest culinary trends at Markthalle Neun, a 19th-century market hall famous for weekly street food parties and global produce from local suppliers. p192

Top : Markthalle Neun, Kreuzberg

Istanbul on the Spree

Berlin goes Bosporus at the bustling canal-side Türkischer Markt, where you can pick through a bonanza of Turkish and Arabic specialties and street food. p201

Above left: Türkischer Markt

Currywurst Cravings

Don't leave town without gobbling a Currywurst, Berlin's cult snack. Top-dog among local sausage kitchens is Konnopke's Imbiss. p148

Above right: Currywurst snack

7 ONLY IN BERLIN

SHANTI HESSE/SHUTTERSTOCK ©

KIRSTYLEE152/SHUTTERSTOCK ©

Few cities do offbeat better than Berlin, a city that bursts with creativity, where thinking outside the box is endemic and conventions are often thrown to the winds. So once you've checked off the blockbuster sights, peel back a few layers to expose Berlin's penchant for quirkiness. We guarantee you'll find a smorgasbord of places and experiences that are truly unique to the German capital.

Bunker Art

Book ahead for face time with works by art-world hotshots displayed at the Sammlung Boros inside a Nazi-era bunker with post-war incarnations as a Soviet POW camp and a fetish techno club. p99

Capital of Spies

Revel in the full-on Berlin panorama when poking around the street art–festooned ruins of the Teufelsberg Spy Station, a Cold War–era US listening post atop a hill built from WWII rubble. p221

Top: Teufelsberg street art.

Airfield Cruising

Cycle down runways, play minigolf in an art installation or kick back in a beer garden on Tempelhofer Feld, a next-gen urban park upcycled from the airfield famous for the 1948-9 Berlin Airlift. p196

Bottom: Cycling on Tempelhofer Feld

What's New

Even three decades after reunification, Berlin is still a metropolis that is constantly on the move. Despite obvious challenges, optimism, resilience and a firm belief in a bright future continue to shape the mood of the city and its people.

Berlin Brandenburg Airport

Berlin's new central airport, Berlin Brandenburg Airport (p296; BER), finally took flight on 31 October 2020 after a costly and embarrassing eight-year delay. It incorporates the old Schönefeld terminal. Tegel airport is now closed and scheduled to be turned into an urban tech campus.

U-Bahn Line U5 Extension

After 10 years in the making, the extension of the U-Bahn line U5 that runs below Unter den Linden between Brandenburger Tor and Alexanderplatz was inaugurated in December 2020.

Humboldt Forum

December 2020 saw the opening of the first phase of the Humboldt Forum (p122) museum and cultural centre inside a replica of the Prussian royal city palace next to Museumsinsel in the heart of the city centre. More openings are scheduled throughout 2021.

Futurium

Peer into the future and come up with strategies on how to shape it at the House of Futures (p100) that opened in a spaceship-like building in late 2019.

LOCAL KNOWLEDGE

WHAT'S HAPPENING

Andrea Schulte-Peevers, Lonely Planet writer

Were it not for the pandemic, these could actually be happy times for Berlin. The start-up scene is booming, Elon Musk is turbo-building a gigafactory that could generate 10,000 jobs right outside the city, and new construction, including entire urban quarters, is sprouting seemingly wherever you look. There are new bike lanes and the state government even passed a rent freeze to keep housing costs from spiralling out of control.

And then there are the blockbuster projects that have come online in 2020. The most anticipated was the Berlin Brandenburg Airport that started operations in October, albeit after an eight-year delay and astronomical cost overrun. Two months later the first U-Bahn trains of the extended U5 line began ferrying passengers to chic new stations below Unter den Linden, thereby closing a major gap in Berlin's central city public transport network. Meanwhile, above ground, doors opened at the Humboldt Forum, which is poised to become an engaging cultural hub set inside the resurrected Prussian city palace.

Corona, take note: Berlin is a resilient beast. Heck, we even have two soccer clubs in the Bundesliga!

Water Fountains

To help cut down on plastic waste, Berliner Wasserbetriebe (Berlin Water Works) has installed over 120 drinking fountains that dispense the city's mineral-rich tap water. Look for them in popular public places, including Kurfürstendamm (p220) and Volkspark Friedrichshain (p206).

James-Simon-Galerie

In July 2019, the central Museum Island entrance building called James-Simon-Galerie (p109), designed by David Chipperfield, opened. For now, it provides access to the Pergamonmuseum and the Neues Museum and also hosts small exhibitions of its own.

Jüdisches Museum

Berlin's zigzagging and zinc-clad Jewish Museum (p180) welcomed its first visitors to its completely overhauled permanent exhibit in August 2020. A new interactive children's museum in a separate building across the street is on stand-by to open as soon as the corona pandemic allows.

Friedrichswerdersche Kirche

After an extensive restoration, the church-turned-museum Friedrichswerdersche Kirche (p95) again started welcoming visitors in October 2020 with a showcase of splendid early-19th-century sculpture.

Palais Populaire

Open since September 2018, Palais Populaire (p95) is an exhibition space in a modernised Prussian royal palace. Sponsored by Deutsche Bank, it presents changing exhibits that span the arc from art to sports.

E-Scooters

Berlin officially legalized e-scooters in June 2019 and, although not everybody likes them, it looks like they are here to stay.

LISTEN, WATCH & FOLLOW

For inspiration and up-to-date news, visit www.lonelyplanet.com/germany/berlin/articles.

Going Local Berlin (www.visitberlin.de/en/going-local-berlin) Free app by Visit Berlin tourism board takes you to cool spots in the city's 12 districts. Available for iOS and Android.

Radio Spätkauf (https://www.radiospaetkauf.com) Irreverent but clued-in English-language news show with an online podcast and blog.

Abandoned Berlin (www.abandonedberlin.com) Website unravels little-known aspects of Berlin's fascinating past one crumbling building at a time.

Pieces of Berlin (www.piecesofberlin.com) Blog and Insta-feed showcasing the lives of ordinary Berliners; reminiscent of 'Humans of New York'.

FAST FACTS

Food trend Sustainable, regional, organic food

Percentage of parks, gardens and forest 25.5

Doner kebabs sold daily 400,000

Population 3.762 million

Museum Closures

The north wing and the Pergamon Altar at the Pergamonmuseum are closed for an extensive facelift until at least 2023. In the meantime, the majesty of this massive antique relic can be enjoyed in the 'Pergamonmuseum. Das Panorama' exhibit (p111) in a custom-built rotunda that pairs a grand photorealistic panorama with original sculptures from the site.

The Bauhaus Archiv's major renovation will likely keep it closed until 2025.

Need to Know

For more information, see Survival Guide (p295)

Currency
Euro (€)

Language
German

Visas
Generally not required for tourist stays of up to 90 days (or at all for EU nationals); some nationalities need a Schengen visa.

Money
Credit card acceptance has skyrocketed, but have some cash on hand as well. ATMs are widespread.

Mobile Phones
Mobile phones operate on GSM900/1800. Local SIM cards can be used in unlocked multiband phones. No roaming charges apply if your phone is registered in another EU country.

Time
Central European Time (GMT/UTC plus one hour)

Tourist Information
Visit Berlin (www.visitberlin.de) has branches at the main train station, BER airport, and the Brandenburg Gate, plus a **call centre** (☎030-2500 2333; ⏰9am-6pm Mon-Fri) for information and bookings.

Daily Costs

Budget: Less than €100

- Dorm bed or peer-to-peer rental: €18–35
- Doner kebab: €3–4
- Club cover: €5–20
- Public transport day pass: €8.60

Midrange: €100–200

- Private apartment or double room: €80–120
- Two-course dinner with wine: €40–60
- Guided public tour: €10–20
- Museum admission: €8–30

Top end: More than €200

- Upmarket apartment or double in top-end hotel: from €180
- Gourmet two-course dinner with wine: €80
- Cabaret ticket: €50–80
- Taxi ride: €25

Advance Planning

Two to three months before Book tickets for the Berliner Philharmonie, the Staatsoper, Sammlung Boros and top-flight events.

One month before Reserve a table at trendy or Michelin-starred restaurants, especially for Friday and Saturday dinners.

Two weeks before Book online tickets for the Reichstag dome, the Neues Museum and the Pergamonmuseum (summer only).

Useful Websites

Lonely Planet (www.lonelyplanet.com/germany/berlin) Destination information, hotel bookings, traveller forum and more.

Visit Berlin (www.visitberlin.de) Official tourist authority info.

BVG (www.bvg.de) Public transport authority site with handy journey planner.

Museumsportal (www.museumsportal-berlin.de) Gateway to the city's museums.

Exberliner (www.exberliner.com) Expat-geared, monthly, English-language Berlin culture magazine.

Resident Advisor (www.residentadvisor.net) Guide to parties and clubs.

WHEN TO GO

July and August are warm but often rainy. May, June, September and October offer plenty of festivals and cooler weather. Winters are cold and quiet.

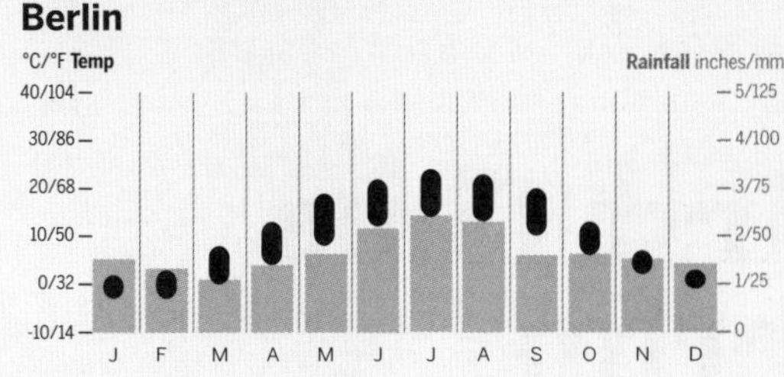

Arriving in Berlin

Berlin Brandenburg Airport FEX Airport Express trains to central Berlin run twice hourly (30 minutes), RE7 and RB14 trains hourly (30 minutes), S9 trains every 20 minutes (45 minutes), all journeys €3.60; taxi to city centre €50 to €60.

Hauptbahnhof Main train station in the city centre near government district and Brandenburg Gate; served by S-Bahn, U-Bahn, tram, bus and taxi.

Zentraler Omnibusbahnhof (ZOB) The central bus station is on the western city centre edge. U-Bahn U2 to city centre from Kaiserdamm station (eg Bahnhof Zoo, eight minutes; Alexanderplatz, 28 minutes) €2.90; taxi to CityWest €15, to Alexanderplatz €28.

For much more on **arrival** see p296

Getting Around

U-Bahn Most efficient way to travel; operates 4am to 12.30am and all night Friday, Saturday and public holidays. From Sunday to Thursday, half-hourly night buses take over in the interim.

S-Bahn Less frequent than U-Bahn trains but with fewer stops, and thus useful for longer distances. Same operating hours as the U-Bahn.

Bus Slow but useful for sightseeing on the cheap, especially lines 100, 200 and 300. Run frequently 4.30am to 12.30am; half-hourly night buses in the interim. MetroBuses (designated eg M19, M41) operate 24/7.

Tram Only in the eastern districts; MetroTrams (designated eg M1, M2) run 24/7.

Bicycle Bike lanes and rental stations abound; bikes allowed in specially marked U-Bahn, S-Bahn and tram carriages.

Taxi Can be hailed, ordered by phone or app, and picked up at ranks.

For much more on **getting around** see p297

Sleeping

Berlin has over 143,000 hotel rooms but the most desirable book up quickly, especially in summer and around holidays, festivals and trade shows; prices soar and reservations are essential during these periods. Otherwise, rates are mercifully low by Western capital standards. Options range from luxurious ports of call to international chains, designer boutique hotels to Old Berlin–style B&Bs, happening hostels to self-catering apartments.

Useful Websites

Lonely Planet (lonelyplanet.com/germany/berlin) Destination information, hotel reviews, traveller forum and more.

Visit Berlin (www.visitberlin.de) Official Berlin tourist office; books rooms at partner hotels with a best-price guarantee.

Boutique Hotels Berlin (www.boutiquehotels-berlin.com) Booking service for about 20 hand-picked boutique hotels.

Berlin30 (www.berlin30.com) Online low-cost booking agency for hotels, hostels, apartments and B&Bs in Berlin.

For much more on **sleeping** see p243

First Time Berlin

For more information, see Survival Guide (p295)

Checklist

➡ Ensure your passport is valid for at least three months past your planned exit date.

➡ Check Covid-19 or other health-related travel requirements.

➡ Check airline baggage restrictions.

➡ Inform your debit-/credit-card company of your upcoming trip.

➡ Organise travel insurance.

➡ Make sure your phone is unlocked and ready for a local SIM card.

➡ Download a translation app.

What to Pack

➡ Good city walking shoes – Berlin is best appreciated on foot.

➡ Umbrella or rain jacket – rain is possible any time of year.

➡ Small daypack.

➡ Travel adapter plug.

➡ Sun hat and sunglasses.

➡ Enough prescription medicine for your entire trip – put it in your carry-on luggage.

Top Tips for Your Trip

➡ Plan on doing most of your sightseeing on foot. To cover larger areas quickly, rent a bicycle. Otherwise, public transport is the best way to get around.

➡ Download the public transport (BVG) app to your phone for planning routes and buying tickets.

➡ There is no curfew, so pace your alcohol intake on bar-hops and in clubs to keep your stamina up.

➡ When picking a place to stay, consider which type of experience you're most keen on – shopping, clubbing, museums, the outdoors, urban cool, partying, history – then choose a neighbourhood to match.

What to Wear

The short answer is: whatever you want. Berlin is an extremely casual city when it comes to fashion. Basically anything goes, including jeans at the opera or a little black dress in a beer garden. Individuality trumps conformity and luxe labels at any time. And leave those high heels at home.

Berlin weather is immensely changeable, even in summer, so make sure you bring layers of clothing. A waterproof coat and sturdy shoes are a good idea for all-weather sightseeing. Winters can get fiercely cold, so be sure you bring your favourite gloves, hat, boots and heavy coat.

Be Forewarned

Berlin is one of the safest capital cities in the world, but that doesn't mean you should let your guard down.

➡ Pickpocketing is on the rise, so watch your belongings, especially in tourist-heavy areas, in crowds and at events.

➡ Bicycle theft is a perennial problem in Berlin. Use a good lock and fasten your bike to a bike rack or a lamp post.

➡ Sign up with Uber or Free Now or carry enough cash or a credit card for a cab ride back to wherever you're staying.

Money

It took fear of catching Covid-19 to break Germany's love affair with cash payments. In Berlin especially, contactless credit- and debit-card use has become widespread, even in restaurants, bars and taxis. Paying by Google Pay and Apple Pay is slowly moving from niche to mainstream.

ATMs are ubiquitous in all central neighbourhoods. Machines do not recognise PIN codes with more than four digits.

Taxes & Refunds

Value-added tax (VAT, *Mehrwertsteuer*) is a 19% sales tax levied on most goods. The rate for food, books and services is 7%. VAT is always included in the price. If your permanent residence is outside the EU, you may be able to partially claim back the VAT you paid on purchased goods.

Tipping

Things are gradually changing but, overall, Germans still consider it rude to leave the tip on the table. Instead, tell the server the total amount you want to pay. If you don't want change back, say *'Stimmt so'* (that's fine).

- **Hotels** Room cleaners €2 per day, porters the same per bag.
- **Restaurants** For good service 10% or more.
- **Bars and pubs** 5% to 10% for table service, rounded to the nearest euro, no or small tip for self-service.
- **Taxis** 10%, always rounding to a full euro.
- **Toilet attendants** €0.50.

Language

You can easily have a great time in Berlin without speaking a word of German. In fact, some bars and restaurants in expat-heavy Kreuzberg and Neukölln have entirely English- (and sometimes Spanish-) speaking staff. Many restaurant and cafe menus are now available in English and German (and sometimes only in English).

Do you accept credit cards?
Nehmen Sie Kreditkarten?
nay·men zee kre·*deet*·kar·ten

Credit cards have become widely accepted in Berlin, but it's still best to enquire first.

2

Which beer would you recommend?
Welches Bier empfehlen Sie?
vel·khes beer emp·*fay*·len zee

Who better to ask for advice on beer than the Germans, whether at a beer garden, hall, cellar or on a brewery tour?

Can I get this without meat?
Kann ich das ohne Fleisch bekommen?
kan ikh das *aw*·ne flaish be·*ko*·men

Even though Berlin has turned into a vegetarian and vegan hot spot, you may still find menus with limited plant-based options.

Do you speak English?
Sprechen Sie Englisch?
shpre·khen zee *eng*·lish

Given Berlin's cosmopolitan tapestry, the answer will most likely be 'yes' but it's still polite not to assume and to ask first.

Do you run original versions?
Spielen auch Originalversionen?
shpee·len owkh o·ri·gi·*nahl*·fer·zi·*aw*·nen

Many movies are dubbed into German. Look for a cinema that shows original version (denoted OV, or OmU with subtitles).

Etiquette

Although Berlin is fairly informal, there are a few general rules worth keeping in mind when meeting strangers.

- **Greetings** Shake hands and say *'Guten Morgen'* (before noon), *'Guten Tag'* (between noon and 6pm) or *'Guten Abend'* (after 6pm). Use the formal *'Sie'* (you) with strangers and only switch to the informal *'du'* and first names if invited to do so. With friends and children, use first names and *'du'*.
- **Asking for help** Germans use the same word – *Entschuldigung* – to say 'excuse me' (to attract attention) and 'sorry' (to apologise).
- **Eating and drinking** At the table, say *'Guten Appetit'* before digging in. Germans hold the fork in the left hand and the knife in the right hand. To signal that you have finished eating, lay your knife and fork parallel across your plate. If drinking wine, the proper toast is *'Zum Wohl'*; with beer it's *'Prost'*.

Perfect Days

Day One

Historic Mitte (p84)

One day in Berlin? Follow this whirlwind itinerary to take in all the key sights. Book ahead for an early lift ride up to the dome of the **Reichstag**, then snap a picture of the **Brandenburg Gate** before exploring the maze of the **Holocaust Memorial** and taking in the contemporary architecture of **Potsdamer Platz**. View the **Berlin Wall remnant** along Niederkirchner Strasse en route to **Checkpoint Charlie**. Ponder the full extent of the Cold War madness before sauntering up Friedrichstrasse to soak up the glory of **Gendarmenmarkt** before your lunch.

Lunch Recharge in the food hall of the Galeries Lafayette (p105).

Museumsinsel & Alexanderplatz (p106)

Follow Unter den Linden east, pop into the brand-new **Humboldt Forum** culture centre, then spend the rest of the afternoon among the antiquities in the **Pergamonmuseum**. After all that heady input, relax over a cold beer while letting the sights pass by on the deck of a **river cruise** on a one-hour spin around Museumsinsel.

Dinner Book ahead for a dinner table at nearby Frea (p133).

Hackescher Markt & Scheunenviertel (p126)

Process your impressions and plan the next day over an expert cocktail at speakeasy-cool **Buck & Breck.**

Day Two

Prenzlauer Berg (p140)

Spend a couple of hours coming to grips with what life in Berlin was like when the Wall still stood by exploring the **Gedenkstätte Berliner Mauer**, a 1.4km-long exhibit that follows the course of the hated barrier. Follow up with a quick spin around **Mauerpark**, then grab a coffee at **Bonanza Coffee Heroes** and poke around the boutiques on Kastanienallee.

Lunch W-Der Imbiss (p149) is a buzzy pit stop on Kastanienallee.

Hackescher Markt & Scheunenviertel (p126)

Stroll down to the Scheunenviertel and explore the narrow warren of this historic Jewish quarter anchored by the glittering resurrected **New Synagogue** and the boutique and cafe-filled **Hackesche Höfe** courtyard ensemble. Check out the latest street art at **Haus Schwarzenberg**, then stroll over to the Spree River for alfresco coffee and cake at the darling cafe **Petit Bijou** with a grand view of the ornate Bode-Museum.

Dinner Head to Kreuzberg for modern German fare at Orania (p188).

Kreuzberg (p178)

After dinner, go bar-hopping around Kottbusser Tor, pulling up for cocktails at stylish **Würgeengel**, beer at raucous **Möbel Olfe** or wine at civilised **Otto Rink**.

WERNER SPREMBERG / SHUTTERSTOCK ©

Bikini Berlin (p226)

MICHAEL KAERCHER / SHUTTERSTOCK ©

Potsdam (p228)

Day Three

City West & Charlottenburg (p214)

Day three starts at **Schloss Charlottenburg**, where the Neuer Flügel (New Wing) and palace garden are essential stops. Take the bus to Zoologischer Garten and meditate upon the futility of war at the **Kaiser-Wilhelm-Gedächtniskirche**, then – assuming it's not Sunday – keep your wallet handy to satisfy your shopping cravings along **Kurfürstendamm** and its side streets, at the **Bikini Berlin** concept mall and at the glorious **KaDeWe** department store.

Lunch Enjoy a gourmet lunch in the KaDeWe (p177) food hall

Neukölln (p194)

Head south to **Tempelhofer Feld** to marvel at how an old airport can be upcycled into a sustainable park and playground. Exiting the park to the east will plunge you into Neukölln. Have a beer or a latte in one of the many cafes in this congenial neighbourhood before taking the U-bahn to Warschauer Strasse. Stroll along the **East Side Gallery**, then cross the Warschauer Brücke to Friedrichshain, perhaps checking out the street art at the **RAW Gelände**.

Dinner Have a delicious animal-free dinner at 1990 Vegan Living (p207).

Friedrichshain (p202)

Wrap the day with a drink or two in one of the many watering holes around Boxhagener Platz, along Simon-Dach-Strasse or along Sonntagstrasse.

Day Four

Potsdam (p228)

There's plenty more to do in Berlin proper, but we recommend you spend the better part of the day exploring the parks and royal palaces in Potsdam, a mere 40-minute S-Bahn ride away. Buy online tickets for your favourite time slot to see **Schloss Sanssouci**, a rococo jewel of a palace. Afterwards, explore the surrounding park and its many smaller palaces at leisure. The **Chinesisches Haus** is a must-see.

Lunch Have lunch at the exotic Drachenhaus (p229) in the park.

Potsdam (p228)

If you're done with your park explorations, head to Potsdam's old town for a spin around the **Holländisches Viertel** (Dutch Quarter) or take a look at the latest art exhibit at the dashing **Museum Barberini** before heading back to Berlin for a well-deserved post-sightseeing drink at **Prater** beer garden.

Dinner Pull up a stool at Prenzlauer Berg's lovely Umami (p149).

Prenzlauer Berg (p140)

After dinner, enjoy a stroll around beautiful Kollwitzplatz. Still got stamina? Turn your evening into a bar-hop, perhaps stopping at **Bryk Bar** or **Becketts Kopf** for fine cocktails.

Month by Month

TOP EVENTS

Berlinale, February

Karneval der Kulturen, May

Christopher Street Day, July

Berlin Marathon, September

Christmas Markets, December

January

New Year's Eve may be wrapped up, but nighttime hot spots show no signs of slowing down. Cold weather invites extended museum visits and foraging at the Grüne Woche (Green Week) food fair.

Tanztage

Held over two weeks at the historic Sophiensaele near Hackescher Markt, the Days of Dance (https://sophiensaele.com) is a contemporary dance festival featuring mostly Berlin-based up-and-coming choreographers and dancers.

Internationale Grüne Woche

Find out about the latest food trends and gorge on global morsels at this nine-day fair (www.gruenewoche.de) of food, agriculture and gardening.

February

Days are still short but Berlin perks up when glamour comes to town during the famous film festival. A full theatre, opera, concert and party schedule also tempts people out of the house.

Transmediale

Digital-media art gets full bandwidth at this edgy festival (www.transmediale.de), which investigates the links between art, culture and technology through exhibitions, conferences, screenings and performances.

Berlinale

Berlin's international film festival (www.berlinale.de) draws stars, starlets, directors, critics and the world's A-to-Z-list celebrities for two weeks of screenings and glamorous parties around town. The best ones go home with a Golden or Silver Bear.

March

Could there be spring in the air? This is still a good time to see the sights without the crowds, but hotel rooms fill to capacity during the big ITB tourism fair.

Internationale Tourismus Börse (ITB)

Take a virtual trip around the globe at the world's largest international travel expo (www.itb-berlin.de); it's trade-only during the week but open to the public at the weekend.

MaerzMusik

'Music' or 'soundscapes'? You decide after a day at this 10-day contemporary music festival (www.berlinerfestspiele.de), which explores a boundary-pushing palette of sounds – from orchestral symphonies to experimental recitals.

April

Life starts moving outdoors as cafe tables appear on pavements and you begin to see budding trees on walks in the park. Hotels get busy over the Easter holidays.

Achtung Berlin

Flicks about Berlin, and at least partly produced in the city, compete for the New Berlin Film Award at this weeklong festival (achtung berlin.de). Screenings are often in the company of writers, directors, producers and actors associated with the movie.

Festtage

Daniel Barenboim, music director of Berlin's internationally renowned Staatsoper Unter den Linden (Berlin State Opera; www.staatsoper-berlin.de), brings the world's finest conductors, soloists and orchestras together for this 10-day highbrow hoedown of gala concerts and operas.

Gallery Weekend

Join collectors, critics and other art aficionados in keeping tabs on the Berlin art scene on a free hop around 40 of the city's best galleries (www.gallery-weekend-berlin.de) over the last weekend in April.

May

Spring has finally arrived, making this a fabulous month to visit Berlin. Time for beer gardens, picnics and walks among blossoming trees. Don't forget your sunglasses! Several public holidays bring in big crowds.

Karneval der Kulturen

Every Whitsuntide (Pentecost; seven weeks after Easter) weekend, the Carnival of Cultures (www.karneval-berlin.de) celebrates Berlin's multicultural tapestry with four days of music, dance, art and culture, culminating in a raucous parade of flamboyantly dressed performers shimmying through the streets of Kreuzberg.

Theatertreffen

The Berlin Theatre Meeting (www.theatertreffen-berlin.de) is a 16-day showcase of new productions by emerging and established German-language ensembles from Germany, Austria and Switzerland.

June

Festival season kicks into high gear around the summer solstice with plenty of alfresco events, thanks to a rising temperature gauge.

Berlin Biennale

This biennial curated forum (p129) for contemporary art explores international trends and invites newcomers to showcase their work around town for about eight weeks. The next is in 2022.

Fête de la Musique

Summer starts with good vibrations thanks to hundreds of free concerts during this global music festival (www.fetedelamusique.de) that started in Paris in 1982. Held each year on 21 June (solstice).

48 Hours Neukölln

For one long weekend Neukölln's multicultural denizens transform shops, courtyards, parks, churches, pavements, galleries, bars and other spaces into an offbeat contemporary art and culture showcase (www.48-stunden-neukoelln.de).

July

Hot summer days send Berliners scurrying to the lakes in town or the surrounding countryside. Gourmets rejoice in the bounty of fresh local produce in the markets. Expect long lines at main sights and attractions.

Classic Open Air Festival

Five nights, five alfresco concerts – from opera to pop – delight an adoring crowd hunkered on bleachers before the palatial backdrop of the Konzerthaus (www.classicopenair.de) on Gendarmenmarkt.

Wassermusik

The Haus der Kulturen der Welt makes waves with this popular series of water-themed concerts (www.hkw.de/wassermusik) held on its roof terrace and combined with related events like markets and movies.

Christopher Street Day

No matter what your sexual persuasion, come out and paint the town pink at this huge pride parade (p70) featuring floats often decorated with queer political statements and filled with naked torsos writhing to electronic beats.

August

More outdoor fun than you can handle, with concerts in parks, daytime clubbing, languid boat

rides, beach-bar partying, lake swimming and a huge beer festival.

Young Euro Classic

Next-gen virutosos perform classical and contemporary music at this festival (www.young-euro-classic.de) created for symphonic youth orchestras. Concerts are held at the Konzerthaus on Gendarmenmarkt.

Holi Festival of Colours

Since 2012 the Holi Festival tour (www.holifestival.com) has made a stop in Berlin. Join in the custom of throwing colourful powder *(gulal)* into the sky and onto each other while dancing to bands and DJs from India and other countries.

Lange Nacht der Museen

Culture meets entertainment during the Lange Nacht der Museen (Long Night of the Museums; www.lange-nacht-der-museen.de) when around 80 museums welcome visitors between 6pm and 2am.

Zug der Liebe

Nonprofit parade (http://zugderliebe.org) with floats and music to demonstrate in favour of love, community and equality and against populism, gentrification and other hot topics.

September

Kids are back in school but there's still plenty of partying to be done and often fine weather to enjoy. As days get shorter, the new theatre, concert and opera season begins.

(Top) Christmas market on Gendarmenmarkt (p91)
(Bottom) Karneval der Kulturen (p25)

FHM / GETTY IMAGES ©

HANOHIKI / SHUTTERSTOCK ©

Berlin Art Week

This contemporary art fair (www.berlinartweek.de) combines art exhibits, fairs and awards with talks, film and tours. It also provides a chance to see private collections, project spaces and artist studios.

Berlin Marathon

Sweat it out with over 40,000 other runners or just cheer 'em on during Germany's biggest street race (www.berlin-marathon.com), which has seen nine world records set since the first race in 1974.

Musikfest Berlin

World-renowned orchestras, choirs, conductors and soloists come together for 21 days of concerts (www.berlinerfestspiele.de) at the Philharmonie and other venues.

October

It's getting nippy again and trees start shedding their summer coats, but Berlin keeps a bright disposition, and not only during the Festival of Lights.

Festival of Lights

For 10 days Berlin is all about 'lightseeing' during this shimmering festival (www.festival-of-lights.de) when historic landmarks such as the Fernsehturm (TV Tower), the Berliner Dom and the Brandenburg Gate sparkle with illuminations, projections and fireworks.

Porn Film Festival

Vintage porn, Japanese porn, indie porn, sci-fi porn – the 'Berlinale' of sex (www.pornfilmfestivalberlin.de) brings alternative skin flicks out of the smut corner and onto the big screen.

Tag der Deutschen Einheit

Raise a toast to reunification on 3 October, the German national holiday celebrated with street parties across town – from the Brandenburg Gate to the Rotes Rathaus (town hall).

November

A great time to visit if you don't like crowds and are keen on snapping up hotel bargains. Weather-wise it's not the prettiest of months, but don't let that darken your mood.

JazzFest Berlin

This top-rated jazz festival (www.jazzfest-berlin.de) has doo-wopped in Berlin since 1964 and presents fresh and big-time talent in dozens of performances all over town.

December

Days are short and cold but the mood is festive, thanks to dressed-up shop windows, illuminated streets and facades, and Christmas markets redolent with the aroma of roast almonds and mulled wine.

Christmas Markets

Pick up shimmering ornaments or indulge in seasonal treats at dozens of Yuletide markets held throughout the city.

Nikolaus

On the night before St Nicholas' Day (6 December) children leave their shoes outside their door to receive sweets if they've been nice, or a stone if they've been naughty; eventually this developed into Santa's international rounds. Germans are pretty attached to the original – all kinds of clubs hold Nikolaus parties, complete with costumed St Nicks.

Silvester

New Year's Eve is the time to hug strangers, coo at fireworks, guzzle bubbly straight from the bottle and generally misbehave. The biggest public bash is at the Brandenburg Gate.

MAY DAY / MYFEST

May Day demonstrations used to be riotous affairs, with heavily armed police and leftist groups facing off in Kreuzberg, complete with flying stones and burning cars. Although an official 'Revolutionary May Day' demonstration still draws as many as 15,000 anticapitalist, antifascist protesters, it's been completely peaceful in recent years. This is due partly to an enormous police presence, and partly to the alternative, largely apolitical Myfest, held in Kreuzberg since 2003. It runs from noon to midnight on 1 May. The actual Revolutionary May Day demonstration starts at 6pm at Lausitzer Platz.

With Kids

Travelling to Berlin with kids can be child's play, especially if you keep a light schedule and involve them in day-to-day planning. There's plenty to do to keep youngsters occupied, from zoos to kid-oriented museums. Parks and imaginative playgrounds abound in all neighbourhoods, as do public pools and swimming lakes.

HANOHIKI / SHUTTERSTOCK ©

Deutsches Technikmuseum (p182)

Museums

Museum für Naturkunde

Meet giant dinosaurs, travel through space back to the beginning of time and find out why zebras are striped in the eye-opening Museum of Natural History (p100).

Science Center Spectrum

Toddlers to teens get to play with, experience and learn about such things as balance, weight, water, air and electricity by pushing buttons, pulling levers and otherwise engaging in dozens of hands-on science experiments (p182).

Deutsches Technikmuseum

Next to the Science Center Spectrum, the collection at the German Museum of Technology (p182) is so vast, it is best to concentrate time and energy on two or three sections that interest your tech-loving kids the most. The one-hour kid-geared audioguide tour provides a good introduction.

Madame Tussauds

Kids of any age are all smiles when posing with the waxen likeness of their favourite pop star or celluloid celebrity (p97).

Legoland Discovery Centre

The milk-tooth set delights in this Lego wonderland (p158) with rides, entertainment and interactive stations.

Computerspielemuseum

Teens can get their kicks in this universe of computer games (p206) – from Pac-Man to World of Warcraft.

Mauermuseum

Teenagers with an interest in history and a decent attention span may enjoy the ingenious homemade contraptions (p98) used to escape from East Germany.

Labyrinth Kindermuseum

Slip into a fantasy world while learning about tolerance, working together and just having fun at this **interactive space** (☎030-8009 31150; www.kindermuseum-labyrinth.de; Osloer Strasse 12; €6.50; ⏱9am-1.30pm Thu, 11am-6pm Fri-Sun, hours vary seasonally; U Pankstrasse).

Parks, Pools & Playgrounds

Park am Gleisdreieck

This family-friendly park (p182) is packed with fun zones, including adventure playgrounds, basketball courts, a huge skate park and a nature garden.

Kollwitzplatz

This square (p144) sports three playgrounds for different age groups, including one with giant wooden toys. All get busy in the afternoon and on weekends. Cafes and ice-cream parlours are just a hop, skip and jump away.

Kinderbad Monbijou

Keep cool on hot days splashing about this family-friendly public **pool** (Map p330, C5; ☎030-2219 0011; www.berlinerbaeder.de; Oranienburger Strasse 78; adult/child €5.50/3.50; ⊙11am-7pm Jun-early Sep; M1, M5, M6, S Hackescher Markt, Oranienburger Strasse) in Hackescher Markt & Scheunenviertel.

Volkspark Friedrichshain

Play in the 'Indian Village', gather your pirate mateys on the boat in the 'harbour' or find your favourite fairy-tale characters at the enchanting Märchenbrunnen (fountain of fairy tales) at this vast city park (p206).

Animals

Zoo Berlin

If the 20,000 furry, feathered and finned friends fail to enchant the little ones, there's also the enormous adventure playground (p223).

Tierpark Berlin

Expect plenty of ooh and aah moments when kids watch baby elephants at play or see lions and tigers being fed at this vast animal **park** (☎030-515 310; www.tierpark-berlin.de; Am Tierpark 125; adult/concession/4-15yr €14.50/9.50/7; ⊙zoo 9am-6.30pm Apr-Sep, to 6pm Mar & Oct, to 4.30pm Nov-Feb, palace 1-5pm Thu-Sat year-round; P; U Tierpark).

Sealife Berlin

At Sealife (p119), little ones get to press their noses against dozens of fish-filled tanks, solve puzzles and admire starfish and sea anemones up close.

Freilichtmuseum Domäne Dahlem

Kids can interact with their favourite barnyard animals, help collect eggs, harvest potatoes or just watch daily farm life unfold at this fun working **farm** (Outdoor Museum Domäne Dahlem; ☎030-666 3000; www.domaene-dahlem.de; Königin-Luise-Strasse 49; grounds free, museum adult/concession/under 18yr €5/3/free; ⊙grounds 7am-10pm May-Sep, to 7pm Oct-Apr, museum 10am-5pm Sat & Sun; P; U Dahlem-Dorf).

Jugendfarm Moritzhof

A farm playground (p147) for kids complete with barnyard animals and courses in basket weaving, forging, felting and other old-timey crafts.

Eating Out

It's fine to eat out as a family any time of day, especially in cafes, bistros, pizzerias and beer gardens. Many offer a limited *Kindermenü* (children's menu) or *Kinderteller* (children's dishes). If they don't, most will be happy to serve half-size portions or prepare a simple meal. Popular dishes include schnitzel, *Pommes mit Ketchup* or *Mayonnaise* (fries with ketchup or mayo), *Nudeln mit Tomatensosse* (noodles with tomato sauce) and *Fischstäbchen* (fish sticks).

Large malls have food courts, while department stores feature self-service cafeterias. Farmers markets have food stalls selling kid-friendly snacks. Bakeries selling scrumptious cakes and sandwiches are plentiful. The most popular snacks-on-the-run are bratwurst in a bun or *Döner Kebab* (sliced meat tucked into a pitta pocket with salad and sauce).

NEED TO KNOW

Public transport Children under six travel free and those between six and 14 pay the reduced *(ermässigt)* fare.

Admission fees Many museums, monuments and attractions are free to anyone under age 18, but the cut-off might also be age 12 or 14.

Supplies Baby food, infant formula, soya and cow's milk, disposable nappies (diapers) and the like are widely available in supermarkets and chemists (drugstores).

Under the Radar Berlin

Berlin is a multifaceted metropolis that is constantly in flux. There's always something new and exciting to discover, so help keep overtourism in check by going beyond the top blockbuster sights and connecting with local life in low-key neighbourhoods and pristine nature spots.

RICHARD NEBESKY/LONELY PLANET ©

Schloss Charlottenburg (p216)

Berlin & Tourism

Until the Covid-19 virus throttled the world, Berlin tourism had grown steadily, clocking in 34 million overnight stays in 2019 – triple the number of 2003. But as is now commonly recognised, while a deluge of visitors may be good for business, it can wreak havoc on a city's social fabric and the environment. In Berlin, the strain of overtourism was especially felt in the party districts of Kreuzberg and Friedrichshain, which led to tensions with the local population. As post-Covid-19 tourism picks up steam, the challenge will be to minimise its impact while keeping the city attractive to visitors.

Some measures to prevent overcrowding are already in place. Most blockbuster attractions, including the Pergamon Museum, the TV Tower, the Reichstag dome, Schloss Charlottenburg and Schloss Sanssouci in nearby Potsdam, have timed entry tickets, which keeps crowds at bay but does require that you plan ahead to book your time slot. Other key sights, such as the Brandenburger Tor, the Holocaust Memorial, the East Side Gallery or the Gedenkstätte Berliner Mauer, are free and outdoors, meaning that they rarely feel crowded.

During prime tourist season – late spring and summer – sights are less impacted during the week than on weekends. And those travelling to Berlin in late autumn or winter will rarely experience queues or crowds.

Zoom in on the Outer Boroughs

Most visitors only spend time in Berlin's central boroughs, an area bounded by the circle line (S-Bahn 41/42). This is, after all, where most of the sightseeing blockbusters are located and where the city's famous party spirit rages in hip clubs and bars until the wee hours and practically nonstop on the weekend. Yet there are plenty of rewards for those who venture to the outer boroughs. Exploring these districts will broaden your understanding of Berlin and its residents and provide you with plenty of authentic and local experiences. Best of all, most are only a quick and easy public transport ride away. The free **Going Local app** published by the tourism authority Visit Berlin has plenty of suggestions.

Cool Alternatives

Instead of getting trapped at kitschy Checkpoint Charlie, rent a bike and follow a stretch of the Berliner Mauerweg (p42), a designated 160km-long trail tracing the course of the erstwhile Berlin Wall. Don't fight for sand space at Badeschiff but keep cool by spreading your towel on one of Berlin's myriad swimming lakes (p238).

Not into sightseeing cruises with 10-language commentary? Rent a kayak and paddle serenely along Berlin's canals, lakes and rivers. Prefer observing animals in the wild instead of the zoo? Head to the idyllic **Tegeler Fliess** nature preserve for encounters with native birds, endangered butterflies and even free-roaming water-buffalo. Skip busy Prater beer garden and hoist a cold mug at one of its chestnut-shaded cousins (p240) by a lake or in the forest instead. And if the mock-medieval Nikolaiviertel leaves you cold, perhaps the cobbled lanes and historic buildings in the old town of Köpenick (p240) won't.

Tracking down the next "it" Neighbourhood

It's easy to follow the crowd down the well-trodden party strips in Kreuzberg, Friedrichshain and Neukölln, but why not channel your pioneer spirit and check out the action in areas away from the spotlight? Cheaper beer is just one bonus.

If you're an urban explorer who likes to stay ahead of the gentrification curve, head to rough-around-the-edges Wedding (p145). The northern borough has a similar multicultural, working-class DNA as Neukölln but, for now, retains its down-to-earth character. Instead of high-concept eateries and third-wave cafes, you'll find cool DIY pubs, restaurants and beer gardens popular with a young, creative crowd. The Sprengelkiez around Tegeler Strasse is a good place to start. Also: lovely old parks abound in the northern reaches, most notably the Volkspark Rehberge with its tree-fringed Plötzensee (p238) swimming lake.

Another neighbourhood coming into focus is **Moabit** just west of the Hauptbahnhof (main train station). An old brewery has been converted into a shopping mall and a historic market hall called Arminius Markthalle (Arminiusstrasse 2-4) is drawing not only locals but clued-in foodies from around town for its produce and bistros. Scout surrounding streets like Wilhelmshavener Strasse or Birkenstrasse for cool shops and libation stations.

Friedrichshain's popularity has spilled over to neighbourhoods in adjacent Lichtenberg, an eastern district characterised by a mix of prefab housing estates and classic old Berlin buildings. An increasingly popular neighbourhood is the **Kaskelkiez**, aka Victoriastadt, east of Ostkreuz train station, which has birthed some interesting shops, cafes and bars.

TOP UNDER THE RADAR ATTRACTIONS

The outer districts also offer up plenty of sights that are pure Insta-gold. Here's a sampling:

➡ Teufelsberg Spy Station (p221) Fabulous Berlin panorama and street art in a Cold War-era listening post.

➡ **Gärten der Welt** (Gardens of the World; ☎030-700 906 720; www.gaertenderwelt.de/en/; Blumberger Damm 44; adult/child €7/free Mar-Oct, €4/free Nov-Feb,; ⏲9am-sunset; P; U Kienberg-Gärten der Welt) Travel around the world one garden at a time surrounded by Berlin's largest prefab housing development.

➡ Zitadelle Spandau (p235) Play hide and seek or catch a concert in Europe's largest Renaissance military fortress.

➡ Deutsch-Russisches Museum (p241) Where Germany's WWII capitulation was signed.

➡ Schloss Cecilienhof (p231) Allied leaders sealed Germany's postwar fate in this Potsdam palace.

➡ Hufeisensiedlung (p282) Check out this and other Unesco-listed Bauhaus social housing estates.

Like a Local

Local life in Berlin is defined to some extent by the enormous influx of neo-Berliners from abroad and other parts of Germany. It's comparatively easy to engage with locals and to participate in their daily lives.

MASSIMO TODARO / SHUTTERSTOCK ©

Brandenburger Tor (p88)

Dining Like a Local

Berliners love to dine out and do so quite frequently, from scarfing down a quick doner at the local kebab joint to indulging in an eight-course tasting menu at a Michelin-starred dining shrine. Eating out is rarely just about getting fed – it is also a social experience. Meeting friends or family over a meal is a great way to catch up, engage in heated discussions or exchange the latest gossip.

Going out for breakfast or brunch is a beloved pastime, especially on weekends. Enjoying a meal out at lunchtime is no longer the domain of desk jockeys and business people on expense accounts, as many restaurants now offer daily specials or value-priced set menus. The traditional German afternoon coffee-and-cake ritual is more the realm of mature generations and not practised widely among Berlin millennials.

The main going-out meal is dinner, with restaurant tables usually filled at 7.30pm or 8pm. Since it's customary to stretch meals to two hours and then linger over cocktails or another glass of wine, restaurants – for now – only count on one seating per table per night. Servers will not present you with the bill until you ask for it.

Partying Like a Local

Most Berliners start the night around 9pm or 10pm in a pub or bar, although among younger people it's common to first meet at someone's home for a few cheap drinks in a ritual called *Vorglühen* (literally 'pre-glowing'). Once out on the town, people either stay for a few drinks at the same place or pop into several spots, before moving on to a club around 1am or 2am at the earliest.

In most pubs and bars, it's common practice to place orders with a server rather than pick up your own drinks at the bar. Only do the latter if that's what everyone does or if you see a sign saying *'Selbstbedienung'* (self-service). Among Germans it is not expected (nor customary) to buy entire rounds for everyone at the table.

Once in the club, how long one stays depends on your inclination and alcohol or whatever consumption. Hardy types stagger out into the morning sunshine, although the most hardcore may last even longer. Since some clubs don't close at all on weekends, it's becoming increasingly popular to start the party in the daytime and go home at, say 11pm, for a normal night's sleep. But don't feel bad if that's not your thing. Partying in Berlin does require some stamina...

Shopping Like a Local

Berliners pretty much fulfil all their shopping needs in their local *Kiez* (neighbourhood). There will usually be three or four supermarkets, including at least one 'Bio' (ie organic) supermarket, within walking distance. Most people don't get all their grocery shopping done in one fell swoop but rather make several smaller trips spread over the course of the week. Since some supermarkets have started home delivery, ordering online is becoming more popular.

For many locals the farmers markets and small specialty shops are the preferred sources of fresh produce and artisanal products like handmade noodles, cheeses, honey, pesto and such. Days start with fresh *Brötchen* (rolls) bought from the bakery around the corner. Nonfood needs such as gifts, flowers, books, hardware and wine are also met locally where possible.

Clothing will come from a mix of places that may include high-street chains, indie boutiques, vintage stores, flea markets and, of course, online shops. Sustainable and eco-conscious brands are making inroads. When Berliners venture out of their neighbourhoods to shop, it's usually to buy big-ticket items like furniture or vehicles, or speciality items not available locally. There are a few big malls in the city centre, such as Mall of Berlin (p169) and Alexa (p125), but generally these are more commonly located in the suburbs.

Living Like a Local

The typical Berlin dwelling is a spacious rented two-bedroom flat on at least the 1st floor of a large early-20th-century apartment building (no one wants to live at street level), probably facing on to a *Hinterhof* (back courtyard) full of bicycles and coloured recycling bins. The apartment itself has very high ceilings, large windows and, as often as not, stripped wooden plank floors. The kitchen will almost invariably be the smallest room in the house and right next to the bathroom. Some kitchens have small pantries and/or storage rooms.

Apartments in new buildings follow a more contemporary layout and usually have an open kitchen facing out to the living-dining room, walk-in closets, guest toilets, lower ceilings and balconies. The fanciest ones also have air-con, which comes in handy as summer temperatures now often exceed 35°C.

Berlin flats are usually nicely turned out with much attention paid to design, though comfort is also considered. At least one item of furniture will come from a certain Swedish furniture chain. Depending on income, the rest may come from the Stilwerk design centre, Polish crafters, a flea market, eBay – or, most likely, any combination thereof.

NEED TO KNOW

For many Berliners, the preferred way of getting around town is by bicycle. Rent your own or make use of the ubiquitous bike-share schemes (p299). Alternatively, and especially in bad weather, take advantage of Berlin's excellent public transport system. For sightseeing on the cheap, hop aboard bus 100, 200 or 300 (p299).

Relaxing Like a Local

Although they are passionate about their city, Berliners also love to get out of town, especially in summer. If they're not jetting off to Mallorca or Mauritius, they will at least try to make it out to a local lake on a sunny day. There are dozens right in town, including the Plötzensee (p238) in Wedding, the Weissensee near Prenzlauer Berg, the vast Müggelsee (p241) in Köpenick and the Wannsee (p238) in Zehlendorf – all easily reached by public transport. Hundreds more are just a quick car or train ride away in the surrounding countryside

D BUSQUETS / SHUTTERSTOCK ©

Strandbad Plötzensee (p238)

of Brandenburg. Everyone's got their favourite body of water and, having staked out the perfect spot, tend to return there time and again. Nude bathing is common (but not compulsory).

With equally easy access to some fabulous parks, Berliners love heading for the greenery to chill with friends and a cold beer, relax in the shade, play frisbee or catch up on their reading. A few parks have areas where barbecuing is permitted.

Sightseeing Like a Local

Most locals – especially more recent arrivals – are very appreciative of Berlin's cultural offerings and keep tabs on the latest museum and gallery openings, theatre productions and construction projects. It's quite common to discuss the merits of the latest play or exhibit at dinner tables.

Although they love being tourists in their own city, Berliners stay away from the big-ticket museums and sights in summer, when the world comes to town. More likely they will bide their time until the cold and dark winter months or visit on late-opening nights with smaller crowds. The annual Lange Nacht der Museen (Long Night of the Museums, usually in August), when dozens of museums stay open past midnight, brings out culture vultures by the tens of thousands.

Local Obsessions

Soccer

Many Berliners live and die by the fortunes of the local soccer team, Hertha BSC, which has seen its share of ups and downs in recent years. After a brief stint in 2. Fussball-Bundesliga (Second Soccer League), the team is now a consistent presence in the Bundesliga premier league. True fans don't quit the team when it's down and, during the season, many will inevitably don their blue-and-white gear to make the trek out to the Olympiastadion (p225) for home games.

It was a minor sensation in 2019 when Berlin's other major club, the 1. FC Union, won promotion to the Bundesliga. The team, which plays in the Alte Försterei stadium in Köpenick, has an especially passionate following in the eastern parts of the city.

The Weather

Many locals are hobby meteorologists who will never pass up a chance to express their opinion on tomorrow's weather or on whether it's been a good summer so far, whether the last winter was mild or brutal, what to expect from the next one, and so on… So if you run out of things to say to a local, get the conversation going again by mentioning the weather. Other popular topics are rising rents or the perceived ineptitude of the local government.

For Free

t's no secret that you can still 'et more bang for your euro n Berlin than in many other Vestern European capitals. Even etter, there are plenty of ways o stretch your budget further y cashing in on some tip-top reebies, including such sights as he Reichstag dome and the Berlin Vall Memorial.

rium (p100)

WERNER SPREMBERG / SHUTTERSTOCK © ARCHITECTS: CHRISTOPH RICHTER & JAN MUSIKOWSKI

History Exhibits

Given that Germany has played a disproportionate role in 20th-century history, it's only natural that there are plenty of memorial sites and exhibits shedding light on various (mostly grim) milestones. Best of all, they're all free.

WWII

Study up on the SS, Gestapo and other organisations of the Nazi power apparatus at the Topographie des Terrors (p96) exhibit, then see the desk where WWII ended with the signing of Germany's unconditional surrender at the Deutsch-Russisches Museum Berlin-Karlshorst (p241). You can stand in the room where the 'Final Solution' was planned at the Haus der Wannsee-Konferenz (p239), get shivers while walking around the Sachsenhausen (p233) concentration camp, then pay your respects to Jewish victims of the Nazis at the Holocaust Memorial (p89). German resistance against the Nazis is the focus of the Gedenkstätte Deutscher Widerstand (p164), the Gedenkstätte Stille Helden (p166) and the Museum Blindenwerkstatt Otto Weidt (p137).

Cold War

The East Side Gallery (p204) may be the longest surviving section of the Berlin Wall, but to get the full picture of the Wall's physical appearance and human impact check out the Gedenkstätte Berliner Mauer (p142) and the Tränenpalast (p97). For an eyeful of what daily life was like behind the Iron Curtain, drop by the new Museum in der Kulturbrauerei (p144). At Checkpoint Charlie (p98), an outdoor exhibit chronicles milestones in Cold War history. For the Cold War years from the point of view of the Western Allies, swing by the AlliiertenMuseum (p237).

Museums & Galleries

Niche Museums

Although the blockbuster state museums do charge admission for adults, a few niche museums don't. Learn about the history of German democracy at the Deutscher Dom (p91), Berlin's equivalent of Oskar Schindler at the Museum Blindenwerkstatt

Otto Weidt (p137) and what the world's future might look like at the new Futurium (p100). The best among the art freebies are Urban Nation Museum (p172), a street art museum, and the Times Art Center Berlin (p130), with Chinese contemporary art. Top corporate art collections are Deutsche Bank's Palais Populaire (p95) and the Daimler Contemporary Berlin (p163). Unusual objects are on view at the Museum der Unerhörten Dinge (p172). Military and airplane buffs should head to the city outskirts for the Militärhistorisches Museum – Flugplatz Berlin-Gatow (p235).

Free under 18

Many museums don't charge admission for curious minds under 18. This includes both public repositories like the Pergamonmuseum (p109), Neues Museum (p111), Gemäldegalerie (p160) and Hamburger Bahnhof (p92) as well as such private institutions as C/O Berlin (p220) and the Käthe-Kollwitz-Museum (p221).

Guided Tours

Many museums and galleries include free multilingual audioguides in the admission price; some also offer free guided tours, although these are usually in German.

Alternative Berlin Tours (p300) and New Berlin Tours (p301) are English-language walking tour companies that advertise 'free' guided tours, although the guides actually depend on tips, so give what you can, keeping in mind that paid tours cost around €20.

Music

Free gigs and music events take place all the time, in pubs, bars, parks and churches. See the listings magazines for what's on during your stay.

Summer Concerts

In summer, many of Berlin's parks and gardens ring out with the free sound of jazz, pop, samba and classical music. Case in point: the lovely Teehaus im Englischen Garten (p168) presents two Sunday concerts (at 4pm and 7pm) in July and August.

NEED TO KNOW

Websites Search for free stuff by date at www.gratis-in-berlin.de.

Discount cards The Museumspass (adult/concession €29/14.50) is good for three days and valid at 30 major and minor museums.

Public wi-fi For the locations of the city's 2000 free public wi-fi hotspots, see www.berlin.de/en/wifi.

Karaoke

The Mauerpark is a zoo-and-a-half on hot summer Sundays, thanks largely to the massively entertaining outdoor Bearpit Karaoke (p146), which sees thousands of spectators cramming into the stone bleachers to cheer and applaud crooners of various talent levels.

Classical

At 1pm on Tuesday from September to mid-June, the foyer of the Berliner Philharmonie (p169) fills with music lovers for free lunchtime chamber-music concerts. At 12.30pm from Tuesday to Saturday, you can enjoy free organ recitals at the Matthäuskirche (p165) in the Kulturforum. The Französischer Dom (p91) has free organ concerts at the same time from Tuesday to Friday.

Rock & Jazz

For one-off free concerts, check the listings magazines (p73). Jazz fans can bop gratis at A-Trane (p226) on Monday and at the late-night jam session after 12.30am on Saturday. On Wednesday, b-Flat (p138) has its own free jam sessions. **Kunstfabrik Schlot** (Map p332, C1; 030-448 2160; www.kunstfabrik-schlot.de; Invalidenstrasse 117, Schlegelstrasse 26; daily; S Nordbahnhof, U Naturkundemuseum) is the go-to freebie several times a week.

TOBIAS ARHELGER / SHUTTERSTOCK ©

Checkpoint Charlie (p98)

The Berlin Wall

It's more than a tad ironic that one of Berlin's most popular tourist attractions is one that no longer exists. For 28 years the Berlin Wall, the most potent symbol of the Cold War, divided not only a city but the world.

The Beginning

Shortly after midnight on 13 August 1961, East German soldiers and police began rolling out miles of barbed wire that would soon be replaced with prefab concrete slabs. Overnight streets were cut in two, transportation between the city halves was halted and East Germans, including commuters, were no longer allowed to travel to West Berlin.

The Berlin Wall was a desperate measure launched by the German Democratic Republic (GDR, East Germany) to stop the sustained brain-and-brawn drain the country had experienced since its 1949 founding. Some 3.6 million people had already headed to western Germany, putting the GDR on the brink of economic and political collapse. The actual construction of the Wall, however, came as a shock to many: only a couple of months before that fateful August day, GDR head of state Walter Ulbricht had declared at a press conference that there were no plans to build a wall.

The Physical Border

Euphemistically called the 'Anti-Fascist Protection Barrier', the Berlin Wall was an instrument of oppression that turned West Berlin into an island of democracy within a sea of socialism. It consisted of a 43km-long inner-city barrier separating West from East Berlin and a 112km border between West

GHOST STATIONS

The Berlin Wall also divided the city's transport system. Three lines (today's U6, U8 and the north–south S-Bahn rails) that originated in West Berlin had to travel along tracks that happened to run beneath the eastern sector before returning to stations back on the western side. Trains slowed down but did not stop at these 'ghost stations' on East Berlin turf, which were closed and patrolled by heavily armed GDR border guards. An exhibit inside the **Nordbahnhof S-Bahn station** describes underground escape attempts and the measures taken by the East German government to prevent them.

Berlin and East Germany. Each reinforced-concrete segment was 3.6m high, 1.2m wide and weighed 2.6 tonnes. In some areas, the border strip included the Spree River or canals.

Continually reinforced and refined over time, the Berlin Wall eventually grew into a complex border-security system consisting of not one, but two, walls: the main wall abutting the border with West Berlin and the so-called hinterland security wall, with the 'death strip' in between. A would-be escapee who managed to scale the hinterland wall was first confronted with an electrified fence that triggered an alarm. After this, he or she would have to contend with guard dogs, spiked fences, trenches and other obstacles. Other elements included a patrol path with lamp posts that would flood the death strip with glaring light at night. Set up at regular intervals along the entire border were 300 watchtowers staffed by guards with shoot-to-kill orders. Only nine towers remain, including the one at Erna-Berger-Strasse (p163) near Potsdamer Platz.

In West Berlin, the Wall came right up to residential areas. Artists tried to humanise the grey concrete scar by covering it in colourful graffiti. The West Berlin government erected viewing platforms, which people could climb to peek across into East Berlin.

Escapes

There are no exact numbers, but it is believed that of the nearly 100,000 GDR citizens who tried to escape, hundreds died in the process, many by drowning, suffering fatal accidents or committing suicide when caught. More than 100 were shot and killed by border guards – the first only a few days after 13 August 1961. Guards who prevented an escape were rewarded with commendations, promotions and bonuses.

The first person to be shot at the Wall was 24-year-old trained tailor Günter Litfin. Construction of the fortification had begun only 11 days earlier when a hailstorm of bullets ripped through his body as he tried to swim to freedom across a 40m-wide canal (the Humboldt Harbour) on 24 August 1961, a Sunday. Since 2003, Günter's legacy is kept with a **memorial exhibit** (030-213 085 123; http://gedenkstaette-guenter-litfin.de; Kieler Strasse 2; 10am-5pm Sat & Sun May-Sep; M5, M8, M10, Schwarzkopfstrasse) FREE in a GDR watchtower near where he was killed.

Another famous incident illustrating the barbarity of the shoot-to-kill order occurred on 17 August 1962 when 18-year-old would-be escapee Peter Fechter was shot and wounded and then left to bleed to death as East German guards looked on. There's a memorial (p93) in his honour on Zimmerstrasse, near Checkpoint Charlie. Several memorials near the Reichstag commemorate the Wall victims: the Gedenkort Weisse Kreuze (p93), the Parlament der Bäume (p93) and the Mauer-Mahnmal (p93) inside the Marie-Elisabeth-Lüders-Haus.

The Gedenkstätte Berliner Mauer (p142) runs along 1.4km of Bernauer Strasse, which was literally split in two by the Berlin Wall, with one side of apartment buildings on the western side and the other in the east. As the barrier was erected, many residents on the eastern side decided to flee spontaneously by jumping into rescue nets or sliding down ropes, risking severe injury and death. Bernauer Strasse was also where several escape tunnels were dug, most famously Tunnel 29 in 1962, so named because 29 people managed to flee to the West before border guards detected the route. Those who were less lucky are commemorated with photographs and names in the emotional 'Window of Remembrance'.

The fact that there was no limit to the ingenuity of would-be escapees is documented at the Mauermuseum (p98) near Checkpoint Charlie. On display are several original contraptions used to flee East

Germany, including a hot-air balloon, a hollow surfboard, a specially rigged car and even a homemade mini-submarine.

The End

The Wall's demise came as unexpectedly as its creation. Once again the GDR was losing its people in droves, this time via Hungary, which had opened its borders with Austria. Thus emboldened, East Germans took to the streets by the hundreds of thousands, demanding improved human rights and an end to the dictatorship of the SED (Sozialistische Einheitspartei Deutschland), the single party in East Germany. A series of demonstrations culminated in a gathering of half a million people on Alexanderplatz on 4 November 1989, vociferously demanding political reform. Something had to give.

It did, on 9 November, when government spokesperson Günter Schabowski announced during a press conference on live TV that all travel restrictions to the West would be lifted. When asked by a reporter when this regulation would come into effect, he nervously shuffled his papers looking for the answer, then responded with the historic words: 'As far as I know, immediately.' In fact, the ruling was not supposed to take effect until the following day, but no one had informed Schabowski.

The news spread through East Berlin like wildfire, with hundreds of thousands heading towards the Wall. Border guards had no choice but to stand back. Amid scenes of wild partying and mile-long parades of GDR-made Trabant cars, the two Berlins came together again.

Today

The dismantling of the border fortifications began almost immediately and by now the city halves have visually merged so perfectly that it takes a keen eye to tell East from West. Fortunately, there's help in the form of a double row of cobblestones with bronze plaques inscribed 'Berliner Mauer 1961–1989' that guides you along 5.7km of the Wall's course. Also keep an eye out for the 32 information panels of the **Berlin Wall History Mile** (www.berlin.de/mauer/en/history/history-mile) set up along the course of the Wall. They draw attention, in four languages, to specific events that took place at each location. Berlin's division, the

edenkstätte Berliner Mauer (p142)

The Berlin Wall

The construction of the Berlin Wall was a unique event in human history, not only for physically bisecting a city but for becoming a dividing line between competing ideologies and political systems. It's this global impact and universal legacy that continues to fascinate people decades after its triumphant tear-down. Fortunately, some of original Wall segments and other vestiges remain, along with museums and memorials, to help fathom the realities and challenges of daily life in Berlin during the Cold War.

Our illustration points out the top highlights you can visit to learn about different aspects of these often tense decades. The best place to start is the ❶ **Gedenkstätte Berliner Mauer**, for an excellent introduction to what the inner-city border looked liked and what it meant to live in its shadow. Reflect upon what you've learned while relaxing along the former death strip, now the ❷ **Mauerpark**, before heading to the emotionally charged exhibit at the ❸ **Tränenpalast**, an actual border-crossing pavilion. Relive the euphoria of the

Tränenpalast
This modernist 1962 glass-and-steel border pavilion was dubbed 'Palace of Tears' because of the many tearful farewells that took place outside the building as East Germans and their Western visitors had to say goodbye.

Brandenburger Tor
People around the world cheered as East and West Berliners partied together atop the Berlin Wall in front of the iconic city gate, which today is a photogenic symbol of united Germany.

Potsdamer Platz
Nowhere was the death strip as wide as on the former no man's land around Potsdamer Platz, from which sprouted a new postmodern city quarter in the 1990s. A few segments of the Wall serve as reminders.

Checkpoint Charlie
Only diplomats and foreigners were allowed to use this border crossing. Weeks after the Wall was built, US and Soviet tanks faced off here in one of the hottest moments of the Cold War.

Wall's demise at the 4 **Brandenburger Tor**, then marvel at the revival of 5 **Potsdamer Platz**, which was nothing but death-strip wasteland until the 1990s. The Wall's geopolitical significance is the focus at 6 **Checkpoint Charlie**, which saw some of the tensest moments of the Cold War. Wrap up by finding your favourite mural motif at the 7 **East Side Gallery**.

It's possible to explore these sights by using a combination of walking and public transport, but a bike ride is the best method for gaining a sense of the former Wall's erratic flow through the central city.

FAST FACTS

Beginning of construction 13 August 1961

Fall of the Wall 9 November 1989

Total length 155km

Height 3.6m

Weight of each segment 2.6 tonnes

Number of watchtowers 300

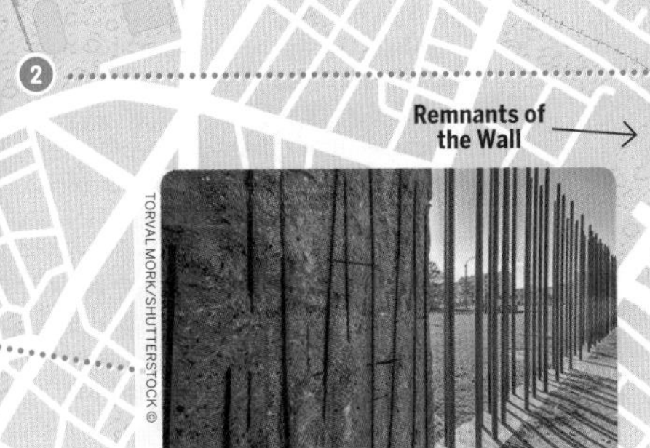

TORVAL MORK/SHUTTERSTOCK ©

Gedenkstätte Berliner Mauer
Germany's central memorial to the Berlin Wall and its victims exposes the complexity and barbaric nature of the border installation, along a 1.4km stretch of the barrier's course.

Mauerpark
Famous for its flea market and karaoke, this popular park actually occupies a converted section of the death strip. A 300m segment of surviving Wall is now an official practice ground for budding graffiti artists.

LINKA A ODOM/GETTY IMAGES ©

East Side Gallery
Paralleling the Spree for 1.3km, this is the longest Wall vestige. After its collapse, more than a hundred international artists expressed their feelings about this historic moment in a series of colourful murals.

EWAIS/SHUTTERSTOCK ©

construction of the Wall, how the Wall fell, and the people who died at the Wall are all addressed.

Only about 2km of the actual concrete barrier still stands today; most famous is the 1.3km stretch that is now the East Side Gallery (p204). But there are plenty of other traces scattered throughout the city, including lamps, patrol paths, fences, perimeter defences, switch boxes and so on. Most are so perfectly integrated they're only discernible to the practised eye. Some help in locating these can be found at www.berlin.de/mauer/en/sites/traces-of-the-wall.

Tours

Insider Tour Berlin (p300), Original Berlin Walks (p300) and New Berlin Tours (p301) offer guided English-language walking tours about and along the Berlin Wall. Fat Tire Bike Tours (p301) and Berlin on Bike (p301) cover the same or more ground by bicycle.

If you're feeling ambitious, rent a bike for a DIY tour of all or part of the 160km-long **Berliner Mauerweg** (Berlin Wall Trail), a signposted walking and cycling path that runs along the former border fortifications, with 40 multilingual information stations posted along the way. For a description and route maps in English, go to www.berlin.de/mauer/en/wall-trail.

The Berlin Wall by Neighbourhood

These original Wall remnants, museums and memorials keep the legacy of the Berlin Wall alive.

➡ **Historic Mitte** Die Mauer – asisi Panorama Berlin, Mauer-Mahnmal im Marie-Elisabeth-Lüders-Haus, BlackBox Kalter Krieg, Brandenburger Tor, Checkpoint Charlie, Gedenkort Weisse Kreuze (White Crosses Memorial Site), Mauermuseum, Parlament der Bäume (Parliament of Trees), Peter Fechter Memorial, Tränenpalast.

➡ **Prenzlauer Berg** Gedenkstätte Berliner Mauer, Mauerpark, Bornholmer Brücke.

➡ **Potsdamer Platz & Tiergarten** Wall remnants at Potsdamer Platz, Wall section at Niederkirchner Strasse (next to Topographie des Terrors), Watchtower Erna-Berger-Strasse.

➡ **Friedrichshain** East Side Gallery.

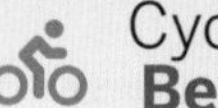

Cycling Tour Berlin Wall

START BORNHOLMER BRÜCKE AT S-BAHN STATION BORNHOLMER STRASSE
END EAST SIDE GALLERY
LENGTH 15KM; 2½ HOURS

This easy ride follows the former course of the Berlin Wall and begins on the Bösebrücke (also known as Bornholmer Brücke) steel bridge. A free outdoor exhibit next to a section of outer wall chronicles the events of 9 November 1989 when the ❶ **Bornholmer Strasse Border Crossing** became the first to open in the city.

Head east on Bornholmer Strasse, turn right on Malmöer Strasse and right again on Behmstrasse. Near the hilltop, cross the street and take the Schwedter Steg footbridge over the railway tracks. Continuing straight takes you to ❷ **Mauerpark** (p144), a popular park built atop the former death strip. A roughly 300m-long section of the inner wall runs along the back of the Friedrich-Ludwig-Jahn-Stadion.

Mauerpark adjoins Bernauer Strasse, home to the ❸ **Gedenkstätte Berliner Mauer** (p142), or Berlin Wall Memorial, a 1.4km-long indoor-outdoor exhibit that's the best place to understand the Wall and how it shaped everyday life. Follow Bernauer Strasse past vestiges of the border installations and escape tunnels, a chapel, a monument and an original section of Wall.

Bernauer Strasse culminates at the ❹ **S-Bahn station Nordbahnhof** (p38), a 'ghost station', for the Wall also divided the city's transportation system. An exhibit inside the station explains the situation in detail.

From Nordbahnhof, continue west on Invalidenstrasse, then head south on Chausseestrasse to Friedrichstrasse. Cross the Spree River and turn right on Reichstagufer to the border crossing pavilion nicknamed ❺ **Tränenpalast** (p97), or Palace of Tears, because of the many tearful goodbyes suffered here. Stop to check out the free exhibit inside before continuing on Reichstagufer.

Turn right on Marshallbrücke, left on Reinhardtstrasse and left again on Schiffbauerdamm. On your left is the ❻ **Parlament der Bäume** (p93), the Parliament of Trees, a garden-like art installation by Ben Wagin to remember those who died at the Wall.

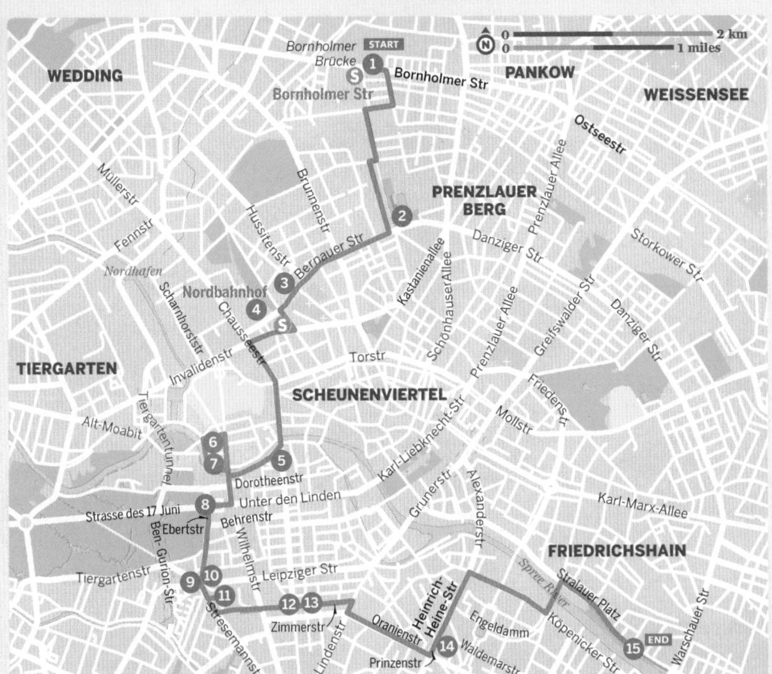

For another Ben Wagin Wall installation, carry your bike down the stairs to the Schiffbauerdamm river promenade and pedal a short stretch to 7 **Marie-Elisabeth-Lüders-Haus** (p94). Lined up in the glass-fronted basement is a row of original Wall segments, each painted with a year and the number of people killed at the border in that year.

Continue on Schiffbauerdamm, turn right on Marshallbrücke and follow Wilhelmstrasse to Unter den Linden. Turn right to arrive at the 8 **Brandenburger Tor** (p88), the Brandenburg Gate, where construction of the Wall began on 13 August 1961. Past the Brandenburger Tor, turn left on Ebertstrasse and head south to 9 **Potsdamer Platz** (p157), which used to be a massive no man's land during the city's division. The death strip was several hundred metres wide here. Outside the S-Bahn station entrance are a few 10 **Berlin Wall segments**.

Continue south on Stresemannstrasse, then hook a left on Erna-Berger-Strasse to get to one of the few remaining 11 **GDR watchtowers** (p163). Guards had to climb up a slim, round shaft via an iron ladder to reach the octagonal observation perch on top.

Backtrack and continue south on Stresemannstrasse, then turn left on Niederkirchner Strasse to get to a 200m-long section of the original outer border wall. Badly scarred by souvenir hunters, it's now protected by a fence.

Keep going east on Niederkirchner Strasse (which becomes Zimmerstrasse) to arrive at 12 **Checkpoint Charlie** (p98), which took its name from the NATO phonetic alphabet. Continue east on Zimmerstrasse, past a 13 **memorial to Peter Fechter** (p93), an 18-year-old would-be escapee who, on 17 August 1962, was shot and wounded and then left to bleed to death by East German guards. Turn right on Axel-Springer-Strasse and left on Oranienstrasse, then left again (at Moritzplatz) onto Heinrich-Heine-Strasse. Just past the intersection with Sebastianstrasse was the 14 **Heinrich-Heine-Strasse** border crossing, used primarily for mail and merchandise and by West Germans.

Follow Heinrich-Heine-Strasse north, turn right on Köpenicker Strasse, left on Engeldamm, cross the Spree, turn right on Stralauer Platz and you'll soon arrive at the 15 **East Side Gallery** (p204), a 1.3km-long stretch of outer wall painted by artists in 1990. The river itself belonged to East Berlin and border guards patrolled the Spree in boats.

Above: GDR Watchtower (p163)

Left: East Side Gallery (p204)

Modern annexe of the Deutsches Historisches Museum (p90) by architect IM Pei

Historical Museums & Memorials

From its humble medieval beginnings, Berlin's history – especially its key role in major events of the 20th century – has created a rich and endlessly fascinating tapestry. It's also extremely well documented in numerous museums, memorial sites and monuments, many of them in original historic locations that are open to the public.

The Evolution of Berlin & Germany

There's no better place to learn about German history from the early Middle Ages to the present than the Deutsches Historisches Museum (p90) in a Prussian armoury in Mitte. Not far away, the Märkisches Museum (p120) zeroes in specifically on the evolution of Berlin from its medieval birth to today's modern metropolis. Berlin's Jewish history gets the spotlight at the Jüdisches Museum (p180).

The Third Reich

Few periods shaped the fate of Berlin as much as its 12-year stint as capital of Nazi Germany. Numerous museums and memorial sites, almost all of them free, make sure that the memory is kept alive. For insight into the sinister machinations of the Nazi state, visit the Topographie des Terrors (p96). Nazi leaders planned the implementation of the so-called 'Final Solution' in a lakeside villa that is now the Haus der Wannsee-Konferenz (p239).

NEED TO KNOW

Tickets

Admission to many museums and memorial sites is free (p35), including Gedenkstätte Berliner Mauer, Topographie des Terrors, and Gedenkstätte Deutscher Widerstand. Major historical museums that charge admission include the Jüdisches Museum, Märkisches Museum, Spy Museum, Deutsches Historisches Museum, Mauermuseum and Schloss Cecilienhof.

Opening Hours

Core museum hours 10am to 6pm, with a number of major venues open until 8pm one day a week.

Closed Monday Märkisches Museum, Ort der Information, Schloss Charlottenburg, Schloss Cecilienhof, Deutsch-Russisches Museum Berlin-Karlshorst, Tränenpalast, AlliiertenMuseum, Urban Nation and Museum in der Kulturbrauerei,

The unfathomable impact of Nazi terror is emotionally documented at the Ort der Information (p89) below the Holocaust Memorial and at the Sachsenhausen concentration camp (p233). Brave locals who tried to stand up against the Nazis are commemorated at the Gedenkstätte Deutscher Widerstand (p164), the Gedenkstätte Stille Helden (p166) and the Museum Blindenwerkstatt Otto Weidt (p137).

When WWII finally came to an end, the German surrender was signed at what is now the Deutsch-Russisches Museum Berlin-Karlshorst (p241), whose exhibits chronicle WWII from the point of view of the Soviet Union. Two giant monuments honour the vast number of Russian soldiers who died in the Battle of Berlin: the Sowjetisches Ehrenmal Treptow (p183) and the Sowjetisches Ehrenmal Tiergarten (p94). To see where the victorious Allies hammered out Germany's postwar fate, visit Schloss Cecilienhof (p231) in nearby Potsdam.

The Cold War

After WWII, Berlin was caught in the crosshairs of the Cold War superpowers – the US and the Soviet Union – as epitomised by the city's division and the construction of the Berlin Wall. The longest surviving vestige of this barrier is the street-art-festooned East Side Gallery (p204). Deepen your understanding of the border fortifications and their human toll at the Gedenkstätte Berliner Mauer (p142) and the Tränenpalast (p97).

Daily life behind the Iron Curtain is documented in interactive fashion at the DDR Museum (p120), while the free Museum in der Kulturbrauerei (p144) follows a comparatively traditional approach to the same subject. Both exhibits also address the role of East Germany's Ministry of State Security (the Stasi) in shoring up the power base of the country's regime. Learn more at the Stasimuseum (p212) and on a guided tour of the Stasi Prison (p212) where regime critics were incarcerated.

Near Checkpoint Charlie (p98), the famous border crossing, you can learn about the daring attempts by East Germans to escape to the West at the privately run Mauermuseum (p98). For a take on the Cold War in Berlin from the perspective of the occupying Western allies, visit the AlliiertenMuseum (p237). Berlin's legacy as the capital of spies is the subject of the German Spy Museum (p163) on Leipziger Platz.

Historical Museums & Memorials by Neighbourhood

- **Historic Mitte** BlackBox Kalter Krieg, Deutsches Historisches Museum, Mauermuseum, Ort der Information, Sowjetisches Ehrenmal Tiergarten, Topographie des Terrors, Tränenpalast, Pergamonmuseum.Das Panorama.
- **Museumsinsel & Alexanderplatz** DDR Museum, Märkisches Museum.
- **Hackescher Markt & Scheunenviertel** Museum Blindenwerkstatt Otto Weidt.
- **Prenzlauer Berg** Gedenkstätte Berliner Mauer, Jüdischer Friedhof Schönhauser Allee, Museum in der Kulturbrauerei.
- **Potsdamer Platz & Tiergarten** Berlin Story Museum, Berlin Wall Museum, Gedenkstätte Stille Helden, Gedenkstätte Deutscher Widerstand, Deutsches Spionage Museum, Die Mauer / The Wall Museum.
- **Kreuzberg** Jüdisches Museum.
- **City West & Charlottenburg** Kaiser-Wilhelm-Gedächtniskirche.
- **Outer Berlin** AlliiertenMuseum, Deutsch-Russisches Museum Berlin-Karlshorst, Gedenkstätte Plötzensee, Haus der Wannsee-Konferenz, Sachsenhausen, Stasi Prison, Stasimuseum, Sowjetisches Ehrenmal Treptow.
- **Potsdam** Schloss Cecilienhof.

Lonely Planet's Top Choices

Gedenkstätte Berliner Mauer (p142) Indoor-outdoor multimedia exhibit vividly illustrates the history, physical appearance and social impact of the Berlin Wall.

Topographie des Terrors (p96) Gripping examination of the origins of Nazism, its perpetrators and its victims, on the site of the SS and Gestapo headquarters.

Jüdisches Museum (p180) Daniel Libeskind's contorted building is a striking backdrop for this thorough survey of the history and cultural heritage of Jews in Germany.

Gedenkstätte und Museum Sachsenhausen (p233) No book or movie comes close to the emotional impact of actually standing in a concentration camp.

Deutsches Historisches Museum (p90) Charts German history in the European context from the Middle Ages to the present, in a former Prussian armoury.

Best in Historic Locations

Stasi Prison (p212) Tours of this infamous jail, which had a starring role in the Academy Award–winning *The Lives of Others*, are sometimes led by former inmates.

Stasimuseum (p212) The headquarters of East Germany's feared and loathed Ministry of State Security are now a museum.

Tränenpalast (p97) Exhibit explains why tears once flowed in this Friedrichstrasse border pavilion, as East Germans said farewell to their loved ones.

Gedenkstätte und Museum Sachsenhausen (p233) North of Berlin, this early concentration camp served as a model for many others.

Best for Jewish Remembrance

Jüdisches Museum (p180) Engagingly laid out chronicle and celebration of 1700 years of Jewish life in Berlin and Germany.

Ort der Information (p89) Chilling exhibit below the Holocaust Memorial examining personal aspects of this unfathomable chapter in human history.

Museum Blindenwerkstatt Otto Weidt (p137) Learn how one heroic man saved many Jewish lives.

Gleis 17 Memorial (p237) Haunting train tracks memorialise the departure point for trains heading to the concentration camps.

Jüdischer Friedhof Schönhauser Allee (p145) Pay your respects to 25,000 Jewish Berliners buried here between 1827 and 1945, including painter Max Liebermann.

Best for Kids

DDR Museum (p120) Experiential and hands-on journey into daily life behind the Iron Curtain.

Mauermuseum (p98) Fascinating collection of ingenious, original contraptions used by East Germans to escape their country.

Freilichtmuseum Domäne Dahlem (p29) Eight hundred years of farming history and traditional crafts in a manor house from 1560.

Best for Historic Milestones

Haus der Wannsee-Konferenz (p239) Get the shivers in the very room where Nazi leaders planned the systematic annihilation of European Jews in January 1942.

Deutsch-Russisches Museum Berlin-Karlshorst (p241) With the stroke of a pen the war in Europe ended on 8 May 1945 with the signing of the German surrender at this former seat of the Soviet Military Administration.

Schloss Cecilienhof (p231) The Potsdam Conference brought Stalin, Truman and Attlee to this pretty palace between 17 July and 2 August 1945 to divvy Germany up into four occupation zones.

Gedenkstätte Deutscher Widerstand (p164) Stand in the rooms where army officer Claus von Stauffenberg and his cohorts planned the ill-fated assassination of Hitler.

Best for Architecture

Jüdisches Museum (p180) Daniel Libeskind's structures are never just buildings; they're also evocative metaphors, as beautifully illustrated by Berlin's Jewish Museum.

Märkisches Museum (p120) This imposing red-brick pile is a clever mash-up of actual historic buildings from the surrounding state of Brandenburg.

Deutsches Historisches Museum (p90) Highlights of this ex-armoury are the baroque dying-warrior sculptures in the courtyard and the modern annexe by IM Pei.

Museum Berggruen (p219)

The Berlin Art Scene

Art aficionados will find their compass on perpetual spin in Berlin. With hundreds of galleries, scores of world-class collections and an estimated 20,000 professional artists, the city has assumed pole position on the global artistic circuit. Perpetual energy, restlessness and experimental spirit combined and infused with an undercurrent of grit are what give this 'eternally unfinished' city its art cred.

te Nationalgalerie (p114)

Major Art Museums

Berlin's most famous art museums are administered by the Staatliche Museen Berlin (Berlin State Museums; www.smb.museum). The main locations:

Gemäldegalerie (p160) Encyclopedic collection of European painting from the 13th to the 18th century – Rembrandt, Caravaggio and Vermeer included; at the Kulturforum.

Alte Nationalgalerie (p114) Neoclassical, Romantic, impressionist and early modernist art, including Caspar David Friedrich, Adolf Menzel and Monet; on Museumsinsel.

Hamburger Bahnhof Museum for Gegenwart (p92) International contemporary art – Warhol to Rauschenberg to Beuys; east of the Hauptbahnhof.

Museum Berggruen (p219) Classical modernist art, mostly Picasso and Klee; near Schloss Charlottenburg.

Sammlung Scharf-Gerstenberg (p219) Surrealist art by Goya, Magritte, Jean Dubuffet, Max Ernst and more; near Schloss Charlottenburg.

Friedrichswerdersche Kirche (p95) European sculpture from the 19th century displayed in a neo-Gothic ex-church by Karl Friedrich Schinkel.

Neue Nationalgalerie (p165) Early-20th-century art, especially German expressionists. It's part of the Kulturforum and is set to emerge from extensive renovation in July 2021.

Aside from these heavy hitters, Berlin teems with smaller museums specialising in a particular artist or genre.

NEED TO KNOW

Tickets

➡ Generally you can buy tickets at the gallery or museum; prebook for the hottest tickets.

➡ Commercial galleries do not charge admission. Most hold *vernissage* (opening) and *finissage* (closing) parties.

➡ The Berlin Museum Pass (€29, concession €14.50) buys admission to about 30 museums and galleries for a three-day period. Available at participating museums and the tourist offices.

Advance Planning

➡ Blockbuster visiting shows often sell out, so it's best to prepurchase tickets online. Same goes for Pergamonmuseum and Neues Museum.

➡ Most private collections require advance registration; reserve months ahead for the Sammlung Boros.

Opening Hours

➡ The big museums and galleries are typically open from 10am to 6pm, with extended viewing one day a week, usually Thursday. Some are closed on Monday.

➡ Commercial galleries tend to be open from noon to 6pm Tuesday to Saturday and by appointment.

➡ The Bauhaus Archiv and parts of the Pergamonmuseum (including the Pergamon Altar itself) are closed for restoration. The Neue Nationalgalerie is expected to reopen in July 2021.

Tours

GoArt! Berlin (www.goart-berlin.de) runs customised tours that demystify Berlin's art scene by opening doors to private collections, artist studios and galleries or by taking you to exciting street-art locations. Also offers art consulting.

Websites

Museumsportal (www.museumsportal.de) Gateway to the city's museums and galleries.

Landesverband Berliner Galerien (www.berliner-galerien.de) For a list and links to Berlin's most important galleries.

SEMMICK PHOTO / SHUTTERSTOCK ©

Above: A mural by artist Tankpetrol at an opening at the Urban Nation Museum (p172)

Below: East Side Gallery (p204)

You can admire the colourful canvases of expressionist artist group Die Brücke in a lovely museum (p236) on the eastern edge of the Grunewald; see the paintings of Max Liebermann while standing in the very studio where he painted them in the Liebermann-Villa am Wannsee (p239); take a survey of a century of Berlin-made art in the Berlinische Galerie (p182), or learn about post-1945 German sculpture in the Kunsthaus Dahlem (p237).

The main exhibition spaces without their own collections are the Gropius Bau (p163) and the Haus der Kulturen der Welt (p94). Both mount superb temporary and travelling art shows, the latter with a special focus on contemporary arts from non-European cultures and societies.

Two museums train the spotlight on women: the Käthe-Kollwitz-Museum (p221), which is dedicated to one of the finest and most outspoken early-20th-century German artists, and the **Das Verborgene Museum** (Hidden Museum; Map p350; ☎030-313 3656; www.dasverborgenemuseum.de; Schlüterstrasse 70; adult/concession €3/1.50; ⏲3-7pm Thu & Fri, noon-4pm Sat & Sun; S Savignyplatz, U Ernst-Reuter-Platz), which champions lesser-known German female artists from the same period.

There are also corporate collections like Palais Populaire (p95) and the Daimler Contemporary (p163) as well as private ones like the Julia Stoschek Collection (p97), Sammlung Hoffmann (p129), Museum Frieder Burda (p129) and, above all, the extraordinary Sammlung Boros (p99).

Commercial Art Galleries

The Galleries Association of Berlin (www.berliner-galerien.de) counts some 340 galleries within the city. In addition, there are at least 200 noncommercial showrooms and off-spaces that regularly show new exhibitions. Although the orientation is global, it's well worth keeping an eye out for the latest works by major contemporary artists living and working in Berlin, including Thomas Demand, Jonathan Meese, Via Lewandowsky, Isa Genzken, Tino Sehgal, Esra Ersen, John Bock and the artist duo Ingar Dragset and Michael Elmgreen.

Galleries cluster in four main areas:

Scheunenviertel (Mitte) Auguststrasse and Linienstrasse were the birthplaces of Berlin's post-Wall contemporary art scene. Some pioneers have since moved on to bigger digs, but key players like Eigen+Art, neugerriemschneider, Galerie Neu and Sprüth Magers remain.

Checkpoint Charlie area (northern Kreuzberg) A number of key galleries hold forth on Zimmerstrasse, Charlottenstrasse, Rudi-Dutschke-Strasse and Markgrafenstrasse, including Galerie Thomas Schulte, Carlier Gebauer, Galerie Barbara Thumm, Galerie Tammen, Kang Contemporary, KOW and Feldbusch, Wiesner, Rudolph.

Potsdamer Strasse & Around (Schöneberg) In recent years, the gritty area around Potsdamer Strasse and Kurfürstenstrasse has emerged as one of Berlin's most dynamic art quarters, with a great mix of established galleries and newcomers. Heavy hitters include Galerie Isabella Bortolozzi, Galerie Thomas Fischer, Jarmuschek + Partner and Klosterfelde Edition.

Around Savignyplatz (Charlottenburg) The traditional gallery district in the western city centre is experiencing a renaissance, with several galleries recently relocating here from Mitte. Standouts include Camera Work, Contemporary Fine Arts, Medhi Chouakri, Galerie Michael Schultz, Galerie Max Hetzler and Galerie Brockstedt.

Street Art & Where to Find It

Stencils, paste-ups, throw-ups, burners and bombings. These are some of the magic words in street art and graffiti, the edgy art forms that have helped shape the aesthetic of contemporary Berlin. A capital of street art, the city is home to Germany's first urban art museum, the Urban Nation Museum (p172) in Schöneberg. Out in the field, Berlin is the canvas of such international heavyweights as Blu, JR, Os Gemeos, Romero, Shepard Fairey and ROA, along with local talent like Alias, El Bocho and XOOOOX. Every night, hundreds of hopeful next-gen artists haunt the streets, staying one step ahead of the police as they aerosol their screaming visions, often within seconds.

TOP THREE BERLIN ART BLOGS

Berlin Art Link (www.berlinartlink.com) Online magazine delving into the contemporary-art scene via studio visits and artist interviews, reviews and event listings.

Street Art Berlin (www.streetartbln.com) Keeps tabs on new works, profiles Berlin artists and posts about events.

ARTatBerlin (www.artatberlin.com) Gallery and museum guide, calendar and map to contemporary art around Berlin.

There's street art pretty much everywhere. The area around U-Bahn station Schlesisches Tor in Kreuzberg has some house-wall-size classics, including Pink Man (p184) by Blu and Yellow Man (p184) by the Brazilian twins Os Gemeos. Skalitzer Strasse is also a fertile hunting ground with Victor Ash's Astronaut (p184) being a highlight (you can even spot it on the northern side of the tracks when riding the above-ground U1). There's also a work by street-art superstar Shepard Fairey called **Make Art Not War** on Mehringplatz.

Across the Spree River in Friedrichshain, the RAW Gelände (p206) is a constantly evolving canvas and even has a dedicated street art gallery, the Urban Spree (p206). Around Boxhagener Platz you'll find works by Boxi, Alias and El Bocho. The facade of the Kino Intimes (p211) is also worth checking out. In Mitte, there's plenty of art underneath the S-Bahn arches along Dircksenstrasse, although the undisputed hub is the courtyard of Haus Schwarzenberg (p137). Prenzlauer Berg has the Mauerpark (p144), where budding artists may legally hone their skills along a section of the Berlin Wall. In the entryway of the dilapidated building at Kastanienallee 86 are works by Alias and El Bocho. You'll also pass by plenty of graffiti when riding the circle S-Bahn line S41/S42.

For a veritable feast in street art, it's also well worth making the trip out to the abandoned spy station on the Teufelsberg (p221).

Several walking tour companies offer street-art tours, including Alternative Berlin Tours (p300) which also runs a hands-on street-art workshop. A good book on the subject is *Street Art in Berlin* by Kai Jakob (2015).

PUBLIC ART

Free installations, sculptures and paintings? Absolutely. Public art is big in Berlin, which happens to be home to the world's longest outdoor mural, the 1.3km-long East Side Gallery (p204). No matter which neighbourhood you walk in, you're going to encounter public art on a grand scale. The Potsdamer Platz area offers especially rich pickings, including works by Keith Haring, Mark di Suvero, Richard Serra, Eduardo Chillida and Frank Stella.

Liebermann-Villa am Wannsee (p239)

The Berlin Art Scene by Neighbourhood

- **Historic Mitte** Sammlung Boros, Hamburger Bahnhof, Akademie der Künste – Pariser Platz, galleries around Checkpoint Charlie, Haus der Kulturen der Welt.
- **Museumsinsel & Alexanderplatz** Alte Nationalgalerie, Altes Museum, Bode-Museum.
- **Hackescher Markt & Scheunenviertel** Museum Frieder Burda, Sammlung Hoffmann, street art, top-notch galleries around Auguststrasse.
- **Potsdamer Platz & Tiergarten** Daimler Contemporary, Gemäldegalerie, Gropius Bau, public art in DaimlerCity.
- **Kreuzberg** Abundant street art; also Berlinische Galerie, König Galerie @ St Agnes Kirche.
- **Friedrichshain** East Side Gallery, street art at RAW Gelände.
- **City West & Charlottenburg** C/O Berlin, galleries around Savignyplatz, Käthe-Kollwitz-Museum, Museum Berggruen, Museum für Fotografie, Sammlung Scharf-Gerstenberg.
- **Grunewald** Street art at Teufelsberg spy station

Lonely Planet's Top Choices

Gemäldegalerie (p160) Sweeping survey of Old Masters from Germany, Italy, France, Spain and the Netherlands from the 13th to the 18th centuries.

Hamburger Bahnhof (p92) Warhol, Beuys and Twombly are among the many legends aboard the contemporary-art express at this former train station.

Sammlung Boros (p99) Book months' ahead for tickets to see this stunning cutting-edge private collection housed in a WWII bunker.

Gropius Bau (p163) First-rate travelling exhibits take up residence in this gorgeous Renaissance-style building.

Best Single-Artist Galleries

Käthe-Kollwitz-Museum (p221) Representative collection of works by Germany's greatest female artist, famous for her haunting depictions of war and human loss and suffering.

Liebermann-Villa am Wannsee (p239) Charming exhibit set up in the lakeside summer home of the great German impressionist and leading Berlin Secession founder Max Liebermann.

Dalí – Die Ausstellung (p163) Private collection showcasing lesser-known drawings, illustrated books and sculptures by the famous Catalan surrealist.

Best by Genre

Museum Berggruen (p219) Picasso, Klee and Giacometti form the heart of this stunning classical-modernist collection sold to the city by the art dealer and collector Heinz Berggruen.

Sammlung Scharf-Gerstenberg (p219) Across from Museum Berggruen, this space delves into the fantastical worlds conjured up by Goya, Max Ernst, Magritte and other giants of the surrealist genre.

Alte Nationalgalerie (p114) This venerable art temple is packed with 19th-century art, including Romantic masterpieces by such genre practitioners as Caspar David Friedrich, Karl Friedrich Schinkel and Carl Blechen.

Brücke-Museum (p236) Forest-framed gem focusing on German expressionism, with works by Karl Schmidt-Rottluff, Ernst Ludwig Kirchner and other members of the Bridge, Germany's first modern-artist group.

Bode-Museum (p114) The biggest names in European sculpture from the early Middle Ages to the 18th century in a palatial setting on Museum Island.

Urban Nation Museum (p172) Germany's first contemporary street art museum.

Best Contemporary Art Galleries

Sammlung Boros (p99) The latest works by established and emerging artists displayed in a labyrinthine WWII bunker.

KW Institute for Contemporary Art (p129) Key art space that champions artistic collaboration and an interdisplinary approach.

Julia Stoschek Collection (p97) Time-based media art in the 1960s-era ex-Czechoslovakian Cultural Institute.

Kindl Centre for Contemporary Art (p196) Interdisciplinary space in the industrials halls of a former brewery.

Schinkel Pavillon (p95) Platform for new art in a striking octagonal GDR-era pavillon.

Times Art Center Berlin (p130) Showcase of contemporary Chinese art with a focus on media and video art sponsored by the nonprofit Guangzhou Times Art Museum.

Best Photographic Exhibits

C/O Berlin (p220) This photographic treasure chest mounts changing exhibits featuring the biggest names in the business, from Germany and beyond.

Museum für Fotografie (p220) Selections from the cache of images that Helmut Newton donated to Berlin share wall space with works by top practitioners from the state museum's collection.

Camera Work (www.camerawork.de) This leading gallery for photography presents icons like Man Ray and Diane Arbus alongside next-gen shutterbug stars like Christian Tagliavini.

Best Art Exhibition Halls

Gropius Bau (p163) Top of the heap with headline-making travelling art exhibits from all fields of creative endeavour.

Haus der Kulturen der Welt (p94) Mounts shows with a special focus on non-European cultures and societies.

Akademie der Künste (p95) Berlin's oldest arts institution (founded in 1696) presents genre-hopping exhibits drawn from its archives in two locations.

Palais Populaire (p95) Presents selections of Deutsche Bank's art collection in a modernised Prussian palace.

Vegan dishes

Dining Out

Berlin's food scene is growing in leaps and bounds and maturing as beautifully as a fine Barolo. Sure, you can still get your fill of traditional German comfort staples, from sausage to roast pork knuckle, but it's the influx of innovative chefs from around the globe that makes eating in the capital such a mouth-watering experience.

Food Trends

As with art and fashion, Berliners are always onto the next hot thing when it comes to food. You'll find plenty of culinary obsessions in the capital.

FOOTPRINT-FRIENDLY REGIONAL CUISINE

Eating healthy while minimising your carbon footprint is sexy, which is why the organic-regional-seasonal trifecta has become an obsession in Berlin. From corner cafes to Michelin-starred restaurants, chefs prefer ingredients that have been harvested, foraged and hunted as close to home as possible. A pioneer of the climate-friendly farm-to-table concept was Michelin-starred Nobelhart & Schmutzig (p102). Indeed, it pushed the envelope even further by banning any ingredient not grown in the region from its kitchens.

Demand for regional ingredients is met by a growing number of farms in the surrounding state of Brandenburg. Apple-fed pork from the Havelland, buffalo mozzarella from Kremmen or wild boar from the Schorfheide now make frequent menu appearances. Some chefs even maintain their own vegetable and herb gardens, while restaurants like Good Bank (p123), Beba (p166) and Layla (p168) grow produce on-site in so-called 'vertical farms'.

Time-tested techniques for preserving seasonal ingredients for future use through pickling, brining and fermentation are also all the rage.

PLANT-BASED PARADISE

A meal featuring meat is so last millennium, which is why vegan (and vegetarian) restaurants are spreading faster than rabbits on Viagra in Berlin. The city has been at the forefront of the plant-based trend for some time now and spawned the world's first all-vegan supermarket chain, Veganz, in 2011. In 2018, Berlin's finest vegetarian temple, Cookies Cream (p102), entered the constellation of Michelin stars. Probably not far behind are Kopps (p132) and Lucky Leek (p149). Taking things one step further is Frea (p133), which opened in 2019 as Berlin's first zero-waste restaurant. For a comprehensive list of vegetarian and vegan restaurants in Berlin, visit www.happycow.net.

LEVANTINE CUISINE

Hummus, shakshuka, kibbe, faroug and other dishes common around the Middle East were practically unknown to German palates until just a few years ago. But thanks to a growing influx of enterprising Israelis and refugees from countries such as Syria, Iran and Iraq, Berlin is now seeing a bountiful crop of restaurants serving this delicious and healthy cuisine, including Kanaan (p148), Café Mugrabi (p186) and Malakeh (p173).

NEW GLOBAL TASTES

Asian cuisines in all their diversity have been riding high in Berlin for a while now, especially when it comes to Vietnamese, Korean and Japanese fare. Now they are getting a run for their money from Chinese cooking, more particularly Szechuan noodles swimming in a bath of sesame chili oil that's often hot enough to make a fire eater choke. See if you can stand the heat at Liu Nudelhaus (p101) in Mitte.

NEED TO KNOW

Opening Hours

Cafes 8am to 8pm

Restaurants 11am to 10pm; some restaurants offer a limited menu until midnight

Fast-food joints 11am to midnight or later

Price Ranges

The following price ranges refer to the average cost of a main course.

€ less than €12

€€ €12–25

€€€ more than €25

Bills & Tipping

- Your bill won't be presented until you ask for it: *'Zahlen, bitte'*.
- It's customary to add 10% or more for good service.
- Tip as you hand over the money, rather than leaving it on the table (as this is considered rude). For example, if your bill comes to €28 and you want to give a €2 tip, say €30. If you have the exact amount and don't need change, just say '*Stimmt so*' (that's fine).

Reservations

Reservations are recommended for all but the most casual restaurants, especially for dinner and at weekends. Book the trendiest places four or more weeks in advance. Many restaurant websites now offer an online booking function.

ODD ANDERSEN / GETTYIMAGES ©

Above: Food truck

Left: Damaskus Konditorie (p198)

Perhaps a safer choice is to visit one of Berlin's growing crop of Georgian restaurants like Der Blaue Fuchs (p148) in Prenzlauer Berg. The country's location at the crossroads of Asia, Europe and the Middle East has resulted in a nuanced cuisine that reflects influences from all these regions.

NON-ALCOHOLIC DRINK PAIRINGS

What goes better with a fine meal then having each course perfectly paired with a glass of wine? Well, some of Berlin's top chefs have come up with non-alcoholic alternatives, for instance homemade juices, kombucha or kefir that pick up or complement the dish's flavours. Try it at such Michelin-starred restaurants as Coda (p199), Einsunternull (p134) and Horvàth (www.restaurant-horvath.de)

SHARING PLATES & CASUAL FINE DINING

These concepts aren't exactly a new trend in most places around the world, but in Germany ordering a bunch of small dishes and putting them in the middle for everyone to tuck in to and help themselves has, until now, not been so common at all.

Neither was the concept of casual fine dining. Stuffy restaurants definitely don't go well with Berlin's idiosyncratic spirit, which is probably why the trend has been embraced with such vengeance.

Eating Like a Local

Formal restaurants with full menus, crisp white linen and fussy servers are (thankfully) a dying breed in Berlin. These days, it's all about casual dining, feeling comfortable with yourself, the food and the environment. A few restaurants are open for lunch and dinner only, but most tend to be open all day. Same goes for cafes, which usually serve coffee and alcohol, as well as light meals, although ordering food is not obligatory.

Berliners tend to linger at the table, so if a place is full at 8pm it's likely that it will stay that way for a couple of hours. Some restaurants are introducing a time limit for seatings (usually two hours), but this is still rare.

English menus are now quite common, and some places (especially those owned by neo-Berliners from the US, UK or around Europe) don't bother with German menus at all. When it comes to paying, sometimes the person who invites pays, but very often Germans split the bill. This might mean everyone chips in at the end of a meal or asks the server to pay separately *(getrennte Rechnung).*

Handy speed-feed shops, called *Imbiss,* serve all sorts of global street food, from sausage-in-a-bun to doner kebab and pizza. Many bakeries serve sandwiches alongside pastries, while some butcher shops (rare as they have become) also offer simple meals for eating on-site or taking away.

Locals love to shop at farmers markets, and nearly every *Kiez* (neighbourhood) runs at least one or two during the week.

Due to the coronavirus pandemic, more and more restaurants now offer home delivery. Ordering and delivery are handled by Lieferando (www.lieferando.com).

TOP FIVE BERLIN FOOD & LIFESTYLE BLOGS

It's no secret that Berlin is a fast-changing city and it's only natural that the food scene is also developing at lightning speed. There are a number of passionate foodies keeping an eye on new developments and generously sharing them on their (English-language) blogs. If you read German, also check out Mit Vergnügen (www.mitvergnuegen.com), Satt und Froh (www.sattundfroh.de) and Berlin Ick Liebe Dir (www.berlin-ick-liebe-dir.de).

Berlin Food Stories (www.berlinfoodstories.com) Excellent up-to-the-minute site by a passionate food lover who keeps tabs on new restaurants and visits each one several times before writing honest, mouth-watering reviews. Also runs food tours – see the website for dates.

Stil in Berlin (www.stilinberlin.de) One of the longest-running city blogs (since 2006), Mary Sherpe's 'baby' keeps track of developments in food, fashion, style and art.

Eatler (www.eatler.de) Irreverent and opinionated blog on restaurant openings and closings and emerging trends.

CeeCee (www.ceecee.cc) Stylish blog on what's hot and what's not across Berlin's culinary and cultural spectrum.

Berlin Loves You (www.berlinlovesyou.com) Tips on where to eat, the best chefs, restaurants and food trucks in town, and everything else about the food scene in Berlin.

Eating by Neighbourhood

Local Specialities

From ceviche to pad thai, you'll find specialities from all over the world in Berlin, but what exactly is 'typical' local fare? Here's a short primer.

Pfannkuchen Known as 'Berliner' in other parts of Germany, these doughnut-like pastries are made from a yeasty dough, stuffed with a dollop of jam, deep fried and tossed in granulated sugar.

Currywurst This classic cult snack, allegedly invented in Berlin in 1949, is a smallish fried or grilled *Wiener* (sausage) sliced into bite-sized ringlets, swimming in a spicy tomato sauce and dusted with curry powder. It's available *'mit'* or *'ohne'* (with or without) its crunchy epidermis and traditionally served on a flimsy plate with a plastic toothpick for stabbing.

Döner Spit-roasted meat may have been around forever, but the idea of serving it in a lightly toasted bread pocket with copious amounts of fresh salad and a healthy drizzle of yogurt-based *Kräuter* (herb), *scharf* (spicy) or *Knoblauch* (garlic) sauce was allegedly invented by a Turkish immigrant in 1970s West Berlin.

Boulette Called *Frikadelle* in other parts of Germany, this cross between a meatball and a hamburger is eaten with a little mustard and an optional dry roll. The name is French for 'little ball' and might have originated during Napoleon's occupation of Berlin in the early 19th century.

Eisbein or Grillhaxe Boiled or grilled pork hock typically paired with sauerkraut and boiled potatoes.

Königsberger Klopse This classic dish may have its origin in Königsberg in eastern Prussia (today's Kaliningrad in Russia), but it has of late made a huge comeback on Berlin menus. It's a simple but elegant plate of golf-ball-sized veal meatballs in a caper-laced white sauce served with a side of boiled potatoes and beetroot.

Lonely Planet's Top Choices

Restaurant Tim Raue (p102) Berlin's top toque is famous for his mash-up of Asian and Western flavours.

Coda (p199) Two Michelin stars for this pioneer of the fine-dining dessert journey with matching drinks.

Ora (p188) Regional-seasonal fare against the stylishly quaint backdrop of a 19th-century pharmacy.

Frea (p133) Zero-waste vegan pioneer in a Scandi-chic setting has hip foodies in a headlock.

Umami (p149) Sharp Indochine nosh for fans of the classics and the innovative amid sensuous lounge decor.

Best By Budget

€

Sironi (p187) Some of the best sourdough ciabatta you'll ever have.

Kantini Berlin (p221) Eat your way around the world at this next-gen food court in the Bikini concept mall.

W-Der Imbiss (p149) Perfect yin and yang of Italian-Indian cooking amid tiki decor.

Burgermeister (p187) Succulent two-handful burgers and fries doused in homemade sauces in a former public latrine.

Street Food Thursday (p186) Global treats at a weekly street-food fair in a 19th-century market hall.

€€

Bonvivant (p175) Creator of the ground-breaking 'vegetarian cocktail bistro' concept.

Barra (p198) A purveyor of unfussy but impeccably crafted comfort food and low-intervention wines.

Ngon (p124) Dip into a pool of pleasurable, authentic and artfully presented Vietnamese dishes in this romantically lit restaurant.

Katz Orange (p134) This stylish 'cat' fancies anything that's regional, seasonal and creative amid chic country decor.

BRLO Brwhouse (p175) Super-creative, flawless craft beer and food pairings in shipping containers with beer garden.

Orania.Restaurant (p188) Culinary magic from three ingredients per plate, plus the signature Xberg Duck.

€€€

Tulus Lotrek (p186) Michelin-standard restaurant serving intensely flavoured fare paired with feel-good flair.

Mine Restaurant (p222) 'Russian Jamie Oliver' jazzes up Berlin's upscale Italian dining scene.

Rutz (p134) Feast like royalty (minus the glitz) at the city's first restaurant to snag three Michelin stars.

Mrs Robinson's (p148) Casual fine dining in a stylishly stripped-down space.

Kin Dee (p176) Elevated and Michelin-decorated Thai fare updated for the 21st century.

Best Middle Eastern

Malakeh (p173) Feistily flavoured Syrian soul food in a cosy lair with living-room flair inspired by the owner's Damascus roots.

Layla (p168) Israeli star chef Meir Adoni's Berlin outpost infuses Middle Eastern dishes with global pizzazz.

Mama Shabz (p186) Neighbourhood charmer serves authentic Pakistani home cooking, pakoras to curries.

Damaskus Konditorei (p198) Bites from this baklava king guarantee a (so-worth-it) sugar rush.

Fes Turkish BBQ (p188) Grill your own meat and veg at this Turkish spin on Korean barbecue.

Café Mugrabi (p186) Simple cafe with top-notch Israeli cuisine inspired by the owner's mom and grandma.

Best Vegan & Vegetarian

Cookies Cream (p102) Clandestine meat-free Michelin kitchen tiptoes between hip and haute.

Kopps (p132) Vegan fine-dining trailblazer has served up healthy, creative and gorgeous dishes since 2011.

Con Tho (p186) At this hip plant-based Vietnamese restaurant trad recipes get a modern riff.

Lucky Leek (p149) Casual fine-dining outpost serving ambitious dishes prone to set off umami fireworks in your mouth.

1990 Vegan Living (p207) Sample the bounty of Vietnamese meatless fare one small plate at a time.

Riverside drinks by the Spree

Bar Open

As one of Europe's primo party playgrounds, Berlin offers a thousand and one scenarios for getting your cocktails and kicks (or wine or beer, for that matter). From cocktail lairs and concept bars, craft-beer pubs to rooftop lounges, the next thirst parlour is usually within stumbling distance.

ssiopeia (p210)

Drinking

Berlin is a notoriously late city: bars stay packed from dusk to dawn, and some clubs don't hit their stride until 4am and stay open nonstop until Monday morning. The lack of a curfew means a tradition of binge drinking was never created, which is why many party folk prefer to pace their alcohol consumption and thus manage to keep going until the wee hours. Of course illegal drugs may also play their part...

Edgier, more underground venues cluster in Kreuzberg, Friedrichshain, Neukölln and, to some extent, parts of Lichtenberg (east of Friedrichshain). Places in Charlottenburg, Mitte and Prenzlauer Berg tend to be more sedate, close earlier and are more suited for date nights than dedicated drinking. Generally, the emphasis here is on style and atmosphere, and some proprietors have gone to extraordinary lengths to come up with creative design concepts.

The line between cafe and bar is often blurred, with many changing stripes as the hands move around the clock. Alcohol, however, is served (and consumed) pretty much all day.

Some bars have happy hours that usually run from 6pm to 9pm, but overall the happy-hour concept isn't as prevalent in Berlin as in other cities. This is partly because drink prices (especially for beer) are still comparatively low. Still, they are creeping up here as well, partly fuelled by a growing demand for quality over quantity, especially when it comes to cocktails, craft beer and wine.

NEED TO KNOW

Opening Hours

- Pubs are open from around noon to midnight or 1am (later on weekends).
- Trendy places and cocktail bars open around 8pm or 9pm until the last tippler leaves.
- Clubs open at 11pm or midnight and start filling up around 1am or 2am.

Costs

Big clubs will set you back €15 or €20, but there are plenty of others that charge between €5 and €12. Places that open a bit earlier don't charge admission until a certain hour, usually 11pm or midnight. Student discounts are virtually unheard of, as are 'Ladies Nights'.

Dress Code

Berlin's clubs are very relaxed. In general, individual style almost always trumps high heels and Armani. Cocktail bars and some disco-style clubs may prefer a more polished look, but in pubs anything goes.

Etiquette

Table service is common, and you shouldn't order at the bar unless you intend to hang out there or there's a sign saying *Selbstbedienung* (self-service). In traditional German pubs, it's customary to keep a tab instead of paying for each round separately. In bars with DJs €1 or €2 is sometimes added to the cost of your first drink. Tip bartenders about 5%, servers 10%. Drinking in public is legal and widely practised, especially around party zones. Try to be civilised about it, though. No puking on the U-Bahn, please!

On the flip side, some of Berlin's late-night convenience stores (called *Spätkauf* or *Späti* for short) cater to the cash-strapped by putting out tables on the sidewalks for patrons to gather and consume their store-bought beverages.

BEER

Predictably, beer is big in Berlin and served almost everywhere all day long. Most places pour a variety of local, national and imported brews, including at least one draught

Drinking & Nightlife by Neighbourhood

beer *(vom Fass)* served in 300mL or 500mL glasses. In summer, drinking your lager as an Alster, Radler or Diesel (mixed with Sprite, Fanta or Coke, respectively) is a popular thirst quencher.

Other German and imported beers are widely available. There's plenty of Beck's and Heineken around, but for more flavour look for Jever Pilsener from northern Germany, Rothaus Tannenzäpfle from the Black Forest, Zywiec from Poland, and Krušovice and Budweiser from the Czech Republic. American Budweiser is practically nonexistent here.

CLASSIC GERMAN BEERS

The most common classic German brews include the following:

Pils (pilsner) Bottom-fermented beer with a pronounced hop flavour and a creamy head.

Weizenbier/Weissbier (wheat beer) Top-fermented wheat beer that's fruity and refreshing. Comes bottled either as *Hefeweizen,* which has a stronger shot of yeast, or the filtered and fizzier *Kristallweizen*.

Berliner Weisse This cloudy, slightly sour wheat beer is typically sweetened with a *Schuss* (shot) of woodruff or raspberry syrup. It's quite refreshing on a hot day, but few locals drink it.

Schwarzbier (black beer, like porter) This full-bodied dark beer is fermented using roasted malt.

Bockbier Strong beer with around 7% alcohol; brewed seasonally. Maibock shows up in May, Weihnachtsbock around Christmas.

CRAFT BEER

Thanks to Germany's famous Reinheitsgebot (Beer Purity Law), which celebrated its 500th anniversary in 2016, the quality of beer has always been high here, which is one of the reasons it took such a long time for the craft-beer craze to reach the country. In recent years, though, it has arrived with a vengeance, leading to a virtual explosion of breweries specialising in handmade suds.

In Berlin, local pioneers such as Heidenpeters, Vagabund, Schoppe Bräu, Eschenbräu and Hops & Barley have been joined by dozens more small breweries. International brands like BrewDog and Mikkeler have also opened their own taprooms in the capital.

To tap deeper into the scene, join an English-language craft-beer tour offered by such outfits as Berlin Craft Beer Experience (p213), Original Berlin Walks (p300) or Alternative Berlin Tours (p300).

WINE

Oenophiles can rejoice as there is finally a respectable crop of wine bars in Berlin. Run by wine enthusiasts, they have an egalitarian rather than elitist mood and pour with a sense of humour and free-spiritedness devoid of snobbery. Since the quality of wine produced in Germany has markedly improved in recent years, you'll now find more Riesling on wine lists than ever before. Other varietals enjoying huge popularity are sauvignon blanc and Grauburgunder (Pinot gris).

Natural wine – or 'low-intervention wine' as some prefer to say – has also made a big splash in trend-conscious bars and restaurants. The quality of these wines, which are made from organically grown grapes with minimal chemical interference, has markedly improved in recent years.

In regular pubs and bars the quality of wine ranges from drinkable to abysmal. In these places, wine is usually served in 200mL glasses and costs from €4 to €6. In better establishments, finer vintages are served in mere 100mL glasses and usually start at €5.

In summer, many Germans like to mix (cheap) white wine with fizzy water, which is called a *Weinschorle.*

Sparkling wine comes in 100mL flutes. Depending on where a place sees itself on the trendiness scale, it will offer German *Sekt,* Italian Prosecco or French *cremant* or *Champagne.*

In winter, and especially at the Christmas markets, *Glühwein* (mulled wine) is a popular beverage to stave off the chill.

A TASTE OF BERLIN

In recent years a flurry of indie boutique beverage purveyors has cropped up in Berlin. Look for them at kiosks, cool bars, pubs and even supermarkets. Here are some of our favourites:

Berliner Brandstifter Berliner Vincent Honrodt is the man behind the Brandstifter Korn, a premium schnapps that gets extraordinary smoothness from a seven-stage filtering process. The company also makes a mean gin.

Original Berlin Cidre (www.obc-cidre.com) OBC is made from 100% German apples by two Berliners, Urs Breitenstein and Thomas Godel. There are three varieties: the dry OBC Strong, the sweet OBC Classic and the fruity OBC Rose.

Adler Berlin Dry Gin Crafted by the **Preussische Spirituosen Manufaktur** (☎030-8057 0307; www.psmberlin.de; Seestrasse 13; 1hr tour per person €10, 4-person minimum, 2hr tour per person €15, 8-person minimum; ⏰shop 9am-7pm Mon-Fri, tours by arrangement; 🚋50, M13) that once served Kaiser Wilhelm II, this creamy and balanced gin is aromatised with juniper, lavender, coriander, ginger and lemon peel.

Our/Berlin (www.ourvodka.com) Made with Berlin water and German wheat, this smooth vodka is distilled in small batches at Flutgraben 2 on the Kreuzberg–Treptow border and sold in stylish bottles right there and in select shops.

Berliner Luft Peppermint schnapps has gained cult status despite tasting like mouthwash. Consumed as a shot, it's a popular method to get blasted fast.

Wostok This Kreuzberg-made certified organic lemonade comes in six flavours, the most famous of which is the pine-scented Tannenwald, based on an original 1973 Soviet softdrink recipe.

COCKTAILS

Dedicated cocktail bars are booming in Berlin and new arrivals continue to elevate the 'liquid art' scene. Classic drinking dens tend to be elegant cocoons with mellow lighting and low sound levels, but of late buzzier cocktail bars with less stuffy ambience have also thrown themselves into the mix. All are helmed by mix-meisters keen on applying their training to both classics and boundary-pushing riffs.

A good cocktail will set you back between €10 and €15. Most bars and pubs serve long drinks and cocktails, too, but of the Sex on the Beach and Cosmopolitan variety. Prices are lower (between €6 and €10) and quality can be hit or miss due to mediocre mixing talents and/or inferior spirits.

Also making appearances in Berlin are sober bars that serve only alcohol-free beer, wine and non-alcoholic cocktails, aka mocktails. A pioneer was Zeroliq (p209) in Friedrichshain, but the chic Bar am Steinplatz (p224) in the namesake hotel in Charlottenburg is also trying to give the concept wings. The jury is still out on whether these non-booze burrows will take root in hedonistic Berlin.

Note that drinks are no longer served with straws for sustainability reasons. If you do get one, it'll likely be made of reusable or compostable materials.

Velvet Bar (p199)

Clubbing

Since the 1990s, Berlin's club culture has taken on near-mythical status and, to no small degree, contributed to the magnetism of the German capital. It has incubated trends and sounds, launched the careers of such internationally renowned DJs as Paul van Dyk, Ricardo Villalobos, Ellen Allien and Paul Kalkbrenner, and put Berlin firmly on the map of global music fans who turn night into day in over 200 clubs in this curfew-free city.

What distinguishes the Berlin scene from other party capitals is a focus on independent, non-mainstream niche venues, run by owners or collectives with a creative rather than a corporate background. The shared goal is to promote a diverse, inclusive and progressive club culture rather than to maximize profit. This is also reflected in a door policy that strives to create a harmonious balance in terms of age, gender and attitude.

Electronic music in its infinite varieties continues to define Berlin's after-dark action, but other sounds like hip-hop, dancehall, rock, swing and funk have also made inroads. The edgiest clubs have taken up residence in power plants, transformer stations, abandoned apartment buildings and other repurposed locations. Most are in Kreuzberg, Friedrichshain and Lichtenberg.

The scene is in constant flux as experienced club owners look for new challenges and a younger generation of promoters enters the scene with new ideas and impetus. Overall, though, rising rents, development, noise complaints and investors focused on profit maximisation have forced many smaller venues to close, thereby threatening Berlin's cult status as one of Europe's most free-wheeling and biggest party hubs.

WHEN TO GO

Whatever club or party you're heading for, don't bother showing up before 1am unless you want to have a deep conversation with a bored bartender. And don't worry about closing times – Berlin's famously long nights have become even later of late and, thanks to a growing number of after-parties

Above: Club der Visionäre (p189)

Right: Monkey Bar (p224)

AJAN ALEN / SHUTTERSTOCK ©

and daytime clubs, not going home until Monday night is definitely an option at weekends. In fact, savvy clubbers put in a good night's sleep, then hit the dance floor when other people head for Sunday church or afternoon tea.

AT THE DOOR

Doors are notoriously tough at Berlin's best clubs, as door staff strive to sift out people that would feel uncomfortable with the music, the vibe or the libertine ways beyond the door. Except at some disco-type establishments, flaunting fancy labels, high heels and glam cocktail dresses can actually get in the way of your getting in. Wear something black and casual. If your attitude is right, age rarely matters. Be respectful in the queue, don't drink and don't talk too loudly (seriously!). Don't arrive wasted. As elsewhere, large groups (even mixed ones) have a lower chance of getting in, so split up if you can. Stag and hen parties are rarely welcome. If you do get turned away, don't argue. And don't worry, there's always another party somewhere…

Party Miles

FRIEDRICHSHAIN

RAW Gelände and Revaler Strasse The skinny-jeanster set invades the gritty venues along the 'techno strip' sprawling out over a former train repair station. Hopscotch from live concert arenas to techno-electro clubs and off-kilter bars.

Ostkreuz Draw a bead on this party zone with several high-octane clubs located within staggering distance of the Ostkreuz train station.

Simon-Dach-Strasse If you need a cheap buzz, head to this well-trodden booze strip popular with field-tripping school groups and stag parties.

KREUZBERG

Kottbusser Tor and Oranienstrasse Grungetastic area perfect for dedicated drink-a-thons with a punky-trashy flair.

Schlesische Strasse Freestyle strip with a potpourri of party stations from beer gardens to concert venues, techno temples to daytime outdoor chill zones.

Skalitzer Strasse Eclectic drag with small clubs and some quality cocktail bars just off it.

NEUKÖLLN

Weserstrasse and around Neukölln's main party drag is packed with an eclectic mix of pubs and bars, from trashy to stylish.

HACKESCHER MARKT & SCHEUNENVIERTEL

Torstrasse This strip draws a globe-spanning roster of monied creatives to style-conscious drinking dens with their well-thought-out bar concepts and drinks made with top-shelf spirits.

NEW FRONTIER: RUMMELSBURG BAY

Displaced by development, rising rents and noise complaints, a growing number of clubs are trading the central districts for locations in suburbs like Lichtenberg, just southeast of Friedrichshain. An area called Rummelsburger Bucht, along the Spree, has emerged as a new frontier, especially for open-air clubs such as **Sisyphos** (☎030-9836 6839; www.sisyphos-berlin.net; Hauptstrasse 15; ⏱hours vary, usually midnight Fri-Sun May-Sep; 🚋21, Ⓢ Ostkreuz). Festival and club-night host **Funkhaus** (☎030-1208 5416; www.funkhaus-berlin.net; Nalepastrasse 18; tours €15; ⏱hours vary; 🚋21) is also nearby. The area is served by tram 21 from Ostkreuz.

Lonely Planet's Top Choices

Velvet Bar (p199) Stylish cocktail laboratory with seasonally influenced concoctions.

Klunkerkranich (p199) Hipster spot with urban garden and great sunset views atop Neukölln shopping centre.

Schleusenkrug (p224) Rambling self-service beer garden by the canal, within sniffing distance of the zoo.

Zeroliq (p209) Sober bar where you can get your kicks with mocktails and alcohol-free beer and wine.

Ankerklause (p200) Been-there-forever beer and breakfast station with views of the swans on Landwehrkanal.

Best Craft-Beer Pubs

Hopfenreich (p189) Berlin's first craft-beer bar has tastings, tap takeovers and guest brewers.

BrewDog (p152) Trendy Mitte flagship with 30 taps dispensing its own and guest draughts.

Vagabund Brauerei (p145) Craft-beer pioneers with a taproom in Wedding.

Hops & Barley (p209) Fabulous unfiltered pilsner, dark and wheat beer poured in a former butcher's shop.

Heidenpeters (p193) Tiny taproom brewed in the cellar of the Markthalle Neun.

Best Cocktail Bars

Buck & Breck (p136) Expertly prepared riffs on classics for grown-ups in a speakeasy-style setting.

Truffle Pig (p199) Follow the pig tracks through a corner pub to this clandestine drinking den.

Würgeengel (p190) Fun crowd keeps the cocktails and conversation flowing in a '50s setting.

Becketts Kopf (p152) Sip on supreme classics and spontaneous inspirations.

Limonadier (p188) Expert classic and Berlin-inspired cocktails in a 1920s-style setting.

Lamm Bar (p151) Unpretentious neighbourhood haunt with industrial interior and big terrace.

Best Wine Bars

Briefmarken Weine (p209) Oenophile den for grown-up Italian wine fanciers.

Otto Rink (p190) For relaxed but demanding wine fans with a penchant for German 7.

Weinerei Forum (p151) Living-room flair with help-yourself and pay-what-you-like honour policy.

Best Rooftop Bars

Klunkerkranich (p199) Hipster spot with urban garden and great sunset views atop Neukölln shopping centre.

Monkey Bar (p224) Trendy West Berlin lair with exotic tiki drinks and a view of the baboons at the Berlin Zoo.

Amano Bar (p134) Bird's-eye views of the Scheunenviertel at the sleek summer edition of the fashionable Amano hotel bar.

Rooftop Terrace (p103) Swish hangout at the Hotel de Rome with full-on view of Berlin's historic centre.

Park Inn Panorama Terrasse (p119) Enjoy a cocktail view with the TV Tower as a backdrop from this bar atop Berlin's highest hotel.

Best Cafes

Kuchenladen (p222) Some of the most tantalising cakes in town in an old-school German coffeehouse setting.

Silo Coffee (p207) Buzzy hipster joint with third-wave coffee and avo toast.

Albatross (p187) Sinful sourdough bread and delectable pastries in this bakery with attached cafe.

Father Carpenter (p136) Top-notch coffee in a hidden courtyard near Hackesche Höfe.

Tadshikische Teestube (p131) Russian tea and food in an original Tajik tearoom gifted to the East Berlin government in the '70s.

Anna Blume (p153) Convivial cafe with a scrumptious cake selection in an art nouveau–inspired setting.

Cafe-Restaurant Wintergarten im Literaturhaus (p222) Take a break from sightseeing over coffee and cake in this sophisticated garden cafe.

Best Late-Nighters

Roses (p191) This 'Queen of Camp' is the ultimate on Kreuzberg's roster of eccentric trash dive bars.

August Fengler (p153) When the party shuts down in Prenzlauer Berg, Fengler keeps going…and going…

Kumpelnest 3000 (p176) Kitschy dive bar in a former brothel; not for the faint of heart.

Best Clubs

Sisyphos (p66) Summer-only party village in retired dog-food factory.

Ritter Butzke (p189) Low-key but high-calibre electro club in ex-factory keeps it real with mostly local DJs and a crowd that appreciates them.

Club der Visionäre (p189) Outdoor spot with willows on an idyllic canal popular for day-to-night partying.

ELEN MARLEN / SHUTTERSTOCK ©

Christopher Street Day (p70)

LGBTIQ+ Berlin

Berlin's legendary liberalism has spawned one of the world's biggest, most divine and diverse LGBTIQ+ playgrounds. Anything goes in 'Homopolis' (and we do mean anything!), from the highbrow to the hands-on, the bourgeois to the bizarre, the mainstream to the flamboyant.

Gay in Berlin

Generally speaking, Berlin's gayscape runs the entire spectrum from mellow cafes, campy bars and cinemas to saunas, cruising areas, clubs with darkrooms and all-out sex venues. In fact, sex and sexuality are entirely everyday matters to the unshockable city folks and there are very few, if any, itches that can't be quite openly and legally scratched. As elsewhere, gay men have more options for having fun, but women, trans and other genders don't have to feel left out.

History

Berlin's emergence as a gay capital has roots in 1897 when sexual scientist Magnus Hirschfeld founded the Scientific Humanitarian Committee, the world's first homosexual advocacy group. Gay life thrived in the wild and wacky 1920s, driven by a demi-monde that drew and inspired writers like Christopher Isherwood, until the Nazis put an end to the fun in 1933. Postwar recovery came slowly, but by the 1970s the scene was firmly re-established, at least in the western city. From 2001 to 2014, Berlin was governed by a gay mayor, Klaus Wowereit. To learn more about Berlin's LGBTIQ+ history, visit the Schwules Museum (p172).

Parties & Clubbing

Berlin's scene is especially fickle and venues and dates may change at any time, so make sure you always check the websites or the listings magazines for the latest scoop. One important alternative queer party space is Südblock (www.suedblock.org) at Kottbusser Tor in Kreuzberg, which is famous for its inclusive programming and diverse clientele.

Note that most of the parties listed below are on hiatus because of the coronavirus pandemic. Some organisers have found ways to keep going while meeting social-distancing requirements, eg by moving the party outdoors. Check the parties' websites for news.

There are also lots of regular parties held in various locations; a selection follows. Unless noted, all are geared towards men.

B:East Party (https://beastparty.berlin) Monthly party for gays and friends with techno, house and disco. Check website for dates and location.

Cafe Fatal All comers descend on SO36 (p189) for the ultimate rainbow tea dance, which goes from 'strictly ballroom' to 'dirty dancing' in a flash. If you can't tell a waltz from a foxtrot, come at 7pm for free lessons. Sundays.

Chantals House of Shame (www.facebook.com/ChantalsHouseofShame) Trash diva Chantal's louche parties have been a beloved institution for over 20 years, not so much for the glam factor as for the over-the-top drag shows and the hotties who love 'em. Thursdays.

CockTail d'Amore (www.facebook.com/cocktail-damoreberlin) Alt-flavoured electro party with indoor and outdoor dancing and partying. First Saturday of the month.

Gayhane Geared towards gay and lesbian Muslims, but everyone's welcome to rock the kasbah when this 'homoriental' party takes over SO36 with Middle Eastern beats and belly dancing. Last Saturday of the month.

Gegen (www.gegenberlin.com) Queer techno party with leftist political undercurrents and wacky art performances. First Friday, alternate months.

Girls Town (www.girlstown-berlin.de) Suse and Zoe's buzzy girl-fest takes over **Gretchen** (Map

NEED TO KNOW

Websites

Gay Berlin4u (www.gayberlin4u.com) Covers all aspects of Berlin's gay scene, in English.

GayCities Berlin (https://berlin.gaycities.com) Offers a basic overview of the scene, in English.

Patroc Gay Guide (www.patroc.de/berlin) Focuses on events but also has some info on venues; in German.

Magazines

Blu (www.maenner.media/regional/blu) Freebie print magazine and e-paper with gay-themed articles and event listings.

L-Mag (www.l-mag.de) Free bimonthly magazine for lesbians in print and online.

Siegessäule (www.siegessaeule.de) Quintessential free weekly Berlin LGBTIQ+ mag distributed online and in print.

Tours

Queer Berlin (p300) Long-running tour company Original Berlin Walks taps into the city's LGBTIQ+ legacy on tours through Kreuzberg and Schöneberg.

Berlinagenten (p301) Customised gay-oriented tours (nightlife, shopping, luxury, history, culinary).

Lügentour (www.luegentour.de) An interactive and humorous walking tour takes you back to the lesbigay scene in 1920s Schöneberg; alas, in German only.

Schröder Reisen Comedy Bus (www.comedy-im-bus.de) Outrageous comedy bus tours led by trash drag royalty Edith Schröder (aka Ades Zabel) and friends.

Help

Mann-O-Meter (☎030-216 8008; www.mann-o-meter.de; Bülowstrasse 106; ⏰5-10pm Mon-Fri, 4-8pm Sat) Gay men's info centre.

Maneo (☎030-216 3336; www.maneo.de; ⏰assault line 5-7pm) Gay victim support centre and gay-attack hotline.

Lesbenberatung (☎030-215 2000; www.lesbenberatung-berlin.de; Kulmer Strasse 20a; ⏰2-5pm Mon & Wed, 10am-4pm Tue, 3-6pm Thu) Lesbian resource centre.

p340; ☎030-2592 2702; www.gretchen-club.de; Obentrautstrasse 19-21; UMehringdamm, Hallesches Tor) in Kreuzberg with down-and-dirty pop, electro, indie and rock. Second Saturday, alternate months, September to May.

GMF (www.gmf-berlin.de) Berlin's premier techno-house Sunday club, last taking place at Ritter Butzke (p189), is known for excessive SM (standing and modelling) with lots of smooth surfaces. Predominantly boyz, but everyone is welcome.

Horse Meat Disco (www.horsemeatdiscoberlin) This classic import from the UK does a bi-monthly shout-out to a dance-crazy queer crowd of all stripes. The music defines eclectic and ranges from disco to house, Afro to funk and punk.

Irrenhouse The name means 'insane asylum', and that's no joke. Party hostess with the mostest trash queen Nina Queer puts on this nutty, naughty monthly event that is not for the faint of heart. Expect the best. Fear the worst. Look up Irrenhouse Berlin on Facebook.

L-Tunes (www.l-tunes.com) Lesbians get their groove on every month in the dancing pits of various locations around town.

Members (www.members-berlin.de) Monthly tech-house party has been running strong since 2013 and often features local DJ royalty like Ellen Allien or Monika Kruse.

Revolver (www.facebook.com/RevolverParty-Global) This London export hosted by Oliver and Gary is a sizzling and sexy party with no special dress code required. Second Friday of the month.

Festivals & Events

Easter Berlin (www.easterberlin.de; various locations; ⌚Mar/Apr) One of Europe's biggest fetish fests whips the leather, rubber, skin and military sets out of the dungeons and into the clubs over the long Easter weekend. It culminates with the crowning of the 'German Mr Leather'.

Lesbisch-Schwules Stadtfest (Lesbigay Street Festival; www.stadtfest.berlin; ⌚Jul; UNollendorfplatz) The Lesbigay City Festival takes over the Schöneberg rainbow village in June, with bands, food, info booths and partying.

Christopher Street Day (www.csd-berlin.de; various locations; ⌚Jul) Later in June, hundreds of thousands of people of various sexual persuasions paint the town pink with a huge semi-political parade and more queens than a royal wedding.

Lesbischwules Parkfest (www.parkfest-friedrichshain.de; Volkspark Friedrichshain; ⌚Aug; 🚌200) The LGBTIQ+ community takes over the Volkspark Friedrichshain for this delightfully noncommercial festival in August.

Folsom Europe (www.folsomeurope.info; ⌚Sep; UNollendorfplatz) The leather crowd returns in early September for another weekend of kinky partying.

Hustlaball (www.hustlaball.de; ⌚Oct) The party year wraps up in October with a weekend of debauched fun in the company of porn stars, go-gos, trash queens, stripping hunks and about 3000 other men who love 'em.

LGBTIQ+ Berlin by Neighbourhood

➡ **Hackescher Markt & Scheunenviertel** Gets a mixed crowd, but its trendy bars and cafes (especially near Hackescher Markt and on Torstrasse) also draw a sizeable contingent of queer customers. (p134)

➡ **Prenzlauer Berg** East Berlin's pink hub before the fall of the Wall has a few surviving bar relics as well as a couple of popular cruising dens and fun stops for the fetish set (eg Stahlrohr). (p151)

➡ **Schöneberg** The area around Nollendorfplatz (Motzstrasse and Fuggerstrasse especially) has been a gay beacon since the 1920s. Institutions like Heile Welt, Tom's and Hafen pull in the punters night after night, and there's also plenty of nocturnal action for the leather and fetish set. (p176)

➡ **Kreuzberg** Hipster central. Things are comparatively subdued in the bars and cafes along main-strip Mehringdamm. Around Kottbusser Tor and along Oranienstrasse the crowd skews younger, wilder and more alternative, and key venues stay open till sunrise and beyond. (p188)

➡ **Neukölln** For a DIY subcultural vibe, head across the canal to Neukölln. (p199)

➡ **Friedrichshain** This area is strangely thin on LGBTIQ+ bars but is still a de rigueur stop on the gay nightlife circuit when the big clubs are open. (p209)

Lonely Planet's Top Choices

GMF (p70) Glamtastic Sunday party with pretty people in stylish and central location.

Roses (p191) Plush, pink, campy madhouse – an essential late-night stop on a dedicated bar hop.

Möbel Olfe (p190) Old furniture shop recast as busy drinking den; standing room only on (unofficial) gay Thursdays.

Heile Welt (p177) Stylish lounge good for chatting and mingling over cocktails.

Best Venues by Day of the Week

Monday

Monster Ronson's Ichiban Karaoke (p209) Loosen those lungs and get louche.

Tom's Bar (p177) Two-for-one drinks.

Kino International (p211) Queer movies during 'Mongay'.

Tuesday

Rauschgold (p189) 'Time Tunnel' retro party.

Möbel Olfe (p190) Comfortably cheerful femme fave.

Wednesday

Himmelreich (p210) Two-for-one drinks.

Thursday

Möbel Olfe (p190) Ma(i)nly men get-together.

Sunday

GMF (p70) Hot-stepping weekend wrap-up.

Cafe Fatal @ SO36 (p189) All-ages tea dance.

Best Gay Bars

Möbel Olfe (p190) Relaxed Kreuzberg joint goes into gay turbodrive on Thursdays; women dominate on Tuesdays.

Himmelreich (p210) This '50s retro lounge is a lesbigay-scene stalwart in Friedrichshain.

Roses (p191) Over-the-top late-night dive with camp factor and strong drinks.

Coven (p136) Stylish Mitte bar with industrial decor and strong drinks.

Sally Bowles (p176) Comfortable and convivial neighbourhood bar with 1920s vibe.

Best Lesbian Bars & Parties

Himmelreich (p210) Women's Lounge on Tuesday brings cool chicks to this comfy Friedrichshain bar.

Möbel Olfe (p190) Pop, disco and rock music get lesbians and their friends into party mood on Tuesday.

L-Tunes (p70) Flirting, dancing and making out at locations around town.

Best for Camp

Rauschgold (p189) Small glitter-glam bar for all-night fun with pop, karaoke and drag shows.

Roses (p191) This pink-fur-walled kitsch institution is an unmissable late-night fuelling stop.

Zum Schmutzigen Hobby (p210) Fabulously wacky party pen in a former fire station.

Konzerthaus Berlin (p103)

Showtime

Berlin's cultural scene is lively, edgy and the richest and most varied of all German-speaking countries. With three state-supported opera houses, five major orchestras – including the world-class Berliner Philharmoniker – scores of theatres, cinemas, cabarets and concert venues, Berlin is replete with entertainment options.

Classical Music

Classical-music fans are truly spoilt in Berlin. Not only is there a phenomenal range of concerts throughout the year, but most of the major concert halls are architectural and acoustic gems of the highest order. Trips to the Philharmonie or the Konzerthaus are a particular treat, and regular concerts are also organised in churches like the Berliner Dom and palaces such as Schloss Charlottenburg.

Top of the pops is, of course, the world-famous Berliner Philharmoniker (p169), which was founded in 1882 and counts Wilhelm Furtwängler, Herbert von Karajan and Simon Rattle among its music directors. Since 2019, Russia-born Kirill Petrenko has continued the tradition.

Berlin's many other orchestras are certainly no musical slouches either. Treat your ears to concerts by the Berliner Symphoniker, the Deutsches Symphonie-Orchester, the Konzerthausorchester and the Rundfunk-Sinfonieorchester Berlin. The city's oldest 'band' is the Berliner Staatskapelle, which was founded in 1570 and later promoted to royal court orchestra by Frederick the Great. Note that most orchestras take a summer hiatus (usually July and August).

Berlin also has two music academies: the prestigious Hochschule für Musik Hanns Eisler (www.hfm-berlin.de) and the new

Barenboim-Said Academy (https://barenboimsaid.de), which supports mainly musicians from North Africa and the Middle East. Students often perform free or low-cost concerts in various venues, including the Pierre Boulez Saal (p103) in Mitte.

Opera

Not many cities afford themselves the luxury of three state-funded opera houses, but then opera has been popular in Berlin ever since the first diva loosened her lungs. Today fans can catch some of Germany's biggest and best performances here. Leading the pack in the prestige department is the Staatsoper Unter den Linden (p96), the oldest among the three, founded by Frederick the Great in 1743. The hallowed hall hosted many world premieres, including Carl Maria von Weber's *Der Freischütz* and Alban Berg's *Wozzeck*. Giacomo Meyerbeer, Richard Strauss and Herbert von Karajan were among its music directors. Since the early 1990s, Daniel Barenboim has swung the baton.

The Komische Oper (p103) opened in 1947 with *Die Fledermaus* by Johann Strauss II and still champions light opera, operettas and dance theatre. Across town in Charlottenburg, the Deutsche Oper Berlin (p226) entered the scene in 1912 with Beethoven's *Fidelio*. It was founded by local citizens keen on creating a counterpoint to the royal Staatsoper.

Live Rock, Pop, Jazz & Blues

Berlin's live-music scene is as diverse as the city itself. There's no Berlin sound as such, but many simultaneous trends, from punk rock to hardcore rap and hip-hop, reggae to sugary pop and downtempo jazz. Music clubs cluster in Kreuzberg, especially around the Schlesisches Tor U-Bahn station, and across the river in Friedrichshain, where the Astra Kulturhaus is a major venue. Some venues segue smoothly from concert to party on some nights. Scores of pubs and bars also host concerts. Jazz fans can look forward to a new Centre for Jazz and Improvised Music to take shape in the Alte Münze (Old Mint) building in Mitte, a project spearheaded by German jazz trumpeter Till Brönner.

International top artists perform at various venues around town, including the following:

NEED TO KNOW

Ticket Bookings

- Early bookings are always advisable and are essential in the case of the Berliner Philharmoniker, the Staatsoper and big-name concerts.
- Most venues now let you book tickets online for free or for a small surcharge using a credit card. You can then print out your ticket or use your smartphone to display a mobile version.

Ticket Agencies

Eventim (www.eventim.de) Mainstream online agency.

Hekticket (www.hekticket.de) Sells half-price tickets for same-day performances between 2pm and 7pm, by phone and online.

Koka 36 (www.koka36.de) Indie ticket agency sells tickets online, by phone and in person.

Theaterkasse Ticket outlets commonly found in shopping malls charge hefty fees.

Discount Tickets

- Some theatres sell unsold tickets at a discount 30 minutes or an hour before shows commence. Some restrict this to students.
- It's fine to buy spare tickets from other theatregoers, but show them to the box-office clerk to make sure they're genuine before forking over any cash.
- The ClassicCard (www.classiccard.de) offers savings for classical-music aficionados under 30.

Resources

Tip (www.tip-berlin.de) Biweekly listings magazine online and in print (in German).

Ex-Berliner (www.ex-berliner.de) Expat-oriented English-language monthly, online and in print.

Gratis in Berlin (www.gratis-in-berlin.de) Online free event listings (in German).

Berlin Bühnen (www.berlin-buehnen.de) Browse by genre (theatre, opera, dance, etc).

Columbiahalle (Map p340; http://columbiahalle.berlin; Columbiadamm 13-21; U Platz der Luftbrücke) Originally a gym for members of the US air force, this hall now packs in up to 3500 people for rock and pop concerts.

Parkbühne Wuhlheide (www.wuhlheide.de; Strasse zum FEZ 4 / An der Wuhlheide; ⌚May-Sep; S Wuhlheide) This 17,000-seat outdoor stage in the shape of an amphitheatre was built in the early 1950s and is a popular venue for German pop and rock concerts.

Mercedez-Benz Arena (p211) Berlin's professional ice hockey and basketball teams play their home games at this state-of-the-art Friedrichshain arena that's also the preferred venue of international entertainment stars.

Olympiastadion (p225) With a seating capacity of nearly 75,000, the storied Olympic Stadium has hosted top music acts, the premier-league soccer team Hertha BSC and even the Pope.

Tempodrom (p169) This midsize hall in an eye-catching tent-shaped building has great acoustics and eclectic programming from concerts to snooker championships.

Waldbühne Berlin (☎tickets 01806 570 070; www.waldbuehne-berlin.de; Glockenturmstrasse 1; ⌚May-Sep; S Pichelsberg) Built for the 1936 Olympics, this 22,000-seat open-air amphitheatre in the woods is a magical place for summer concerts.

Film

In other parts of the world, small indie cinemas and art-houses may be a dying breed thanks to the rise in streaming services, but not so in Berlin. Of course, there are plenty of stadium-style megaplexes with the latest sound and technology. Many locals, however, are actually fiercely loyal to their neighbourhood theatres and often fight to keep them alive and out of the clutches of developers. Many venues now double as cafes or bars, thereby not only supplementing their revenue but also giving patrons a handy spot for post-screening philosophising.

Mainstream Hollywood movies are dubbed into German, but numerous theatres also show flicks in their original language, denoted in listings by the acronym 'OF' *(Originalfassung)* or 'OV' *(Originalversion)*; those with German subtitles are marked 'OmU' *(Original mit Untertiteln).*

Food and drink may be taken inside the auditoriums, although you are of course expected to purchase your beer and popcorn at the theatre. Almost all cinemas also add a sneaky *Überlängezuschlag* (overrun supplement) of €0.50 to €1.50 for films longer than 90 minutes. There's also a surcharge for 3D movies plus a rental fee if you don't have your own 3D glasses. Seeing a flick on a *Kinotag* (film day, usually Monday or Tuesday) can save you a couple of euros.

Theatre

With more than 100 stages around town, theatre is a mainstay of Berlin's cultural scene. Add in a particularly active collection of roaming companies and experimental outfits and you'll find there are more than enough offerings to satisfy all possible tastes. Kurfürstendamm in Charlottenburg and the area around Friedrichstrasse in Mitte (the 'East End') are Berlin's main drama drags, but there are off-stages scattered through all Berlin districts.

OUTDOOR CINEMAS

From May to September, alfresco screenings are a popular tradition, with classic and contemporary flicks spooling off in *Freiluftkinos* (open-air cinemas). Come early to stake out a good spot and bring pillows, blankets and snacks. Films are usually screened in their original language with German subtitles, or in German with English subtitles.

Here's a shortlist of our favourite summertime movie haunts:

Freiluftkino Insel im Cassiopeia (p211) Indie movies next to a beer garden and bunker-turned-climbing wall on the RAW Gelände in Friedrichshain.

Freiluftkino Friedrichshain (p211) Vast amphitheatre-style venue at Volkspark Friedrichshain with drink-and-snack kiosk.

Freiluftkino Kreuzberg (p192) Presents movies in the original language in the courtyard of Kunstquartier Bethanien arts centre.

Open-air Kino Central (p137) Tiny space tucked into the final courtyard of nonprofit arts centre Haus Schwarzenberg in the Scheunenviertel.

Most plays are performed in German, naturally, but several of the major stages – including Schaubühne (p224), Deutsches Theater (p104) and Gorki (p104) – use English surtitles in some of their productions. There's also the English Theatre Berlin (p189), which has some pretty innovative productions often dealing with such socio-political themes as racism, identity and expat-related issues.

Many theatres are closed on Monday and from mid-July to late August.

The **Berliner Theatertreffen** (Berlin Theatre Meeting; www.theatertreffen-berlin.de), in May, is a three-week-long celebration of new plays and productions that brings together top ensembles from Germany, Austria and Switzerland.

Live Comedy

Stand-up comedy isn't much of a tradition here. In Berlin, though, belly laughs have become a staple on the entertainment circuit thanks in large part to the city's vast expat community. People from all over the world fuel a lively English-language comedy scene with everything from stand-up to sketch and musical comedy being performed around town, but especially in the main expat-burg of Neukölln. An excellent source for locations and upcoming events is www.comedyinenglish.de.

Cabaret

The light, lively and lavish variety shows of the Golden Twenties have been undergoing a revival in Berlin. Get ready for an evening of dancers and singers, jugglers, acrobats and other entertainers. A popular venue is the Bar Jeder Vernunft (p224) and its larger sister Tipi am Kanzleramt (p104) whose occasional reprise of the musical *Cabaret* plays to sell-out audiences. In the heart of the 'East End' theatre district, Friedrichstadt-Palast (p138) is Europe's largest revue theatre and the realm of leggy dancers and Vegas-worthy technology. The nearby Chamäleon (p138) is considerably more intimate. Travelling shows camp out at the lovely Wintergarten Varieté (p177) in Schöneberg.

These 'cabarets' should not be confused with *Kabarett*, which are political and satirical shows with monologues and skits.

Dance

With independent choreographers and youthful companies consistently promoting experimental choreography, Berlin's independent dance scene is thriving as never before. The biggest name in choreography is Sasha Waltz, whose company Sasha Waltz & Guests has a residency at the cutting-edge Radialsystem V (p210). Other indie venues include the **Sophiensaele** (Map p330; 030-283 5266; www.sophiensaele.com; Sophienstrasse 18; most tickets €10-15; M1, S Hackescher Markt, U Weinmeisterstrasse), **Dock 11** (Map p334; 030-448 1222; www.dock11-berlin.de; Kastanienallee 79; M1, U Eberswalder Strasse) and Hebbel am Ufer (p191). The last of these, in cooperation with Tanzwerkstatt Berlin, organises **Tanz im August** (www.tanzimaugust.de), Germany's largest contemporary dance festival, which attracts loose-limbed talent and highly experimental choreography from around the globe.

In the mainstream, the Staatsballett Berlin (Berlin State Ballet) performs both at the Staatsoper and at the Deutsche Oper Berlin.

Entertainment by Neighbourhood

- **Historic Mitte** Tops for classical music and opera. (p103)
- **Hackescher Markt & Scheunenviertel** Cabaret, comedy, cinema, theatre. (p137)
- **Prenzlauer Berg** Live music, comedy. (p153)
- **Potsdamer Platz & Tiergarten** Art-house cinema, casino. (p169)
- **Schöneberg** Cabaret, indie cinema. (p177)
- **Kreuzberg** Live music, art-house cinemas, comedy. (p191)
- **Neukölln** Live music, off-theatre, art-house cinemas, comedy. (p200)
- **Friedrichshain** Live music, outdoor cinema, comedy. (p210)
- **City West & Charlottenburg** Theatre, opera, jazz and indie screens. (p224)

Lonely Planet's Top Choices

Berliner Philharmoniker (p169) One of the world's top orchestras within its own 'cathedral of sound'.

Staatsoper Unter den Linden (p96) Top-ranked opera house.

Babylon (p137) Diverse and intelligent film programming in a 1920s building.

Radialsystem V (p210) Experimental and offbeat performances.

Schaubühne (p224) Thought-provoking contemporary plays in a repurposed 1920s Streamline Moderne cinema; with English surtitles.

Best Live-Music Venues

Tempodrom (p169) An eccentric midsized tent-shaped structure with great acoustics, an intimate ambience and eclectic programming.

Waldbühne Berlin (p74) Berliner Philharmoniker to the Rolling Stones: they've all rocked this enchanting outdoor amphitheatre near the Olympic Stadium.

Best Classical-Music Venues

Berliner Philharmonie (p169) The one and only. Enough said.

Konzerthaus Berlin (p103) Schinkel-designed concert hall festooned with fine sculpture; a festive backdrop for fine symphonies.

Berliner Dom (p120) Former royal court church presents concerts, sometimes played on the famous Sauer organ.

Pierre Boulez Saal (p103) Midsize venue designed by Frank Gehry that hosts mostly chamber-music concerts.

Best Experimental Performance

Radialsystem V (p210) Gets bragging rights for its cutting-edge, genre-defying productions, especially in dance.

Hebbel am Ufer (p191) Boundary-pushing and poly-genre productions that challenge preconceptions.

Sophiensaele (p75) Presents collaborative mash-ups of dance, theatre, performance and music in the banqueting hall of a 1905 crafts workshop.

Best Free Entertainment

Bearpit Karaoke (p146) A huge crowd turns out to sing and cheer on Sunday at the Mauerpark.

Berliner Philharmonie (p169) Free Tuesday lunchtime concerts in the foyer of this famous concert hall.

A-Trane jazz jam (p226) Mondays bring down the house in this well-established jazz club.

Französischer Dom organ recitals (p91) Short lunch break in a historic church at 12.30pm Tuesday to Friday.

Teehaus im Englischen Garten (p168) Jazz to hip-hop concerts on summer Sundays at this charming Tiergarten beer garden.

Best Cabaret

Chamäleon (p138) Historic variety theatre in the Hackesche Höfe presents mesmerising contemporary spins on acrobatics, dance, theatre, magic and music.

Bar Jeder Vernunft (p224) An art nouveau mirrored tent provides a suitably glam backdrop for high-quality entertainment.

Tipi am Kanzleramt (p104) There's not a bad seat in the house at this festive dinner theatre in a tent on the edge of the Tiergarten park.

Best Cinemas

Babylon (p137) Art-house cinema in protected 1920s Bauhaus building with restored theatre organ.

Arsenal (p169) Arty fare from around the world in the original language, often with English subtitles.

Freiluftkino Friedrichshain (p211) Classics, indies, documentaries and blockbusters under the stars in the vast Volkspark Friedrichshain.

Kino International (p211) Legendary GDR-era cinema with glamorous 1960s interior and a bar with views of Karl-Marx-Allee.

Best Theatre

English Theatre Berlin (p189) Innovative and often provocative productions by Berlin's English-language theatre.

Berliner Ensemble (p138) Theatre that premiered Brecht's *Threepenny Opera* is still rocking audiences today.

Gorki (p104) 'Post-migrant' theatre with multicultural cast picks up on works that address upheavals and transitions in society; with English surtitles.

DANILOVI / GETTY IMAGES ©

Boutiques in Hackesche Höfe (p130)

Treasure Hunt

Berlin is a great place to shop, and we're definitely not talking malls and chains. The city's appetite for the individual manifests in small neighbourhood boutiques and buzzing markets that are a pleasure to explore. Shopping here is as much about visual stimulus as it is about actually spending your cash.

Where to Shop

Berlin's main shopping boulevard is Kurfürstendamm (Ku'damm) in the City West and Charlottenburg, which is largely the purview of mainstream retailers (from H&M to Prada). Its extension, Tauentzienstrasse, is anchored by KaDeWe, continental Europe's largest department store. Standouts among the city's dozens of other shopping centres are the concept mall Bikini Berlin and the vast LP12 Mall of Berlin at Leipziger Platz.

Getting the most out of shopping in Berlin, though, means venturing off the high street and into the *Kieze* (neighbourhoods). This is where you'll discover a cosmopolitan cocktail of indie boutiques stirred by the city's zest for life, envelope-pushing energy and entrepreneurial spirit.

Home-Grown Designers

Michael Michalsky may be the capital's best-known fashion export, but it is Berlin-born Claudia Skoda who is considered so iconic that the Kunstbibliothek dedicated a special exhibition to her in 2020.

Other fashion-forward local designers include C.Neeon, Anna von Griesheim, Firma Berlin, Esther Perbandt, C'est Tout, Kostas

NEED TO KNOW

Opening Hours

➡ Malls, department stores and supermarkets open from 10am to 8pm or 9pm; a few supermarkets are open 24 hours.

➡ Boutiques and other smaller shops have flexible hours, usually from 11am to 7pm weekdays, and to 4pm or 5pm Saturday.

Taxes & Refunds

If your permanent residence is outside the EU, you may be able to partially claim back the 19% value-added tax (VAT, *Mehrwertsteuer*) you have paid on goods purchased in stores displaying the 'Tax-Free for Tourists' sign.

Late-Night Shopping

➡ One handy feature of Berlin culture is the *Spätkauf* (*Späti* in local vernacular), which are small neighbourhood stores stocked with the basics and open from early evening until 2am or later.

➡ Some supermarkets stay open until midnight; a few are open 24 hours.

Sunday Shopping

➡ Stores are closed on most Sundays, except for some bakeries, flower shops and souvenir shops.

➡ Shops and supermarkets in major train stations (Hauptbahnhof, Ostbahnhof, Friedrichstrasse) are open late and on Sunday.

➡ Shops may also open from 1pm to 8pm on two December Sundays before Christmas and on a further six Sundays throughout the year (usually around major events like the Berlinale film festival). Exact dates change annually and are set by the Berlin Senate.

Murkudis, Kaviar Gauche, Potipoti and Leyla Piedayesh. In typical Berlin style, they walk the line between originality and contemporary trends in a way that more mainstream labels do not.

In keeping with the zeitgeist, Berlin has also produced its share of ethical and eco-minded fashion brands, including Hund-Hund, Folksdays, Slowmo, Car e., UVR Connected, Ken Panda!, Dzaino, Myrka Studios, The Tribe Berllin, and jovoo.

For accessories, look for eyewear by ic! Berlin and Mykita, bags by Liebeskind and Tausche, shoes by Trippen, and hats by Fiona Bennett and Rike Feurstein.

Flea Markets

Flea markets are like urban archaeology: you'll need plenty of patience and luck when sifting through other people's cast-offs, but oh, the thrill when you finally unearth a piece of treasure! Berlin's numerous hunting grounds set up on weekends (usually Sunday) year-round – rain or shine – and are also the purview of fledgling local fashion designers and jewellery makers. The most famous market is the weekly Flohmarkt im Mauerpark (p153) in Prenzlauer Berg, which is easily combined with a visit to nearby Trödelmarkt Arkonaplatz (p154).

Shopping by Neighbourhood

➡ **Historic Mitte** (p104) Souvenir shops on Unter den Linden; top-flight retailers, concept stores and galleries on and around Friedrichstrasse.

➡ **Museumsinsel & Alexanderplatz** (p125) Eastern Berlin's mainstream shopping hub (Alexanderplatz), plus a weekend collectables market, souvenirs in Nikolaiviertel.

➡ **Hackescher Markt & Scheunenviertel** (p138) Covetable international labels alongside local designers and accessories in chic boutiques and concept stores.

➡ **Prenzlauer Berg** (p153) Fashionable boutiques and accessories on Kastanienallee, children's stores around Helmholtzplatz and famous Mauerpark flea market.

➡ **Potsdamer Platz & Tiergarten** (p169) One big mall and little else.

➡ **Schöneberg** (p177) Indie shops along Goltzstrasse and Akazienstrasse; designer stores on Potsdamer Strasse.

➡ **Kreuzberg** (p192) Vintage fashion and streetwear along with music and accessories, all in indie boutiques.

➡ **Neukölln** (p201) Eclectic owner-run shops, local designers, music, low-key concept stores.

➡ **Friedrichshain** (p211) Indie boutiques around Boxhagener Platz, site of a Sunday flea market; antique market at Ostbahnhof.

➡ **City West & Charlottenburg** (p226) Mainstream on Kurfürstendamm, indie boutiques in the side streets, concept stores at Bikini Berlin, and homewares on Kantstrasse.

Lonely Planet's Top Choices

KaDeWe (p177) The ultimate consumer temple has seemingly everything every heart desires.

Bikini Berlin (p226) Edgy shopping in a revitalised 1950s landmark building near Zoo Station.

Dussmann – Das Kulturkaufhaus (p104) The mother lode of books and music with high-profile author readings and signings.

Hallesches Haus (p192) Arbiter of contemporary cool homewares in a former post office with integrated lunch cafe.

Folkdays (p192) Young label for chic and fair products straight from indigenous artesans from all corners of the world.

Best Fashion & Accessories

lala Berlin (p139) Big city fashion label that reflects the idiosyncractic Berlin spirit.

IC! Berlin (p125) Unbreakable and stylish eyewear for the fashion-forward.

Trippen (p139) Handmade designer footwear that's sustainable, ergonomic and stylish.

Loveco (p211) Berlin pioneering concept store for eco-friendly, vegan clothing and shoes for women and men.

Zweimalschön (p153) One of Berlin's best-stocked and best-value charity shops.

DearGoods (p153) Germany's first all-vegan boutique has you looking – and feeling – good.

Best Bookshops

Taschen Store Berlin (p226) The flagship store of this publisher of gorgeous coffee-table books has swoon-worthy decor.

Another Country (p193) Quirkily run English-language bookstore-library-community living room.

Do You Read Me?! (p139) Handpicked selection of indie magazines and books on photography, design, art, fashion and literature.

Hundt Hammer Stein (p138) Expertly curated literary bookshop run by well-read staff.

Curious Fox (p201) Congenial Neukölln hang-out with new and used English-language lit.

Best Flea Markets

Flohmarkt im Mauerpark (p153) The mother of all markets is overrun but still a good show for secondhand and local designer stuff.

Nowkoelln Flowmarkt (p201) This internationally flavoured market is also a showcase of local creativity.

Flohmarkt Boxhagener Platz (p212) Fun finds abound at this charmer on a leafy square.

RAW Flohmarkt (p213) Bargains galore at this little market on the grounds of a railway repair station turned party zone.

Best Farmers Markets

Markt am Winterfeldtplatz (p177) Local institution with quality produce alongside artsy-crafty stuff and global snack stands.

Türkischer Markt (p201) Bazaar-like canal-side market with bargain-priced produce and Mediterranean deli fare.

Kollwitzplatzmarkt (p154) Posh player with top-quality produce, artisanal cheeses and pasta, homemade pesto and other exquisite morsels.

Wochenmarkt Boxhagener Platz (p213) Lively and colourful neighbourhood meet-up with a great selection of unusual foods and snack stands.

Markthalle Neun (p192) Thrice-weekly market brings regional bounty to a historic market hall.

Best Malls & Department Stores

Bikini Berlin (p226) The city's first concept mall, with hip stores and views of the monkeys at Berlin Zoo.

Mall of Berlin (p169) Huge high-end shopping quarter with around 300 stores alongside apartments, a hotel and offices.

KaDeWe (p177) The largest department store in continental Europe.

Best One-of-a-Kind

1. Absinth Depot Berlin (p139) Make your acquaintance with the Green Fairy at this quaint Old Berlin–style shop.

Käthe Wohlfahrt (p226) Where it's Christmas 365 days of the year so you can stock up on things that shine and glitter in July.

Other Nature (p192) This woman-owned alternative sex shop stocks toys, tutorials and tips on how to tickle your fancy – or whatever.

Sugafari (p153) Take a trip around candy world at this sweet and colourful shop packed with global sugary treats.

Frau Tonis Parfum (p104) Bring home a fragrant memory of Berlin custom-mixed at this elegant perfume boutique.

Explore Berlin

BERLIN'S TOP EXPERIENCES

Neighbourhoods at a Glance

❶ Historic Mitte p84

A cocktail of culture, commerce and history, Mitte packs in plenty of blockbuster sights: the Reichstag, Brandenburg Gate, the Holocaust Memorial, Gendarmenmarkt and Checkpoint Charlie are all within its confines. Cutting through it all are the grand boulevard of Unter den Linden and posh shopping street Friedrichstrasse.

❷ Museumsinsel & Alexanderplatz p106

This is sightseeing central thanks to Museumsinsel (with the unmissable Pergamonmuseum), the Berliner Dom and the spanking new Humboldt Forum culture centre. Nearby, learn about life under socialism in the DDR Museum, then scale the Fernsehturm (TV Tower) for a bird's-eye view of Berlin.

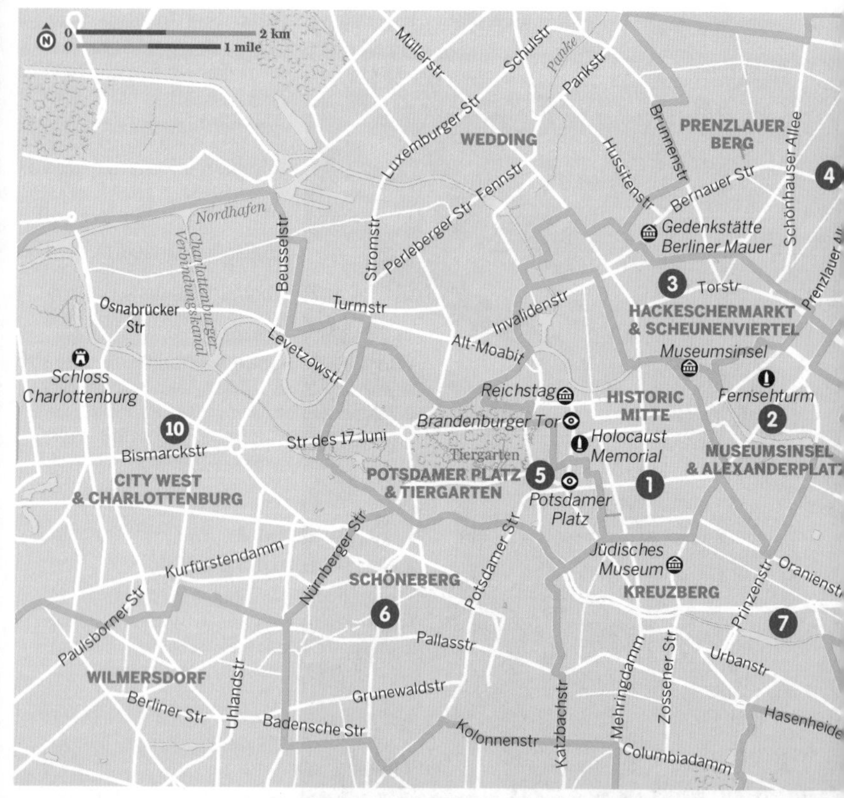

❸ Hackescher Markt & Scheunenviertel p126

The Scheunenviertel's greatest charms reveal themselves in the labyrinth of lanes fanning out from Oranienburger Strasse and Rosenthaler Strasse. A distinctive feature of the quarter is its *Höfe* – interlinked courtyards filled with cafes and shops.

❹ Prenzlauer Berg p140

A charismatic residential neighbourhood filled with cafes, historic buildings and indie boutiques. On Sunday the world descends on Mauerpark for flea marketeering. The key sight is the Gedenkstätte Berliner Mauer, a 1.4km-long exhibit about the Berlin Wall.

❺ Potsdamer Platz & Tiergarten p155

Forged from ground bisected by the Berlin Wall in the 1990s, Potsdamer Platz is a showcase of contemporary architecture. Steer towards the nearby Kulturforum museums, especially the Gemäldegalerie, and the world-class Berliner Philharmonie. Tiergarten park invites a break from sightseeing.

❻ Schöneberg p170

Berlin's traditional gay quarter, largely residential Schöneberg has had an influx of new-concept restaurants, cafes and galleries, especially along Potsdamer Strasse. Main sights are the Urban Nation street-art museum and the KaDeWe department store.

❼ Kreuzberg p178

Big-ticket sights are the Jüdisches Museum and the Deutsches Technikmuseum, but Kreuzberg is best understood as a hub of alternative Berlin. The western area, around Bergmannstrasse, has a more genteel air.

❽ Neukölln 194

Traditionally dominated by Turkish and Middle Eastern populations, Neukölln has become the favourite landing pad for Western expats, fuelling dynamic creative and party scenes. Tempelhofer Feld, a vast airfield turned park, offers a handy hangover antidote. Sights include a brewery upcycled into an exhibition space.

❾ Friedrichshain p202

Famous for high-profile GDR-era relics such as the longest surviving stretch of the Wall (the East Side Gallery), the socialist boulevard Karl-Marx-Allee and the former Stasi headquarters, Friedrichshain also stakes its reputation on having Berlin's most rambunctious nightlife scene, appealing indie boutiques and a popular Sunday flea market.

❿ City West & Charlottenburg p214

Charlottenburg is a big draw for shopaholics, royal groupies and art-lovers. Its main sightseeing attraction is Schloss Charlottenburg, with its park and adjacent art museums. The City West area, around Zoologischer Garten (Zoo Station), is bisected by the Kurfürstendamm, Berlin's famous shopping boulevard.

Historic Mitte

GOVERNMENT QUARTER & NORTHERN TIERGARTEN | BRANDENBURGER TOR & UNTER DEN LINDEN | FRIEDRICHSTRASSE & CHECKPOINT CHARLIE | HAUPTBAHNHOF & AROUND | GENDARMENMARKT

Neighbourhood Top Five

❶ **Brandenburger Tor** (p88) Snapping a selfie with this famous landmark and symbol of German reunification.

❷ **Gendarmenmarkt** (p91) Taking in the architectural symmetry of this gorgeous square before indulging in a gourmet meal at one of the stellar restaurants in its vicinity.

❸ **Holocaust Memorial** (p89) Soaking in the stillness and presence of uncounted souls at this haunting site before gaining an insight into the horrors of the Holocaust at the underground exhibit.

❹ **Reichstag** (p86) Standing in awe of history at Germany's government building, then pinpointing the sights while meandering up its landmark glass dome.

❺ **Museum für Naturkunde** (p100) Sizing yourself up next to giant dinos in the city's Museum of Natural History.

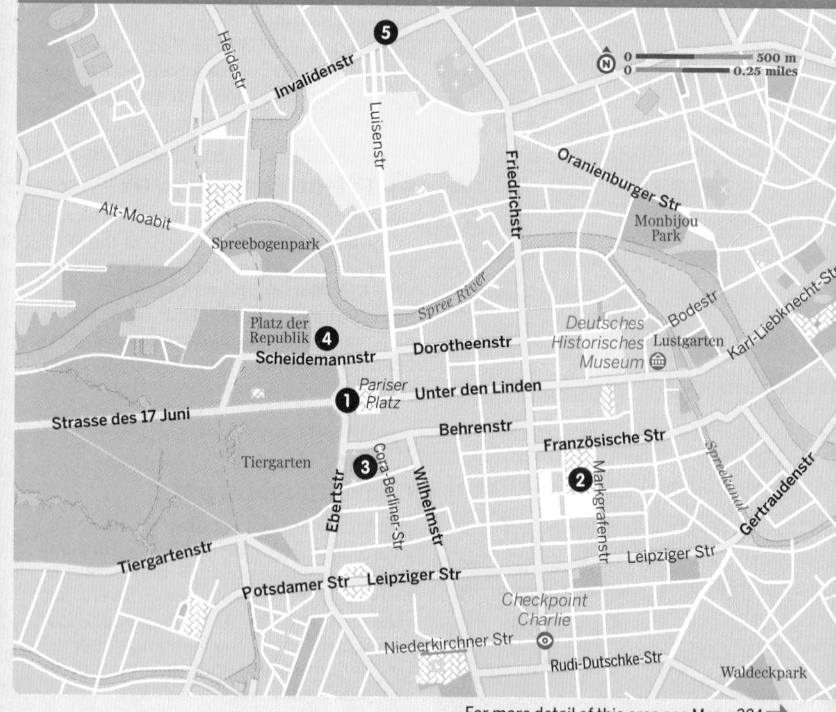

For more detail of this area see Map p324

Explore Historic Mitte

With a high concentration of sights within a walkable area, the most historic part of Berlin is naturally a prime port of call for first-time visitors. Book ahead for access to the Reichstag dome (p87), then snap a picture of Brandenburger Tor (p88) and pay tribute to lost souls at the Holocaust Memorial (p89). Dip into Berlin's Prussian past on a stroll along grand Unter den Linden.

Friedrichstrasse, which bisects Unter den Linden, runs north into the 'East End' theatre district and south to Checkpoint Charlie. Gendarmenmarkt (p91), Berlin's most beautiful square, is just one block east and is surrounded by ritzy restaurants and fancy shops. Its Konzerthaus (p103) provides sophisticated after-dark diversion, but aside from a few posh bars this area is pretty devoid of nightlife. There's a bit more going on near the theatres north of Friedrichstrasse train station, especially on Schiffbauerdamm on the northern bank of the Spree.

Contemporary-art fanciers should also head north of the river to the Sammlung Boros (p99), in a WWII bunker, and the Hamburger Bahnhof (p92), in a converted railway station. Nearby, the Museum für Naturkunde (p100) draws families with its famous dinosaurs.

Local Life

Highbrow culture Music fans are drawn to this part of town to take in a performance at the Staatsoper Berlin (p103), the Konzerthaus Berlin (p103) and the Pierre Boulez Saal (p103), as well as opera at the Komische Oper (p103).

Power of words Self-titled 'cultural department store' Dussmann (p104) is El Dorado for bookworms. There's a huge music selection, plus free readings and other events.

Getting There & Away

Bus Buses 100, 245 and 300 run along most of Unter den Linden from Alexanderplatz.

S-Bahn S1 and S2/25 stop at Brandenburger Tor and Friedrichstrasse.

U-Bahn Stadtmitte (U2, U6) and Hausvogteiplatz (U2) are convenient for Gendarmenmarkt. The new U5 runs below Unter den Linden.

Tram The M1 and 12 travel down Friedrichstrasse en route between Museumsinsel and Prenzlauer Berg.

Lonely Planet's Top Tip

There is definitely a mystique to Checkpoint Charlie, so by all means drop by to take a look. However, in order to truly understand what it was like to cross between West and East Berlin, swing by the excellent – and free – exhibit in the Tränenpalast (p97), the former border-crossing pavilion on Friedrichstrasse.

Best Places to Eat

- India Club (p101)
- Liu Nudelhaus (p101)
- Cookies Cream (p102)
- Restaurant Tim Raue (p102)

For reviews, see p100.

Best Places to Drink

- Bar Tausend (p103)
- Rooftop Terrace (p103)
- Crackers (p102)
- Berliner Republik (p102)

For reviews, see p103.

Best Places to Shop

- Dussmann – Das Kulturkaufhaus (p104)
- Rausch Schokoladenhaus (p104)
- Frau Tonis Parfum (p104)

For reviews, see p104.

PISAPHOTOGRAPHY / SHUTTERSTOCK ©

TOP EXPERIENCE

CLIMB TO THE DOME OF THE REICHSTAG

It's been burnt, bombed, rebuilt, buttressed by the Berlin Wall, wrapped in fabric and finally turned into the modern home of the German parliament by Norman Foster: the Reichstag is one of Berlin's most iconic buildings. Its most eye-catching feature is its glistening glass dome, which draws more than three million visitors each year.

Dome

Resembling a giant glass beehive, the sparkling cupola is open at the top and bottom and sits right above the plenary chamber as a visual metaphor for transparency and openness in politics. A lift whisks you to the rooftop terrace, from where you can easily pinpoint such sights as the curvaceous House of World Cultures and the majestic Berliner Dom (Berlin Cathedral) or marvel at the enormous dimensions of Tiergarten park. To learn more about these and other landmarks, the Reichstag building and the workings of parliament, pick up a free multilingual audioguide as you exit the lift. The commentary starts automatically as you mosey up the dome's 230m-long ramp, which spirals around a mirror-clad cone that deflects daylight down into the plenary chamber.

Main Facade

Stylistically, the monumental west-facing main facade borrows heavily from the Italian Renaissance, with a few neobaroque elements thrown into the mix. A massive staircase leads up to a portico curtained by six Corinthian columns and topped by the dedication 'Dem Deutschen Volke' (To the German People), which wasn't added until 1916. The

DON'T MISS

- Views from the rooftop
- The facade
- Audioguide tour of the dome
- Gerhard Richter's *Birkenau* installation

PRACTICALITIES

- Map p324, C4
- ☎030-2273 2152
- www.bundestag.de
- Platz der Republik 1, Visitors Centre, Scheidemannstrasse
- admission free
- ⏲lift 8am-midnight, last entry 9.45pm, Visitors Centre 8am-8pm Apr-Oct, to 6pm Nov-Mar
- 🚌100, S Brandenburger Tor, Hauptbahnhof, U Brandenburger Tor, Bundestag

bronze letters were designed by Peter Behrens, one of the pioneers of modern architecture, and cast from two French cannons captured during the Napoleonic Wars of 1813–15. The original dome, made of steel and glass and considered a high-tech marvel at the time, was destroyed during the Reichstag fire in 1933.

Home of the Bundestag

Today, the Reichstag is the anchor of the federal-government quarter built after reunification. The Bundestag, Germany's parliament, has hammered out its policies here since moving from the former West German capital of Bonn to Berlin in 1999. The parliament's arrival followed a complete architectural revamp masterminded by Norman Foster, who preserved only the building's 19th-century shell and added the landmark glass dome.

Historic Milestones

The grand old structure was designed by Paul Wallot and completed in 1894, when Germany was still a constitutional monarchy known as the Deutsches Reich (German Empire) – hence the building's name. Home of the German parliament from 1894 to 1933 and again from 1999, the hulking building will likely give you more flashbacks to high-school history than any other Berlin landmark. On 9 November 1919, parliament member Philipp Scheidemann proclaimed the German republic from one of its windows. In 1933, the Nazis used a mysterious fire as a pretext to seize dictatorial powers. A dozen years later, victorious Red Army troops raised the Soviet flag on the bombed-out building, which stood damaged and empty on the western side of the Berlin Wall throughout the Cold War. In the late 1980s, megastars including David Bowie, Pink Floyd and Michael Jackson performed concerts on the lawn in front of the building.

The Wall collapsed soon thereafter, paving the way for German reunification, which was enacted here in 1990. Five years later, the Reichstag made headlines once again when artist couple Christo and Jeanne-Claude wrapped the massive structure in silvery fabric. It had taken an act of the German parliament to approve the project, which was intended to mark the end of the Cold War and the beginning of a new era. For two weeks starting in late June 1995, visitors from around the world flocked to Berlin to admire this unique sight. Shortly after the fabric came down, Norman Foster set to work.

An extensive **photographic exhibit** at the bottom of the dome captures many of these historic moments.

TAKE A

Book at le ahead for a Dachgartenr Käfer (p101) o Reichstag roof

For snacks and beer, report to the **Restaurant Populär** (Map p324; ☎030-2065 4737; www.berlin-pavillon.de; Scheidemannstrasse 1; dishes €4.50-9; ⏰8am-9pm; 🚌100, S Brandenburger Tor, U Brandenburger Tor, Bundestag), a Frisbee toss away at the edge of Tiergarten park.

VISITING THE DOME

Free reservations for visiting the Reichstag dome must be made at www.bundestag.de and are available for the current and following two months. Prepare to show picture ID, pass through a metal detector and have your belongings X-rayed. Guided tours and lectures can also be booked via the website. If you haven't prebooked, swing by the **Visitors' Centre** (Map p324; ☎030-2273 2152; www.bundestag.de; Scheidemannstrasse; ⏰8am-8pm Apr-Oct, to 6pm Nov-Mar; 🚌100, S Brandenburger Tor, U Bundestag) in a nearby kiosk to enquire about remaining tickets for that day or the following two.

ANDREY_POPOV / SHUTTERSTOCK ©

TOP EXPERIENCE

MARVEL AT THE BRANDENBURGER TOR

Brandenburg Gate is Berlin's most famous – and most photographed – landmark. Trapped right behind the Berlin Wall during the Cold War, it went from symbol of division to epitomising German reunification when the hated barrier fell in 1989. It now serves as a photogenic backdrop for raucous New Year's Eve parties, concerts, festivals and mega-events, including FIFA World Cup finals.

Commissioned by Prussian king Friedrich Wilhelm II, the gate was completed in 1791 as a symbol of peace and a suitably impressive entrance to the grand boulevard Unter den Linden. Architect Carl Gotthard Langhans looked to the Acropolis in Athens for inspiration for this elegant triumphal arch, which is the only surviving one of 18 city gates that once ringed historical Berlin.

Crowning Brandenburg Gate is the *Quadriga*, Johann Gottfried Schadow's famous sculpture of a winged goddess piloting a chariot drawn by four horses. After trouncing Prussia in 1806, Napoleon kidnapped the lady and held her hostage in Paris until she was freed by a gallant Prussian general in 1815. Afterwards, the goddess, who originally represented Eirene (the goddess of peace), was promoted to Victoria (the goddess of victory) and equipped with a new trophy designed by Karl Friedrich Schinkel: an iron cross wrapped into an oak wreath and topped with a Prussian eagle.

The gate lords it over elegant Pariser Platz, which was completely flattened in WWII, then spent the Cold War trapped just east of the Berlin Wall. Look around now: the US, French and British embassies, banks and a luxury hotel have returned to their original sites and once again frame the bustling plaza, just as they did during its 19th-century heyday.

DON'T MISS

- *Quadriga*
- View from Pariser Platz at sunset

PRACTICALITIES

- Brandenburg Gate
- Map p324, D4
- Pariser Platz
- S Brandenburger Tor, U Brandenburger Tor

TOP EXPERIENCE

LEARN AT THE HOLOCAUST MEMORIAL

The Denkmal für die ermordeten Juden Europas (Memorial to the Murdered Jews of Europe) was officially dedicated in 2005. Colloquially known as the Holocaust Memorial, it's Germany's central memorial to the Nazi-planned genocide during the Third Reich. For the football-field-size space, New York architect Peter Eisenman created 2711 sarcophagus-like concrete stelae (slabs) of equal size but various heights, rising in sombre silence from undulating ground.

You're free to access this massive concrete maze at any point and make your individual journey through it. At first it may seem austere, even sterile. But take time to feel the coolness of the stone and contemplate the interplay of light and shadow, then stumble aimlessly among the narrow passageways, and you'll soon connect with a metaphorical sense of disorientation, confusion and claustrophobia.

For context, visit the subterranean **Ort der Information** (Information Centre; 030-2639 4336; www.stiftung-denkmal.de; audioguide €3; 10am-6pm Tue-Sun, last admission 45min before closing) FREE, which movingly lifts the veil of anonymity from some of the six million Holocaust victims. A graphic timeline of Jewish persecution during the Third Reich is followed by a series of rooms documenting the fates of individuals and families. The most visceral is the darkened **Room of Names**, where the names and years of birth and death of Jewish victims are projected onto all four walls while a solemn voice reads their short biographies. Poignant and heart-wrenching, these exhibits leave no one untouched. Not recommended for children under 14. Audioguides and audio translations of exhibit panels are available. Free guided tours in German daily at 3pm and in English on Friday, Saturday and Sunday at 11am.

DON'T MISS

- Field of stelae
- Ort der Information
- Room of Names

PRACTICALITIES

- Map p324, D5
- 030-263 9430
- www.stiftung-denkmal.de
- Cora-Berliner-Strasse 1
- audioguide €3
- 24hr
- S Brandenburger Tor, U Brandenburger Tor

TOP EXPERIENCE

VISIT THE DEUTSCHES HISTORISCHES MUSEUM

If you're wondering what Germans have been up to for the past 1500 years, take a spin around this engaging museum in the baroque Zeughaus, formerly the Prussian arsenal. Upstairs, displays concentrate on the period from the 6th century to the end of WWI in 1918, while the ground floor tracks the 20th century until the fall of the Berlin Wall.

Permanent Exhibit

The permanent exhibit addresses all the major milestones in German history in a European context and examines political history as it was shaped by rulers. The timeline begins with the coronation of Charlemagne, the founding of the Holy Roman Empire and everyday life in the Middle Ages. It then jumps ahead to Martin Luther and the Reformation, the bloody Thirty Years' War and its aftermath, Napoleon and the collapse of the Holy Roman Empire in 1806, and the founding of the German Empire in 1871. WWI, which brought the end of the monarchy and led to the Weimar Republic, is a major theme, as of course are the Nazi era and the Cold War. The exhibit ends with reunification and the withdrawal of Allied troops from Germany.

Displays are a potpourri of documents, paintings, books, dishes, textiles, weapons, furniture, machines and other objects ranging from the sublime to the trivial. One of the oldest objects is a 3rd-century Roman milestone. There's also splendid medieval body armour for horse and rider and a bicorn felt hat worn by Napoleon during the Battle of Waterloo. Among the more unusual objects is a pulpit hourglass, which was introduced after the Reformation to limit the length of sermons to one hour. A startling highlight is a big globe that originally stood in the Nazi Foreign Office, with a bullet hole where Germany should be. Among the newer objects is a 1985 Robotron PC 1715, the first PC made in East Germany.

The Building

The rose-coloured Zeughaus, which was used as a weapons depot until 1876, was a collaboration between four architects: Johann Arnold Nering, Martin Grünberg, Andreas Schlüter and Jean de Bodt. Completed in 1730, it is the oldest building along Unter den Linden and a beautiful example of secular baroque architecture. This is thanks in no small part to Schlüter's magnificent sculptures, especially the heads of dying soldiers, their faces contorted in agony, that grace the facades in the glass-covered courtyard. Although intended to represent vanquished Prussian enemies, they actually make more of a pacifist statement in the eyes of modern viewers.

IM Pei Bau

High-calibre temporary exhibits take up a spectacular contemporary annexe designed by Chinese American architect IM Pei. Fronted by a glass spiral, it's an uncompromisingly geometrical space, made entirely from triangles, rectangles and circles, yet imbued with a sense of lightness achieved through an airy atrium and generous use of glass.

DON'T MISS

- Schlüter's sculptures in the courtyard
- IM Pei Bau
- GDR-era Robotron personal computer
- Painting of Martin Luther by Lucas Cranach the Elder
- Nazi globe

PRACTICALITIES

- German Historical Museum
- Map p324, G4
- 030-203 040
- www.dhm.de
- Unter den Linden 2
- permanent exhibit free, IM Pei Bau adult/concession/under 18yr €8/4/free
- 10am-6pm
- 100, 245, 300, U Hausvogteiplatz, S Hackescher Markt

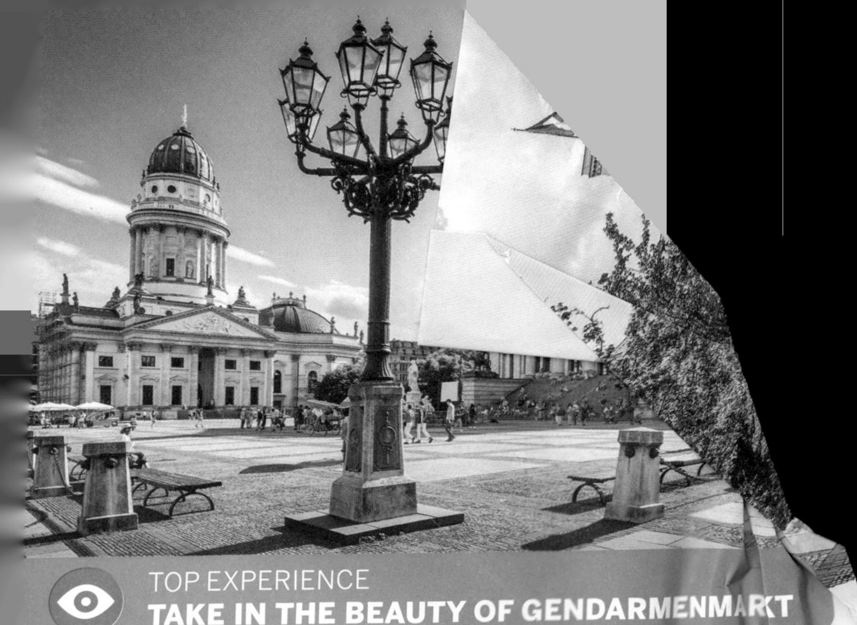

TOP EXPERIENCE

TAKE IN THE BEAUTY OF GENDARMENMARKT

The graceful Gendarmenmarkt is widely considered Berlin's prettiest public square and – surrounded by luxury hotels, fancy restaurants and bars – shows off the city at its ritziest. It was laid out around 1690 and named after the Gens d'Armes, an 18th-century Prussian regiment of French Huguenots who settled here after being expelled from France in 1685.

The **Französischer Dom** (www.franzoesischer-dom.de; church free; church noon-5pm Tue-Sun) FREE was built by Huguenot refugees and consists of two buildings: the 1705 Französische Fredrichstadtkirche (French Church), a copy of the Huguenots' mother church in Charenton; and the soaring domed tower (closed for renovation), which was added by Carl von Gontard in 1785. The church hosts free short organ recitals at 12.30pm Tuesday to Friday, plus a 30-minute version at 3pm on Tuesday.

DON'T MISS

- Free organ recital in the Französische Fredrichstadtkirche
- Concert at the Konzerthaus

PRACTICALITIES

- Map p324, F5
- U Unter den Linden, Stadtmitte

The **Deutscher Dom** (030-2273 0431; www.bundestag.de/deutscherdom; 10am-7pm Tue-Sun May-Sep, to 6pm Oct-Apr) FREE wasn't much of a looker until it was crowned by its own Gontard-designed galleried dome in 1785. Built as the Neue Kirche (New Church) between 1702 and 1708 for German-speaking congregants, it is now home to an exhibit charting Germany's path to parliamentary democracy. English audioguides and tours are available.

One of Karl Friedrich Schinkel's finest buildings, the 1821 Konzerthaus (p103) rose from the ashes of Carl Gotthard Langhans' Schauspielhaus (National Theatre). Schinkel kept the surviving walls and columns and added a grand staircase leading to a raised columned portico. The building is fronted by an elaborate sculpture of 18th-century poet and playwright Friedrich Schiller. For a look inside this beacon of Berlin highbrow culture, catch a concert or take a free 30-minute walk-through tour, offered almost daily.

CLAUDIO DIVIZIA/SHUTTERSTOCK ©

TOP EXPERIENCE

APPRECIATE ART AT HAMBURGER BAHNHOF

Berlin's main contemporary-art museum occupies the mid-19th-century Hamburger Bahnhof railway station, whose late-neoclassical grandeur is an impressive foil for this Aladdin's cave of paintings, sculptures and installations. The inventory spans the entire arc of post-1950 artistic movements, from conceptual art and pop art to minimal art, Arte Povera and Fluxus.

Seminal works by such headliners as Andy Warhol, Cy Twombly, Anselm Kiefer, Robert Rauschenberg and Bruce Nauman are presented in changing configurations. On permanent display in the west wing are large-scale sculptures by Joseph Beuys, the ultimate artistic-boundary pusher. Behind the historic main building, the 300m-long industrial Rieckhallen galleries present selections from the minimal art collection of Friedrich Christian Flick, but only until September 2021; the investment company that owns the halls plans to demolish them to make room for office buildings.

Trains first rolled through the Hamburger Bahnhof in 1846, but after only 32 years the station had become too small and was repurposed first as office space and then as a transport museum. After WWII the building lingered empty for decades until architect Josef Paul Kleihues converted it into a contemporary exhibition space. He kept the elegant exterior, which at night is bathed in the light of a Dan Flavin installation. The interior was gutted and turned into modern minimalist galleries that flank the lofty central hall with its exposed iron girders.

DON'T MISS

- Andy Warhol's *Chairman Mao* (1975)
- Anselm Kiefer's *Volkszählung* (*Census*; 1991)
- Joseph Beuys' *The End of the Twentieth Century* (1983)

PRACTICALITIES

- Map p324, C1
- 030-266 424 242
- www.smb.museum
- Invalidenstrasse 50-51
- adult/concession/under 18yr €10/5/free, 4-8pm 1st Thu of month free
- 10am-6pm Tue, Wed & Fri, to 8pm Thu, 11am-6pm Sat & Sun
- M5, M6, M8, M10, S Hauptbahnhof, U Hauptbahnhof

NEUE WACHE MEMORIAL

Map p324 (New Guardhouse; Unter den Linden 4; ⏲10am-6pm; 🚌100, 245, 300) FREE This temple-like neoclassical structure (1818) was Karl Friedrich Schinkel's first important Berlin commission. Originally a royal guardhouse and a memorial to the victims of the Napoleonic Wars, it is now Germany's central memorial for the victims of war and dictatorship. Its sombre and austere interior is dominated by Käthe Kollwitz' heart-wrenching *Pietà*-style sculpture of a mother cradling her dead soldier son.

SCHLOSSBRÜCKE BRIDGE

Map p324 (Palace Bridge; Unter den Linden; 🚌100, 245, 300) Marking the transition from Unter den Linden to Museumsinsel, the Palace Bridge is considered to be among Berlin's prettiest. Designed by Karl Friedrich Schinkel in the 1820s, it is decorated with eight marble sculptures depicting the life and death of a warrior. Alas, empty royal coffers kept them from being chiselled until the late 1840s, a few years after the master's death.

DZ BANK NOTABLE BUILDING

Map p324 (www.dzbank.de; Pariser Platz 3; S Brandenburger Tor, U Brandenburger Tor) FREE In keeping with Berlin's conservative building regulations, architect Frank Gehry realised his trademark deconstructivist style behind the facade of the DZ Bank on Pariser Platz. Lidded by a curving glass roof whose shape has been compared to a whale, the building is dominated by a vast amorphous sculpture that's actually a conference room. You're free to dip into the foyer for a peek.

SITE OF HITLER'S BUNKER HISTORIC SITE

Map p324 (cnr In den Ministergärten & Gertrud-Kolmar-Strasse; ⏲24hr; S Brandenburger Tor, U Brandenburger Tor) Berlin was burning and Soviet tanks advancing relentlessly when Adolf Hitler shot himself in the head on 30 April 1945 in his bunker near the Reich chancellery. His long-time female companion, Eva Braun, whom he had married just hours earlier, died by his side from a cyanide pill. Today, a parking lot covers the site, revealing its dark history only via an information panel with a diagram of the vast bunker network, construction data and the site's post-WWII history.

The interior was blown up and sealed off by the Soviets in 1947. The 2004 movie *The Downfall* vividly chronicles Hitler's last days in the Führerbunker. For a 1:25 scale model of the bunker, visit the nearby exhibit 'Hitler – how could it happen' (p163).

MADAME TUSSAUDS MUSEUM

Map p324 (☎01806-545 800; www.madametussauds.com/berlin; Unter den Linden 74; adult/child €25/20.50; ⏲10am-6pm Mon-Fri, to 7pm Sat & Sun, last entry 1hr before closing; 🚌100, S Brandenburger Tor, U Brandenburger Tor) No celebrity in town to snare your stare? Don't fret: at this legendary wax museum, the world's biggest pop stars, Hollywood legends, sports heroes and historical icons stand still – very still – for you to snap their picture. Sure, it's an expensive haven of kitsch and camp, but where else can you take a selfie with Nicki Minaj, find your perfect make-up with Kendall Jenner or ride a bike with ET? Avoid queues and save money by buying tickets online.

⊙ Friedrichstrasse & Checkpoint Charlie

TRÄNENPALAST MUSEUM

Map p324 (☎030-467 777 911; www.hdg.de; Reichstagufer 17; ⏲9am-7pm Tue-Fri, 10am-6pm Sat & Sun; 🚋M1, 12, S Friedrichstrasse, U Friedrichstrasse) FREE During the Cold War, tears flowed copiously in this glass-and-steel border-crossing pavilion where East Berliners had to bid adieu to family visiting from West Germany – hence its 'Palace of Tears' moniker. The exhibit uses original objects (including the claustrophobic passport-control booths and a border auto-firing system), photographs and historical footage to document the division's social impact on the daily lives of Germans on both sides of the border.

JULIA STOSCHEK COLLECTION GALLERY

Map p324 (☎030-921 062 460; www.jsc.art; Leipziger Strasse 60; adult/under 18yr €5/free; ⏲noon-6pm Sat & Sun; 🚌200, 265, U Hausvogteiplatz, Stadtmitte) The Czechoslovakian Cultural Institute is a time capsule from the 1960s, but the time-based media art displayed within is truly cutting edge. There are usually several parallel group and solo exhibitions drawn from private collector Julia Stoschek's trove of international video, film, sound, computer and augmented and virtual-reality art.

The scope ranges from contemporary classics by Marina Abramović and Isa Genzken to work by up-and-comers like Bunny Rogers and Bjarne Melgaard.

MUSEUM FÜR KOMMUNIKATION BERLIN MUSEUM

Map p324 (☎030-202 940; www.mfk-berlin.de; Leipziger Strasse 16; adult/concession/under 17yr €6/3/free; ⏰11am-8pm Tue, 11am-5pm Wed-Fri, 10am-6pm Sat & Sun; 🚌200, Ⓤ Mohrenstrasse, Stadtmitte) Three cheeky robots welcome you to this elegant neo-baroque museum, which takes you on an entertaining romp through the evolution of communication, from smoke signals to smartphones. Admire such rare items as a Blue Mauritius stamp or one of the world's first telephones, test milestones in communication techniques, or ponder the impact of information technology on our daily lives.

FRIEDRICHSTADTPASSAGEN ARCHITECTURE

Map p324 (Friedrichstrasse, btwn Französische Strasse & Mohrenstrasse; ⏰10am-8pm Mon-Sat; Ⓟ; Ⓤ FStadtmitte) This trio of shopping complexes (called *Quartiere*), which was built during the post-reunification construction-boom years, never really managed to trigger the revival of southern Friedrichstrasse as a luxury retail spine and now finds itself partly facing bankruptcy. It's still worth checking out the striking interiors, especially the shimmering glass funnel inside the Jean Nouvel–designed Galeries Lafayette (p105). Next door, Quartier 206 is an art deco–style symphony in coloured marble, while John Chamberlain's crushed-car tower anchors Quartier 205.

MAUERMUSEUM MUSEUM

Map p324 (Haus am Checkpoint Charlie; ☎030-253 7250; www.mauermuseum.de; Friedrichstrasse 43-45; adult/concession €14.50/9.50, audioguide €5; ⏰9am-10pm; Ⓤ Kochstrasse) The Cold War years, especially the history and horror of the Berlin Wall, are engagingly, if haphazardly, documented in this privately run tourist magnet. Open since 1961, the ageing exhibit is still strong when it comes to telling the stories of escape attempts to the West. Original devices used in the process, including a hot-air balloon, a one-person submarine and a BMW Isetta, are crowd favourites.

TOP EXPERIENCE
PASS THROUGH CHECKPOINT CHARLIE

Checkpoint Charlie was the principal gateway for foreigners and diplomats between the two Berlins from 1961 to 1990. Since it was the third Allied checkpoint to open, it was named 'Charlie' in reference to the third letter of the NATO phonetic alphabet (alfa, bravo, charlie...). The only direct Cold War–era confrontation between the US and the Soviet Union took place on this very spot, when tanks faced off shortly after the Wall went up, nearly triggering a third world war. A simple **plaque** affixed to a pile of sandbags in front of a replica army guardhouse commemorates this tense moment.

Alas, little else indicates Checkpoint Charlie's historical importance, as the site has been allowed to degenerate into a tacky tourist trap. Souvenir shops and fast-food restaurants line Friedrichstrasse and young men dressed as American or Soviet border guards pose with tourists for tips. A rare redeeming aspect is the free **open-air gallery** that uses photos and documents to illustrate milestones in Cold War history, as does the **BlackBox Kalter Krieg**. Although a bit pricey, Yadegar Asisi's **Die Mauer – asisi Panorama Berlin** helps you visualise the site during the Wall years.

DON'T MISS

- Open-air gallery
- Die Mauer – asisi Panorama Berlin

PRACTICALITIES

- Map p324, F7
- cnr Zimmerstrasse & Friedrichstrasse
- admission free
- ⏰24hr
- Ⓤ Kochstrasse

BUNKER ART: SAMMLUNG BOROS

A Nazi-era bunker serves as the backdrop to the **Sammlung Boros** (Boros Collection; Map p324; www.sammlung-boros.de; Reinhardtstrasse 20; adult/concession €18/10; 10am-6.30pm Fri-Sun; M1, S Friedrichstrasse, U Oranienburger Tor, Friedrichstrasse), the sublime private collection of contemporary art amassed by advertising guru Christian Boros, who acquired the behemoth in 2003. Selections change every few years and currently include installations by Katja Novitskova, digital paintings by Avery Singer and photo series by Peter Piller. Book online (weeks, if not months, ahead) to join a guided tour (also in English) and to pick up fascinating nuggets about the building's surprising other peacetime incarnations.

Tours begin with an introduction to the exhibit and the building against the noisy backdrop of a clattering blackboard by Belgian artist Kris Martin called *Mandi III*. Leading the group past preserved original fittings, pipes, steel doors and vents, guides provide enough thought fodder, context and explanations about the artworks to help even the uninitiated tame their bewilderment.

Built for 2000 people, the bunker's dank rooms crammed in twice as many during the heaviest air raids towards the end of WWII. After the shooting stopped, the Soviets briefly used it as a POW prison before it assumed a more benign role as a fruit-and-vegetable storeroom in East Berlin, a phase that spawned the nickname 'Banana Bunker'. In the 1990s the claustrophobic warren hosted some of Berlin's naughtiest techno raves and fetish parties.

DIE MAUER – ASISI PANORAMA BERLIN — MUSEUM

Map p324 (030-695 808 601; www.die-mauer.de; Friedrichstrasse 205; adult/concession/child €10/8/4; 11am-6pm, last entry 5.30pm; U Kochstrasse, Stadtmitte) Artist Yadegar Asisi is famous for creating bafflingly detailed monumental photographic panoramas. Right next to Checkpoint Charlie, 'Die Mauer' transports visitors to the divided city on a cloudy day in the 1980s. Standing on a platform, you get to peek from the western side of the Wall across the 'death strip' into East Berlin and contemplate what life was like in the shadow of barbed wire and guard towers. Sound and light intensify the mood of bleakness and oppression.

Some 200 photographs of real people complement this fictitious scene.

BLACKBOX KALTER KRIEG — MUSEUM

Map p324 (030-216 3571; www.bfgg.de; Friedrichstrasse 47; adult/concession €5/3.50; 11am-4pm; U Kochstrasse) This small exhibit right by Checkpoint Charlie provides an easily accessible chronicle of the Cold War using photographs, maps, memorabilia, and original footage and recordings. It also explains how the Berlin Wall fitted into the conflict and how proxy wars in Korea and Vietnam fuelled the tension between the US and the Soviet Union.

TRABI MUSEUM — MUSEUM

Map p324 (030-3020 1030; www.trabi-museum.com; Zimmerstrasse 14-15; adult/under 12yr €5/free; 10am-5pm; U Kochstrasse) If you were lucky enough to own a car in East Germany, it would most likely have been a Trabant (Trabi for short), a tinny two-stroker whose name ('satellite' in English) was inspired by the launch of the Soviet Sputnik in 1956. They've all but disappeared from the streets, but they get star treatment in this small exhibit. Curiosities include rare wooden and racing versions, as well as a camper-van model.

DETLEV ROHWEDDER BUILDING — HISTORIC BUILDING

Map p324 (Bundesfinanzministerium; Leipziger Strasse 5-7; closed to the public; U Kochstrasse) The GDR was founded in 1949 in this behemoth that housed Hermann Göring's Reich Air Ministry during the Nazi years and now serves as the home of the Federal Ministry of Finance. It's closed to the public, but the 20m-long mural along Leipziger Strasse, made of Meissen porcelain tiles by GDR artist Max Lingner in 1950 for what was then East Germany's House of Ministries, is worth a look.

It's an idealised depiction of strong and optimistic East Germans looking forward to a bright future under socialism.

Hauptbahnhof & Around

HAMBURGER BAHNHOF – MUSEUM FÜR GEGENWART MUSEUM

See p92.

★FUTURIUM MUSEUM

Map p324 (House of Futures; ☎030-408 189 777; www.futurium.de; Alexanderufer 2; ⏰10am-6pm Wed & Fri-Mon, to 8pm Thu; 👪; 🚊M5, M8, M10, SHauptbahnhof, UHauptbahnhof) FREE The future is now at the Futurium, an exhibition space that landed in a suitably spaceship-like structure on the Spree River in late 2019. Divided into three 'thinking spaces' called Nature, People and Technology, it seeks to inspire all of us to participate in the debate on how we are going to – and, more importantly, how we want to – live in the coming decades.

Exhibits address possible scenarios for all the buzzing issues of today, such as globalisation, overpopulation, overconsumption, sustainability, artificial intelligence and big data, in relatively random and often interactive fashion. There's also a workshop lab in the basement with a 3D printer and a laser cutter, and a rooftop sky walk for slowing down your spinning head.

TIERANATOMISCHES THEATER MUSEUM

Map p324 (☎030-209 312 870; www.tieranatomisches-theater.de; North Campus, Humboldt University, Philippstrasse 13, House 3; ⏰2-6pm Tue-Sat; 🚌147, 245, UOranienburger Tor) FREE Brandenburg Gate architect Carl Gotthard Langhans designed the neoclassical Veterinary Anatomy Theatre in 1790; note the animal skulls adorning the sleek facade. The elegant domed auditorium where horses and cows were once dissected now showcases experimental exhibits that create a dialogue between scientific exploration and art.

EATING

Historic Mitte is awash with swanky restaurants where the decor is fabulous, the crowds cosmopolitan and the menus stylish. Sure, some places may be more sizzle than substance, but the see-and-be-seen punters don't seem to mind.

TOP EXPERIENCE
EXPLORE THE MUSEUM FÜR NATURKUNDE

Fossils and minerals don't quicken your pulse? Well, how about Oskar, a 13m-high *Giraffatitan*, the *Guinness Book*–certified world's tallest mounted dino? At Berlin's Museum of Natural History, the plant-munching Jurassic superstar is joined by a dozen other extinct buddies, including a ferocious *Allosaurus* and a spiny-backed *Kentrosaurus*, all of them about 150-million-year-old migrants from Tanzania. The same hall also showcases an ultra-rare fossilised *Archaeopteryx*, a primeval bird. Back in the house from mid-2021 will be Tristan, the *T. rex*, who has been on loan in Copenhagen.

Beyond the dinosaurs you can journey deep into space or clear up such age-old mysteries as why zebras are striped and why peacocks have such beautiful feathers. An unexpected highlight are the massively magnified insect models – wait until you see the mind-boggling anatomy of an ordinary house fly! You'll also pass through a creepy but artistically illuminated dark gallery of ethanol-preserved creatures used for research.

A crowd favourite among the taxidermic animals is Knut, the polar bear whose birth at Berlin Zoo in 2006 caused global 'Knutmania'. The cuddly giant died suddenly in 2011.

DON'T MISS

- Tristan the *T. rex*
- Knut the stuffed polar bear

PRACTICALITIES

- Museum of Natural History
- Map p324, D1
- ☎030-8891 408 591
- www.museumfuernaturkunde.berlin
- Invalidenstrasse 43
- adult/concession incl audioguide €8/5
- ⏰9.30am-6pm Tue-Fri, 10am-6pm Sat & Sun
- 🚊M5, M8, M10, 12, UNaturkundemuse

Government Quarter

DACHGARTENRESTAURANT KÄFER GERMAN €€€

Map p324 (☎030-226 2999; www.feinkost-kaefer.de/berlin; Platz der Republik, enter via West Portal/West C; breakfast from €20.50, 3-course dinner €69, additional courses €10; ⏱9am-1pm & 7-11pm; 🚌100, U Bundestag, S Brandenburger Tor) While politicians debate treaties and taxes in the plenary hall below, you can enjoy breakfast and dinner tasting menus with a regional bent at the restaurant on the Reichstag rooftop. For security reasons, reservations must be made at least two days in advance; they include access to the landmark Reichstag dome. Original picture ID required for entry.

Brandenburger Tor & Unter den Linden

★**INDIA CLUB** NORTH INDIAN €€

Map p324 (☎030-2062 8610; www.india-club-berlin.com; Behrenstrasse 72; mains €18-27; ⏱6-11pm; 🌶; S Brandenburger Tor) No need to book a flight to Mumbai or London: authentic northern Indian cuisine has finally landed in Berlin. Thanks to top toque Manish Bahukhandi, curries here are like culinary poetry, the 24-hour marinated tandoori chicken silky and succulent, and the stuffed cauliflower an inspiration.

The dark mahogany furniture is enlivened by splashes of colour in the plates, the chandeliers and the servers' uniforms.

EINSTEIN UNTER DEN LINDEN AUSTRIAN €€

Map p324 (☎030-204 3632; www.einstein-udl.com/en; Unter den Linden 42; mains €18-29; ⏱8am-10pm Mon-Fri, 9am-10pm Sat & Sun; 🚌200, 300, S Brandenburger Tor, Friedrichstrasse, U Brandenburger Tor, Friedrichstrasse) A coffee house with big-city flair, this cosmopolitan spot is great for scanning the power crowd for famous politicians, artists or actors – discreetly, please – while noshing on Wiener schnitzel, homemade apple strudel and other Austrian staples. Also a good spot for an afternoon break over coffee and divine cakes or a post-sightseeing drink, in summer outside with a view of Brandenburg Gate.

Gendarmenmarkt

GOODTIME THAI €€

Map p324 (☎030-2007 4870; www.goodtime-berlin.de; Hausvogteiplatz 11; mains €12.50-25; ⏱noon-midnight; 🌶; U Hausvogteiplatz) Sweep on down to this busy dining room with a garden courtyard for fragrant Thai and Indonesian dishes. Creamy curries, succulent shrimp and roast duck all taste flavourful and fresh, if a bit easy on the heat to accommodate German stomachs. If you like it hot, order Api Sapi (aka 'beef in hell').

AUGUSTINER AM GENDARMENMARKT GERMAN €€

Map p324 (☎030-2045 4020; www.augustiner-braeu-berlin.de; Charlottenstrasse 55; mains €7.50-30, lunch special €6.40; ⏱10am-10pm; U Unter den Linden, Stadtmitte) Tourists, concertgoers and hearty-food lovers rub shoulders at rustic tables in this Bavarian-style beer hall. Sausages, roast pork and pretzels provide rib-sticking sustenance, with only a token salad offered for non-carnivores. Service can be uneven. Good-value weekday lunch specials.

BORCHARDT INTERNATIONAL €€€

Map p324 (☎030-8188 6262; www.borchardt-restaurant.de; Französische Strasse 47; dinner mains €20-40; ⏱11.30am-midnight; U Unter den Linden) Mick Jagger, George Clooney and Robert Redford are among the celebs who have tucked into dry-aged steaks and plump oysters in the marble-pillared dining hall of this see-and-be-seen Berlin institution, established in 1853 by a caterer to the Kaiser. No dish, however, moves as fast as the Wiener schnitzel, a wafer-thin slice of breaded veal fried to crisp perfection.

Friedrichstrasse & Checkpoint Charlie

★**LIU NUDELHAUS** CHINESE €

Map p324 (☎0178 668 4572; https://chengduweidao.de; Kronenstrasse 72; mains €9.50-11.50; ⏱11.30am-3pm Sun-Thu, 11.30am-3pm & 5-8.30pm Fri & Sat; U Stadtmitte, Mohrenstrasse) Liu does a roaring trade in food from the southwestern Chinese province of Sichuan, famous for its pandas and its palate-numbing dishes. Must-try: the Sichuan Zajiang noodles bathing in a bold chili-oil sauce. Come before 12.30pm or after 2pm to avoid the lunchtime rush.

Caution: unless you're auditioning as a fire-eater, don't go past '1' on its spice scale.

ISHIN
JAPANESE €

Map p324 (030-2067 4829; www.ishin.de; Mittelstrasse 24; sushi platter €8.50-15, bowl €5.60-12.20; noon-8pm Mon-Sat; S Friedrichstrasse, U Friedrichstrasse) Look beyond the cafeteria-style get-up to discover sushi glory at fair prices. The combination platters are ample and affordable, especially during happy hour (all day Wednesday and Saturday, and until 4pm on other days). If you're not in the mood for raw fish, tuck into a steaming donburi (rice bowl) topped with meat, fish and/or veg.

GANYMED
FRENCH €€

Map p324 (030-2859 9046; www.ganymed-brasserie.de; Schiffbauerdamm 5; mains €15-45; noon-2.30pm & 5-10pm) Ganymed has pole position on Berlin's longest riverside terrace, but it's the stucco ceilings, leather banquettes and hand-painted murals that make this well-established brasserie such a welcoming port of call. The French menu is just as tastefully composed and heavy on the classics, from bouillabaisse to chateaubriand and coq au vin, best paired with a Gallic wine, *bien sûr*.

BERLINER REPUBLIK
GASTROPUB €€

Map p324 (030-3087 2293; www.die-berliner-republik.de; Schiffbauerdamm 8; mains €10-23; 10am-5am; ; S Friedrichstrasse, U Friedrichstrasse) Just as in a mini stock exchange, the price of beer (18 varieties on tap!) fluctuates with demand after 5pm at this tourist-geared riverside pub. Everyone goes Pavlovian when a heavy brass bell rings, signalling rock-bottom prices. A full menu of home-style Berlin and German fare provides sustenance. In summer, seats on the terrace are the most coveted.

★COOKIES CREAM
VEGETARIAN €€€

Map p324 (030-680 730 448; www.cookiescream.com; Behrenstrasse 55; 5-course menu €79, additional courses €10; 5-11pm Tue-Sat; ; U Unter den Linden) In 2017 this perennial local favourite became Berlin's first flesh-free restaurant to enter the Michelin pantheon, on its 10th anniversary no less. Its industrial look and clandestine location are as unorthodox as the tasty compositions of head chef Stephan Hentschel. The entrance is off the service alley of the Westin Grand Hotel (past the chandelier; ring the bell).

★RESTAURANT TIM RAUE
ASIAN €€€

Map p324 (030-2593 7930; www.tim-raue.com; Rudi-Dutschke-Strasse 26; 4-course lunch €88, additonal courses €15, 8-course dinner €218; noon-3pm & 6.30pm-midnight Wed-Sat; U Kochstrasse) Now here's a double-Michelin-starred restaurant we can get our mind around. Unstuffy ambience and stylishly understated design with walnut and Vitra chairs are a perfect counterpoint to Berlin-born Tim Raue's brilliant Asian-inspired plates. Each dish shines the spotlight on a few choice ingredients. His interpretation of Peking duck is an absolute classic.

The restaurant has been in the top 50 list of the world's best restaurants since 2016 and Raue has also been featured in an episode of *Chef's Table*. Book at least a couple of weeks in advance for dinner.

CRACKERS
INTERNATIONAL €€€

Map p324 (030-680 730 488; www.crackersberlin.com; Friedrichstrasse 158; mains €20-70; 6.30pm-1am; U Unter den Linden) With Crackers, Berlin nightlife impresario Heinz 'Cookie' Gindullis transformed his legendary nightclub, Cookies, into a cosmopolitan gastro-cathedral with a ceiling as lofty as the food. Push open the heavy gate to arrive in a seductively lit space, and prepare to indulge in a journey of smart and sassy dishes made with sustainably harvested, raised or caught provisions.

It's also a good spot to pop in for late-night cocktails.

NOBELHART & SCHMUTZIG
INTERNATIONAL €€€

Map p324 (030-2594 0610; www.nobelhartundschmutzig.com; Friedrichstrasse 218; 10-course menu Tue & Wed €105, Thu-Sat €130; 6.30pm-midnight Tue-Sat; U Kochstrasse) 'Vocally local' is the motto at the Michelin-starred restaurant of top sommelier and culinary provocateur Billy Wagner. Snagging a seat at the kitchen counter to look on as your 10-course dinner is prepared is on many a foodie's bucket list. All ingredients, without exception, hail from producers in and around Berlin and the nearby Baltic Sea – hence, no pepper or lemons.

DRINKING & NIGHTLIFE

Since Historic Mitte isn't much of a residential area, bars and nightlife cater mostly to visitors and are often confined to the hotels. Notable exceptions are a few riverside haunts along Schiffbauerdamm, off Friedrichstrasse, which are also popular with the post-theatre crowd.

BÖSE BUBEN BAR — BAR

Map p324 (030-2759 6909; www.boesebubenbar.de; Marienstrasse 18; 10am-midnight; S Friedrichstrasse, U Friedrichstrasse, Oranienburger Tor) Cosy and crammed with books, vintage furnishings and memorabilia, the 'Bad Boy Bar' is a cafe by day (breakfast until 2pm, homemade cakes!) and a dimly lit anti-hipster haunt for wine and chat in the evening. Despite the name, it actually attracts a most civilised – shall we say intellectual – local crowd. Occasional readings and concerts.

ROOFTOP TERRACE — BAR

Map p324 (030-460 6090; www.roccofortehotels.com; Behrenstrasse 37, Hotel de Rome; 2-11pm May-Sep; ; 100, 200, TXL, U Hausvogteiplatz) A hushed, refined ambience reigns at the rooftop bar of the exclusive Hotel de Rome (p247), where you can keep an eye on the Fernsehturm, the opera house and the historic city centre beyond. It's a chill spot for an afternoon coffee break, a sunset cocktail or a romantic glass of champagne under the starry sky.

BAR TAUSEND — BAR

Map p324 (030-2758 2070; www.tausendberlin.com; Schiffbauerdamm 11; 7pm-late Thu-Sat; M1, S Friedrichstrasse, U Friedrichstrasse) No sign, no light, just an anonymous steel door tucked under a railway bridge leads to one of Berlin's chicest clandestine bars. A mirrored ceiling, a giant light installation resembling an eye and conversation-friendly sounds from soul to house give the tunnel-shaped space a glam, grown-up vibe. The cocktails are inspired by hip districts of the world's metropolises.

And for all you cineasts: in the TV series *Babylon Berlin* Bar Tausend stood in for the decadent nightclub Der Holländer.

ENTERTAINMENT

STAATSOPER BERLIN — OPERA

Map p324 (030-2035 4240; www.staatsoper-berlin.de; Unter den Linden 7; tickets €8-180; ; 100, 245, 300, U Unter den Linden) Berlin's most famous opera company performs at the venerable neoclassical Staatsoper Unter den Linden. Its repertory includes works from four centuries along with concerts and classical and modern ballet, all under the musical leadership of Daniel Barenboim. Some performances are shortened to appeal to families.

KOMISCHE OPER — OPERA

Map p324 (Comic Opera; tickets 030-4799 7400; www.komische-oper-berlin.de; Behrenstrasse 55-57; tickets €12-94; 100, 147, 245, 300, U Unter den Linden) The smallest among Berlin's trio of opera houses is also its least stuffy, even if its flashy neo-baroque auditorium might suggest otherwise. Productions are innovative and unconventional – yet top quality – and often reinterpret classic (and sometimes obscure) pieces in zeitgeist-capturing ways. Seats feature an ingenious subtitling system in English, Turkish and other languages.

KONZERTHAUS BERLIN — CLASSICAL MUSIC

Map p324 (tickets 030-203 092 101; www.konzerthaus.de; Gendarmenmarkt 2; tickets €10-84; U Stadtmitte) This lovely classical-music venue – a Schinkel design from 1821 – counts the top-ranked Konzerthausorchester Berlin as its 'house band' but also hosts visiting soloists and orchestras in three halls. For a midday sightseeing break, check the schedule for weekly 45-minute 'Espresso Concerts' costing €8, including one (you guessed it) espresso.

PIERRE BOULEZ SAAL — CONCERT VENUE

Map p324 (tickets 030-4799 7411; www.boulezsaal.de; Französische Strasse 33d; tickets €10-65; 100, 245, 300, U Hausvogteiplatz) Open since 2017, this intimate concert hall was designed by Frank Gehry and conceived by Daniel Barenboim as a venue to promote dialogue between cultures through music. The musical line-up spans the arc from classical to jazz, electronic to Middle Eastern music.

Performers include top-flight international artists, and students of the affiliated Barenboim-Said Academy, as well as the Boulez Ensemble.

GORKI THEATRE

Map p324 (030-2022 1115; www.gorki.de; Am Festungsgraben 2; tickets €10-34; 100, 200, TXL, M1, 12, S Friedrichstrasse, U Friedrichstrasse) The smallest of Berlin's four state-funded stages sees itself as a 'post-migrant theatre'. The international ensemble cast puts on classic and original productions, often with an interdisciplinary approach, that examine such issues as integration, identity, transition and discrimination. All performances have English subtitles.

DEUTSCHES THEATER THEATRE

Map p324 (030-2844 1225; www.deutschestheater.de; Schumannstrasse 13; tickets €5-48, students €6-9; M1, U Oranienburger Tor) Steered by Max Reinhardt from 1905 until 1932, the DT still ranks among Germany's top stages. Now under artistic director Ulrich Khuon, the repertoire includes classical and contemporary plays that reflect the issues and big themes of today. Plays are also performed in the adjacent Kammerspiele and at the 70-seat Box. Some performances have English surtitles.

TIPI AM KANZLERAMT CABARET

Map p324 (tickets 030-3906 6550; www.tipi-am-kanzleramt.de; Grosse Querallee; tickets €30-53; 100, S Hauptbahnhof, U Bundestag) Tipi stages a year-round program of professional cabaret, dance, acrobatics, musical comedy and magic shows starring German and international acts. It's all presented in a festively decorated cabaret-style tent set up on the edge of Tiergarten park. Pre-show dinner is available.

ADMIRALSPALAST PERFORMING ARTS

Map p324 (tickets 030-2250 7000; www.admiralspalast.theater; Friedrichstrasse 101; M1, S Friedrichstrasse, U Friedrichstrasse) This beautifully restored 1920s 'palace' stages crowd-pleasing musicals, shows, comedy and concerts in its glamorous historic grand hall. Many performances are suitable for non-German speakers, but do check ahead. Ticket prices vary.

SHOPPING

There are some souvenir shops along Unter den Linden and around Checkpoint Charlie, but for fancy fashion and accessories, make a beeline for Friedrichstrasse, with its high-end boutiques and the Galeries Lafayette department store.

DUSSMANN – DAS KULTURKAUFHAUS BOOKS

Map p324 (030-2025 1111; www.kulturkaufhaus.de; Friedrichstrasse 90; 9am-10pm Mon-Fri, to 11.30pm Sat; ; S Friedrichstrasse, U Friedrichstrasse) It's easy to lose track of time in this cultural playground with wall-to-wall books (including an extensive English section), DVDs and CDs, leaving no genre unaccounted for. Bonus points for the downstairs cafe, the vertical garden, and the performance space used for free concerts, political discussions and high-profile book readings and signings.

★ **FRAU TONIS PARFUM** PERFUME

Map p324 (030-2021 5310; www.frau-tonis-parfum.com; Zimmerstrasse 13; 10am-6pm Mon-Sat; U Kochstrasse) Follow your nose to this scent-sational made-in-Berlin perfume boutique, where a 'scent test' reveals if you're the floral, fruity, woody or oriental type, to help you choose a matching fragrance.

Bestsellers include the sensual 'Oud Weiss' and the maritime 'Aventure'. Individualists can have their own customised blend created in a one-hour session (€160, including 50mL eau de parfum; reservations required).

DIE ESPRESSIONISTEN COFFEE

Map p324 (030-3640 9494; www.espressionisten.de; Zimmerstrasse 90; 9am-6pm Mon-Fri, 10am-6pm Sat; U Kochstrasse) If you worship at the altar of the espresso gods, this elegant shrine should be on your itinerary. Floor to ceiling and wall to wall, it's packed with objects of desire for hobby baristas, from pots to scales to tamping stations and, of course, its custom-roasted beans. Sample them at the in-store coffee bar.

RAUSCH SCHOKOLADENHAUS CHOCOLATE

Map p324 (030-757 880; www.rausch.de; Charlottenstrasse 60; 10am-7pm Mon-Sat, from 11am Sun; U Stadtmitte) If the Aztecs regarded chocolate as the elixir of the gods, then this emporium of truffles and pralines must be heaven. The shop features Instaworthy replicas of Berlin landmarks such as Brandenburg Gate, while upstairs you can create your own custom chocolate bar or sip sinful drinking chocolate in the cafe with a view of Gendarmenmarkt.

GALERIES LAFAYETTE DEPARTMENT STORE

Map p324 (☎030-209 480; www.galerieslafayette.de; Friedrichstrasse 76-78; ⊙10am-8pm Mon-Sat; UUnter den Linde, Stadtmitte) Stop by the Berlin branch of the exquisite French fashion emporium, if only to check out the show-stealing interior (designed by Jean Nouvel, no less), centred on a huge glass cone shimmering with kaleidoscopic intensity. Around it wrap three circular floors filled with fancy fashions, fragrances and accessories, while gourmet treats await in the basement food hall.

RITTER SPORT BUNTE SCHOKOWELT CHOCOLATE

Map p324 (☎030-2009 5080; www.ritter-sport.de; Französische Strasse 24; ⊙10am-6pm Mon-Sat; 👪; UUnter den Linde, Stadtmitte) Fans of Ritter Sport's colourful square chocolate bars can pick up limited-edition, organic, vegan and diet varieties in addition to all the classics at this flagship store. Upstairs, a free exhibit explains the journey from cocoa bean to finished product, but kids are more enchanted by the chocolate kitchen, where staff create your own personalised bars.

VIELFACH – DAS KREATIVKAUFHAUS GIFTS & SOUVENIRS

Map p324 (☎030-9148 4678; www.geschenke-berlin.com; Zimmerstrasse 11; ⊙noon-5pm Mon-Sat; UKochstrasse) Pick up unique gifts or souvenirs handmade in Germany at this showroom where artists and designers can rent shelf space to display beauty products, jewellery, bags, ceramics, photographs and lots of other pretty things.

ANTIK- UND BUCHMARKT AM BODEMUSEUM MARKET

Map p324 (www.antik-buchmarkt.de; Am Kupfergraben; ⊙10am-5pm Sat & Sun; 🚊M1, 12, SHackescher Markt, UHackescher Markt) This book and collectibles market has about 60 vendors in a gorgeous setting with Museumsinsel as a backdrop. Bookworms have plenty of boxes to sift through, alongside a smattering of furniture, toys, coins, bric-a-brac and old photographs.

SPORTS & ACTIVITIES

TRABI SAFARI DRIVING

Map p324 (☎030-3020 1030; www.trabi-safari.de; Zimmerstrasse 97; adult/child under 18yr from €49/free; ⊙ticket shop 10am-5pm; UKochstrasse) Catch the *Good Bye, Lenin!* vibe on daily tours of Berlin with you driving or riding as a passenger in a convoy of GDR-made Trabant (Trabi) cars, with live commentary (in English by prior arrangement) piped into your vehicle. The 'compact' tour lasts 1¼ hours, the 'XXL' tour 2¼ hours; both travel to both eastern and western Berlin.

WELTBALLON BERLIN BALLOONING

Map p324 (☎030-5321 5321; www.air-service-berlin.de; Zimmerstrasse 95; adult/concession/child 3-10yr €25/20/12; ⊙10am-10pm Apr-Sep; UKochstrasse) Drift up but not away for about 15 minutes aboard this helium-filled balloon, which remains tethered to the ground as it lifts you noiselessly 150m into the air for panoramas of the historic city centre. Your pilot will help you pinpoint all the key sights. Confirm ahead, as flights are cancelled in poor weather. Up to 30 people fit onto the enclosed platform.

Museumsinsel & Alexanderplatz

ALEXANDERPLATZ | HUMBOLDT FORUM & NIKOLAIVIERTEL

Neighbourhood Top Five

❶ **Pergamonmuseum** (p109) Time-travelling through ancient Greece and Babylon to the Middle East at this glorious museum.

❷ **Neues Museum** (p111) Making a date with Nefertiti and her royal entourage at this stunningly rebuilt repository.

❸ **Humboldt Forum** (p122) Getting a first look at Berlin's much-anticipated new cultural centre as it gradually opens throughout 2021 in the reconstructed Prussian city palace.

❹ **Berlin by Boat** (p123) Letting the sights drift by while enjoying cold drinks on the deck of a Spree River tour boat.

❺ **DDR Museum** (p120) Dipping behind the Iron Curtain at this interactive exhibit with its virtual Trabi ride and fully furnished GDR-era apartment.

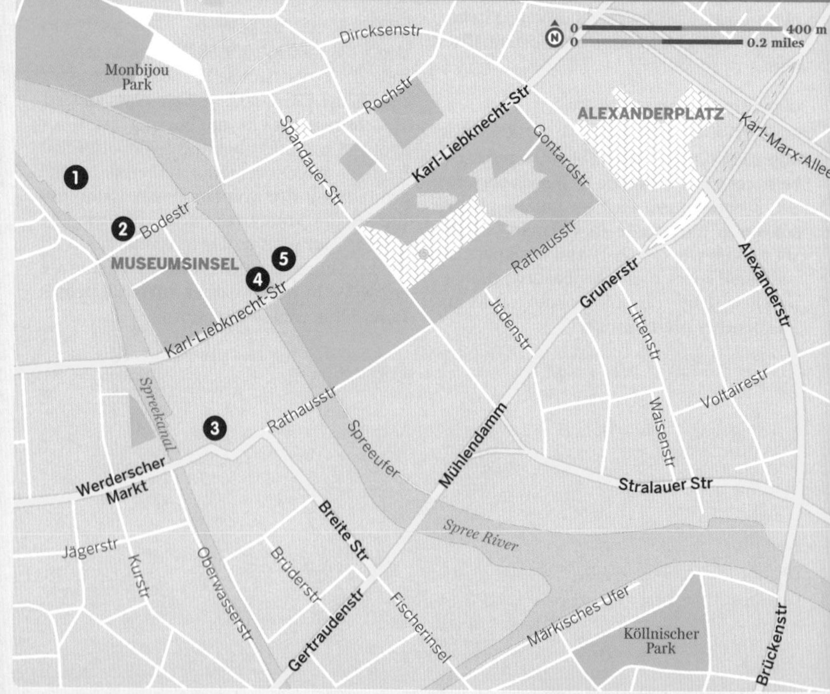

For more detail of this area see Map p328

Explore Museumsinsel & Alexanderplatz

This historic area packs most of eastern Berlin's trophy sights into a compact frame and is best explored on foot in the daytime when museums and shops are open. A good place to start is on vast and amorphous Alexanderplatz, a mainstream shopping hub that's lorded over by the 368m-high Fernsehturm (p118).

The open area west of the Fernsehturm links up with the Nikolaiviertel (p120), Berlin's medieval birthplace, which was first torn down, then rebuilt by the East German government. The surrealism of this pseudo-quaint quarter can be a hoot, but don't expect to find too many Berliners patronising the pricey cafes and souvenir shops.

Better save your energy for the stunning treasures of the five museums on Museumsinsel (Museum Island). If time is an issue, focus on the Pergamonmuseum (p109), with its monumental antiquities, or the ancient Egyptian collection at the Neues Museum (p111). For more recent history, take a spin around the DDR Museum (p120), which engagingly captures facets of daily life in East Germany.

Relax during a one-hour boat ride (p123) through the historic centre or by hanging out on the Lustgarten lawn in front of the Berliner Dom (p120) before checking out the brand-new Humboldt Forum (p122) cultural centre.

Local Life

Late-night openings The best time to visit Museumsinsel without the crowds is on Thursday evening, when all five museums stay open until 8pm.

Shopping Big shopping centres are scarce in central Berlin, which probably explains the local popularity of the Alexa (p125) megamall.

Get a wurst on the go For a quick belly filler, grab a bratwurst in a bun from one of the ambulatory sausage kitchens on Alexanderplatz.

Getting There & Away

Bus Buses 100, 245 and 300 travel along Unter den Linden from Alexanderplatz; bus 100 goes to Zoo station via Tiergarten.

S-Bahn S5, S7 and S75 converge at Alexanderplatz.

Tram M4, M5 and M6 connect Alexanderplatz with Hackescher Markt. M2 goes to Prenzlauer Berg.

U-Bahn U2, U5 and U8 stop at Alexanderplatz. Newly extended U5 continues below Unter den Linden.

Lonely Planet's Top Tip

Heading up the Fernsehturm (TV Tower) may give you bragging rights for having been atop Germany's tallest structure, but for fabulous views on a budget and cocktails with the tower as a backdrop, head to the nearby Panorama Terrasse (p119) atop the Park Inn Hotel.

Best Places to Eat

- Ngon (p124)
- Good Bank (p123)
- Brauhaus Georgbraeu (p124)
- Zur Letzten Instanz (p124)
- Dolores (p123)

For reviews, see p123.

Best Views

- Fernsehturm (p118)
- Park Inn Panorama Terrasse (p119)
- Berliner Dom (p120)

For reviews, see p118.

Best Non-Museum Sights

- Berliner Dom (p120)
- Fernsehturm (p118)
- St Marienkirche (p119)
- Nikolaiviertel (p120)

For reviews, see p118.

BPK / PIERRE ADENIS ©

TOP EXPERIENCE
DISCOVER TREASURES AT MUSEUMSINSEL

Walk through ancient Babylon, meet an Egyptian queen or be mesmerised by Monet's landscapes. Welcome to Museumsinsel, Berlin's famous treasure trove of 6000 years' worth of art, artefacts, sculpture and architecture from Europe and beyond. Spread across five grand museums built between 1830 and 1930, the complex covers the northern half of the Spree island where Berlin's settlement began in the 13th century.

Berlin's Louvre

The first repository to open was the Altes Museum (Old Museum), completed in 1830 next to the Berliner Dom and the Lustgarten park. Today it presents Greek, Etruscan and Roman antiquities. Behind it, the Neues Museum (New Museum) showcases the Ägyptisches Museum (Egyptian Museum), most famously the bust of Queen Nefertiti, and also houses the Museum für Vor- und Frühgeschichte (Museum of Pre- and Early History). The temple-like Alte Nationalgalerie (Old National Gallery) trains the focus on 19th-century European art. The island's top draw is the Pergamonmuseum, with its monumental architecture from ancient worlds, including the namesake Pergamon Altar. The Bode-Museum, at the island's northern tip, is famous for its medieval sculptures.

Museumsinsel Master Plan

In 1999 the Museumsinsel repositories collectively became a Unesco World Heritage Site. The distinction was at least partly achieved because of a master plan for the renovation and modernisation of the complex, led by British architect David Chipperfield and

DON'T MISS

- Ishtar Gate
- Bust of Nefertiti
- Berliner Goldhut
- *Praying Boy*
- Sculptures by Tilman Riemenschneider
- Paintings by Caspar David Friedrich

PRACTICALITIES

- Map p328, A3
- 030-266 424 242
- www.smb.museum
- day tickets for all 5 museums & Pergamon Panorama adult/concession/under 18yr €19/9.50/free
- hours vary
- 100, 245, 300, M1, 12, S Hackescher Markt, Friedrichstrasse, U Friedrichstrasse

expected to be completed in 2026. Except for the Pergamon, whose exhibits are currently being reorganised, the restoration of the museums themselves has been completed. For more details see www.museumsinsel-berlin.de.

James-Simon-Galerie

Museumsinsel's central entrance building, the James-Simon-Galerie on Bodestrasse, opened in July 2019 and was named for an early-20th-century German-Jewish patron and philanthropist. Designed by David Chipperfield, the colonnaded building contains the ticket office, a cafe and shop, and space for smaller temporary exhibits. It currently provides direct access to the Pergamonmuseum, the Neues Museum and the partly completed Archaeological Promenade, a subterranean walkway that will ultimately link all the island's museums except the Alte Nationalgalerie.

Pergamonmuseum

The **Pergamonmuseum** (pictured left; adult/concession/under 18yr €12/6/free; ⏱10am-6pm Tue, Wed & Fri-Sun, to 8pm Thu) opens a fascinating window onto the ancient world. Completed in 1930, the three-wing complex presents a rich feast of classical sculpture and monumental architecture from Greece, Rome, Babylon and the Middle East in three collections: the Collection of Classical Antiquities, the Museum of the Ancient Near East and the Museum of Islamic Art. Most of the pieces were excavated and spirited to Berlin by German archaeologists around the turn of the 20th century.

The Pergamonmuseum is the fourth treasure chest on Museumsinsel to undergo extensive, gradual restoration that will leave some sections closed for years. The north wing and the hall containing the namesake Pergamon Altar will be off-limits until at least 2023. During the second phase, the south wing will be closed and a fourth wing facing the Spree River will be constructed so that in future all parts of the museum can be experienced on a continuous walk, possibly by 2026.

Vorderasiatisches Museum

Entering the Pergamonmuseum via the James-Simon-Galerie, the Museum of the Ancient Near East is the first collection you encounter. Its undisputed highlight is the **Ishtar Gate**, the **Processional Way** leading to it and the facade of the king's **throne hall**, all dating back to Babylon during the reign of Nebuchadnezzar II (604–562 BCE). They are sheathed in radiant blue glazed bricks and adorned with ochre reliefs of strutting lions, bulls and dragons representing Babylonian gods. They're so striking that you can almost hear the roaring and fanfare as the procession rolls into town.

TAKE A BREAK

Cu29 (Map p328; www.cu-berlin.de; Eiserne Brücke; dishes €7-15; ⏱noon-6pm Tue, Wed & Fri-Sun, to 8pm Thu) at the James-Simon-Galerie serves elevated cafe fare on the riverside terrace and in the stylish copper-ceilinged interior.

Sweet cafe Petit Bijou (p124) dispenses drinks and snacks – in summer enjoy them from the terrace with a view of the Bode-Museum.

The Pergamonmuseum was purpose built between 1910 and 1930 to house the massive volume of ancient art and archaeological treasures excavated by German teams at such sites as Babylon, Assur, Uruk and Miletus. Designed by Alfred Messel, the building was constructed by his close friend Ludwig Hoffmann following Messel's death, and was later badly pummelled in WWII. Lots of objects were whisked to the Soviet Union as war booty, but many were returned in 1958.

PERGAMONMUSEUM

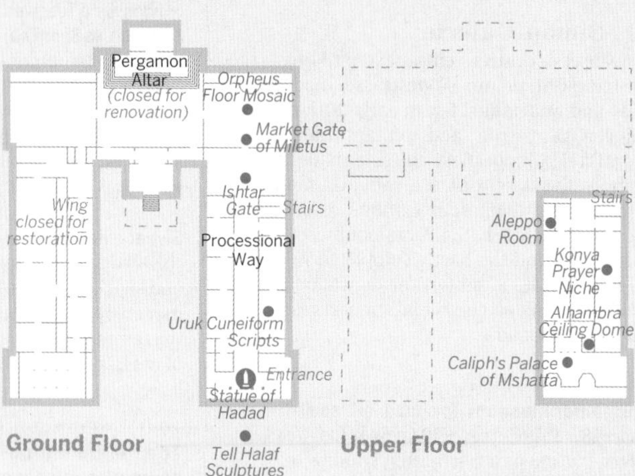

But before you reach the Ishtar Gate, stop by the giant sculptures from a 1st-millennium-BCE palace in **Tell Halaf** (Syria) in the first room and marvel at the fact that they were reconstructed from 27,000 fragments. The colossal statue of the weather god **Hadad** (775 BCE) is another focal point in room 1, as are the small clay tablets with **cuneiform scripts** detailing transactions and agreements in room 5. Found in Uruk (Iraq), they date to the late 4th millennium BCE and are considered among the earliest written documents.

Antikensammlung

The Antikensammlung (Collection of Classical Antiquities) presents artworks from ancient Greece and Rome here and at the Altes Museum. While the Pergamon Altar is closed to the public, the main sight is the 2nd-century-CE **Market Gate of Miletus**, right behind the Ishtar Gate on the ground floor. Merchants and customers once flooded through the splendid 17m-high gate into the bustling market square of this wealthy Roman trading town in modern-day Turkey. A strong earthquake levelled much of the town in the early Middle Ages, but German archaeologists dug up the site between 1903 and 1905 and managed to put the puzzle back together. The richly decorated marble gate blends Greek and Roman design features and is the world's single largest monument ever to be reassembled in a museum.

Also from Miletus is a beautifully restored **floor mosaic** starring Orpheus, from ancient Greek mythology, whose lyre playing charmed even the beasts surrounding him. It originally graced the dining room of a 2nd-century Roman villa.

Museum für Islamische Kunst

In the Museum of Islamic Art, upstairs, top billing belongs to the facade from the **Caliph's Palace of Mshatta** (8th century, room 9) in today's Jordan, which was a gift to Kaiser Wilhelm II from Ottoman sultan Abdul Hamid II. A masterpiece of early Islamic architecture, it depicts animals and mythical creatures frolicking peacefully amid a riot of floral motifs in an allusion to the Garden of Eden.

Other rooms feature fabulous ceramics, carvings, glasses and other artistic objects as well as an 11th-century turquoise **prayer niche** from a mosque in Konya, Turkey, and an intricately patterned cedar-and-poplar **ceiling dome** from the Alhambra in Spain's Granada.

Capping a tour of the museum is the **Aleppo Room** (room 16). Guests arriving in this richly painted, wood-panelled reception room would have had no doubt as to the wealth and power of its owner, a Christian merchant in 17th-century Aleppo, Syria. The paintings depict Christian themes and courtly scenes like those portrayed in Persian book illustrations, suggesting a high level of religious tolerance.

Pergamonmuseum. Das Panorama

While the Pergamon Altar is off limits, you can still grasp its impressive beauty at the exhibit called **Pergamonmuseum. Das Panorama** (Am Kupfergraben 2; adult/concession/under 18yr €12/6/free, combination ticket with Pergamonmuseum €19/9.50/free; 10am-6pm Tue-Sun) in a purpose-built rotunda opposite the Bode-Museum. Inside is a 360-degree panorama by Iranian artist and architect Yadegar Asisi that presents a vivid photorealistic snapshot of the city of Pergamon in 129 CE under the rule of Roman emperor Hadrian. Also on display are 80 Pergamon masterpieces from the Antikensammlung, including a colossal head of Heracles and a big piece from the famous Telephos frieze.

Neues Museum

David Chipperfield's reconstruction of the bombed-out **Neues Museum** (New Museum; Bodestrasse 1-3; adult/concession/under 18yr €12/6/free; 10am-6pm Tue, Wed & Fri-Sun, to 8pm Thu; 100, 245, 300, M1, 12, S Hackescher Markt, Friedrichstrasse, U Friedrichstrasse) is the residence of Queen Nefertiti, the showstopper of the **Ägyptisches Museum** alongside the equally enthralling **Museum für Vor- und Frühgeschichte**. As if piecing together a giant jigsaw puzzle, the British architect incorporated every original shard, scrap and brick he could find into the new building. This brilliant blend of the historic and the modern creates a dynamic space that beautifully juxtaposes massive stairwells and domed rooms with muralled halls and high ceilings.

The entrance is via the James-Simon-Galerie.

TOP TIPS

- Avoid culture fatigue by focusing on just two of the five museums in a single day.
- If you plan to visit more than one museum, save money by buying the combination ticket (€19, concession €9.50), good for one-day admission to all five museums and the Panorama.
- Admission is free for those under 18.
- Make use of the excellent multilingual audioguides included in the admission price.
- In good weather, the lawns of the Lustgarten, outside the Altes Museum, are an inviting spot to chill.

Pergamon was the capital of the Kingdom of Pergamon, which reigned over vast stretches of the eastern Mediterranean in the 3rd and 2nd centuries BCE. Inspired by Athens, its rulers, the Attalids, turned their royal residence into a major cultural and intellectual centre. Draped over a 330m-high ridge were grand palaces, a library, a theatre and glorious temples dedicated to Trajan, Dionysus and Athena.

Ägyptisches Museum

The Egyptian Museum occupies three floors in the northern wing of the Neues Museum. Most visitors come here for an audience with the eternally gorgeous Egyptian queen **Nefertiti**. Her bust was created around 1340 BCE by the court sculptor Thutmose. Extremely well preserved, the sculpture was part of the treasure trove unearthed around 1912 by a Berlin expedition of archaeologists who were sifting through the sands of Armana, the royal city built by Nefertiti's husband, King Akhenaten (r 1353–1336 BCE).

Another famous work is the so-called **Berlin Green Head** – the bald head of a priest carved from smooth green stone. Created around 400 BCE in the Late Egyptian Period, it shows Greek influence and is unusual in that it is not an actual portrait of a specific person but an idealised figure meant to exude universal wisdom and experience.

Museum für Vor- und Frühgeschichte

Highlights within this collection are the **Trojan antiquities** discovered by archaeologist Heinrich Schliemann in 1870 near Hisarlik in modern-day Turkey. However, most of the elaborate jewellery, ornate weapons and gold mugs on display are replicas because the originals became Soviet war booty after WWII and remain in Moscow. Exceptions are the three humble-looking 4500-year-old silver jars proudly displayed in their own glass case.

One floor up the grand staircase, in the Bacchus Hall, awaits another head turner: the bronze **Xanten Youth** surrounded by items from the **Barbarian Treasure of Neupotz** buried in the Rhine in the 3rd century. The iron tools, shackles, cauldrons and silverware provide important insight into daily life in the Roman-occupied Rhineland.

The exhibit on the top floor travels back even further to the Stone, Bronze and Iron Ages. Highlights include the 45,000-year-old **fossilised skull** of an 11-year-old Neanderthal boy found in 1909 in Le Moustier. Crowds also surround the 3000-year-old **Berliner Goldhut** (Berlin Gold Hat, room 305). Resembling a wizard's hat, it is covered in elaborate bands of astronomical symbols and must indeed have struck the Bronze Age people as something magical. It's one of only four of its kind unearthed worldwide.

Altes Museum

Architect Karl Friedrich Schinkel pulled out all the stops for the grand neoclassical **Altes Museum** (Old Museum; adult/concession/under 18yr €10/5/free; ⏲10am-6pm Tue, Wed & Fri-Sun, to 8pm Thu), which was the first exhibition space to open on Museumsinsel in 1830. A curtain of fluted columns gives way to a Pantheon-inspired rotunda that's the focal point of a prized antiquities collection. In the downstairs galleries, sculptures, vases, tomb reliefs and jewellery shed light on various facets of life in ancient Greece, while upstairs the focus is on the Etruscans and Romans. Top draws include the *Praying Boy* bronze sculpture, Roman silver vessels and portraits of Caesar and Cleopatra.

Greeks

This chronologically arranged exhibit on the ground floor spans all periods in ancient Greek art from the 10th to the 1st centuries BCE. Among the oldest items is a collection of bronze helmets, but it's the monumental statues and elaborate vases that show the greatest artistry.

Among the first eye-catchers is the strapping **Kouros of Didyma** (room 2), a nude male with a Mona Lisa smile and a great mop of hair. In the next gallery, all eyes are on the **Berlin Goddess**, a beautifully preserved funerary statue of a wealthy young woman in a fancy red dress. The finely carved **Seated Goddess of Tarent** (room 9) is another highlight.

Ägyptisches Museum

The biggest crowd pleaser is the **Praying Boy** (room 5), an idealised young male nude sculpted in Rhodes around 300 BCE and brought to Berlin by Frederick the Great in 1747. Both Napoleon and Stalin took a fancy to the pretty boy and temporarily abducted him as war booty to Paris and Moscow, respectively. Today, his serene smile once again radiates beneath the museum's soaring **rotunda**, which is lidded by a grand coffered and frescoed ceiling. Light filters through a central skylight illuminating 20 large-scale statues representing a who's who of ancient gods, including Nike, Zeus and Fortuna.

Etruscans & Romans

The museum's Etruscan collection is one of the largest outside Italy and contains some stunning pieces. Admire a circular shield from the grave of a warrior alongside amphorae, jewellery, coins and other items from daily life dating back as far as the 8th century BCE. Learn about the Etruscan language by studying the **tablet from Capua** and about funerary rites by examining the highly decorated **cinerary urns** and **sarcophagi**.

Adjacent rooms are dedicated to the Romans. There's fantastic sculpture, a stunning 1st-century 70-piece silver table service called the **Hildesheim Treasure** and busts of Roman leaders, including Caesar and Cleopatra. An adults-only **erotic cabinet** (behind a closed door) brims with not-so-subtle depictions of satyrs, hermaphrodites and giant phalli.

ART FOR THE PEOPLE

Museumsinsel is a product of the late-19th-century fad among European royalty to open their private collections to the public. The Louvre in Paris, the British Museum in London, the Prado in Madrid and the Glyptothek in Munich all date back to this period. In Berlin, Friedrich Wilhelm III and his successors followed suit.

Looking like a baptismal font for giants, the massive granite basin outside the Altes Museum was designed by Karl Friedrich Schinkel and carved from a single slab by Christian Gottlieb Cantian. It was considered an artistic and technical feat back in the 1820s. The original plan to install it in the museum's rotunda had to be ditched when the bowl ended up being too massive to fit into the site allocated for it. Almost 7m in diameter, it was carved in situ from a massive boulder in Brandenburg and transported via a custom-built wooden railway to the Spree and from there by barge to Berlin.

Bode-Museum

Mighty and majestic, the **Bode-Museum** (cnr Am Kupfergraben & Monbijoubrücke; adult/concession/under 18yr €10/5/free) has pushed against the northern tip of Museumsinsel like a proud ship's bow since 1904. The gloriously restored neo-baroque beauty presents sculpture, paintings, coins and Byzantine art in mostly naturally lit galleries.

The beautifully proportioned building features sweeping staircases, interior courtyards, frescoed ceilings and marble floors that give it palatial grandeur. The tone is set in the grand domed entrance hall with Andreas Schlüter's monumental sculpture of Great Elector Friedrich Wilhelm on horseback. An Italian Renaissance-style basilica featuring a glazed terracotta sculpture by Luca della Robbia leads to a smaller domed, rococo-style hall with marble statues of Frederick the Great and his generals. The galleries radiate from both sides of this axis and continue upstairs.

Skulpturensammlung

The highlight of the Bode-Museum is its famous collection of European sculpture from the early Middle Ages to the late 18th century, with a special focus on the Italian Renaissance. There are priceless masterpieces, such as Donatello's **Pazzi Madonna**, Giovanni Pisano's **Man of Sorrows** relief and Antonio Canova's **Dancer**. Staying on the ground floor, you can cruise from the Italians to the Germans by admiring the 12th-century **Gröninger Empore**, a church gallery from a former monastery that is considered a major work of the Romanesque period.

Most of the German sculptures are upstairs, including a clutch of works by the late-Gothic master carver Tilman Riemenschneider. Highlights include the exquisite **St Anne and Her Three Husbands** as well as the **Four Evangelists**. Compare Riemenschneider's emotiveness to that of his contemporaries Hans Multscher and Nicolaus Gerhaert van Leyden, whose work is also displayed here.

New since 2019 is the **James-Simon-Kabinett**, a room that shows paintings, sculpture and furniture from the private collection of this major art donor. A highlight is Andrea Mantegna's **Madonna with the Sleeping Child**.

A selection of paintings from the Gemäldegalerie (p160) displayed among the sculptures adds another layer of visual appeal.

Museum für Byzantinische Kunst

Before breaking for coffee at the elegant cafe, pop back down to the ground floor, where the Museum of Byzantine Art takes up just a few rooms off the grand domed foyer. It presents fine works of Late Antique and Byzantine art from the 3rd to the 15th centuries. The elaborate Roman sarcophagi, the ivory carvings and the mosaic icons point to the high level of artistry in these early days of Christianity.

Münzsammlung

Coin collectors will get a kick out of the Numismatic Collection on the 2nd floor. With half a million coins – and counting – it's one of the largest of its kind in the world, even if only a small fraction can be displayed at one time. The oldest farthing is from the 7th century BCE and displayed in a special case alongside the smallest, largest, fattest and thinnest coins.

Alte Nationalgalerie

The Greek temple-style **Alte Nationalgalerie** (Old National Gallery; Bodestrasse 1-3; adult/concession/under 18yr €10/5/free; ⏲10am-6pm Tue, Wed & Fri-Sun, to 8pm Thu), open since 1876, is a three-storey showcase of first-rate 19th-century European

ltes Museum (p112) and Lustgarten

art. It was a tumultuous century, characterised by revolutions and industrialisation that brought about profound changes in society. Artists reacted to the new realities in different ways. While German Romantics like Caspar David Friedrich sought solace in nature and Nazarenes like Anselm Feuerbach turned to religious subjects, the epic canvases of Adolf Menzel and Franz Krüger glorified moments in Prussian history, and the impressionists focused on light and aesthetics.

On the 1st floor, Johann Gottfried Schadow's **Statue of Two Princesses** and a bust of Johann Wolfgang von Goethe are standout sculptures. The painter Adolph Menzel also gets the star treatment – look for his famous **A Flute Concert of Frederick the Great at Sanssouci**, showing the king playing the flute at his Potsdam palace.

The 2nd floor shows impressionist paintings by famous French artists including Claude Monet, Edgar Degas, Paul Cézanne, Pierre-Auguste Renoir and Édouard Manet; Manet's **In the Conservatory** is considered a masterpiece. Among the Germans, there's Arnold Böcklin's **Isle of Death** and several canvases by Max Liebermann.

Romantics rule the top floor, where all eyes are on Caspar David Friedrich's mystical landscapes and the Gothic fantasies of Karl Friedrich Schinkel. Also look for key works by Carl Blechen and portraits by Philipp Otto Runge and Carl Spitzweg.

LUSTGARTEN

The Lustgarten (Pleasure Garden), as the patch of green fronting the Altes Museum is called, has seen many makeovers. It started as a royal kitchen garden and became a military exercise ground before being turned into a pleasure garden by Schinkel. The Nazis held mass rallies here; the East Germans ignored it. Restored to its Schinkel-era appearance, it's now a favourite resting spot for footsore tourists.

The banker JHW Wagener was an avid collector of art and arts patron who, in 1861, bequeathed his entire collection of 262 paintings to the Prussian state to form the basis of a national gallery. Just one year later, William I commissioned Friedrich August Stüler to design a suitable museum. He came up with the Alte Nationalgalerie, an imposing temple-like structure perched on a pedestal and fronted by a curtain of Corinthian columns. The entrance is reached via a sweeping double staircase crowned by a statue of Friedrich Wilhelm IV on horseback.

Museumsinsel

A HALF-DAY TOUR

Navigating around this five-museum treasure repository can be daunting, so we've created this itinerary to help you find the must-see highlights while maximising your time and energy. You'll need at least four hours and a Museumsinsel ticket for entry to all museums.

Start in the Altes Museum, where you can admire the roll call of antique gods guarded by a perky bronze statue called the ❶ **Praying Boy**, the poster child of a prized collection of antiquities. Next up, head to the Neues Museum for your audience with the ❷ **Bust of Queen Nefertiti**, the star of the Egyptian collection atop the grand central staircase.

One more floor up, don't miss the dazzling Bronze Age ❸ **Berliner Goldhut** (room 305). Leaving the Neues Museum, turn left for the Pergamonmuseum. With the namesake altar off-limits until at least 2023, the first major sight you'll see is the ❹ **Ishtar Gate**. Upstairs, pick your way through the Islamic collection, past carpets, prayer niches and a caliph's palace facade to the intricately painted ❺ **Aleppo Room**.

Jump ahead to the 19th century at the Alte Nationalgalerie to zero in on paintings by ❻ **Caspar David Friedrich** on the 3rd floor and precious sculptures such as Schadow's ❼ **Statue of Two Princesses** on the 1st floor. Wrap up your explorations at the Bode-Museum, reached in a five-minute walk. Admire the foyer with its equestrian statue of Friedrich Wilhelm, then feast your eyes on European sculpture without missing masterpieces by ❽ **Tilman Riemenschneider**.

FAST FACTS

Oldest object 700,000-year-old Paleolithic hand axe at Neues Museum

Newest object A piece of barbed wire from the Berlin Wall at Neues Museum

Oldest museum Altes Museum, 1830

Most popular museum on Museumsinsel Neues Museum (777,000 visitors)

Total Museumsinsel visitors (2017) 2.33 million

Sculptures by Tilman Riemenschneider (Bode-Museum)
Dazzling detail and great emotional expressiveness characterise the wooden sculptures by late-Gothic master carver Tilman Riemenschneider, as in his portrayal of *St Anne and Her Three Husbands* from around 1510.

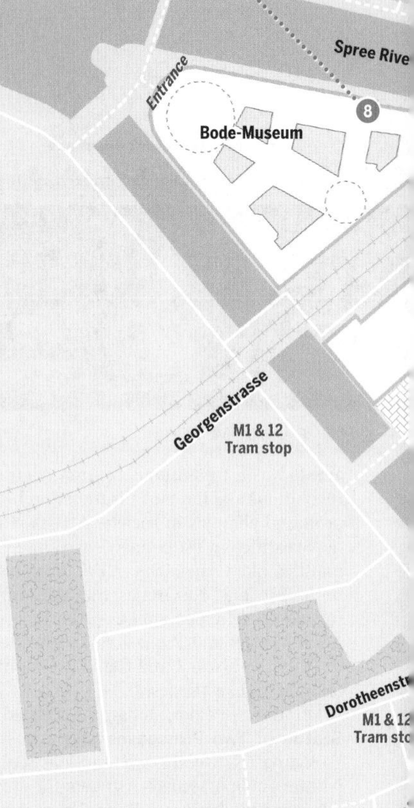

VLADIMIR WRANGEL/SHUTTERSTOCK © - AUTHORIZED BY BPK-BILDAGENTUR

Bust of Queen Nefertiti (Room 210, Neues Museum)
In the north dome, fall in love with Berlin's most beautiful woman – the 3330-year-old Egyptian queen Nefertiti, she of the long, graceful neck and timeless good looks.

Aleppo Room (Room 16, Pergamonmuseum)

A highlight of the Museum of Islamic Art, this richly painted, wood-panelled reception room from a Christian merchant's home in 17th-century Aleppo, Syria, combines Islamic floral and geometric motifs with courtly scenes and Christian themes.

Ishtar Gate (Room 9, Pergamonmuseum)

Draw breath as you enter the 2600-year-old city gate to Babylon, which has soaring walls sheathed in radiant blue-glazed bricks and adorned with ochre reliefs of strutting lions, bulls and dragons representing Babylonian gods.

Spree River

Alte Nationalgalerie

Entrance

Neues Museum

Entrance

Entrance

Bodestrasse

Altes Museum

Entrance

Berliner Dom

Lustgarten

Paintings by Caspar David Friedrich (Top Floor, Alte Nationalgalerie)

A key artist of the romantic period, Caspar David Friedrich put his own stamp on landscape painting with his dark, moody and subtly dramatic meditations on the boundaries of human life versus the infinity of nature.

Statue of Two Princesses (1st Floor, Alte Nationalgalerie)

Johann Gottfried Schadow captures Prussian princesses (and sisters) Luise and Friederike in a moment of intimacy and thoughtfulness in this double marble statue, created in 1795 at the height of the neoclassical period.

Berliner Goldhut (Room 305, Neues Museum)

Marvel at the Bronze Age artistry of the Berlin Gold Hat, a ceremonial gold cone embossed with ornamental bands that is believed to have been used in predicting the best times for planting and harvesting.

Praying Boy (Room 5, Altes Museum)

The top draw at the Old Museum is the *Praying Boy*, ancient Greece's 'Next Top Model'. The life-size bronze statue of a young male nude is the epitome of physical perfection and was cast around 300 BC in Rhodes.

SERBI / SHUTTERSTOCK ©

TOP EXPERIENCE

ADMIRE THE CITY FROM THE FERNSEHTURM

No matter where you are in Berlin, look up and chances are you'll see the Fernsehturm. The TV Tower – Germany's tallest structure – is as iconic to the city as the Eiffel Tower is to Paris and has been soaring 368m high (including the antenna) since 1969. Pinpoint city landmarks from the panorama platform at 203m (with Bar 203) or from the upstairs Sphere restaurant (207m; p124) – views are stunning on clear days.

Ordered by East German government leader Walter Ulbricht in the 1950s, the tower was built not only as a transmitter for radio and TV programs but also as a demonstration of the GDR's strength and technological prowess. However, it ended up becoming a bit of a laughing stock when it turned out that, when struck by the sun, the steel sphere below the antenna produced the reflection of a giant cross. This inspired a popular joke (not appreciated by the GDR leadership) that the phenomenon was the 'Pope's revenge' on the secular socialist state for having removed crucifixes from churches.

The tower's rocketlike shape was inspired by the space race of the 1960s and in particular the launch of the first satellite, the Soviet Sputnik. The tower is made up of the base, the 250m-high shaft, the 4800-ton sphere and the 118m-high antenna. Its original location was supposed to be the Müggelberg hills on the city's southeastern edge. Construction had already begun when the authorities realised that the tower would be in the flight path of the planned airport at nearby Schönefeld. Ulbricht then decided on its current location.

DON'T MISS

- Observation deck
- Sunset cocktails at Bar 203

PRACTICALITIES

- TV Tower
- Map p328, C3
- ☎030-247 575 875
- www.tv-turm.de
- Panoramastrasse 1a
- adult/child €18.50/9.50, fast track online ticket €22.50/13
- 9am-midnight Mar-Oct, 10am-midnight Nov-Feb, last ascent 11.30pm
- 100, 200, 300, U Alexanderplatz, S Alexanderplatz

SIGHTS

It's practically impossible to visit Berlin without spending time in this area. Explore the city's beginnings in the Nikolaiviertel, then check out the Humboldt Forum in the reconstructed Berlin City Palace, skip around superb museums, take a river cruise and keep an eye on it all from atop the Fernsehturm (TV Tower).

MUSEUMSINSEL — MUSEUM

See p108.

Alexanderplatz

FERNSEHTURM — LANDMARK

See p118.

PARK INN PANORAMA TERRASSE — VIEWPOINT

Map p328 (☎030-238 90; www.parkinn-berlin.de/en/panorama-terrace; Alexanderplatz 7; €4; ⏲noon-10pm Apr-Sep, to 6pm Oct-Mar; U Alexanderplatz, S Alexanderplatz) For sweeping city views at eye level with the Fernsehturm, head up to the rooftop Panorama Terrasse, the open-air lounge of the Park Inn hotel, some 120m above Alexanderplatz. Grab a sunlounger and relax with a cold beer or a glass of bubbly. There's a lift, of course, but it's stairs for the last five floors.

If you're lucky, you might even get to look on as gutsy base-flyers prepare to leap off the edge of the building in a controlled fall using a special winch system usually used by stuntpeople.

ST MARIENKIRCHE — CHURCH

Map p328 (St Mary's Church; www.marienkirche-berlin.de; Karl-Liebknecht-Strasse 8; ⏲10am-6pm Apr-Dec, to 4pm Jan-Mar; 🚌100, 200, 245, 300, S Hackescher Markt, Alexanderplatz, U Alexanderplatz, Rotes Rathaus) This Gothic brick gem has welcomed worshippers since the early 14th century, making it one of Berlin's oldest surviving churches. A 22m-long *Dance of Death* fresco in the vestibule inspired by a 15th-century plague leads to a relatively plain interior enlivened by numerous other art treasures. The oldest is the 1437 bronze baptismal font buttressed by a trio of dragons. The baroque alabaster pulpit by Andreas Schlüter from 1703 is another eye-catcher.

ROTES RATHAUS — HISTORIC BUILDING

Map p328 (Berlin Town Hall; ☎030-9026 2032; www.berlin.de/berliner-rathaus; Rathausstrasse 15; ⏲9am-6pm Mon-Fri; S Alexanderplatz, U Alexanderplatz, Klosterstrasse) FREE The Rotes Rathaus (Red Town Hall), a red-brick neo-Renaissance pile completed in 1869, is the seat of Berlin's governing mayor. Outside, note the terracotta frieze that illustrates historic Berlin milestones until 1871. Except during special events, much of the town hall is open to the public – pick up a brochure with a self-guided tour in the foyer and also check out the free special exhibits.

The moniker 'red', by the way, was inspired by the brick facade and not (necessarily) the political leanings of its occupants. In the neo-noir TV series *Babylon Berlin,* the Rotes Rathaus stands in for the police headquarters nicknamed the 'Red Castle'.

NEPTUNBRUNNEN — FOUNTAIN

Map p328 (Rathausplatz; 🚌100, 200, 245, U Rotes Rathaus, Alexanderplatz, S Alexanderplatz) This elaborate fountain was designed by Reinhold Begas in 1891 and depicts Neptune holding court over a quartet of buxom beauties symbolising the rivers Rhine, Elbe, Oder and Vistula. Kids get a kick out of the water-squirting turtle, seal, crocodile and snake.

SEALIFE BERLIN — AQUARIUM

Map p328 (☎0180-666 690 101; www.visitsealife.com; Spandauer Strasse 3; adult/child €19/15; ⏲10am-6pm, last admission 5pm; 🚌100, 200, 245, S Hackescher Markt, Alexanderplatz) Smile-inducing seahorses, ethereal jellyfish, sleek skates and a marine dinosaur skeleton that can be 'reanimated' are some of the crowd favourites among the 5000 denizens of this rambling aquarium. It takes you on a journey from the source of the Spree River to the North Sea and on to tropical waters. Tickets are cheaper online.

BLOCK DER FRAUEN — MEMORIAL

Map p328 (Block of Women; Rosenstrasse; S Hackescher Markt, Alexanderplatz, U Alexanderplatz) A reddish sandstone memorial in a small park on Rosenstrasse called *Block der Frauen* by Jewish-German artist Inge Hunzinger (1915–2009) pays tribute to the non-Jewish German women who peacefully but tenaciously protested against the planned deportation of their Jewish husbands who had been detained near this site in 1943.

It was a rare, courageous – and ultimately successful – act of defiance against the Nazi regime.

Humboldt Forum & Nikolaiviertel

BERLINER DOM CHURCH

Map p328 (Berlin Cathedral; ticket office 030-2026 9136; www.berlinerdom.de; Am Lustgarten; adult/concession/under 18yr €7/5/free; hours vary, usually 9am-8pm Apr-Sep, to 7pm Oct-Mar; 100, 247, 300, S Hackescher Markt, U Rotes Rathaus) Pompous yet majestic, the Italian Renaissance–style former royal court church (1905) does triple duty as house of worship, museum and concert hall. Inside it's gilt to the hilt and outfitted with a lavish marble-and-onyx altar, a 7269-pipe Sauer organ and elaborate royal sarcophagi. Climb up the 267 steps to the gallery for glorious city views.

For more dead royals, albeit in less extravagant coffins, drop below to the crypt. Skip the cathedral museum unless you're interested in the building's construction. The sanctuary has great acoustics and is often used for classical concerts, sometimes played on the famous organ. Multilingual audioguides cost €3.

NIKOLAIVIERTEL AREA

Map p328 (btwn Rathausstrasse, Breite Strasse, Spandauer Strasse & Mühlendamm; 24hr; U Klosterstrasse) FREE Commissioned by the East German government to celebrate Berlin's 750th birthday, the twee Nicholas Quarter is a half-hearted attempt at recreating the city's medieval birthplace around its oldest surviving building, the 1230 Nikolaikirche. The maze of cobbled lanes is worth a quick stroll, while several olde-worlde-style restaurants provide sustenance.

MÄRKISCHES MUSEUM MUSEUM

Map p328 (030-2400 2162; www.stadtmuseum.de; Am Köllnischen Park 5; adult/concession/under 18yr €7/4/free; noon-6pm Tue-Fri, 10am-6pm Sat & Sun; U Märkisches Museum) BerlinZEIT, the permanent exhibit at this regional history museum, offers a compact and engaging introduction to Berlin for first-time visitors. Budget about an hour to learn about historic milestones and key protagonists that shaped the city on its journey from medieval trading village to

TOP EXPERIENCE

GO BACK IN TIME AT THE DDR MUSEUM

How did regular East Germans spend their day-to-day lives? The 'touchy-feely' DDR Museum does an entertaining job of pulling back the Iron Curtain on an extinct society.

In hands-on fashion you'll learn how, under socialism, kids were put through collective potty training, engineers earned little more than farmers, and everyone, it seems, went on nudist holidays. You get to rummage through school bags, open drawers and cupboards or watch TV in a 1970s living room. And it's not only kids who love squeezing behind the wheel of a Trabant (Trabi) car for a virtual drive through an East Berlin *Plattenbauten* (prefab concrete-slab housing estate). Another highlight is a walk through a recreated 1980s apartment found inside those massive structures.

The more sinister sides of life in the GDR are also addressed, including chronic supply shortages, surveillance by the Stasi (secret police) and the Sozialistische Einheitspartei Deutschlands (SED) party's monopoly on power. You can stand in a recreated prison cell, or imagine what it was like to be in the cross hairs of a Stasi officer's sights by sitting on the victim's chair in a tiny, windowless interrogation room.

DON'T MISS

- Trabi ride
- Recreated 1980s apartment
- Stasi interrogation room

PRACTICALITIES

- GDR (East Germany) Museum
- Map p328, B4
- 030-847 123 731
- www.ddr-museum.de
- Karl-Liebknecht-Strasse 1
- adult/concession €9.80/6
- 9am-9pm
- 100, 247, 300, S Hackescher Markt

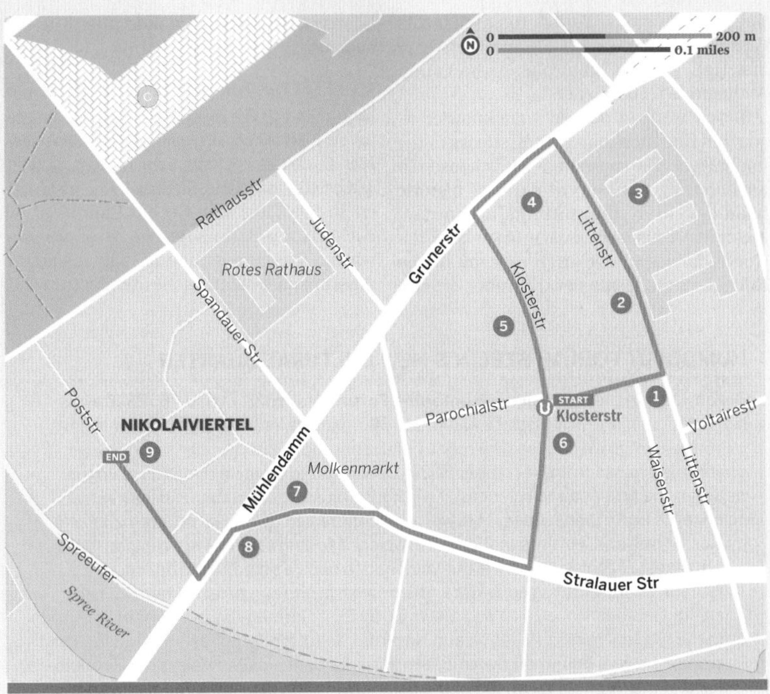

Neighbourhood Walk
Back to the Roots: History Ramble

START KLOSTERSTRASSE U-BAHN
END NIKOLAIVIERTEL
LENGTH 1.3KM; ONE HOUR

This walk charts Berlin's history from its medieval beginnings to the 20th century. From U-Bahn Klosterstrasse, walk east on Parochialstrasse. Note Berlin's oldest restaurant, 1 **Zur Letzten Instanz** (p124), which has been serving pork knuckle for nearly 400 years, then turn left on Littenstrasse and stop at a crude 8m-long pile of boulders and bricks. This is what's left of 2 **Stadtmauer**, the city wall built around 1250 to protect the first settlers from marauders. Looming above is the monumental 3 **Justizgebäude Littenstrasse**, a 1912 courthouse with a grand art nouveau foyer – feel free to pop in and take a look.

On your left, the Gothic 4 **Franziskaner Klosterkirche** (Franciscan Monastery Church) was once a prestigious school and is now used for cultural events. Follow Littenstrasse north, turn left on Grunerstrasse and left again on Klosterstrasse. The big building on your right is 5 **Altes Stadthaus** (Old City Hall); its distinctive 87m-high domed tower is crowned by the goddess Fortuna. Continue on Klosterstrasse to the 17th-century 6 **Parochialkirche**, at once graceful and monumental. Designed by the same architect as Schloss Charlottenburg, it was burnt out in WWII and, though restored, deliberately still reveals the scars of war.

Turn right on Stralauer Strasse, which leads to 7 **Molkenmarkt**, Berlin's oldest square, once a thriving marketplace. The ornate building at No 2 is the 8 **Alte Münze**, the old mint, now a space for art and cultural projects. Reichsmark, GDR Mark, Deutsche Mark and euro coins were all minted here until 2006. Note the decorative frieze depicting the evolution of metallurgy and minting.

Across the street, the 9 **Nikolaiviertel** may look medieval, but it's a product of the 1980s, built by the East German government to celebrate Berlin's 750th birthday. The 1230 Nikolaikirche and a handful of small museums are worth a visit.

today's metropolis. Period rooms like the Gothic Hall, the Guild Hall and the Weapons Hall provide atmospheric eye candy. Audioguide recommended.

If you want to deepen your knowledge, you will find more objects and stories in the upper level. The museum itself is housed in an imposing mash-up of parts of historic buildings from the surrounding region, including a bishop's palace tower and the Gothic gables of a church. A copy of the Roland statue, a medieval symbol of civic liberty and freedom, stands guard at the entrance.

MUSEUM NIKOLAIKIRCHE MUSEUM

Map p328 (☎030-2400 2162; www.stadtmuseum.de; Nikolaikirchplatz; adult/concession/under 18yr €5/3/free; ⏱10am-6pm Fri-Sun; 🚌M48, Ⓤ Klosterstrasse, Rotes Rathaus) Reconstructed in 1987, the late-Gothic Church of St Nicholas was Berlin's first house of worship when it was consecrated in 1230. It's now a museum documenting the architecture and

HUMBOLDT FORUM: BERLIN'S NEW CULTURAL QUARTER

Seven years in the making, the **Humboldt Forum** (Map p328; ☎030-265 9500; www.humboldtforum.org; Schlossplatz; 🚌100, 247, 300, Ⓤ Rotes Rathaus) FREE, Berlin's new culture and science hub inside a replica of the baroque Prussian city palace, began opening in phases from December 2020. Conceived to create a dynamic dialogue between the arts and the sciences, it will house museums, exhibits, an interactive science lab and other spaces. This will be accompanied by a lively program of performances, films and lectures that explore topical issues in science, art, religion, politics and business. Admission is free, but you need to book a timed ticket online.

Although barely damaged in WWII, the original grand city palace where Prussian rulers had resided since 1443 was blown up by East Germany's government in 1950 to drop the final curtain on Prussian and Nazi rule. To further emphasise the point, the communist rulers built their own modernist parliament – called Palast der Repubilk (Palace of the Republic) – on top of the palace ruins 26 years later. Riddled with asbestos, this building too had a date with the wrecking ball in 2006. Construction of the Humboldt Forum kicked off in 2013.

The 800-year history of the site is documented in a **permanent exhibit,** whose highlights include a 28m-long video panorama, vestiges of a medieval monastery and the original palace, and sculptures that once graced the demolished palace's facade.

A small exhibit introduces the complex's namesakes, Age of Enlightenment thinkers and brothers **Alexander and Wilhelm Humboldt**. With their curiosity and gift for examining the world from fresh perspectives, they greatly advanced cultural and scientific thought in the early 19th century.

After Nature, the first exhibit of the university-run Humboldt Lab, is a space where the public can engage with the sciences to gain a better understanding of this increasingly complex world. The exhibit takes an unflinching look at the catastrophic effects human behaviour has had on the global environment, from species loss to climate change.

An edgy immersive exhibition called **Berlin Global** examines the city of Berlin and its connections with the world in seven thematic rooms: Revolution, Free Space, Boundaries, Entertainment, War, Fashion and Interconnection.

The **Ethnological Museum** and the **Asian Art Museum** were relocated here from their Cold War–era home in the suburb of Dahlem. Their combined collections include a trove of 20,000 objects from Africa, Asia, Oceania and the Americas that illustrates the story of the world's cultures and arts through the ages.

The quince-yellow Schloss 2.0 comes with a price tag of €663 million – the federal government footed most of the bill. With the exception of the Spree-facing facade, the palace's shell is a copy of Andreas Schlüter's 17th-century original palace. Italian architect Franco Stella designed the modernist interior.

The central square, called **Schlüterhof**, and a colonnaded pathway (**Passage**) that runs through the entire building are accessible 24/7. A cupola, controversially crowned by a golden cross, graces the main entrance.

BEST OF BERLIN BY BOAT

A lovely way to experience Berlin from April to October – and take a break from museum-hopping – is on the open-air deck of a river cruiser. Several companies run relaxing Spree spins through the city centre from landing docks on the eastern side of Museumsinsel, for example outside the **DDR Museum** (Map p328; S Alexanderplatz, Hackescher Markt, U Alexanderplatz) and from the **Nikolaiviertel** (Map p328; 100, 200, TXL, U Alexanderplatz, S Alexanderplatz). Sip refreshments while a guide showers you with anecdotes (in English and German) as you glide past grand old buildings and museums, beer gardens and the government quarter. The one-hour tour costs around €17.

history of the church and the surrounding Nikolaiviertel. Grab the free audioguide for the scoop on the octagonal baptismal font and the triumphal cross, or to find out why the building is nicknamed the 'pantheon of prominent Berliners'.

There's a free 30-minute organ recital on Friday at 5pm. At other times, head up to the gallery for close-ups of the organ, a sweeping view of the interior and a chance to listen to recorded church hymns.

HANF MUSEUM BERLIN MUSEUM

Map p328 (Hemp Museum; 030-242 4827; www.hanfmuseum.de; Mühlendamm 5; adult/concession €4.50/3; 10am-8pm Tue-Fri, noon-8pm Sat & Sun; U Klosterstrasse, Rotes Rathaus) Unique in Germany, this eight-room exhibit examines the many uses of hemp; surveys its cultural, practical, medicinal and religious significance over time and in various societies; and addresses its legal status.

STAATSRATSGEBÄUDE HISTORIC BUILDING

Map p328 (Schlossplatz 1; 100, 200, TXL, U Hausvogteiplatz) This hulking building served as the seat of the GDR's State Council from 1964 until 1990 and is mainly noteworthy for incorporating the arched entry portal of the original, demolished Berlin City Palace into its facade. It was from the portal's balcony that Karl Liebknecht proclaimed Germany a 'free socialist republic' on 9 November 1918.

EATING

With its abundant fast-food outlets, Alexanderplatz isn't exactly a foodie haven, although there's a respectable self-service cafeteria in the Galeria Kaufhof (p125). Otherwise, try the food court in the Alexa mall (p125), the traditional German restaurants in the Nikolaiviertel or head straight to the Scheunenviertel for better options.

Alexanderplatz

GOOD BANK HEALTH FOOD €

Map p328 (030-3302 1410; www.good-bank.de; Rosa-Luxemburg-Strasse 5; mains €6-10; 11.30am-10pm; U Alexanderplatz, S Alexanderplatz) Good Bank made headlines as the country's first 'vertical-farm-to-table restaurant' for growing lettuces right in its tunnel-shaped space. The freshly harvested leaves find their destiny in an array of eclectic salads and colourful organic rice- or quinoa-based bowls. A great lunch option.

DOLORES CALIFORNIAN €

Map p328 (030-2809 9597; www.dolores-online.de; Rosa-Luxemburg-Strasse 7; burritos from €5.50; 11.30am-9pm; U Alexanderplatz, S Alexanderplatz) Dolores hasn't put a foot wrong since introducing the California-style burrito to Berlin. Pick your favourites from among the marinated meats (or soy meat), rice, beans, veggies, cheeses and homemade salsas, and the cheerful staff will build it on the spot. Goes perfectly with an *agua fresca* (Mexican-style lemonade).

HOFBRÄUHAUS BERLIN GERMAN €€

Map p328 (030-679 665 520; www.hofbraeu-wirtshaus.de/berlin; Karl-Liebknecht-Strasse 30; sausages €7-13, mains €10-24; noon-midnight Mon-Thu, noon-1am Fri, 10am-midnight Sun; S Alexanderplatz, U Alexanderplatz) Popular with coach tourists and field-tripping teens, this giant beer hall with 2km of wooden benches doesn't have the patina of the Munich original, but it does serve the same litre-size mugs of beer and big plates piled high with gut-busting German fare.

The roast pork, sausage salad and *Weisswurst* (veal sausage) are perennial menu favourites. A brass band and Dirndl- and Lederhosen-clad staff add further faux-authenticity.

SPHERE INTERNATIONAL €€€

Map p328 (030-247 575 875; www.tv-turm.de/en/bar-restaurant; Panoramastrasse 1; mains €10-33; 10am-10pm; ; 100, 200, 300, U Alexanderplatz, S Alexanderplatz) Berlin's highest restaurant may not take demanding taste buds for a spin, but it will take you around in a full circle within one hour. The revolving dining room, 207m up the iconic Fernsehturm (p118), delivers classic Berlin and international cuisine along with sweeping city views.

Nikolaiviertel

NGON VIETNAMESE €€

Map p328 (0174-192 3359; www.ngonberlin.com; Rathausstrasse 23; mains €12-22; 5pm-midnight Mon-Thu, noon-midnight Fri-Sun; U Alexanderplatz, Rotes Rathaus) Ngon is Berlin's first authentic Vietnamese restaurant to spotlight all layers of the country's culinary tradition, from mild in the north to spicy in the middle and fruity-sweet in the south. Move from creatively filled rolls to rich beef *pho* and the unmissable 'Tofu is on Fire' (a veg-seafood-tofu medley), all gorgeously presented in a sensuously lit setting with private-villa flair.

ZUR LETZTEN INSTANZ GERMAN €€

Map p328 (030-242 5528; www.zurletztenin stanz.com; Waisenstrasse 14-16; mains €14-26; noon-midnight Tue-Sun; U Klosterstrasse) With its folksy Old Berlin charm, this rustic restaurant has been an enduring hit since 1621 and has fed everyone from Napoleon and Charlie Chaplin to Angela Merkel. Although geared to tourists, it serves quality regional rib-stickers such as grilled pork knuckle or meatballs in caper sauce. In summer the beer garden beckons.

In winter the seats around the green-tiled stove are the cosiest.

BRAUHAUS GEORGBRAEU GERMAN €€

Map p328 (030-242 4244; www.brauhaus-georgbraeu.de; Spreeufer 4; mains €7-16; noon-midnight; U Alexanderplatz, Rotes Rathaus) Solidly on the tourist track, this old-style gastropub churns out its own light and dark Georg-Braeu beer, which can even be ordered by the metre (12 glasses at 0.2L). In winter the woodsy beer hall is perfect for tucking into hearty Berlin-style fare, while in summer tables in the riverside beer garden are golden.

A perennial menu favourite is the boiled pork knuckle *(Eisbein)*, served with sauerkraut, mushy peas, potatoes, a small beer and a schnapps for €14.20.

ZUM NUSSBAUM GERMAN €€

Map p328 (030-242 3095; Am Nussbaum 3; mains €8-16; noon-midnight; U Klosterstrasse) This cute little inn is a faithful replica of the 1507 original, a favourite watering hole of writers and artists, including the caricaturist Heinrich Zille, until it was destroyed in WWII. Today, laden with platters of classic local fare, it does a roaring trade with global nomads searching for a slice of Old Berlin.

MOBILE WURST

They're all over Alexanderplatz – the Grillwalkers, or what we cheekily call 'Self-Contained Underpaid Bratwurst Apparatus', aka SCUBA. Picture this: guys with a mobile gas grill strapped around their bellies upon which sizzling bratwursts wait for customers. At €1.90 a pop, squished into a roll and slathered with mustard or ketchup, those crunchy wieners are going fast.

DRINKING & NIGHTLIFE

Aside from a few tourist-oriented bars on Alexanderplatz and inside a clutch of hotels, there are few imbibing stations to be found in this area. For beer and Old Berlin flair, head to the restaurants in the Nikolaiviertel. For better options altogether, take the short stroll over to the Scheunenviertel.

PETIT BIJOU CAFE €

Map p330 (030-3088 2073; www.petitbijou.de; Monbijoustrasse 1; dishes €7-18; 10am-8pm; M1, M5, S Oranienburger Strasse) This little jewel of a cafe has an enviable perch on the riverbank with a happiness-inducing view

THE NEW U5

In December 2020, exactly 10 years after the ground-breaking ceremony, the latest segment of Berlin's subway network kicked into operation. The 2.2km-long extension of the U5 line added three new stations between Alexanderplatz and Brandenburg Gate. This means that it is now possible to travel from Hauptbahnhof (the main train station) straight to Friedrichshain and outer suburbs in eastern Berlin.

The design of each of the stations reflects its above-ground surroundings. The Rotes Rathaus station, for instance, was inspired by the vaulted ceilings of the city's medieval town hall, remnants of which were discovered during tunnel construction. The Unter den Linden station, which is near Humboldt University, has a science theme. The most spectacular is the Museumsinsel station (which won't open until 2021), whose tracks will be lidded by a midnight-blue starry-sky ceiling.

of the Bode-Museum. Park yourself outside under a lemon-yellow umbrella for a scrumptious breakfast, an energy-restoring juice or latte, or perhaps a post-sightseeing *aperitivo.*

BRAUFACTUM BERLIN CRAFT BEER

Map p328 (030-8471 2959; www.braufactum-alexanderplatz.de; Memhardstrasse 1; noon-late; U Alexanderplatz, S Alexanderplatz) With its urban-contempo looks and big terrace, this craft-beer outpost shakes up the gastro wasteland of Alexanderplatz. Aside from the dozen house brews like the subtly sweet-bitter India Pale Ale Progusta and the whisky-barrel-matured Barrel 1, the blackboard menu also features suds from other breweries. Solid pub grub (€7 to €10) helps keep brains in balance.

ALLEGRETTO GRAN CAFE CAFE

Map p328 (030-308 777 517; http://allegretto-grancaffe.de; Anna-Louisa-Karsch-Strasse 2; mains €10-20; noon-9pm Mon-Fri, 10am-9pm Sat & Sun; ; 100, 200, 245, S Hackescher Markt) Grab a terrace table at this modern cafe and combat sightseeing fatigue with coffee and cake, a light lunch or traditional German mains while enjoying terrific views of the Spree and the Berliner Dom.

SHOPPING

Alexanderplatz is the hub of mainstream shopping in the eastern centre. From tights to electronics, it's easy to pick up a rainbow of goods in this fairly compact area. Main draws are big box stores like Primark, TK Maxx and Decathlon, the Galeria Kaufhof department store and the massive Alexa shopping mall. Souvenir and trinket collectors should check out the little shops in the Nikolaiviertel.

ALEXA MALL

Map p328 (www.alexacentre.com; Grunerstrasse 20; 10am-9pm Mon-Sat; S Alexanderplatz, U Alexanderplatz) Power shoppers love this XXL mall, which cuts a rose-hued presence near Alexanderplatz and features the predictable range of high-street retailers. Good food court for a bite on the run.

GALERIA KAUFHOF DEPARTMENT STORE

Map p328 (030-247 430; www.galeria.de; Alexanderplatz 9; 10am-8pm Mon-Wed, to 9pm Thu-Sat; S Alexanderplatz, U Alexanderplatz) A full makeover by Josef Paul Kleihues turned this former GDR-era department store into a glitzy retail cube, complete with a glass-domed light court and a sleek travertine skin that glows green at night. There's little you won't find on the five football-field-size floors, including a gourmet supermarket on the ground floor.

IC! BERLIN FASHION & ACCESSORIES

Map p328 (030-220 666 055; www.ic-berlin.de; Münzstrasse 5; noon-6pm Mon-Sat; ; U Weinmeisterstrasse) The flagship store of this Berlin-based but internationally famous eyewear maker stocks more than 500 featherweight frames with their signature klutz-proof, screw-less hinges. If needed, there's an optician on-site to assess your prescription, and coffee and a sofa for chilled shopping. Ask about its free factory tours.

Hackescher Markt & Scheunenviertel

HACKESCHER MARKT AREA | TORSTRASSE & AROUND

Neighbourhood Top Five

❶ **Hackesche Höfe** (p130) Exploring fashion boutiques, shops, galleries and cafes in this charismatic courtyard maze.

❷ **Neue Synagoge** (p128) Admiring the exotic architecture and studying up on the quarter's Jewish history at this local landmark.

❸ **KW Institute for Contemporary Art** (p129) Keeping tabs on the latest developments in the art world at this groundbreaking exhibit space.

❹ **Haus Schwarzenberg** (p137) Picking your favourite street-art motif and checking out the exhibits in this funky vestige of pre-reunification Berlin.

❺ **Boutique hopping** (p138) Roaming the warren of lanes in search of cool threads and accessories in local and international stores.

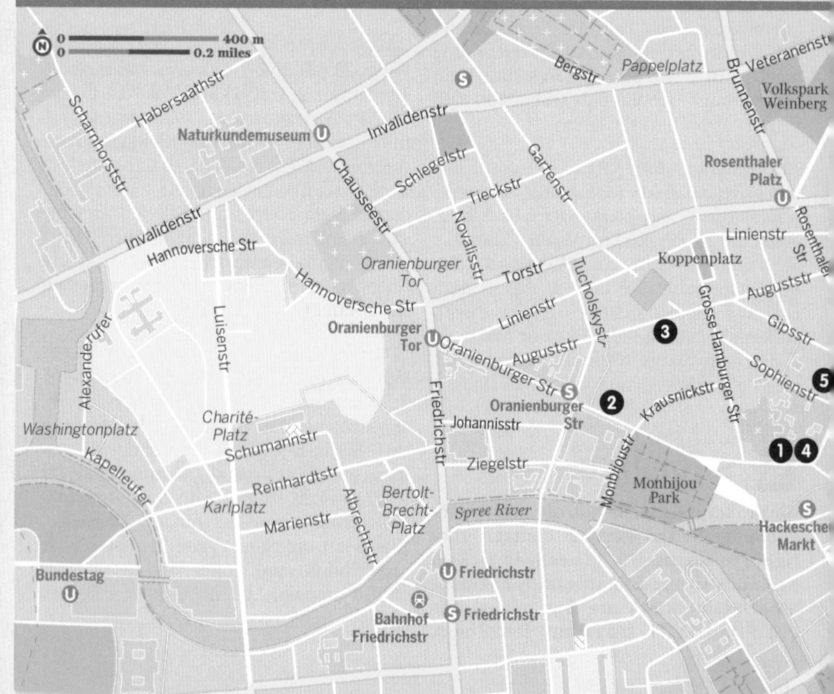

For more detail of this area see Maps p330 and p332

Explore Scheunenviertel

The Scheunenviertel, one of Berlin's oldest neighbourhoods, has morphed into a grown-up cosmopolitan district dappled with respected local and international designer boutiques, third-wave coffee shops and often boundary-pushing restaurants. A good place to embark on an aimless wander around its web of narrow lanes is the historic Hackesche Höfe (p130) courtyard ensemble. Don't start before midmorning, though, as the streets are still very quiet until then.

Art fanciers, too, have plenty to look forward to in the Scheunenviertel. Exploring the galleries and exhibit spaces along Auguststrasse and its side streets can easily take the better part of an afternoon.

Not to be missed is the rebuilt Neue Synagoge (p128) on Oranienburger Strasse. Its gleaming dome is a poignant reminder of the revival of Berlin's Jewish community, which has its hub here in the Scheunenviertel.

More change is afoot on Oranienburger Strasse, where construction of an urban quarter called Am Tacheles is under way. The quarter will incorporate the former Kunsthaus Tacheles, a famous artists squat in a dilapidated pre-WWII department store between 1990 and 2012. Not far away, another huge development, the Forum an der Museumsinsel, is taking shape in a cluster of historic brick buildings that was originally used by the post office and the Charite hospital.

Local Life

Shopping Find out what keeps Berlin designers' sewing machines humming by prowling the backstreets for the shops of fashion-forward local labels.

Bar-hopping Play it cool when joining hotties and hopefuls for a classy buzz in Torstrasse's door-staff-guarded booze burrows.

Chilling in Monbijoupark Grab a cold beverage and a blanket and catch some rays with a view of the Berliner Dom at this pint-sized riverside park.

Getting There & Away

U-Bahn Weinmeisterstrasse (U8) is the most central station. For Torstrasse, get off at Rosenthaler Platz (U8), Rosa-Luxemburg-Platz (U2) or Oranienburger Tor (U6).

S-Bahn Hackescher Markt (S5, S7, S75) and Oranienburger Strasse (S1, S2, S25) stations are both good jumping-off points.

Tram M1 runs from Museumsinsel (Museum Island) to Prenzlauer Berg and stops throughout the Scheunenviertel.

Bus No 142 links Hauptbahnhof with Ostbahnhof via Torstrasse.

Lonely Planet's Top Tip

On a sunny summer day, spend a mood-enhancing spell in the Weinbergspark, a compact patch of green just north of Rosenthaler Platz. Once covered by vineyards, it's now a lovely spot to spread a blanket by the little pond, sniff out the rose garden with its beer-dispensing kiosk (p136) or enjoy Austrian cuisine in a 1950s pavilion.

Best Places to Eat

- Rutz (p134)
- Katz Orange (p134)
- Frea (p133)
- KWA (p131)
- Kopps (p132)

For reviews, see p131.

Best Places to Drink

- Buck & Breck (p136)
- Torbar (p136)
- Rosengarten (p136)
- Melody Nelson (p136)

For reviews, see p134.

Best Places to Shop

- Bonbonmacherei (p138)
- Paper & Tea (p139)
- Kauf Dich Glücklich (p139)
- Do You Read Me?! (p139)

For reviews, see p138.

TOP EXPERIENCE

TAKE IN HISTORY AT THE NEUE SYNAGOGE

The gleaming gold dome of the Neue Synagoge is the most visible symbol of Berlin's revitalised Jewish community. The original 1866 building was once Germany's largest synagogue but was badly hit by bombing raids in WWII. Its contemporary reincarnation is not so much a house of worship (although prayer services do take place) as a museum and place of remembrance.

For the original synagogue, architect Eduard Knoblauch looked to the Alhambra in Granada for inspiration, which explains the exotic Moorish design elements. Today's version replicates the elaborate facade and the shiny dome but is otherwise modern on the inside. Consecrated on Rosh Hashanah in 1866, the building seated 3200 people, making it Germany's largest synagogue at the time.

During the 1938 Kristallnacht (Night of the Broken Glass) pogroms, local police chief Wilhelm Krützfeld prevented a gang of SA (Sturmabteilung, a militia of the Nazi party) troopers from setting it on fire, an act of civil courage commemorated by a plaque affixed to the main facade. The German Wehrmacht used the synagogue as a warehouse until bombs levelled it in 1943. After the war, the ruin lingered until reconstruction began in 1988 on the 50th anniversary of Kristallnacht.

Rededicated in 1995, today's Neue Synagoge houses the **Centrum Judaicum**, a memorial and exhibition space that's also a centre of Berlin's Jewish community. In addition to temporary presentations, the permanent exhibit 'Open ye the Gates' features architectural fragments and objects recovered from the ruins of the building before its reconstruction. They include a Torah scroll and an eternal lamp, and help tell the history of the building and the people associated with it.

DON'T MISS

- The facade
- The dome
- Torah scroll

PRACTICALITIES

- Map p330, B4
- ☎030-8802 8300
- www.centrumjudaicum.de
- Oranienburger Strasse 28-30
- adult/concession €7/4.50, audioguide €3
- 10am-6pm Mon-Fri, to 7pm Sun Apr-Sep, 10am-6pm Sun-Thu & 10am-3pm Fri Oct-Mar
- M1, U Oranienburger Tor, S Oranienburger Strasse

SIGHTS

Art, architecture, Jewish history and new urban development characterise the Scheunenviertel. Start your explorations at the Hackesche Höfe courtyard ensemble, then meander the narrow lanes, perhaps with a focus on Grosse Hamburger Strasse, Auguststrasse and Alte Schönhauser Strasse.

NEUE SYNAGOGE — SYNAGOGUE

See p128.

JÜDISCHE MÄDCHENSCHULE — HISTORIC BUILDING

Map p330 (Jewish Girls' School; www.maedchenschule.org; Auguststrasse 11-13; ⏲hours vary; 🚊M1, S Oranienburger Strasse, U Oranienburger Tor) FREE With its red-brick facade broken up by horizontal window bands, the former Jewish Girls' School is a prime example of 1920s New Objectivity architecture. Forcibly closed by the Nazis in 1942, it again served as a school until 1996 before being rebooted as a cultural and culinary hub in 2012. Plenty of original design features have survived, including classroom lights and the richly tiled hallways leading to two restaurants and three art spaces. Its Jewish architect, Alexander Beer, perished at Theresienstadt concentration camp.

MUSEUM FRIEDER BURDA – SALON BERLIN — MUSEUM

Map p330 (☎030-2404 7404; www.museum-frieder-burda.de/en/salon-berlin; Auguststrasse 11-3; ⏲noon-6pm Thu-Sat; 🚊M1, U Oranienburger Tor, S Oranienburger Strasse) FREE This petite exhibition and project space in the historic Jüdische Mädchenschule presents highlights from the main Frieder Burda Museum in Baden-Baden, often in dialogue with international contemporary art.

KW INSTITUTE FOR CONTEMPORARY ART — GALLERY

Map p330 (☎030-243 4590; www.kw-berlin.de; Auguststrasse 69; adult/concession €8/6, 6-9pm Thu free; ⏲11am-7pm Mon, Wed & Fri-Sun, to 9pm Thu; 🚊M1, S Oranienburger Strasse, U Oranienburger Tor) Founded in the early 1990s in an old margarine factory, nonprofit KW played a key role in turning the Scheunenviertel into Berlin's first major post-Wall art district. It continues to stage boundary-pushing exhibits that reflect the latest – and often radical – trends in contemporary art.

KW's founding director, Klaus Biesenbach, also inaugurated the **Berlin Biennale** (www.berlinbiennale.de; ⏲Jun-Sep even-numbered years) in 1998. The courtyard Café Bravo (p136) in a glass pavilion by Dan Graham makes for a stylish culture break.

HECKMANN-HÖFE — HISTORIC SITE

Map p330 (www.heckmannhoefe.de; Oranienburger Strasse 32; ⏲24hr; 🚊M1, S Oranienburger Strasse) FREE For a retreat from the urban frenzy, skip on over to this idyllic 19th-century courtyard complex that links Oranienburger Strasse with Auguststrasse. Aside from boutiques, restaurants and a theatre, it also shelters the adorable Bonbonmacherei (p138), an old-fashioned candy kitchen and shop.

Construction of the complex began in 1799 and continued in the 19th century when its then-owner, a timber merchant, added a horse barn and a coach house. In 1905 it became the headquarters of the Heckmann company that specialised in building distilleries.

When entering from Auguststrasse, gaze upwards for a photogenic view of the dome of the Neue Synagoge.

SAMMLUNG HOFFMANN — GALLERY

Map p330 (☎030-2849 9120; www.sammlung-hoffmann.de; Sophienstrasse 21, Sophie-Gips-Höfe, 2nd courtyard, entrance C; tours adult/concession €10/8; ⏲11am-4pm Sat; U Weinmeisterstrasse) Blink and you'll miss the doorway leading to the Sophie-Gips-Höfe, a former sewing-machine factory built around a trio of courtyards linking Sophienstrasse and Gipsstrasse. In the second courtyard, Erika Hoffmann resides, surrounded by high-calibre contemporary art that she and her late husband Rolf collected for decades. On Saturdays she opens her home for 90-minute tours (book ahead online or by phone). Children under 10 not allowed.

FRIEDHOF GROSSE HAMBURGER STRASSE — CEMETERY

Map p330 (☎030-880 280; www.jg-berlin.org; Grosse Hamburger Strasse 26; ⏲7.30am-5pm Mon-Thu, to 2.30pm Fri, 8am-5pm Sun Apr-Sep, 7.30am-4pm Mon-Thu, to 2.30pm Fri, 8am-4pm Sun Oct-Mar; 🚊M1, S Hackescher Markt, U Weinmeisterstrasse) What looks like a small park is in fact Berlin's oldest Jewish cemetery, destroyed by the Nazis in 1943. Some 2700 people were buried here between 1672 and 1827, including the philosopher Moses

Mendelssohn. There's a symbolic tombstone in his honour. A sarcophagus filled with destroyed gravestones stands mute witness to all the interred residents.

TIMES ART CENTER BERLIN GALLERY

Map p330 (☎030-2478 1038; www.timesartcenter.org; Brunnenstrasse 9; ⊙noon-7pm Tue-Sat) FREE Contemporary Chinese art has thus far pretty much flown under the radar in Western countries, a shortcoming the private, nonprofit Guangzhou Times Art Museum set out to change by opening its first European branch in Berlin in 2018. On three suitably austere floors, curators mount several boundary-pushing shows annually, with a focus on multimedia and video art.

BRECHT-WEIGEL MUSEUM MUSEUM

Map p332 (☎030-200 571 844; www.adk.de/de/archiv/museen/brecht-weigel-museum; Chausseestrasse 125; tours adult/concession €5/2.50; ⊙tours half-hourly 10-11.30am & 2-3.30pm Tue, 10-11.30am & 5-6.30pm Thu, 10-11.30am Wed & Fri, 10am-3.30pm Sat, hourly 11am-6pm Sun; UOranienburger Tor, Naturkundemuseum) Playwright Bertolt Brecht lived in this apartment from 1953 until his death in 1956. Tours (in German) take you inside his office, a large library, and the tiny bedroom where he died. Decorated with Chinese artwork, the rooms have been left as though he'd briefly stepped out, leaving his hat and woollen cap hanging on the door.

Downstairs are the cluttered quarters of his actress wife, Helene Weigel, who lived here until 1971. The couple are buried in the adjacent Dorotheenstädtischer Friedhof. The museum offers tours of the cemetery at 2.30pm on Wednesday.

DOROTHEENSTÄDTISCHER FRIEDHOF I CEMETERY

Map p332 (☎030-461 7279; http://evfbs.de/tickets; Chausseestrasse 126; entry free, chapel tours adult/concession €10/5; ⊙8am-4pm Jan & Dec, to 5pm Feb & Nov, to 6pm Mar & Oct, to 8pm May-Aug; UOranienburger Tor, Naturkundemuseum) This compact 18th-century cemetery is the place of perpetual slumber for a veritable roll call of famous Germans, including philosophers GWF Hegel and Johann Gottlieb Fichte, architect Karl Friedrich Schinkel, sculptor Christian Daniel Rauch and writers Bertolt Brecht and Heinrich Mann. A map by the entrance shows grave locations. The burial chapel harbours an ethereal

TOP EXPERIENCE
WANDER THROUGH THE HACKESCHE HÖFE

The Hackesche Höfe is the largest and most famous of the courtyard ensembles peppered throughout the Scheunenviertel. Built in 1907, it lingered through the city's division before undergoing a total makeover in the mid-1990s. In 1996 the eight interlinked courtyards reopened to great fanfare with a congenial mix of cafes, galleries, indie boutiques and entertainment venues. The main entrance off Rosenthaler Strasse leads to **Court I**, prettily festooned with ceramic tiles by art-nouveau architect August Endell. One of Berlin's best cabarets, the **Chamäleon Theatre** (p138), is located here in a historic art-nouveau ballroom. It presents a fun and innovative mix of acrobatics, music, dance and comedy – no German skills required! Cinephiles flock upstairs to the **Hackesche Höfe Kino** (p138), an art-house cinema in the same building.

Shoppers can look forward to galleries and the flagship shops of Berlin designers. If you're a fan of the little characters on Berlin traffic lights, stock up on souvenirs at **Ampelmann Berlin** (p139) in Court V. Court VII leads off to the **Rosenhöfe**, a frilly art nouveau–inspired courtyard with a sunken rose garden and tendril-like balustrades.

DON'T MISS

- Endell's art-nouveau facade in Court I
- Berlin designer boutiques such as Trippen
- Rosenhöfe

PRACTICALITIES

- Hackesche Courtyards
- Map p330, D4
- ☎030-2809 8010
- www.hackesche-hoefe.com
- M1, SHackescher Markt, UWeinmeisterstrasse

light installation by James Turrell that can be seen on hour-long guided tours. Check times and buy tickets online.

A wander around the cemetery brings you face to face with many artistic tombstones. Schinkel, in fact, designed his own. Dramatist Heiner Müller joined the illustrious group in 1995; fans still leave cigars for him. There's also a memorial to resistance fighters killed by the Nazis in the aftermath of the failed assassination attempt on Hitler on 20 July 1944.

EATING

The Scheunenviertel packs in so much culinary variety you could eat your way around the world in a day. Practically all tastes, budgets and food neuroses are catered for in restaurants ranging from comfy neighbourhood joints to big-city dining shrines, health-nut havens to ho-hum tourist traps, plus several Michelin-starred establishments.

Hackescher Markt Area

★KWA — MIDDLE EASTERN €

Map p330 (030-3552 9966; www.eatkwa.de; Gipsstrasse 2; mains €8-17; noon-10pm Sun-Thu, to 11pm Fri & Sat; U Rosenthaler Platz, Weinmeisterstrasse) Kebab with Attitude has upped the ante in the Berlin *Döner* stakes by using only free-range, sustainable beef and chicken and hand-stacking it onto the giant skewer. Skip the fancy versions with mango or truffle and keep it classic with crisp cabbage and salad. Excellent homemade sauces and *ayran* (Turkish yogurt drink). Conclusion: pricey but worth it.

BEETS & ROOTS — INTERNATIONAL €

Map p330 (www.beetsandroots.de; Grosse Hamburger Strasse 38; mains €6-13; 11am-9pm Mon-Fri, noon-8pm Sat & Sun; M1, M5, S Oranienburger Strasse, U Rosenthaler Platz) If you're after a quick, healthy food pick-me-up, this small but growing Berlin chain has you covered. Its colourful salads, wraps and bowls are all prepared to order and include vegan, dairy- and gluten-free options. Top picks include the Japanese salmon bowl with pulled salmon, edamame and yuzu dressing and the chipotle-meatball wrap. Check the website for other locations.

PETIT BIJOU — CAFE €

Map p330 (030-3088 2073; www.petitbijou.de; Monbijoustrasse 1; dishes €7-18; 10am-8pm; M1, M5, S Oranienburger Strasse) This little jewel of a cafe has an enviable perch on the riverbank with a happiness-inducing view of the Bode-Museum. Park yourself outside under a lemon-yellow umbrella for a scrumptious breakfast, an energy-restoring juice or latte, or perhaps a post-sightseeing *aperitivo*.

TADSHIKISCHE TEESTUBE — RUSSIAN €

Map p330 (030-204 1112; www.tadshikische-teestube.de; KunstHof, Oranienburger Strasse 27; mains €7-12; 4-11pm Mon-Fri, noon-11pm Sat & Sun; M1, S Oranienburger Strasse) Treat yourself to a Russian tea ceremony complete with silvery samovar, biscuits and vodka, or tuck into hearty Russian *blini* (pancakes) or *vareniki* (dumplings) while reclining amid plump pillows, hand-carved sandalwood pillars and heroic murals in this original Tajik tearoom. The authentic space was gifted by the Soviets to the East German government in 1974. Cash only.

DISTRICT MÔT — VIETNAMESE €

Map p330 (030-2008 9284; www.district-mot.com; Rosenthaler Strasse 62; dishes €6.50-21.50; noon-midnight; ; M1, U Rosenthaler Platz) At this colourful mock-Saigon street-food parlour, patrons squat on tiny plastic stools around wooden tables where rolls of toilet paper irreverently stand in for paper napkins. The warm glass-noodle salad in any variation is a dependable pick, but it's the De La Sauce *bao* burger that has collected the accolades.

HOUSE OF SMALL WONDER — FUSION €

Map p332 (030-2758 2877; www.houseofsmallwonder.de; Johannisstrasse 20; mains €8-21; 9am-10pm; ; U Oranienburger Tor, S Oranienburger Strasse, Friedrichstrasse) A wrought-iron staircase spirals up to this day-to-night oasis where potted plants and whimsical decor create a relaxed backyard-garden feel. The food is mostly Japanese riffs on international comfort food, like the *mentaiko* spaghetti, the millefeuille *katsu* or the Okinawan taco rice. Also a popular spot for brunch or just coffee and home-baked pastries like the matcha roulade.

MURET LA BARBA — ITALIAN €€

Map p330 (030-2809 7212; www.muretlabarba.de; Rosenthaler Strasse 61; mains €15-31; 11am-midnight Mon-Fri, noon-midnight Sat &

STUMBLING UPON HISTORY

If you lower your gaze you'll see them all over town, but nowhere are they more concentrated than in the Scheunenviertel: small brass paving stones in front of house entrances. Called **Stolpersteine** (stumbling blocks), they are part of a nationwide project by Berlin-born artist Gunter Demnig and are essentially mini-memorials honouring the people (usually Jews) who lived in the respective houses before being killed by the Nazis. The engravings indicate the person's name, birth year, year of deportation, the name of the concentration camp where they were taken and the date they perished.

Sun; M1, U Rosenthaler Platz) This wine shop and bar-restaurant combo exudes the kind of rustic authenticity that instantly transports the cognoscenti to Italy. Feast on feisty antipasti, cheese and salami or tuck into hearty pastas or meaty mains made with top ingredients imported from the motherland. Every wine is available by the glass or bottle.

★KOPPS — VEGAN €€

Map p330 (030-4320 9775; www.kopps-berlin.de; Linienstrasse 94; 3-course lunch €15, 3-course dinner menu €48, additional courses €8, 4-course brunch €25; noon-2pm & 5.30-9.30pm Sun-Thu, 5.30-10.30pm Fri & Sat; ; M1, U Rosenthaler Platz) If you're in the mood for plant-based fine dining, call the Kopps! From turnips to carrots, the cosmo-comfy Scheunenviertel kitchen has been coaxing maximum flavour out of the vegetable kingdom long before vegan went mainstream. The beautiful nosh is matched by a wine list heavy on natural and organic bottles. Loyal locals practically mob the place on weekends for brunch.

REMI — EUROPEAN €€

Map p330 (030-2759 3090; www.remi-berlin.de; Torstrasse 48; mains €15-24; noon-3pm & 6-10pm Tue-Sat; U Rosa-Luxemburg-Platz) The design of this modern and airy brasserie mixes and matches materials, from the burgundy granite bar and two-tone chairs to the eye-catching light sculpture. And the modern European food fashioned in the open kitchen from small-footprint ingredients is just as eclectic. Lunches are light and peppy, dinners more complex and combinable into four-course menus.

NIGHT KITCHEN — MEDITERRANEAN €€

Map p330 (030-2357 5075; www.nightkitchenberlin.com; Oranienburger Strasse 32; small plates €5-23, Dinner with Friends per person €42 or €56; 5-11pm; ; M1, M5, S Oranienburger Strasse, U Oranienburger Tor) This smartly seductive bistro is often packed with punters hungry for modern Med spins inspired by the mothership in Tel Aviv. You're free to order à la carte, but the guiding concept here is 'Dinner with Friends', a chef-collated meal designed for sharing with your posse. Sit inside at the wrap-around bar or al fresco in the candlelit garden and patio.

CLÄRCHENS BALLHAUS — GERMAN €€

Map p330 (030-555 785 440; https://claerchensball.haus; Auguststrasse 24; mains €11-22; 5-11pm Mon-Thu & Sun, 5pm-1am Fri, noon-1am Sat; M1, S Oranienburger Strasse) The glitter walls are gone and so are the beloved cross-generational dance parties. Since Clärchens changed owners in 2019, the venerable early-20th-century ballroom has mostly become a restaurant serving modern reinterpretations of traditional Berlin cuisine as well as Sunday brunch in the charmingly morbid Spiegelsaal (Mirror Hall) upstairs. In summer, the beer garden beckons.

SCHWARZWALDSTUBEN — GERMAN €€

Map p330 (030-2809 8084; www.schwarzwaldstuben-berlin.com; Tucholskystrasse 48; mains €7.50-19.50; noon-midnight Mon-Fri, 9am-11pm Sat & Sun; M1, S Oranienburger Strasse, U Oranienburger Tor) Fancy a *Hansel and Gretel* moment? Join the other 'lost kids' for satisfying slow food from the southwest German regions of Baden and Swabia. Tuck into gut-filling plates of *Kässpätzle* (mac 'n' cheese), *Maultaschen* (ravioli-like pasta), crispy *Flammkuchen* (Alsatian pizza) or a giant schnitzel with fried potatoes. Dine inside amid rustic forest decor or grab a sidewalk table. Cash only.

MOGG — DELI €€

Map p330 (0176 6496 1344; www.moggmogg.com; Auguststrasse 11-13; mains €10-16; noon-9pm; ; M1, M5, S Oranienburger Strasse) At Berlin's first New York–style Jewish deli, home-cured and smoked pastrami on rye feeds tummy and soul in an arty 1930s-inspired setting with purple-topped benches and Finnish designer chairs. The menu also features non-traditional deli picks like chicken-liver brûlée and seared salmon with shaved-fennel salad. The creamy New York cheesecake is among the best in town.

GRILL ROYAL
STEAK €€€

Map p332 (☎030-2887 9288; www.grillroyal.com; Friedrichstrasse 105b; steaks €34-155; ⊙5-11pm; 📶; S Friedrichstrasse, U Friedrichstrasse) With its airy dining room, original look-at-me art, polyglot staff and open kitchen, Grill Royal ticks all the boxes of a true metropolitan restaurant. A platinum card is a handy accessory if you want to slurp your oysters and tuck into aged prime steaks in the company of A-listers, power politicians, pouty models and 'trustafarians'.

Riverside tables are the place to be in fine weather.

ZENKICHI
JAPANESE €€€

Map p332 (☎030-2463 0810; www.zenkichi.de; Johannisstrasse 20; 7-course tasting menu €75-105; ⊙5.30-11pm; 🖉; U Oranienburger Tor, Friedrichstrasse, S Friedrichstrasse) Romance runs high at this lantern-lit subterranean *izakaya* (Japanese pub), which serves faithfully executed gourmet Japanese fare in cosy alcoves with black-lacquer tables shielded by bamboo blinds for extra privacy. Only set menus are available – perfect to sample the complexity of flavours and textures and ideally paired with premium pure-rice sake imported from artisanal Japanese brewers.

PAULY SAAL
FRENCH €€€

Map p330 (☎030-3300 6070; www.paulysaal.com; Auguststrasse 11-13; 3/4/5-course menu €85/105/125; ⊙7-10pm Wed-Sat; 🚊M1, S Oranienburger Strasse, U Oranienburger Tor) Since taking the helm at this Michelin-starred outpost, Dirk Gieselmann has given the menu a traditional French workout while following the seasonal-regional-organic credo. Only multicourse menus are served, even at lunch. The venue itself – in the edgy-art-decorated gym of a former Jewish girls' school (p129) in a Bauhaus building – is simply stunning. On balmy days, the tables beneath the old schoolyard's trees are mighty tempting, too.

Torstrasse & Around

DALUMA
HEALTH FOOD €

Map p330 (☎030-2095 0255; www.daluma.de; Weinbergsweg 3; dishes €6-10; ⊙8am-8pm Mon-Fri, 9am-7pm Sat, 10am-7pm Sun; 🚊M1, M8, M10, U Rosenthaler Platz) A pioneer of the detox trend in Berlin, Daluma serves up power smoothies, build-your-own bowls and wholesome cereals amid purist decor tempered by herringbone flooring and potted plants. In summer the outdoor benches invite lingering. Also stocks its own small line of skincare and nutritional supplements.

DADA FALAFEL
MIDDLE EASTERN €

Map p332 (☎030-2759 6927; www.facebook.com/dadafalafel; Linienstrasse 132; dishes €3.50-8.50; ⊙noon-8pm Mon-Fri, to 6pm Sat; 📶🖉; 🚊M1, U Oranienburger Tor) After just one bite of Dada's freshly prepared falafel or *shawarma* doused with a tangy homemade sauce, you too will understand why there's always a queue of local loyalists at this teensy outpost with adjacent dining space–gallery and summer terrace.

ROSENTHALER GRILL UND SCHLEMMERBUFFET
MIDDLE EASTERN €

Map p330 (☎030-283 2153; www.rosenthaler-grill.de; Torstrasse 125; dishes €3-8; ⊙24hr; 🚊M1, 12, U Rosenthaler Platz) Veteran family-run *Döner* and kebab joint with homemade sauces and bread, indoor-outdoor seating and nonstop service for early birds, night owls and everyone in-between. Also does respectable grilled chicken and pizza.

STORE KITCHEN
INTERNATIONAL €

Map p330 (☎030-405 044 550; www.thestorex.com/berlin; Torstrasse 1; dishes €6-14; ⊙10am-7pm Mon-Sat; 📶; U Rosa-Luxemburg-Platz) This is the kind of impossibly trendy place that had food fanciers excited the moment it opened inside hipper-than-thou lifestyle and fashion temple The Store, on the ground floor of Soho House. Head here if you crave breakfast, salads, sandwiches and light meals that capture the latest global food trends while using the produce of local suppliers.

★FREA
VEGAN €€

Map p330 (☎030-9839 6198; www.frea.de; Torstrasse 180; mains €17-18; ⊙5.30pm-midnight; 🖉; 🚌142, U Rosenthaler Platz) As a completely vegan and zero-waste restaurant, Frea pushes new boundaries in ethical and ultra-sustainable eating. From sourdough bread to chocolate, everything's made in-house from regional ingredients; food scraps are composted and returned to the growers as fertiliser. Dishes like pumpkin-potato-filled agnolotti may be modest in size but pack a big flavour punch. Note the cool lampshades made from fungi.

★KATZ ORANGE INTERNATIONAL €€

Map p330 (030-983 208 430; www.katzorange.com; Bergstrasse 22; mains €18-25; 6-11pm; M8, U Rosenthaler Platz) With its thoughtful farm-to-table menu, stylish country flair and top-notch cocktails, the 'Orange Cat' hits a gastro grand slam. It will have you purring for such perennial favourites as Duroc pork that's been slow-roasted for 12 hours (nicknamed 'candy on bone'). The setting in a castle-like former brewery is stunning, especially in summer when the patio opens.

CECCONI'S ITALIAN €€

Map p330 (030-405 044 680; www.cecconisberlin.com; Torstrasse 1; mains €14-35; noon-3pm & 6-11pm Mon-Fri, 11am-3pm & 6-11pm Sat & Sun; ; M2, M4, M5, M6, M8, U Rosa-Luxemburg-Platz) Within members-only Soho House but open to all, Cecconi's exhibits metropolitan flair with red-leather booths, marble floors, an open kitchen and a suitably sophisticated clientele. Aside from pasta, pizza and risotto dishes – some pimped up with lobster and black truffle – the menu also checks the superfoods box with its quinoa and black-kale salads.

★RUTZ GERMAN €€€

Map p332 (030-2462 8760; www.rutz-restaurant.de; Chausseestrasse 8; 6/8-course menu €180/220; 6-11pm Tue-Sat; U Oranienburger Tor) At the top of an illuminated onyx staircase sits Rutz, Berlin's first restaurant awarded three Michelin stars. It's the realm of Marco Müller, whose 'Inspiration' menus showcase his dedication to creativity and quality. Exquisite wine or nonalcoholic-drink parings ensure that you'll remember your meal long after paying the – significant – bill.

EINSUNTERNULL INTERNATIONAL €€€

Map p332 (030-2757 7810; www.einsunternull.com; Hannoversche Strasse 1; 6-course dinner menu €139; 6-11pm Thu-Mon; ; M1, U Oranienburger Tor) The name means 'one below zero', but the food at Michelin-starred Einsunternull is actually happening hot. Adventurous palates get to embark on a radically regional, product-focused journey that draws upon such time-tested techniques as preservation and fermentation. A vegetarian menu and nonalcoholic-drink pairings are available.

TO THE BONE STEAKHOUSE €€€

Map p330 (030-4073 3440; http://tothebone.bonita.berlin; Torstrasse 96; antipasti €11-16, steaks per 100g from €9; 6-11pm Mon-Sat, bar to 1am Mon-Thu, to 3am Fri & Sat; ; U Rosenthaler Platz) If you love meat *and* Italian food, this hip joint is your kinda place. Sip a potent Negroni while scanning art by Gerhard Richter and Frank Thiel and anticipating super-aromatic, organic cuts of beef straight from Italy. The kitchen also puts ample creativity into the antipasti: the succulent bone marrow with oxtail confit is a mainstay.

DRINKING & NIGHTLIFE

The Scheunenviertel has plenty of bars to match the demands of its creative, international and well-heeled residents and visitors. Torstrasse is an especially fertile hunting ground, but there are also some cute wine bars, gay haunts and offbeat watering holes tucked into the quiet side lanes.

Hackescher Markt Area

AMANO BAR BAR

Map p330 (030-809 4150; www.amanogroup.de/de/eat-and-drink/amano-bar; Auguststrasse 43; 5pm-late; ; M1, M8, 12, U Rosenthaler Platz) This glamorous vixen at the budget-hip Hotel Amano (p249) juxtaposes a cool green-marble bar with warm furnishings and lighting and attracts global sophisticates with both classic and original libations. DJs on Friday and Saturday. From May to September it expands to the rooftop terrace for great sunset-watching.

AUFSTURZ PUB

Map p330 (030-2804 7407; www.aufsturz.de; Oranienburger Strasse 67; noon-late; ; M1, M5, U Oranienburger Tor, S Oranienburger Strasse) Mingle in the warm glow of this old-school pub teeming with global DNA and serving some 100 beers on tap and in the bottle, plus 40 whiskies and a line-up of belly-filling pub grub. There's local art on the wall and changing gigs in the basement club to boot.

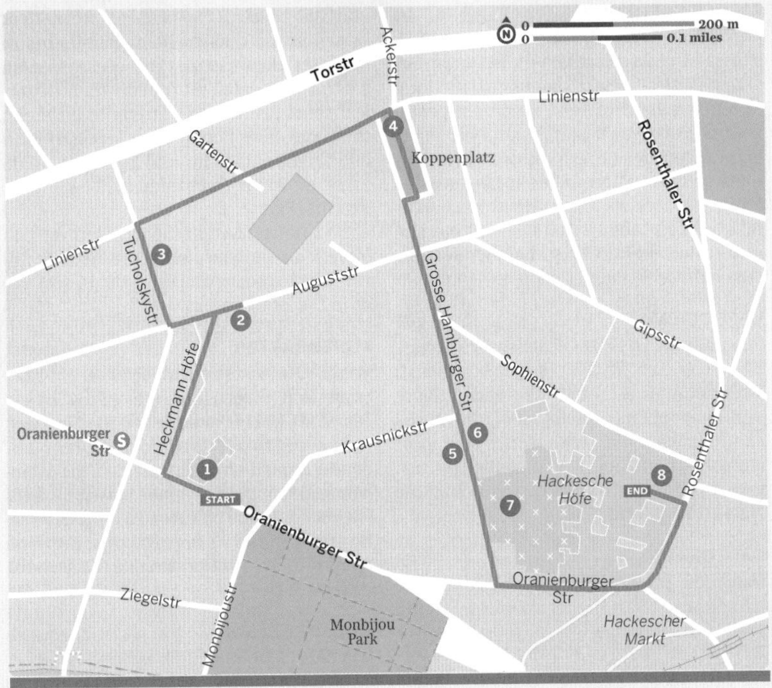

Neighbourhood Walk
Traces of Jewish Life in the Scheunenviertel

START NEUE SYNAGOGE
END HAUS SCHWARZENBERG
LENGTH 1.5KM; ONE TO THREE HOURS

This easy walk takes you past vestiges, memorials and revitalised sites of Jewish life throughout the Scheunenviertel. Start at the rebuilt 1 **Neue Synagoge** (p128), inaugurated in 1866 as Germany's largest Jewish house of worship and now a museum and community centre. Take the Heckmann Höfe to Auguststrasse and turn right to find yourself at the 2 **Jüdische Mädchenschule** (p129), a Bauhaus-style Jewish girls' school turned gallery and restaurant space.

Double back on Auguststrasse, then turn right on Tucholskystrasse, perhaps stopping for a bite at the kosher 3 **Beth Cafe** at No 40. Turn right on Linienstrasse and continue to Koppenplatz, with Karl Biedermann's art installation 4 **Der Verlassene Raum** (The Deserted Room). It consists of a table and two chairs, one knocked over as a symbol of Jewish residents being forced to flee suddenly from their homes.

Follow Grosse Hamburger Strasse south and note facades still scarred by bullet and shrapnel holes along the walkway leading to the baroque Sophienkirche. Further on, look on your right for the 5 **Missing House**, Christian Boltanski's 1990 memorial installation on the site of a bombed-out apartment building. Signs bearing the names of its former residents are affixed to the facades of the adjacent buildings. The structure opposite, at No 27, was a 6 **Jewish Boys' School**. The Nazis turned it and the adjacent Jewish seniors' home into a deportation centre in 1942. The home was destroyed in a bombing raid shortly before the war ended, but the school building survived and became a vocational school in GDR times. Just south, the 7 **Friedhof Grosse Hamburger Strasse** (p129) was Berlin's first Jewish cemetery. Outside is a memorial stone to the deported Jews as well as a sculpture by Will Lammert showing 13 fatigued women.

The tour concludes at street-art-decorated 8 **Haus Schwarzenberg** (p137), which harbours two small museums dealing with the fate of Jews under the Nazis.

FATHER CARPENTER CAFE

Map p330 (www.fathercarpenter.com; Münzstrasse 21; ⏲9am-6pm Mon-Fri, 10am-6pm Sat; UWeinmeisterstrasse) Thanks to its location in a quiet courtyard, Father Carpenter isn't a place you'll simply stumble upon. Yet among the coffee cognoscenti it's very much a destination for its locally roasted Fjord java, cakes from Albatross bakery in Kreuzberg and season-inspired hot and cold dishes (€5 to €13). A handy refuelling stop halfway through a shopping spree.

CAFE CINEMA CAFE

Map p330 (☎030-280 6415; Rosenthaler Strasse 39; ⏲10am-3am; 📶; 🚊M1, SHackescher Markt) This dimly lit cafe with its wooden tables and movie-themed memorabilia has lured chatty boho types with coffee and beer since 1990, making it one of the few surviving pre-gentrification places around the Hackescher Markt.

CAFÉ BRAVO CAFE

Map p330 (www.cafe-bravo.de; Auguststrasse 69; ⏲9am-late Mon-Fri, 11am-late Sat & Sun; 📶; 🚊M1, SOranienburger Strasse, UOranienburger Tor) Is it art? Is it a cafe? Is it a bar? Answer: it's all three. This glass-chrome-concrete pavilion in the quiet and pretty courtyard of the KW Institute for Contemporary Art (p129) was dreamed up by US artist Dan Graham and is a suitably arty refreshment stop on any Scheunenviertel saunter. It serves breakfast, cakes and light meals, and cocktails at night.

COVEN BAR

Map p330 (☎01511 498 2524; www.thecovenberlin.com; Kleine Präsidentenstrasse 3; ⏲8pm-2am Sun-Thu, 9pm-3am Fri & Sat; 📶; 🚊M1, M4, M5, M6, SHackescher Markt) Steel frames, industrial lamps, hard edges – this particular witches' lair has a decidedly stylish, masculine look and feel. Strong and creative drinks, some made with homemade liqueurs and garden-fresh ingredients, make seasoned imbibers of all stripes and sexual persuasions happy.

Torstrasse & Around

★BUCK & BRECK COCKTAIL BAR

Map p330 (☎0176 3231 5507; Brunnenstrasse 177; ⏲7pm-4am; 🚊M1, URosenthaler Platz) Liquid maestro Gonçalo de Sousa Monteiro and his baseball-cap-wearing team treat grown-up patrons to libational flights of fancy in their clandestine cocktail salon with sophisticated yet friendly flair. Historical short drinks are a strength, including the eponymous bubbly-based cocktail Buck and Breck, named for mid-19th-century US president James Buchanan and his VP John Breckinridge.

It's often packed to capacity, but you can leave your number and someone will call you when space opens up at the 14-seat bar or in the lounge area.

ROSENGARTEN BEER GARDEN

Map p330 (www.rosengarten-berlin.de; ⏲3-10pm or later Mon-Fri, noon-10pm or later Sat & Sun Apr-Sep; 🚊M1, M13, URosenthaler Platz) Hemmed in by roses, this little outdoor bar/beer garden in a pavilion at the edge of the Weinbergspark, opposite Weinbergsweg 13, doles out cocktails and culture to a chilled, eclectic crowd in the warmer months. Run by a nonprofit, it's a tradition going back to the 19th century.

MELODY NELSON COCKTAIL BAR

Map p332 (☎0177 744 6751; www.melodynelson.de; Novalisstrasse 2; ⏲7pm-2am Mon-Thu, to 4am Fri & Sat; 🚊M1, M5, 12, UOranienburger Tor) Everything here speaks of refinement, but without an iota of stuffiness: the dim lighting, the plush leather and velvet seating, the carpeted floors and the luxe cocktails. It helps that '60s icon Jane Birkin is gazing at you from behind the bar. The menu features plenty of innovative concoctions, but we're partial to well-crafted classics like a whisky sour or a mint julep.

The name references a song Serge Gainsbourg wrote for Birkin in 1971.

TORBAR BAR

Map p330 (☎030-5520 2582; www.torbar.berlin; Torstrasse 183; ⏲7pm-2am Wed & Thu, to 3.30am Fri & Sat; UOranienburger Tor) This buzzy restaurant-bar owned by Dieter Meier, one half of the 1980s Swiss proto-techno duo Yello, is always packed with beautiful people keen for a good time and quality cocktails like the signature Firefly (mezcal, Campari, pineapple, lime).

Keep an eye on passers-by through the floor-to-ceiling windows or sidle up to the long bar with its complexion-friendly lighting.

MIKKELER CRAFT BEER

Map p330 (☎0176 8314 1103; Torstrasse 102; ⏰5pm-midnight; ⓤRosenthaler Platz) Mikkeler – the name stands for Mikkel Borg Bjergsø and Kristian Klarup Keller – dispenses elevated craft beer that the two Danes have been brewing since 2006. In their first beer salon in Germany, their two dozen signature and guest brews on tap are best enjoyed over free-flowing conversation at the bar amid minimalist Scandinavian-woodsy surroundings.

ENTERTAINMENT

★**BABYLON** CINEMA

Map p330 (☎030-242 5969; www.babylonberlin.de; Rosa-Luxemburg-Strasse 30; tickets €7-10; ⓤRosa-Luxemburg-Platz) This top-rated indie screens a smart line-up of cinematic expression, from experimental German films and international art-house flicks to themed retrospectives and other stuff you'd never catch at the multiplex. For silent movies, including a free show at midnight on Saturday, the historic theatre organ is put

HAUS SCHWARZENBERG

A dingy-looking tunnel right beside the sparkling Hackesche Höfe leads to **Haus Schwarzenberg** (Map p330; www.haus-schwarzenberg.org; Rosenthaler Strasse 39; ⏰courtyard 24hr; 🚋M1, ⓈHackescher Markt) FREE, a hub of subculture in one of the last unrenovated buildings in this heavily gentrified area. Its facades are an ever-evolving street-art canvas, while several offbeat venues, plus a couple of Jewish-themed exhibits, are tucked behind its walls.

Eschschloraque Rümschrümp (www.eschschloraque.de; 2nd courtyard; ⏰6pm-1am Sun-Tue, 3pm-1am Wed-Sat) A project by the artists collective Dead Chickens, this subculture survivor is filled with metal monster sculptures and hosts concerts, parties and performance art beyond the mainstream – from Dada burlesque to Balkan post-punk concerts. Small beer garden.

Monsterkabinett (www.monsterkabinett.de; 2nd courtyard; tours adult/concession €8/5; ⏰tours 6.30-9.30pm Wed & Thu, 4.30-9.30pm Fri & Sat) If you want to meet 'Püppi' the techno-loving go-go dancer or 'Orangina' the twirling six-legged doll, you'll need to descend a steep spiral staircase for a short tour of Hannes Heiner's surrealist underground world. Inspired by his dreams, the artist has assembled a menagerie of mechanical robot-creatures in a computer-controlled art and sound installation that will entertain, astound and perhaps even frighten you just a little bit.

Kino Central (☎030-2859 9973; www.kino-central.de; 2nd courtyard; adult/concession €9.50/8.50) This teensy alternative cinema has a stealth location in the back of the graffiti-festooned courtyard of Haus Schwarzenberg. It screens international art-house flicks, usually in the original language with German subtitles. In summer the screenings move al fresco into the courtyard.

Museum Blindenwerkstatt Otto Weidt (Museum Otto Weidt Workshop for the Blind; ☎030-2576 2629; www.museum-blindenwerkstatt.de; 1st courtyard; ⏰10am-8pm) Standing up to the Nazi terror took unimaginable courage, but one man who did so was Otto Weidt. The broom and brush maker saved many of his deaf and blind Jewish employees from deportation and death by organising false papers, bribing Gestapo officials and hiding people in the back of his workshop. This small exhibit in the original workshop tells the story of Weidt and the people he saved.

Anne Frank Zentrum (☎030-288 865 600; www.annefrank.de; 1st courtyard; adult/concession/family €6/3.50/14; ⏰10am-6pm Tue-Sun) The diary Anne Frank penned while hiding from the Nazis in Amsterdam is one of the most iconic books of the 20th century. The heart of this exhibit is 'All About Anne', which charts her short life from her childhood in Germany to her death from typhus at the concentration camp Bergen-Belsen in 1945. Interactive stations allow you to explore how Anne's fate relates to you and today's world.

through its paces. Also hosts film festivals, readings and concerts.

CHAMÄLEON CABARET

Map p330 (☎030-400 0590; www.chamaeleonberlin.com; Rosenthaler Strasse 40/41; tickets €37-59; M1, M4, M5, M6, S Hackescher Markt, U Weinmeisterstrasse) A marriage of art-nouveau charms and high-tech theatre trappings, this intimate venue in a 1920s-style ballroom is a prime address for sophisticated 'contemporary circus' shows with a blend of comedy, acrobatics, music, juggling and dance – often in sassy, sexy and unconventional fashion. Sit at the bar, at bistro tables or in comfy armchairs.

BERLINER ENSEMBLE THEATRE

Map p332 (☎030-2840 8155; www.berliner-ensemble.de; Bertolt-Brecht-Platz 1; tickets €8-53; U Friedrichstrasse, Oranienburger Tor, S Friedrichstrasse) The company founded by Bertolt Brecht in 1949 is based at the neo-baroque theatre called Theater am Schiffbauerdamm, where his *Threepenny Opera* premiered in 1928. Artistic director Oliver Reese and his ensemble keep the master's legacy alive while also exploring new theatrical frontiers.

FRIEDRICHSTADT-PALAST BERLIN PERFORMING ARTS

Map p332 (☎030-2326 2326; www.palast.berlin; Friedrichstrasse 107; tickets €20-190; M1, U Oranienburger Tor, S Friedrichstrasse, Oranienburger Strasse) Europe's largest revue theatre has been putting on the glitz for well over a century. Night after night its huge ensemble delights audiences with visually stunning Vegas-style shows featuring leggy dancers, singing, sublime costuming, a high-tech stage and fabulous special effects and artistry. Productions are innovative and highly entertaining and don't require German skills.

B-FLAT LIVE MUSIC

Map p330 (☎030-283 3123; www.b-flat-berlin.de; Dircksenstrasse 40; tickets €12-15; ⏲8pm-1am Sun-Thu, 8.30pm-2am Fri & Sat; M1, M4, M5, M6, U Weinmeisterstrasse, S Hackescher Markt) Cool cats of all ages flock to this beloved jazz and acoustic-music venue, where you'll sit within spitting distance of the stage. The eclectic line-up features a global roster of performers and the gamut of genres, be it blues, soul and funk or tunes from folk and flamenco to modern and experimental. Wednesday's free jam session often brings down the house.

HACKESCHE HÖFE KINO CINEMA

Map p330 (☎030-283 4603; www.hoefekino.de; Rosenthaler Strasse 39; tickets €7.50-10.50; M1, S Hackescher Markt) This five-screen indie cinema, upstairs in Court I of the Hackesche Höfe complex, presents a well-curated mix of European art-house movies, documentaries and indie films from the USA, many of them in their original language with German, and sometimes also English, subtitles.

SHOPPING

Along Rosenthaler Strasse, Alte Schönhauser Strasse, Neue Schönhauser Strasse, Münzstrasse, Mulackstrasse and inside the Hackesche Höfe are plenty of options for seekers of the latest fashion and accessories. Contemporary art galleries line Linienstrasse, Auguststrasse and their side streets.

BONBONMACHEREI FOOD

Map p330 (☎030-4405 5243; www.bonbonmacherei.de; Heckmann Höfe, Oranienburger Strasse 32; ⏲noon-7pm Wed-Sat Sep-Jun; M1, S Oranienburger Strasse) The aroma of peppermint and liquorice wafts through this old-fashioned basement candy kitchen whose owners use antique equipment and time-tested recipes to churn out souvenir-worthy bonbons from sweet and sour to spicy. Be sure to try their signature leaf-shaped *Berliner Maiblätter,* made with woodruff. Mix and match your own bag.

Call ahead for timings if you want to look on as they're whipping up the next candy batch.

HUNDT HAMMER STEIN BOOKS

Map p330 (☎030-2345 7669; www.hundthammerstein.de; Alte Schönhauser Strasse 23/24; ⏲11am-7pm Mon-Sat; U Weinmeisterstrasse) Kurt von Hammerstein has a nose for good literature beyond the bestseller lists. Feel free to browse through this stylish lair with word candy from around the world or ask the affable owner to match a tome to your taste. There's a sizeable English selection, quality books for tots and a sprinkling of travel guides as well.

KAUF DICH GLÜCKLICH
FASHION & ACCESSORIES

Map p330 (☎030-2887 8817; www.kaufdichgluecklich-shop.de; Rosenthaler Strasse 17; ⊙11am-8pm Mon-Sat; UWeinmeisterstrasse) What began as a waffle cafe and vintage shop has turned into a small emporium of indie concept boutiques, with this branch as the flagship. The rambling store presents a Berlin-eclectic mix of reasonably priced on-trend clothing, home accessories, books and cosmetics from its own KDG collection and other hand-picked labels, many from Scandinavia.

PAPER & TEA
TEA

Map p330 (www.paperandtea.com; Alte Schönhauser Strasse 50; ⊙11am-7.30pm Mon-Sat; URosa-Luxemburg-Platz) Drink in the calming Zen atmosphere in this apothecary-style concept store that stocks dozens of hand-selected whole-leaf and hand-processed tea varieties from Asia and Africa (many of them organic), along with teapots, utensils and cups. If you're bewildered, the expertly schooled 'teaists' will be happy to dole out advice.

DO YOU READ ME?!
BOOKS

Map p330 (☎030-6954 9695; www.doyoureadme.de; Auguststrasse 28; ⊙10am-7.30pm Mon-Sat; M1, M5, SOranienburger Strasse, URosenthaler Platz) Trend chasers could probably spend hours flicking through this gallery-style assortment of cool, obscure and small-print magazines from around the world. There's a distinct focus on fashion, design, architecture, music, art and contemporary trends, and knowledgeable staff to help you navigate, if needed.

TRIPPEN FLAGSHIP STORE
SHOES

Map p330 (☎030-2839 1337; www.trippen.com; Hackesche Höfe, Courts IV & VI, Rosenthaler Strasse 40/41; ⊙11am-7pm Mon-Sat; M1, SHackescher Markt) Forget about 10cm heels! Berlin-based Trippen's shoes are designed with human anatomy in mind, yet they have absolutely nothing in common with orthopaedic loafers. The combo of avant-garde design and prime materials has racked up plenty of international awards.

LALA BERLIN
FASHION & ACCESSORIES

Map p330 (☎030-2009 5363; www.lalaberlin.com; Alte Schönhauser Strasse 3; ⊙11am-7pm Mon-Sat; URosa-Luxemburg-Platz) Ex-MTV editor Leyla Piedayesh makes spot-on urban fashion that beautifully reflects Berlin's sassy, unconventional and bohemian spirit. Originally known for knitwear, her flagship boutique showcases the latest designs that look good on both the twig thin and the generously upholstered.

AMPELMANN BERLIN
GIFTS & SOUVENIRS

Map p330 (☎030-4472 6438; www.ampelmann.de; Hackesche Höfe, Court V, Rosenthaler Strasse 40/41; ⊙10am-8pm Mon-Sat, 1-6pm Sun; M1, SHackescher Markt, UWeinmeisterstrasse) It took a vociferous grassroots campaign to save the little Ampelmann, the endearing fellow on East German pedestrian traffic lights. Now the beloved cult figure and global brand graces an entire shop's worth of T-shirts, fridge magnets, pasta, onesies, umbrellas and other knick-knacks.

This branch in the Hackesche Höfe is the original one. Check the website for additional branches around town.

SCHWARZER REITER
ADULT

Map p330 (☎030-4503 4438; www.schwarzer-reiter.de; Torstrasse 3; ⊙noon-8pm Mon-Sat; M2, M8, URosa-Luxemburg-Platz) If you worship at the altar of hedonism, you'll appreciate the wide range of luxe erotica and kink couture in this classy shop decked out in sensuous black and purple. Beginner and advanced pleasure needs can be fulfilled, from rubber-ducky vibrators to harnesses and hardcore toys.

1. ABSINTH DEPOT BERLIN
FOOD & DRINKS

Map p330 (☎030-281 6789; www.erstesabsinthdepotberlin.de; Weinmeisterstrasse 4; ⊙2pm-midnight Mon-Fri, 1pm-midnight Sat; UWeinmeisterstrasse) Vincent Van Gogh, Henri de Toulouse-Lautrec and Oscar Wilde are among the fin-de-siècle artists who drew inspiration from the 'green fairy', as absinthe is also known. This quaint little shop has over 100 varieties of the potent stuff and an expert owner who'll happily help you pick out the perfect bottle for your own mind-altering rendezvous.

Prenzlauer Berg

MAUERPARK & NORTHERN PRENZLAUER BERG | KOLLWITZPLATZ & SOUTHERN PRENZLAUER BERG

Neighbourhood Top Five

❶ **Gedenkstätte Berliner Mauer** (p142) Coming to grips with the absurdity of a divided city at this memorial exhibit that follows the course of a 1.4km-long stretch of the Berlin Wall.

❷ **Mauerpark** (p144) Spending a sunny Sunday digging for flea-market treasures and cheering on karaoke crooners in this popular park reclaimed from a section of the Berlin Wall death strip.

❸ **Kulturbrauerei** (p144) Catching a concert, movie or street-food market at this venerable red-brick brewery turned cultural centre.

❹ **Kollwitzplatz** (p144) Taking a ramble around this leafy square and its side streets lined with beautiful town houses, convivial cafes and indie boutiques.

❺ **Schloss Schönhausen** (p152) Checking out the palace where both Fidel Castro and Frederick the Great's wife have slept, followed by a spin around the lovely park.

For more detail of this area see Map p334

Explore Prenzlauer Berg

Once a neglected backwater, Prenzlauer Berg went from rags to riches after reunification to emerge as one of Berlin's most desirable and well-heeled neighbourhoods.

The one must-see sight is the Gedenkstätte Berliner Mauer (p142), the city's best place to understand the layout and impact of the Berlin Wall. The 1.4km-long indoor-outdoor exhibit actually starts in the adjoining district of Wedding but ends in Prenzlauer Berg near the Mauerpark. This patch of green wrested from the Berlin Wall death strip hosts a hugely popular Sunday flea market and outdoor karaoke.

Generally speaking, Prenzlauer Berg's ample charms reveal themselves in subtler, often unexpected ways and are best experienced on a leisurely daytime meander. The prettiest area, and a good place to start, is around Kollwitzplatz (p144), which is packed with congenial cafes and indie boutiques selling custom jewellery, Berlin-made fashions or organic baby clothing.

Also pop by the Kulturbrauerei (p144), a brewery turned culture centre, to admire its fortresslike red-brick architecture. A good time to visit here is during the Sunday street-food market.

Local Life

Outdoor quaffing Celebrate summer by bagging a beverage at a *Späti* (convenience market) and watching the sunset from the hilly slope in the Mauerpark.

Shopping Follow the locals to the *Kiez'* (neighbourhood's) charismatic indie boutiques. Kastanienallee, Stargarder Strasse and the Kollwitzplatz area offer especially good pickings.

Quality quick feeds Favourites for foodies on the run include Habba Habba (p148) for Middle Eastern wraps and Konnopke's Imbiss (p148) for *Currywurst.*

Getting There & Away

U-Bahn The U2 stops at Schönhauser Allee, Eberswalder Strasse and Senefelderplatz en route to Alexanderplatz, Potsdamer Platz and western Berlin.

Tram The M1 links Museumsinsel and Prenzlauer Berg via the Scheunenviertel, Kastanienallee and Schönhauser Allee. The M10 links Hauptbahnhof with Friedrichshain via Danziger Strasse.

S-Bahn Ringbahn (Circle Line) trains S41 and S42 stop at Schönhauser Allee, Prenzlauer Allee, Greifswalder Strasse, Landsberger Allee and Storkower Strasse.

Lonely Planet's Top Tip

On Saturday, pick up farm-fresh produce and artisanal products before joining locals for gourmet snacks and a glass of bubbly at the bountiful farmers market on Kollwitzplatz (p154).

Best Places to Eat

- Lucky Leek (p149)
- Umami (p149)
- Mrs Robinson's (p148)
- W-Der Imbiss (p149)
- Holy Everest (p148)

For reviews, see p147.

Best Places to Drink

- Prater Garten (p151)
- Bryk Bar (p152)
- Weinerei Forum (p151)
- BrewDog (p152)
- Lamm Bar (p151)

For reviews, see p151.

Best Places to Shop

- Flohmarkt im Mauerpark (p153)
- Sugafari (p153)
- Zweimalschön (p153)
- DearGoods (p153)
- Goldhahn und Sampson (p154)

For reviews, see p153.

TOP EXPERIENCE

LEARN AT THE GEDENKSTÄTTE BERLINER MAUER

For an insightful primer on the Berlin Wall, visit this 1.4km-long outdoor memorial, which explains the physical layout of the barrier and the death strip, how the border fortifications were enlarged and perfected over time, and what impact they had on the daily lives of people on both sides of the Wall.

The memorial exhibit extends along Bernauer Strasse, one of the streets that played a pivotal role in Cold War history. The Berlin Wall ran along its entire length, with one side of the street located in West Berlin and the other in East Berlin. The exhibit is divided into four sections with overarching themes. Integrated within are an original section of the Wall, vestiges of the border installations, a chapel and a monument. Multimedia stations, photographs, 'archaeological windows' and markers provide context, details and anecdotes about events that took place along here.

Gartenstrasse to Ackerstrasse

This is the most important segment of the memorial. It focuses on explaining how the Berlin Wall restricted citizens' freedom of movement and secured the East German government's power. An emotional highlight is the **Window of Remembrance**, where photographic portraits give identity to would-be escapees who lost their lives at the Wall, one of them only six years old. Some spaces have deliberately been left empty in case more victims are identified. The park-like area surrounding the installation was once part of the adjacent cemetery.

DON'T MISS

- Exhibit at the Documentation Centre and view from its tower
- Remembrance service at the Chapel of Reconciliation
- National Monument to German Division

PRACTICALITIES

- Berlin Wall Memorial
- Map p334, A6
- 030-213 085 166
- www.berliner-mauer-gedenkstaette.de
- Bernauer Strasse, btwn Schwedter & Gartenstrasse
- admission free
- visitor & documentation centre 10am-6pm Thu-Sun, open-air exhibit 8am-10pm
- S Nordbahnhof, Bernauer Strasse, Eberswalder Strasse

Near Ackerstrasse the **National Monument to German Division** consists of a 70m section of original Berlin Wall bounded by two rusted steel flanks and embedded in an artistic representation of the border complex. Walk down Ackerstrasse to enter the monument from the back. Through slits in the inner wall (which were not there originally), you can glimpse the former death strip, complete with a guard tower, a security-patrol path and the lamps that bathed it in fierce light at night.

Documentation Centre

Across the street from the National Monument to German Division, a former parish hall now houses a two-floor Documentation Centre. The **exhibit** – called '1961/1989. The Berlin Wall' – provides a concise and engaging overview of the Wall and answers such questions as why it was built and what led to its collapse. It also uses artefacts, documents and videos to depict life in divided Berlin. Use the information you've gleaned to picture the barrier as it once was when you stand atop the adjacent **viewing platform** (open noon to 5pm Thursday to Sunday). From here, you'll also have a bird's-eye view of the monument directly below.

Ackerstrasse to Brunnenstrasse

In this section, the linear exhibit focuses on the division's human toll and especially on the daring and desperate escapes that took place along Bernauer Strasse. Just past Ackerstrasse, the modern **Chapel of Reconciliation** stands in the spot of an 1894 brick church detonated in 1985 to make room for a widening of the border strip. A 15-minute remembrance service for Wall victims is held at noon Tuesday to Friday. Other information stations deal with the physical construction of the Wall and the continuous expansion of the border complex.

Brunnenstrasse to Schwedter Strasse

In the final section, info stations and exhibits must skirt private property and new apartment buildings and are mostly restricted to a narrow strip along the former border-patrol path. Information stations address such topics as West Germany's take on the Berlin Wall, what life was like for an East German border guard and the eventual fall of the Wall in 1989. A highlight is the dramatic story of the world-famous **Tunnel 29**, which ran for 135m below Bernauer Strasse and helped 29 people escape from East Berlin in September 1962.

TAKE A BREAK

Head to **Ost-West Cafe** (Map p334; ☎030-4677 6016; https://ost-west-cafe.business.site; Brunnenstrasse 53; dishes €4.50-9; ⊙8am-8pm; 📶; U Bernauer Strasse) for simple international dishes amid Cold War-era-themed decor.

Castle (p152) is a great local joint for processing your impressions over pizza and cold craft beer. Free wi-fi and beer garden.

Guards at the barrier and along the intra-German border were authorised by the GDR government to shoot at citizens trying to escape *from* its own territory. In Berlin alone, an estimated 90 people were killed between 1961 and 1989. Guards received bonuses for their actions.

TOP TIPS

- Start your visit in the visitor centre across from Nordbahnhof S-Bahn station and work your way east.
- Pick up a free map and watch the introductory film at the visitor centre.
- For a self-guided tour, go to www.berliner-mauer.mobi.
- If you have limited time, spend it in the first section between Gartenstrasse and Ackerstrasse.

SIGHTS

Prenzlauer Berg may not have any blockbuster sights, but there are still plenty of gems scattered throughout the district. The prettiest area is around Kollwitzplatz. Further north is the eastern terminus of the Gedenkstätte Berliner Mauer, the city's most important exhibit on the Wall. It stretches for 1.4km between Nordbahnhof and Mauerpark.

GEDENKSTÄTTE BERLINER MAUER — MEMORIAL

See p142.

MAUERPARK — PARK

Map p334 (www.mauerpark.info; btwn Bernauer Strasse, Schwedter Strasse & Gleimstrasse; M1, M10, 12, U Eberswalder Strasse) One of Berlin's most popular parks, Mauerpark was forged from a section of Berlin Wall death strip and is now regularly swarmed by thousands of locals and visitors on Sunday for its genial flea market, outdoor karaoke and overall free-spirited vibe. It's cleaned up nicely after a makeover and has also doubled in size.

Up a slope (great for sunset watching), a 300m-long Berlin Wall segment is now an officially sanctioned practice ground for graffiti artists. Behind here loom the floodlights of the badly ageing **Friedrich-Ludwig-Jahn-Sportpark** (Jahnsportpark@seninnDS.berlin.de; Cantianstrasse 24), the stadium where Stasi chief Erich Mielke used to cheer on his beloved Dynamo Berlin football (soccer) team. Just north of here is the **Max-Schmeling-Halle** (030-4430 4430; www.max-schmeling-halle.de; Falkplatz 1), a venue for concerts, competitions and sports events.

ZEISS GROSSPLANETARIUM — PLANETARIUM

Map p334 (030-4218 4510; www.planetarium.berlin; Prenzlauer Allee 80; adult €9-10.50, concession €7-8.50; M2, S Prenzlauer Allee) It was the most advanced planetarium in East Germany at its opening in 1987, and its 2016 renovation upped the scientific, technology and comfort ante once again. At one of Europe's most modern and beautiful space theatres, you can delve into the mysteries not only of the cosmos but of science in general. Many programs are in English, some are set to music and others are geared to children. Tickets are available online.

KOLLWITZPLATZ — SQUARE

Map p334 (; U Senefelderplatz) OK, so it's triangular, but Kollwitzplatz is still the prettiest square in Prenzlauer Berg. The leafy park in its centre is tot heaven, with three playgrounds plus a bronze sculpture of the artist Käthe Kollwitz, who used to live nearby. Cafes and restaurants invite lingering, but for the full-on local vibe, swing by the farmers markets (p154) on Thursday and Saturday.

TCHOBAN FOUNDATION – MUSEUM FÜR ARCHITEKTURZEICHNUNG — MUSEUM

Map p334 (Museum for Architectural Drawing; 030-4373 9090; www.tchoban-foundation.de; Christinenstrasse 18a; adult/concession €5/3; 2-7pm Mon-Fri, 1-5pm Sat & Sun; M1, 12, U Senefelderplatz) Fans of edgy contemporary architecture should swing by this private museum housed in a striking sculptural pile of relief-decorated concrete cubes topped by a glass-encased top floor. Changing exhibits showcase examples of the dying art form of architectural drawings from the collection of Sergei Tchoban, the foundation's St Petersburg-born founder, or from such renowned repositories as Vienna's Albertina or London's Sir John Soane's Museum.

Danish-Icelandic artist Olafur Eliasson has his studio next door.

KULTURBRAUEREI — CULTURAL CENTRE

Map p334 (030-4435 2170; www.kulturbrauerei.de; btwn Schönhauser Allee, Knaackstrasse, Eberswalder Strasse & Sredzkistrasse; P; M1, U Eberswalder Strasse) The fanciful red-and-yellow brick buildings of this 19th-century brewery have been upcycled into a cultural powerhouse with a small village's worth of venues, from concert and theatre halls to nightclubs, dance studios, a multiplex cinema and a free GDR-history museum. The main entrances are on Knaackstrasse and Sredzkistrasse.

On Sunday foodies fill up on global treats at the Street Food Auf Achse (p149) market, while in December the old buildings make a romantic backdrop for a Swedish-style Lucia Christmas market.

MUSEUM IN DER KULTURBRAUEREI — MUSEUM

Map p334 (030-467 777 911; www.hdg.de; Knaackstrasse 97; 9am-6pm Tue-Fri, 10am-6pm Sat & Sun; P; M1, M10, 12, U Eberswalder

WORTH A DETOUR

SPOTLIGHT ON WEDDING

Amorphous, multiethnic and rough around the edges – Wedding is a draw for urban explorers of neighbourhoods that are not yet in the full grip of gentrification. Sights are fairly scarce, but if you're keen on offbeat, down-to-earth locals and improvised DIY bars and creative venues, you'll find them in this working-class northern district.

Sights

Myth of Germania – Vision & Crime (Map p334; ☎030-4991 0517; www.berliner-unterwelten.de; cnr Badstrasse & Behmstrasse; adult/concession €6/3; ⏲11am-5pm, last entry 4pm) What would look Berlin like if the Nazis had won the war? This multimedia exhibit presents Hitler's megalomaniacal vision of the 'World Capital of Germania' and examines the crimes against humanity it would have taken to turn it into reality. A key exhibit is the amazing 3D model of the city centre originally made for 2004 movie *The Downfall*. The entrance is inside Gesundbrunnen subway station. Tickets available online.

Eating

Pförtner Cafe (☎030-5036 9854; www.pfoertner.co; Uferstrasse 8-11; mains lunch €5.50-10, dinner €12-18; ⏲9am-11pm Mon-Fri, from 11am Sat; UPankstrasse) This artsy-funky cafe occupies the gatehouse of a bus-repair station turned artists studios. Rustic, market-fresh local dishes scrawled on a blackboard feed resident creatives and visitors from breakfast until night. In summer the terrace is a sweet spot for homemade cakes and Italian coffee.

Drinking

Vagabund Brauerei Taproom (☎030-5266 7668; www.vagabundbrauerei.com; Antwerpener Strasse 3; ⏲5pm-late Mon-Fri, 1pm-late Sat & Sun; ; USeestrasse) American friends Tom, Matt and David became Berlin craft-beer pioneers when they started their small-batch brewery in 2011. In their earthy-chic taproom they pour a changing line-up of suds, from double and triple Indian pale ales to wheat beer and sour beer (Gose).

Entertainment

Silent Green Kulturquartier (☎030-1208 2210; www.silent-green.net; Gerichtstrasse 35; SWedding, UWedding, Leopoldplatz) A historic Wedding crematorium has been rebooted as an unusual cultural-event space that presents mostly experimental music, dance and other performances in the former mourning hall with its striking acoustics. A bit creepy, perhaps? But oh so Berlin. In the daytime, on-site cafe Mars serves lunch and beverages.

Strasse) FREE Original documents, historical footage and objects (including a camper-style Trabi car) illustrate daily life under socialism in East Germany in themed rooms in this government-curated exhibit. As you wander the halls, you'll realise the stark contrast between the lofty aspirations of the socialist state and the sobering realities of material shortages, surveillance and oppression its people had to endure.

The exhibit also addresses the various paths individuals took to cope with their circumstances.

JÜDISCHER FRIEDHOF SCHÖNHAUSER ALLEE CEMETERY

Map p334 (☎030-441 9824; www.jg-berlin.org; Schönhauser Allee 22; ⏲8am-4pm Mon-Thu, 7.30am-1pm Fri; USenefelderplatz) Berlin's second Jewish cemetery opened in 1827 and hosts some 25,000 dearly departed, including the artist Max Liebermann and the composer Giacomo Meyerbeer. It's a pretty place with dappled light filtering through big old chestnuts and linden trees and a sense of melancholy emanating from ivy-draped graves and toppled tombstones. The

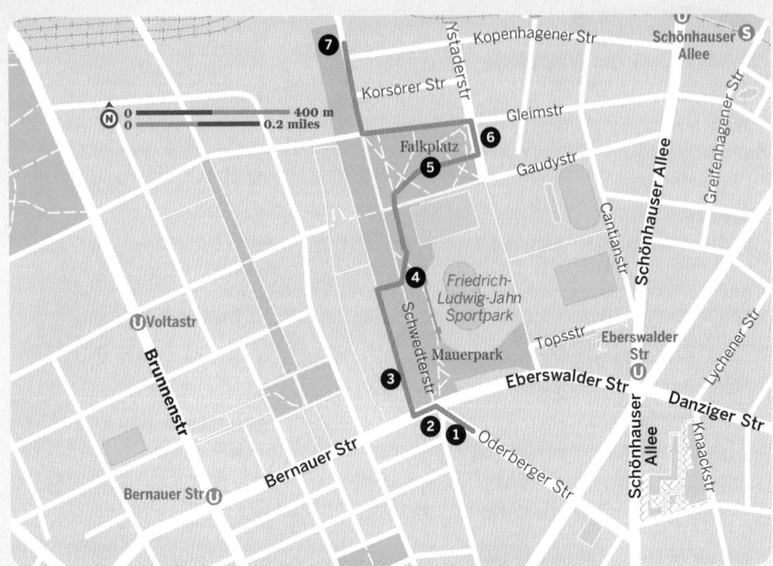

Local Life
Sundays Around the Mauerpark

Locals, expats and tourists – everyone flocks to the Mauerpark on Sunday. Doubled in size in 2020, it's an energetic urban tapestry where a flea market, karaoke and bands provide entertainment, and people gather for barbecues, basketball and boules. A graffiti-covered section of the Berlin Wall recalls the time when the park was part of the death strip separating East and West Berlin.

1 Bright Beginnings

Start your day on Oderberger Strasse, which is lined with restaurants and cafes, including **Bonanza Coffee Heroes** (www.bonanzacoffee.de; Oderberger Strasse 35; 8.30am-7pm Mon-Fri, 10am-7pm Sat & Sun;). While sipping a cuppa, admire the beautiful facades of the restored 19th-century town houses that were saved from demolition in the late '70s when the street still dead-ended at the Berlin Wall.

2 Confronting Cold War History

During the Cold War, East met West at Bernauer Strasse, now paralleled by a 1.4km-long linear multimedia memorial exhibit (p142) that vividly illustrates the realities of life with the Berlin Wall. Its eastern terminus is here at Schwedter Strasse. Even walking just a short stretch west on Bernauer Strasse offers eye-opening insights.

3 Urban Archaeology

After this dose of history, hit the Flohmarkt im Mauerpark (p153) for some quality hunting and gathering. Afterwards, fortify yourself at a street-food stall or drag your loot to a market beer garden to chill out in the sun.

4 Bearpit Karaoke

On most summer Sundays, Berlin's best free entertainment kicks off around 3pm when Joe Hatchiban sets up his custom-made mobile **karaoke** (www.bearpitkaraoke.com; around 3-8pm Sun spring-autumn) FREE unit in the Mauerpark's amphitheatre. Join the crowds in cheering and clapping for eager crooners ranging from giggling 11-year-olds to Broadway-calibre belters.

5 Falkplatz

Studded with ancient chestnut, oak, birch, ash and poplar trees, this leafy park was a parade ground for Prussian soldiers back in the 19th century and used to grow vegeta-

LINKA A ODOM / GETTY IMAGES ©

Festival at Mauerpark

bles right after WWII. Today, it's a great place to relax and watch kids frolicking around the sea-lion fountain or searching for other animal sculptures tucked among the shrubs.

❻ Burgermania

New York meets Berlin at expat favourite **Bird** (www.thebirdinberlin.com; Am Falkplatz 5; burgers €10-14.50, steaks from €22.50; ⏲6-10pm Mon-Thu, 4-11pm Fri, noon-11pm Sat, noon-10pm Sun; 📶), whose dry-aged steaks, burgers and hand-cut fries might just justify the hype.

❼ Northern Mauerpark

Not even all locals know that the Mauerpark continues north of the Gleimstrasse tunnel. In this much quieter section, you'll find an enchanting birch grove; the **Jugendfarm Moritzhof** (www.jugendfarm-moritzhof.de; Schwedter Strasse 90; ⏲1-6pm Tue-Sat Oct-Mar, to 6.30pm Apr-Sep, from noon school holidays) farm playground; and daredevils scaling the **Schwedter Nordwand** (www.alpinclub-berlin.de; Schwedter Strasse) climbing wall.

nicest and oldest have been moved to the Lapidarium by the main entrance.

Liebermann's tomb is next to his family's crypt, roughly in the centre along the back wall. Men must cover their heads upon entering the cemetery; pick up a free skullcap by the entrance.

GETHSEMANEKIRCHE CHURCH

Map p334 (☎030-445 7745; https://ekpn.de/vier-kirchen/gethsemane; Stargarder Strasse 77; ⏲10am-6pm Mon-Fri May-Sep, hours vary Oct-Apr; 🚋M1, Ⓤ Schönhauser Allee, Ⓢ Schönhauser Allee) This 1893 neo-Gothic church was a hotbed of dissent in the final days of the GDR and thus a thorn in the side of the Stasi, which, as late as October 1989, brutally quashed a peaceful gathering outside its portals. Artworks include a copy of Ernst Barlach's 1928 *Geistkämpfer* (Ghost Fighter) sculpture outside the church, which also hosts concerts and other cultural events in addition to Sunday service at 11am.

A short prayer meeting in support of unjustly imprisoned people worldwide takes place daily at 6pm.

EATING

Prenzlauer Berg has an exceptionally high density of neighbourhood restaurants catering to the demanding and well-travelled palates of its international residents. Even without any Michelin shrines, there's still lots of high-calibre chowing down to be done.

Mauerpark & Northern Prenzlauer Berg

EISPATISSERIE HOKEY POKEY ICE CREAM €

Map p334 (☎0176-8010 3080; www.hokey-pokey.de; Stargarder Strasse 72; ⏲noon-10pm May-Sep, changes seasonally; 🚋M1, Ⓤ Schönhauser Allee, Ⓢ Schönhauser Allee) The debate over Berlin's best ice cream may have local foodies in a headlock, but there's no doubt that Hokey Pokey is a strong contender. People brave rock-star-worthy lines to get their fix of these creamy orbs of goodness created by a master patissier with a knack for adventurous new flavour combos.

ATAYA CAFFE VEGAN €

Map p334 (☎030-3302 1041; www.atayacaffe.de; Zelter Strasse 6; mains €9-11, Sun brunch €14;

noon-4pm Tue-Thu, noon-4pm & 6-10pm Fri & Sat, 11am-4pm Sun; M2, Prenzlauer Berg) This cheerfully decorated living-room-style zero-waste cafe way off the tourist track is the lovechild of Elisabetta and Bachir Niang, who have poured their hearts and cash into feeding plant-based-food fans with yummy mindful fare from their homelands of Sardinia and Senegal. Specialities include Mafè, a peanut-infused vegetable stew, and the homemade ravioli. The all-you-can-eat Sunday brunch is fast becoming a local tradition.

HABBA HABBA — MIDDLE EASTERN €

Map p334 (030-3674 5726; www.habba-habba.de; Kastanienallee 15; dishes €5.50-11; 11am-11pm; ; M1, 12, Eberswalder Strasse) This tiny *Imbiss* (snack bar) makes yummy wraps with a twist, like the one stuffed with tangy pomegranate-marinated chicken and nutty freekeh (green wheat) in a minty yogurt sauce. Take 'em away or score a seat on the elevated porch for casting an eye on passing folk. Vegetarian and vegan versions are available, too.

KONNOPKE'S IMBISS — GERMAN €

Map p334 (030-442 7765; www.konnopke-imbiss.de; Schönhauser Allee 44a; sausages €1.80-3.50; 11am-6pm Mon-Fri, noon-6pm Sat; ; M1, M10, M13, Eberswalder Strasse) Brave the inevitable queue at this famous sausage kitchen, ensconced in the same spot below the U-Bahn viaduct since 1930, but now equipped with a heated pavilion, an English menu and a vegan sausage option. The 'secret' tomato sauce topping its *Currywurst* comes in a five-tier heat scale from mild to wild.

DER BLAUE FUCHS — GEORGIAN €€

Map p334 (030-2607 4244; https://derblauefuchs.metro.bar; Knaackstrasse 43; mains €11-19.50; 4-11pm Tue-Thu, noon-11pm Fri-Sun; ; Senefelder Platz) In a soft-toned ambience accented by hand-painted 1920s wallpaper and GDR-era lamps, you can feast on such Georgian palate teasers as *gebjalia* (pesto-filled mozzarella rolls) or the richly nuanced *chakapuli* (veal stew). Just be careful not to fill up on the classic – and highly addictive – *khachapuri* (cheese-filled bread). There's a kids' play corner.

KANAAN — MIDDLE EASTERN €€

Map p334 (01590 134 8077; www.kanaan-berlin.de; Schliemannstrasse 15; mains lunch & brunch €4-15, dinner €20; 6-10pm Wed & Thu, noon-10pm Fri-Sun; ; M1, Schönhauser Allee, Schönhauser Allee) In this feel-good venture, an Israeli biz whiz and a Palestinian chef have teamed up to bring a progressive blend of vegan and vegetarian Middle Eastern street fare to Berlin. The hummus is divine, especially when pimped up with garlic-lemon sauce and marinated vegetables.

HOLY EVEREST — NEPALESE €€

Map p334 (030-2630 0423; www.facebook.com/holyeverest; Gleimstrasse 54; momos €6-7, mains €11-20; noon-4pm Mon, noon-4pm & 5-11pm Sun & Tue-Thu, noon-4pm & 5pm-midnight Fri & Sat; ; M1, Schönhauser Allee, Schönhauser Allee) Helmed by a Himalayan Sherpa, Holy Everest melds Nepalese street-food culture with pro techniques and good food karma. Must-orders are the momos, creatively filled dumplings fried in chilli sauce or served with tangy tomato chutney, and the lentil-based *dal bhat* stew (the national dish). Everything tastes genuine, fresh and inflected with a medley of Ayurvedic spices. Many dishes are vegan.

ODERQUELLE — GERMAN €€

Map p334 (030-4400 8080; www.oderquelle.de; Oderberger Strasse 27; mains €13-20; 5-11pm Mon-Sat, noon-11pm Sun; M1, 12, Eberswalder Strasse) It's always fun to pop by this woodsy stalwart on Oderberger Strasse to see what inspired the chef today. Most likely it'll be a well-crafted German dish like schnitzel with roast potatoes or roast duck with red cabbage. Best tables: on the pavement, so you can keep an eye on the parade of passers-by.

ZUM SCHUSTERJUNGEN — GERMAN €€

Map p334 (030-442 7654; www.zumschusterjungen.com; Danziger Strasse 9; mains €10-19; 11am-midnight; Eberswalder Strasse) Tourists, expats and locals descend upon this old-school gastropub where rustic Berlin charm is doled out with as much abandon as the delish home cooking. Big platters of goulash, roast pork and *sauerbraten* feed both tummy and soul, as do the regionally brewed Berliner Schusterjunge pilsner and Märkischer Landmann black beer.

MRS ROBINSON'S — INTERNATIONAL €€€

Map p334 (030-5462 2839; www.mrsrobinsons.de; Pappelallee 29; 4/5/6-course menu €62/65/75; 6-11pm Thu-Mon; ; 12,

WORTH A DETOUR

EXPLORING BERLIN'S UNDERBELLY

After you've checked off Brandenburg Gate and the TV Tower, why not explore Berlin's dark and dank underbelly? Join **Berliner Unterwelten** (030-4991 0517; www.berliner-unterwelten.de; Brunnenstrasse 105; adult/concession €12/10; hours vary; S Gesundbrunnen, U Gesundbrunnen) on its 1½-hour 'Dark Worlds' tour of a WWII underground bunker and pick your way through a warren of claustrophobic rooms, past heavy steel doors, hospital beds, helmets, guns, boots and lots of other wartime artefacts. Listen in horror and fascination as guides bring alive the stories of the thousands of ordinary Berliners cooped up here, cramped and scared, as the bombs rained down on the city. Other tours explore a Cold War nuclear bomb shelter, Berlin Wall escape tunnels and other intriguing sites.

Tickets must be purchased online. No children under seven.

Berliner Unterwelten are also the folks behind the exhibit Myth of Germania – Vision & Crime (p145) that deals with Hitler's plan for Berlin as the 'world capital of Germania'.

U Eberswalder Strasse) When Ben Zviel and Samina Raza launched their minimalist casual fine-dining parlour (white-brick walls, polished wooden tables) in 2016, they immediately garnered the attention of the local culinary cognoscenti. Treating sustainably sourced seasonal and local fare with respect and time-tested techniques, their intensely flavoured dishes beautifully capture the city's adventurous and experimental spirit. Only natural wines feature on the wine list.

Kollwitzplatz & Southern Prenzlauer Berg

★UMAMI VIETNAMESE €

Map p334 (030-2886 0626; www.umami-restaurant.de; Knaackstrasse 16; most mains €7.80; noon-11pm; ; M2, U Senefelderplatz) A mellow 1950s lounge vibe and an inspired menu of Indochine home cooking divided into 'regular' and 'vegetarian' choices are the main draws at this restaurant with an expansive sidewalk terrace. Leave room for its cupcake riff (called 'popcake'). The six-course family meal is a steal at €23 for two, plus €10 per additional person.

★W-DER IMBISS FUSION €

Map p334 (030-4435 2206; www.w-derimbiss.de; Kastanienallee 49; dishes €5-20; noon-10pm Sun-Thu, to 11pm Fri & Sat; ; M1, U Rosenthaler Platz) The self-described home of 'indo-mexi-cal-ital' fusion, W is always busy as a beehive with fans of its signature naan pizza freshly baked in the tandoor oven and decorated with anything from avocado to smoked salmon. Other standouts are the fish tacos, the thali curry spread and the tandoori salmon.

Enjoy it all amid cheerful tiki decor alongside a healthy spirulina-laced apple juice. There's a second branch in Schöneberg at Nollendorfstrasse 10.

STREET FOOD AUF ACHSE STREET FOOD €

Map p334 (www.streetfoodaufachse.de; Kulturbrauerei, btwn Schönhauser Allee, Knaackstrasse, Eberswalder Strasse & Sredzkistrasse; noon-6pm Sun late Jan–mid-Nov) On Sunday the Kulturbrauerei (p144) gets mobbed by hungry folk keen on a first-class culinary journey at economy prices. Dozens of mobile kitchens set up in the courtyard of this 19th-century red-brick brewery turned cultural complex, and there's a beer garden as well as occasional live music and other entertainment.

It's even open in winter, when fire pits warm hands and hearts.

★LUCKY LEEK VEGAN €€

Map p334 (030-6640 8710; www.lucky-leek.com; Kollwitzstrasse 54; mains €21, 3/4/5-course tasting menus €39/50/63; 6-10pm Wed-Sun; ; U Senefelderplatz) Josita Hartanto has a knack for coaxing maximum flavour out of the vegetable kingdom and for boldly combining ingredients in unexpected ways. Hers is one of the best vegan kitchens in town and is especially lovely in summer, when seating expands to a leafy pavement terrace. If you're sitting inside, ask for an upstairs table next to the orangutan.

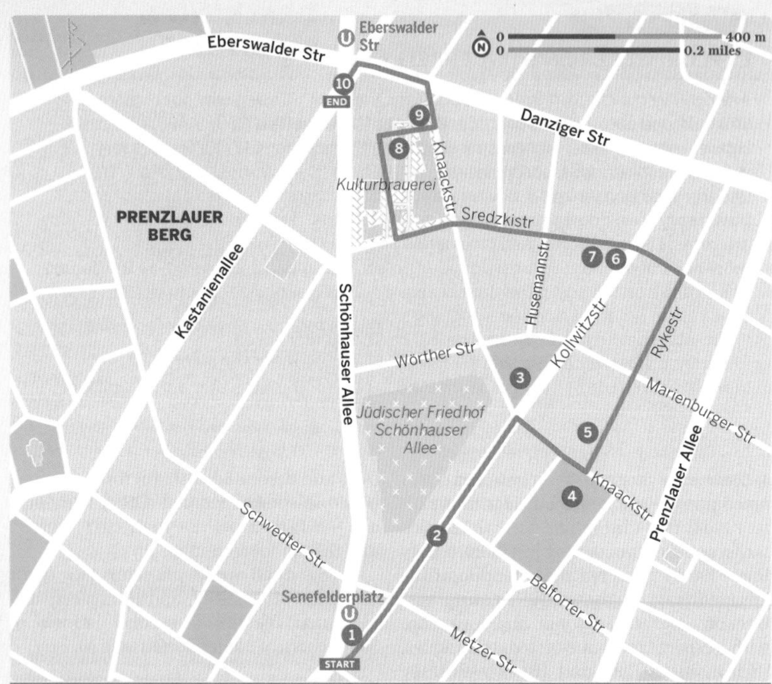

Neighbourhood Walk
Poking Around Prenzlauer Berg

START SENEFELDER PLATZ
END KONNOPKE'S IMBISS
LENGTH 1.2KM; 1½ HOURS

Start out at 1 **Senefelder Platz**, a patch of green named for Alois Senefelder, who invented lithography. Note the marble statue with his name chiselled in mirror writing, just as it would be using his printing technique. Head northeast on 2 **Kollwitzstrasse**, where the huge LPG organic supermarket and the ultra-deluxe Palais KolleBelle apartment complex are solid indicators of the neighbourhood's upmarket demographics.

You'll soon arrive at 3 **Kollwitzplatz** (p144), a square named for artist Käthe Kollwitz, who lived here with her husband for over 40 years while tending to the destitute. A bronze statue in the square's central park and a plaque on the blue building at Kollwitzstrasse 58 honour her legacy.

Follow Knaackstrasse to Rykestrasse, past a row of cafes, and note the circular 4 **Wasserturm**, Berlin's oldest water tower (1877), which is now honeycombed with flats. In Nazi Germany its machine room went through a sinister stint as a prison and torture centre. Follow Rykestrasse, noting the handsome facades of its restored town houses. At No 53 is the 5 **Synagoge Rykestrasse**, which survived WWII and once again hosts Shabbat services.

Continue on Rykestrasse to Sredzkistrasse, perhaps stopping for a cuppa and delicious homemade cakes at 6 **Anna Blume** (p153) and a browse at the 7 **Bücher Tauschbaum**, a free book exchange made from tree trunks.

Further up on the right looms the sprawling 8 **Kulturbrauerei** (p144), a brewery turned cultural complex. Admire the gorgeous architecture, whose turrets and towers conjure visions of a fairy-tale fortress. In its northern wing, the free 9 **Museum in der Kulturbrauerei** (p144) invites you to get an eyeful of daily life in East Germany.

Exit the Kulturbrauerei onto Knaackstrasse and turn left on Danziger Strasse to wrap up your walk with a *Currywurst* from cult kitchen 10 **Konnopke's Imbiss** (p148).

CHUTNIFY INDIAN €€

Map p334 (030-4401 0795; www.chutnify.com; Sredzkistrasse 43; mains €10-17; noon-3pm & 6-10pm Tue-Fri, noon-10pm Sat & Sun; ; M2, M10, U Eberswalder Strasse) Aparna Aurora's haunt spices up Berlin's bland Indian-food scene with adroitly spiced South Indian street food. Her specialities are dosas (a type of savoury rice-lentil crêpe) filled with flavour-packed curries and stews, but it's well worth exploring what's behind such lesser-known dishes as *vada* and *idli*.

Stake out some turf in the cheerfully decorated brick-walled dining room or at a pavement table.

DER HAHN IST TOT! FRENCH, GERMAN €€

Map p334 (030-6570 6756; www.der-hahn-ist-tot.de; Zionskirchstrasse 40; 4-course dinner €25; 6.30-11pm Tue-Sun; ; M1, 12, U Senefelderplatz, Rosenthaler Platz) A French children's ditty inspired the curious name, which translates as 'The rooster is dead!'. At this homey restaurant the deceased bird is turned into French country stew *coq au vin* and features as a main-course option on the weekly-changing four-course dinners (one of them meat free) that shine a spotlight on the best of French and German rural cooking.

STANDARD – SERIOUS PIZZA PIZZA €€

Map p334 (030-4862 5614; www.standard-berlin.de; Templiner Strasse 7; pizza €8.50-15; 5-11pm Tue-Fri, 1-11pm Sat & Sun; ; U Senefelderplatz) The name is the game: serious Neapolitan-style pizza *truly* is the standard at this modern parlour, where the dough is kneaded daily and the bases are topped with San Marzano tomatoes from the heel of Vesuvius and super-creamy fior di latte cheese. Best of all, they're tickled to perfection in a ferociously hot cupola furnace.

AUSSPANNE GERMAN €€

Map p334 (030-4430 5199; www.deutsches-restaurant.berlin; Kastanienallee 65; mains €16-22; 4-11pm Tue-Sat; ; M1, 12, U Senefelderplatz, Rosenthaler Platz) Rustic, cosy and decorated with wood, mirrors and vintage enamel signs, Ausspanne pairs Old Berlin flair with fresh and imaginative modern-German cooking. The seasons keep the menu in flux, but perennial favourites like Königsberger Klopse (veal dumplings in caper sauce) never go out of fashion.

DRINKING & NIGHTLIFE

Going out in Prenzlauer Berg is focused on low-key locals' bars and cafes, with many lining Lychener Strasse, Schliemannstrasse and Dunckerstrasse (nicknamed 'LSD') south of Helmholtzplatz. There's also a good crop on Kastanienallee, including Berlin's oldest beer garden, Prater.

★PRATER GARTEN BEER GARDEN

Map p334 (030-448 5688; www.pratergarten.de; Kastanienallee 7-9; snacks €2.50-7.50; noon-late Apr-Sep; ; M1, 12, U Eberswalder Strasse) Berlin's oldest beer garden has seen beer-soaked days and nights since 1837 and is still a charismatic spot for guzzling a custom-brewed Prater pilsner beneath the ancient chestnut trees (self-service). Note that it will be closed for renovation until at least July 2021.

In foul weather, in winter or to sample modern German and regional plates, report to the adjacent Prater Gaststätte beer hall.

WEINEREI FORUM WINE BAR

Map p334 (www.weinerei.com; Fehrbelliner Strasse 57; 10am-midnight; ; M1, 12, U Rosenthaler Platz) Serving homemade cakes and light meals by day, this living-room-style cafe turns into a wine bar after 8pm. It works on the honour principle: you 'rent' a wine glass for €2, then taste as much vino as you like and in the end decide what you want to pay. Please be fair to keep this fantastic concept going.

The concept is run by the nearby wine shop and all bottles are available for purchase.

★LAMM BAR COCKTAIL BAR

Map p334 (030-4467 5366; www.lammbar.de; Wisbyer Strasse 1; 6pm-2am Mon-Sat; M1, 50, U Schönhauser Allee, S Schönhauser Allee) It's well worth the pilgrimage to northern Prenzlauer Berg to spend a relaxed evening on the spacious terrace or in the industrial-minimal interior of this fab cocktail bar with neighbourly flair. Best of all, every drink on the seasonally changing menu can be ordered in full size (Lamm) or as a smaller version (Lämmchen, ie little lamb). Perfect for the indecisive.

WORTH A DETOUR

SCHLOSS SCHÖNHAUSEN

Surrounded by a lovely park, **Schloss Schönhausen** (☎030-3949 2625; www.spsg.de; Tschaikowskistrasse 1; adult/concession €6/5; ⏲10am-5.30pm Tue-Sun Apr-Oct, 10am-4pm Sat & Sun Nov-Mar; P; 🚋M1) packs a lot of history into its pint-sized frame. Originally a country estate of Prussian nobles, it became the summer residence of Frederick II's estranged wife Elisabeth Christine, then fell into a long slumber after her death in 1797. The Nazis stored 'degenerate' art in the by then neglected structure, which became the seat of East Germany's first president, Wilhelm Pieck, in 1949, before serving as the GDR government's guesthouse for state visitors.

After yet another mega-makeover, the palace sparkles in renewed splendour. Tours take in the downstairs rooms, whose furniture and wallpaper reflect the style of the 18th century when the queen had her private quarters here. More interesting – largely for their uniqueness – are the upstairs rooms where East German fustiness is alive in the heavy furniture of Pieck's 1950s office and in the baby-blue bedspread in the Gentlemen's Bedroom where Fidel Castro, Nicolae Ceauşescu and Muammar Gaddafi once slept. After your tour, it's well worth exploring the lovely gardens surrounding the palace.

To get to the palace, which is in Pankow just north of Prenzlauer Berg, catch tram M1 to the Tschaikowskistrasse stop, then walk about 300m east on Tschaikowskistrasse.

BRYK BAR — COCKTAIL BAR

Map p334 (☎030-2246 8055; www.bryk-bar.com; Rykestrasse 18; ⏲4pm-late; 🚋M2, M10, Ⓢ Prenzlauer Allee) Both vintage and industrial elements contribute to the unhurried, dapper ambience at this darkly lit cocktail lab. Bar chef Frank Grosser whips unusual ingredients into such experimental liquid teasers as the rum-based Kamasutra with a Hangover that's topped with white chocolate–horseradish foam. The free dill popcorn is positively addictive.

Also on the hit list: a gin and tonic made with BRYK Gin, a potent juniper juice created by the bar's founders and snazzily bottled in charcoal-grey ceramic.

CAFE CHAGALL — BAR

Map p334 (☎030-441 5881; www.cafe-chagall.com; Kollwitzstrasse 2; ⏲10am-1am or later; Ⓤ Senefelderplatz) Proof that the boho spirit isn't dead in Prenzlauer Berg, Chagall gets flooded with a congenial mix of locals, expats and visitors. They come for cold drinks served by staff who make everyone feel welcome. Separate smoking room in back, big pavement terrace in summer and Russian food from the affiliated restaurant next door.

BREWDOG — CRAFT BEER

Map p334 (☎030-4847 7770; www.brewdog.com; Ackerstrasse 29; ⏲noon-midnight Sun-Thu, to 2am Fri & Sat; 🚋12, M5, M8, Ⓤ Bernauer Strasse) Scottish cult beer-maker BrewDog now brings its fine suds to Berlin. Its modern-industrial flagship with brick walls and dark wood has some 30 taps dispensing its own draughts (try the Punk IPA) alongside a rotating roster of German and global guest pours. The pizza (€10 to €12) pairs well with the amber fluid.

CASTLE — PUB

Map p332 (☎0151 6767 6757; www.thecastleberlin.de; Invalidenstrasse 129; ⏲2pm-1am Mon-Thu, 2pm-2am Fri, 1pm-1am Sun; 📶; 🚋M5, M8, M10, 12, Ⓢ Nordbahnhof) Ben and Gekko's 'castle' is a comfortable lair that has just the right amount of contemporary cool without hitting the hipster needle. With a choice of 20 beers on tap and 20 gins to build drinks from, you're never far from a good time here. If you're hungry, load up on the cheese-laden homemade pizza.

BECKETTS KOPF — COCKTAIL BAR

Map p334 (☎030-4403 5880; www.becketts-kopf.de; Pappelallee 64; ⏲7pm-2am; 🚋12, Ⓢ Schönhauser Allee, Ⓤ Schönhauser Allee) Past Samuel Beckett's portrait, the art of cocktail-making is taken very seriously. Since 2004, the husband-and-wife owners have constantly upped the mixology ante by giving special twists to classic cocktails and by whipping up idiosyncratic concoctions that truly stimulate all the senses. Most of the spirits they use come from small suppliers.

ANNA BLUME CAFE €

Map p334 (030-4404 8749; www.cafe-anna-blume.de; Kollwitzstrasse 83; breakfast €4-13, mains €8-15; 9am-midnight; M2, M10, U Eberswalder Strasse) Potent java, tantalising cakes, weekly-changing hot dishes, and flowers from the attached shop perfume the art nouveau interior of this corner cafe named for a 1919 Dadaist poem by German artist Kurt Schwitters. In fine weather the terrace offers primo people-watching. Great for breakfast (served any time), especially if you order the tiered tray for two.

AUGUST FENGLER BAR

Map p334 (www.augustfengler.de; Lychener Strasse 11; from 7pm Mon-Sat; M1, U Eberswalder Strasse) With its flirty vibe, wallet-friendly drink prices and pretension-free crowd, this old-school but all-ages institution (since 1936!) scores a trifecta on the key ingredients for a good night out. Different DJs kick into gear after 10pm Tuesday to Saturday, playing an eclectic sound mix from '80s to funk, indie to rock.

Foosball, table tennis and dancing til the wee hours..

ENTERTAINMENT

LICHTBLICK KINO CINEMA

Map p334 (030-4405 8179; www.lichtblick-kino.org; Kastanienallee 77; tickets €7-7.50; M1, U Eberswalder Strasse) With space for only 32 cineastes, there's not a bad seat in the Lichtblick, one of Berlin's smallest cinemas. It's run by a collective and known for its eclectic programming of retrospectives, political documentaries, Berlin-made movies and global avant-garde fare, sometimes screened in the presence of directors or actors.

SHOPPING

Kastanienallee is the main shopping drag and popular for Berlin-made fashions and streetwear. Indie stores also line Stargarder Strasse and the streets around Helmholtzplatz, especially lower Dunckerstrasse. Note that most shops don't open until 11am or noon. On Sunday, cool-hunters should steer to the Mauerpark and Arkonaplatz to forage for flea-market treasure. For everyday needs, stop by the Schönhauser Allee Arcaden mall right by the eponymous U-/S-Bahn station.

★ FLOHMARKT IM MAUERPARK MARKET

Map p334 (www.flohmarktimmauerpark.de; Bernauer Strasse 63-64; 9am-6pm Sun; M1, M10, 12, U Eberswalder Strasse) Join the throngs of thrifty trinket hunters, bleary-eyed clubbers and excited tourists sifting for treasure at this always-busy flea market with cult status, in a spot right where the Berlin Wall once ran. Source new favourites among retro threads, local-designer T-shirts, vintage vinyl and offbeat stuff. Street-food stands and the beer gardens **Mauersegler** (030-9788 0904; www.mauersegler-berlin.de; 10am-late May-Oct;) and Schönwetter provide sustenance.

★ DEARGOODS FASHION & ACCESSORIES

Map p334 (030-9838 9926; www.deargoods.com; Schivelbeiner Strasse 35; 11am-8pm Mon-Fri, to 6pm Sat; U Schönhauser Allee) This was Germany's first all-vegan fashion boutique when it opened in 2012. It now has branches in other cities but remains uncompromisingly married to its original concept. Shop with a clear conscience for threads and accessories made from eco-friendly organic materials that will have you looking – and feeling – great.

★ SUGAFARI FOOD

Map p334 (030-9560 9713; www.sugafari.com; Kopenhagener Strasse 69; 2-7.30pm Tue-Fri, 11am-6pm Sat; M1, U Schönhauser Allee, S Schönhauser Allee) Take a trip around the world one candy at a time in this happiness-inducing cornucopia of sugary treats. No matter whether you're a homesick expat, nostalgic for your favourite childhood sweets or curious about Ma Hwa Cookies from China or a Bon Bon Bum lolly from Colombia, you'll find it in this sweet little shop (or its online store).

ZWEIMALSCHÖN VINTAGE

Map p334 (030-4431 95290; www.zweimalschoen.de; Danziger Strasse 22; 11am-8pm Mon-Sat; U Eberswalder Strasse) Thumb your nose at fast fashion and forage for covetable local and international clothing labels (for men and women), bags, household stuff, books and jewellery at this friendly charity shop run by the nonprofit Deutsche

Kleiderstiftung. Quality is high and prices reasonable. All proceeds support social projects worldwide.

GOLDHAHN UND SAMPSON FOOD

Map p334 (☎030-4119 8366; www.goldhahnundsampson.de; Dunckerstrasse 9; ⏰8am-8pm Mon-Fri, 9am-8pm Sat; 🚋12, Ⓤ Eberswalder Strasse) Harissa paste, additive-free red miso and crusty German bread are among the global pantry stockers at this stylish gourmet gallery. Owners Sascha and Andreas travel the world to source all items, most of them rare, organic and from small artisanal suppliers. For inspiration, nose around the cookbook library or join up for a class at the on-site cooking school.

KOLLWITZPLATZMARKT MARKET

Map p334 (cnr Kollwitzstrasse & Wöhrter Strasse; ⏰noon-7pm Thu Apr-Dec, to 6pm Thu Jan-Mar, 9am-4pm Sat; Ⓤ Senefelderplatz) At the edge of lovely and leafy Kollwitzplatz, this posh farmers market has everything you need to put together a gourmet picnic or meal. Velvety gorgonzola, juniper-berry smoked ham, crusty sourdough bread and home-made pesto are among the exquisite morsels scooped up by well-heeled locals.

The Thursday edition is all organic, while the Saturday market also features handicrafts. Locals love to cap a spree with a snack or a glass of wine right in the marketplace or in one of the numerous surrounding cafes.

SAINT GEORGES ENGLISH BOOKSHOP BOOKS

Map p334 (☎030-8179 8333; www.saintgeorgesbookshop.com; Wörther Strasse 27; ⏰11am-8pm Mon-Fri, to 7pm Sat; 📶; 🚋M2, Ⓤ Senefelderplatz) Laid-back and low-key, Saint Georges bookshop is a sterling spot to track down new and used English-language fiction and non-fiction. The selection includes plenty of rare and out-of-print books as well as a big shelf of literature by German and international authors translated into English.

TA(U)SCHE FASHION & ACCESSORIES

Map p334 (☎030-4030 1770; www.tausche.de; Raumerstrasse 8; ⏰11am-7pm Mon-Fri, to 6pm Sat; 🚋12, Ⓤ Eberswalder Strasse) Heike Braun and Antje Strubels now sell their messenger-style bags and backpacks with easily exchangeable flaps around the world, but this is the shop where it all began. Produced entirely in Germany, bags come in 12 sizes and your choice of over 200 cool and colourful flaps that zip off and on in seconds (or design your own).

TRÖDELMARKT ARKONAPLATZ MARKET

Map p334 (www.troedelmarkt-arkonaplatz.de; Arkonaplatz; ⏰10am-4pm Sun; 🚋M1, M10, Ⓤ Bernauer Strasse) Surrounded by cafes perfect for carbo-loading, this smallish flea market on a leafy square lets you ride the retro frenzy with plenty of groovy furniture, accessories, clothing, vinyl and books, including some East German vintage items. It's easily combined with a visit to the famous Flohmarkt im Mauerpark (p153).

RATZEKATZ TOYS

Map p334 (☎030-681 9564; www.ratzekatz.de; Raumerstrasse 7; ⏰10am-6pm Mon-Sat; 🚋12, Ⓤ Eberswalder Strasse) Packed with quality playthings, this adorable shop made headlines a few years ago when Angelina Jolie and son Maddox picked out a Jurassic Park's worth of dinosaurs. Even without the celeb glow, it's a fine place to source toys for all age groups – from babies to teens.

Potsdamer Platz & Tiergarten

POTSDAMER PLATZ | KULTURFORUM | TIERGARTEN & DIPLOMATENVIERTEL

Neighbourhood Top Five

❶ **Gemäldegalerie** (p160) Perusing an Aladdin's cave of Old Masters, from Rembrandt to Vermeer.

❷ **Sony Center** (p157) Stopping for a beer and people-watching beneath the magnificent canopy of this svelte glass-and-steel landmark designed by Helmut Jahn.

❸ **Panoramapunkt** (p158) Catching Europe's fastest lift to take in Berlin's impressive cityscape and enjoy refreshments in the sky.

❹ **Tiergarten** (p165) Getting lost amid the lawns, trees and paths of this city park with its ponds, monuments and beer gardens.

❺ **Gedenkstätte Deutscher Widerstand** (p164) Admiring the brave people who stood up to the Nazis at this memorial exhibit in the offices where the 20 July 1944 assassination attempt on Hitler was plotted.

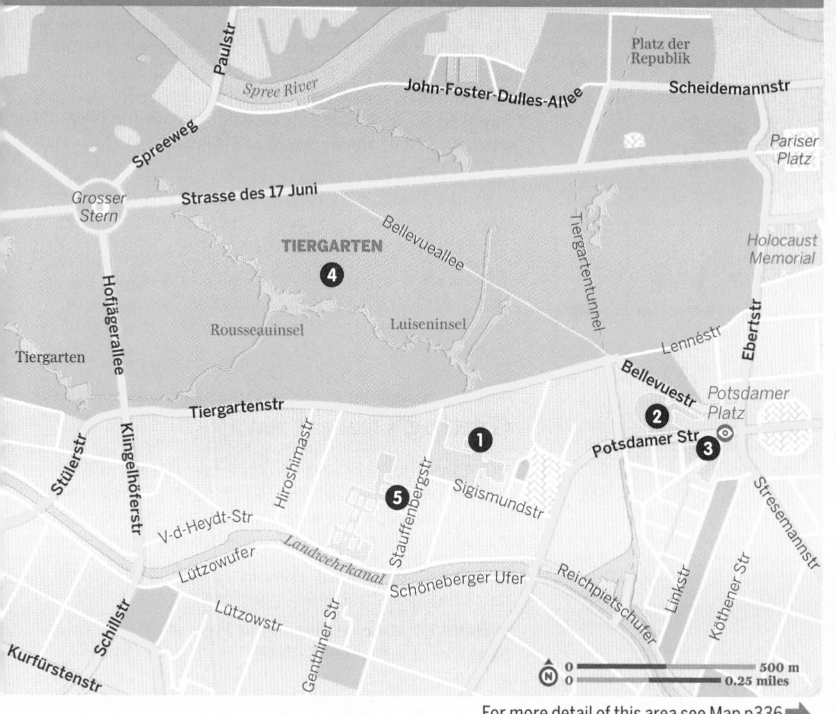

For more detail of this area see Map p336

Lonely Planet's Top Tip

From September until June, join hundreds of classical-music fans – from students to tourists to desk jockeys – for free one-hour chamber concerts on Tuesday at 1pm in the foyer of the Berliner Philharmonie.

Best Places to Eat

- Layla (p168)
- Beba (p166)
- Ki-Nova (p166)
- Mabuhay (p166)

For reviews, see p166.

Best Places to Drink

- Café am Neuen See (p168)
- Solar Lounge (p168)
- Barn (p168)

For reviews, see p168.

Best Architecture

- Sony Center (p157)
- Berliner Philharmonie (p165)
- Gropius Bau (p163)

For reviews, see p157.

Explore Potsdamer Platz & Tiergarten

Despite the name, Potsdamer Platz is not actually a square but an entire city quarter, forged in the 1990s from terrain once bisected by the Berlin Wall. A collaborative effort by the world's finest architects, it is considered a showcase of urban renewal. The area itself is rather compact and quickly explored – unless you stick around to see Berlin from above from the Panoramapunkt (p158) or dive into German film history at the Museum für Film und Fernsehen (p158).

Arty types should saunter over to the Kulturforum complex, a cluster of stellar museums that zeroes in on art, music and design. Seeing them all would easily keep you busy for a day, so if time is tight, stick to the Old Masters in the Gemäldegalerie (p160). Follow up with a leafy respite in the vast Tiergarten (p165), Berlin's equivalent to New York's Central Park, perhaps stopping for refreshments at Café am Neuen See (p168). South of the park, the Diplomatenviertel (p166; Diplomatic Quarter) is another visual plum for aficionados of contemporary architecture. The main attraction east of Potsdamer Platz is the huge Mall of Berlin (p169) on octagonal Leipziger Platz square.

Local Life

Tiergarten When the sun is out, Berliners just want to get outdoors to the sweeping lawns, shady paths and romantic corners of the Tiergarten (p165) park, followed up with pizza and a cold brew at the beer garden of Café am Neuen See (p168).

Beer-garden concerts On Sundays in July and August, the Teehaus im Englischen Garten (p168) turns into a big garden party with free rock, pop and jazz concerts (www.konzertsommer-berlin.de).

Traffic light The clock-tower-shaped replica of Europe's first traffic light, from 1924, at the corner of Potsdamer Platz and Stresemannstrasse is a popular meeting point.

Getting There & Away

Bus Line 200 links with Zoologischer Garten and Alexanderplatz; 300 with the East Side Gallery; M41 with Hauptbahnhof, Kreuzberg and Neukölln; and M29 with Kreuzberg and Charlottenburg via Checkpoint Charlie.

S-Bahn S1 and S2 link Potsdamer Platz with Unter den Linden and the Scheunenviertel.

U-Bahn U2 stops at Potsdamer Platz and Mendelssohn-Bartholdy-Park.

TOP EXPERIENCE
EXPLORE POTSDAMER PLATZ

The rebirth of the historic Potsdamer Platz was Europe's biggest building project of the 1990s, a showcase of urban renewal masterminded by such top international architects as Renzo Piano and Helmut Jahn. An entire city quarter sprouted on terrain once divided by the Berlin Wall, and today it houses offices, theatres and cinemas, hotels, apartments and museums.

Until WWII sucked all life out of the area, Potsdamer Platz was Berlin's traffic, entertainment and commercial hub. Its modern reinterpretation is again divided into three sections, of which the **Sony Center** is the flashiest and most visitor friendly, with a central plaza canopied by a glass roof that erupts in changing colours after dark. Segments of the **Berlin Wall** stand at the corner of Potsdamer Strasse and Ebertstrasse. Across Potsdamer Strasse, **Daimler City** has big hotels, a shopping mall, sprinkles of public art, and entertainment venues that host movie premieres and galas during the Berlinale film festival in February. The **Beisheim Center**, home to the Ritz-Carlton Hotel, is modelled after classic American skyscrapers.

DON'T MISS

- Panoramapunkt
- Museum für Film und Fernsehen
- Berlin Wall remnants

PRACTICALITIES

- Map p336, G5
- Alte Potsdamer Strasse
- 200, 300, M41, S Potsdamer Platz, U Potsdamer Platz

Sony Center

Designed by Helmut Jahn, the visually dramatic **Sony Center** (www.potsdamer-platz.net) is fronted by a 26-floor glass-and-steel tower that's the tallest building on Potsdamer Platz. It integrates rare relics from Potsdamer Platz' prewar era, such as a section of the facade of the **Hotel Esplanade** (visible from Bellevuestrasse) and the opulent **Kaisersaal**, whose 75m move to its current location required some technological wizardry. The heart of the Sony Center is a plaza canopied by a tent-like glass roof with supporting beams radiating like bicycle spokes. The plaza and its many cafes lend themselves to hanging out and people-watching.

TAKE A BREAK

Take time out with a single-origin cuppa or a coffee-based cocktail at the Barn (p168), inside the historic Haus Huth.

Restore energy with a colourful, health-focused lunch at Ki-Nova (p166), an upbeat cafe with sidewalk tables.

In WWII 80% of Potsdamer Platz was destroyed and it plunged into a coma, only to be bisected by the Berlin Wall in 1961. Today, a double row of cobblestones indicates the course of the Wall, and a few segments (p157) outside the northern Potsdamer Platz train station entrance feature explanatory texts about other Wall-related memorial sites.

TOP TIPS

- Check out the Berlin Wall segments outside the Potsdamer Platz S-Bahn station entrance.
- Admission to the Museum für Film und Fernsehen (p158) is free from 4pm to 8pm Thursdays.
- An original Berlin Wall guard tower (p163) is just a short walk away on Erna-Berger-Strasse (off Stresemannstrasse).

Museum für Film und Fernsehen

From silent movies to sci-fi, Germany's long and illustrious film history gets the star treatment at the engaging **Museum für Film und Fernsehen** (Museum for Film & Television; ☎030-300 9030; www.deutsche-kinemathek.de; Potsdamer Strasse 2; adult/concession €8/5, 4-8pm Thu free; ⏲10am-6pm Wed & Fri-Mon, to 8pm Thu). The tour kicks off with an appropriate sense of drama as it sends you through a dizzying mirrored walkway that conjures visions of *The Cabinet of Dr Caligari.* Major themes include pioneers and early divas, silent-era classics such as Fritz Lang's *Metropolis,* Leni Riefenstahl's ground-breaking Nazi-era documentary *Olympia,* German exiles in Hollywood, and post-WWII movies. Stealing the show, as she did in real life, is femme fatale Marlene Dietrich, whose glamour lives on through her original costumes, personal finery, photographs and documents. The **TV exhibit** upstairs has more niche appeal but is still fun if you always wanted to know what *Star Trek* sounds like in German.

Make use of the excellent audioguide (€2) as you work your way through various themed galleries.

The museum is part of the Filmhaus, which also harbours a film school, the Arsenal cinema (p169), a library and a museum shop.

Legoland Discovery Centre

The **Legoland Discovery Centre** (☎01806-6669 0110; www.legolanddiscoverycentre.de/berlin; Potsdamer Strasse 4; €19.50; ⏲10am-7pm Wed-Sun, last admission 5pm) is an indoor amusement park made entirely of those little coloured plastic building blocks that many of us grew up with. Cute but low tech, it's best suited to kids aged three to eight. Skip the promotional introductory film and head straight to adventure stations such as Ninjago, where you train as a Ninja and brave a laser labyrinth, or Merlin's Magic Carousel to become a wizard's apprentice. Other thrills include the 4D cinema (with tactile special effects), a slo-mo ride through the Dragon's Castle, and building a Lego racing car. Grown-ups will have fun marvelling at a Berlin in miniature at Miniland, which uses more than two million Lego bricks to recreate major landmarks.

The website has ticket deals and combination tickets with other attractions.

Panoramapunkt

Europe's fastest lift, **Panoramapunkt** (☎030-2593 7080; www.panoramapunkt.de; Potsdamer Platz 1; adult/concession €7.50/6, without wait €11.50/9; ⏲11am-7pm Apr-Oct, to 5pm Nov-Mar) yo-yoes up and down the red-brick postmodern Kollhof Tower in 20 sec-

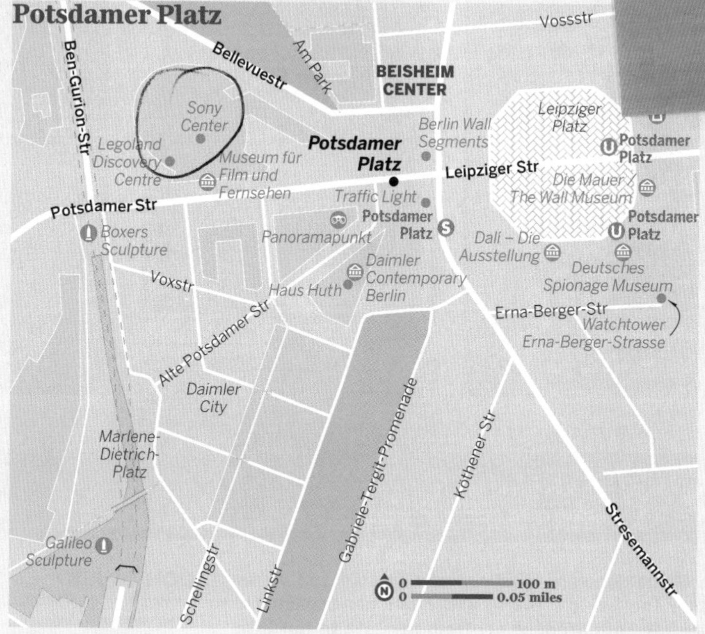

onds. From the bi-level viewing platform at a lofty 100m, you can pinpoint the sights, make a java stop in the 1930s-style glass-fronted cafe, enjoy sunset from the terrace and check out the exhibit that peels back the layers of the quarter's history.

Art at Daimler City

Daimler City is a postmodern urban landscape dotted with large-scale abstract sculptures that explore the relationship between art and urban space. A self-guided tour might start with Keith Haring's **Boxers**, which shows two cut-steel stick figures – one blue, one red – seemingly punching each other out. Or are they embracing each other? You decide! From here, walk south to the so-called Piano Lake, accented by Mark di Suvero's **Galileo**, an abstract jumble of rusted steel T-beams assembled into a gravity-defying sculpture.

The sculptures are part of the Daimler Art Collection, which also maintains a quiet, loft-style gallery, the Daimler Contemporary Berlin (p163), nearby. Curators mount several exhibits yearly, drawing from the corporation's rich collection of international abstract, conceptual and minimalist art. It's on the top floor of the historic Haus Huth, a rare surviving building from pre-WWII Potsdamer Platz. Ring the bell to be buzzed in.

TOP EXPERIENCE
ADMIRE ART AT THE GEMÄLDEGALERIE

The Gemäldegalerie (Gallery of Old Masters) ranks among the world's finest and most comprehensive collections of European art from the 13th to the 18th centuries. Expect to feast your eyes on masterpieces by Titian, Goya, Botticelli, Holbein, Gainsborough, Canaletto, Hals, Rubens, Vermeer and many other Old Masters. The gallery also hosts high-profile visiting exhibits featuring works by the great artists of this period.

Collection Overview

The Gemäldegalerie's opening in a purpose-built Kulturforum space in 1998 marked the happy reunion of a collection separated by the Cold War for half a century. Some works had remained at the Bode-Museum in East Berlin, the rest went on display in the West Berlin suburb of Dahlem. Today, about 1500 paintings span the arc of artistic vision over five centuries. Dutch and Flemish painters, including Rembrandt, are especially well represented, as are exponents of the Italian Renaissance. Another focus is on German artists from the late Middle Ages, and there's also a sprinkling of British, French and Spanish masters.

East Wing: German, Dutch & Flemish Masters

The exhibit kicks off with religious paintings from the Middle Ages and moves quickly to the Renaissance and works by two of the era's most famous artists: Albrecht Dürer and Lucas Cranach the Elder. A standout in Room

DON'T MISS

- Rembrandt Room (Room X)
- *Amor Victorius* (Room XIV)
- *Dutch Proverbs* (Room 7)
- *Fountain of Youth* (Room III)

PRACTICALITIES

- Map p336, E5
- 030-266 424 242
- www.smb.museum/gg
- Matthäikirchplatz
- adult/concession/under 18yr €10/5/free
- 10am-6pm Tue, Wed & Fri, to 8pm Thu, 11am-6pm Sat & Sun
- 200, 300, M41, M48, M85, S Potsdamer Platz, U Potsdamer Platz

2 is Dürer's portrait of **Hieronymus Holzschuher** (1526), a Nuremberg patrician, career politician and strong supporter of the Reformation. Note how the artist brilliantly homes in on his friend's features with the utmost precision, down to the furrows, wrinkles and thinning hair.

One of Cranach's finest works is **Fountain of Youth** (1546) in Room III, which illustrates humankind's yearning for eternal youth. Crones plunge into a pool and emerge as dashing hotties – no need for plastic surgeons! The transition is also reflected in the landscape, which is stark and craggy on the left and lush and fertile on the right.

Another remarkable portrait awaits in Room 4. **Portrait of a Young Woman** (1470) by Petrus Christus depicts an intriguing woman with almond-shaped eyes and porcelain skin, gazing at us with a blend of sadness and skepticism. It was the artist's only work featuring a woman.

A main exponent of the Dutch Renaissance was Pieter Bruegel the Elder, who here is represented with the dazzling **Dutch Proverbs** (1559) in Room 7. The moralistic yet humorous painting crams more than 100 proverbs and idioms into a single seaside-village scene. While some point up the absurdity of human behaviour, others unmask its imprudence and sinfulness. Some sayings are still in use today, among them 'swimming against the tide' and 'armed to the teeth'.

North Wing: Dutch 17th-Century Paintings

The first galleries in the north wing feature some exceptional portraits, most notably Frans Hals' **Malle Babbe** (1633) in Room 13. Note how Hals ingeniously captures the character and vitality of his subject 'Crazy Barbara' with freely wielded brushstrokes. Hals met the rosy-cheeked woman with the near-demonic grin in the workhouse for the mentally ill where his son Pieter was also a resident. The tin mug and owl are symbols of Babbe's fondness for a tipple.

Another eye-catcher is **Woman with a Pearl Necklace** (1662) in Room 18, a famous painting by Dutch realist Jan Vermeer. It depicts a young, well-dressed woman facing a small window and a mirror while fastening a pearl necklace around her neck, an intimate moment beautifully captured with characteristic soft brushstrokes.

A highlight of the north wing is the octagonal Room X, which is dedicated to Rembrandt and dominated by the large-scale **Mennonite Minister Cornelis Claesz Anslo** (1641), which shows the preacher in conversation with his wife. The huge open Bible

TAKE A BREAK

The friendly Chez Ahmet kiosk on Potsdamer Strasse has cold drinks, *Currywurst* and Turkish snacks from 10am to 8pm.

The building housing this encyclopaedic collection was the last Kulturforum museum to open, in 1998. Designed by Munich firm Hilmer & Sattler, it is a postmodern interpretation of the clear lines and stark symmetry of Karl Friedrich Schinkel's era. The entrance sits atop a sloping piazza, while the permanent galleries radiate from a football-field-size hall used for temporary exhibits.

TOP TIPS

- Take advantage of the excellent free audioguide to get the low-down on selected works.
- Note that the room-numbering system is quite confusing, as both Latin (I, II, III) and Arabic numbers (1, 2, 3) are used.
- A tour of all 72 rooms covers almost 2km, so allow at least a couple of hours for your visit and wear comfortable shoes.

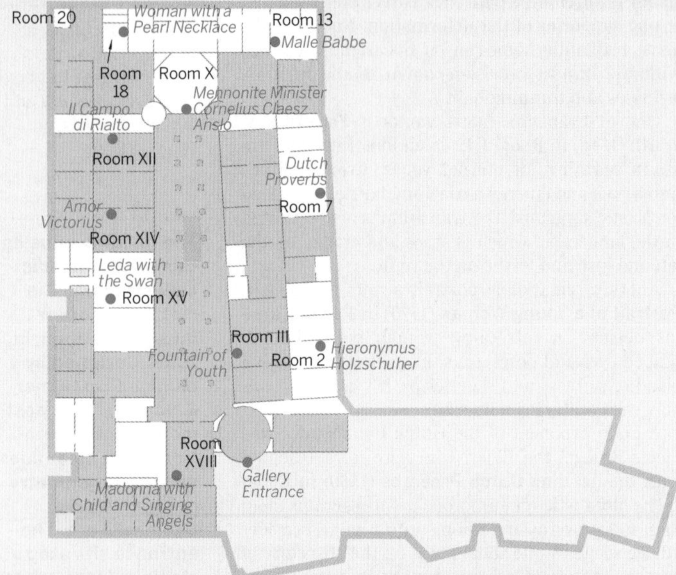

and his gesturing hand sticking out in almost 3D style from the centre of the painting are meant to emphasise the strength of his religious convictions. Also note Rembrandt's small self-portrait next to it.

West Wing: Italian Masterpieces

The first galleries in the west wing stay in the 17th and 18th centuries. Crowds often form before Canaletto's **Il Campo di Rialto** (1758–63) in Room XII, which depicts the arcaded main market square of the artist's home town, Venice, with stunning precision and perspective. Note the goldsmith shops on the left, the wig-wearing merchants in the centre and the stores selling paintings and furniture on the right.

Older by 150 years is Caravaggio's delightful **Amor Victorius** (1602–03) in Room XIV. Wearing nothing but a mischievous grin, a pair of black angel wings and a fistful of arrows, this cheeky Amor means business. Note the near photographic realism achieved by the dramatic use of light and shadow.

The next galleries travel back to the Renaissance, when Raphael, Titian and Correggio dominated Italian art. Correggio's **Leda and the Swan** (1532) in Room XV is worth a closer look. Judging by her blissed-out expression, Leda is having a fine time with that swan, who, according to Greek mythology, is none other than Zeus himself. The erotically charged nature of this painting apparently so incensed its one-time owner Louis of Orleans that he cut off Leda's head with a knife. It was later restored.

Lest you think that all West Wing paintings have a naughty subtext, let us draw your attention to Sandro Botticelli's **Madonna with Child and Singing Angels** (1477) in Room XVIII. This circular painting (a format called a *tondo*) shows Mary flanked by two sets of four wingless angels. It's an intimate moment that shows the Virgin tenderly embracing – perhaps even about to breastfeed – her child. The white lilies are symbols of her purity. Note that mother and child have the same hazel eyes.

SIGHTS

Sights in this compact area are handily clustered around Potsdamer Platz itself and in the adjacent Kulturforum museum complex. The Diplomatic Quarter is just west of here, the Tiergarten park to the north. It's all easily explored on foot.

Potsdamer Platz

POTSDAMER PLATZ — AREA

See p157.

★GROPIUS BAU — GALLERY

Map p336 (☎030-254 860; www.gropiusbau.de; Niederkirchner Strasse 7; adult/concession/under 16yr €15/10/free; ⊙10am-7pm Fri-Wed, to 9pm Thu; P; 🚌M41, S Potsdamer Platz, U Potsdamer Platz) With its mosaics, terracotta reliefs and airy atrium, this Italian Renaissance-style exhibit space named for its architect (Bauhaus founder Walter Gropius' great-uncle) is a celebrated venue for high-calibre art and cultural exhibits. Whether it's a David Bowie retrospective, the latest works of Ai Weiwei or an ethnological exhibit on the mysteries of Angkor Wat, it's bound to be well curated and engrossing.

The Berlin state parliament convenes in the stately neo-Renaissance structure (the Abgeordnetenhaus) across the street.

DEUTSCHES SPIONAGE MUSEUM — MUSEUM

Map p336 (German Spy Museum; ☎030-398 200 451; www.deutsches-spionagemuseum.de; Leipziger Platz 9; adult/concession €12/8; ⊙10am-8pm, last entry 7pm; 🚌200, M41, M48, M85, S Potsdamer Platz, U Potsdamer Platz) High-tech and interactive, this private museum not only documents the evolution of spying from ancient Egypt to the 20th century but also displays hundreds of ingenious tools of the trade, including a lipstick pistol, shoe bugs and an ultra-rare Enigma cipher machine. You learn about some famous spies, get to encrypt a message, detect bugging devices and take a lie-detector test. A hit with kids of all ages is the wicked laser labyrinth.

The exhibit also addresses hot-button issues of our times: big data as well as data security, rights in the surveillance society, and issues surrounding social media.

DALÍ – DIE AUSSTELLUNG — GALLERY

Map p336 (www.daliberlin.de; Leipziger Platz 7; adult/concession €12.50/9.50, with tour €19.50/14; ⊙noon-6pm, last entry 5pm; 🚌200, M41, M48, M85, S Potsdamer Platz, U Potsdamer Platz) If you only know Salvador Dalí as the painter of melting watches, burning giraffes and other surrealist imagery, this private collection will likely open new perspectives on the man and his work. Here, the focus is on his graphics, illustrations, sculptures, drawings and films, with highlights including etchings on the theme of Tristan and Isolde and epic sculptures like *Surrealist Angel*, as well as the *Don Quixote* lithographs.

DIE MAUER / THE WALL MUSEUM AM LEIPZIGER PLATZ — MUSEUM

Map p336 (☎030-6296 8599; www.berlinwallexpo.de; Leipziger Platz 11; adult/concession €10/8; ⊙11am-6pm; U Potsdamer Platz, S Potsdamer Platz) Anti-tank barriers made from railroad tracks, uniforms, communication equipment and a disc-shaped GDR flag from a former border checkpoint are among the exhibits in Berlin's newest museum about the history of the Wall.

GDR WATCHTOWER ERNA-BERGER-STRASSE — MEMORIAL

Map p336 (Erna-Berger-Strasse; 🚌M41, U Potsdamer Platz, S Potsdamer Platz) Imagine what it was like to be a Berlin Wall border guard as you climb up the iron ladder of one of the few remaining watchtowers. The octagonal observation perch of this 1971 model was particularly cramped. The design was later replaced by larger square towers.

DAIMLER CONTEMPORARY BERLIN — GALLERY

Map p336 (☎030-2594 1421; www.art.daimler.com; 4th fl, Haus Huth, Alte Potsdamer Strasse 5; ⊙11am-6pm; 🚌200, 300, M41, S Potsdamer Platz, U Potsdamer Platz) FREE Escape the city bustle at this quiet, loft-style gallery where the Daimler corporation shares selections from its considerable collection of international abstract, conceptual and minimalist art with the public. It's on the top floor of the historic Haus Huth, a rare surviving building from pre-WWII Potsdamer Platz. Ring the bell to be buzzed in.

BERLIN STORY BUNKER — MUSEUM

Map p340 (☎030-2655 5546; www.berlinstory.de; Schöneberger Strasse 23a; adult/concession Hitler exhibit €12/9, Berlin Story Museum €6/4.50; ⊙10am-7pm, last entry 5.30pm; 🚌M29, M41, S Anhalter Bahnhof) This multimedia exhibit 'Hitler – how could it happen', atmospherically set on three floors inside a WWII air-raid shelter, does a thorough job of documenting Hitler's rise and his impact on Germany and the world. A highlight is the 1:25 scale model of the bunker where Hitler committed suicide. Located in the same building is the Berlin Story Museum, which chronicles milestones in city history in a one-hour audio tour.

Kulturforum

GEMÄLDEGALERIE GALLERY

See p160.

KUNSTGEWERBEMUSEUM MUSEUM

Map p336 (Museum of Decorative Arts; 030-266 424 242; www.smb.museum; Matthäikirchplatz; adult/concession/under 18yr €8/4/free; 10am-6pm Tue-Fri, 11am-6pm Sat & Sun; 200, M41, M48, M85, S Potsdamer Platz, U Potsdamer Platz) This prized collection of European design, fashion and decorative arts from the Middle Ages to today is part of the Kulturforum museum cluster. You can feast your eyes on exquisitely ornate medieval reliquaries and portable altars or compare Bauhaus classics to contemporary designs by Philippe Starck and Ettore Sottsass. Pride of place goes to the Fashion Gallery, with classic designer outfits and accessories from the past 150 years.

Open for guided tours only until further notice because of the Covid-19 pandemic.

KUPFERSTICHKABINETT GALLERY

Map p336 (Museum of Prints & Drawings; 030-266 424 242; www.smb.museum/kk; Matthäikirchplatz; adult/concession €6/3; 10am-6pm Tue, Wed & Fri, to 8pm Thu, 11am-6pm Sat & Sun; 200, 300, M29, M41, M48, M85, S Potsdamer Platz, U Potsdamer Platz) One of the world's largest and finest collections of art on paper, this gallery shelters a bonanza of hand-illustrated books, illuminated manuscripts, drawings and prints produced mostly in Europe from the 14th century onward. Artists represented include Albrecht Dürer, Rembrandt, Karl Friedrich Schinkel, Pablo Picasso, Alberto Giacometti and Gerhard Richter. Among its most prized possessions are Sandro Botticelli's illustrations for Dante's *Divine Comedy*. Alas, these fragile works don't do well under light, which is why only a tiny fraction of the collection is shown at a time.

TOP EXPERIENCE

REMEMBERING THE RESISTANCE

If you've seen the movie *Valkyrie* you know the story of Claus von Stauffenberg, the poster boy of the German resistance against Hitler and the Third Reich. The very rooms where senior army officers led by Stauffenberg plotted their bold but ill-fated assassination attempt on the Führer on 20 July 1944 are now home to the **Gedenkstätte Duetscher Widerstand** (German Resistance Memorial Centre). The building itself, the historic Bendlerblock, harboured the Wehrmacht high command from 1935 to 1945 and is today the seat of the German defence ministry.

Aside from the Stauffenberg-led coup, the centre also documents the efforts of many other Germans who risked their lives opposing the Third Reich for ideological, ethical, religious or military reasons. Most were just regular folks, such as Hans and Sophie Scholl of the White Rose student group, or the craft-maker Georg Elser; others were prominent citizens like the artist Käthe Kollwitz and the theologian Dietrich Bonhoeffer.

In the yard, a sculpture marks the spot where Stauffenberg and three of his co-conspirators were executed right after the failed coup.

DON'T MISS

- Stauffenberg exhibit (rooms 8 to 11)
- White Rose exhibit (room 15)

PRACTICALITIES

- Map p336, D5
- 030-2699 5000
- www.gdw-berlin.de
- Stauffenbergstrasse 13-14
- admission free
- 9am-6pm Mon-Fri, 10am-6pm Sat & Sun
- 200, M29, M48, M85, S Potsdamer Platz, U Potsdamer Platz, Kurfürstenstrasse

MUSIKINSTRUMENTEN-MUSEUM MUSEUM

Map p336 (Musical Instruments Museum; ☎030-2548 1178; www.simpk.de; Tiergartenstrasse 1; adult/concession/under 18yr €6/3/free; ⏲9am-5pm Tue, Wed & Fri, to 8pm Thu, 10am-5pm Sat & Sun; 🚌200, 300, M41, Ⓢ Potsdamer Platz, Ⓤ Potsdamer Platz) This darling museum is packed with fun, precious and rare sound machines, including the glass harmonica invented by Ben Franklin, a flute played by Frederick the Great, and Johann Sebastian Bach's harpsichord. Stop at the listening stations to hear what some of the more obscure instruments sound like.

There are also plenty of old trumpets, bizarre bagpipes and even a talking walking stick. A crowd favourite is the Mighty Wurlitzer (1929), an organ with more buttons and keys than a troop of beefeaters, that's cranked up at noon on Saturday and at 3pm on Sunday (€3) as well as during silent-movie screenings. Classical concerts, many free, take place year-round (ask for a schedule or check the website). Enter the museum via Ben-Gurion-Strasse.

NEUE NATIONALGALERIE GALLERY

Map p336 (www.smb.museum; Potsdamer Strasse 50; ⏲closed until Jul 2021; 🚌200, M49, M48, M85, Ⓤ Potsdamer Platz, Ⓢ Potsdamer Platz) After five years of renovations led by architect David Chipperfield, the New National Gallery and its prized collection of early-20th-century art is set to reopen in July 2021. The building itself is a late masterpiece by Ludwig Mies van der Rohe. All glass and steel and squatting on a raised platform, it brings to mind a postmodern Buddhist temple. Check online for details.

BERLINER PHILHARMONIE ARCHITECTURE

Map p336 (☎030-2548 8156; www.berliner-philharmoniker.de; Herbert-von-Karajan-Strasse 1; tours adult/concession €5/3; ⏲tours 1.30pm Sep-Jun; 🚌200, 300, M29, M41, M48, M85, Ⓢ Potsdamer Platz, Ⓤ Potsdamer Platz) A masterpiece of organic architecture, Hans Scharoun's honey-coloured 1963 concert venue is the iconic home base of the prestigious Berliner Philharmoniker (p169). The auditorium feels like the inside of a finely crafted instrument and boasts supreme acoustics and excellent sight lines from every seat.

MATTHÄUSKIRCHE CHURCH

Map p336 (Church of St Matthew; ☎030-262 1202; www.stiftung-stmatthaeus.de; Matthäikirchplatz; ⏲11am-6pm Tue-Sun; 🚌200, 300, M29, M41, M48, M85, Ⓢ Potsdamer Platz, Ⓤ Potsdamer Platz) FREE Standing a bit lost and forlorn within the Kulturforum, the Friedrich August Stüler–designed Matthäuskirche (1846) is a beautiful neo-Romanesque confection with alternating bands of red and ochre brick and a light-flooded, modern sanctuary filled with artworks and temporary exhibits. A nice time to visit is for the free 20-minute organ recitals at 12.30pm Tuesday to Saturday. Views from the tower are free but only so-so.

Tiergarten & Diplomatenviertel

★TIERGARTEN PARK

(Strasse des 17 Juni; 🚌100, 200, Ⓢ Potsdamer Platz, Brandenburger Tor, Ⓤ Brandenburger Tor) Berlin's rulers used to hunt boars and pheasants in the rambling Tiergarten until garden architect Peter Lenné landscaped the grounds in the 19th century. Today it's one of the world's largest urban parks, popular for strolling, jogging, picnicking, frisbee tossing and, yes, nude sunbathing and gay cruising (especially around the Löwenbrücke). It is bisected by a major artery, the Strasse des 17 Juni. Walking across the entire park takes at least an hour, but even a shorter stroll has its rewards.

SIEGESSÄULE MONUMENT

Map p336 (Victory Column; Grosser Stern, Strasse des 17 Juni; adult/concession €3.50/3; ⏲9.30am-6.30pm Mon-Fri, to 7pm Sat & Sun Apr-Oct, 9.30am-5pm Mon-Fri, to 5.30pm Sat & Sun Nov-Mar; 🚌100, Ⓤ Hansaplatz, Ⓢ Bellevue) Like the arms of a starfish, five roads merge into the Grosser Stern roundabout at the heart of the huge Tiergarten (p165) park. The Victory Column at its centre celebrates 19th-century Prussian military triumphs and is crowned by a gilded statue of the goddess Victoria. Today it is also a symbol of Berlin's gay community. Climb 285 steps for sweeping views of the park.

The column stood in front of the Reichstag until the Nazis moved it here in 1938 to make room for their Germania urban-planning project. The pedestal was added at the time, bringing the column height to 67m. Film buffs might remember the Goddess of Victory on top from a key scene in Wim Wenders' 1985 flick *Wings of Desire.*

KULTURFORUM COMBO TICKET

A Kulturforum area ticket costs €16 (concession €8) and includes same-day admission to the Gemäldegalerie (p160), the Kunstgewerbemuseum (p164), the Kupferstichkabinett (p164) and the Musikinstrumenten-Museum (p165). Admission to all museums is free to anyone under 18.

GEDENKSTÄTTE STILLE HELDEN MUSEUM

Map p336 (Silent Heroes Memorial Center; 030-263 923 822; www.gedenkstaette-stille-helden.de; Stauffenbergstrasse 13-14; 9am-6pm Mon-Fri, 10am-6pm Sat & Sun; 200, M29, M48, M85, U Potsdamer Platz, Kurfürstenstrasse, S Potsdamer Platz) FREE The Silent Heroes Memorial Center is dedicated to ordinary Germans who found the courage to help their persecuted Jewish neighbours through such actions as providing food, hiding people or obtaining fake ID cards. Using documents, photographs and objects, the exhibit illustrates both successful and failed rescue attempts.

DIPLOMATENVIERTEL AREA

Map p336 (Diplomatic Quarter; M29, 200, S Potsdamer Platz, U Potsdamer Platz) In the 1920s, a quiet villa-studded colony south of the Tiergarten evolved into Berlin's embassy quarter. After WWII the obliterated area remained in a state of quiet decay while the embassies all set up in the West German capital of Bonn. After reunification, many countries rebuilt on their historic lots, accounting for some of Berlin's boldest new architecture, which can be nicely explored on a leisurely wander.

AKADEMIE DER KÜNSTE CULTURAL CENTRE

Map p336 (Academy of Arts; 030-200 572 000; www.adk.de; Hanseatenweg 10; admission varies, last 4hr Tue free; building 10am-8pm, exhibit hours vary; S Bellevue, U Hansaplatz) The Academy of Arts has a pedigree going back to 1696, but its cultural programming is solidly rooted in the now and tomorrow. It shows exhibitions, organises concerts, lectures, discussions and readings, and hosts film screenings and theatre and dance performances.

EATING

The best restaurants on Potsdamer Platz are in the hotels. For a quick nibble, head to the food court on the 2nd floor of the Mall of Berlin (p169). The beer gardens tucked within Tiergarten park also serve food and are destinations in their own right.

MABUHAY INDONESIAN €

Map p336 (030-265 1867; www.mabuhay.juisyfood.com; Köthener Strasse 28; mains €6-13; noon-3pm & 5-9.30pm Mon-Fri, 5-9.30pm Sat; ; U Mendelssohn-Bartholdy-Park) Tucked into a concrete courtyard, this hole-in-the-wall place scores a one for looks and a 10 for the food. Usually packed (especially at lunchtime), it delivers Indonesian food with authentic flair at itty-bitty prices. The heat meter has been adjusted for German tastes, but the spicing of such dishes as gado gado or curry rendang is still feisty and satisfying.

BEBA ISRAELI €€

Map p336 (0157 3190 7076; www.bebarestaurant.com; Niederkirchnerstrasse 7; small plates €7, mains €12-15; 11.30am-6pm Mon & Tue, to 8pm Thu & Fri, 10.30am-7pm Sat & Sun; ; M41, U Potsdamer Platz, S Potsdamer Platz) In its mirror-lidded dining room inside the grand Gropius Bau, Beba crystallises the complex flavours of the Jewish diaspora into a single tasty menu. Whether you choose vegan sabich from Iraq, Tunisian fish and chips or Polish mushroom-and-barley soup, it'll be delicious and laced with herbs freshly picked in the vertical indoor garden. Cakes are by local legend Cynthia Barcomi.

KI-NOVA INTERNATIONAL €€

Map p336 (030-2546 4860; www.ki-nova.de; Potsdamer Strasse 2; mains €9-15; 11.30am-10pm Mon-Fri, noon-10pm Sat; ; 200, 300, M41, U Potsdamer Platz, S Potsdamer Platz) The name of this lunchtime favourite hints at the concept: 'ki' is Japanese for energy and 'nova' Latin for new. 'New energy' in this case translates into health-focused yet comforting bites starring global and regional ingredients. The contemporary interior radiates urban warmth, with heavy plank tables, a black-tiled bar, movie stills and floor-to-ceiling windows.

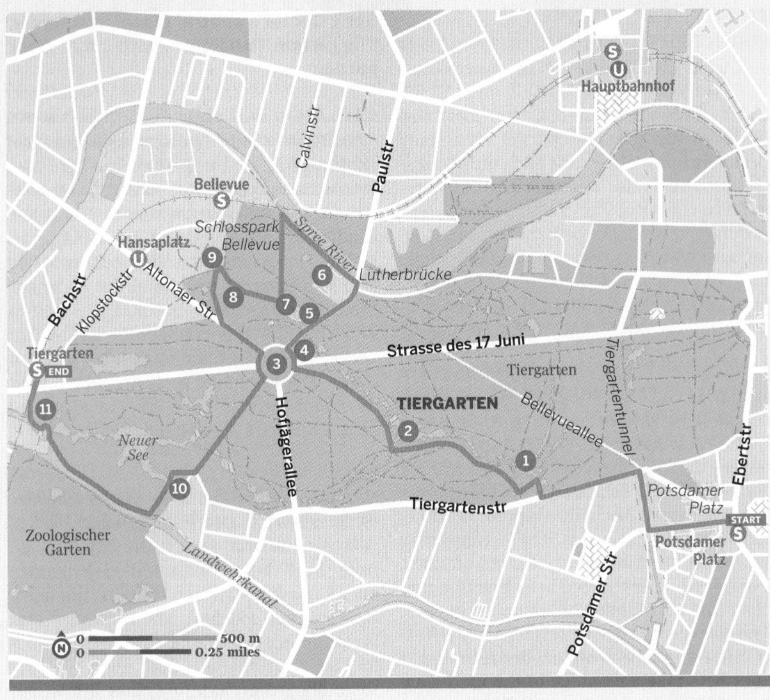

Neighbourhood Walk
A Leisurely Tiergarten Meander

START POTSDAMER PLATZ
END TIERGARTEN S-BAHN STATION
LENGTH 5KM; TWO HOURS

A ramble around Tiergarten delivers a relaxing respite from sightseeing. From Potsdamer Platz, make your way to 1 **Luiseninsel**, an enchanting gated garden dotted with statues and flower beds. Not far away is 2 **Rousseauinsel**, a memorial to 18th-century French philosopher Jean-Jacques ('Back to Nature') Rousseau. It was modelled after his actual burial site near Paris and placed on a teensy island in a sweet little pond.

At the heart of the park, engulfed by traffic, the imposing 3 **Siegessäule** (p165) is crowned by a gilded statue of the goddess Victoria and commemorates Prussian military triumphs enforced by Iron Chancellor Otto von Bismarck. Nearby, the colossal 4 **Bismarck Denkmal**, a monument to the man, shows him flanked by statues of Atlas (with the world on his back), Siegfried (wielding a sword) and Germania (stomping a panther).

Following Spreeweg north takes you past the oval 5 **Bundespräsidialamt**, the offices of the German president, to the presidential residence in 6 **Schloss Bellevue** (closed to public), a snowy-white neoclassical royal palace built for the younger brother of Frederick the Great in 1785.

Follow the path along the Spree, then turn left into the 7 **Englischer Garten**, created in the '50s in commemoration of the 1948 Berlin Airlift. At its heart, overlooking a pretty pond, the thatched-roof 8 **Teehaus im Englischen Garten** (p168) hosts free summer concerts. Check out the latest art exhibit at the nearby 9 **Akademie der Künste** (p166), on the edge of the Hansaviertel, a modernist quarter that emerged from a 1957 building exhibition.

Walk south back through the park, crossing Altonaer Strasse and Strasse des 17 Juni, to arrive at the Neuer See with 10 **Café am Neuen See** (p168) at its south end. Stroll north along the Landwehrkanal via the 11 **Gaslaternenmuseum**, an open-air collection of 90 historic gas lanterns, and wrap up your tour at Tiergarten S-Bahn station.

TEEHAUS IM ENGLISCHEN GARTEN INTERNATIONAL **€€**

Map p336 (☎030-3948 0400; www.teehaus-tiergarten.com; Altonaer Strasse 2; mains €8.50-28.50; ⏲noon-11pm Tue-Sat, from 10am Sun; ; SBellevue, UHansaplatz) Not even many Berliners know about this enchanting reed-thatched teahouse tucked into the north-western corner of Tiergarten park. It's best in summer, when the beer garden overlooking an idyllic pond seats up to 500 people for cold beers and a global roster of simple, tasty dishes from steamed artichoke to schnitzel. Breakfast is served on Sunday.

FACIL INTERNATIONAL **€€€**

Map p336 (☎030-590 051 234; www.facil.de; 5th fl, Mandala Hotel, Potsdamer Strasse 3; 1/2/3-course lunch €23/44/62, 4- to 8-course dinner €132-208; ⏲noon-2pm & 7-10pm Mon-Fri; P; 200, SPotsdamer Platz, UPotsdamer Platz) With two Michelin stars to its name, Michael Kempf's fare is hugely innovative yet devoid of unnecessary flights of fancy. Enjoy it while ensconced in a sleek Donghia chair and surrounded by a bamboo garden. The glass ceiling can be retracted for alfresco dining in fine weather. Budget-minded gourmets take advantage of the lunchtime menu. Vegetarian menu available.

LAYLA MIDDLE EASTERN **€€€**

Map p340 (☎0151 2256 3654; www.layla-restaurant.com; Möckernstrasse, cnr Hallesche Strasse; 6 sharing dishes per person €55; ⏲6-10pm Fri & Sat; SAnhalter Bahnhof) Israeli star chef Meir Adoni's fine-casual Berlin haunt takes your taste buds on a wild ride with its richly nuanced postmodern mash-up of European and Middle Eastern dishes. The sharing-is-caring concept is perfect for loading up on Yemenite brioche, smoked-eggplant carpaccio, spicy Lebanese pancakes and other treats streaming from the open kitchen.

DRINKING & NIGHTLIFE

Potsdamer Platz is hardly a dynamic nightlife area, although there are some nice bars in the hotels. For a bit more action, head to the places ringing the Sony Center's central plaza. In summer, Tiergarten beckons with its beer gardens.

CAFÉ AM NEUEN SEE BEER GARDEN

(☎030-254 4930; www.cafeamneuensee.de; Lichtensteinallee 2; ⏲restaurant 9am-11pm, beer garden 11am-midnight; ; 200, UZoologischer Garten, SZoologischer Garten, Tiergarten) Cradled by old trees and overlooking an idyllic Tiergarten lake, this country-style cafe gets jammed year-round for its sumptuous breakfasts and seasonal fare (€10 to €26), but it really comes into its own in beer-garden season. Enjoy a micro-vacation over a cold one and a pretzel or pizza, then take your sweetie for a spin in a rowing boat. Children's playground, too.

SOLAR LOUNGE BAR

Map p336 (☎0163 765 2700; www.solar-berlin.de; Stresemannstrasse 76; ⏲6pm-2am Thu-Sat; SAnhalter Bahnhof) Watch the city light up from this 17th-floor glass-walled sky lounge above a posh restaurant. With its dim lighting, leather couches, giant swings and breathtaking panorama, it's a great spot for sunset drinks or a date night. Getting there aboard an exterior glass lift is half the fun. The entrance is behind the Pit Stop auto shop. Cool factor: the 'DJ elevator' that yo-yos between the bar and the restaurant.

BARN COFFEE

Map p336 (www.thebarn.de; Alte Potsdamer Strasse 5; ⏲10am-5pm; 200, 300, M41, UPotsdamer Platz, SPotsdamer Platz) One of Berlin's most prominent third-wave coffeeshops, the Barn serves its single-origin java plus coffee-based cocktails in the hallowed halls of the historic Haus Huth at Potsdamer Platz. Note the granite bar, the floating oak bench and the Eames chairs.

STUE BAR BAR

Map p336 (☎030-311 7220; www.so-berlin-das-stue.com; Stue hotel, Drakestrasse 1; ⏲noon-1am Sun-Thu, to 2am Fri & Sat; 100, 106, 200) In the Stue hotel (p250), light installations and animal sculptures pave the way to this glam bar where serious mixologists give classic cocktails from the 1920s and '30s a contemporary makeover. There's also an impressive line-up of whiskies and vermouths.

ENTERTAINMENT

Heads up: if all goes to plan, the world-famous Cirque du Soleil will begin a residency in the Theater am Potsdamer Platz on 16 September 2021.

BERLINER PHILHARMONIKER — CLASSICAL MUSIC

Map p336 (☎tickets 030-2548 8999; www.berliner-philharmoniker.de; Herbert-von-Karajan-Strasse 1; tickets €25-138; 🚌200, 300, M41, M29, M48, M85, SPotsdamer Platz, UPotsdamer Platz) One of the world's most famous orchestras, the Berliner Philharmoniker is based at the Philharmonie, Hans Scharoun's iconic 1960s building whose unusual shape makes for optimal acoustics. Kirill Petrenko has been chief conductor since 2018.

ARSENAL — CINEMA

Map p336 (☎030-2695 5100; www.arsenal-berlin.de; Sony Center, Potsdamer Strasse 2; tickets €8.50; 🚌200, 300, M48, SPotsdamer Platz, UPotsdamer Platz) The antithesis of popcorn culture, this arty twin-screen cinema features a bold global flick schedule that hopscotches from Japanese satire to Brazilian comedy to German road movies. Many films have English subtitles.

TEMPODROM — LIVE MUSIC

Map p340 (☎tickets 01806 554 111; www.tempodrom.de; Möckernstrasse 10; SAnhalter Bahnhof) The white tent-shaped Tempodrom is a midsize venue with super-eclectic programming that may feature a salsa congress, an Iggy Pop concert, a magic show and a children's musical all in the same month.

SPIELBANK BERLIN — CASINO

Map p336 (☎030-255 990; www.spielbank-berlin.de; Marlene-Dietrich-Platz 1; €2; ⏲slots 11am-5am, tables 3pm-3am, poker from 5.45pm Mon-Fri, 3.45pm Sat & Sun; 🚌200, SPotsdamer Platz, UPotsdamer Platz) Vegas it ain't, but there are still plenty of opportunities to challenge Lady Luck over a game of poker, roulette or blackjack at this casino. The poker floor is the largest in Germany. Bring ID; no entry for those under 18. There's no formal dress code, although men must wear long pants and closed shoes.

> **LOCAL KNOWLEDGE**
>
> **CONCERTS IN THE PARK**
>
> In July and August, the lovely Teehaus im Englischen Garten presents free concerts – jazz, pop, funk, soul, hip hop – in its beer garden at 4pm and 7pm every Sunday. Details at www.konzertsommer-berlin.de.

SHOPPING

MALL OF BERLIN — MALL

Map p336 (www.mallofberlin.de; Leipziger Platz 12; ⏲10am-8pm Mon-Sat; 📶👪; 🚌200, 300, M48, UPotsdamer Platz, SPotsdamer Platz) This sparkling retail quarter is tailor-made for black-belt mall rats. More than 270 shops vie for your euros, including flagship stores by Karl Lagerfeld, Hugo Boss, Liebeskind, Marc Cain, Muji and other international high-end brands, alongside the usual high-street chains like Mango and H&M. Kids love the giant indoor slide on the 2nd floor. Free mobile-phone recharge stations in the basement and on the 2nd floor.

SPORTS & ACTIVITIES

LIQUIDROM — SPA

Map p340 (☎030-258 007 820; www.liquidrom-berlin.de; Möckernstrasse 10; per 2hr/4hr/day Mon-Fri €17.50/22.50/27.50, Sat & Sun €20/25/30, sauna extra €2.50; ⏲9am-midnight Sun-Thu, to 1am Fri & Sat; UMöckernbrücke, SAnhalter Bahnhof) Soothing, sensual and slightly surreal, Liquidrom centres on a domed indoor pool where you can float in warm saltwater while listening to 'liquid sound' – classical to electronic music – that's piped in underwater. Four saunas and a Japanese-style outdoor pool provide additional chill zones, and massages can be booked too. No bathing suits may be worn in the sauna.

Schöneberg

Neighbourhood Top Five

❶ **KaDeWe** (p177) Getting lost in the historic maze of high-end wares and a mind-boggling food hall in continental Europe's largest department store.

❷ **Urban Nation Museum** (p172) Gaining an appreciation for the heroes of street art in this beautiful new private museum.

❸ **Markt am Winterfeldtplatz** (p177) Joining food-lovers and professional chefs at this bustling and colourful farmers market, held twice weekly.

❹ **Flohmarkt am Rathaus Schöneberg** (p177) Jostling with bargain-seekers on their hunt for deals and collectables at this flea market next to the town hall famous for JFK's 'Ich bin ein Berliner' speech.

❺ **Schwules Museum** (p172) Diving deep into the history of queer Berlin through exhibits, events and extensive archives.

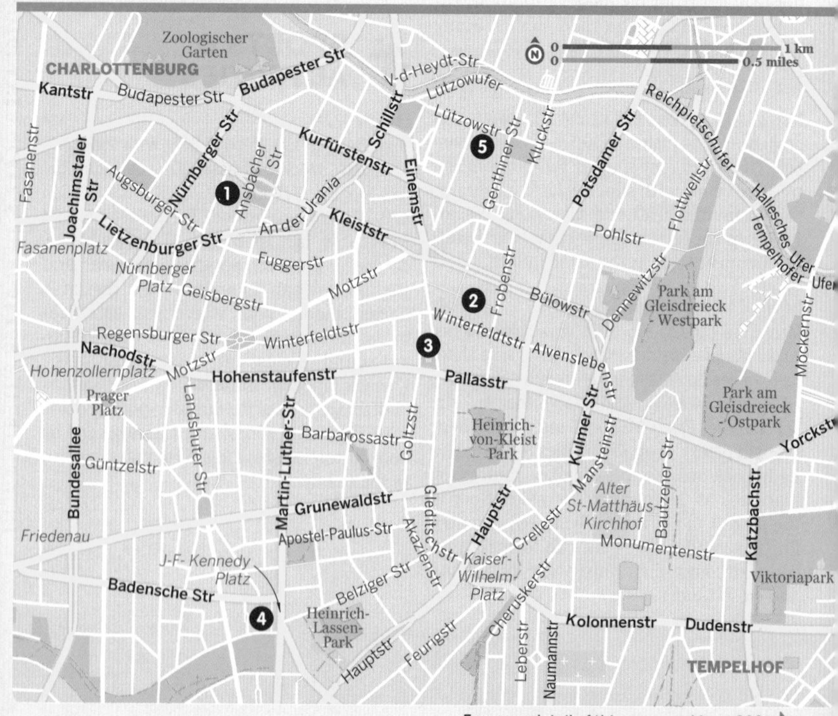

For more detail of this area see Map p339

Explore Schöneberg

Schöneberg's multifaceted character is best experienced like a fine wine: in sips, not gulps. In other words: on foot. A good place to start is at the KaDeWe department store (p177), one of the city's most tempting retail attractions. From here it's just a short hop (or single U-Bahn stop) to Nollendorfplatz, which makes an ideal launch pad for a neighbourhood stroll via Winterfeldtplatz and boutique- and cafe-lined Goltzstrasse and Akazienstrasse down to bustling Hauptstrasse, where David Bowie bunked back in the 1970s.

Back around Nollendorfplatz, the gay crowd has partied here since the 1920s, cheered on by the ghost of British novelist Christopher Isherwood, who lived here during the Weimar years. One local gal who liked to hang out with the 'boyz' was Marlene Dietrich. She's buried in southern Schöneberg, not far from the town hall (p172) where John F Kennedy gave his morale-boosting 'Ich bin ein Berliner' speech back in 1963.

But times are a-changing even in Schöneberg. Catch a glimpse of the new by dropping into Urban Nation (p172), a street-art museum that has injected a dose of hipness into the 'hood. But even more important are the developments on Potsdamer Strasse. Start a leisurely saunter in the late afternoon to explore edgy galleries, boutiques and restaurants now tucked among the Turkish grocers, penny stores and sex shops.

Local Life

Luxe lunch Slurp oysters and bubbly or nibble on designer vegan doughnuts at KaDeWe's gourmet floor, stylishly updated in 2019.

Urban archaeology Get up early for the best deals and cool finds at the flea market at Rathaus Schöneberg, where JFK proclaimed himself a Berliner.

Marketeering Join hobby and amateur cooks in sourcing seasonal bounty and artisanal goodies at the bustling Saturday market on Winterfeldtplatz.

Getting There & Away

U-Bahn Nollendorfplatz is the main hub, served by U1, U2, U3 and U4.

Bus M19 travels west to Kurfürstendamm and east to Mehringdamm in Kreuzberg, M29 goes from Ku'damm via Potsdamer Platz and Checkpoint Charlie to Hermannplatz.

S-Bahn S1 and S2 go to central Berlin via Yorckstrasse; the circle line S41/S42 and the S45 stop at Schöneberg and Innsbrucker Platz stations.

Lonely Planet's Top Tip

A stroll around Berlin's oldest farmers market (p177), on Winterfeldtplatz, is a joy, but for more exotic flair and flavours (and rock-bottom prices) head to its raucous and often overlooked cousin on Crellestrasse, held Wednesday and Saturday from 10am to 3pm.

Best Places to Eat

- Bonvivant Cocktail Bistro (p175)
- Kin Dee (p176)
- Rocket + Basil (p173)
- Malakeh (p173)
- Taverna Ousia (p175)

For reviews, see p173.

Best Places to Drink

- Stagger Lee (p176)
- Sally Bowles (p176)
- Green Door (p176)
- BRLO Brwhouse (p175)

For reviews, see p176.

Best Places to Shop

- KaDeWe (p177)
- Markt am Winterfeldtplatz (p177)
- Winterfeldt Schokoladen (p174)
- Flohmarkt am Rathaus Schöneberg (p177)

For reviews, see p177.

SIGHTS

Though devoid of blockbuster sights, Schöneberg has a few niche museums (street art to gay history) that are worth your while. It will also bring out the groupie in you, provided you're a fan of JFK, the Brothers Grimm or Marlene Dietrich (p289).

URBAN NATION MUSEUM — MUSEUM

Map p339 (www.urban-nation.com; Bülowstrasse 7; 10am-6pm Tue & Wed, noon-8pm Thu-Sun; M19, U Nollendorfplatz) FREE Creating a museum for street art may be akin to caging a wild animal. Yet, this showcase of works by top urban artists pulls the genre out from the underpasses and abandoned buildings and makes it accessible to a wider audience. Through changing exhibits, the beautiful bi-level space designed by Graft architects introduces key players and styles – stencils to paste-up to sculpture. Even the facade doubles as an ever-changing canvas.

SCHWULES MUSEUM — MUSEUM

Map p339 (Gay Museum; 030-6959 9050; www.schwulesmuseum.de; Lützowstrasse 73; adult/concession €9/3; 2-6pm Mon, Wed, Fri & Sun, to 8pm Thu, to 7pm Sat; M29, 100, U Nollendorfplatz, Kurfürstenstrasse) In a former print shop, this nonprofit museum is one of the largest and most important cultural institutions documenting LGBTIQ culture around the world, albeit with a special focus on Berlin and Germany. It presents changing exhibits on gay icons, artists, gender issues and historical themes and also hosts film screenings and discussions to keep things dynamic. Ask about guided English-language tours.

MUSEUM DER UNERHÖRTEN DINGE — MUSEUM

Map p339 (Museum of Unheard of Things; 0175 410 9120, 030-781 4932; www.museumderuner hoertendinge.de; Crellestrasse 5-6; 3-7pm Wed-Fri; U Kleistpark, S Julius-Leber-Brücke) FREE 'Every object has a story' could be the motto of Robert Albrecht's kooky collection of curiosities. In this tiny museum, the artist and writer displays everyday objects like artworks, be they a broken-off arm of a Chinese lucky cat or a rusty rose. Each item is accompanied by a laminated text where Albrecht blends fiction and reality to tell its story. A mind-bending spoof? An exercise in irony? Perhaps, but this 'museum' will surely challenge your perception of the ordinary. The name, by the way, is a delightful pun in German, since '*unerhört*' can mean both 'unheard of' and 'incredible'.

DAVID BOWIE APARTMENT — HISTORIC SITE

Map p339 (Hauptstrasse 155; closed to the public; U Kleistpark) A memorial plaque marks the house where the late David Bowie and his buddy Iggy Pop bunked in the late '70s. The seven-room flat was on the 1st floor; Pop later moved into his own digs across the back courtyard.

ALTER ST MATTHÄUS KIRCHHOF — CEMETERY

Map p339 (Old St Matthew Cemetery; 030-781 1850; www.zwoelf-apostel-berlin.de; Grossgörschenstrasse 12-14; 8am-dusk; S Yorckstrasse, U Yorckstrasse) One of Berlin's prettiest cemeteries, St Matthäus was a favourite final resting place for Berlin's 19th-century bourgeoisie. It brims with the often artistic gravestones and mausoleums of bankers, artists, scientists and captains of industry, including the Brothers Grimm.

KLEISTPARK — PARK

Map p339 (Potsdamer Strasse; U Kleistpark) This romantic little park is dominated by the richly ornamented sandstone Königskolonnaden (Royal Colonnades), a pair of rococo arcades designed in 1780 by Brandenburg Gate architect Carl von Gontard. They originally stood in the Mitte district but were moved because of road construction in 1910.

KAMMERGERICHT — HISTORIC SITE

Map p339 (Courthouse; 030-901 50; Elssholzstrasse 30-31; 7.25am-4.20pm Mon-Wed, to 6pm Thu, to 2.35pm Fri; U Kleistpark) Today the highest court in the state of Berlin, the Kammergericht was the site of the notorious show trails of the Nazi Volksgerichthof (People's Court) against participants – real and alleged – in the July 1944 assassination attempt on Hitler. About 110 people were handed their death sentences by the fanatical ruling judge Roland Freisler.

RATHAUS SCHÖNEBERG — HISTORIC SITE

Map p339 (John-F-Kennedy-Platz; U Rathaus Schöneberg) The town hall of Schöneberg was the seat of the West Berlin government from 1948 to 1990. Internationally, though, it is best remembered for a single day in

1963 when US President John F Kennedy expressed his solidarity with Germany in a speech on the balcony that concluded with the now legendary words: *'Ich bin ein Berliner'*.

EATING

Tucked into Schöneberg's quiet residential streets is a virtual United Nations of neighbourhood eateries serving up everything from Turkish to Indian and Nepalese to Peruvian. Good options abound on Potsdamer Strasse, Winterfeldtstrasse, Motzstrasse, Goltzstrasse and Akazienstrasse. For some culinary flights of fancy, head to the 6th-floor food hall of the KaDeWe department store (p177). On Wednesday and Saturday a bustling farmers market (p177) sets up on Winterfeldtplatz.

★JONES ICE CREAM — ICE CREAM €

Map p339 (☎0171 833 5780; www.jonesicecream.com; Goltzstrasse 3; per scoop €2.50; ⊙noon-7pm; UElsenacher Strasse) French Dessert Champion of 2006 Gabrielle Jones now regales Berliners with her mouth-watering artisanal ice cream, made with prime ingredients and served in cones that are freshly baked on-site. If salted butter caramel or whisky and pecan don't tempt you, maybe one of her triple-chocolate cookies will.

WITTY'S BIOLAND IMBISS — GERMAN €

Map p339 (www.wittys-berlin.de; Wittenbergplatz 5; sausages €3.70; ⊙10am-midnight Mon-Sat, 11am-midnight Sun; UWittenbergplatz) This 'doggeria' opposite the KaDeWe department store has been serving organic sausages since 2003. However, adding a serving of its crispy French fries topped with homemade mayo, peanut or garlic sauce quickly ruins the illusion that this is anything like a guilt-free meal (but it's so worth it!).

JOSEPH-ROTH-DIELE — GERMAN €

Map p339 (☎030-2636 9884; www.joseph-roth-diele.de; Potsdamer Strasse 75; mains €8-14; ⊙10am-11pm Mon-Thu, to midnight Fri; UKurfürstenstrasse) Named for an Austrian Jewish writer, this wood-panelled salon time warps you back to the 1920s, when Roth used to live next door. Walls decorated with bookshelves and quotations from his works draw a literary, chatty crowd, especially at lunchtime, when two daily-changing €5.95 specials (one vegetarian) supplement the hearty menu of German classics. Pay at the counter.

> **LOCAL KNOWLEDGE**
>
> **TURKISH BATHING DELIGHT**
>
> An exotic flair embraces you at **Sultan Hamam** (Map p339; ☎030-2175 3375; www.sultanhamamberlin.de; Bülowstrasse 57; 3/5hr sessions €19/25; ⊙women 11am-10pm Tue, Thu, Fri & Sun, 10am-10pm Sat, men 2-10pm Mon, mixed 11am-10pm Wed; SYorckstrasse, UBülowstrasse), a traditional Turkish bathhouse that's geared to women, with a colourfully tiled sauna, a steam room and a relaxation room. For that extra-clean feeling, book a treatment package, such as the popular 'Sabun', which includes a full-body scrub, a soaping and a 30-minute massage (€72). The website has details (also in English).

ROCKET + BASIL — MIDDLE EASTERN €

Map p339 (☎0176-6176 7845; www.rocketandbasil.com; Lützowstrasse 22; mains €6-15; ⊙11am-9pm Tue-Fri, 9am-9pm Sat, 9am-4pm Sun) Rocket and Basil are the pets of Sophia and Xenia, German-Iranian sisters who grew up in Australia and now regale curious diners with their next-gen take on Persian cooking. Made-with-love salads, sandwiches, *khoresht* (stews) and classics like *fesenjan* (pomegranate chicken) are a Technicolor riot on the plate and flavour bursts on the palate.

FRÜHSTÜCK 3000 — BREAKFAST €€

Map p339 (☎030-4366 6659; https://fruehstueck3000.com; Bülowstrasse 101; breakfast €10-16; ⊙8am-5pm Mon-Fri, from 9am Sat & Sun; UNollendorfplatz) After doing pop-ups in some of Berlin's most happening restaurants, this anytime-breakfast place has found a permanent home near Nollendorfplatz. Greet the day – whenever that may be – with creative sweet or savoury variations on anything from pancakes and French toast to Vietnamese rice soup, shakshuka or a cheese-and-charcuterie platter.

MALAKEH — SYRIAN €€

Map p339 (☎0176-2216 0998; Potsdamer Strasse 153; dishes €12-22; ⊙3-11pm Tue-Fri, noon-11pm

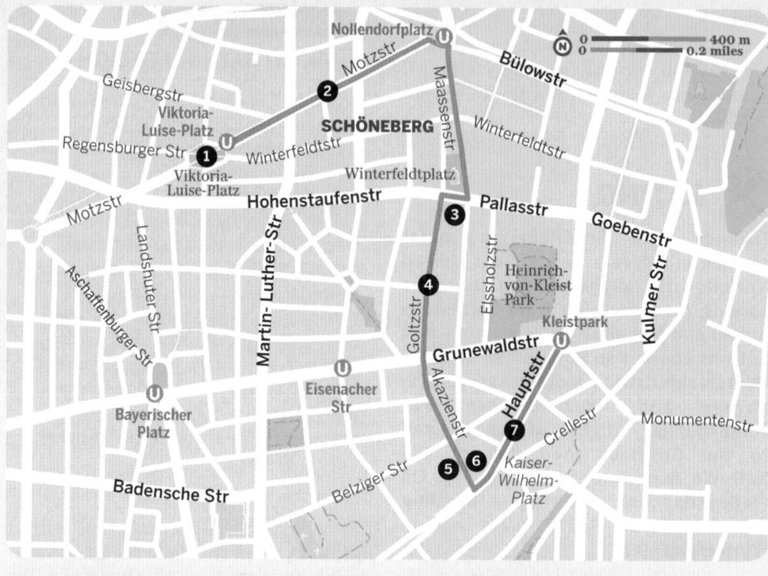

Local Life
Saunter Around Schöneberg

Schöneberg flaunts a mellow middle-class identity but has a radical pedigree rooted in the squatter days of the '80s. Stroll from bourgeois Viktoria-Luise-Platz through Berlin's traditional gay quarter and along streets squeezed tight with cafes and boutiques to bustling Hauptstrasse. The best days for this walk are Wednesday and Saturday, when a farmers market sets up on Winterfeldtplatz.

1 Viktoria-Luise-Platz
Soak up the laid-back vibe of Schöneberg's prettiest **square**, a classic baroque-style symphony of flower beds, big old trees, a lusty fountain and benches where locals swap gossip. The hexagonal square is framed by inviting cafes and historic town houses whose facades, with their sculpture and ornamentation, invite closer inspection, especially those at numbers 7, 12 and 12a.

2 Nollendorfplatz & the 'Gay Village'
In the early 20th century, Nollendorfplatz was a bustling urban square filled with cafes, theatres and people on parade. Then, as now, it was also the gateway to Berlin's **historic gay quarter**, where British writer Christopher Isherwood penned *Berlin Stories* (the inspiration for *Cabaret*) while living at Nollendorfstrasse 17. Rainbow flags still fly proudly, especially along Motzstrasse and Fuggerstrasse.

3 Chocophile Alert
Winterfeldt Schokoladen (☎030-2362 3256; www.winterfeldt-schokoladen.de; Goltzstrasse 23; ⏰10am-7pm Mon-Fri, to 6pm Sat, noon-6pm Sun) stocks a vast range of international handmade gourmet chocolates, all displayed in the original oak fixtures of a 19th-century pharmacy, which doubles as a cafe. Kosher, raw and gluten-free chocolates are among the more unusual choices.

4 Boutique Hopping
Goltzstrasse and its continuation Akazienstrasse teem with indie boutiques selling everything from vintage clothing to slinky underwear, fragrant olive oil to handmade jewellery, exotic teas to cooking supplies. No high-street chain in sight! Wedged in between are charismatic restaurants and cafes, many with pavement terraces.

5 Double Eye
Local coffee-lovers are addicted to the award-winning espresso of **Double Eye** (☎0179 456 6960; Akazienstrasse 22; ⏰8.30am-6.30pm Mon-Fri, 9am-6.30pm Sat), which is why no one seems to mind the inevitable out-the-door queue. Since there are few seats, this is more of a grab-and-go cafe.

6 Möve im Felsenkeller
An artist hang-out since the 1920s, woodsy **Möve im Felsenkeller** (☎030-781 3447; Akazienstrasse 2; ⏰4pm-1am Mon-Sat) is where Jeffrey Eugenides penned his 2002 bestseller *Middlesex*. A stuffed seagull dangling from the ceiling keeps an eye on patrons seeking inspiration from the six beers on tap.

7 Hauptstrasse
Chic boutiques give way to grocers and doner-kebab shops along main artery Hauptstrasse. The Turkish supermarket **Öz-Gida** (☎030-7871 5291; www.ozgida.de; Hauptstrasse 16; ⏰8am-8pm Mon-Sat) is known citywide for its fish and seafood, olives, quality halal meats and fresh-baked goods. In the '70s, David Bowie and Iggy Pop shared a pad at Hauptstrasse 155.

Sat & Sun; 🖉; Ⓤ Bülowstrasse) Malakeh Jazmati's eclectic dining room is as welcoming as a hug from an old friend. The self-taught chef from Damascus had her own TV food show in Jordan before decamping to Berlin in 2015. Now she feeds her feistily flavoured soul food to Berliners, homesick Syrians and clued-in tourists. We heartily recommend the yoghurt-based lamb stew *shakrieh*. No alcohol.

★BRLO BRWHOUSE INTERNATIONAL €€
Map p339 (☎030-5557 7606; www.brlo-brwhouse.de; Schöneberger Strasse 16; mains from €18; ⏰restaurant 5-11pm Tue-Fri, noon-11pm Sat & Sun, beer garden noon-midnight Apr-Sep; 📶👪; Ⓤ Gleisdreieck) The house-crafted suds flow freely at this shooting star among Berlin's craft breweries. Production, taproom and restaurant are housed in 38 shipping containers fronted by a big beer garden with sand box and views of Gleisdreieckpark. Shareable dishes are mostly vegetable-centric, although missing out on the meat prepared to succulent perfection in a smoker would be a shame.

TAVERNA OUSIA GREEK €€
Map p339 (☎030-216 7957; www.taverna-ousies.de; Grunewaldstrasse 54; small plates €3.50-16.50, mains €11-24; ⏰5-11pm Wed-Mon; Ⓤ Bayerischer Platz) You'll be as exuberant as Zorba at this easy-going yet top-rated Greek restaurant. Build a meal with the hot or cold appetisers or go for such substantial mains as the melt-in-your-mouth *spalla* (red-wine stewed lamb shoulder) or the nicely spiced *loukaniko* (homemade rustic sausage). The country-style decor, complete with stone floor and rural knick-knacks, oozes Hellenic charm.

★BONVIVANT COCKTAIL BISTRO VEGETARIAN €€
Map p339 (☎0176-6172 2602; https://bonvivant.berlin; Goltzstrasse 32; dishes €9-16; ⏰6pm-1am Tue-Sun; 🖉; Ⓤ Nollendorfplatz) 🌿 Bonvivant catapulted to culinary toast of the town thanks to its boundary-pushing 'vegetarian cocktail bistro' concept. The chilled corner space dishes out veg-based slow food tied to nature and the seasons, alongside exceptional cocktails composed by Yvonne Rahm, Germany's best bartender of 2018.

STICKS'N'SUSHI JAPANESE €€
Map p339 (☎030-2610 3656; www.sticksnsushi.berlin; Potsdamer Strasse 85; bites €4-30;

⌚noon-midnight Tue-Sun; 📶; Ⓤ Kurfürstenstrasse) At Germany's first branch of Danish cult chain Sticks'n'Sushi, sushi and yakitori get a creative twist that results in eye-candy small plates like Shake Tataki (flambéed salmon) or Kushi Katzu (panko-encrusted duck breast). It's all served in a dining room whose cathedral ceilings, giant chandeliers and spiral staircase engender cosmopolitan cosiness.

★KIN DEE — THAI €€€

Map p339 (☎030-215 5294; www.kindeeberlin.com; Lützowstrasse 81; tasting menu €65; ⌚6-10pm Tue-Sat; 📶; Ⓤ Kurfürstenstrasse) Kin Dee's opening created an instant buzz in 2017 and it took only two years for the Michelin testers to give it a star. Owner-chef Dalad Kambhu fearlessly catapults classic Thai dishes into the 21st century, often by using locally grown ingredients. The menu consists of eight to 10 sharing dishes, giving you maximum exposure to her creativity. Essential order: the octopus *krapao*.

IRMA LA DOUCE — FRENCH €€€

Map p339 (☎030-2300 0555; www.irmaladouce.de; Potsdamer Strasse 102; mains €28-43; ⌚6-10pm; 🚌M48, M85, Ⓤ Kurfürstenstrasse) Although named for the 'hooker with a heart of gold' heroine in a Billy Wilder comedy, there's nothing shady about Irma La Douce. At this brasserie near Potsdamer Platz, a glass of champagne is the overture to a symphony of next-gen French cuisine served in a sensuous 1920s-style setting. Expect plenty of unconventional flavour pairings, impeccable service and sublime wines.

DRINKING & NIGHTLIFE

Dapper drinking has long been fashionable in Schöneberg, which delivers a slew of fine cocktail bars for elevated drinking. The area around Nollendorfplatz is the traditional LGBTIQ party quarter (especially Motzstrasse and Fuggerstrasse). Around the corner, bars on Maassenstrasse are popular with rowdy weekend warriors. For classier joints, steer towards the mellow side streets or to nicely gentrifying Potsdamer Strasse.

STAGGER LEE — COCKTAIL BAR

Map p339 (☎030-2903 6158; www.staggerlee.de; Nollendorfstrasse 27; ⌚7pm-2am; Ⓤ Nollendorfplatz) Belly up to the polished wooden bar or plop down on chocolate-hued Chesterfield sofas at this cocktail saloon oozing Wild West sophistication. Barkeeps mix and pour both the tried-and-true and the adventurous-experimental with abandon and a focus on whisky and tequila.

The name channels a 19th-century St Louis murderer immortalised in song by everyone from Nick Cave to The Clash.

SALLY BOWLES — BAR

Map p339 (☎030-2083 8269; www.sally-bowles.de; Eisenacher Strasse 2; ⌚6pm-1am Tue-Sun; 🚌M19, M29, Ⓤ Nollendorfplatz) The star of *Cabaret* is the namesake of this congenial bar that draws a friendly, unpretentious crowd. Owners Nadine and Sebastian searched high heaven, flea markets and classified ads to create a cosy 1920s look and vibe that is perfect for a chill evening of cocktails and chat.

VICTORIA BAR — COCKTAIL BAR

Map p339 (☎030-2575 9977; www.victoriabar.de; Potsdamer Strasse 102; ⌚6pm-late; Ⓤ Kurfürstenstrasse) Original art decorates this discreet cocktail lounge whose motto is the 'Pleasure of Serious Drinking'. It's favoured by a grown-up, artsy crowd. If you want to feel like an insider, order the off-menu 'Hilde' (vodka and Champagne), created in memory of German singer-actor Hildegard Knef. Happy hour runs from 6pm to 9pm and all night on Sunday.

GREEN DOOR — COCKTAIL BAR

Map p339 (☎030-215 2515; www.greendoor.de; Winterfeldtstrasse 50; ⌚6pm-2am Sun-Thu, to 3am Fri & Sat; Ⓤ Nollendorfplatz) A long line of renowned mixologists has presided over this softly lit bar behind the eponymous green door – a nod to Prohibition-era speakeasies. Amid walls sheathed in gingham and '70s swirls, you can choose from more than 500 cocktails, including some potent house concoctions.

KUMPELNEST 3000 — BAR

Map p339 (☎030-261 6918; www.kumpelnest3000.com; Lützowstrasse 23; ⌚7pm-5am or later; Ⓤ Kurfürstenstrasse) A former brothel, this trashy bat cave started out as an art project and is kooky and kitsch enough to feature in a 1940s Shanghai noir thriller.

Famous for its wild, debauched all-nighters, it attracts a hugely varied crowd, including the occasional celebrity.

HEILE WELT GAY & LESBIAN

Map p339 (☎030-2191 7507; www.facebook.com/heileweltbar; Motzstrasse 5; ⏰7pm-3am; Ⓤ Nollendorfplatz) Chic yet loungey, the 'Perfect World' gets high marks for its chatty vibe, flirt factor and handsome laddies (and the occasional lady). It's a great whistle stop before launching into a raunchy night, but it gets packed in its own right the higher the moon rises in the sky.

TOM'S BAR GAY

Map p339 (☎030-213 4570; www.tomsbar.de; Motzstrasse 19; ⏰10pm-6am; Ⓤ Nollendorfplatz) Erotic artist Tom of Finland inspired the name of this been-here-forever men-only bar, although you don't have to look as buff as his subjects to feel comfortable here. It's cruisy, with most people tempted to check out the action in the labyrinthine darkroom. On Monday drinks are two-for-one.

HAFEN GAY

Map p339 (☎030-211 4118; www.hafen-berlin.de; Motzstrasse 19; ⏰from 7pm; Ⓤ Nollendorfplatz) This 'Harbour' has been a friendly stop to dock at for about 30 years and remains a good place to ease into the night with dancing, theme parties, drinking and flirting. Monday wouldn't be the same without Hendryk Ekdahl's hilarious Quizz-o-rama quiz show.

ENTERTAINMENT

WINTERGARTEN VARIETÉ CABARET

Map p339 (☎030-588 433; www.wintergarten-variete.de; Potsdamer Strasse 96; ticket prices vary; Ⓤ Kurfürstenstrasse) This sumptuous cabaret venue with its sparkling starry-sky ceiling features changing variety shows, concerts, acrobats, magicians and other entertainers. Shows are suitable for non-German speakers.

SHOPPING

Schöneberg's big retail draw is the KaDeWe, one of Europe's grandest department stores. A stroll from Nollendorfplatz to Hauptstrasse, via Maassenstrasse, Goltzstrasse and Akazienstrasse, takes you past lots of small independent shops selling everything from clothing to books to gifts. On Saturday the farmers market on Winterfeldtplatz brings in fans and foodies from throughout the city.

★KADEWE DEPARTMENT STORE

Map p339 (www.kadewe.de; Tauentzienstrasse 21-24; ⏰10am-8pm Mon-Thu & Sat, to 9pm Fri; Ⓤ Wittenbergplatz) Continental Europe's largest department store has been going strong since 1907 and boasts an assortment so vast that a pirate-style campaign is the best way to plunder its bounty. If pushed for time, at least hurry up to the updated 6th-floor gourmet food hall.

The name, by the way, stands for Kaufhaus des Westens (department store of the West).

MARKT AM WINTERFELDTPLATZ MARKET

Map p339 (Winterfeldtplatz; ⏰8am-2pm Wed, to 4pm Sat; Ⓤ Nollendorfplatz) The market on ho-hum Winterfeldtplatz is a favourite of foodies and chefs. Wednesday and Saturday it bristles with farm-fresh fare and food and flower stalls. Along with seasonal produce (most of it local and organic), you'll find handmade cheeses, cured meats, and tubs spilling over with olives, local honey and spicy Turkish sausage. The much larger Saturday edition also has arty-crafty stalls.

ACNE STUDIOS FASHION & ACCESSORIES

Map p339 (☎030-2636 6909; www.acnestudios.com; Potsdamer Strasse 87; ⏰11am-6pm; Ⓤ Kurfürstenstrasse) The opening of the flagship store of Sweden's cutting-edge fashion brand adds a further dose of hipness to gentrifying Potsdamer Strasse.

FLOHMARKT AM RATHAUS SCHÖNEBERG MARKET

Map p339 (John-F-Kennedy-Platz; ⏰8am-4pm Sat & Sun; Ⓤ Rathaus Schöneberg) Pro and amateur vendors mix it up at this neighbourhood market, where prices are fair and bargaining skills are easily honed. Though not the trendiest of markets, it still offers an enticing mix of bric-a-brac, vintage vinyl and preloved anything right below the town hall where JFK gave his famous 'Ich bin ein Berliner' speech.

Kreuzberg

BERGMANNKIEZ & WESTERN KREUZBERG | KOTTBUSSER TOR & EASTERN KREUZBERG

Neighbourhood Top Five

❶ **Jüdisches Museum** (p180) Stepping back into the fascinating history of Jews in Germany at this Daniel Libeskind–designed architectural masterpiece.

❷ **Deutsches Technikmuseum** (p182) Exploring this vast temple to technology, from trains to planes to automobiles.

❸ **Park am Gleisdreieck** (p182) Relaxing or exercising in a huge natural expanse ingeniously forged from a 19th-century railroad crossing.

❹ **Kotti Bar-Hop** (p190) Soaking up the punky-funky alt-feel of eastern Kreuzberg.

❺ **Street-Food Thursday** (p186) Eating your way around the world at the weekly street-food party.

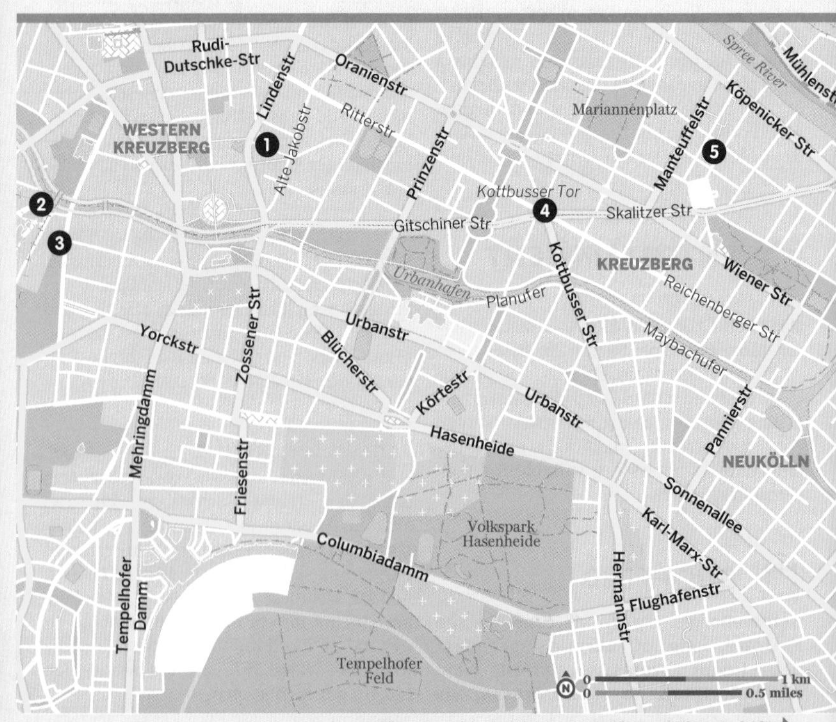

For more detail of this area see Maps p340 and p342

Explore Kreuzberg

Kreuzberg is an epicentre of free-wheeling, multicultural and alternative Berlin and an energising combo of urban grit and hipster haven. There are two quite distinct areas. The western half has an upmarket, genteel air. It is one of Berlin's most charismatic neighbourhoods, thanks to beautifully restored 19th-century houses and a bevy of owner-operated indie stores, restaurants, cafes and bars, especially along Bergmannstrasse. Kreuzberg's two big-ticket sights, the Jewish Museum and the German Museum of Technology, are not far from here.

Eastern Kreuzberg (between Moritzplatz and Schlesisches Tor) has a pedigree as Berlin's traditional 'Turkish quarter'. More recently, it has been 'discovered', first by students, artists and global nomads, drawn by cheap rents and the area's unbridled spirit, and now by real-estate developers seeking to cash in on the hype. Although the district's soul is under attack, you can still track down fabulous street art, fight a hangover with a greasy doner kebab, browse vintage stores and find out for yourself why eastern Kreuzberg is known as a nightcrawler's paradise.

Local Life

Bar-hopping Kreuzberg delivers some of Berlin's best night-time action, especially around Kottbusser Tor and along Skalitzer Strasse and Schlesische Strasse.

Shopping Delightfully devoid of high-street chains, the shops around here are all about individual style. Join locals in putting together that inimitable outfit from vintage shops, local designers, streetwear boutiques, pop-up shops and flea markets.

Chilling The locals don't live to work here. Heck, they may not work at all, which is why they have plenty of time to hang in green oases such as Park am Gleisdreieck (p182), Viktoriapark (p183) and Görlitzer Park or to wave to the swans on the Landwehrkanal.

Getting There & Away

Bus No 140 goes from Bergmannkiez to Tempelhofer Feld, M29 links up with Tiergarten, Schöneberg and Charlottenburg, 165 comes through en route from Mitte to Treptower Park.

U-Bahn Kreuzberg is connected to Charlottenburg and Friedrichshain by the U1, to Neukölln and Mitte by the U8 and to Schöneberg by the U7.

Lonely Planet's Top Tip

Kreuzberg is bisected by the pretty Landwehrkanal, much of which is lined by leafy trees and paralleled by a path that's perfect for strolling, jogging or bicycling. In summer, the grassy patch at the Urbanhafen invites lounging, while foodies gravitate to restaurant row along the Paul-Lincke-Ufer.

Best Places to Eat

- Tulus Lotrek (p186)
- Con Tho (p186)
- Ora (p188)
- Fes Turkish BBQ (p188)
- Orania.Restaurant (p188)

For reviews, see p185.

Best Places to Drink

- Birgit & Bier (p189)
- Limonadier (p188)
- Würgeengel (p190)
- Möbel Olfe (p190)
- Otto Rink (p190)

For reviews, see p188.

Best Places to Shop

- Folkdays (p192)
- VooStore (p192)
- Hallesches Haus (p192)
- Other Nature (p192)

For reviews, see p192.

MARC31 / SHUTTERSTOCK ©

TOP EXPERIENCE

FACE HISTORY AT THE JÜDISCHES MUSEUM

In a landmark building by Daniel Libeskind, Berlin's Jewish Museum has, since 2001, chronicled Jewish life, history and culture in Germany from the early Middle Ages via the Enlightenment to the present.

The Building

Libeskind's architectural masterpiece (which he titled *Between the Lines*) has been interpreted as a 3D metaphor for the tortured history of the Jewish people. Its zigzag shape symbolises a broken Star of David; its silvery titanium-zinc walls are sharply angled; and instead of windows, there are only small gashes piercing the gleaming facade.

The Axes

The museum consists of two buildings. The entrance is via a stately baroque structure that once housed the Prussian supreme court. From here a steep, dark and winding staircase leads down to the Libeskind building, where three intersecting walkways called 'axes' represent the experiences of Jews in the 20th century. The **Axis of Emigration** leads to the maze-like Garden of Exile, which consists of 49 tilted concrete columns; Russian willow oak, a symbol of hope, sprouts from each. The **Axis of the Holocaust** ends in the tomb-like 'void' that stands for the loss of Jewish life, culture and humanity in Europe. Only the **Axis of Continuity**, which represents the present and the future, leads to the actual exhibits, but it too is a cumbersome journey up a sloping walkway and several steep flights of stairs.

DON'T MISS

- Axis of the Holocaust
- *Shalekhet – Fallen Leaves* installation
- 'Catastrophe' Room

PRACTICALITIES

- Jewish Museum
- Map p340, D2
- ☎030-2599 3300
- www.jmberlin.de
- Lindenstrasse 9-14
- adult/concession/under 18yr €8/3/free, audioguide €3
- 10am-7pm
- U Hallesches Tor, Kochstrasse

Permanent Exhibit

Relaunched in August 2020, the museum's new two-floor core exhibit traces 1700 years of Jewish history, traditions, trials and triumphs in Germany. Divided into five chapters, it kicks off in the early Middle Ages, when Jewish communities first emerged in northwestern Europe. From here, it moves through the Enlightenment and the Nazi years all the way to the present-day revival of Jewish life in Germany.

Themed areas introduce aspects of Jewish culture and religion, such as music, prayer, the Torah and the Sabbath, using a mix of original objects, art installations, interactive games, listening pods and other forms of modern museum curation.

Throughout, the exhibit stresses the interrelations between Jewish and Christian communities over time. The Third Reich section, called 'Catastrophe', unravels the anatomy of the Nazi state. Its backbone is a wall installation of nearly 1000 anti-Jewish laws and policies passed between 1933 and 1945.

Art Installations

The late Menashe Kadishman's **Shalekhet – Fallen Leaves** (pictured left) is a poignant standout in the museum's art collection. More than 10,000 open-mouthed faces cut from rusty iron plates lie arbitrarily scattered on the floor in an ocean of silent screams. The effect is exacerbated by the space itself: a Memory Void on the ground floor (first door as you ascend the staircase).

Your route to Shalekhet passes through Dresden-born artist Via Lewandowsky's **Gallery of the Missing**, which consists of irregularly shaped black glass sculptures. Each contains an acoustic description of a missing or destroyed object relating to German-Jewish culture, such as the *Encyclopaedia Judaica,* whose composition came to a sudden halt at the letter 'L' in 1934.

The permanent exhibit features **Shevirat ha-Kelim** (Breaking of the Vessels), a room-size installation by German contemporary artist Anselm Kiefer that interprets a cosmic concept of the Kabbalah, the most famous form of Jewish mysticism.

Children's World ANOHA

In a former flower-market hall opposite the main museum, ANOHA is the Jewish Museum's new interactive children's museum. Geared to kids from three to 10 years old, it centres on a gigantic wooden Noah's Ark that kids can board and help 'steer' from the past into the future, accompanied by 150 artist-created animals made from recycled materials. Elsewhere, kids can learn about topics such as sustainability and natural resources.

TAKE A BREAK

The **museum cafe** in the glass courtyard offers light lunches, cakes and hot and cold beverages.

At the nearby Berlinische Galerie, **Cafe Dix** (Map p340; ☎030-2392 4109; www.cafe-dix.berlin; Alte Jakobstrasse 124-128; mains €6-10; ⏰10am-6pm Wed-Mon; Ⓤ Kochstrasse, Moritzplatz) serves salads, German dishes and cakes.

Tickets are also valid for reduced admission on the same day and the next two days to the Berlinische Galerie (p182), a survey of 150 years of Berlin art that's located just 500m away.

TOP TIPS

- Rent the audioguide (€3) for a more in-depth experience.
- Guided tours (in German, €3) take place at 3pm on Saturday and at 11am on Sunday.
- Budget at least two hours to visit the museum, and wear comfortable footwear.
- The garden behind the museum has deckchairs for relaxing and taking in the architecture.

SIGHTS

Kreuzberg's blockbuster sights are the Jewish Museum and the German Museum for Technology, but you'll also find lots of smaller niche museums, especially when it comes to art. Also keep your eyes peeled for edgy street art by local and global players. For Tempelhofer Feld, see the Neukölln chapter (p194).

Bergmannkiez & Western Kreuzberg

JÜDISCHES MUSEUM — MUSEUM

See p180.

★BERLINISCHE GALERIE — GALLERY

Map p340 (Berlin Museum of Modern Art, Photography & Architecture; ☎030-7890 2600; www.berlinischegalerie.de; Alte Jakobstrasse 124-128; adult/concession/child under 18yr €12/9/free; ⌚10am-6pm Wed-Mon; UHallesches Tor, Kochstrasse) This gallery in a converted glass warehouse is a superb spot for taking stock of Berlin's art scene since 1870. Downstairs, temporary exhibits highlight contemporary artists and trends, often in unconventional or even controversial fashion. Two crossover floating staircases lead upstairs to the permanent exhibit, with canvas candy from such art-world rock stars as Otto Dix, Jeanne Mammen and Georg Baselitz.

If you have a ticket from the nearby Jewish Museum (p180), you only pay the concession price if visiting on the same or the next two days. The deal also works the other way round.

★DEUTSCHES TECHNIKMUSEUM — MUSEUM

Map p340 (German Museum of Technology; ☎030-902 540; https://technikmuseum.berlin; Trebbiner Strasse 9; adult/concession/child under 18yr €8/4/after 3pm free; ⌚9am-5.30pm Tue-Fri, 10am-6pm Sat & Sun, last entry 4pm; P 👪; UGleisdreieck, Möckernbrücke) A roof-mounted 'candy bomber' (the plane used in the 1948 Berlin Airlift) is merely the overture to this enormous and hugely engaging shrine to technology. Fantastic for kids, the giant museum includes the world's first computer, an entire hall of vintage locomotives, and exhibits on aerospace and navigation in a modern annexe. At the adjacent Science Center Spectrum (p182), entered on the same ticket, kids can participate in hands-on experiments.

It's easy to spend a full day here, especially if you also explore the vast museum park with its wind- and watermills, brewery and smithy. Check the schedule for demonstrations and workshops. Three cafes provide sustenance and you're also free to bring your own picnic (tables provided). For a more in-depth experience, download the Deutsches Technikmuseum app, which includes the audio tour 'Technical Revolutions' (available in English) as well as a children's audio tour.

SCIENCE CENTER SPECTRUM — SCIENCE CENTRE

Map p340 (☎030-9025 4284; https://technikmuseum.berlin/spectrum; Möckernstrasse 26; adult/concession/under 18yr €8/4/free after 3pm; ⌚9am-5.30pm Tue-Fri, 10am-6pm Sat & Sun, last entry 4pm; P; UMöckernbrücke, Gleisdreieck) Why is the sky blue? Can you see heat? Any why does a plane stay up in the sky? Kids (and grown-ups!) can find the answers to these and other timeless questions in this annexe of the Deutches Technikuseum. The four-floor space is filled with 150 hands-on scientific experiments divided into eight themes, including Electricity & Magnetism, Music & Sound and Light & Vision. Accessible only with prior registration during the coronavirus pandemic.

PARK AM GLEISDREIECK — PARK

Map p340 (www.gruen-berlin.de/gleisdreieck; cnr Obentrautstrasse & Möckernstrasse; ⌚24hr; UMöckernbrücke, Gleisdreieck, Yorckstrasse, SYorckstrasse) FREE Berliners crave green open spaces, and this vast park reclaimed from a former railway junction between 2011 and 2014 is the latest in a string of urban oases. An active railway track still separates the sprawling grounds into the wide-open **Westpark**, with expansive lawns and play zones for kids, and the **Ostpark**, with a nature discovery area, a half-pipe, a little maple and oak forest and an outdoor dance floor.

Historic relics such as tracks, signals and ramps are smoothly integrated throughout. There are numerous entrances – getting off at Gleisdreieck U-Bahn station will put you right in the thick of the Westpark. For the Ostpark, Yorckstrasse S-Bahn station is closest.

WORTH A DETOUR

TREPTOWER PARK & THE SOVIET WAR MEMORIAL

Southeast of Kreuzberg, the former East Berlin district of Treptow gets its character from the Spree River and two parks: Treptower Park and Plänterwald. Both are vast sweeps of expansive lawns, shady woods and tranquil riverfront, and have been popular for chilling, tanning, picnicking, jogging or just strolling around for well over a century. In summer, Stern + Kreis (p301) operates cruises from landing docks just south of the Treptower Park S-Bahn station. A bit further south, you'll pass the **Insel der Jugend** (030-8096 1850; www.inselberlin.de; Alt-Treptow 6; P; S Plänterwald, Treptower Park), a pint-size island reached via a 1915 steel bridge that was the first of its kind in Germany. In summer there's a cafe, boat rentals, movie screenings, concerts and parties. The restaurant is open year-round.

Nearby awaits Treptower Park's main sight: the gargantuan **Sowjetisches Ehrenmal Treptow** (Soviet War Memorial; 24hr; Treptower Park) FREE, which stands above the graves of 5000 Soviet soldiers killed in the 1945 Battle of Berlin. Inaugurated in 1949, it's a sobering testament to the immensity of Russia's wartime losses. Coming from the S-Bahn station, you'll first be greeted by a statue of **Mother Russia** grieving for her dead children. Beyond, two mighty walls fronted by soldiers kneeling in sorrow flank the gateway to the memorial itself; the red marble used here was supposedly scavenged from Hitler's ruined chancellery. Views open up to an enormous sunken lawn lined by **sarcophagi** representing the then 16 Soviet republics, each decorated with war scenes and Stalin quotations. The epic dramaturgy reaches a crescendo at the **mausoleum**, topped by a 13m statue of a Russian soldier clutching a child, his sword resting melodramatically on a shattered swastika. The socialist-realist mosaic within the plinth shows grateful Soviets honouring the fallen.

South of here, near the *Karpfenteich* (carp pond), is the **Archenhold-Sternwarte** (Archenhold Observatory; 030-4218 4510; www.planetarium.berlin; Alt-Treptow 1; tours & demonstrations adult/child €7/5, exhibit free; 5.30-8pm Fri, 1.30-8pm Sat, 11.30am-5.30pm Sun; P; 165, 166, 265, S Plänterwald), Germany's oldest astronomical observatory. It was here in 1915 that Albert Einstein gave his first public speech in Berlin about the theory of relativity. The observatory's pride and joy is its 21m-long refracting telescope, the longest in the world, built in 1896 by astronomer Friedrich Simon Archenhold. Check the website for demonstrations of this giant of the optical arts. Exhibits on the ground floor are a bit ho-hum but still impart fascinating nuggets about the planetary system, astronomy in general and the history of the observatory. Kids love having their picture taken next to a huge meteorite chunk.

Speaking of kids… Generations of East Germans still have fond memories of the Kulturpark Plänterwald, the country's only amusement park, created in 1969 and privatised and renamed **Spreepark** (030-700 906 710; www.spreepark.berlin; Kiehnwerderallee 1-3; tours adult/child €5/3; tours weekends & public holidays Apr-Oct, in English 1pm Sat; ; S Plänterwald) in 1990. Dwindling visitor numbers forced it into bankruptcy in 2001, leaving the Ferris wheel and carousels standing still ever since. The grounds became off-limits, which didn't stop urban adventurers from trespassing and frolicking among the abandoned dinosaurs and dragons. In January 2016 the job of reanimating the park was assigned to Grün Berlin, a private nonprofit affiliated with the state of Berlin, which has created other public park spaces such as Tempelhofer Feld. It plans to revive the Ferris wheel, the Eierhäuschen restaurant and other relics, as well as adding new artistic and cultural attractions. An information kiosk provides details on what's being planned. Guided tours are available from April to October.

VIKTORIAPARK PARK

Map p340 (btwn Kreuzbergstrasse, Methfesselstrasse, Dudenstrasse & Katzbachstrasse; 24hr; U Platz der Luftbrücke) Take a break in this unruly, rambling park draped over the 66m-high Kreuzberg hill, Berlin's highest natural elevation. It's crowned by a spire-like monument topped by an iron cross that, 100 years later, inspired Kreuzberg's name ('Kreuz' being German for 'cross'). Designed by Karl Friedrich Schinkel, it commemorates Napoleon's defeat at

ICONIC MURALS OF KREUZBERG

Astronaut Mural (Map p342; Mariannenstrasse; UKottbusser Tor) One of Berlin's best-known works of street art is this monumental stencil-style piece inspired by the US–Soviet space race and created by Victor Ash as part of the 2007 Backjumps urban-art festival. It's near Skalitzer Strasse.

Pink Man Mural (Map p342; Falckensteinstrasse 48; USchlesisches Tor) The most famous Berlin work by Italian artist Blu depicts a monster-like creature composed of hundreds of writhing pink naked bodies. Crouching on its finger is a lone scared white individual that's about to be devoured.

Rounded Heads Mural (Map p342; Oppelner Strasse 46-47; USchlesisches Tor) *Rounded Heads* is a house-size mural by internationally renowned Berlin street artist Nomad that shows a faceless person embracing a hooded character.

Yellow Man Mural (Map p342; Oppelner Strasse 3; USchlesisches Tor) This wall-size street mural showing a bizarrely dressed, seemingly genderless, yellow-skinned figure is a signature work by Os Gemeos, aka identical twins Otavio and Gustavo Pandolfo, from São Paulo, Brazil.

Waterloo in 1815. The park is also home to a vineyard, lawns for chilling, the Golgatha (p188) beer garden and an artificial waterfall.

Tumbling down a rock-lined canal, the waterfall empties into a pool anchored by a fountain featuring a frisky Neptune frolicking with an ocean nymphet.

LUFTBRÜCKENDENKMAL MEMORIAL

Map p340 (Berlin Airlift Memorial; Platz der Luftbrücke; P; UPlatz der Luftbrücke) Nicknamed *Hungerharke* (Hunger Rake), the Berlin Airlift Memorial right outside the former Tempelhof Airport honours those who participated in keeping the city fed and free during the 1948 Berlin Blockade. A trio of spikes represents the three air corridors used by the Western Allies, while a plinth bears the names of the 79 people who died in this colossal effort.

Kottbusser Tor & Eastern Kreuzberg

FHXB FRIEDRICHSHAIN-KREUZBERG MUSEUM MUSEUM

Map p342 (030-5058 5258; www.fhxb-museum.de; Adalbertstrasse 95a; noon-6pm Tue-Thu, 10am-8pm Fri-Sun; UKottbusser Tor) FREE The ups and downs of one of Berlin's most colourful administrative districts – Kreuzberg and Friedrichshain – are chronicled in this converted red-brick factory. The permanent exhibit, which zeros in on Kreuzberg's radical legacy, is complemented by changing presentations that don't shy away from such hot-button issues as immigration and gentrification.

WERKBUND ARCHIV – MUSEUM DER DINGE MUSEUM

Map p342 (Werkbund Archive – Museum of Things; 030-9210 6311; www.museumderdinge.de; Oranienstrasse 25, 3rd fl; adult/concession/under 18yr €6/4/free; noon-7pm Thu-Mon; UKottbusser Tor) To the uninitiated, this obscure museum in a former factory may look like a *Wunderkammer* of random objects: pots, pans, cigarette cases, keychains, detergent boxes, all crammed into glass-fronted cabinets. The clued-in know that its actual mission is to portray the evolution of product design after the advent of industrial manufacturing and mass production.

The collection is based on the archive of the Deutscher Werkbund, an influential association of artists, architects and designers established in 1907 with the goal of integrating traditional arts and crafts with industrial mass-production techniques. It was an important precursor to the 1920s Bauhaus movement and counted Walter Gropius and Peter Behrens among its main proponents.

KÜNSTLERHAUS BETHANIEN GALLERY

Map p342 (030-616 9030; www.bethanien.de; Kottbusser Strasse 10; 2-7pm Tue-Sun; UKottbusser Tor) FREE A former light-fixture factory on bustling Kottbusser Strasse has been reincarnated as an artistic sanctuary and creative cauldron for emerging artists from around the globe. Founded in 1975, the nonprofit has launched the careers of hundreds of artists through its artist-in-residence program. Exhibits showcase their work, as well as that of former residents and other artists.

KUNSTQUARTIER BETHANIEN ARTS CENTRE
Map p342 (www.kunstquartier-bethanien.de; Mariannenplatz 2; 10am-8pm Sun-Wed, to 10pm Thu-Sat; U Kottbusser Tor) FREE It took an alliance of squatters and conservationists to save this grand, twin-towered 1840s hospital from demolition in the early 1970s. Rebooted as an intercultural hub of indie art and culture, it's home to some two dozen institutions from across the creative spectrum – from theatre to dance, music to visual arts. A key player is the **Kunstraum Kreuzberg/Bethanien** gallery, whose exhibits reflect the centre's activist and socially conscious bent.

Also on the premises is the original pharmacy where poet Theodor Fontane worked in 1848–49. It is open from 2pm to 5pm on Tuesday but can be easily appreciated through the glass door (ground floor, turn right).

RAMONES MUSEUM MUSEUM
Map p342 (030-6128 5399; www.ramones museum.com; Oberbaumstrasse 5; cafe-bar free, museum €5, with drink €7; 10am-10pm; U Schlesisches Tor) They sang 'Born to Die in Berlin', but the legacy of pioneering punk band the Ramones is kept very much alive in this quirky vegan cafe-bar-shrine. Sip a cold beer while walking down memory lane in this jam-packed treasure trove of band memorabilia, including signed album covers, posters, photographs and branded merch from T-shirts to socks.

MOLECULE MAN MONUMENT
Map p342 (An den Treptowers 1; S Treptower Park) Although monumental, the *Molecule Man* sculpture by American artist Jonathan Borofsky appears to float above the Spree River and cuts an especially photogenic figure at sunset. The three 2D bodies about to embrace each other are meant to symbolise the post-Wall reunion of the three bordering districts of Kreuzberg, Friedrichshain and Treptow.

EATING

Kreuzberg is among Berlin's most exciting and diverse foodie districts, with some of the best eating done in low-key neighbourhood restaurants, global kitchens and canal-side cafes. But the area also fields a growing share of high-end restaurants, including three decorated with Michelin stars. Markthalle Neun (p192), ground zero for Berlin's street-food craze, is still going strong, and vegan cafes continue to pop up at an impressive rate.

Bergmannkiez & Western Kreuzberg

CURRY 36 GERMAN €
Map p340 (030-2580 088 336; www.curry36.de; Mehringdamm 36; snacks €2-6; 9am-11pm; U Mehringdamm) Day after day, night after night, a motley crowd – cops, cabbies, office jockeys, tourists etc – wait their turn at this popular *Currywurst* snack shop that's been frying 'em up since 1981. No matter if you're tempted by the classic, organic or vegan versions, you're in for some of the tastiest wieners in town.

CHURCH TO GALLERY CONVERSION

If art is your religion, a pilgrimage to church turned gallery **König Galerie @ St Agnes Kirche** (Map p340; 030-2610 3080; www.koeniggalerie.com; Alexandrinenstrasse 118-121; 10am-6pm Tue-Sat, from noon Sun; U Prinzenstrasse) is a must. Tucked into a nondescript part of Kreuzberg, this decommissioned Catholic church, designed in the mid-1960s by architect and city planner Werner Düttmann, is a prime example of Brutalist architecture in Berlin. In 2012 it was leased by gallerist Johann König and converted into a spectacular space that presents interdisciplinary, concept-oriented and space-based art.

The interior is stark but stunning, with its lofty hall lit only by a few slits and skylights. Soaring next to the nearly windowless, brooding structure is a square bell tower made of solid concrete.

LOCAL KNOWLEDGE

STREET FOOD PARTIES

Street-Food Thursday (www.markthalleneun.de; Eisenbahnstrasse 42-43; ⏲5-10pm Thu; U Görlitzer Bahnhof) Every Thursday evening since 2013, this Berlin institution has seen a couple of dozen aspiring chefs set up their stalls in Markthalle Neun (p192), a historic Kreuzberg market hall, and serve delicious global street food. Order your favourites, lug them to a communal table and gobble them up with a glass of Heidenpeters, a craft beer brewed right on the premises.

Bite Club (www.biteclub.de; ⏲5pm-late Fri May-Sep or Oct; S Treptower Park, U Schlesisches Tor) Going strong since 2013, the Bite Club outdoor street-food fiesta is a mighty tasty spot to keep tabs on tomorrow's global food trends. To keep things in flux, regular stands and trucks are joined by aspiring newbies as well as craft-beer, wine and whisky purveyors. Check the website or Facebook for the current location.

HINTERLAND — GERMAN €

Map p340 (☎030-9843 8447; www.hinterlandprovisions.com; Gneisenaustrasse 67; dishes €6-11; ⏲noon-3pm Tue-Fri, 11am-3pm Sat, 6-11pm Tue-Sat; U Südstern) Fresh country flair breezes through this darling bistro helmed by Madeline McLean, who has built relationships with regional farmers to ensure that only fresh, organic and sustainable provisions land on your plate. Hinterland's second pillar is natural wine, available by the glass and by the bottle, along with local beers and specialty cocktails.

VAN LOON — INTERNATIONAL €€

Map p342 (☎030-692 6293; www.vanloon.de; Carl-Herz-Ufer 5; breakfast €5-16.50, mains €13-22; ⏲10am-10pm Wed-Sat, to 6pm Sun; U Prinzenstrasse) This retired Dutch cargo ship moored on the Landwehrkanal is a delightful greet-the-day spot, with sumptuous breakfasts served on the sun deck until 3pm. At night, candles and a crackling fire are conducive to romantic dinners over the famous fish soup, gravlax with potato cakes or smoked barbecue ribs.

★TULUS LOTREK — INTERNATIONAL €€€

Map p342 (☎030-4195 6687; www.tuluslotrek.de; Fichtestrasse 24; 6/8-course tasting menu €130/160; ⏲6-11pm Thu-Mon; U Südstern) This next-gen Michelin-starred restaurant has all you could wish for: fantastic food, to-die-for wines and conversation-sparking design, all wrapped into a feel-good vibe of disarming irreverence. Meisterchef Max Strohe fearlessly blends a global range of products into intensely aromatic and intellectually ambitious food with soul. The secret ingredient to Tulus Lotrek's success, though, is the forever-smiling Ilona Scholl, the quintessential host.

Kottbusser Tor & Eastern Kreuzberg

★CAFÉ MUGRABI — ISRAELI €

Map p342 (☎030-2658 5400; www.cafemugrabi.com; Görlitzer Strasse 58; mains €6.50-13; ⏲11am-9pm Wed-Mon; U Görlitzer Bahnhof) Feel-good Café Mugrabi ticks all the boxes of meatless Levantine classics, including finger-lickin' hummus, tangy shakshuka and roasted cauliflower. It's often filled to the hilt, but the team remains remarkably chill under pressure. In summer, grab a table with a view of Görlitzer Park. Most dishes can be made vegan.

★CON THO — VIETNAMESE €

Map p342 (☎030-2245 6122; http://con-tho-restaurant.de; Hasenheide 16; dishes €3.50-9; ⏲noon-midnight; U Hermannplatz) Punctuated by bamboo and paper lanterns, Con Tho ('rabbit' in Vietnamese) is a feel-good vegan-vegetarian burrow that gives traditional recipes a contempo workout. Dip into a pool of mouthwatering goodness with the 'happy to share' small plates, or pick your favourite rice bowl, stuffed rice-flour crêpe or lemongrass-annatto-based soup.

MAMA SHABZ — PAKISTANI €

Map p342 (www.mamashabz.com; Reichenberger Strasse 61a; mains €7.50-10; ⏲noon-9pm Tue-Sat) A London transplant with family roots in Pakistan, Shabz Syed quickly won over Berliners with delectables from her mom's treasure box of time-tested recipes. In her cheerful pint-size kitchen dhal, masalas, pakoras, samosas and other street-food-style treats cycle on and off the menu to keep regulars in a state of anticipation.

SIRONI BAKERY €

Map p342 (www.facebook.com/sironi.de; Markthalle Neun, Eisenbahnstrasse 42; snacks from €2.50; 8am-8pm Mon-Wed, Fri & Sat, to 10pm Thu; U Görlitzer Bahnhof) The focaccia and ciabatta are as good as they get without taking a flight to Italy, thanks to Alfredo Sironi, who hails from the Boot and now treats Berlin bread-lovers to his habit-forming carb creations. Watch the flour magicians whip up the next batch in his glass bakery right in the iconic Markthalle Neun (p192), then order a piece to go.

ALBATROSS BAKERY & CAFE BAKERY €

Map p342 (0176 8009 7982; info@albatrossberlin.com; Graefestrasse 66-67; pastries €1.50-3; 8am-7pm; U Schönleinstrasse) Albatross is a beloved bakery and cafe specialising in habit-forming pastries (killer cinnamon rolls!), sourdough bread and some of Berlin's best buttery croissants. Locals of all stripes flock to this hip outpost for a flat-white coffee, a cardamom croissant or whatever else is on the menu on the day.

ANNELIES BREAKFAST €

Map p342 (www.anneliesberlin.com; Görlitzer Strasse 68; dishes €7.50-10; 10am-5pm Mon, Wed-Fri, to 6pm Sat & Sun; ; U Görlitzer Bahnhof) A gem of a breakfast bistro, Annelies puts zeitgeist-compatible twists on morning classics with intensely palate-pleasing results. Temptations like scrambled eggs crowned by smoked egg yolk and kohlrabi kimchi, or beets and blackberries with amaranth granola, yoghurt and herbs pack enough punch to tide you over until the early afternoon.

COCOLO RAMEN X-BERG JAPANESE €

Map p342 (030-9833 9073; www.kuchi.de; Graefestrasse 11; ramen €10-12; noon-10pm Mon-Sat; ; U Kottbusser Tor) For some of Berlin's champion Japanese soups, follow locals to this well-established parlour where homemade noodles, fresh vegetables and toppings from egg to wakame bathe in a richly flavoured pork broth.

HENNE GERMAN €

Map p342 (030-614 7730; www.henne-berlin.de; Leuschnerdamm 25; half chicken €9.80; 5-11pm Tue-Sun; M29, 140, 147, U Moritzplatz, Kottbusser Tor) This Old Berlin institution operates on the KISS (keep it simple, stupid!) principle: milk-fed chicken spun on the rotisserie for moist yet crispy perfection. That's all it's been serving for over a century, alongside tangy potato and white-cabbage salads. Eat under the linden trees or in the cosy 1907 dining room that's resisted the tides of time. Reservations are essential.

MASANIELLO ITALIAN €

Map p342 (030-692 6657; www.masaniello.de; Hasenheide 20; pizza €8-11.50; noon-11pm Wed-Mon; U Hermannplatz) The tables are almost too small for the wagon-wheel-size certified-Neapolitan pizzas tickled by wood fire at Luigi and Pascale's old-school pizza institution. On Friday and Saturday the pies get competition from the grilled fresh-fish platters that are perfect for sharing with your posse. On balmy summer nights, the spacious, flowery terrace practically transports you to Italy.

BURGERMEISTER BURGERS €

Map p342 (030-403 645 320; www.burger-meister.de; Oberbaumstrasse 8; burgers €3.50-7; 11am-1am Mon-Wed, 11am-2am Thu-Sat, noon-midnight Sun; U Schlesisches Tor) It's green, ornate, a century old and...it used to be a toilet. Fast forward to 2006, when the original branch of this fast-growing Berlin burger franchise opened in this unlikely location beneath the elevated U-Bahn tracks. There's always a wait for the plump all-beef patties tucked between a brioche bun – but it's so worth it!

See the website for details on branches at Kottbusser Tor, Potsdamer Platz and Zoo station and in Prenzlauer Berg.

GOLDIES FAST FOOD €

Map p342 (030-7478 0320; www.goldies-berlin.de; Oranienstrasse 6; mains €5-11; 12.30-10pm; U Görlitzer Bahnhof) Having worked in some of Germany's most celebrated Michelin-starred kitchens, Vladislav Gachyn, with buddy Kajo Hiesl, started Goldies with a mission to perfect the humble French fry. Now they have locals flocking to their upbeat joint for fries gussied up with homemade sauces or loaded with eclectic toppings such as pulled duck, roast beef or baked eggplant.

TA'CABRÓN TAQUERÍA MEXICAN €

Map p342 (030-3266 2439; Skalitzer Strasse 60; mains €7-9; 1-11pm Sun-Thu, to midnight Fri & Sat; ; U Schlesisches Tor) Joaquín Robredo's tiny but cheerfully painted outpost feeds fans with the kind of food his mum used to make back home in Culiacán. Tacos, burritos and quesadillas bulge with such finger-lickin' fillings as *cochinita pibil* (spicy pulled pork) and chicken *mole* (in chocolate-based sauce), while the salsa packs a respectable punch. Soy-based riffs available. For refreshing liquid accompaniment, try a *michelada* (beer with spices and lime).

★ORA EUROPEAN €€

Map p342 (030-5486 1070; http://ora.berlin; Oranienplatz 14; 2/3/4-course dinner €35/42/49, lunch incl 1 glass wine €19; 5.30pm-midnight Wed, 12.30pm-midnight Thu-Sat, 4-11pm Sun; UKottbusser Tor) A 19th-century pharmacy has been splendidly rebooted as a stylishly casual wine restaurant. The antique wooden medicine cabinets are now the back bar, where craft beer and cocktails are dispensed to those with an appreciation for the finer things in life. The daily calibrated modern brasserie menu is a composition of whatever trusted regional suppliers deliver that morning.

★FES TURKISH BBQ TURKISH €€

Map p342 (030-2391 7778; http://fes-turkishbbq.de; Hasenheide 58; meze €4-11, meat from €16; 5-11pm Tue-Sun; USüdstern) If you like a communal DIY approach to dining, gather your friends for a grill-fest at this contemporary Turkish restaurant. Give strips of marinated chicken, beef fillet and tender lamb the perfect tan on the electric grill sunk right into your rustic wooden table while you spread a rainbow of homemade meze onto the freshly baked bread – pure bliss! Book a few days ahead on weekends.

★ORANIA.RESTAURANT INTERNATIONAL €€

Map p342 (030-6953 9680; https://orania.berlin/restaurant; Oranienstrasse 40; dishes €16-20; lunch noon-3pm, dinner 6-10pm; UMoritzplatz) Punctilious artisanship meets boundless creativity at cosmo-chic Orania.Restaurant, where a small army of chefs fusses around culinary wunderkind Philipp Vogel in the shiny open kitchen. Only three ingredients find their destiny in each dish, inspired by global flavours rather than food fads. Must try: Vogel's magic 'Xberg Duck', which deconstructs the bird into four delectable courses (€54, two-person minimum). The bar is a great spot for pre- and post-dinner drinks, often accompanied by conversation-friendly live jazz, soul or piano music.

FREISCHWIMMER INTERNATIONAL €€

Map p342 (030-6107 4309; www.freischwimmer-berlin.com; Vor dem Schlesischen Tor 2; mains brunch & lunch €8-12, dinner €10-22; noon-late Mon-Fri, from 10am Sat & Sun; ; STreptower Park, USchlesisches Tor) In fine weather, few places are more idyllic than this rustic 1930s boathouse turned canal-side chill zone. The menu runs from meat and fish cooked on a lava-rock grill to crisp salads, *Flammkuchen* (Alsatian pizza) and seasonal specials. It's also a popular Sunday brunch spot.

MAX UND MORITZ GERMAN €€

Map p342 (030-6951 5911; www.maxundmoritzberlin.de; Oranienstrasse 162; mains €9-20; 5-11pm Wed-Mon; ; UMoritzplatz) The patina of yesteryear hangs over this ode-to-old-school gastropub, named for the cheeky Wilhelm Busch cartoon characters. Since 1902, it has packed hungry diners and thirsty drinkers into its rustic tile-and-stucco-ornamented rooms for sudsy home brews and granny-style Berlin fare. A menu favourite is the *Königsberger Klopse* (veal meatballs in caper sauce).

DRINKING & NIGHTLIFE

Bergmannkiez & Western Kreuzberg

GOLGATHA BEER GARDEN

Map p340 (030-785 2453; www.golgatha-berlin.de; Dudenstrasse 48-64; 9am-late Apr-Sep; ; SYorckstrasse, UPlatz der Luftbrücke) This beer-garden institution in idyllic Viktoriapark (p183) draws a changing cast of characters all day long: families for the adjacent playground, digital nomads for the free wi-fi, the after-work crowd for sunset rays on the rooftop terrace, chatty types for beer and bratwursts in the evening, and party folk to dance till morning. After 10pm, enter the park from Katzbachstrasse.

LIMONADIER COCKTAIL BAR

Map p340 (0170 601 2020; www.limonadier.de; Nostitzstrasse 12; from 6pm Tue-Sat; UMehringdamm) Top-shelf spirits, home-made bitters, liqueurs and lemonades – plus a deep cache of drink-slinging know-how and imagination – make for a night of sophisticated drinking at this locally adored cocktail cavern bathed in a sensuous 1920s vibe. Go local and order a house creation such as the fruity-spicy Berlin at Night or the gin-based Kreuzberg Spritz.

A big stylised painting of Harry Johnson, whose 1882 bartenders' manual is still the profession's 'bible', keeps an eye on imbibers. Happy hour 7pm to 8pm.

RAUSCHGOLD GAY & LESBIAN

Map p340 (030-9227 4178; www.rauschgold.berlin; Mehringdamm 62; from 8pm; ; UMehringdamm) German for tinsel, Rauschgold's name is the game at this shimmering queer lair that normally hosts outlandish theme parties, drag-queen shows, karaoke contests, potent cocktails, and singalong hits from the '60s to today spun by local DJs. Everyone is welcome.

Kottbusser Tor & Eastern Kreuzberg

CLUB DER VISIONÄRE CLUB

Map p342 (030-6951 8942; www.clubdervisionaere.com; Am Flutgraben 1; from 3pm Mon-Fri, 2pm Sat & Sun; STreptower Park, USchlesisches Tor) It's cold beer, crispy pizza and fine electro at this summertime day-to-night-and-back-to-day chill and party playground in an old canal-side boat shed. Park yourself beneath the weeping willows, stake out some turf on the upstairs deck or hit the tiny dance floor. In winter, CDV moves to the historic *Hoppetosse* boat moored nearby.

SO36 CLUB

Map p342 (030-6140 1306; www.so36.de; Oranienstrasse 190; UKottbusser Tor) This legendary club began as an artist squat in the early 1970s and soon evolved into Berlin's seminal punk venue, known for wild concerts by the Dead Kennedys, Die Ärzte and Einstürzende Neubauten. Hugely beloved, it's hanging in there with pandemic-adapted programming, including an indoor beer garden and readings.

RITTER BUTZKE CLUB

Map p342 (https://club.ritterbutzke.com; Ritterstrasse 24; UMoritzplatz) Ritter Butzke has evolved from illegal club to Kreuzberg party-circuit fixture. Even during the coronavirus pandemic, it's working hard to come up with concepts to keep the joint alive. Check the website or Facebook.

BIRGIT & BIER BEER GARDEN

Map p342 (0162 694 1825; www.birgit.berlin; Schleusenufer 3; hours vary; 165, 265, N65, STreptower Park, USchlesisches Tor) Enter through the iron gate and embark on a magical mystery tour that'll have you chilling in the funky beer garden, taking selfies on a huge Hollywood swing, lounging in a retired carousel or dancing under the disco ball.

An eclectic roster of events, including outdoor cinema, deep-flow music yoga and party nights, pretty much guarantees a good time.

HOPFENREICH PUB

Map p342 (030-8806 1080; www.hopfenreich.de; Sorauer Strasse 31; from 4pm; USchlesisches Tor) Since 2014, Berlin's first dedicated craft-beer bar has been plying punters with a changing roster of nearly two dozen global ales, IPAs and other brews on tap – both known and obscure. It's all served with street-cred flourish in a corner pub near the Schlesische Strasse party mile.

Tastings, tap takeovers and guest brewers keep things in flux.

MADAME CLAUDE PUB

Map p342 (030-8411 0859; www.madameclaude.de; Lübbener Strasse 19; from 6pm Fri & Sat; USchlesisches Tor) Gravity is upended at this David Lynchian booze burrow, where the furniture dangles from the ceiling and the moulding is on the floor. The name honours a famous French prostitute – *très apropos* given the place's bordello pedigree.

ENTERTAINMENT

Bergmannkiez & Western Kreuzberg

ENGLISH THEATRE BERLIN THEATRE

Map p340 (030-691 1211; www.etberlin.de; Fidicinstrasse 40; M19, UPlatz der Luftbrücke) Berlin's oldest English-language theatre puts on an engaging roster of in-house productions, plays by international visiting troupes, concerts, comedy, dance and cabaret by local performers. Quality is often

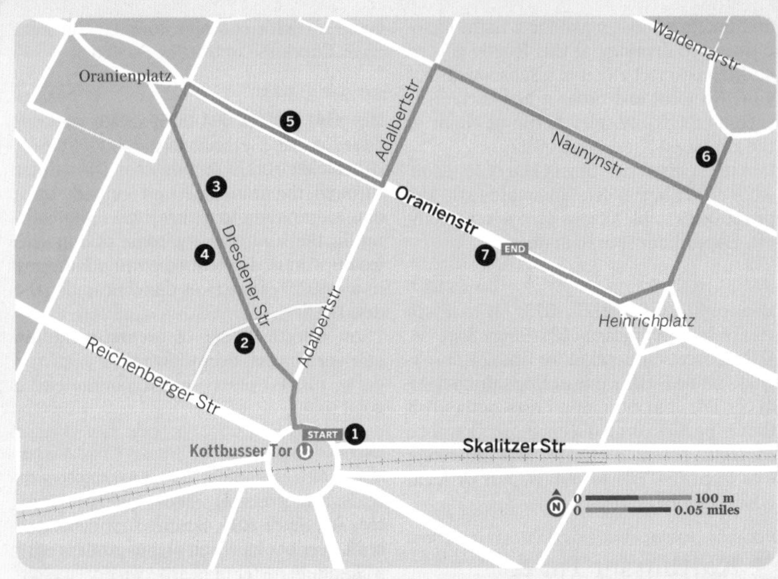

Local Life
Kotti Bar-Hop

Noisy, chaotic and sleepless, the area around Kottbusser Tor U-Bahn station (Kotti, for short) defiantly retains the alt-punky feel that's defined it since the 1970s. More gritty than pretty, this beehive of snack shops, cafes, pubs and bars delivers high-octane night-time action and is tailor-made for bar-hopping. Note that smoking is permitted in most places.

❶ Elevated Speakeasy

Pull up the steel door and head up a grotty staircase to arrive at **Fahimi Bar** (☎030-6165 6003; www.fahimibar.de; Skalitzer Strasse 133; ⊙from 6pm), a speakeasy oozing understated glamour. A generously sized U-shaped backlit bar flanked by shiny bar stools anchors the dimly lit space accented by dark wood, steel and concrete. The barstaff make mean cocktails, and DJs fuel the fun on select nights.

❷ Funky Saloon

Tucked behind a pile of Turkish kebab shops, grocers and *shisha* bars, **Möbel Olfe** (☎030-2327 4690; www.moebel-olfe.de; Reichenberger Strasse 177; ⊙6-11pm Tue-Sun) is a queer-leaning saloon that channels the area's alternative vibe with boho decor, strong Polish beers and a chatty crowd. It's a popular gathering spot for lesbians on Tuesday and gay men on Thursday.

❸ Grape Delights

A charming lair with woodsy fixtures and a bar covered in slate, **Otto Rink** (☎0163 706 8369; www.ottorink.de; Dresdener Strasse 124; ⊙6pm-2am) is an easygoing place to discover just how wonderful German wines can be. Friendly staff will happily help you find your favourite. After 5pm on Sunday, budget oenophiles invade for *Restetrinken* (leftover drinking), when glasses from open bottles cost a mere €4.

❹ 1950s Cocktail Cave

For a swish night out, point your compass to **Würgeengel** (☎030-615 5560; www.wuergeengel.de; Dresdener Strasse 122; ⊙from 7pm), a stylish art deco–style cocktail bar with operatic chandeliers and shiny black-glass surfaces. The name pays homage to the surreal 1962 Luis Buñuel movie *Exterminating Angel*.

Möbel Olfe

5 Luscious Lair

Luzia (www.facebook.com/luziabar; Oranienstrasse 34; ⏲from noon Tue-Sun) is an excellent place to get the party started with a few beers or long drinks. Vintage decor gets contempo sass from a mural by street artist Chin Chin, while tables behind the panoramic windows are great people-watching perches.

6 Medicine in a Glass

Get your hands on a potent Penicillin cocktail at charming **Apotheken Bar** (☎030-6951 8108; www.facebook.com/apothekenbar; Mariannenplatz 6; ⏲5-11pm Tue-Sat) in a retired 150-year-old pharmacy. Shelves and drawers that once held pills and potions have become the well-stocked back bar, but the drink menu features the best of the past and today.

7 Den of Debauchery

A mash-up of trash, camp and fun, **Roses** (☎030-615 6570; Oranienstrasse 187; ⏲10pm-6am) is a beloved pit stop on the Kreuzberg party scene, especially among LGBTIQ+ people and friends. Don't let the furry walls and the predominance of pink distract you: this place takes drinking seriously until the early hours.

high and the cast international. Most tickets cost €16.50.

HEBBEL AM UFER THEATRE

Map p340 (HAU 1; ☎030-259 0040; www.hebbel-am-ufer.de; Stresemannstrasse 29; tickets €8-30; UHallesches Tor) One of Germany's most avant-garde indie theatres has a mission to explore changes in the social and political fabric of society, often by blurring the lines between theatre, dance, music and visual art. Performances are held in this 1907 art nouveau theatre called Hau 1 (the main venue), as well as in two smaller venues nearby, HAU 2 and HAU 3.

YORCKSCHLÖSSCHEN LIVE MUSIC

Map p340 (☎030-215 8070; www.yorckschloesschen.de; Yorckstrasse 15; tickets €4-8; ⏲from 6pm; UMehringdamm) Cosy and knick-knack laden, this Kreuzberg institution has plied an all-ages, all-comers crowd of jazz- and blues-lovers with tunes and booze for over 30 years. Toe-tapping bands invade several times a week, but there's also a pool table, a beer garden, Kreuzberger beer on tap and European soul food served till late.

☆ Kottbusser Tor & Eastern Kreuzberg

FREILUFTKINO KREUZBERG OUTDOOR CINEMA

Map p342 (☎030-2936 1628; www.freiluftkino-kreuzberg.de; Mariannenplatz; tickets €8.50; ⏲daily May-early Sep; UKottbusser Tor) This beloved open-air cinema screens international current-season, classic and cult flicks in digital quality on the courtyard lawn behind the Kunstquartier Bethanien (p185) arts centre. All movies are presented in the original language with German subtitles; German movies have English subtitles.

All screenings take place rain or shine.

FSK-KINO CINEMA

Map p342 (☎030-614 2464; www.fsk-kino.de; Segitzdamm 2; adult/concession €8/7; 🚌M29, 140, UKottbusser Tor) This sweet little art-house theatre run by a collective since 1988 presents handpicked quality films, often with a political or feminist bent, in the original language.

BALLHAUS NAUNYNSTRASSE THEATRE

Map p342 (☎030-7545 3725; www.ballhausnaunynstrasse.de; Naunynstrasse 27; tickets

SEX & THE CITY

Insomnia (www.insomnia-berlin.de; Alt-Tempelhof 17-19; UAlt-Tempelhof) is a deliciously decadent Berlin nightlife fixture in a 19th-century ballroom. While the full-on erotic party nights are on hiatus, it is still open for some action, including weekend party live streams, bar and lounge evenings with DJs, shows, BDSM and fetish evenings and whatever else owner-hostess Dominique dreams up. The website has details.

It's about 2.5km south of Mehringdamm and the Bergmannkiez.

adult/concession €14/8; UKottbusser Tor) This fringe theatre in a repurposed 19th-century ballroom presents cutting-edge and often provocative intercultural plays with a focus on the perspectives of Black people, people of colour and gay people. Many actors have a migrant background. Some performances have English subtitles.

MUSIK & FRIEDEN LIVE MUSIC

Map p342 (☎030-2391 9994; www.musikundfrieden.de; Falckensteinstrasse 48; USchlesisches Tor) Although the line-up is much compromised because of the coronavirus pandemic, this easy-going live-music club still puts on the occasional socially distanced concert, from indie-alternative to punk.

SHOPPING

Kreuzberg has a deliciously eclectic shopping scene, with zero malls or international high-street chain branches. Bergmannstrasse in the more mellow and upscale western part of the district and funky Oranienstrasse near Kotti are the main drags for owner-run boutiques, with plenty of local character. Kottbusser Damm is the heart of a Turkish neighbourhood, with vendors selling everything from billowing bridal gowns to roasted nuts and gooey baklava.

★FOLKDAYS FASHION & ACCESSORIES

Map p342 (☎030-9362 6094; www.folkdays.com; Manteuffelstrasse 19; ⏲noon-7pm Mon-Fri, to 6pm Sat; UGörlitzer Bahnhof) The folks from Folkdays travel the world to build relationships with skilled artisans who produce contemporary fashion, accessories and homewares using time-tested techniques passed down through generations. Whether you fall in love with an alpaca sweater from Peru, handwoven baskets from Morocco or recycled brass earrings from Kenya, you can be sure it's fair trade at its finest.

★HALLESCHES HAUS HOMEWARES

Map p340 (www.hallescheshaus.com; Tempelhofer Ufer 1; ⏲10am-7pm Wed-Sun; 📶; UHallesches Tor) Design fans will go ga-ga at this pretty pad packed with mod whimsies for the home. From teapots to terrariums, everything gets a zany twist in this vaulted loft space converted from an old post office. The in-store cafe serves locally roasted coffee, baked goods and light meals at lunchtime, much of it organic and local.

★VOOSTORE FASHION & ACCESSORIES

Map p342 (☎030-6165 1112; www.vooberlin.com; Oranienstrasse 24; ⏲10am-8pm Mon-Sat; UKottbusser Tor) Kreuzberg's first concept store presents its covetables in an old backyard locksmith shop off gritty Oranienstrasse. In suitably austere-chic surrounds, it stocks fashion-forward designer threads and accessories, along with cool books, gadgets, mags and spirits. The in-house Companion Cafe serves speciality coffees and tea from its own micro-farm.

OTHER NATURE ADULT

Map p340 (☎030-2062 0538; www.other-nature.de; Mehringdamm 79; ⏲noon-6pm Mon-Sat; UMehringdamm, Platz der Luftbrücke) At this alternative sex shop with a feminist, queer and sex-positive slant, you can stock up on vegan condoms, Kegel balls, menstrual cups, dildos in all shapes, sizes and materials, and other fun stuff presented in a non-sexist environment. Owner Sara is happy to offer advice on any and all subjects.

MARKTHALLE NEUN MARKET

Map p342 (☎030-6107 3473; www.markthalleneun.de; Eisenbahnstrasse 42-43; ⏲noon-6pm Mon-Wed & Fri, noon-10pm Thu, 10am-6pm Sat; UGörlitzer Bahnhof) This delightful 1891 market hall with its iron-beam-supported ceiling was saved by dedicated locals in

2009. Not only do local and regional producers present their wares but also, on Street-Food Thursday (p186), they're joined by aspiring or semipro chefs, who set up their stalls to serve delicious snacks from around the world. There's even an on-site craft brewery, Heidenpeters.

HARD WAX MUSIC

Map p342 (030-6113 0111; www.hardwax.com; 3rd fl, door A, 2nd courtyard, Paul-Lincke-Ufer 44a; noon-8pm Mon-Sat; U Kottbusser Tor) This well-hidden record shop, in business since 1989, is a seminal stop for fans of electronic music in all its permutations.

ANOTHER COUNTRY BOOKS

Map p340 (030-6940 1160; www.anothercountry.de; Riemannstrasse 7; noon-6.30pm Wed-Sat; ; U Gneisenaustrasse) Run by the eccentric Sophie Raphaeline, this nonprofit outfit is more a library and boho hangout than a bookshop. Pick a tome from around 20,000 used English-language books – classic lit to science fiction – and, if you want, sell it back, minus a €1.50 borrowing fee. It also puts on events, with a focus on the LGBTIQ+ community and people of colour.

MARHEINEKE MARKTHALLE FOOD

Map p340 (www.meine-markthalle.de; Marheinekeplatz; 8am-8pm Mon-Fri, to 6pm Sat; U Gneisenaustrasse) This nicely renovated historic market hall is like a giant deli where vendors offer everything from organic sausage to handmade cheese, artisanal honey and other delicious bounty, both local and international. Take a break from shopping with a glass of Prosecco or a snack.

SPORTS & ACTIVITIES

BADESCHIFF SWIMMING

Map p342 (0162 545 1374; www.arena-berlin.de; Eichenstrasse 4; adult/concession €6.50/3.50; from 8am May-Sep; 265, Treptower Park, U Schlesisches Tor) Take an old river barge, fill it with water, moor it in the Spree and – voila! – you get an artist-designed urban lifestyle pool that's a popular swim-and-chill spot. With music blaring, a sandy beach, wooden decks, lots of hot bods and a bar to fuel the fun, the vibe is distinctly 'Ibiza on the Spree'.

Come early on scorching days, as it's often filled to capacity by noon. Alternatively, show up for sunset, night-time parties or concerts. Yoga, stand-up paddle boarding (SUP) and massage treatments are also available.

Neukölln

Neighbourhood Top Five

1 Tempelhofer Feld (p196) Flying a kite, cycling, picnicking or simply being slothful at this airfield turned open-air park and playground.

2 Türkischer Markt (p201) Immersing yourself in multicultural bounty on a crawl through the canal-side Turkish-German market.

3 Kindl Centre for Contemporary Art (p196) Opening your mind to edgy new art concepts in this private exhibition space in a former brewery.

4 Rixdorf (p196) Slowing down and embarking on a time-warp stroll through one of the oldest neighbourhoods in Berlin.

5 Körnerpark (p196) Catching some rays or a concert while sprawled on the lawn of this baroque-style garden forged from a gravel pit.

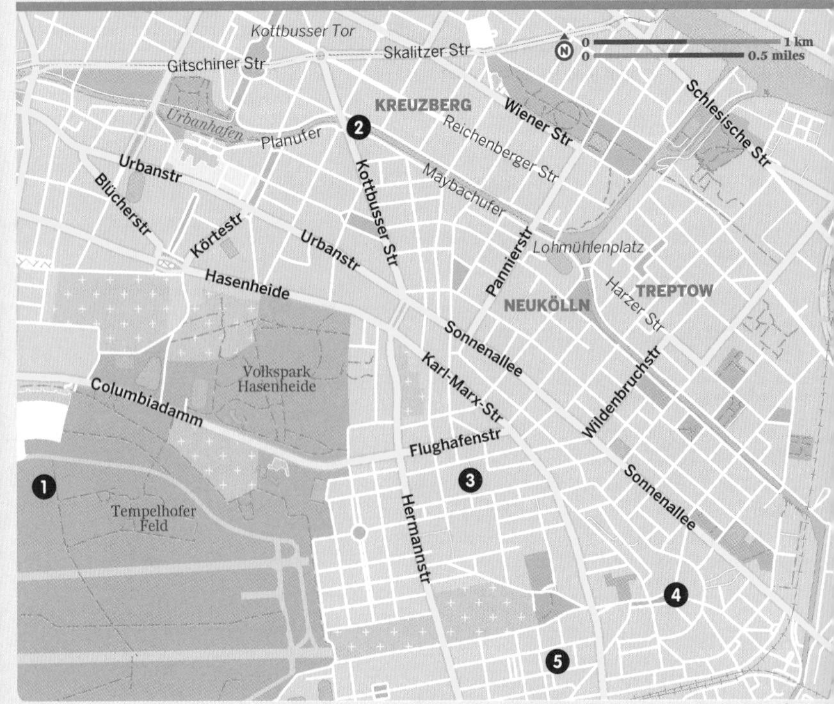

For more detail of this area see Map p344

Explore Neukölln

Once only making headlines for its high crime levels and poorly performing schools, Neukölln has catapulted from ghetto-gritty to funkytown-hip over the last decade. Fuelled by an enormous influx of young, creative neo-Berliners (especially from Spain, the UK, the US, Australia and Italy), the district sees new bars, performance spaces and galleries open up almost daily. An exciting culinary scene has also emerged, including a two-Michelin-star restaurant.

The action centres on the northern *Kieze* (neighbourhoods) between the Landwehrkanal and the circle line S-Bahn tracks. To the west lies the unbeatable Tempelhofer Feld (p196), a vast urban park created on the airfield of the former Tempelhof airport that had a starring role in the 1948–49 Berlin Airlift. The two main commercial ribbons, Karl-Marx-Strasse and Sonnenallee, are home to Neukölln's Middle Eastern and Turkish communities and great for getting your doner or shawarma fix.

Away from the hubbub, Berlin's largest district also delivers some surprising discoveries, including hidden parks and gardens, a palace and even a Unesco World Heritage Site, the 1920s Hufeisensiedlung (p282) housing estate.

Local Life

Marketeering Put together a yummy picnic from olives, feta, crusty bread and produce at the bazaar-like canalside Türkischer Markt (p201).

Sunset views Wind down the day with a cold drink parked under a sun sail at the Klunkerkranich (p199) rooftop roost.

Parks Let the wind clear your brain's cobwebs (or hangover) on an extended stroll around Tempelhofer Feld (p196) or leafy Volkspark Hasenheide (p197).

Getting There & Away

Bus M41 connects Hauptbahnhof with Neukölln via Potsdamer Platz; M29 comes in from Charlottenburg, Schöneberg and Kreuzberg; 171 goes to Treptow.

S-Bahn The Ringbahn (Circle Line) S41/S42 stops at Sonnenallee, Neukölln and Hermannstrasse.

U-Bahn Schönleinstrasse, Hermannplatz and Boddinstrasse (all on the U8) as well as Rathaus Neukölln and Karl-Marx-Strasse (U7) are key stops.

Lonely Planet's Top Tip

Not your parents' minigolf course, Nuture Mini Art Golf on Tempelhofer Feld (p196) is a wonderfully wacky interactive art installation, put together from recycled materials by a team of 18 international artists. It's a fun way to spend a couple of hours in good weather. Enter from Columbiadamm.

Best Places to Eat

- Barra (p198)
- Coda (p199)
- Cafe Jacques (p198)
- Berlin Burger International (p197)
- eins44 (p199)

For reviews, see p197.

Best Places to Drink

- Velvet Bar (p199)
- Truffle Pig (p199)
- Geist im Glas (p199)
- Klunkerkranich (p199)

For reviews, see p199.

Best Places to Shop

- Türkischer Markt (p201)
- Shio Store (p201)
- Curious Fox (p201)
- Nowkoelln Flowmarkt (p201)

For reviews, see p201.

SIGHTS

Most people don't venture to Neukölln because of its sights. Pity, because there are a few surprising – and very worthy – gems, including a baroque garden in a gravel pit and a medieval village. Note that the vast Tempelhof Airport turned outdoor playground is covered in this chapter, even though most of it is actually in Kreuzberg.

KINDL CENTRE FOR CONTEMPORARY ART — ARTS CENTRE

Map p344 (030-832 159 120; www.kindl-berlin.com; Am Sudhaus 3; adult/under 18yr €5/free; noon-8pm Wed, to 6pm Thu-Sun; U Boddinstrasse, Rathaus Neukölln) In the 1920s Expressionist-style industrial halls of the former Kindl brewery, this nonprofit presents changing international contemporary art exhibits augmented by lectures, meet-the-artist gatherings, readings and other educational programs. The coolest room is the Kesselhaus (boiler room), whose cathedral-like dimensions make it ideal for large-scale and site-specific installations. A cafe serves snacks and drinks, in summer outside in the beer garden.

KÖRNERPARK — GARDENS

Map p344 (030-5682 3939; www.körnerpark.de; Schierker Strasse 8; park 24hr, gallery 10am-8pm Tue-Sun; S Neukölln, U Neukölln) FREE This sunken neo-baroque century-old garden comes with a secret: strolling past the balustrades, sculptures, flower beds and cascading fountain, you're actually standing atop a reclaimed gravel pit. Ponder this as you sip a coffee in the cafe or check out the latest exhibit in the gallery. In summer join locals for free film nights or alfresco classical, jazz and world-music concerts.

RIXDORF — AREA

Map p344 (Richardplatz; S Berlin-Neukölln, U Karl-Marx-Strasse, Neukölln) Weavers from Bohemia first settled in quiet Rixdorf, a tiny historic village centred on Richardplatz, in the early 18th century. Some of the

TEMPELHOFER FELD: AIRPORT-TURNED-URBAN PLAYGROUND

In Berlin history, Tempelhof Airport is a site of legend. It was here in 1909 that aviation pioneer Orville Wright ran his first flight experiments, managing to keep his homemade flying machine in the air for a full minute. The first Zeppelin landed the same year and in 1926 Lufthansa's first scheduled flight took off for Zurich. The Nazis held massive rallies on the airfield and enlarged the smallish terminal into a massive semicircular compound measuring 1.23km from one end to the other. Designed by Ernst Sagebiel, it was constructed in only two years and is still one of the world's largest freestanding buildings. Despite its monumentalism, Sagebiel managed to inject some pleasing design features, especially in the grand art deco–style departure hall.

After the war, the US Armed Forces took over the airport and expanded its facilities, installing a power plant, a bowling alley and a basketball court. In 1948–49, the airport saw its finest hours during the Berlin Airlift. After the now-decommissioned Tegel Airport opened in 1975, passenger volume declined, and flight operations stopped in 2008 following much brouhaha and (initially) against the wishes of many Berliners. That sentiment changed dramatically when the airfield opened as a public **park** (Map p340; www.gruen-berlin.de/tempelhofer-feld; sunrise-sunset; ; U Paradestrasse, Boddinstrasse, Leinestrasse, Tempelhof, S Tempelhof) FREE, a wonderfully noncommercial and creative open-sky space where cyclists, bladers and kite-surfers whisk along the tarmac. Fun zones include a beer garden (p200) near Columbiadamm, barbecue areas, an artsy minigolf course, art installations, abandoned aeroplanes and an urban gardening project.

The Tempelhof airport building, meanwhile, is being turned into a cultural and creative space. Plans include moving the Allied Museum (p237) currently based in Dahlem, opening the tower to the public and creating a 1.2km-long Geschichtsgalerie (History Gallery) on the airport rooftop. English-language **tours** (Map p340; 030-200 037 441; www.thf-berlin.de; Platz der Luftbrücke 5; tours adult/concession €16.50/11; English tours 1.30pm Thu-Sun; U Platz der Luftbrücke) of both airport and airfield are available.

original buildings still survive, including a **blacksmith** (Richardplatz 28), a farmhouse and the 15th-century **Bethlehemskirche** (Richardplatz 22), but in recent years the area has become increasingly hip and gentrified and now teems with cafes, bars and creative spaces.

PUPPENTHEATER-MUSEUM BERLIN
MUSEUM

Map p344 (Puppet Theatre Museum; ☎030-9837 8131; www.puppentheater-museum.de; rear bldg, Karl-Marx-Strasse 135; adult/child €5/4, shows from €5.50; ⏱1-5pm Tue-Sun; UKarl-Marx-Strasse) At this little museum you'll enter a fantasy world inhabited by adorable hand puppets, marionettes, shadow puppets, stick figures and all manner of dolls, dragons and devils from around the world. Many of them hit the stage singing and dancing during shows that enthral both the young and the young at heart.

VOLKSPARK HASENHEIDE
PARK

Map p344 (www.volkspark-hasenheide.de; ⏱24hr; UHermannplatz) This rambling park links Neukölln with Kreuzberg and was originally the royal family's rabbit preserve (hence the name: 'rabbit heath'). After WWII it became a public park, and it remains a popular hangout for neighbourhood folks, with playgrounds, an outdoor cinema, an animal sanctuary and the lovely Hasenschänke cafe-beer garden. The 68m-high Rixdorfer Höhe is another of Berlin's rubble mountains built from wartime debris.

SCHLOSS BRITZ
PALACE

(☎030-6097 9230; www.schlossbritz.de; Alt-Britz 73; museum adult/concession €3/2; ⏱noon-6pm Tue-Sun; UParchimer Allee, then bus M46) This 18th-century country estate, with its frilly neo-Renaissance facade and surrounding park, once served as the residence of Prussian ministers and high-ranking court officials. Today it's a nice place for strolls, picnics or summer concerts in the park, or to catch a glimpse of the lifestyle of a well-to-do Berlin family in the late 19th century by taking in the museum's five period rooms.

EATING

Thanks to the influx of expats from all corners of the world, plus the huge long-time resident Middle Eastern and Turkish population, Neukölln has evolved into Berlin's most dynamic and diverse cuisine terrain. The scene is growing increasingly sophisticated – and yes, there's even a double-Michelin-starred restaurant.

★BERLIN BURGER INTERNATIONAL
BURGERS €

Map p344 (☎0160 482 6505; www.berlinburgerinternational.com; Pannierstrasse 5; burgers €8-10.70; ⏱noon-10pm Mon-Wed, to 11pm Thu-Sun; ✍; UHermannplatz) The folks at BBI know that size matters – at least when it comes to burgers. These bulging and sloppy contenders require both hands and your full attention. Everything's prepared fresh, including the chili-cheese fries and the coleslaw. Recommended: the El Gordonita, topped with guacamole, sweet-potato chips and Irish cheddar. Paper towels are supplied. You'll need 'em.

AZZAM
LEBANESE €

Map p344 (☎030-6097 7541; Sonnenallee 54; mains €4-6; ⏱8am-1am; 🚌M41, UHermannplatz, Rathaus Neukölln) Unpretentious Azzam transplants Beirut's palpable energy and convivial vibes to Neukölln's gritty Sonnenallee. The food is just as authentic and it's the reason the joint is usually as busy as a beehive. Drop by for the heavenly hummus, crispy falafel or crunchy *fatteh* – an addictive mash-up of fried pita bits, cashews and chickpeas drizzled with yoghurt. Bonus: free pickles and pita bread.

TWO PLANETS
VEGAN €

Map p344 (www.facebook.com/twoplanetsberlin; Hermannstrasse 230; mains €6.50; ⏱9am-6pm; ✍; UBoddinstrasse) Priding itself on its self-proclaimed 'dope ass toasts', Two Planets serves up simple but delicious vegan food in a trendy and welcoming setting on Neukölln's bustling Hermannstrasse. The coffee, which is available with cow's milk or plant-based substitutes, is exquisitely prepared and full of flavour, and the banana bread is too legit to quit.

Beetroot lattes and matcha lattes are also available for the Instagrammers.

LA STELLA NERA
VEGAN €

Map p344 (☎030-2394 9708; www.lastellanera.de; Leykestrasse 18; pizza €5.50-12; ⏱5-11pm Tue-Fri, 1-11pm Sat & Sun; ✍; ULeinestrasse) At this cosy collective the Neapolitan-style pizza gets topped with fresh veggies, herbs and vegan cheese and crisped up in a wood-fired oven. The atmosphere inside is typical Neukölln – vibrant and cosy, with an eclectic mix of diners. Try the *panelle* (Sicilian chickpea fritters) as a starter.

DAMASKUS KONDITOREI — BAKERY €

Map p344 (030-7037 0711; www.damaskus-konditorei-emissa.com; Sonnenallee 93; snacks from €2; 9am-10pm Mon-Sat, noon-8pm Sun; M41, U Rathaus Neukölln) Of all the Middle Eastern bakeries in Neukölln, Damaskus stands out for its truly artistic and rave-worthy pastries. The shop is run by a Syrian family who had to leave behind their thriving bakery and resettle in Germany. Try the buttery baklava with walnuts or pistachios, or the signature *halawa* (creamy rosewater-and-cheese pockets).

KNÖDELWIRTSCHAFT — GERMAN €

Map p344 (030-9660 0459; https://knoedelwirtschaft.de; Fuldastrasse 33; mains €9-15; 5-10pm Mon-Fri, 4-10pm Sat & Sun; M41, U Rathaus Neukölln) OK, the translation 'German bread dumplings' may not make the uninitiated salivate, but one bite of *Knödel* at this cosy lair may quickly make you a convert. Order the traditional versions stuffed with cheese or speck, or try the walnut-and-goat-cheese variation. One order gets you two dumplings with Parmesan, butter and a small salad.

BRAMMIBAL'S DONUTS — BAKERY €

Map p344 (030-2394 8455; www.brammibalsdonuts.com; Maybachufer 8; doughnuts from €2.50; 10am-8pm Mon-Sat, 11am-7pm Sun; U Schönleinstrasse) Locals can often be seen queuing out the door for fresh vegan doughnuts in tantalising flavours from cookie dough to cranberry pecan to caramel apple crunch. This is the original branch, but there are now several others around town – check the website.

FRÄULEIN FROST — ICE CREAM €

Map p344 (030-9559 5521; www.fräulein-frost.de; Friedelstrasse 38; per scoop €1.40-1.70; noon-6pm or later; ; U Schönleinstrasse) Sure, there are vanilla, strawberry and chocolate, but ordering these would be missing the point of this popular ice-cream parlour. Fräulein Frost is all about experimentation, as reflected in such courageous – and delectable – concoctions as GuZiMi, which stands for Gurke-Zitrone-Minze (cucumber-lemon-mint). Heart-shaped hot waffles are served in winter.

CITY CHICKEN — MIDDLE EASTERN €

Map p344 (030-624 8600; www.facebook.com/citychickenberlin; Sonnenallee 59; half-chicken plate €8.50; 11am-2am; U Rathaus Neukölln) There's chicken and then there's City Chicken, an absolute cult destination when it comes to juicy birds sent through the rotisserie for the perfect tan. All chicken orders are served with creamy hummus, vampire-repelling garlic sauce and salad. Sit outside for the full-on Neukölln street-life immersion. There's also a full menu of other Middle Eastern dishes, including tabbouleh, halloumi and felafel.

★BARRA — EUROPEAN €€

Map p344 (030-8186 0757; www.barraberlin.com; Okerstrasse 2; dishes €4-27; 6.30-10.30pm Fri-Mon, noon-2pm Sun; U Leinestrasse) Named for a Scottish island, Barra is a favourite with foodies and off-duty chefs for its elevated comfort food. Sit next to the bar or at the long communal table in the back and start putting together a small-plate menu featuring pioneering flavour pairings made with choice seasonal ingredients. The chocolate mousse with cardamon and olive oil is a revelation.

★CAFE JACQUES — MEDITERRANEAN €€

Map p344 (030-694 1048; http://cafejacques.de; Maybachufer 14; mains €12.50-19.50; noon-10pm; U Schönleinstrasse) Like a fine wine, this French-Mediterranean darling keeps improving with age. Candlelit wooden tables and art-festooned brick walls feel as welcoming as an old friend's embrace. Owner Ahmad is an impeccable host who'll happily advise you on the perfect wine to match to your blackboard-menu pick. Expect a rotating festival of tantalising dishes, often with unexpected flavour combinations. Cash only.

CHICHA — PERUVIAN €€

Map p344 (030-6273 1010; www.chicha-berlin.de; Friedelstrasse 34; mains €10-14.50; 6pm-midnight Wed-Sun; U Schönleinstrasse) What began as a regular appearance at Berlin's street-food fairs has evolved into a cheerful permanent nosh spot serving Peruvian classics, most famously creative spins on ceviche (marinated raw fish). Dishes pair perfectly with a tangy pisco sour and the mood-enhancing decor.

LA BOLOGNINA — ITALIAN €€

Map p344 (030-5563 4454; www.facebook.com/LaBologninaNeukoelln; Donaustrasse 107;

mains €8-14; ⌚5-11pm Tue-Sat; ⓤRathaus Neukölln) This petite place represents pasta perfection. From tagliatelle to ravioli, all noodles are homemade and paired with sauces that hum with the spirit of Italy. Also try the *piadine* (stuffed flatbreads).

★CODA DESSERTS €€€

Map p344 (☎030-9149 6396; http://coda-berlin.com; Friedelstrasse 47; weekday/weekend 7-course tasting menu €138/148, 4-course late-night menu €83/93; ⌚7.30-11pm Thu, 6.30pm-late Fri & Sat; ✎; ⓤHermannplatz) In this cosy *boîte*, dessert is not an afterthought but the star of the show. A sweet tooth isn't necessary to dig Coda's sensual fine-dining experience, though – chef René Frank favours *umami* (savoury) notes, natural ingredients and labour-intensive techniques for well-rounded flavour. The Michelin testers loved it so much they gave him two stars.

Book ahead for the seven-course 7pm tasting menu or the four-course 10pm menu, both served with paired drinks.

EINS44 EUROPEAN €€€

Map p344 (☎030-6298 1212; www.eins44.com; 3rd courtyard, Elbestrasse 28/29; mains €22-28; ⌚5-10pm; 📶; 🚌M41, 104, 166, ⓤRathaus Neukölln) This casual fine-dining outpost in a late-19th-century distillery serves meals with robust flavours and a strong native identity, composed largely with seasonally hunted and gathered ingredients. Competing with the kitchen compositions is the lofty dining room's industrial charm, accented by black-and-white metro tiles, metal lamps and hefty beechwood tables.

DRINKING & NIGHTLIFE

Neukölln may well have eclipsed Kreuzberg and Friedrichshain as party central. Clubs are still thin on the ground, but there's such a wealth of cafes, pubs and bars that you could probably go to a different one every day of the year.

★VELVET BAR COCKTAIL BAR

Map p344 (www.velvet-bar-berlin.de; Ganghoferstrasse 1; ⌚7pm-late Wed-Mon; ⓤRathaus Neukölln) This first-rate drinking den is the perfect spot for an evening of paced imbibing. Boutique spirits, seasonal ingredients and unusual techniques (involving a centrifuge or an ultrasonic bath) conspire to create cocktails that are like alchemy in a glass.

No surprise that Velvet snagged Germany's 'Bar of the Year' title in 2019, just a year and a half after its opening.

★TRUFFLE PIG COCKTAIL BAR

Map p344 (☎0176 3433 8558; http://trufflepigberlin.de; Reuterstrasse 47; ⌚8am-late Wed-Sat; 🚌M41, ⓤHermannplatz, Schönleinstrasse) No need to ferret through dirt, but a little intuition will help you find clandestine cocktail lair Truffle Pig. Hint: push the fire-alarm button at the back of the Kauz & Kiebitz craft-beer pub to gain access to this complexion-friendly realm of elevated imbibing designed by the same studio as club legend Berghain.

★KLUNKERKRANICH BAR

Map p344 (www.klunkerkranich.org; Karl-Marx-Strasse 66; €3-6, before 4pm free; ⌚4pm-2am, open earlier summer; 📶; ⓤRathaus Neukölln) The Insta-perfect views are only the overture at this constantly evolving and always packed cafe-bar-club-garden-culture-venue in the sky. Thanks to two cosy huts hosting concerts, poetry slams, movies and even a Christmas market, Klunkerkranich is worth a trip even on cold and rainy days. Find it on the top parking deck of the Neukölln Arcaden shopping mall.

To get there, take the lift just inside the mall's side entrance marked 'Bibliothek/Post' on Karl-Marx-Strasse. There's often a line; families and seniors don't have to wait.

GEIST IM GLASS BAR

Map p344 (☎0152 5135 3816; www.facebook.com/geistimglas; Lenaustrasse 27; ⌚6-11pm Mon-Fri, 10am-3pm & 6-11pm Sat & Sun; ⓤHermannplatz) Weekends wouldn't be the same without Aishah Bennett's soul-restoring brunches (buttermilk pancakes, Bloody Marys, bottomless filter coffee!). But, frankly, swinging by this seductively lit, cabin-style lair is a clever endeavour any night. Get comfortable with immaculate cocktails and well-curated craft-beer and wine selections. Quality is tops and prices are fair.

ZOSSE BAR

Map p344 (www.facebook.com/ZosseBar; Richardstrasse 37; ⌚6pm-midnight Tue-Thu, 6pm-3am Fri, 4pm-3am Sat, 4-11.45pm Sun; ⓤKarl-Marx-Strasse) Follow a cobbled alleyway to this cosy drinking den in an old blacksmith shop in historic Rixdorf. Whether it's cocktails by the wood-burning stove in winter or a cold beer in the summertime garden, Zosse is a chill place to transition from tourist-track frenzy to night-time relaxation. Bonus: free popcorn.

Zosse is an old German word for 'horse'.

HERR LINDEMANN COCKTAIL BAR

Map p344 (www.facebook.com/BarHerrLindemann; Richardplatz 16; ⏲6pm-late; UKarl-Marx-Strasse) Delicious cocktails with healing properties? We're so there! 'There' is Herr Lindemann, a stylish bar with industrial-meets-nature design, a terrace for those balmy summer nights and a herbalicious menu of mood enhancers. The aromatic palette of herbs hails from owner Peter Edinger's own garden and finds its destiny in inspired and smoothly balanced drinks.

Feeling frisky? Try the signature Ziegenpeter, which is made with horny-goat-weed infused rum!

ANKERKLAUSE PUB

Map p344 (☎030-693 5649; www.ankerklause.de; Kottbusser Damm 104; ⏲4pm-late Mon, from 10am Tue-Sun; USchönleinstrasse) Ahoy there! Drop anchor at this nautical-kitsch tavern in an old harbour master's shack to give the classic jukebox a workout over cold beers and surprisingly good German pub fare. The best seats are on the Landwehrkanal-facing terrace, where you can wave at swans and boats puttering past. A cult pit stop from breakfast until the wee hours.

LUFTGARTEN BEER GARDEN

Map p344 (☎0152 2255 9174; www.luftgarten-berlin.de; Tempelhofer Feld; ⏲from 11am Apr-Oct; UBoddinstrasse) Kick back with a cold brew and a grilled sausage and watch the action on the tarmac in this breezy beer garden at the northern edge of the vast Tempelhofer Feld (p196), an airfield turned public park. Enter from Columbiadamm.

THELONIOUS COCKTAIL BAR

Map p344 (☎030-5561 8232; www.facebook.com/theloniousbarberlin; Weserstrasse 202; ⏲6pm-1am or later; UHermannplatz) Well-mannered patrons pack this narrow burrow named for American jazz giant Thelonius Monk, embraced by the mellow soundscape and complexion-friendly lighting. Owner Laura Maria, who travelled the world before returning to her Neukölln roots, is the consummate host and creator of a drinks menu that ticks all the boxes, from the classic to the adventurous.

TIER BAR

Map p344 (www.tier.bar; Weserstrasse 42; ⏲from 6pm; 🚌M41, URathaus Neukölln) Tier was the first serious cocktail bar on the Weserstrasse strip, and it still draws global hipsters with its vintage design and good drinks from a pedigreed bar staff. Note that it's not shy about turning away groups of over six people or enforcing the 'no photos' policy. Customers must be at least 21.

☆ ENTERTAINMENT

★COMEDY CAFÉ BERLIN COMEDY

Map p344 (CCB; www.comedycafeberlin.com; Roseggerstrasse 17; ⏲7-11pm Wed-Sun; 🚌Geygerstrasse, UKarl-Marx-Strasse) This vivacious bar offers stand-up and improv shows in English five nights a week, with many free shows and a lot of varied performances from Berlin's burgeoning English comedy scene. In addition to laughs, there are super-cheesy toasties, a great selection of spirits, and craft beer on tap.

NEUKÖLLNER OPER THEATRE

Map p344 (☎tickets 030-6889 0777; www.neukoellneroper.de; Karl-Marx-Strasse 131; UKarl-Marx-Strasse) Neukölln's refurbished 1930s ballroom has an anti-elitist crossover line-up of intelligent musical theatre, original productions and new interpretations of offbeat classics. Many performances pick up on contemporary themes or topics relevant to Berlin (eg migration, gentrification); some are suitable for non-German speakers.

WOLF KINO CINEMA

Map p344 (☎030-921 039 333; www.wolfberlin.org; Weserstrasse 59; adult/concession €9/8; 🚌M41, 104, 166, URathaus Neukölln) The antidote to binge-streaming is crowdfunded Wolf, a two-screen bastion of international indie cinema tucked into a former brothel. After taking in a quirky flick, pull up a chair in the attached cafe-bar for drinks and deep discussions with fellow cineasts. With any luck, you might even get to meet the film-maker(s).

IL KINO CINEMA

Map p344 (☎030-6290 3878; www.ilkino.de; Nansenstrasse 22; tickets adult/concession €7/5; ⊙cafe-bar 9.30am-1am Mon-Thu, to 3am Fri, 1pm-3am Sat, 11am-1am Sun; 📶; Ⓤ Schönleinstrasse) Run by the Italian documentary filmmaker Carla Molino and friends, this 52-seat indie cinema with quality sound, projection and seating presents a smartly curated all-day program of international off-grid movies in the original language. Afterwards, the cosy cafe-bar invites post-screening conversation.

SHOPPING

For cool 'only-in-Berlin' shopping discoveries, hit the side streets (especially along Weserstrasse and around Schönleinstrasse U-Bahn station), which brim with owner-run galleries, designer shops, and stores selling vintage, vinyl and ecofashion. Find great produce at the twice-weekly Turkish market and pick up a shisha, spices or baklava in the Middle Eastern shops on Sonnenallee. For your everyday needs, hit the Neukölln Arcaden mall, next to Rathaus Neukölln U-Bahn station.

★TÜRKISCHER MARKT MARKET

Map p344 (Turkish Market; www.tuerkenmarkt.de; Maybachufer; ⊙11am-6.30pm Tue & Fri; Ⓤ Schönleinstrasse) This bazaar-like market along the Landwehrkanal is sure to bring a gleam to foodies' eyes. Join global hipsters, pram-pushing parents and curious tourists for a bewildering bounty of seasonal fruit and veg, Middle Eastern specialities and everything from fabric to organic teas. Popularity has pushed up selection and quality along with prices, but late in the day bargains still abound.

SHIO STORE FASHION & ACCESSORIES

Map p344 (www.shiostore.com; Weichselstrasse 59; ⊙noon-7pm; Ⓤ Schönleinstrasse) Kate Pinkstone tailors chic, timeless and sustainable pieces from linen, organic cotton jersey and upcycled cotton in her studio located right behind her elegantly minimalist store. There's also the Shio Upcycled line, where she breathes new life into secondhand clothing foraged at flea markets and thrift shops.

NEUZWEI VINTAGE

Map p344 (www.neuzwei.com; Weserstrasse 53; ⊙9am-7pm Tue, 1-7pm Wed-Sat; 🚌M41, 104, 166, Ⓤ Rathaus Neukölln) Hop on the slow-fashion train at Neuzwei, a top pick among Berlin vintage boutiques. Owner Barbara Molnar looks high and low for classic luxe fashions of yesteryear that have you looking fab in no time. Labels include Laura Lombardi, Prada and Issey Miyake. She also designed the store furniture.

CURIOUS FOX BOOKS

Map p344 (☎030-5266 4791; www.curiousfox.de; Flughafenstrasse 22; ⊙2-7pm Mon, noon-7pm Tue-Fri, noon-6pm Sat; Ⓤ Rathaus Neukölln) This sweet little bookshop not only stocks quality new and used English-language literature but hosts all sorts of events, from quiz nights to poetry readings and a book club.

KOLLATERALSCHADEN FASHION & ACCESSORIES

Map p344 (☎030-5308 1062; www.kollateralschaden.com; Bürknerstrasse 11; ⊙11am-7pm Mon-Fri, to 6pm Sat; Ⓤ Schönleinstrasse) Owner Philippe Werhahn studied fashion in Milan and has dedicated himself to creating timeless and classic clothing from chemical-free fabrics. All the T-shirts, sweaters and dresses feature the special and ultra-comfortable 'Kolla sleeve'.

NOWKOELLN FLOWMARKT MARKET

Map p344 (www.nowkoelln.de; Maybachufer; ⊙10am-5pm 2nd & 4th Sun of month Mar-Dec; Ⓤ Kottbusser Tor, Schönleinstrasse) This flea market sets up twice monthly along the scenic Maybachufer and delivers secondhand bargains galore, along with handmade threads and jewellery.

SPORTS & ACTIVITIES

STADTBAD NEUKÖLLN SWIMMING

Map p344 (☎030-2219 0011; www.berlinerbaeder.de; Ganghoferstrasse 3; adult €3.50-5.50, concession €2-3.50; ⊙hours vary; 🚌104, Ⓤ Rathaus Neukölln, Karl-Marx-Strasse) This gorgeous bathing temple from 1914 wows swimmers with mosaics, frescos, marble and brass. There are two pools (19m and 25m) and a Russian-Roman bath with sauna (€16). Check the schedule for opening hours. Mondays are reserved for women; Sunday nights are nude swimming.

Friedrichshain

Neighbourhood Top Five

❶ **East Side Gallery** (p204) Confronting the ghosts of the Cold War at the world's longest outdoor artwork on a 1.3km-long vestige of the Berlin Wall.

❷ **RAW Gelände** (p206) Partying till sunrise and beyond in the rough-around-the-edges bars, clubs and concert venues occupying the grounds of this former train-repair station.

❸ **Flea market** (p212) Foraging for treasure at this Sunday sell-a-thon on Boxhagener Platz, followed by brunch in a nearby cafe.

❹ **Karl-Marx-Allee** (p205) Marvelling at the monumental socialist architecture of the apartment buildings lined up along this grand Cold War–era boulevard.

❺ **Volkspark Friedrichshain** (p206) Chilling over a beer, a barbecue or an open-air movie in Berlin's oldest public park.

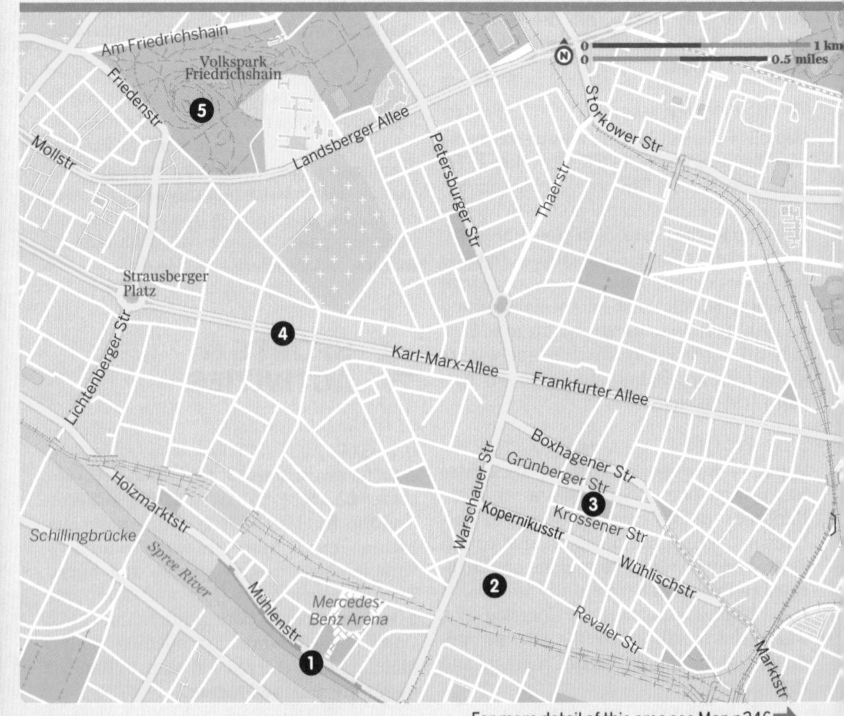

For more detail of this area see Map p346

Explore Friedrichshain

Friedrichshain is the only central district where major vestiges of the GDR have survived. The prime sight is the East Side Gallery (p204), the longest surviving stretch of the Berlin Wall, closely followed by Karl-Marx-Allee (p205), a grand boulevard that is the epitome of Stalinist pomposity. To delve deep into the extinct country's sinister underbelly, swing by the HQ of the Stasi, the GDR's omnipresent secret police, or head out to the adjacent district of Hohenschönhausen and its Stasi Prison (p212), where regime critics wound up.

In recent years Friedrichshain has been fully engulfed by turbo-gentrification, especially in the area along the East Side Gallery, which has sprouted office towers, a shopping mall and an entertainment quarter anchored by the Mercedes-Benz-Arena.

The district truly comes into its own at night. From late afternoon onward, waves of international party pilgrims stream out to the happy-hour bars around Simon-Dach-Strasse, later moving on to RAW Gelände (p206) and the electro clubs around Ostkreuz or the netherworld of Berghain/Panorama Bar (p209).

Local Life

Marketeering Forage for vintage finds at flea markets on Boxhagener Platz (p212), at the RAW Flohmarkt (p213) and at Ostbahnhof (p213) – urban archaeology at its finest.

Picnic in the park Berlin's long summer evenings are perfect for chilling in the rambling Volkspark Friedrichshain (p206), whether it involves a barbecue or a sunset with a six-pack.

Riverside chilling Ring in day's end with pizza and beer at the Holzmarkt (p207) creative village on the Spree or on the lawn behind the East Side Gallery.

Getting There & Away

S-Bahn Ostbahnhof and Warschauer Strasse are handy for the East Side Gallery; Warschauer Strasse and Ostkreuz for Boxhagener Platz and Revaler Strasse. Ringbahn (circle line) trains S41 and S42 stop at Frankfurter Allee and Ostkreuz.

U-Bahn U1 goes west as far as Charlottenburg; U5 links with Hauptbahnhof.

Tram M10 and M13 link Warschauer Strasse with Prenzlauer Berg.

Bus Handy lines are 300 to Alexanderplatz and Potsdamer Platz; 200 to Volkspark Friedrichshain from Mitte; 240 from Ostbahnhof to Boxhagener Platz.

Lonely Planet's Top Tip

Mostly in summer – but sometimes at other times – the arches of the fanciful Oberbaumbrücke between Kreuzberg and Friedrichshain, as well as gritty, noisy Warschauer Brücke above the railway tracks, become essentially an open-air stage. A good place to get the party started for free.

Best Places to Eat

- 1990 Vegan Living (p207)
- Khwan (p208)
- Michelberger (p208)
- Hako Ramen am Boxi (p207)
- Futura (p208)

For reviews, see p206.

Best Places to Drink

- Hops & Barley (p209)
- Tentación (p209)
- Krass Böser Wolf (p209)
- Zeroliq (p209)

For reviews, see p209.

Best Places to Shop

- Flohmarkt am Boxhagener Platz (p212)
- Loveco (p211)
- Prachtmädchen (p213)
- UVR Connected (p213)

For reviews, see p211.

TOP EXPERIENCE

WALK ALONG THE EAST SIDE GALLERY

In 1989, after 28 years, the Berlin Wall, that grim divider of humanity, was finally torn down. Most of it was quickly dismantled, but along Mühlenstrasse, a 1.3km stretch became the East Side Gallery, the world's largest open-air mural strip. Today it's a memorial to the fall of the Wall and the peaceful reunification that followed.

After the Wall fell, 118 artists from 21 countries translated the era's euphoria and optimism into a mix of political statements, drug-induced musings and artistic satire. Look out for Birgit Kinder's *Test the Rest,* showing a Trabi bursting through the Wall, and Thierry Noir's bright cartoon faces, called *Homage to the Young Generation.* Perhaps the most famous piece is *My God, Help Me to Survive This Deadly Love* (pictured above), by Dmitri Vrubel. It shows East German and Soviet leaders Erich Honecker and Leonid Brezhnev locked in a kiss of socialist brotherhood.

Alas, the elements, taggers and disrespectful tourists getting a kick out of signing their favourite picture continue to take a toll on this historic landmark, which has had to be restored twice. The East Side Gallery has also come under attack from property developers. Riverside construction caused several sections of the wall to be moved, despite big protests that were even joined by David Hasselhoff and Roger Waters.

Guided tours on the Wall's history and the murals run on Saturday. Register at infomobil@stiftung-berliner-mauer.de at least a day ahead. Also on weekends, between 2pm and 5pm, multilingual speakers from the Berlin Wall Foundation that now maintains the Gallery stand by to answer your burning Wall-related questions. The foundation also runs the excellent Gedenkstätte Berliner Mauer (p142) in Prenzlauer Berg/Wedding.

DON'T MISS

- Taking a picture in front of your favourite mural.
- Sunset drinks on the riverside lawn behind the East Side Gallery.

PRACTICALITIES

- Map p346, C7
- www.eastsidegalleryberlin.de
- Mühlenstrasse, btwn Oberbaumbrücke & Ostbahnhof
- tours adult/concession €3.50/2.50
- 24hr
- U Warschauer Strasse, S Ostbahnhof, Warschauer Strasse

SIGHTS

This notorious party district also has a serious side, especially when it comes to blockbuster vestiges of the GDR era such as the East Side Gallery, Karl-Marx-Allee and the Stasi HQ. These key sights are all pretty spread out and best reached by public transport or bicycle.

EAST SIDE GALLERY — LANDMARK

See p204.

BOXHAGENER PLATZ — SQUARE

Map p346 (Boxhagener Platz; 24hr; P; 240, S Warschauer Strasse, U Samariterstrasse, Warschauer Strasse) The heart of Friedrichshain, 'Boxi' is a lovely, leafy square with benches and a playground. It's framed by restored 19th-century buildings harbouring trend-conscious cafes, artisanal shops, bakeries and fair-fashion boutiques. The area is busiest during the Saturday farmers market (p213) and on Sunday, when a flea market (p212) brings in folks from all over town.

KARL-MARX-ALLEE — STREET

Map p346 (U Strausberger Platz, Weberwiese, Frankfurter Tor) FREE It's easy to feel like Gulliver in the Land of Brobdingnag when walking down monumental Karl-Marx-Allee, one of Berlin's most impressive GDR-era relics. Built between 1952 and 1960, the 90m-wide boulevard runs for 2.3km between Alexanderplatz and Frankfurter Tor and is a fabulous showcase of East German architecture. A considerable source of national pride back then, it provided modern flats for comrades and served as a backdrop for military parades.

Some of the finest East German architects of the day (Hartmann, Henselmann, Hopp, Leucht, Paulick and Souradny) collaborated on KMA's construction, looking to Moscow for inspiration. There, Stalin favoured a style that was essentially a socialist reinterpretation of good old-fashioned neoclassicism. In East Berlin, Prussian building master Karl Friedrich Schinkel was the stylistic godfather, rather than Walter Gropius and the functional modernist aesthetic embraced in West Berlin.

TOP FIVE EAST SIDE GALLERY MURALS

You'll most likely find your own favourite among the 100 or so murals, but here's our take:

It Happened in November (Kani Alavi) A wave of people being squeezed through a breached Wall in a metaphorical rebirth reflects Alavi's recollection of the events of 9 November 1989. Note the different expressions on the faces, ranging from hope, joy and euphoria to disbelief and fear.

Test the Rest (Birgit Kinder) A favourite with photographers, Kinder's painting shows a GDR-era Trabant car (known as a Trabi) bursting through the Wall with its licence plate reading 'November 9, 1989'. It was originally called *Test the Best,* but the artist renamed her work after the image's 2009 restoration.

Homage to the Young Generation (Thierry Noir) This Berlin-based French artist has done work for Wim Wenders and U2, but he's most famous for these cartoon-like heads. Naive, simple and boldly coloured, they symbolise the new-found freedom that followed the Wall's collapse. Noir was one of the few artists who had painted the western side of the Wall before its demise.

Detour to the Japanese Sector (Thomas Klingenstein) Born in East Berlin, Klingenstein spent time in a Stasi prison for dissent before being extradited to West Germany in 1980. This mural was inspired by his childhood love for Japan, where he ended up living from 1984 to the mid-'90s.

My God, Help Me to Survive This Deadly Love (Dmitri Vrubel) The gallery's best-known painting – showing Soviet and GDR leaders Leonid Brezhnev and Erich Honecker locking lips with eyes closed – is based on an actual photograph taken by French journalist Remy Bossu during Brezhnev's 1979 Berlin visit. This kind of kiss between men was an expression of mutual respect in socialist countries.

Living here was considered a privilege; in fact, for a long time there was no better standard of living in East Germany. Flats featured such luxuries as central heating, lifts, tiled baths and built-in kitchens; facades were swathed in Meissen tiles.

COMPUTERSPIELEMUSEUM MUSEUM

Map p346 (Computer Games Museum; ☎030-6098 8577; www.computerspielemuseum.de; Karl-Marx-Allee 93a; adult/concession €9/6; ⏱10am-8pm; U Weberwiese) No matter if you grew up with Nimrod, Pac-Man, World of Warcraft or no games at all, this well-curated museum takes you on a fascinating trip down computer-game memory lane while putting the industry's evolution into historical and cultural context. Colourful and engaging, it features interactive stations amid some 300 original exhibits, including an ultra-rare 1972 Pong arcade machine and its twisted modern cousin, the 'PainStation' (must be over 18 to play…).

An eye-catching feature is the Wall of Hardware, composed of over 50 classics, including an Apple II, an Atari and a 1996 PlayStation. The Milestones installation provides high-tech background on dozens of seminal games such as Pac-Man, SimCity and Tomb Raider.

RAW GELÄNDE CULTURAL CENTRE

Map p346 (Revaler Strasse 99; S Warschauer Strasse, Ostkreuz, U Warschauer Strasse) FREE This jumble of derelict buildings is one of the last subcultural bastions in central Berlin. It began life in 1867 as a train repair station ('Reichsbahn-Ausbesserungs-Werk', aka RAW) and remained in operation until 1994. Since 1999 the graffiti-slathered grounds have been a thriving offbeat sociocultural centre for creatives of all stripes. They also harbour clubs, bars, an indoor skate park, a 'beach' club, a bunker turned climbing wall and a Sunday flea market.

Changes are afoot, however, as the land was bought by an investor in 2015 and the district government green-lit its partial development in 2019, albeit with the proviso that 10% of the area must continue to be set aside for sociocultural ventures.

Search for 'RAW-Gelaende' on Facebook.

URBAN SPREE ARTS CENTRE

Map p346 (☎030-7407 8597; www.urbanspree.com; RAW Gelände, Revaler Strasse 99; ⏱gallery & bookshop 2-7pm Wed-Fri, noon-7pm Sat & Sun

TOP EXPERIENCE

RELAX IN VOLKSPARK FRIEDRICHSHAIN

Berlin's oldest public park has provided relief from urbanity since 1840 but has been hilly only since the late 1940s, when wartime debris was piled here to create two 'mountains' – **Mont Klamott** is the taller, at 78m. Diversions include expansive lawns, tennis courts, a half-pipe, the outdoor cinema **Freiluftkino Friedrichshain** (p211) and a couple of good beer gardens, including **Schoenbrunn** (p208), by a little pond. Kids in tow? Head for the themed playgrounds and enchanting 1913 **Märchenbrunnen** fountain, where frolicking turtle and frog sculptures are flanked by Cinderella, Snow White and other Brothers Grimm stars.

Along Friedenstrasse, the sculpture **Denkmal der Spanienkämpfer** pays respect to the German communists who died in the Spanish Civil War (1936–39) fighting for the International Brigades. The **Friedhof der Märzgefallenen** is a cemetery for the victims of the revolutionary riots of March 1848, as well as for the fallen of the 1918 November Revolution. Finally, there's the **Denkmal des Polnischen Soldaten und des deutschen Antifaschisten**, a memorial to the joint fight against the Nazis by the Polish communist underground army and German communist resistance fighters.

DON'T MISS

- Märchenbrunnen
- Schoenbrunn
- Freiluftkino Friedrichshain

PRACTICALITIES

- Map p346, B1
- btwn Am Friedrichshain, Friedenstrasse, Danziger Strasse & Landsberger Allee
- ⏱24hr
- 🚌142, 200, 🚋M5, M6, M8, M10

Nov-Mar, to 6pm Apr-Oct; M10, U Warschauer Strasse, S Warschauer Strasse) Keep tabs on the latest trends in urban culture at this grassroots arts space in the RAW Gelände compound. Comprising a gallery, a bookshop, artist studios and a concert room, it's especially fun in summer when the beer garden opens, street-food container units open and an eclectic line-up of festivals keeps revellers coming back. The building's facade doubles as an 'Artist Wall', with new urban artworks going up every month or so.

HOLZMARKT — AREA

Map p346 (www.holzmarkt.com; Holzmarktstrasse 25; U Jannowitzbrücke) The Holzmarkt urban village on the Spree is a perpetually evolving creative campus that beautifully embodies Berlin's visionary spirit. Drop by to poke around buildings handcrafted from wood and recycled materials, dance in the world's smallest disco, and watch the boats on parade with a cold beer from the on-site brewery or while tucking into gourmet food at trashy-arty Katerschmaus (p208).

OBERBAUMBRÜCKE — BRIDGE

Map p346 (Oberbaumstrasse; S Warschauer Strasse, U Schlesisches Tor, Warschauer Strasse) With its jaunty towers and turrets, crenellated walls and arched walkways, the Oberbaumbrücke (1896) gets our nod for being Berlin's prettiest bridge. Linking Kreuzberg and Friedrichshain across the Spree, it smoothly integrates a steel centre span by Spanish bridgemeister Santiago Calatrava. Suspended below the elevated railway bridge, Thomas Goldberg's neon installation *Rock, Paper, Scissors* is a popular shutterbug motif.

Added bonus: great sunsets over the city centre with the TV Tower and a nice view upriver where you'll spot, in the distance, the giant aluminium sculpture called Molecule Man (p185) by American artist Jonathan Borofsky. In summer, street musicians and artists often turn the bridge into an impromptu party zone.

EATING

Friedrichshain does bars best, but times are changing. To be sure, you'll still find plenty of quick-feed shops, but evolving demographics also translate into a United Nations of restaurants catering to folks with deeper pockets and more sophisticated palates. And with a growing crop of vegan outlets, vegetarians, too, should be in meat-free heaven.

★1990 VEGAN LIVING — VEGAN €

Map p346 (030-8561 4761; www.restaurant-1990.de; Krossener Strasse 19; small plates €4.20, mains €9.90; noon-10.30pm Mon-Sat, 1-10.30pm Sun; M10, M13, U Samariterstrasse, Warschauer Strasse) Serving a vibrant range of small and large bowls, this family-run Vietnamese joint channels the unassuming, buzzy vibe of the streets of Hanoi. Inside you'll be embraced by an array of imported knick-knacks, while outside tables give you a full-on view of the Boxhagener Platz action.

SILO COFFEE — CAFE €

Map p346 (www.silo-coffee.com; Gabriel-Max-Strasse 4; dishes €6-12; 9.30am-3.30pm Mon-Fri, to 5pm Sat & Sun; M10, M13, U Warschauer Strasse, S Warschauer Strasse) If you've greeted the day with bloodshot eyes, get back in gear at this Aussie-run coffee and brunch joint favoured by Friedrichshain's hip and international crowds. Beans from local Fjord Coffee Roasters ensure possibly the best flat white in town, while sourdough from Sironi (Markthalle Neun) adds scrumptiousness to the poached-egg avo toast.

HAKO RAMEN AM BOXI — JAPANESE €

Map p346 (030-8442 6700; www.hakoramen.com; Boxhagener Strasse 26; mains €9-12; noon-10pm; M10, 21, U Samariter Strasse) This cosy ramen spot is full of authentic Japanese flair and the wafting smell of rich broths. Sit at the bar or grab a table to enjoy a warming, savoury noodle bowl based on pork, chicken or vegan broth. (p.s. *hako* translates as 'box' – appropriate, given the location.)

VÖNER — VEGAN €

Map p346 (www.voener.de; Boxhagener Strasse 56; dishes €3.50-6.50; 2-7pm Sun-Fri, noon-10pm Sat; S Ostkreuz) Vöner stands for 'vegan doner kebab' and is a spit-roasted blend of wheat protein, vegetables, soy meal, herbs and spices. It was dreamed up more than 20 years ago by Holger Frerichs, a one-time resident of a so-called *Wagenburg*, a countercultural commune made up of old vans, buses and caravans. The alt-spirit lives on in his original Vöner outlet.

★KHWAN THAI, BARBECUE €€

Map p346 (☎0152 5902 1331; http://khwanberlin.com; RAW Gelände, Revaler Strasse 99; plates €6-23; ⏲6-11.30pm Wed-Sat, 11am-3pm & 5-10.30pm Sun; ; M10, M13, UWarschauer Strasse, SWarschauer Strasse) For some of the best northern Thai barbecue this side of Chiang Mai, pounce on this rustic warehouse ensconced – for now – among the clubs and bars on the RAW Gelände (p206) strip. Your senses will be hooked by the aromatic smoke (*khwan* in Thai) wafting from the wood-fire pit, where flames lick chicken, pork, fish and vegetables to succulent perfection.

FUTURA PIZZA €€

Map p346 (☎030-9839 4408; www.futurapizza.com; Bänschstrasse 91; pizza €8.50-14; ⏲6-11pm Tue-Fri, 5-11pm Sat & Sun; UFrankfurter Allee) Berlin's obsession with Neapolitan pizza shows no sign of abating, and Futura has kicked up the quality another notch. Certified *pizzaiolo* Allesandro Leonardi, covered in tattoos, puts a premium on top ingredients to decorate pies that are good to the last crumb. If possible, save room for the pistachio tiramisu.

FISCHSCHUPPEN SEAFOOD €€

Map p346 (☎030-9147 6207; www.facebook.com/Fischschuppen; Boxhagener Strasse 68; mains €6-24; ⏲noon-10.30pm; SOstkreuz) This shop-restaurant gets salty flair not only from its big selection of sustainably caught, fresh fish but also from its ship-cabin-like wooden walls, big aquarium and fishy mural. To sample the full bounty of lakes and sea, order the mixed grilled-fish platter. Alternatively, to fill up on a budget, get your hands greasy with a serving of fish 'n' chips.

SPÄTZLE & KNÖDEL GERMAN €€

Map p346 (☎030-2757 1151; www.spaetzleknoedel.de; Wühlischstrasse 20; mains €9-16; ⏲4-10pm Mon-Fri, 3-10pm Sat & Sun; USamariterstrasse) This elbows-on-the-table gastropub provides a southern German comfort-food fix, including roast pork with dark-beer gravy, goulash with red cabbage and, of course, the eponymous *Spaetzle* (German mac 'n' cheese) and *Knödel* (dumplings). Bonus: Bavarian Riegele, Maisel and Weihenstephan beers on tap.

SCHOENBRUNN AUSTRIAN €€

Map p346 (☎030-453 056 525; www.schoenbrunn.net; Am Schwanenteich, Volkspark Friedrichshain; mains €16-23, pizza €9-12; ⏲restaurant noon-10pm Mon-Fri, 10am-10pm Sat & Sun Mar-Nov, beer garden 4pm-midnight Mon-Fri, from noon Sat & Sun Apr-Sep; ; 200, 240, M4, M5, M6, M8) Watch snow-white swans drift around their pond in the middle of Volkspark Friedrichshain (p206) while tucking into Austrian fare with Mediterranean touches. If you're not in the mood for the formal restaurant, report to the beer garden for a cold one paired with pizza or sausage. Breakfast (€6 to €12) is served until 2pm on weekends.

★MICHELBERGER INTERNATIONAL €€€

Map p346 (☎030-2977 8590; www.michelbergerhotel.com; Warschauer Strasse 39; dinner tasting menu €32; ⏲8am-1pm & 6-10pm; ; SWarschauer Strasse, UWarschauer Strasse) Ensconced in one of Berlin's coolest hotels (p251), Michelberger makes creative dinners from whatever its local organic farmers, hunters and foragers have supplied that day. Both vegans and omnivores can be accommodated. Sit inside the lofty, white-tiled restaurant or in the breezy courtyard.

SKYKITCHEN & SKYBAR INTERNATIONAL €€€

Map p346 (☎030-4530 532 620; www.skykitchen.berlin; Landsberger Allee 106; 6-course dinner €119; ⏲6-11pm Tue-Sat; ; 21, M4, M5, M6, M8, M10, SLandsberger Allee) Book early to snag a window table facing the TV Tower for a romantic dinner at this unpretentious Michelin-starred restaurant. On the 12th floor of the Andel's hotel, champion chef (and genuine Berliner!) Alexander Koppe deftly injects global finesse into classic German fare using top-flight ingredients. The bar does a stellar job to match the fabulous food. Vegetarian menu available too.

KATERSCHMAUS EUROPEAN €€€

Map p346 (☎0152-2941 3262; www.katerschmaus.de; Holzmarktstrasse 25; mains €21-45; ⏲1-11pm Tue-Sat; ; UJannowitzbrücke, SJannowitzbrücke) This kitty (*Kater* is a male cat in German) is sleek and rustic-chic and hides out riverside in a carefully designed ramshackle space on the Holzmarkt (p207) cultural playground. It inclines towards ingredients from regional suppliers and will have you purring for its wicked crème brûlée.

DRINKING & NIGHTLIFE

Along with Kreuzberg, Friedrichshain is Berlin's seminal fun and party zone, with hot-stepping venues centred on the RAW Gelände cultural centre (p206), along Simon-Dach-Strasse and around the Ostkreuz train station. The neighbourhood is also usually home to the city's best techno-electro clubs.

HOPS & BARLEY
MICROBREWERY

Map p346 (030-2936 7534; www.hopsandbarley-berlin.de; Wühlischstrasse 22/23; 5pm-late Mon-Fri, from 3pm Sat & Sun; M13, U Warschauer Strasse, S Warschauer Strasse) Conversation flows as freely as the unfiltered pilsner, malty *Dunkel* (dark) and fruity *Weizen* (wheat) produced right here at one of Berlin's oldest craft breweries (since 2008). The pub is inside a former butcher's shop and still has the tiled walls to prove it. For variety, the brewmeisters also produce weekly blackboard specials and potent unfiltered cider.

Two beamers project football (soccer) games.

TENTACIÓN
BAR

Map p346 (030-2393 0401; www.tentacion-mezcalothek.de; Scharnweberstrasse 32; 5-11pm Wed-Sat, noon-8pm Sun; U Samariterstrasse) Resisting temptation can be tough. Forget about it when visiting Tentación (Spanish for 'temptation'); its main ammo is the Latin American cult spirit mezcal, which reportedly has psychedelic qualities. The tiny parlour dispenses a huge selection of the wicked potion along with Mala Vida, the owner-brewed craft beer. A small menu of feisty Oaxacan munchies is on stand-by for the peckish.

KRASS BÖSER WOLF
BAR

(0157 3966 2585; www.krassboeserwolf.de; Markgrafendamm 36; 6pm-3am Mon-Sat; S Ostkreuz) Although the name translates roughly as 'very mean wolf', this dimly lit lair is actually a friendly imbibing spot. Pop by to wind down the day with a cold beer from the tap or rev things up a notch with one of the classic or original cocktails.

BRIEFMARKEN WEINE
WINE BAR

Map p346 (030-4202 5292; www.briefmarkenweine.eu; Karl-Marx-Allee 99; 7pm-midnight Mon & Wed-Sat, 5pm-midnight Tue; U Weberwiese) For *dolce vita* right on socialist-era Karl-Marx-Allee, head to this charmingly nostalgic Italian wine bar ensconced in a former stamp shop. The original wooden cabinets cradle a hand-picked selection of Italian bottles that complement a snack menu of yummy cheeses, prosciutto and salami, plus a pasta dish of the day. Best to book ahead.

ZEROLIQ
BAR

Map p346 (0157 9237 4581; www.zeroliq.com; Boxhagener Strasse 104; 5pm-midnight Thu-Sat; U Samariterstrasse) Keep your brain clear and sensitise your taste buds by sipping cocktails sans alcohol at aptly named Zeroliq. Aside from serving nearly three dozen booze-free craft beers, it also pours de-alcoholised wines and vegan mocktails that won't make you miss the real thing. Try the Summer in Berlin or the Zeroligroni.

MONSTER RONSON'S ICHIBAN KARAOKE
KARAOKE

Map p346 (030-8975 1327; www.karaoke-monster.de; Warschauer Strasse 34; 7-11pm Tue, Thu & Fri, 2-11pm Sat & Sun; S Warschauer Strasse, U Warschauer Strasse) Knock back a couple of brewskis if you need to loosen your nerves before belting out your best Adele or Lady Gaga at this mad, great karaoke joint. Shy types can book a private booth for music and mischief.

Currently it rents only private karaoke cabins for up to 12 persons. All must be from one household, couples or families.

BERGHAIN AS ART SPACE

Only world-class spin-masters heat up **Berghain** (Map p346; www.berghain.de; Am Wriezener Bahnhof; Fri-Mon; S Ostbahnhof), the hedonistic bass-junkie hellhole inside a labyrinthine former power plant. With clubs closed for COVID, it has been converted into an art-exhibition hall for an open-ended run. On view are edgy works by top contemporary artists such as Elmgreen & Dragset, Olafur Eliasson and Katharina Grosse. For tickets and more information, see http://studio.berlin.

CASSIOPEIA CLUB

Map p346 (www.cassiopeia-berlin.de; Gate 2, RAW Gelände, Revaler Strasse 99; ⏲from 7pm or later Tue-Sun; M10, M13, U Warschauer Strasse, S Warschauer Strasse) No wild dance-a-thons during the pandemic, but this delightfully trashy venue is trying to keep alive by only hosting corona-compatible events such as quiz nights and spoken-word sessions, and beaming others (DJ sets and concerts) straight to you via livestream.

HAUBENTAUCHER CLUB

Map p346 (www.haubentaucher.berlin; RAW Gelände, Revaler Strasse 99, Gate 1; admission varies, usually €6; ⏲noon-late Mon-Fri, from 11am Sat & Sun May-Sep; 📶; M10, M13, U Warschauer Strasse, S Warschauer Strasse) Behind brick walls on the graffiti-festooned RAW Gelände (p206) hides this ingenious urban beach club for day-to-night partying amid industrial charm and Med flair. At its heart is a good-size heated outdoor swimming pool flanked by a sun deck of white stone and wooden planks. For shade, retreat to the vine-festooned garden lounge.

On occasion, events in the adjacent bar-and-club hall carry the party into the night.

CRACK BELLMER BAR

Map p346 (☎030-3198 7929; www.crackbellmer.de; RAW Gelände, Revaler Strasse 99; ⏲5pm-late Thu-Sat; M10, M13, U Warschauer Strasse, S Warschauer Strasse) In the RAW (p206) compound, behind the requisite street-art-festooned facade, awaits this bar-club combo with vintage sofas, lofty ceilings and chandeliers. Popular for pre-party warm-ups, post-party nightcaps and any time in between.

SÜSS WAR GESTERN BAR

Map p346 (Wühlischstrasse 43; ⏲8pm-late Mon-Sat; M13, U Warschauer Strasse, Samariterstrasse, S Warschauer Strasse, Ostkreuz) A machine-gun-toting rabbit is the ironic mascot of this long-running DJ bar with well-mixed cocktails (try the eponymous Süss War Gestern with real ginger, ginger ale and whisky), loud house, and a crowd of locals, newcomers and visitors.

GROSSE FREIHEIT 114 GAY

Map p346 (☎0163 683 1601; www.grosse-freiheit-114.de; Boxhagener Strasse 114; ⏲7pm-late Wed & Sat; U Frankfurter Tor) Named for a lane in Hamburg's red-light district where the Beatles cut their teeth, Grosse Freiheit is a popular men-only harbour for a drink and meet-up, complete with darts, a jukebox and darkrooms.

The campy nautical decor is reminiscent of the way most 1980s films portrayed gay bars. On Wednesday drinks are two-for-one.

HIMMELREICH GAY & LESBIAN

Map p346 (☎030-2936 9292; www.himmelreich-berlin.de; Simon-Dach-Strasse 36; ⏲5pm-2am or later Mon-Sat, 4pm-1am or later Sun; M13, M10, S Warschauer Strasse, U Warschauer Strasse) This candle-lit and pretence-free drinking cove is a great place to launch or wrap up a night on the razzle – or any time in between, quite frankly. Try the Prosit Beer, especially brewed for Himmelreich, while keeping an eye on the parade of folks from the sidewalk terrace. There's also an impressive selection of gin-based long drinks and a wicked organic cider. On Wednesday many drinks are two-for-one.

ZUM SCHMUTZIGEN HOBBY GAY

Map p346 (☎030-3646 8446; www.facebook.com/zumschmutzigenhobby; RAW Gelände, Revaler Strasse 99, Gate 2; ⏲6pm-late; M10, M13, S Warschauer Strasse, U Warschauer Strasse) Although founder and trash-drag deity Nina Queer has moved on to other pastures, this living-room-size, deliciously kitsch and wacky party den in a former fire station is still swarmed nightly. Predominantly gay, but everyone welcome.

☆ ENTERTAINMENT

THE WALL COMEDY CLUB COMEDY

Map p346 (www.thewallcomedy.com; Grünberger Strasse 84; ⏲7pm-1am Mon-Wed, to 3am Thu-Sat; M13, U Samariterstrasse) Hosts an eclectic roster of English-language stand-up comedy showcases every night, featuring international touring talent as well as some funny German comics. If you dare, sign up for Tuesday's open-mic night.

RADIALSYSTEM V PERFORMING ARTS

Map p346 (☎tickets 030-288 788 588; www.radialsystem.de; Holzmarktstrasse 33; 📶; S Ostbahnhof) 'Space for arts and ideas' is the motto of this progressive performance space in a 19th-century riverside pump station. Its programming blurs the boundaries between the arts to nurture new forms of creative expression: contemporary dance meets medieval music, poetry meets pop tunes, painting meets digital.

The pleasant cafe-bar with a riverside terrace opens from 10am on event days.

KINO INTERNATIONAL CINEMA

Map p346 (☎030-2475 6011; www.yorck.de; Karl-Marx-Allee 33; tickets €7.50-10; USchillingstrasse) The East German film elite once held its movie premieres in this 1960s cinema, whose glamorous array of chandeliers and glitter curtains is a show in itself. Today it presents smartly curated international indie hit flicks daily, usually in the original language with German subtitles.

The panorama bar is great for pre- or post-screening libations. The Monday 10pm time slot is reserved for gay-themed movies.

FREILUFTKINO FRIEDRICHSHAIN CINEMA

Map p346 (☎030-2936 1629; www.freiluftkino-berlin.de; Volkspark Friedrichshain; tickets €8.50; ⏰mid-May–mid-Sep; 🚊M5, M6, M8, M10) Cradled by Volkspark Friedrichshain (p206), this open-air cinema has seating for 1500 on comfortable benches with backrests, plus a lawn with space for 300 more film fans. A kiosk sells drinks and snacks, and you're free to bring a picnic. Unless flagged otherwise, movies are dubbed into German.

KINO INTIMES CINEMA

Map p346 (www.kino-intimes.de; Boxhagener Strasse 107; adult/concession €6.90/4.90; 🚊21, UFrankfurter Tor) Saved from extinction by a local initiative in 2019, this petite flick palace has presented movies since the silent era and, though now renovated, is still a delightful vintage venue to catch the latest art-house movies. Its facade is an ever-evolving canvas of street art.

FREILUFTKINO INSEL IM CASSIOPEIA CINEMA

Map p346 (☎030-3512 2449; www.freiluftkino-insel.de; RAW Gelände, Revaler Strasse 99; tickets €8.50; ⏰around 9.30pm Mon, Tue, Thu & Sun May-Sep; 🚊M10, M13, SWarschauer Strasse, UWarschauer Strasse) Part of the Cassiopeia beer garden and club complex in the RAW Gelände, this 350-seat outdoor cinema shows an eclectic roster of indie movies in their original language with German or English subtitles.

WORTH A DETOUR

LITTLE HANOI: DONG XUAN CENTER

A sprawling cluster of six industrial halls repurposed from a Cold War–era factory for carbon products, today **Dong Xuan Center** (☎030-5515 2038; www.dongxuan-berlin.de; Herzbergstrasse 128-139, Lichtenberg; ⏰10am-8pm Wed-Mon; 🚊M8) is the cultural, culinary and commercial hub of Berlin's sizeable Vietnamese community. Each building is lined with long corridors where vendors sell the gamut of imports from the motherland: clothing, plastic flowers, produce and sacks of rice. Even if you're not buying, it's fun to browse and wrap up a visit with a bowl of authentic *pho* soup.

MERCEDES-BENZ ARENA LIVE MUSIC

Map p346 (☎tickets 030-206 070 8899; www.mercedes-benz-arena-berlin.de; Mühlenstrasse 12-30; SOstbahnhof, Warschauer Strasse, UWarschauer Strasse) The jewel among Berlin's multiuse indoor venues, this 17,000-seat arena regularly welcomes international entertainment royalty from Dua Lipa to Andrea Bocelli. It's also home turf for the city's professional ice-hockey team, the Eisbären Berlin, and basketball team, Alba Berlin.

SHOPPING

Friedrichshain has come along in the shopping department, with increasingly chic indie clothing boutiques, concept stores, eco-fashions and lifestyle accessories sprinkled around Boxhagener Platz (especially Wühlischstrasse) and along Sonntagstrasse and its side streets near Ostkreuz station.

★LOVECO FASHION & ACCESSORIES

Map p346 (www.loveco-shop.de; Sonntagstrasse 29; ⏰noon-10pm Mon-Fri, 11am-7pm Sat; SOstkreuz) Lovable Loveco gets a big eco-nod of approval for its huge selection of vegan, sustainable and fair-trade clothing and accessories by local and international labels such as Armed Angels, People Tree and

WORTH A DETOUR

STASI SIGHTS IN EAST BERLIN

In East Germany, the walls had ears. Modelled after the Soviet KGB, the GDR's Ministerium für Staatssicherheit (Ministry for State Security, Mfs or 'Stasi' for short) was founded in 1950. It was secret police, central intelligence agency and bureau of criminal investigation all rolled into one. Called the 'shield and sword' of the SED (the sole East German party), it put millions of GDR citizens under surveillance in order to protect the SED leadership and suppress internal opposition. By the end, the Stasi had 91,000 official full-time employees and 189,000 IMs (inoffizielle Mitarbeiter, unofficial informants). The latter were regular folks recruited to spy on their coworkers, friends, family and neighbours. There were also 3000 IMs in West Germany.

When the Wall fell, the Stasi fell with it. Thousands of citizens stormed the Mfs headquarters in January 1990, putting an end to the shredding of documents that revealed the full extent of institutionalised surveillance and repression. The often cunningly low-tech surveillance devices (hidden in watering cans, rocks, even neckties) are among the exhibits in the **Stasimuseum** (030-553 6854; www.stasimuseum.de; Haus 1, Normannenstrasse 20; adult/concession €8/6, tour additional €2; 10am-6pm Mon-Fri, 11am-6pm Sat & Sun, English tours 3pm Mon, Thu & Sat; U Magdalenenstrasse), which occupies the fortress-like ministry headquarters. A highlight is the 'lion's den', the stuffy offices and private quarters of Erich Mielke, Stasi head for an incredible 32 years, from 1957 until the bitter end. Other rooms introduce the ideology, rituals and institutions of East German society. Information panels are partly in English. For a more in-depth experience, join a tour or get the audioguide (€2).

Victims of the Stasi often ended up in the **Stasi prison** (Gedenkstätte Berlin-Hohenschönhausen; 030-9860 8230; www.stiftung-hsh.de; Genslerstrasse 66; tours adult/concession €6/3, exhibit free; tours in English 11.45am, 2.15pm & 3.45pm, more frequent German tours 10am-4pm, exhibit 9am-6pm; P; M5) in Lichtenberg, a few kilometres from the headquarters. The prison, too, is now a memorial site today and is, if anything, even creepier than the museum. **Prison tours**, sometimes led by former detainees, reveal the full extent of the cruelty perpetrated upon thousands of suspected political opponents, many utterly innocent. If you've seen the Academy Award–winning film *The Lives of Others*, you may recognise many of the settings. A free **exhibit** uses photographs, objects and media stations to document the lives of those behind bars as well as the Stasi staff that kept them there.

Old maps of East Berlin show a blank spot where the prison is: officially, it did not exist. In reality, the compound had three incarnations. Right after WWII the Soviets used it to process prisoners (mostly Nazis, or suspected Nazis) destined for the gulag. More than 3000 detainees died here due to atrocious conditions – usually by freezing in their unheated cells – until the Western Allies intervened in October 1946.

The Soviets then made it a regular prison, dreaded especially for its 'U-Boat', an underground tract of damp, windowless cells outfitted only with a wooden bench and a bucket. Prisoners were subjected to interrogations, beatings, sleep deprivation and water torture. Everybody signed a confession sooner or later.

In 1951 the Soviets handed the prison over to the Stasi, who adopted its mentors' methods. Prisoners were locked up in the U-Boat until a new, much bigger cell block was built, with prisoner labour, in the late '50s. Psycho-terror now replaced physical torture: inmates suffered total isolation and sensory deprivation. Only the collapse of the GDR put an end to the horror.

LovJoi. All pieces are handpicked by owner Christina and beautifully presented in the stylish store with its signature swing.

See the website for locations of branches in Kreuzberg and Schöneberg.

FLOHMARKT BOXHAGENER PLATZ MARKET

Map p346 (Boxhagener Platz; 10am-6pm Sun; M13, S Warschauer Strasse, U Warschauer Strasse, Samariterstrasse) Wrapped around leafy Boxhagener Platz, this fun flea market is just a java whiff away from oodles of convivial cafes. Although the presence of pro vendors has grown, there are still plenty of regular folks here to unload their spring-cleaning detritus at bargain prices.

PRACHTMÄDCHEN FASHION & ACCESSORIES

Map p346 (☎030-9700 2780; www.prachtmaedchen.de; Wühlischstrasse 28; ⏱noon-7pm Mon-Fri, 11am-6pm Sat; 🚋M13, SWarschauer Strasse, UWarschauer Strasse) Low-key and friendly, this pioneer on Wühlischstrasse (aka Friedrichshain's 'fashion mile') is great for kitting yourself out head to toe with affordable threads and accessories by grown-up streetwear labels and still-under-the-radar newcomers.

UVR CONNECTED FASHION & ACCESSORIES

Map p346 (www.uvr-connected.de; Gärtnerstrasse 5; ⏱noon-7pm Mon-Fri, 11am-7pm Sat; 🚋M10, M13, USamariterstrasse, Warschauer Strasse, SWarschauer Strasse) This Berlin-based label designs urban fashions for grown-up men and women with a penchant for classic styles and subdued colours. Also stocks other 'it' brands, such as Bench, Ben Sherman, Minimum and Selected. Plenty of accessories too.

WOCHENMARKT BOXHAGENER PLATZ MARKET

Map p346 (Boxhagener Platz; ⏱9am-3.30pm Sat; 🚋M10, M13, USamariterstrasse, Frankfurter Tor) This popular farmers market brings out the entire neighbourhood for fresh fare along with homemade liqueurs, international cheeses, exotic spices, smoked fish, hemp muesli, purple potatoes and other culinary delights. There are plenty of snack stands, along with crafts and gift items, many of them handmade.

STRAWBETTY CLOTHING

Map p346 (☎030-8999 3663; www.strawbetty.com; Wühlischstrasse 25; ⏱noon-7pm Mon-Fri, 11am-6pm Sat; 🚋M13, UWarschauer Strasse, SWarschauer Strasse, Ostkreuz) No matter if you're a dedicated rockabella or just want to look good at the next theme party, this boutique will kit you out with petticoats, sailor dresses, capri pants, boleros and other feminine vintage threads. It also stocks the right bag, hat and jewellery to perfect the fashion time warp.

SOMETIMES COLOURED VINTAGE

Map p346 (☎030-2935 2075; www.facebook.com/sometimescoloured; Grünberger Strasse 90; ⏱noon-7pm Tue-Sat; USamariterstrasse) As its name implies, most threads sold at this secondhand boutique are in subdued colours, whether it's jet black, charcoal grey or midnight blue. All are washed, in great condition and include contemporary labels (Adidas, Cos, The Kooples). For genuine vintage gems, visit sister store King Kong Vintage on the same street.

RAW FLOHMARKT MARKET

Map p346 (www.rawflohmarkt.de; RAW Gelände, Revaler Strasse 99; ⏱8am-5pm Sun; 🚋M10, M13, SWarschauer Strasse, UWarschauer Strasse) Bargains abound at this smallish flea market right on the grounds of RAW Gelände (p206), a train repair station turned party village. It's wonderfully free of professional sellers, meaning you'll find everything from the proverbial kitchen sink to 1970s go-go boots. There are toilet blocks for trying things on, and street-food stalls and a beer garden provide handy post-shopping pit stops.

GROSSER ANTIKMARKT OSTBAHNHOF ANTIQUES

Map p346 (Erich-Steinfurth-Strasse; ⏱9am-5pm Sun; SOstbahnhof) If you're after antiques and collectables, head to this sprawling market outside the Ostbahnhof's north exit. Up to 150 vendors hawk yesteryear's collectables. Forage for Iron Curtain–era relics, old coins, gramophone records, books, stamps, jewellery and bric-a-brac, but don't expect clothing or recent knick-knacks.

SPORTS & ACTIVITIES

BERLIN CRAFT BEER EXPERIENCE WALKING

Map p346 (☎01577 921 6971; www.berlincraftbeerexperience.com; tours €46; ⏱2pm Mon & Wed-Sat; UWarschauer Strasse, SWarschauer Strasse) Beer aficionado Cliff Kinchen has been leading insightful three- to four-hour tours of the Berlin craft-beer scene since 2014. Tours drop in at three stops (pubs or breweries) around Friedrichshain and/or Kreuzberg, and include at least five sud samples and a hot snack. Book online. Tours depart from Warschauer Strasse U-Bahn station.

City West & Charlottenburg

KURFÜRSTENDAMM & AROUND | SAVIGNYPLATZ & KANTSTRASSE

Neighbourhood Top Five

❶ **Schloss Charlottenburg** (p216) Marvelling at the pomposity of Prussian royal life, then relaxing with a picnic by the carp pond in the palace park.

❷ **Teufelsberg** (p221) Exploring awesome street art inside a ruined Cold War–era spy station on top of a hill built from WWII debris.

❸ **Kaiser-Wilhelm-Gedächtniskirche** (p220) Considering the horrors of war at this majestically ruined 19th-century church.

❹ **Zoo Berlin** (p223) Communing with creatures ranging from apes to zebras at the world's most species-rich animal park, founded in the mid-19th century.

❺ **Bikini Berlin** (p226) Shopping for idiosyncratic Berlin fashions and accessories at this architecturally stunning concept mall with interesting food options to boot.

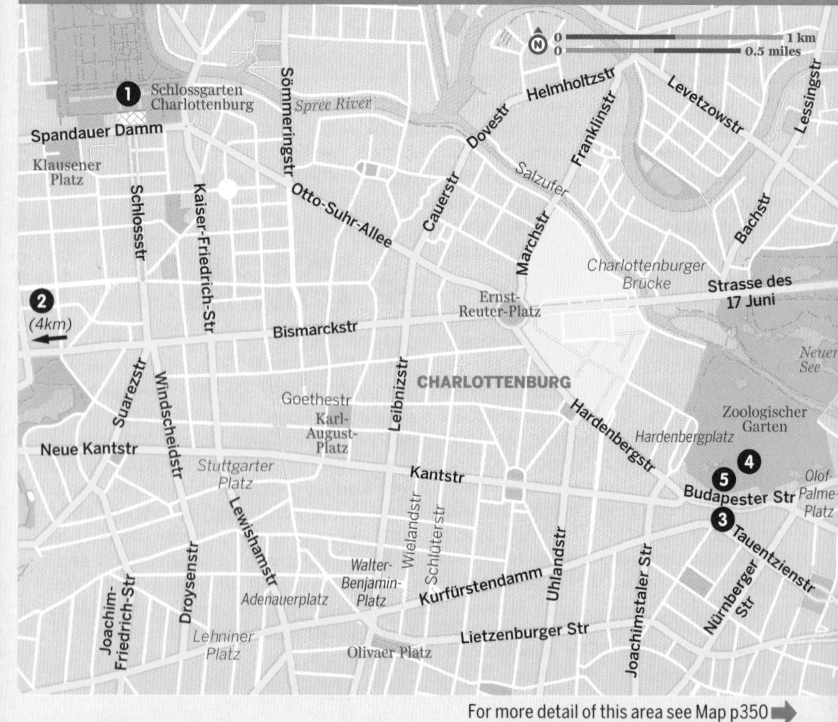

For more detail of this area see Map p350

Explore City West & Charlottenburg

West Berlin's commercial hub during the city's Cold War–era division, Charlottenburg still counts its famous shopping boulevard, the Kurfürstendamm (p220), among its biggest drawcards. Fashionable boutiques mix it up with high-street chains and department stores along this strip and its leafy side streets. It continues east as Tauentzienstrasse, leading to the humongous KaDeWe (p177) department store.

Recent construction and revitalisation characterise the City West area around the landmark Kaiser-Wilhelm-Gedächtniskirche (p220), a ruined church turned anti-war memorial. Nearby, elephants trumpet and pandas cuddle in the famous Zoo Berlin (p223), a sure-fire hit with kids.

After satisfying your shopping urges, head out to must-see Schloss Charlottenburg (p216) for a look at the lifestyles of Prussian royalty. Tour the fancifully decorated living quarters, then relax with a stroll in lushly landscaped gardens. In fine weather, consider bringing a picnic. A trip to the palace is easily combined with a spin around the trio of excellent art museums nearby.

Local Life

Shopping Shop till you drop at high-street chains and high-fashion boutiques along Ku'damm (p220) and its side streets or at the Bikini Berlin (p226) concept mall.

The Asian mile Find your favourite among the authentic eateries in Berlin's Little Asia (p222) along Kantstrasse.

Cafe hang-outs Take an afternoon break with a cappuccino and sinful cakes at the classic Kuchenladen (p222) or in the garden of the cafe at the Literaturhaus (p222).

Getting There & Away

Bus Bus 100 and 200 both depart from Zoologischer Garten. M19 and M29 travel along Kurfürstendamm. Lines 109 and M45 go to Schloss Charlottenburg.

S-Bahn S5 and S7 link to Hauptbahnhof and Alexanderplatz via Zoologischer Garten and link with the circle line S41/S42 at Westkreuz.

U-Bahn Uhlandstrasse, Kurfürstendamm and Wittenbergplatz stations (U1) put you right in shopping central. The U2 passes through Zoologischer Garten.

Lonely Planet's Top Tip

Leaving from Bahnhof Zoologischer Garten, buses 100 and 200 pass many blockbuster sights (including Potsdamer Platz and the Reichstag) on their route through the central city to Alexanderplatz.

Best Places to Eat

- Mine Restaurant (p222)
- Madame Ngo (p222)
- Kantini Berlin (p221)
- Christopher's (p223)
- Kuchenladen (p222)

For reviews, see p221.

Best Places to Drink

- Schleusenkrug (p224)
- Diener Tattersall (p224)
- Monkey Bar (p224)
- Bar Zentral (p224)
- Bar am Steinplatz (p224)

For reviews, see p223.

Best Shopping

- Bikini Berlin (p226)
- Manufactum (p226)
- Stilwerk (p226)
- Taschen Store Berlin (p226)

For reviews, see p226.

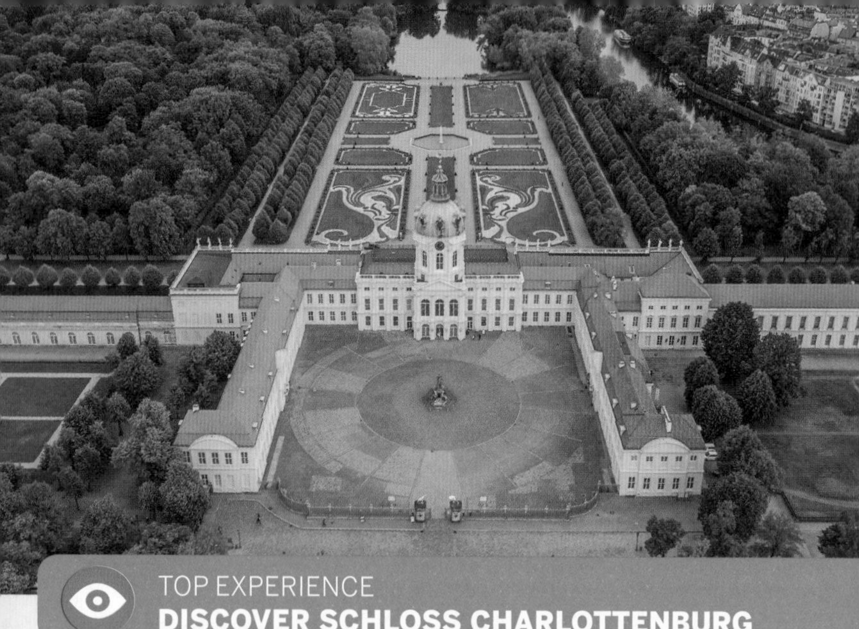

TOP EXPERIENCE

DISCOVER SCHLOSS CHARLOTTENBURG

This exquisite baroque palace is the best place in Berlin to soak up the grandeur of the Hohenzollern clan, who ruled Brandenburg and later Prussia from 1415 to 1918. A visit is especially pleasant in summer, when you can fold a stroll around the garden into a day of peeking at treasures and lavishly furnished period rooms reflecting centuries of royal tastes and lifestyles.

The palace started out rather modestly, as a petite summer retreat built for Sophie-Charlotte, wife of Elector Friedrich III, and was expanded in the mode of Versailles after the elector's promotion to king in 1701. Subsequent royals dabbled with the compound, most notably Frederick the Great, who added the spectacular Neuer Flügel. Reconstruction of the Schloss after its WWII drubbing was completed in 1966.

The grand complex consists of the main palace and three smaller structures scattered about the sprawling **Schlossgarten Charlottenburg** (Charlottenburg Palace Park; donation €2; ⏲8am-dusk) FREE, which is part formal French baroque garden, part unruly English landscape and all idyllic playground. Hidden among the shady paths, flower beds, lawns, mature trees and carp pond are the sombre Mausoleum, the playful Belvedere and the elegant Neuer Pavillon.

Altes Schloss

Also known as the Nering-Eosander Building after its two architects, the **Altes Schloss** (Old Palace; adult/concession €12/8; ⏲10am-5.30pm Tue-Sun Apr-Oct, to 4.30pm Tue-Sun Nov-Mar) is the central, and oldest, section of the palace, and is fronted by Andreas Schlüter's grand equestrian statue of the Great Elector (1699). Inside, the baroque living quarters of Friedrich I and Sophie-Charlotte are an extravaganza in stucco and brocade. After a comprehensive restoration, you can now again swoon over the **Oak Gallery**, a wood-panelled festival hall draped in family

DON'T MISS

- Frederick the Great's apartments in the Neuer Flügel
- Schlossgarten Charlottenburg
- Neuer Flügel's paintings by French 18th-century masters

PRACTICALITIES

- off Map p350
- ☎030-320 910
- www.spsg.de
- Spandauer Damm 10-22
- varies by bldg, day pass to all open bldgs adult/concession €17/13
- ⏲hrs vary by building
- 🚌M45, 109, 309, Ⓤ Richard-Wagner-Platz, Sophie-Charlotte-Platz

portraits; the charming **Oval Hall** overlooking the park; Friedrich I's bedchamber, with its grand bed and the first-ever bathroom in a baroque palace; and the **Palace Chapel**, with its trompe l'œil arches. The king's passion for precious china is reflected in the dazzling **Porcelain Cabinet**, smothered in nearly 3000 pieces of Chinese and Japanese blue ware. Upstairs, an exhibition charts the rise of the Hohenzollern dynasty from Brandenburg electors to German emperors. Also here is the **Silver Vault**, a pirate ship's worth of royal tableware and silverware.

Neuer Flügel

Dreamed up by Frederick the Great and masterminded in 1746 by the period's star architect Georg Wenzeslaus von Knobelsdorff, the **Neuer Flügel** (New Wing; adult/concession incl tour or audioguide €12/8; ⌚10am-5.30pm Tue-Sun Apr-Oct, to 4.30pm Nov-Mar) extension of the Old Palace contains not only the private quarters of the king and his successors but also a pair of dazzling festival halls from the rococo period: the confection-like **White Hall** and the mirrored and gilded **Golden Gallery**. Also on view is a prized collection of paintings by Watteau, Pesne and other French 18th-century masters. Frederick the Great's nephew and successor King Friedrich Wilhelm II added a summer residence with Chinese and Etruscan design elements as well as the neoclassical **Winter Chambers**. Later his daughter-in-law, the popular Queen Luise, moved into the latter. Note her stunning bedroom with furniture by Karl Friedrich Schinkel.

Neuer Pavillon

Returning from a trip to Italy, Friedrich Wilhelm III (r 1797–1848) commissioned Karl Friedrich Schinkel to design the **Neuer Pavillon** (New Pavilion; adult/concession €4/3; ⌚10am-5.30pm Tue-Sun Apr-Oct, noon-4pm Tue-Sun Nov-Mar) as a summer retreat modelled on neoclassical Italian villas. Today, the mini-palace shows off Schinkel's many talents as architect, painter and designer, while also presenting sculpture by Christian Daniel Rauch and master paintings by such Schinkel contemporaries as Caspar David Friedrich and Eduard Gaertner.

Belvedere

The late-rococo Belvedere palace, with its distinctive cupola, got its start in 1788 as a private sanctuary for Friedrich Wilhelm II. The exhibit will be closed until the end of 2021, but even from the outside the building is still worth a gander.

Mausoleum

The 1810 temple-shaped **Mausoleum** (adult/concession €3/2; ⌚10am-5.30pm Tue-Sun Apr-Oct) was conceived as the final resting place of Queen Luise, and was twice expanded to make room for other royals, including Kaiser Wilhelm I and his wife, Augusta. Their marble sarcophagi are exquisitely sculpted works of art. More royals are buried in the crypt (closed to the public).

TAKE A BREAK

A good option for a hearty meal and a cold beer is **Brauhaus Lemke am Schloss** (☎030-3087 8979; www.lemke.berlin; Luisenplatz 1; mains €7-15; ⌚5-9.30pm Mon & Tue, 1-9.30pm Wed-Fri, noon-9.30pm Sat & Sun; 🚌M45, 109, 309, Ⓤ Richard-Wagner-Platz), not far from the palace.

From April to October, a lovely way to travel to or from the palace is on the Spree River cruise operated by Reederei Bruno Winkler (p301). Boats usually make the trip twice daily from landing docks at Bahnhof Friedrichstrasse/Reichstagsufer (Map p324) to the palace boat landing just outside the east corner of the park. You can also travel the other way or do a round trip.

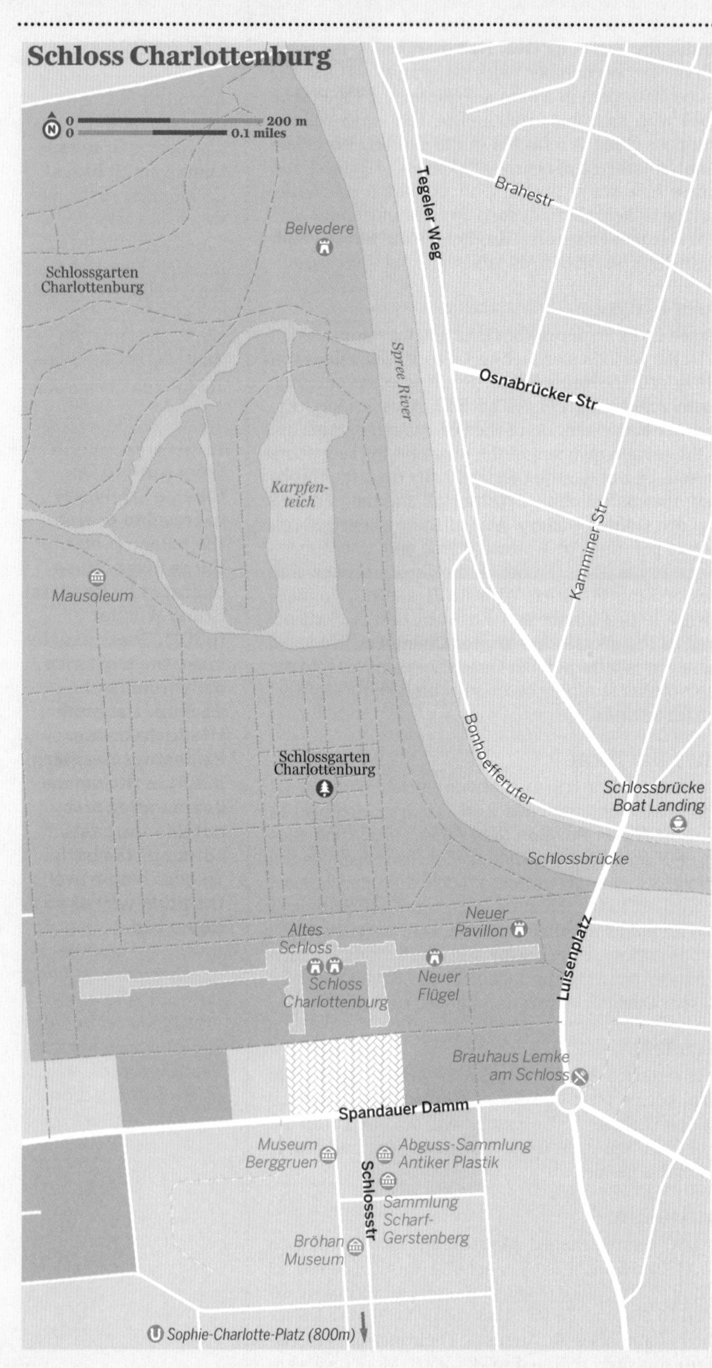
Schloss Charlottenburg
0 200 m
0 0.1 miles
Belvedere
Schlossgarten
Charlottenburg
Tegeler Weg
Brahestr
Spree River
Osnabrücker Str
Karpfen-
teich
Kamminer Str
Mausoleum
Bonhoefferufer
Schlossgarten
Charlottenburg
Schlossbrücke
Boat Landing
Schlossbrücke
Neuer
Pavillon
Altes
Schloss
Luisenplatz
Schloss
Charlottenburg
Neuer
Flügel
Brauhaus Lemke
am Schloss
Spandauer Damm
Museum
Berggruen
Abguss-Sammlung
Antiker Plastik
Schlossstr
Sammlung
Scharf-
Gerstenberg
Bröhan
Museum
Sophie-Charlotte-Platz (800m)

Sammlung Scharf-Gerstenberg

The **Scharf-Gerstenberg Collection** (☎030-266 424 242; Schlossstrasse 70; adult/concession incl Museum Berggruen €12/6; ⌚10am-6pm Tue-Fri, from 11am Sat & Sun) is a splendid lineup of 250 years of surrealist art based on the private collection of the late insurance mogul Otto Gerstenberg. Standouts include Goya's spooky etchings and the creepy dungeon scenes by Italian engraver Giovanni Battista Piranesi. Perhaps even more disturbing is Hans Bellmer's erotically charged *La Poupée* (The Doll, 1936). Upstairs is superb work by René Magritte and Max Ernst, including the former's *Gaspard de la nuit* (1965) and the latter's *Triumph of Love* (1937).

Museum Berggruen

The intimate **Museum Berggruen** (☎030-266 424 242; www.smb.museum/mb; Schlossstrasse 1; adult/concession incl Sammlung Scharf-Gerstenberg €12/6; ⌚10am-6pm Tue-Fri, from 11am Sat & Sun) is for fans of 20th-century art, notably the work of Pablo Picasso, Paul Klee, Henri Matisse and Alberto Giacometti. Its basis is the exceptional private collection of art dealer and collector Heinz Berggruen. In the domed main building – a stately Prussian officers' casino – the focus is on Picasso, with works from all key phases. Standouts include the *Seated Harlequin* from the early rose period and bold cubist canvases such as *Nude Reclining*. In an extension connected via a glass walkway it's off to Klee's poetic world, Matisse's paper cut-outs and Giacometti's sculptures. In the garden, note the monumental double sculpture *United Enemies* by contemporary German artist Thomas Schütte.

Bröhan Museum

The **Bröhan Museum** (☎030-3269 0600; www.broehan-museum.de; Schlossstrasse 1a; adult/concession/under 18yr €8/5/free; ⌚10am-6pm Tue-Sun) spotlights art nouveau, art deco and functionalist furniture and design that rocked the aesthetics from the late 19th century until the 1930s. Its permanent exhibit displays covetable chairs, tables, teapots and other objects by key protagonists, including Hector Guimard, Peter Behrens, Josef Hoffmann and Wilhelm Wagenfeld. Works by Berlin Secession artists complement the exhibits. Changing displays take over the two upper floors and may also temporarily displace the permanent exhibit on the ground floor.

Abguss-Sammlung Antiker Plastik

If you are a fan of antique sculpture or simply enjoy studying naked guys who are missing noses or other bodily protrusions, make the **Abguss-Sammlung Antiker Plastik** (Antique Plaster-Cast Collection; ☎030-342 4054; www.abguss-sammlung-berlin.de; Schlossstrasse 69b; ⌚2-5pm Thu-Sun) FREE a stopover. It has plaster-cast copies of works spanning 3500 years, created by cultures as diverse as the Minoans, Romans and Byzantines, allowing you to trace the evolution of this ancient art form.

TOP TIPS

- Sold online, the 'Charlottenburg+' ticket (adult/concession €17/13) is a day pass valid for one-day admission to every open palace or building (special exhibits usually excepted).
- Avoid weekends, especially in summer, when queues can be long.
- Art aficionados should check out the three museums on Schlossstrasse, right across from the Altes Schloss.
- Large bags and luggage can be checked for free in the cloakroom in the Altes Schloss.

Feel like a member of the Prussian court during the Berliner Residenz Konzerte (www.residenzkonzerte.berlin), a series of concerts held by candlelight with musicians dressed in powdered wigs and historical costumes playing works by baroque and early classical composers. Various packages are available, including one featuring a pre-concert dinner.

SIGHTS

Concentrate your sightseeing in the City West around Zoologischer Garten and along the famous Kurfürstendamm boulevard, Berlin's major shopping strip. From here it's about 3.5km northwest to western Berlin's top sight: Schloss Charlottenburg, the grand 18th-century Prussian park-and-palace ensemble.

SCHLOSS CHARLOTTENBURG — PALACE

See p216.

KURFÜRSTENDAMM — AREA

Map p350 (Kurfürstendamm; U Kurfürstendamm, Uhlandstrasse) The 3.5km Kurfürstendamm is a ribbon of commerce that began as a bridle path to the royal hunting lodge in the Grunewald forest. In the early 1870s, Otto von Bismarck, the Iron Chancellor, decided that the capital of the newly founded German Reich needed its own representative boulevard, which he envisioned as even bigger and better than Paris' Champs-Élysées. Today it is Berlin's busiest shopping strip, especially towards its eastern end.

★C/O BERLIN — GALLERY

Map p350 (☎030-284 441 662; www.co-berlin.org; Hardenbergstrasse 22-24; adult/concession/child under 18yr €10/6/free; ⏲11am-8pm; P; S Zoologischer Garten, U Zoologischer Garten) Founded in 2000, C/O Berlin is the capital's most respected private, non-profit exhibition centre for international photography. It is based at the iconic Amerika Haus, which served as a US cultural and information centre from 1957 until 2006. C/O's roster of highbrow exhibits regularly features the art form's international elite, including Annie Leibovitz, Stephen Shore, Nan Goldin and Anton Corbijn.

MUSEUM FÜR FOTOGRAFIE — GALLERY

Map p350 (☎030-266 424 242; www.smb.museum/mf; Jebensstrasse 2; adult/concession €10/5; ⏲11am-7pm Tue, Wed & Fri-Sun, to 8pm Thu; S Zoologischer Garten, U Zoologischer Garten) A former Prussian officers' casino now showcases the artistic legacy of Helmut Newton (1920–2004), the Berlin-born *enfant terrible* of fashion and lifestyle photography, with the two lower floors dedicated to his life and work as well as to the artistic

TOP EXPERIENCE
KAISER-WILHELM-GEDÄCHTNISKIRCHE

One of Berlin's most photographed landmarks, the Kaiser-Wilhelm-Gedächtniskirche is actually a ruin, albeit an impressive one. Allied bombing on 23 November 1943 left only the husk of the west tower of this magnificent neo-Romanesque church, built in honour of Kaiser Wilhelm I, standing. Now an antiwar memorial, the original was designed by Franz Schwechten and completed in 1895. Historic photographs in the **Gedenkhalle** (Hall of Remembrance) help you visualise its former grandeur. The hall also contains remnants of elaborate mosaics depicting heroic moments from Wilhelm I's life, among other scenes.

Note the marble reliefs, liturgical objects and two symbols of reconciliation: an icon cross donated by the Russian Orthodox church and a copy of the Cross of Nails from Coventry Cathedral, which was destroyed by Luftwaffe bombers in 1940.

In 1961 a bell tower and **octagonal church** designed by Egon Eiermann were completed next to the ruined tower; the striking church has glowing midnight-blue glass walls and a golden statue of Christ 'floating' above the altar. Also note the *Stalingrad Madonna* (a charcoal drawing) against the north wall.

DON'T MISS

- Memorial hall mosaics
- Blue glass walls

PRACTICALITIES

- Kaiser Wilhelm Memorial Church
- Map p350, G5
- ☎030-218 5023
- www.gedaechtniskirche.com
- Breitscheidplatz
- admission free
- ⏲church 10am-6pm, memorial hall noon-5.30pm
- U Zoologischer Garten, Kurfürstendamm, S Zoologischer Garten

WORTH A DETOUR

TEUFELSBERG: SPIES TO STREET ART

The 121.1m-high Teufelsberg in the Grunewald forest has a forbidding name (Devil's Mountain) and a fascinating history. The Nazis' plan to build a military training school here got quite literally buried by WWII rubble piled on top of it until 1972. During the Cold War, the US military erected the **Teufelsberg Spy Station** (www.teufelsberg-berlin.de; Teufelschaussee; tickets €5, with photo permission €10, tours €15; ⌚11am-sunset Wed-Sun, last entry 1hr before sunset; S Heerstrasse) atop the hill to keep an ear on the East Germans and Soviets. The derelict compound is now an awesome street-art gallery with mesmerising Berlin views.

output of photographic compatriots, such as his wife, Alice Springs. On the top floor, the barrel-vaulted **Kaisersaal** (Emperor's Hall) forms a grand backdrop for changing international photography exhibits.

KÄTHE-KOLLWITZ-MUSEUM MUSEUM

Map p350 (☎030-882 5210; www.kaethe-kollwitz.de; Fasanenstrasse 24; adult/concession/under 18yr €7/4/free, audioguide €3; ⌚11am-4pm; U Uhlandstrasse) Käthe Kollwitz (1867–1945) was a famous early-20th-century artist whose social and political awareness lent a tortured power to her lithographs, graphics, woodcuts, sculptures and drawings. This four-floor exhibit in a charming 19th-century villa kicks off with an introduction to this extraordinary woman, who lived in Berlin for 52 years, before presenting a life-spanning selection of her work, including the powerful anti-hunger lithography *Brot!* (Bread!, 1924) and the woodcut series *Krieg* (War, 1922–23).

Note that the museum is set to move to the theatre at Schloss Charlottenburg in late 2022.

MAHNMAL AM BREITSCHEIDPLATZ MEMORIAL

Map p350 (Breitscheidplatz; 🚌100, 200, U Zoologischer Garten, S Zoologischer Garten) This simple memorial honours the victims of the terror attack of 19 December 2016 when a man drove a truck into the crowd at the Christmas market held every year on Breitscheidplatz. The rampage left 12 people dead and scores injured. Unveiled on the event's first anniversary, the memorial consists of a golden crack that runs down the steps leading up to the Kaiser Wilhelm Memorial Church, with the names of the dead chiselled into the front of the steps.

EATING

The dining quality in Charlottenburg is dependably high and the number of trailblazing kitchens is growing steadily. Savignyplatz exudes the relaxed and bustling vibe of an Italian piazza on balmy summer nights, while Kantstrasse is lined with many excellent Asian eateries. Of late, several successful Mitte and Prenzlauer Berg restaurants have opened branches in the district, including W-Der Imbiss and Burgermeister.

Kurfürstendamm & Around

CURRY WOLF GERMAN €

Map p350 (☎030-3214 0262; https://curry-wolf.de; Rankestrasse 36; sausages €3-4; ⌚9am-10pm Mon-Sat, from 10am Sun; U Kurfürstendamm) If shopping on Kurfürstendamm has left you hungry like a wolf, this snack shack in a tree-lined side street makes for a tasty refueling stop. The secret weapon is the sauce – fittingly called 'Opium' – that gets people hooked. To prevent withdrawal, you can even take home a wurst in a mason jar.

KANTINI BERLIN INTERNATIONAL €

Map p350 (www.bikiniberlin.de/de/kantini_und_restaurant; Bikini Berlin, Budapester Strasse; dishes €4-26; ⌚10am-8pm Mon-Sat; 🌶 👪; U Zoologischer Garten, S Zoologischer Garten) This next-gen food court at the stylish Bikini Berlin shopping mall has Instaworthy looks thanks to its mash-up of industrial edge and playful design touches, including potted plants, candy-coloured furniture and Berlin Zoo views. The 14 outlets pick up on international food trends – ramen to bibimbap to poke bowls – often with high quality.

LOCAL KNOWLEDGE

BERLIN'S LITTLE ASIA

It's not quite Chinatown, but if you're in the mood for the flavours of Asia, head to Kantstrasse between Savignyplatz and Wilmersdorfer Strasse. The strip is chock-a-block with the city's densest concentration of authentic Chinese, Vietnamese and Thai restaurants, including the perennially popular Good Friends. At lunchtime most offer value-priced specials, perfect for filling up on the cheap.

★MADAME NGO VIETNAMESE €€

Map p350 (☎030-6027 4585; http://madame-ngo.de; Kantstrasse 30; mains €9-17; ⊙noon-10pm) Set up in a former pharmacy, Madame Ngo's *pho*-nomenal soups may be just what the doctor ordered. Swimming in a rich bone broth are tender chicken bits, various cuts of beef or a vegetable medley. Calling itself a Hanoi-style brasserie, Madame's also plays with French colonial influences, such as pâté, *crevettes* (shrimp) *de Paris* and fried quail.

NENI INTERNATIONAL €€

Map p350 (☎030-120 221 200; www.neniberlin.de; Budapester Strasse 40; mains €6-30; ⊙noon-11pm; 🛜✍; 🚌100, 200, ⓈZoologischer Garten, ⓊZoologischer Garten) This bustling greenhouse-style dining hall at the 25hours Hotel Bikini Berlin (p252) presents a spirited menu of meant-to-be-shared dishes inspired by Mediterranean, Iranian and Austrian cuisines. Top billing goes to the homemade falafel, the Jerusalem platter, the pulled-beef sandwich and the *knafeh* (a spirit-soaked dessert). The 10th-floor views of the zoo and the rooftops are a bonus.

MR HAI SHABUKI JAPANESE €€

Map p350 (☎030-8862 8136; www.mrhai.de; Olivaer Platz 9; nigiri/maki from €3.30, sushi platters €15.50-29; ⊙noon-10pm; 🚌M19, 109, ⓊAdenauerplatz, Uhlandstrasse) Purists can stick to classic *nigiri* and *maki*, but been-here-forever Mr Hai is mostly about expanding your sushi horizons. Unconventional morsels, composed like little works of art, may feature kimchi, pork, mozzarella or cream cheese; others are flambéed or deep-fried.

CAFÉ-RESTAURANT WINTERGARTEN IM LITERATURHAUS INTERNATIONAL €€

Map p350 (☎030-882 5414; http://cafe-im-literaturhaus.de; Fasanenstrasse 23; mains €8-16; ⊙9am-midnight; ✍; ⓊUhlandstrasse) The hustle and bustle of Ku'damm is only a block away from this genteel late-19th-century villa with attached literary salon and bookshop. Tuck into dreamy cakes or seasonal bistro cuisine amid Old Berlin decor in the gracefully stucco-ornamented rooms or, if weather permits, in the idyllic garden. Breakfast is served until 2pm.

★MINE RESTAURANT ITALIAN €€€

Map p350 (☎030-8892 6363; www.minerestaurant.de; Meinekestrasse 10; mains €21-29; ⊙5.30-10pm; ⓊUhlandstrasse) Italian restaurants may be a dime a dozen, but Mine's style, menu and service blend together as perfectly as a Sicilian stew. Helmed by Mikhail Mnatsakanov, the son of a Russian TV celebrity chef, it presents feistily flavoured next-gen fare from around the Boot by riffing on traditional recipes in innovative ways. The wine list makes even demanding oenophiles swoon.

Savignyplatz & Kantstrasse

★KUCHENLADEN CAFE €

Map p350 (☎030-3101 8424; www.derkuchenladen.de; Kantstrasse 138; cakes €2.50-4.50; ⊙10am-8pm Tue-Sun, noon-8pm Mon; ⓈSavignyplatz) No one can resist the siren call of this classic cafe, whose homemade cakes are like works of art wrought from flour, sugar and cream. From cheesecake to carrot cake to the ridiculously rich Sachertorte, it's all delicious down to the last crumb.

ALI BABA ITALIAN €

Map p350 (☎030-881 1350; www.alibaba-berlin.de; Bleibtreustrasse 45; dishes €4.50-15.50; ⊙noon-midnight; ✍; ⓈSavignyplatz) In business for more years than there are robbers in the eponymous fairy tale, Ali Baba is a bustling port-of-call with local cult status thanks to cheap and simple but delicious thin-crust pizzas, heaps of pasta and crusty homemade bread for sopping up the juices, all at bargain prices. Separate vegan pizza menu.

LON MEN'S NOODLE HOUSE €

Map p350 (030-3151 9678; https://lon-mens-noodle-house.business.site; Kantstrasse 33; dishes €6-10; noon-10pm Wed-Mon; ; SSavignyplatz, UWilmersdorfer Strasse) If you're pining for hot soup to stave off the chills, shoehorn your way inside Lon Men's, a time-tested, spectacularly unhip purveyor of soul-soothing noodle bowls. A Kantstrasse institution, it's famous for its chili wontons but also has tempting daily specials and plenty of meat-free options.

GOOD FRIENDS CHINESE €€

Map p350 (030-313 2659; www.goodfriends-berlin.de; Kantstrasse 30; 2-course weekday lunch €7-7.70, dinner mains €11-20; noon-11pm; SSavignyplatz) Good Friends is widely considered to be Berlin's best Cantonese restaurant. The ducks dangling in the window are merely an overture to a menu long enough to confuse Confucius, including plenty of authentic homestyle dishes (on a separate menu). If steamed chicken feet prove too challenging, you can always fall back on sweet-and-sour pork or fried rice with shrimp.

CHRISTOPHER'S INTERNATIONAL €€€

Map p350 (030-2435 6282; www.christophers.online; Mommsenstrasse 63; mains €20-27, 4/5-course menu €65/75; 6pm-midnight Mon-Sat; ; SSavignyplatz) This casual fine-dining lair delivers the perfect trifecta: fabulous food, wine and long drinks. Order the multi-course menu to truly experience the genius of kitchen champion Christopher Kümper, who creates globally inspired and regionally sourced symphonies of taste and texture. Or keep it casual with just a bite and a gin and tonic.

DRINKING & NIGHTLIFE

Today's Charlottenburg may no longer be the giddy party pit of the Golden Twenties, but that's not to say that a good time can't be had. You'll find it in fancy cocktail bars (many of them in hotels), lovably nostalgic Old Berlin pubs and a couple of jazz and mainstream dance clubs.

TOP EXPERIENCE

ZOO BERLIN & AQUARIUM

Berlin's zoo holds a triple record as Germany's oldest, most species rich and most popular animal park. It has its origins in 1844, when Friedrich Wilhelm IV donated land plus animals from the royal family's private reserve. More recently, the zoo gained international fame when the polar-bear cub Knut, born here in 2006, was successfully hand-raised by a zookeeper after his mother had abandoned him. Sadly, Knut died from brain inflammation in 2011. The zoo's current biggest heartthrobs are Meng Meng and Jiao Qing, a pair of adorable pandas on loan from China. Feeding sessions are a major visitor magnet – pick up a schedule at the ticket counter. The California sea lions usually elicit the biggest cheers.

The adjacent **Aquarium** (www.aquarium-berlin.de; 9am-6pm) presents exotic fish, amphibians and reptiles in darkened halls and glowing tanks. Its tropical Crocodile Hall could be the stuff of nightmares, but jellyfish, iridescent poison frogs and a real-life 'Nemo' should bring smiles to most youngsters' faces.

The zoo's architecture deserves a special mention, especially the exotic Elephant Gate. The main entrance is the Lion Gate on Hardenbergplatz.

DON'T MISS

- Panda enclosure
- Great apes
- Crocodile Hall

PRACTICALITIES

- Map p350, G3
- 030-254 010
- www.zoo-berlin.de
- Hardenbergplatz 8
- adult/child €16/8, with aquarium €22/11
- 9am-6.30pm Apr-Sep, to 6pm Mar & Oct, to 4.30pm Nov-Feb, last entry 1hr before closing
- 100, 200, SZoologischer Garten, UZoologischer Garten, Kurfürstendamm

BAR AM STEINPLATZ COCKTAIL BAR

Map p350 (030-554 4440; http://barsteinplatz.com; Steinplatz 4; 4pm-late; U Ernst-Reuter-Platz) This liquid playground at the art deco Hotel am Steinplatz (p252) has made history several times, most recently as Germany's first alcohol-free hotel-based cocktail bar. Mix-meister Willi Bittorf combines nonalcoholic distillates with kombucha, rose water, syrups, herbs and juices to create guilt- and hangover-free libations. Handy and hygienic: the menu is printed on the tables. Craft beer and wine (with alcohol) are served as well.

SCHLEUSENKRUG BEER GARDEN

Map p350 (030-313 9909; www.schleusenkrug.de; Müller-Breslau-Strasse; noon-midnight Mon-Sat, from 11am Sun; S Zoologischer Garten, Tiergarten, U Zoologischer Garten) Sitting pretty at the edge of Tiergarten park, next to a canal lock, Schleusenkrug has a charming 1950s interior but truly rocks beer-garden season. People from all walks of life hunker over big mugs and comfort food – from grilled sausages to *Flammkuchen* (Alsatian pizza) and weekly specials (mains €9 to €17). Breakfast is served until 2pm.

BAR ZENTRAL COCKTAIL BAR

Map p350 (030-3743 3079; www.barzentral.de; Lotte-Lenya-Bogen 551; 5pm-late; S Zoologischer Garten, U Zoologischer Garten, Kurfürstendamm) 'Disappear here', beckons a blue neon sign at this top libation station run by two local bar gurus. Heed the call at the long wooden bar to pick through the palette of expertly crafted classics and newfalutin potions. The decor is both elegant and understated, and there are terrace tables for raising a pinkie al fresco on balmy evenings.

MONKEY BAR BAR

Map p350 (030-120 221 210; www.monkeybarberlin.de; Budapester Strasse 40; noon-2am; ; S Zoologischer Garten, U Zoologischer Garten) On the 10th floor of the 25hours Hotel Bikini Berlin (p252), this mainstream-hip 'urban jungle' delivers fabulous views of the city and Berlin Zoo, while the menu gives prominent nods to rum-based concoctions (great mai tai!) and has an inspired line-up of mocktails. Come early for chilled sundowners on the terrace. Different DJs spin nightly Friday to Sunday, from 4pm.

DIENER TATTERSALL PUB

Map p350 (030-881 5329; www.diener-berlin.de; Grolmanstrasse 47; 6pm-2am Mon-Sat; S Savignyplatz) In business for over a century, this Old Berlin haunt was taken over by German heavyweight champion Franz Diener in the 1950s and became one of West Berlin's iconic artist pubs. From Billy Wilder to Harry Belafonte, they all came for beer and *Bulette* (meat patties) and left behind signed black-and-white photographs that grace Diener's walls to this day.

☆ ENTERTAINMENT

BAR JEDER VERNUNFT CABARET

Map p350 (030-883 1582; www.bar-jeder-vernunft.de; Schaperstrasse 24; admission varies; U Spichernstrasse) Life's still a cabaret at this intimate 1912 mirrored art-nouveau tent theatre, one of Berlin's most beloved venues for sophisticated song-and-dance shows, comedy and *chansons* (songs). Sip a glass of bubbly while relaxing at a candlelit cafe table or in a curvy red-velvet booth bathed in flickering candlelight that's reflected in the mirrors. Many shows don't require German-language skills.

SCHAUBÜHNE THEATRE

Map p350 (030-890 023; www.schaubuehne.de; Kurfürstendamm 153; tickets €7-49; U Adenauerplatz) In a converted 1920s expressionist cinema by Erich Mendelsohn, Schaubühne is a top German stage for experimental, contemporary theatre, usually with a critical and analytical look at current social and political issues. The ensemble is directed by Thomas Ostermeier and includes many top names from German film and TV. Some performances feature English or French subtitles.

ZOO PALAST CINEMA

Map p350 (01805-222 966; www.zoopalast.premiumkino.de; Hardenbergstrasse 29a; tickets €11-19; 100, 200, S Zoologischer Garten, U Zoologischer Garten) Old-school glamour meets state-of-the-art technology and comfort at this rejuvenated grand cinema, which screens mostly 2D and 3D blockbusters (dubbed into German) in seven fancily appointed theatres. Check out the cool 1950s foyer. International stars can often be seen sashaying down the red carpet during the **Berlinale film festival** (www.berlinale.de; Feb).

WORTH A DETOUR

OLYMPIASTADION & AROUND

The main attraction in far-western Berlin is the **Olympiastadion** (Olympic Stadium; 030-2500 2322; https://olympiastadion.berlin; Olympischer Platz 3; adult/concession self-guided tour €8/5.50, tours from €11/9.50; 9am-7pm Apr-Jul, Sep & Oct, to 8pm Aug, 10am-4pm Nov-Mar; P; S Olympiastadion, U Olympiastadion). Even though it was put through a total modernisation for the 2006 FIFA World Cup, it's hard to ignore the fact that this massive coliseum-like stadium was built by the Nazis for the 1936 Olympic Games. The bombastic bulk of the structure remains but has been softened by the addition of a spidery oval roof, a blue tartan track, snazzy VIP boxes, and top-notch sound, lighting and projection systems. It can seat up to 75,000 people, be it for the local Bundesliga (premier league) Hertha BSC football (soccer) team, Bruce Springsteen or the Pope.

On nonevent days you can explore the stadium on your own, with a multimedia guide (€2) or on a guided tour. Tours (some in English) run several times daily and take you into areas that are otherwise off-limits, including the locker rooms, warm-up areas and VIP sections. Access the stadium via the visitors centre at the Osttor (eastern gate).

To truly appreciate the grandeur of the stadium, head west past the Maifeld parade grounds to the outdoor viewing platform of the 77m-high **Glockenturm** (Olympic Bell Tower; 030-305 8123; www.glockenturm.de; Am Glockenturm; adult/child €4.50/3; 10am-6pm Apr-Oct; P; S Pichelsberg), which was also built for the 1936 Olympics. En route you'll pass a replica of the Olympic bell (the damaged original is displayed south of the stadium). In the foyer, an exhibit chronicles the ground's history, including the 1936 games, with panels in German and English. A documentary features rare original footage of the Nazi era.

The concrete monolith jutting skywards south of the stadium was Swiss-French architect Le Corbusier's contribution to the 1957 International Building Exhibition (Interbau). An architectural cult classic, the **Corbusierhaus** (gallery 030-8974 2310; www.corbusierhaus.org; Flatowallee 16; P; U Olympiastadion) was the fourth in a series of large-scale residential complexes he called *Unité d'Habitation* (Housing Unit). A gallery in staircase B presents exhibits on postwar Berlin architecture.

About 1km east is the **Georg Kolbe Museum** (030-304 2144; www.georg-kolbe-museum.de; Sensburger Allee 25; adult/concession/under 18yr €7/5/free; 10am-6pm; P; S Heerstrasse), dedicated to one of Germany's most influential early-20th-century sculptors (1877–1947). A member of the Berlin Secession, Kolbe distanced himself from traditional sculpture and became a chief exponent of the idealised nude, which later found favour with the Nazis. The museum in his former studio and home mounts several exhibits per year with a focus on sculpture by Kolbe and his contemporaries, often juxtaposed with works by contemporary artists. Built in the late 1920s, it consists of two rectangular brick buildings flanking a tranquil sculpture garden. The charming **Cafe Benjamine**, named for Kolbe's wife, makes for a lovely sightseeing respite.

About 2km southeast of the stadium, overlooking the trade fairgrounds, looms another Berlin landmark, the 147m-high **Funkturm** (Radio Tower; 030-3038 1905; www.funkturm-messeberlin.de; Messedamm 22; adult/concession platform €6/3, restaurant €3/2; platform 2-10pm Tue-Fri, 11am-10pm Sat & Sun, seasonal variations; P; U Kaiserdamm, S Messe Nord/ICC). The filigree structure bears an uncanny resemblance to Paris' Eiffel Tower and looks especially attractive when lit up at night. It started transmitting signals in 1926; nine years later the world's first regular TV program was broadcast from here. From the viewing platform at 126m or the restaurant at 55m, you can enjoy sweeping views of the Grunewald forest and the western city, as well as the **AVUS**, Germany's first car-racing track, which opened in 1921. The Nazis made it part of the autobahn system, which it still is today.

DEUTSCHE OPER BERLIN OPERA

Map p350 (German Opera Berlin; ☎030-3438 4343; www.deutscheoperberlin.de; Bismarckstrasse 35; tickets €20-180; U Deutsche Oper) Founded by Berlin burghers in 1912 as a counterpoint to the royal opera on Unter den Linden, the Deutsche Oper presents a classic 19th-century opera repertory from Verdi and Puccini to Wagner and Strauss, all sung in their original languages. For contemporary, experimental and cross-cultural productions, check out what's on at the Tischlerei, the opera's joinery turned studio space.

A-TRANE JAZZ

Map p350 (☎030-313 2550; www.a-trane.de; Bleibtreustrasse 1; tickets €10-20; ⏰8-11pm or later; S Savignyplatz) Herbie Hancock and Diana Krall are among the many world-class musicians who have graced the stage of this intimate jazz club. Mostly, though, it's top emerging global talent bringing their A-game to the A-Trane. Entry is free on Monday, when pianist Andreas Schmidt and his band get everyone's toes tapping. Concerts start promptly at 8pm. A cafe provides pre-concert sustenance.

SHOPPING

Kurfürstendamm and Tauentzienstrasse are chock-a-block with outlets of international chains flogging fashion and accessories. Further west on Ku'damm are the more high-end boutiques such as Hermès, Cartier and Bulgari. Kantstrasse is the go-to zone for home designs. Connecting side streets, such as Bleibtreustrasse and Schlüterstrasse, house upscale indie and designer boutiques, bookshops and galleries, while Bikini Berlin features cutting-edge concept and flagship stores.

★**BIKINI BERLIN** MALL

Map p350 (☎030-5549 6455; www.bikiniberlin.de; Budapester Strasse 38-50; ⏰shops 10am-8pm Mon-Sat, bldg 9am-8pm Mon-Sat; 📶; 🚌100, 200, U Zoologischer Garten, S Zoologischer Garten) Germany's first concept mall opened in 2014 in a smoothly rehabilitated 1950s architectural icon nicknamed 'Bikini' because of its design: 200m-long upper and lower sections separated by an open floor, now chastely covered by a glass facade. Inside are three floors of urban indie boutiques, short-lease pop-up 'boxes' for chic up-and-comers, and an international street-food court.

★**MANUFACTUM** HOMEWARES

Map p350 (☎030-2403 3844; www.manufactum.de; Hardenbergstrasse 4-5; ⏰10am-8pm Mon-Fri, to 6pm Sat; U Ernst-Reuter-Platz) 🍃 Long before sustainable became a buzzword, this shop (the brainchild of a German Green Party member) stocked traditionally made quality products from around the world, many of which have stood the test of time. Cool finds include hand-forged iron pans by Turk, lavender soap from a French monastery and fountain pens by Lamy.

★**TASCHEN STORE BERLIN** BOOKS

Map p350 (☎030-8872 0929; www.taschen.de; Schlüterstrasse 39; ⏰11am-6pm; 🚌109, M19, M29, U Uhlandstrasse) Taschen publishes some of the hippest books under the sun on art, architecture, design and related fields. This five-room flagship store feels more like a gallery and is worth visiting not only for a browse but for the impossibly chic Italian design, especially the wooden bookcases and the geometric tile floors.

STILWERK HOMEWARES

Map p350 (☎030-315 150; www.stilwerk.de/berlin; Kantstrasse 17; ⏰10am-7pm Mon-Sat; S Savignyplatz) This four-storey temple of good taste will have devotees of the finer things itching to redecorate. Everything you could possibly want for home and hearth is here, from key rings to grand pianos to vintage lamps. It's all housed in a striking modern building anchored by an open atrium clad in natural stone, maple and glass.

KÄTHE WOHLFAHRT ARTS & CRAFTS

Map p350 (☎0800 409 0150; www.kaethe-wohlfahrt.com; Kurfürstendamm 225-226; ⏰11am-5pm Mon-Sat; U Kurfürstendamm) With its mind-boggling assortment of traditional German Yuletide decorations and ornaments, this shop lets you celebrate Christmas year-round. It's accessed via a ramp that spirals around an 8m-high ornament-laden Christmas tree.

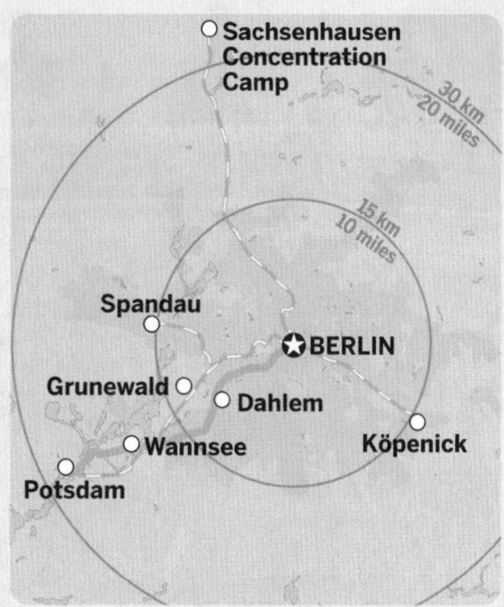

Day Trips from Berlin

TOP EXPERIENCE

EXPLORE POTSDAM & SCHLOSS SANSSOUCI

Potsdam, on the Havel River just 25km southwest of central Berlin, is the capital and crown jewel of the federal state of Brandenburg. Easily reached by S-Bahn, the former Prussian royal seat is the most popular day trip from Berlin, luring visitors with its splendid gardens and palaces, which garnered Unesco World Heritage status in 1990.

Headlining the roll call of royal pads is Schloss Sanssouci, the private retreat of Friedrich II (Frederick the Great), who was also the mastermind of Potsdam's other fabulous parks and palaces. Miraculously, most survived WWII with nary a shrapnel wound. When the shooting stopped, the Allies chose Schloss Cecilienhof for the Potsdam Conference of August 1945 to lay the groundwork for Germany's postwar fate.

Schloss & Park Sanssouci

This glorious park and array of palaces is what happens when a king has good taste, plenty of cash and access to the finest architects and artists of the day. Sanssouci was dreamed up by Frederick the Great (1712–86) and is anchored by the eponymous palace, his favourite summer retreat, a place where he could be *'sans souci'* (without cares).

Schloss Sanssouci

The biggest stunner, and what everyone comes to see, is Schloss Sanssouci. Designed by Georg Wenzeslaus von Knobelsdorff in 1747, the rococo gem sits daintily above vine-draped terraces with the king's grave nearby.

Standouts on the tour (guided or self-guided) include the **Konzertsaal** (Concert Hall), whimsically decorated with vines, grapes and even a cobweb where sculpted spiders frolic. The king himself gave flute recitals here. Also note the intimate **Bibliothek** (library), lidded by a gilded sunburst ceiling, where the king would seek solace amid 2000 leather-

DON'T MISS

- Schloss Sanssouci
- Chinesisches Haus
- View of Sanssouci palace from the fountain at the foot of the vineyard terrace
- Grottensaal and Marmorsaal at Neues Palais

PRACTICALITIES

- ☎0331-969 4200
- www.spsg.de
- Maulbeerallee
- day pass to all palaces adult/concession €19/14
- ⏲varies by palace
- 🚌614, 650, 692, 695, 697

bound tomes ranging from Greek poetry to the latest releases by his friend Voltaire. Another highlight is the **Marmorsaal** (Marble Room), an elegant white-Carrara-marble symphony modelled after the Pantheon in Rome. As you exit the palace, note the **Ruinenberg**, a pile of fake classical ruins looming in the distance.

Bildergalerie

The **Picture Gallery** (Gallery of Old Masters; Im Park Sanssouci 4; adult/concession €6/5; ⏲10am-5.30pm Tue-Sun May-Oct) shelters Frederick the Great's prized collection of Old Masters, including such pearls as Caravaggio's *Doubting Thomas,* Anthony van Dyck's *Pentecost* and several works by Peter Paul Rubens. Behind the rather plain facade hides a sumptuous symphony of gilded ornamentation, yellow and white marble and a patterned stone floor that is perhaps just as impressive as the closely hung paintings covering nearly every inch of wall space.

Neue Kammern

The **New Chambers** (New Chambers; Park Sanssouci; adult/concession incl tour or audioguide €6/5; ⏲10am-5.30pm Tue-Sun Apr-Oct), built by Knobelsdorff in 1748, were originally an orangery and later converted into a guest palace. The interior drips with rococo opulence, most notably the square **Jasper Hall**, drenched in precious stones and lidded by a Venus fresco, and the **Ovidsaal**, a grand ballroom with gilded wall reliefs depicting scenes from Ovid's *Metamorphosis.*

Chinesisches Haus

The 18th-century fad for the Far East is strongly reflected in the adorable **Chinese House** (Am Grünen Gitter; adult/concession €4/3; ⏲10am-5.30pm Tue-Sun May-Oc). The cloverleaf-shaped pavilion is among the park's most photographed buildings thanks to its enchanting exterior of exotically dressed, gilded figures shown sipping tea, dancing and playing musical instruments amid palm-shaped pillars. Inside is a precious collection of Chinese and Meissen porcelain.

Orangerieschloss

Modelled after an Italian Renaissance villa, the 300m-long, 1864-built **Orangery Palace** (Orangery Palace; An der Orangerie 3-5; adult/concession €6/5, tower €3/2; ⏲10am-5.30pm Tue-Sun May-Oct, 10am-5.30pm Sat & Sun Apr) was the favourite building project of Friedrich Wilhelm IV – a passionate Italophile. Its highlight is the **Raffaelsaal** (Raphael Hall), which brims with 19th-century copies of the famous painter's masterpieces. The greenhouses are still used for storing potted plants in winter. The tower can be climbed for so-so views.

TAKE A BREAK

Right in the park, **Drachenhaus** (☎0331-505 3808; www.drachenhaus.de; Maulbeerallee 4; mains €10-23; ⏲11am-7pm daily Apr-Oct, noon-6pm Tue-Sun Nov, Dec & Mar, noon-6pm Sat & Sun Jan & Feb; 👪; 🚌695) is a pagoda-style miniature palace serving coffee, cakes and seasonal cuisine.

For international favourites, head to **Potsdam Zur Historischen Mühle** (☎0331-281 493; www.moevenpick-restaurants.com; Zur Historischen Mühle 2; mains €14-25; ⏲11am-8pm; P 👪; 🚌614, 650, 695), with beer garden and children's playground.

The S7 makes the trip from central Berlin, as do regional trains (eg from Berlin Hauptbahnhof). All arrive at Potsdam Hauptbahnhof; some continue to Potsdam Charlottenhof and Potsdam Park Sanssouci stations. Bus lines 614, 650, 692, 695 and 697 go from Potsdam Hauptbahnhof straight to Schloss Sanssouci.

Historische Mühle

This reconstructed 18th-century Dutch-style **windmill** (Historic Windmill; ☎0331-550 6851; Maulbeerallee 5; adult/concession €4/3; ⊙10am-6pm Apr-Oct) contains exhibits about the history of the mill and mill technology, and offers a close-up look at the grinding mechanism and a top-floor viewing platform. According to legend, Frederick the Great ordered its owner to demolish the original mill because of the clattering. He relented, however, when the miller refused and threatened to go to court.

Neues Palais

The final palace commissioned by Frederick the Great, the **New Palace** (New Palace; Am Neuen Palais; adult/concession incl tour or audioguide €6/5; ⊙10am-5.30pm Tue-Sun Apr-Oct, 10am-4.30pm Wed-Mon Nov-Mar) has made-to-impress dimensions, a central dome and a lavish exterior capped with a parade of sandstone figures. The interior attests to the 18th century's high level of artistry and craftwork. Ceiling frescoes, gilded stucco ornamentation, ornately carved wainscotting and fanciful wall coverings sit alongside paintings (by Antoine Pesne, for example) and elaborately crafted furniture. The palace was built in just six years, largely to demonstrate the undiminished power of the Prussian state following the bloody Seven Years' War (1756–63). The king himself rarely stayed here, preferring the intimacy of Schloss Sanssouci and using it for representational purposes only. Only the last German Kaiser, Wilhelm II, used it as a residence, until 1918.

After extensive restoration, most of the building's highlights are once again accessible, including the shell-festooned **Grottensaal** (Grotto Hall) festival hall and the magnificent **Marmorsaal** (Marble Hall), where visitors walk across a raised pathway to protect the precious marble floor, illuminated by eight massive crystal chandeliers. The redone **Unteres Fürstenquartier** (Lower Royal Suite) consists of a concert room, an oval-shaped chamber, an antechamber and a dining room with walls sheathed in red silk damask with gold-braided trim.

The pair of lavish buildings behind the palace is called the **Communs**. It originally housed servants and the kitchens and is now part of Potsdam University.

Restoration is still under way at the **Schlosstheater** (Palace Theatre), which will keep it closed for some time.

Schloss Charlottenhof

The jewel of Park Charlottenhof, this small **palace** (Charlottenhof Palace; Geschwister-Scholl-Strasse 34a; tours adult/concession €6/5; ⊙tours 10am-5.30pm Tue-Sun May-Oct) started out as a baroque country manor before being expanded by Karl Friedrich Schinkel for Friedrich Wilhelm IV in the late 1820s. The building is modelled on classical Roman villas and features a Doric portico and a bronze fountain. Landscape architect Peter Joseph Lenné designed the surrounding gardens, creating a harmonious blend of architecture and nature.

Römische Bäder

Karl Friedrich Schinkel, aided by his student Ludwig Persius, dreamed up the so-called **Roman Baths** (adult/concession €5/4; ⊙10am-5.30pm Tue-Sun May-Oct) in Park Charlottenhof. Despite the name, it's actually a romantic cluster of 15th-century Italian country-estate buildings, complete with vine-draped pergola. The entire ensemble is in poor condition and is expected to close soon for restoration.

Museum Barberini

The original Barberini Palace was a baroque Roman palazzo commissioned by Frederick the Great and bombed in WWII. Since January 2017, a majestic replica called **Museum Barberini** (☎0331-236 014 499; www.museum-barberini.com; Alter Markt, Humboldtstrasse 5-6; adult weekday/weekend €16/18, concession/under 18yr daily €10/free; ⊙10am-7pm Wed-Mon, 1st Thu of month to 9pm, last entry 1hr before closing) has added a new jewel to Potsdam's already bursting cultural landscape. It houses a private

chloss Cecilienhof

art museum funded by German software impresario Hasso Plattner, and mounts three high-calibre exhibits per year with an artistic arc that spans Old Masters to French impressionists to GDR-era artists.

Schloss Cecilienhof

An English-style country palace, **Schloss Cecilienhof** (Im Neuen Garten 11; special exhibit until Oct 2021 adult/concession €14/10; ⏲10am-5.30pm Tue-Sun Apr-Oct, to 4.30pm Nov-Mar) was completed in 1917 for Crown Prince Wilhelm and his wife, Cecilie, as the last residence built by the Hohenzollern clan. It's mostly famous for hosting the 1945 Potsdam Conference where Stalin, Truman and Churchill (and later his successor Clement Attlee) hammered out Germany's postwar fate and incidentally laid the foundation for the Cold War. Until October 2021, a special multimedia exhibit takes you back to these history-making days.

KGB Prison

Now the Memorial Leistikowstrasse, Potsdam's central remand prison for Soviet Counter Intelligence – colloquially known as the **KGB prison** (☎0331-201 1540; www.gedenkstaette-leistikowstrasse.de; Leistikowstrasse 1; ⏲10am-6pm Tue-Sun) FREE – is a particularly sinister Cold War relic. All sorts of real or alleged crimes could land you here, including espionage, desertion, insubordination or Nazi complicity. Using letters, documents, photographs, personal items and taped interviews, exhibits outline the fate of individuals.

TOP TIPS

- Book your timed ticket to Schloss Sanssouci online to avoid wait times and/or disappointment.
- Avoid visiting on Monday, when most palaces are closed.
- The sanssouci+ ticket, a one-day pass to palaces in Potsdam, costs €19 (concession €14) and is sold online and at each building.
- Picnicking is permitted throughout the park, but cycling is limited to Ökonomieweg and Maulbeerallee.
- Note that palaces are fairly well spaced – it's almost 2km between the Neues Palais and Schloss Sanssouci.

A relaxing way to enjoy Potsdam is from the deck of a cruise boat operated by Schifffahrt in Potsdam (www.schifffahrt-in-potsdam.de). The most popular trip is the 90-minute Schlösserundfahrt palace cruise (€18); there's also a two-hour tour to Lake Wannsee (€19) and a three-hour trip around several Havel lakes (€20). Boats depart from the Lange Brücke docks below the Mercure Hotel. English commentary available.

Potsdam

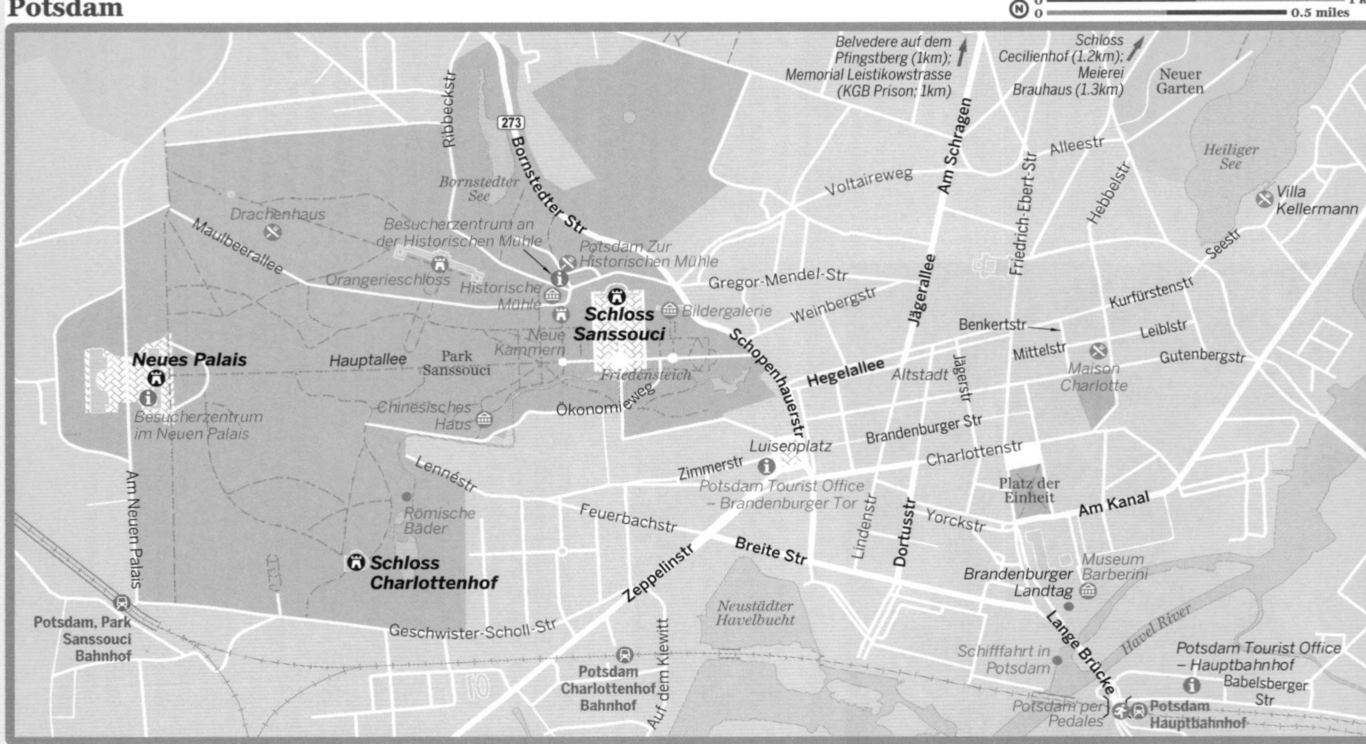
0
0
1 km
0.5 miles
Belvedere auf dem Pfingstberg (1km); Memorial Leistikowstrasse (KGB Prison; 1km)
Schloss Cecilienhof (1.2km); Meierei Brauhaus (1.3km)
Neuer Garten
Heiliger See
Villa Kellermann
273
Ribbeckstr
Bornstedter Str
Bornstedter See
Am Schragen
Alleestr
Voltaireweg
Friedrich-Ebert-Str
Hebbelstr
Seestr
Drachenhaus
Maulbeerallee
Besucherzentrum an der Historischen Mühle
Potsdam Zur Historischen Mühle
Orangerieschloss
Historische Mühle
Gregor-Mendel-Str
Jägerallee
Kurfürstenstr
Schloss Sanssouci
Bildergalerie
Weinbergstr
Benkertstr
Leiblstr
Neue Kammern
Mittelstr
Gutenbergstr
Neues Palais
Hauptallee
Park Sanssouci
Schopenhauerstr
Hegelallee
Altstadt
Jägerstr
Maison Charlotte
Friedensteich
Chinesisches Haus
Ökonomieweg
Besucherzentrum im Neuen Palais
Brandenburger Str
Luisenplatz
Charlottenstr
Zimmerstr
Potsdam Tourist Office – Brandenburger Tor
Lennéstr
Platz der Einheit
Am Kanal
Am Neuen Palais
Römische Bäder
Feuerbachstr
Lindenstr
Dortustr
Yorckstr
Breite Str
Schloss Charlottenhof
Museum Barberini
Brandenburger Landtag
Zeppelinstr
Neustädter Havelbucht
Lange Brücke
Havel River
Potsdam, Park Sanssouci Bahnhof
Geschwister-Scholl-Str
Schifffahrt in Potsdam
Potsdam Tourist Office – Hauptbahnhof
Babelsberger Str
Potsdam Charlottenhof Bahnhof
Auf dem Kiewitt
Potsdam per Pedales
Potsdam Hauptbahnhof

EATING & DRINKING IN POTSDAM

Meierei Brauhaus (☎0331-704 3211; www.meierei-potsdam.de; Im Neuen Garten 10; mains €7-15; ⊙noon-8pm Tue-Sun; 🚌603 to Höhenstrasse) The Berlin Wall once ran right past this brewpub, where the beer garden invites you to count the boats sailing on the Jungfernsee in summer. The hearty German dishes are a perfect match for the delicious craft beers, including the classic *Helles* (pale lager) and seasonal suds brewed on the premises.

Maison Charlotte (☎0331-280 5450; www.maison-charlotte.de; Mittelstrasse 20; Flammkuchen €9.50-15.50, 3/4-course menus €49/59; ⊙noon-10pm Wed-Mon; 🚌604, 609, 638, 🚋92, 96) There's a rustic lyricism to the French country cuisine in this darling Dutch Quarter bistro, whether your appetite runs towards a simple *Flammkuchen* (Alsatian pizza), Breton fish soup or a multi-course menu. Bon vivants on a budget come for the daily lunch special (€7.50), which includes a glass of wine; it's best enjoyed on the patio in summer.

Villa Kellermann (☎0331-2004 6540; https://villakellermann.de; Mangerstrasse 34; mains €23-32, 3-course dinner €62; ⊙6-10pm Wed-Sun, noon-2pm Sat & Sun; 🚋92, 93, 96) This gorgeous 1914 villa with a tumultuous history and eclectic decor feels a bit like your rich old uncle's country house. It's a smart, grown-up spot where culinary wunderkind Tim Raue has created a menu that gives regional dishes an exciting next-gen spin. The veal meatballs with beetroot and mashed potatoes are a perennial bestseller. Sublime wine list, to boot.

Sachsenhausen Concentration Camp

Explore

Sachsenhausen was built by prisoners and opened in 1936 as a prototype for other concentration camps. By 1945 about 200,000 people had passed through its sinister gates, initially mostly political opponents, but later also Roma, gay people, Jews and, after 1939, POWs from Eastern Europe, especially the Soviet Union. Tens of thousands died here from hunger, exhaustion, illness, exposure, medical experiments and executions. Thousands more succumbed during the death march of April 1945, when the Nazis evacuated the camp in advance of the Red Army. Note the memorial plaque to these victims as you walk towards the camp (at the corner of Strasse der Einheit and Strasse der Nationen).

Top Tip

➡ Between mid-October and mid-March, avoid visiting on a Monday, when all indoor exhibits are closed.

Getting There & Away

S-Bahn & Regional Train The S1 makes the trip three times hourly from central Berlin (eg Friedrichstrasse station) to Oranienburg (ABC ticket €3.60, 45 minutes). Hourly regional RE5 trains leaving from Hauptbahnhof and RB12 trains from Ostkreuz are faster (ABC ticket €3.60, 25 minutes). The camp is about 2km from the Oranienburg train station. Turn right onto Stralsunder Strasse, right on Bernauer Strasse, left on Strasse der Einheit and right on Strasse der Nationen. Alternatively, bus 804 makes hourly trips from the station straight to the site (use the same ticket as for the train, seven minutes).

Need to Know

➡ **Area Code** ☎03301

➡ **Location** About 35km north of central Berlin.

SIGHTS

The permanent exhibit of what is officially called **Gedenkstätte und Museum Sachsenhausen** (Memorial & Museum Sachsenhausen; ☎03301-200 200; www.sachsenhausen-sbg.de; Strasse der Nationen 22, Oranienburg;

⌚8.30am-6pm mid-Mar–mid-Oct, to 4.30pm mid-Oct–mid-Mar, museums closed Mon mid-Oct–mid-Mar; P; S Oranienburg) FREE is spread over 13 buildings, with each section explaining its historical purpose and the events that took place there. Unless you're on a guided tour, pick up an audioguide (€3) at the visitor centre to get a better grasp of this huge site. For an introduction to the camp's history, watch the 30-minute film shown in the former Prisoners' Kitchen.

Just beyond the perimeter, the **Neues Museum** (New Museum) introduces Sachsenhausen's precursor, the nearby Oranienburg concentration camp, set up in a repurposed brewery in March 1933. Proceed to **Tower A**, the entrance gate, cynically labelled, as at Auschwitz, Arbeit Macht Frei (Work Sets You Free). Inside is a stomach-turning exhibit on the arbitrary and sadistic brutality meted out by SS officers on camp inmates using eight case studies.

Beyond here is the roll-call area, with barracks and other buildings fanning out beyond. Off to the right, two restored barracks illustrate the abysmal living conditions prisoners endured. **Barrack 38** has an exhibit on Jewish inmates, while **Barrack 39** graphically portrays daily life at the camp. Famous inmates in the next-door prison included Hitler's would-be assassin Georg Elser and the anti-Nazi minister Martin Niemöller, author of the widely quoted 'First They Came...' poem.

The memorial's largest exhibit in the **infirmary barracks** on the other side of the roll-call area illustrates the camp's poor medical care, its response to infectious diseases, and the horrific medical experiments and crimes performed on prisoners, including the castration of homosexuals.

Moving towards the centre, the **Prisoners' Kitchen** chronicles key moments in the camp's history. Exhibits include instruments of torture, the original gallows that stood in the roll-call area and, in the cellar, heart-wrenching artwork scratched into the wall by prisoners.

The most sickening displays, though, are in the exhibit about **Station Z**, which was separated from the rest of the grounds and consisted of a firing-squad site, four cremation ovens and a gas chamber. The most notorious mass executions took place in autumn 1941, when more than 13,000 Soviet POWs were executed here in the course of four weeks.

In the far right corner, a modern building and two original barracks house the **Soviet Special Camp Museum**, which documents Sachsenhausen's stint as Speciallager No 7, a German POW camp run by the Soviets from 1945 until 1950. About 60,000 people were held here; some 12,000 of them died, mostly of malnutrition and disease. After 1950, Soviet and East German military used the grounds for another decade until the camp became a memorial site in 1961.

EATING & DRINKING

A cafe in the Neues Museum serves sandwiches, cakes and hot and cold beverages. There's also a bistro in the parking lot outside the visitor centre. You're allowed to bring food and drink with you. There are cafes, bakeries and small markets outside Oranienburg train station.

Spandau

Explore

Spandau is a charming mash-up of green expanses, rivers, industry and almost rural residential areas wrapped around a medieval core famous for its 16th-century bastion, the Zitadelle Spandau (Spandau Citadel). Older than Berlin by a few years, Spandau sits at the confluence of the Havel and the Spree and thrived as an independent city for nearly eight centuries; it only became part of Berlin in 1920. To this day, its people still talk about 'going to Berlin' when they head to any other city district. Nearly all sights are handily clustered in and around the Altstadt. The suburb of Gatow, with the Military History Museum, is about 10km south of here.

The Best...

➡ **Sight** Zitadelle Spandau

➡ **Place to Eat** Satt und Selig (p236)

Top Tip

In summer, big international acts like Billy Idol, Lana Del Rey and Limp Bizkit gig to appreciative audiences al fresco during the

Citadel Music Festival (www.citadel-music-festival.de). Year-round concerts take place in the Gothic Hall.

Getting There & Away

U-Bahn The recommended route is via the U7, which travels from central Berlin to Spandau in about 30 minutes (€2.90, AB tariff) and stops at the Zitadelle, the Altstadt and the Rathaus.

S-Bahn The S3 makes the trip to central Spandau in 30 to 40 minutes.

Need to Know

- **Area Code** 030
- **Location** About 13km northwest of central Berlin.
- **Tourist Office** (030-333 9388; www.visitspandau.de; Breite Strasse 32; noon-5pm Tue-Sat; S Spandau, U Altstadt Spandau)

SIGHTS

★ZITADELLE SPANDAU CASTLE

(Spandau Citadel; 030-354 9440; www.zitadelle-berlin.de; Am Juliusturm 64; adult/concession €4.50/2.50, audioguide €2; 10am-5pm Fri-Wed, 1-8pm Thu, last entry 30min before closing; U Zitadelle) The 16th-century Spandau Citadel, on a little island in the Havel River, is considered to be one of the world's best-preserved Renaissance fortresses. With its moat, drawbridge and arrowhead-shaped bastions, it is also a veritable textbook in military architecture. These days, the impressive complex multitasks as museum, exhibit space, cultural venue and wintering ground for thousands of bats. Climb the 30m-high Julius Tower for sweeping views. Top international artists perform at the Citadel Music Festival in summer.

There are permanent exhibits on the history of the fortress, of Spandau in general and of political monuments that were once part of Berlin's urban landscape. A bizarre highlight is the head of the Lenin statue that once graced Platz der Vereinten Nationen in Friedrichshain.

NIKOLAIKIRCHE CHURCH

(Church of St Nicholas; 030-322 944 555; www.nikolai-spandau.de; Reformationsplatz 6; tower €2; noon-4pm Mon-Fri, 11am-3pm Sat, 11.30am-4pm Sun, tower tours 12.30pm Sat, 12.30pm 1st & 3rd Sun Apr-Oct; U Altstadt Spandau) The Gothic Church of St Nicholas is famous for hosting Brandenburg's first public Lutheran-style service back in 1539, under elector Joachim II, whose bronze statue stands outside the church. Inside, treasures include a baptismal font (1398), a baroque pulpit (1714) and an 8m-high late-Renaissance altar (1582).

Also note the cannonball lodged in the northern church wall that commemorates the attack on the Spandau citadel in 1813.

GOTISCHES HAUS HISTORIC BUILDING

(030-354 9440; www.gotischeshaus.de; Breite Strasse 32; 10am-6pm Mon-Sat, noon-6pm Sun, closed Mon Oct-Mar; U Altstadt Spandau) FREE Whoever built the Gothic House in the 15th century must have been flush with cash; it's made of stone, not wood as was customary in those times. The well-preserved Altstadt gem is one of the oldest surviving residential buildings in Berlin. It houses an art gallery, a Spandau history exhibit and the tourist office (note the ornate net-ribbed vaulted ceiling).

WORTH A DETOUR

MILITARY AVIATION HISTORY ON THE RUNWAY

Run by the Bundeswehr (German armed forces), the **Militärhistorisches Museum – Flugplatz Berlin-Gatow** (Museum of Military History – Airfield Berlin-Gatow; 030-3687 2601; www.mhm-gatow.de; Am Flugplatz Gatow 33; 10am-6pm Tue-Sun; P; 135) spreads its wings over a military airfield used by both the Nazis and the British Royal Air Force. The permanent exhibit in Hangar 3 examines the evolution of military aviation in Germany from 1884 to the present day. Outside, dozens of fighter jets, bombers, reconnaissance aircraft, helicopters and air defence systems – mostly from the Cold War era – litter the runway, including a Russian MiG-21 and an Antonov An-14.

The museum is about 10km south of central Spandau. Take bus 135 from S- or U-Bahn Rathaus Spandau to 'Kurpromenade', then walk for 1km.

EATING & DRINKING

SATT UND SELIG INTERNATIONAL €€

(☎030-3675 3877; www.sattundselig.de; Carl-Schurz-Strasse 47; mains €9-20; ⏲9am-11pm; 👪; Ⓤ Altstadt Spandau) In a baroque half-timbered house in the historic centre, this local favourite gets things right from morning to night. The breakfast selection is legendary, the cakes homemade and the main dishes (including steaks from the lava grill) creative, fresh and ample. In summer, terrace tables spill out onto the pedestrian zone. Kids' menu available.

BRAUHAUS SPANDAU GERMAN €€

(☎030-353 9070; www.brauhaus-spandau.de; Neuendorfer Strasse 1; mains €10-19; ⏲10am-midnight Sun-Thu, to 1am Fri & Sat; Ⓤ Altstadt Spandau) In good weather there are few nicer places to while away a few hours in central Spandau than in the tree-canopied beer garden of this rustic brewpub located in a historical red-brick building. Always on tap is its Spandauer Havelbräu, which goes well with its hearty German pub grub. Breakfast is served until 2pm.

Grunewald & Dahlem

Explore

Berlin's most upper-crust neighbourhoods, Dahlem and Grunewald are packed with cultural and natural appeal. Set between their leafy streets and lavish villa colonies (for instance around Grunewald S-Bahn station) are gardens, parks, palaces and a sprinkling of museums, most of them with an art focus. After WWII, the area was part of the American sector, a legacy reflected in such institutions as the AlliiertenMuseum (Allied Museum) and the hulking US consulate. The Grunewald forest, a vast fresh-air refuge criss-crossed by paths and dotted with lakes extending all the way west to the Havel River, offers a respite from the city. Wild boars, deer and other animals make their home here.

The Best...

- **Sight** Brücke-Museum
- **Place to Eat & Drink** Luise (p238)

Top Tip

Berlin's vast **botanical gardens** (☎030-8385 0100; www.bgbm.org; Königin-Luise-Strasse 6-8; adult/concession €6/3; ⏲gardens 9am-8pm, greenhouses to 7pm; Ⓟ; Ⓢ Botanischer Garten) boast 22,000 plant species and are an inspirational spot to reconnect with nature.

Getting There & Away

U-Bahn The U3 meanders through this area; key stops are Dahlem-Dorf for the museums and Krumme Lanke for easy access to lakes and the southern Grunewald forest.

S-Bahn The S1 skirts southern Dahlem, while the S7 runs straight through the Grunewald forest.

Need to Know

- **Area Code** ☎030
- **Location** About 11km southwest of central Berlin.

SIGHTS

BRÜCKE-MUSEUM GALLERY

(☎030-831 2029; www.bruecke-museum.de; Bussardsteig 9; adult/concession/under 18yr €6/4/free, with Kunsthaus Dahlem €8/5/free; ⏲11am-5pm Wed-Mon; Ⓟ; Ⓤ Oskar-Helene-Heim, then bus 115 or X10 to Pücklerstrasse) In 1905 Karl Schmidt-Rottluff, Erich Heckel and Ernst Ludwig Kirchner founded Germany's first modern-art group, called Die Brücke (The Bridge). Rejecting traditional techniques taught in the academies, they experimented with bright, emotional colours and warped perspectives that paved the way for German expressionism and modern art in general. Schmidt-Rottluff's personal collection forms the core of this lovely presentation of expressionist art.

David Bowie was a frequent visitor to the Brücke-Museum during his Berlin years in the mid-'70s. Heckel's painting *Roquairol* inspired the cover of his *Heroes* album.

TRACKS OF DEATH

Starting in 1941, more than 50,000 Jewish Berliners were deported from Gleis 17 (platform 17) next to the S-Bahn station Grunewald. Some 186 trains left for Theresienstadt, Riga, Lodz and Auschwitz, carrying their Jewish cargo like cattle to the slaughter. It's now the **Mahnmal Gleis 17** (Platform 17 Memorial; www.memorialmuseums.org; Am Bahnhof Grunewald; ⌚24hr; Ⓢ Grunewald). Along the platform's edge, plaques record the departure dates, the number of people transported and the destination of each train. It's quiet here, with only the trees rustling in the breeze, but the silence speaks loudly.

A visit here is easily combined with the nearby Kunsthaus Dahlem.

KUNSTHAUS DAHLEM GALLERY

(☎030-8322 7258; www.kunsthaus-dahlem.de; Käuzchensteig 8; adult/concession/under 19yr €6/4/free, with Brücke-Museum €8/5/free; ⌚11am-5pm Wed-Mon; Ⓟ; Ⓤ Oskar-Helene-Heim, then bus 115 or X10) This small museum presents postwar modernist works created in West and East Germany, especially between the end of WWII in 1945 and the construction of the Berlin Wall in 1961. While western artists embraced abstraction during these early Cold War years, social realism emerged as the guiding principle in the east. Housed in the monumental studio of Third Reich–era sculptor Arno Breker, themed short- and long-term exhibits, mostly of sculpture, zero in on this often overlooked period in art history.

There's a lovely museum cafe with a terrace where you can indulge in coffee and cake or a light meal.

Combination tickets with the nearby Brücke-Museum (of German expressionist art) are available.

ALLIIERTENMUSEUM BERLIN MUSEUM

(Allied Museum; ☎030-818 1990; www.alliiertenmuseum.de; Clayallee 135; ⌚10am-6pm Tue-Sun; Ⓟ; 🚌115, X83, Ⓤ Oskar-Helene-Heim) FREE The original Checkpoint Charlie guardhouse, a Berlin Airlift plane and a reconstructed spy tunnel are among the top exhibits at the Allied Museum. The permanent exhibit documents historical milestones and the challenges faced by the Western Allies during the Cold War. It covers the Allied victory, the early years of occupation and the Berlin Airlift, then jumps headlong into the Cold War years when Berlin was a major spy capital, ending with reunification and the withdrawal of Allied forces in 1994.

The first part of the exhibit is housed in the former Outpost cinema for US troops. An original piece of the Berlin Wall sits in the yard. All signage is in English, French and German.

'BERLIN BRAIN' LIBRARY ARCHITECTURE

(Philological Library of the Free University; ☎030-8385 8888; www.fu-berlin.de/sites/philbib; Habelschwerdter Allee 45; ⌚9am-10pm Mon-Fri, 10am-8pm Sat & Sun; Ⓤ Thielplatz) FREE British architect Norman Foster was the brain behind the 'Berlin Brain', a cranial-shaped 2005 masterpiece of modern architecture that houses the Philological Library at the **Freie Universität Berlin** (Free University Berlin). Inside are four floors sheltered within a naturally ventilated, bubble-like enclosure draped in aluminium and glazed panels. An inner membrane of translucent glass fibre filters the daylight, while scattered transparent openings allow momentary glimpses of sky.

GRUNEWALDTURM TOWER

(Havelchaussee 61; adult/concession €5/2.50; ⌚10am-10pm; Ⓟ; 🚌218) With its dainty turrets and red bricks, the 55m neo-Gothic Grunewald tower has dreamy 'Rapunzel' looks even if it was built to mark the 100th birthday of decidedly unromantic Wilhelm I. That's him in marble in the domed hall. Some 200 steps lead up to a viewing platform for a grand woods-and-river panorama. A restaurant provides sustenance.

The tower was designed by Franz Schwechten, who was also the architect of the Gedächtniskirche (Memorial Church) in Charlottenburg and the Kulturbrauerei in Prenzlauer Berg.

EATING & DRINKING

LINDWERDER GERMAN €€

(☎030-2007 6949; www.lindwerder.de; Havelchaussee 43; mains €13-35; ⌚noon-10pm Wed-Sun; 🅿; 🚌218) A visit to this lovely restaurant on a teensy island is the perfect antidote to urban overwhelm. Feel the stress melt away as you count the water lilies from your terrace table while downing a cold one, munching homemade cakes or tucking into German fare from local pike-perch to hearty goulash. A little ferry (€2 return) will get you there.

LUISE INTERNATIONAL €€

(☎030-841 8880; www.luise-dahlem.de; Königin-Luise-Strasse 40-42; pizza €8-13, mains €10-25; ⌚11am-11pm Mon-Thu, 11am-midnight Fri, 10am-midnight Sat, 10am-11pm Sun; 📶👪; 🅄Dahlem-Dorf) This cafe-restaurant-beer-garden combo is a Dahlem institution with a long menu likely to please everyone from saladheads to schnitzel fiends to pizza punters. Scrumptious breakfasts are served until noon, and there are seven beers on tap to enjoy beneath the chestnut trees. Children can romp around on a playground and pick from their own menu.

Wannsee

Explore

Leafy Wannsee, Berlin's southwesternmost suburb, is named for the enormous Wannsee lake, which is really just a bulge in the Havel River. In fine weather it's a fantastic place to leave the city bustle behind. You can cruise around the lake, walk in the forest, visit an enchanting island, tour a Prussian palace, and work on your tan at the Strandbad Wannsee, a lakeside lido with a long sandy beach, or at one of the area's other quick-dip spots. At the western edge of the lake (and easily reached by bus) are a couple of major sights, one linked to the Nazis and one to the painter Max Liebermann.

LOCAL KNOWLEDGE

SPLISH, SPLASH – FAVOURITE SWIMMING LAKES

Berlin summers have been getting hotter in recent years. Fortunately, the city and surrounding countryside are dotted with hundreds of lakes. So when the mercury soars, do as the locals do and kick back by the water. Just don't be shocked by the scores of bathers letting it all hang out...

Our top four natural splash zones:

Schlachtensee This popular lake in Zehlendorf even has a namesake S-Bahn station (S1), making it easy to get to and therefore often crowded. Spread out on the lawn or follow the shoreline path to find a more secluded spot under the trees. A short walk gets you to a restaurant with beer garden.

Strandbad Plötzensee (☎030-8597 6425; www.strandbad.ploetzensee.de; Nordufer 26; adult/concession €6/3; ⌚9am-8pm Mon-Fri, to 10pm Sat & Sun May-Aug, from 10am Sep; 🚋M13, 50) In the district of Wedding, this privately run lido on a natural lake has a broad, sandy beach, expansive lawns, pizza, cocktails and the occasional concert. It's a short walk from tram station Virchow-Klinikum, the terminus of lines M13 and 50.

Strandbad Wannsee (☎030-2219 0011; www.berlinerbaeder.de/baeder/strandbad-wannsee; Wannseebadweg 25; €3.80; ⌚10am-7pm May & Sep, 9am-8pm Jun-Aug, last entry 1hr before closing; 🅂Nikolassee) With its 1.2km-long ribbon of golden sand, Berlin's most famous lakeside beach has delighted aquaphiles for more than a century. You can rent a traditional wicker beach chair called a *Strandkorb*. Active types can pick from the gamut of water sports.

Liepnitzsee Out in Wandlitz in Brandenburg, this lake is a bit harder to reach but so worth it! Clean, crystal-clear water, an island to swim to, and mature trees for chilling in the shade await. Rent a car for the 50km drive, or bring a bicycle and take the S2 to Bernau, then pedal 10km to the lake.

The Best...

➜ **Sight** Liebermann-Villa am Wannsee

➜ **Place to Eat & Drink** Loretta am Wannsee (p240)

Top Tip

For cruising on the cheap, catch the 20-minute ride on public-transport ferry F10 from Wannsee to the Spandau suburb of Alt-Kladow (tariff AB, €2.90).

Getting There & Away

S-Bahn Take S1 or S7 from central Berlin to Wannsee, then walk or continue by bus, depending on where you're headed.

Need to Know

➜ **Area Code** 030

➜ **Location** About 25km southwest of central Berlin.

SIGHTS

LIEBERMANN-VILLA AM WANNSEE MUSEUM

(030-8058 5900; www.liebermann-villa.de; Colomierstrasse 3; adult/concession/under 18yr €10/6/free, multimedia guide €3; 10am-6pm Wed-Mon Apr-Sep, 11am-5pm Wed-Mon Oct-Mar; S Wannsee, then bus 114) This lovely lakefront villa was the summer retreat of German impressionist painter and Berliner Secession founder Max Liebermann from 1909 until his death in 1935. Liebermann loved the lyricism of nature and often painted the gardens as seen through the window of his barrel-vaulted upstairs studio. A selection of these works is displayed in these very rooms, while downstairs you'll find a timeline charting milestones in the life of the Liebermann family and the villa itself.

Afterwards, drink in the entrancing views of the beautiful gardens spilling into Lake Wannsee over coffee and cake from the villa's **Cafe Max**, which has seating in the Liebermann family dining room and on the flower-flanked terrace.

PFAUENINSEL PARK

(Peacock Island; 0331-969 4200; www.spsg.de; Nikolskoer Weg; return ferry adult/child €4/3; ferry 10am-6pm Apr-Oct, to 4pm Nov-Mar; S Wannsee, then bus 218) 'Back to nature' was the dictum in the 18th century, so Friedrich Wilhelm II had this little Havel island turned into an idyllic playground, perfect for retreating from state affairs and for frolicking with his mistress in a snowy-white fairy-tale **palace** (closed for renovation). For added romance, he brought in a flock of peacocks that gave the island its name; you'll find the eponymous birds strutting their stuff to this day.

Even with the palace closed, Pfaueninsel makes for a lovely excursion. A standout among the smattering of other buildings is the **Meierei,** a dairy farm in the shape of a ruined Gothic monastery at the island's northern end.

Pfaueninsel is a nature preserve, so there's no smoking, cycling or swimming. There are no cafes or restaurants, but picnicking is allowed. The island is about 4km northwest of Wannsee S-Bahn station, from where bus 218 goes to the ferry dock several times hourly.

HAUS DER WANNSEE-KONFERENZ MEMORIAL

(030-805 0010; www.ghwk.de; Am Grossen Wannsee 56-58; 10am-6pm; S Wannsee, then bus 114) FREE In January 1942 a group of 15 high-ranking Nazi officials met in a stately villa near Lake Wannsee to hammer out the details of the 'Final Solution': the systematic deportation and murder of European Jews. The 13-room exhibit (in German and English) in the very rooms where discussions took place illustrates the sinister meeting; it also examines the racial policies and persecution leading up to it and such issues as how aware ordinary Germans were of the genocidal actions.

You can study the actual minutes of the meeting (taken by Adolf Eichmann) and look at photographs of those involved, many of whom lived to a ripe old age. The site is about 2.5km northwest of Wannsee S-Bahn station and served from there by bus 114 several times hourly.

SCHLOSS GLIENICKE PALACE

(0331-969 4200; www.spsg.de; Königstrasse 36; adult/concession €6/5; 10am-5.30pm Tue-Sun Apr-Oct, to 4pm Sat & Sun Nov-Mar; P; S Wannsee, then bus 316) Glienicke Palace is the result of a rich royal kid travelling to Italy and falling in love with the country. Prince Carl of Prussia (1801–83) was only 21 when he returned to Berlin giddy with

BOATING ON THE WANNSEE

From April to mid-October, **Stern + Kreisschiffahrt** (030-536 3600; www.sternundkreis.de; Ronnebypromenade; 2hr cruise adult/child €14.50/7.25; Apr-Oct; S Wannsee) operates two-hour cruises around seven lakes, departing from the same landing docks near Wannsee S-Bahn station as the public ferry to Kladow. The website has tickets and times.

dreams of building his own Italian villa, so he hired starchitect du jour Karl Friedrich Schinkel to turn an existing garden estate into an elegant, antique-looking compound. You can visit the richly decorated interior with its marble fireplaces, sparkling chandeliers, gold-framed paintings and fine furniture.

The turquoise bedroom of the princess and the midnight-blue library are especially memorable. Schinkel not only expanded the mansion but added a smaller guesthouse (the 'Casino') and two charming pavilions, the **Kleine Neugierde** ('Small Curiosity') and **Grosse Neugierde** ('Great Curiosity'). The latter sits in an especially scenic spot overlooking the Havel River, Schloss Babelsberg and the outskirts of Potsdam. The palace is about 6km west of S-Bahn station Wannsee and served several times hourly by bus 316.

EATING & DRINKING

LORETTA AM WANNSEE GERMAN €€

(030-8010 5333; http://loretta-berlin.de; Kronprinzessinnenweg 260; beer-garden snacks €2.50-11, restaurant mains €14-26; noon-10pm or later; P; S Wannsee) Robust Bavarian cooking is the focus of the menu at this traditional but updated restaurant where the enchanting beer garden has a view of Wannsee lake in the distance. Have a grilled sausage or a crisp salad, or go the whole hog with *Grillhaxe* (pork leg) braised in black beer. König Pilsner, Augustiner Helles and Erdinger Urweisse are on tap.

It's about 300m south of Wannsee S-Bahn station.

RESTAURANT SEEHAASE INTERNATIONAL €€

(030-8049 6474; www.restaurant-seehaase.de; Am Grossen Wannsee 58/60; mains €10-22; noon-8pm Mon-Thu, to 9pm Fri, 11am-9pm Sat, 11am-8pm Sun; P; S Wannsee, then bus 114) Most of the Wannsee waterfront lots are in private hands, so the Seehaase with its lake views is predictably popular. The menu covers all the bases from breakfast to pasta, and *Flammkuchen* (Alsatian pizza) to grilled fish and meat, plus a few dishes calibrated to kids' tastes.

It's close to the Haus der Wannsee-Konferenz (p239).

Köpenick

Explore

The southeastern Berlin suburb of Köpenick was founded around 1240, making it only three years younger than the capital itself. It's famous for its handsome baroque palace, a picturesque Altstadt and a trio of superlative natural assets: Berlin's largest lake (Müggelsee), biggest forest (Köpenicker Stadtforst) and highest natural elevation (Müggelberge, 115m). A leisurely ramble, relaxed boat ride or cooling dip in the water quickly restores balance to a brain overstimulated by life in the city or too much sightseeing.

Many of the cobblestone streets in the Altstadt still follow their medieval layout. The main street, Alt-Köpenick, is lined with baroque beauties and the historic Rathaus.

Urban trend-spotters, meanwhile, might want to keep an eye on developments in Oberschöneweide, a former industrial area northwest of central Köpenick that's slowly showing up on the radar of artists and digital creatives.

The Best...

- **Sight** Schloss Köpenick
- **Place to Eat & Drink** Ratskeller Köpenick (p242)

Top Tip

For a more in-depth understanding of Köpenick's history, take a self-guided tour with the help of a multimedia audioguide (€5) dispensed by the tourist office.

Getting There & Away

S-Bahn For the Altstadt, take the S3 to S-Bahn station Köpenick, then walk 1.5km south along Bahnhofstrasse or take tram 62 to the Schloss Köpenick. For the Müggelsee continue on the S3 to Friedrichshagen and then take tram 60 or walk 1.5km south on Bölschestrasse.

Need to Know

- **Area Code** ☎030
- **Location** About 16km southeast of central Berlin.
- **Tourist Office** (☎030-6548 4348; www.tkt-berlin.de; Alt-Köpenick 31-33; 9am-6pm Mon-Fri, 10am-1pm Sat; 62, S Köpenick)

SIGHTS

SCHLOSS KÖPENICK — PALACE

(Museum of Decorative Arts; ☎030-266 424 242; www.smb.museum; Schlossinsel 1; adult/concession/under 18yr €6/3/free; 11am-6pm Tue-Sun Apr-Sep, to 5pm Thu-Sun Oct-Mar; 62, S Köpenick) Berlin's only surviving baroque palace, on a little island off the Altstadt, houses a branch of Berlin's **Kunstgewerbemuseum** (Museum of Decorative Arts). It's a rich and eclectic collection of furniture, tapestries, porcelain, silverware, glass and other frilly objects from the Renaissance, baroque and rococo periods. Note the elaborate ceiling paintings and stucco ornamentation. Highlights include four lavishly panelled rooms and the recreated **Wappensaal** (Coat of Arms Hall).

It was in this very hall in 1730 that a military court sentenced Crown Prince Friedrich (later Frederick the Great) and his friend Hans Katte to death for attempted desertion. The future king was eventually spared but forced by his father, the 'Soldier King', to watch his friend's beheading.

RATHAUS KÖPENICK — HISTORIC BUILDING

(Town Hall; Alt-Köpenick 21; 8am-6pm; 62, S Köpenick) FREE With its frilly turrets, soaring tower and stepped gable, Köpenick's town hall exudes fairy-tale charm but is actually more famous for an incident that happened back in 1906. An unemployed cobbler named Wilhelm Voigt, costumed as an army captain, marched upon the town hall, arrested the mayor, confiscated the city coffers and disappeared with the loot. Although quickly caught, Voigt became a celebrity for his chutzpah. A bronze statue and an exhibit recall the story, which is re-enacted every summer.

GROSSER MÜGGELSEE — LAKE

(60, S Friedrichshagen) At 4km long and 2.5km wide, the Müggelsee is Berlin's largest lake. Hemmed in by forest on two sides, it's hugely popular for swimming and boating on hot summer days. It's easily reached by public transport in less than an hour from central Berlin.

WORTH A DETOUR

DEUTSCH-RUSSISCHES MUSEUM BERLIN-KARLSHORST

On 8 May 1945, the madness of six years of WWII in Europe ended when Field Marshal Wilhelm Keitel signed Nazi Germany's unconditional surrender in this building, which was then the headquarters of the Soviet army. Today the **Deutsch-Russisches Museum Berlin-Karlshorst** (German-Russian Museum Berlin-Karlshorst; ☎030-5015 0810; www.museum-karlshorst.de; Zwieseler Strasse 4; 10am-6pm Tue-Sun; S Karlshorst) houses a memorial exhibit that charts this fateful day and the events leading up to it from both the Russian and German perspectives.

Documents, photographs, uniforms and knick-knacks illustrate such topics as the Hitler–Stalin Pact, the daily grind of life as a WWII Soviet soldier and the fate of Soviet civilians during wartime. You can stand in the great hall where the surrender was signed and see the office of Marshal Zhukov, the first Soviet supreme commander after WWII when the building was the seat of the Soviet Military Administration. Outside is a battery of Soviet weapons, including a howitzer canon and the devastating Katyuscha multiple rocket launcher, also known as the 'Stalin organ'.

The museum is a 10- to 15-minute walk from the S-Bahn station; take the Treskowallee exit, then turn right onto Rheinsteinstrasse.

The Müggelpark on its north shore has restaurants and beer gardens as well as the landing docks of **Reederei Kutzker** (☎03362-6251; www.reederei-kutzker.de; Müggelseedamm, Müggelpark; 1hr tours €8; ⏲tours Apr-early Oct; 🚊60, Ⓢ Friedrichshagen), which runs lake tours several times daily.

For a walk in the woods, head to the other side of the Spree via the nearby Spreetunnel. **Seebad Friedrichshagen** (☎030-645 5756; www.seebad-friedrichshagen.de; Müggelseedamm 216; adult/concession €5.50/3; ⏲10am-7pm May-Aug; 🚊60, Ⓢ Friedrichshagen) is the closest public lake beach and has boat rentals; it's about 300m east of the Müggelpark.

EATING & DRINKING

RATSKELLER KÖPENICK — GERMAN €€

(☎030-655 5178; www.ratskeller-koepenick.de; Rathaus, Alt-Köpenick 21; mains €9-19; ⏲11am-11pm Tue-Sat, to 10pm Sun; 🚊62, 68, Ⓢ Köpenick) The olde-worlde ambience at this vaulted cellar-warren in Köpenick's historic town hall (p241) is fun, and the menu full of classic rib-stickers (try the smoked pork knuckle) alongside healthier, seasonal and meatless selections. Many ingredients are locally sourced. Reservations advised for the Friday and Saturday live-jazz nights.

KROKODIL — MEDITERRANEAN €€

(☎030-6588 0094; www.der-coepenicker.de; Gartenstrasse 46-48; mains €8.50-19; ⏲4-11pm Mon-Fri, 3pm-midnight Sat, noon-11pm Sun; Ⓟ; 🚊62, 68, Ⓢ Köpenick) The seasonal fare at this urban getaway is delish, but even more memorable is the idyllic setting on the Dahme River some 700m south of the Altstadt. Join locals in capping a day of lounging and swimming at Krokodil's sandy beach with sundowners or an al fresco dinner. The attached **guesthouse** (☎030-6588 0094; www.hotel-pension-berlin.eu; Gartenstrasse 46-48; tw from €99; 🚭📶; 🚊62, 62 Schlossplatz Köpenick) has 15 nicely decorated rooms.

From S-Bahn station Köpenick take tram 62 or 68 to Schlossplatz, then walk east on Müggelheimer Strasse for 300m and turn south on Kietz for another 400m.

Sleeping

Berlin offers the gamut of places to unpack your suitcase. Just about every international chain now has an offering in the German capital, but more interesting options that better reflect the city's verve and spirit abound. You can sleep in a former bank, boat or factory, in the home of a silent-movie diva or in a 'flying bed'.

Hotels

With around 143,000 beds in almost 800 properties, Berlin has more beds than New York and even more are scheduled to come online in the coming years. You'll find the entire range of hotels in Berlin, from no-frills cookie-cutter chains to all-out luxury abodes with top-notch amenities and fall-over-backwards service.

The best beds often sell out early, so make reservations, especially around major holidays, cultural events and trade shows. Most properties can be booked directly on their website, usually with a best-price guarantee.

Most smaller and midsize hotels are now entirely nonsmoking; a few of the larger ones (especially the international chains) still set aside rooms or entire floors for smokers.

BOUTIQUE, DESIGNER & ART HOTELS

Berlin being an art- and design-minded city, it's not surprising that there's a large number of smaller indie hotels catering to the needs of savvy urban nomads with at least a midrange budget. Properties often integrate distinguished architecture with a customised design concept that projects a sense of place and tends to appeal to creative spirits and travellers searching for an authentic and localised experience. There's usually great emphasis on the latest tech trends and on such lifestyle essentials as iPod docks and brand-name espresso machines and sound systems. The antithesis of cookie-cutter chains, these types of abodes are sprinkled around the city but are especially prevalent in the Mitte district. Many have succeeded in cultivating the local community with hip rooftop lounges, cocktail bars, progressive restaurants, chic spas and pop-up parties and events.

CHAIN HOTELS

Practically all international hotel chains now have one or multiple properties in Berlin. Since most conform to certain standards of decor, service and facilities, they're great for people who enjoy predictability and privacy (or simply want to use up those frequent flyer points). Most have several categories of comfort, from cramped singles to high-roller suites, with rates reflecting size and amenities. Prices generally fluctuate dramatically, with last-minute, weekend or low-occupancy bargains a possibility.

Besides the international chains, there are also some Berlin-based contenders, including Amano (www.amanogroup.de) and Meininger (www.meininger-hotels.com) and German chains like Motel One (www.motelone.com) and Leonardo (www.leonardo-hotels.com).

Hostels

Berlin's hostel scene is as vibrant as ever and consists of both classic backpacker hostels with large dorms and a communal spirit to modern 'flashpacker' crash pads catering to wallet-watching city-breakers. Quite common by now are hostel-hotel hybrids that have a standard similar to budget hotels. Many also have private quarters with bathrooms and even apartments with kitchens. You'll find them in all districts, but especially

SMOKING

Smoking rooms are a dying breed. Some larger properties and chain hotels may still have set aside floors with rooms where smoking is permitted. Smaller independent hotels and hostels usually don't allow smoking in rooms and often impose fines on those who light up anyway. By law, there's no smoking in indoor public areas.

in Mitte, Kreuzberg and Friedrichshain, putting you within stumbling distance of bars and clubs.

Dorm beds can be had for as little as €10, but the better places now charge twice as much or more for dorms with fewer beds and en suite bathroom. Dorms tend to be mixed, though some hostels also offer women-only units. Hostels have no curfew and staff tend to be savvy, multilingual and keen to help with tips and advice.

Short-Term Holiday Rentals

Renting a furnished flat is a hugely popular – and economical – lodging option. The benefit of space, privacy and independence makes flats especially attractive to families and small groups. In 2016, the state government introduced a law that categorically barred locals from renting their flat to short-term holidaymakers through such platforms as Airbnb. However, after the regulations were softened in 2018, the supply of legal short-term rental apartments has again grown significantly. The highest concentration can be found in northern Neukölln, Kreuzberg, Mitte and Prenzlauer Berg.

If you're planning to stay in Berlin for a month or longer, renting a room or an apartment might be the most sensible option. Try the online platform www.housinganywhere.com.

B&Bs

Nostalgic types seeking old Berlin flavour should check into a charismatic B&B, called *Hotel-Pension* or simply *Pension*. But you'd better do it quickly because these types of abodes are a dying breed! *Pensions* typically occupy one or several floors of a historic residential building. The cheapest rooms may have shared facilities. You'll still find a few of these time warps in the western district of Charlottenburg, around Kurfürstendamm.

Rates

Fierce competition has kept prices low compared to other capital cities in Europe. Prices spike during major trade shows, festivals and public holidays, when early reservations are essential. Hotels geared to business travellers often have good deals at weekends. In winter, prices often plummet outside holidays, with five-star rooms costing as little as €120. Throughout the year, the lowest rates of the week are for Sunday nights.

Amenities

Midrange options generally offer the best value for money. Expect clean, comfortable and decent-sized rooms with at least a modicum of style, a private bathroom, TV and wi-fi. Top-end hotels provide the full spectrum of international-standard amenities and perhaps a scenic location, designer decor or historical ambience. Budget places are generally hostels or other simple establishments where bathrooms may be shared.

Overall, rooms tend to be on the small side. You'll usually find that BBC and CNN are the only English-language channels on TV (nearly all foreign shows and films are dubbed into German) and that air-con is a rare commodity. Fans or cooling units may be provided on particularly scorching summer days.

Wi-fi is commonplace and almost always free, but in rare cases access may be restricted to public areas. Few hotels have their own parking lot or garage, and even if they do, space will be limited and the cost as high as €30 per day. Public garages are widely available, but also cost a pretty penny.

Lonely Planet's Top Choices

Orania.Berlin (p250) Gorgeous urban-chic pad for individualists and style lovers with top-rated restaurant and live music.

Michelberger Hotel (p251) Fun base with eccentric design, party pedigree and unpretentious attitude that beautifully captures the Berlin vibe.

S/O Berlin Das Stue (p250) Charismatic refuge from the urban bustle with understated grandeur and the Tiergarten park as a front yard.

Hotel am Steinplatz (p252) Golden 1920s glamour still radiates from the walls of this revivified art deco jewel.

Best By Budget: €

Grand Hostel Berlin Classic (p250) Connect to the magic of yesteryear at this historic lair imbued with both character and modern amenities.

EastSeven Berlin Hostel (p249) Friendly and low-key hostel with communal vibe ideal for solo travellers.

Hostel One80° (p247) Vast next-gen hostel with hotel-style comforts and amenities.

Best By Budget: €€

Orania.Berlin (p250) Culturally minded style pad with superb restaurant and live concerts.

Arte Luise Kunsthotel (p247) Sleep in artist-designed rooms sprawled across a historic building.

Almodóvar Hotel (p251) Solid eco-cred pairs with mod-cons and rooftop sauna.

Adina Apartment Hotel Berlin Checkpoint Charlie (p247) Ideal base for budget-conscious space-craving self-caterers.

Best By Budget: €€€

S/O Berlin Das Stue (p250) This chic and quiet outpost next to the Tiergarten park counts a spa and a Michelin restaurant among its assets.

Hotel am Steinplatz (p252) Reincarnated art deco gem with top-notch bar and restaurant.

Hotel de Rome (p247) Posh player in former bank building with rooftop bar and bank-vault pool and spa.

Best Cool Factor

Michelberger Hotel (p251) Zeitgeist-capturing crash pad with funky industrial DIY aesthetics and popular restaurant.

25hours Hotel Bikini Berlin (p252) Inner-city playground with easy access to top shopping and rooms overlooking the Berlin Zoo.

nhow Berlin (p251) Karim Rashid–designed riverside hotel with guitar rentals and recording studio.

Hüttenpalast (p250) Quirky abode where you can bed down in an old-school camper van or a regular room.

Best Hostels

Circus Hostel (p248) This Berlin classic is a superb launch pad for fun-seekers and culture cravers.

Grand Hostel Berlin Classic (p250) Historic lair with nostalgic flair and zeitgeist-compatible comforts.

EastSeven Berlin Hostel (p249) Small, personable and spotless crash pad, perfect for making new friends.

NEED TO KNOW

Price Ranges

The following price ranges refer to a standard double room with private bathroom during high season but outside of major events, holidays or trade-show periods. Rates include 7% VAT but not the 5% city tax. Breakfast is sometimes included, but more often than not is an optional extra.

€	less than €90
€€	€90–€180
€€€	more than €180

City Tax

Value-added tax (VAT; 7%) has long been included in room rates, but since 1 January 2014 an additional 5% 'city tax' is payable on the net room rates, ie excluding VAT and fees for amenities and services. The tax is added to the hotel bill. Business travellers are exempt from this tax.

Which Floor?

In Germany, 'ground floor' refers to the floor at street level. The 1st floor (what would be called the 2nd floor in the US) is the floor above that.

Where to Stay

NEIGHBOURHOOD	FOR	AGAINST
Historic Mitte	Close to major sights like Reichstag and Brandenburger Tor; great transport links; mostly high-end hotels; Michelin-starred and other top restaurants; close to theatre, opera and classical concert venues	Touristy, expensive, pretty dead at night
Museumsinsel & Alexanderplatz	Supercentral sightseeing quarter; easy transport access; close to blockbuster sights and mainstream shopping; large and new hotels	Noisy, busy and dusty thanks to major construction; hardly any nightlife
Scheunenviertel	Hipster quarter; trendy, historic, central; brims with boutique and designer hotels; indie and trendy chain shopping; international eats and strong cafe scene; top galleries and some street art	Pricey, busy in daytime, noisy, no parking, touristy
Prenzlauer Berg	Well-heeled, clean, charming residential area; lively cafe and restaurant scene; indie boutiques and Mauerpark flea market	Limited late-night action, few essential sights
Potsdamer Platz & Tiergarten	Urban flair in Berlin's only high-rise quarter; cutting-edge architecture; high-end international hotels; top museums, Philharmonie and multiplex cinemas; next to huge Tiergarten city park	Limited eating options; pricey; practically no street life at night
Kreuzberg	Vibrant arty, underground and multicultural party quarter; great bar-hopping and clubbing; high-octane vibe; great foodie scene; excellent street art	Gritty, noisy and busy; U-Bahn ride(s) away from major sights
Neukölln	Vibrant nightlife, international flair and restaurants; busy cafe scene; young population; close to Tempelhofer Feld	Grimy, noisy, lots of traffic, no parking
Friedrichshain	Student and young family quarter; bubbling nightlife; superb Cold War–era sights	Limited sleeping options; not so central for sightseeing; transport difficult in some areas
City West & Charlottenburg	The former heart of 'West Berlin'; great shopping on Kurfürstendamm; stylish lounges, 'Old Berlin' bars and quality restaurants; best range of good-value lodging; historic B&Bs	Sedate; far from key sights and happening nightlife

Historic Mitte

★**ADINA APARTMENT HOTEL BERLIN CHECKPOINT CHARLIE** APARTMENT €€
Map p324 (030-200 7670; www.adinahotels.com; Krausenstrasse 35-36; studio/1-bedroom apt from €109/139; U Hausvogteiplatz, Spittelmarkt) Adina's contemporary studios and one- and two-bedroom apartments with full kitchens are tailor-made for cost-conscious families, anyone in need of elbow room, and self-caterers (a supermarket is a minute away). Roomy studios with kitchenette are also available. The spa area with its 17m-long indoor pool and sauna helps combat post-flight fatigue. Optional breakfast is €15. See the website for other Adina properties in town.

★**MINILOFT MITTE BERLIN** APARTMENT €€
Map p324 (030-847 1090; www.miniloft.com; Hessische Strasse 5; apt €135-185; U Naturkundemuseum) These stunning lofts close to the main train station spread across a historic building and an adjoining modern annex and were created by their architect-owners with lots of energy-saving features. Units are light-flooded and come with stylishly minimalist furnishings and petite but thoughtfully equipped kitchenettes. Those in the old wing are quieter but not accessible by lift. Two-night minimum.

ARTE LUISE KUNSTHOTEL BOUTIQUE HOTEL €€
Map p324 (030-284 480; www.luise-berlin.com; Luisenstrasse 19; d from €109, with shared bathroom from €55; S Friedrichstrasse, U Friedrichstrasse) At this 'gallery with rooms' each of the 50 units is designed by a different artist who receives royalties whenever it's rented. All sport high ceilings, oak floors and wonderfully imaginative, poetic or bizarre decor – we're especially fond of number 107 with its giant bed. For cash-strapped art fans there are smaller rooms with shared baths. Avoid rooms facing the train tracks.

COSMO HOTEL BERLIN HOTEL €€
Map p324 (030-5858 2222; www.cosmo-hotel.de; Spittelmarkt 13; d €99-244; U Spittelmarkt) Despite its ho-hum location on a busy street, this privately owned hotel scores high for comfort, design and a 'with it' vibe. The lobby, with its extravagant lamps and armchairs, sets the tone for crisply angular rooms with silvery design accents and floor-to-ceiling windows. Suites have a balcony. The excellent breakfast buffet is €20.

HOTEL DE ROME LUXURY HOTEL €€€
Map p324 (030-460 6090; www.roccofortehotels.com; Behrenstrasse 37; d from €265; 100, 245, 300, U Hausvogteiplatz) A delightful alchemy of history and contemporary flair, this luxe contender in a 19th-century bank has sumptuously furnished, oversized rooms with extra-high ceilings, marble baths and heated floors. Wind down in the pool and spa area (a former vault), over cocktails in the bar or, in summer, on the rooftop terrace with historic Berlin views. Optional breakfast is €39.

HOTEL ADLON KEMPINSKI LUXURY HOTEL €€€
Map p324 (030-226 10; www.kempinski.com; Unter den Linden 77, Pariser Platz; r from €320; S Brandenburger Tor, U Brandenburger Tor) The Adlon has been Berlin's most high-profile defender of the grand tradition since 1907. The striking lobby with its signature elephant fountain is a mere overture to the full symphony of luxury awaiting in spacious, amenity-laden rooms and suites with timelessly regal decor. The snazziest ones overlook the Brandenburg Gate. Optional breakfast is €48. A top-notch spa with indoor pool and a double-Michelin-star restaurant add 21st-century cool. To soak up the ambience on a budget, have a drink in the lobby by the elephant fountain or a snack at the coffee shop.

Museumsinsel & Alexanderplatz

HOSTEL ONE80° HOSTEL €
Map p328 (030-2804 4620; www.one80hostels.com; Otto-Braun-Strasse 65; dm €10-30; S Alexanderplatz, U Alexanderplatz) With its designer sofas, ambient music and industrial-chic public areas, One80° is a next-gen lifestyle hostel. There's space for over 700 people in cheerfully painted dorms (some with private bathroom) sleeping four to eight in comfy bunk beds with individual reading lamps and two electrical outlets each. Optional breakfast is €7.20. Minimum age 18.

MOTEL ONE BERLIN-HACKESCHER MARKT HOTEL €€
Map p328 (030-2005 4080; www.motel-one.de; Dircksenstrasse 36; d from €90;

SAlexanderplatz, UAlexanderplatz) If you value location over luxury, this budget designer chain comes with excellent crash-pad credentials. Smallish rooms feature sleek touches (granite bathroom with rain showers and organic amenities, air-con) that are normally the reserve of posher players. Major sights, good restaurants and trendy shopping are just steps away. Check the website for the other Berlin locations. Optional breakfast is €11.50.

RADISSON BLU HOTEL HOTEL **€€**

Map p328 (030-238 280; www.radissonblu.com/hotel-berlin; Karl-Liebknecht-Strasse 3; d from €180; P; 100, 200, 245, SHackescher Markt, URotes Rathaus) At this swish and supercentral contender, you quite literally sleep with the fishes, thanks to the lobby's 25m-high tropical aquarium. Streamlined design radiates urban poshness in the 427 rooms and throughout the two restaurants and various social nooks. Thoughtful perks include a 24/7 spa with pool and sauna. Optional breakfast is €30.

CAPRI BY FRASER APARTMENT **€€**

Map p328 (030-20 07 70 1888; https://berlin.capribyfraser.com; Scharrenstrasse 22; r from €146; P; 200 248, 265, USpittelmarkt) These 143 self-catering studios and one-bedroom apartments close to Nikolaiviertel are a sweet fusion of substance and style. Smartly laid-out rooms come with plenty of closet space, device docks and kitchenettes, and there's a guest laundry, bar and restaurant on site. In the jazzily coloured lobby, a glass floor covers medieval foundations unearthed during construction. Optional breakfast is €15.

PARK INN BY RADISSON BERLIN ALEXANDERPLATZ HOTEL **€€**

Map p328 (030-238 90; www.parkinn-berlin.de; Alexanderplatz 7; d from €130; P; SAlexanderplatz, UAlexanderplatz) Views, views, views! Berlin's tallest hotel has got them. Right on Alexanderplatz, this sleek tower is honeycombed with 1012 modern and stylish rooms (some rather snug) sporting charcoal-and-white hues, panoramic windows, wooden floors and noiseless air-con. For superb sunsets, snag a room facing the Fernsehturm (TV Tower). Optional breakfast is €19.

Great rooftop panorama terrace (p119) with bar and lounge chairs.

HOTEL INDIGO ALEXANDERPLATZ HOTEL **€€**

Map p328 (030-505 0860; www.hotelindigoberlin.com/alex; Bernhard-Weiss-Strasse 5; d from €120; ; SAlexanderplatz, UAlexanderplatz) Sophisticated, efficient and supercentral, this mod designer hotel spoils you with amenities normally reserved for pricier abodes (fluffy bathrobes, smartphone docks, kettle). Contemporary rooms feature designer furniture, floor-to-ceiling windows, plank flooring and citrusy colour accents; standard ones are rather snug. Breakfast is €19.

ART'OTEL BERLIN MITTE HOTEL **€€**

Map p328 (030-240 620; www.artotels.de; Wallstrasse 70-73; d from €122; P; UMärkisches Museum) This boutique hotel wears its 'art' moniker with justifiable swagger: original works by renowned contemporary German artist Georg Baselitz decorate rooms and public areas. Suites have extra-cool bathrooms and those on the 6th floor even boast small balconies. The hotel is docked to the rococo Ermelerhaus, which harbours a modern Mediterranean restaurant. Optional breakfast is €14.

Scheunenviertel

★**CIRCUS HOSTEL** HOSTEL **€**

Map p330 (030-2000 3939; www.circus-berlin.de; Weinbergsweg 1a; dm from €19, d without/with bathroom €58/75; @; URosenthaler Platz) Clean, cheerfully painted singles, doubles and dorms (sleeping four to 10) plus abundant shared facilities, helpful staff and a great location are among the factors that have kept Circus at the top of the hostel heap for two decades. It has a cute on-site cafe (with €5 breakfast until 1am) and a basement bar with its own microbrewery and fun events.

HONIGMOND BOUTIQUE HOTEL BOUTIQUE HOTEL **€€**

Map p332 (030-284 4550; www.honigmond.de; Tieckstrasse 11; d €160; P@; UOranienburger Tor) This delightful hotel in a century-old building scores high, not for being particularly lavish, but for its familiar yet elegant ambience. Rooms sparkle with old-timey glory, complete with patterned wallpaper, wooden floors and framed oil paintings. The nicest are in the new wing and flaunt their historic features – ornate stucco ceilings, frescoes – to maximum effect. Also check out the charming nearby sister property, Honigmond Garden.

HOTEL AMANO HOTEL €€

Map p330 (030-809 4150; www.amanogroup.de; Auguststrasse 43; d from €120; P; Rosenthaler Platz) This sleek designer hotel has efficiently styled, mod-con-laden rooms, where white furniture teams up with oak floors and grey hues to create crisp cosiness. For space-cravers there are apartments in three sizes and with kitchens. Optional breakfast is €15.

The on-site Amano Bar (p134), in summer on the rooftop, is a local favourite.

FLOWER'S BOARDINGHOUSE MITTE APARTMENT €€

Map p330 (030-2804 5306; www.flowersberlin.de; Mulackstrasse 1; studio/1-bedroom apt from €85/115; reception 9am-2pm; P; Weinmeisterstrasse, Rosa-Luxemburg-Platz) Self-caterers won't miss many comforts of home in these 21 breezy self-catering apartments available in three sizes – L, XL and XXL – the last being a split-level unit with fabulous views over the rooftops. Units come with open kitchens; rates include a small breakfast (rolls, coffee, tea) that you pick up at reception.

BOUTIQUE HOTEL I31 BOUTIQUE HOTEL €€

Map p332 (030-338 4000; www.hotel-i31.de; Invalidenstrasse 31; d from €88; P; M5, M6, M8, M10, Naturkundemuseum) This contemporary contender has modern, if smallish, rooms in soothing colours and various relaxation zones, including a sauna, a sunny terrace and a small garden with sun lounges. Nice touch: the minibar with free soft drinks. For a special experience, stay in a converted shipping container framed by a leafy terrace. Breakfast is €17.

CASA CAMPER BOUTIQUE HOTEL €€€

Map p330 (030-2000 3410; www.casacamper.com; Weinmeisterstrasse 1; d incl breakfast €150-190; ; Weinmeisterstrasse) Catalan shoemaker Camper has translated its concept of chic yet sensible footwear into this style-pit for trend-conscious global nomads. Good-sized rooms come with colour-splashed walls, day-lit bathrooms with natural amenities, and beds that invite hitting the snooze button. Minibars are eschewed for a top-floor lounge with stellar views and free 24/7 hot and cold snacks and drinks.

Prenzlauer Berg

★EASTSEVEN BERLIN HOSTEL HOSTEL €

Map p334 (030-9362 2240; www.eastseven.de; Schwedter Strasse 7; dm/d from €25/65; @; Senefelderplatz) Excellent for solo travellers, this small indie hostel has personable staff who go out of their way to make all feel welcome. It's not a party hostel but you can still make friends while chilling in the lounge or garden (hammocks!), firing up the barbecue or hanging out in the 24-hour kitchen. Brightly painted dorms feature comfy pine beds and lockers. You must be 18 to stay unless with a parent.

★BRILLIANT APARTMENTS APARTMENT €€

Map p334 (030-8061 4796; www.brilliant-apartments.de; Oderberger Strasse 38; apt from €109; ; M1, 12, Eberswalder Strasse) These 11 stylish and modern self-catering studios and two-bedroom apartments have full kitchens, plenty of design cachet and neat historic touches such as exposed red-brick walls and wooden floors. Four have balconies, one a little garden. The location puts you in the middle of a neighbourhood filled with cafes, restaurants and boutiques and close to the Mauerpark.

Apartments facing out back are quieter. Three-night minimum stay most times.

HOTEL ODERBERGER HOTEL €€

Map p334 (030-780 089 760; www.hotel-oderberger.de; Oderberger Strasse 56/57; d incl breakfast from €129; P; M1, 12, Eberswalder Strasse) These stately public baths established in a neo-Renaissance building in 1902 have been recycled into a modern hotel that smoothly integrates original tiles, lamps, doors and other design details. Its most distinctive asset is the actual swimming pool (access €4) in a cathedral-like hall, which can be turned into an event space. An excellent restaurant and cosy bar invite winding down.

HOTEL KASTANIENHOF HOTEL €€

Map p334 (030-443 050; www.kastanienhof.berlin; Kastanienallee 65; d from €95; P@; M1, 12 to Zionskirchstrasse, Rosenthaler Platz, Senefelderplatz) Right on Kastanienallee with its cafes, restaurants and boutiques, this family-run traditional charmer has caring staff and 35 traditionally furnished rooms decked out in natural colours and pairing historical touches with a good range of mod cons. The cheapest are located in the attic; the nicest feature air-con. Optional breakfast is €11.

LINNEN GUESTHOUSE €€
Map p334 (030-4737 2440; www.linnenberlin.com; Eberswalder Strasse 35; d from €120; ; U Eberswalder Strasse) This 'boutique inn' brims with charisma in each of its five idiosyncratically furnished (and TV-less) rooms. The tiniest is No 4, which gets forest-cabin flair from wooden walls and bird feeders, while the largest is the Suite with burgundy walls and balcony. There are also apartments. The downstairs area serves breakfast, sandwiches and cakes until 6pm. Various minimum-stay periods.

Potsdamer Platz & Tiergarten

SCANDIC BERLIN POTSDAMER PLATZ HOTEL €€
Map p336 (030-700 7790; www.scandichotels.com; Gabriele-Tergit-Promenade 19; d from €115; P; U Mendelssohn-Bartholdy-Park) This Scandinavian import gets kudos for its central location and spacious rooms with box-spring beds, parquet floors, panoramic windows with blackout curtains and for going the extra mile when it comes to being green. Distinctive features include the good-sized 8th-floor gym-with-a-view, honey from the rooftop beehive and free bikes. Optional (partly organic) breakfast is €17.

MÖVENPICK HOTEL BERLIN AM POTSDAMER PLATZ HOTEL €€
Map p336 (030-230 060; www.moevenpick.com; Schöneberger Strasse 3; d from €115; P @; S Anhalter Bahnhof) This snazzy Green Globe–certified hotel smoothly marries contemporary boldness with the industrial flair of the listed Siemenshöfe factory. Rooms vamp it up with cheerful colours and sensuous olive-wood furniture, while the courtyard restaurant is lidded by a retractable glass roof for al-fresco dining. Light sleepers should ask about the special 'Sleep' rooms. Optional breakfast is €24.

GRIMM'S POTSDAMER PLATZ HOTEL €€
Map p339 (030-258 0080; www.grimms-hotel.de; Flottwellstrasse 45; d from €90; P; U Mendelssohn-Bartholdy-Park) The fairy tales of the Brothers Grimm inspired the name and decor of this cosmopolitan crash pad, which is mercifully uncluttered and kitsch-free. The 110 rooms feature the latest upscale touches such as extra-long mattresses, wooden floors and an eco-conscious heating and cooling system. The Finnish sauna (€12 fee) and rooftop terrace are popular regeneration areas. Optional breakfast is €11.

★S/O BERLIN DAS STUE BOUTIQUE HOTEL €€€
Map p336 (030-311 7220; www.das-stue.com; Drakestrasse 1; d from €340; P @; 100, 106, 200) This charismatic refuge in a 1930s Danish diplomatic outpost flaunts understated grandeur and has the Tiergarten park as a front yard. A crocodile sculpture flanked by sweeping staircases leads the way to a bar, a Michelin-starred restaurant and sleekly furnished, oversized rooms (some with terrace or balcony). The elegant spa has a pool, a sauna and top-notch massages. Optional breakfast €35.

Kreuzberg

★GRAND HOSTEL BERLIN CLASSIC HOSTEL €
Map p340 (030-2009 5450; www.grandhostel-berlin.de; Tempelhofer Ufer 14; dm €19-24, tw €83, tw without bathroom €58, incl breakfast; @; U Möckernbrücke) Cocktails in the library bar? Check. Canal views? Yep. Ensconced in a fully renovated 1870s building, the 'five-star' Grand Hostel is one of Berlin's most supremely comfortable, convivial and atmospheric hostels. The good-value private rooms have twin beds, purple carpet and wooden night stands.

Also check out its Grand Hostel Urban at Sonnenallee 6 in the heart of Neukölln.

HÜTTENPALAST HOSTEL €
Map p344 (030-3730 5806; www.huettenpalast.de; Hobrechtstrasse 66; d campervans & cabins €70-100, hotel €70-160; check-in 9am-6pm or by arrangement; ; U Hermannplatz) This indoor campground in an old vacuum-cleaner factory is an unusual place to hang your hat, even by Berlin's standards. It has hotel-style rooms (spiffed up in 2020) with private bath, but who wants those when you can sleep in a romantic wooden hut with rooftop terrace or in a snug vintage caravan?

★ORANIA.BERLIN HOTEL €€
Map p342 (030-6953 9680; www.orania.berlin; Oranienstrasse 40; d from €190; ;

ⓤMoritzplatz) This gorgeous hotel in a sensitively restored 1913 building wraps everything that makes Berlin special – culture, class and culinary acumen, infused with a freewheeling cosmopolitan spirit – into one tidy package. Warmth radiates from the open lobby bar, whose stylish furniture, sultry lighting and open fireplace exude living-room flair. Catch shuteye in 41 comfy rooms that mix retro and modern touches.

Berlin bands lure a local crowd to the bar and the upstairs salon. The restaurant (p188) is tops as well.

HOTEL JOHANN HOTEL €€

Map p340 (030-225 0740; www.hotel-johann-berlin.de; Johanniterstrasse 8; d from €97; P; ⓤPrinzenstrasse) This 33-room hotel consistently tops the popularity charts, thanks to its eager-to-please service, homey ambience and good-sized rooms with wooden flooring, uncluttered modern design and occasional historic flourishes. The small garden is perfect for summery breakfasts, while happening Bergmannstrasse and the Jüdisches Museum are both 1km away. Breakfast €13.

Neukölln

HOTEL PRENS BERLIN HOTEL €

Map p344 (030-887 759 960; www.hotel-prens.com; Kottbusser Damm 102; d €60-105; P; ⓤSchönleinstrasse) A great find if you're not in need of buckets of space, this small private hotel puts you smack dab in the heart of dynamic Neukölln, within stumbling distance of the canal and a United Nations of bars and restaurants. Rooms won't win any design awards but are clean and comfortable and come with soundproof windows. Breakfast is €8.50.

Friedrichshain

EASTERN COMFORT HOSTELBOAT HOSTEL €

Map p346 (030-6676 3806; www.eastern-comfort.com; Mühlenstrasse 73; dm/d from €16/58; reception 8am-midnight; ⓤWarschauer Strasse, ⓢWarschauer Strasse) Let the Spree River murmur you to sleep while you're snugly ensconced in this two-boat floating hostel right by the East Side Gallery. Cabins are trimmed in wood and sweetly snug (except for '1st class'); most have their own shower and toilet. Make new friends in the lounge bar that hosts parties and events. Optional breakfast is €8.

Cabins are also available on the sister boat on the Kreuzberg side of the Spree.

★MICHELBERGER HOTEL HOTEL €€

Map p346 (030-2977 8590; www.michelbergerhotel.com; Warschauer Strasse 39; d from €105; P; ⓤWarschauer Strasse, ⓢWarschauer Strasse) Offering the ultimate in creative places to stay, Michelberger perfectly encapsulates Berlin's offbeat DIY spirit without being self-consciously cool. Rooms don't hide their factory pedigree, but are comfortable and come in sizes suitable for lovebirds, families or rock bands. Staff are friendly and clued-up, and the restaurant (p208) is popular with both guests and locals. Optional breakfast is €20.

ALMODÓVAR HOTEL HOTEL €€

Map p346 (030-692 097 080; www.almodovarhotel.de; Boxhagener Strasse 83; d from €129; P; 21, M13, ⓢOstkreuz) A certified organic hotel, Almodóvar is perfect for keeping your healthy ways while travelling. A yoga mat is a standard amenity in the 60 rooms with modern-rustic natural rosewood furniture, sky-blue accent walls and iPod docking stations. The rooftop sauna will heat you up on cold days. Breakfast is €19.50.

NHOW BERLIN DESIGN HOTEL €€

Map p346 (030-290 2990; www.nhow-hotels.com; Stralauer Allee 3; d from €138; P; ⓢWarschauer Strasse, ⓤWarschauer Strasse) This riverside behemoth bills itself as a 'music and lifestyle' hotel and underscores the point by offering two recording studios and e-guitar rentals. The look is definitely dynamic, with a sideways tower jutting out over the Spree and Karim Rashid's digi-pop-pink design. Get a Spree-facing room for maximum Berlin feeling. Nice restaurant-bar with water-facing terrace.

City West & Charlottenburg

HOTEL-PENSION FUNK B&B €

Map p350 (030-882 7193; www.hotel-pensionfunk.de; Fasanenstrasse 69; d with/without bathroom, incl breakfast from €82/52; P; ⓤUhlandstrasse, Kurfürstendamm) This charismatic B&B in the former home of silent-movie siren Asta Nielsen takes you back to the Golden Twenties. Stuffed with art-nouveau furniture and decor, it's perfect if you value old-fashioned charm over mod cons. The 14 rooms vary quite significantly; if size matters, call and bring up the subject when booking. Cheaper rooms have partial or shared facilities.

★25HOURS HOTEL BIKINI BERLIN
DESIGN HOTEL €€

Map p350 (030-120 2210; www.25hours-hotels.com; Budapester Strasse 40; d €110-250; P ; 100, 200, S Zoologischer Garten, U Zoologischer Garten) The 'urban jungle' theme of this lifestyle outpost in the iconic 1950s Bikini Haus plays on its location between the zoo and main shopping district. Rooms are thoughtfully cool with clever design touches; the best face the animal park. Quirks include an on-site bakery, free bikes and Mini cars, a 'jungle-sauna' with zoo view and a Jogging Corner. Breakfast is €23. The rooftop Monkey Bar (p224) and Neni (p222) restaurant draw a good local crowd as well.

★SIR SAVIGNY
BOUTIQUE HOTEL €€

Map p350 (030-323 015 600; www.hotel-sirsavigny.de; Kantstrasse 144; d from €140; ; S Savignyplatz) Global nomads with a hankering for style and sophistication would be well advised to point their compass to this cosmopolitan hotel. Each of the 44 rooms exudes delightfully risqué glamour and teems with mod cons and graphic art. Beds are fab and the library a compact but inspired gathering spot. Breakfast is €22.50.

★LOUISA'S PLACE
BOUTIQUE HOTEL €€

Map p350 (030-631 030; www.louisas-place.de; Kurfürstendamm 160; ste from €137-250; P ; M19, M29, U Adenauerplatz) The all-suite Louisa's, in a charismatic 1904 building, is the kind of place that dazzles with class rather than glitz. The family-friendly suites with full kitchens brim with individual character, high ceilings and elegantly traditional furnishings. Though small, the pool provides a refreshing dip after a session in the sauna or on the treadmill. Optional breakfast is €26.

HOTEL ART NOUVEAU
B&B €€

Map p350 (030-327 7440; www.hotelartnouveau.de; Leibnizstrasse 59; d €89-149; @; 109, M19, M29, U Adenauerplatz, Wilmersdorfer Strasse, S Savignyplatz) A quaint birdcage lift drops you off at this arty B&B whose wood-floored, colour-drenched and stylishly furnished rooms skimp neither on space nor charisma. Space cravers should book the 'superior' category or a spacious suite. Bonus points for the superb beds, the breakfast buffet (€12) and the honour bar.

HENRI HOTEL
BOUTIQUE HOTEL €€

Map p350 (030-884 430; www.henri-berlin.com; Meinekestrasse 9; d from €108; P @; U Kurfürstendamm) Enter a belle-époque time warp while soaking up personal flair, modern comforts and an urban setting close to top restaurants and shopping. Rooms come in three sizes and comfort categories: petite Kabinett, classical Les Chambres and the ritzy Salon. Stuccoed ceilings, parquet floors and late-19th-century furniture create a delightful retro vibe. Full breakfast is €16.

HOTEL OTTO
HOTEL €€

Map p350 (030-5471 0080; www.hotelotto.com; Knesebeckstrasse 10; d from €92; P ; U Ernst-Reuter-Platz) Otto would feel like 'just' a business hotel were it not for cool perks like fair-trade beauty products and complimentary afternoon coffee and cake. Rooms are contemporary, functional and derive an extra dimension from colour accents and tactile fabrics. Small rooms really are tiny. The slow-food breakfast (€18), served till noon, is best enjoyed on the leafy rooftop terrace.

★HOTEL AM STEINPLATZ
HOTEL €€€

Map p350 (030-554 4440; www.hotelsteinplatz.com; Steinplatz 4; r €100-290; P @; M45, 245, U Ernst-Reuter-Platz) Vladimir Nabokov and Romy Schneider were among the guests of the original Hotel am Steinplatz, which got a second lease of life in 2013, a century after it first opened. Rooms in this elegant art deco jewel reinterpret the 1920s in contemporary style with sleek lamps, ultra-comfy beds and device-docking stations. Classy bar (p224) and restaurant, too. The optional breakfast costs €35.

Berliner Philharmonie (p165)

Understand Berlin

History

Berlin has long been in the cross-hairs of history: it staged a revolution, was headquartered by fascists, bombed to bits, ripped in half and finally reunited – all just in the 20th century! An accidental capital whose medieval birth was a mere blip on the map of history, Berlin puttered along in relative obscurity until becoming the royal capital of Prussia in 1701. It was only in fairly recent times that it significantly impacted on world history.

Medieval Berlin

Berlin's medieval birthplace, around the Nikolaikirche, was devastated during WWII bombing raids. Today's 'Nikolaiviertel' is actually a replica of the quarter, dreamed up by the East German government in celebration of the city's 750th anniversary in 1987.

The discovery of an oak beam suggests that Berlin may have roots going back to 1183 but, for now, history records that the city was officially founded in 1237 by itinerant merchants as twin trading posts called Berlin and Cölln. The modest settlements flanked the Spree River in an area just southwest of today's Alexanderplatz. It was a profitable spot along a natural east–west trade route, about halfway between the fortified towns of Köpenick to the southeast and Spandau to the northwest whose origins can be traced to the 8th century. The tiny settlements grew in leaps and bounds and, in 1307, merged into a single town for power and protection. As the centre of the March (duchy) of Brandenburg, it continued to assert its political and economic independence and even became a player in the Hanseatic League in 1360.

Such confidence did not sit well with Sigismund, king of the Germans, who, in 1411, put one of his cronies, Friedrich von Hohenzollern, in charge of Brandenburg, thereby ushering in five centuries of uninterrupted rule by the House of Hohenzollern.

Reformation & the Thirty Years' War

The Reformation, kick-started in 1517 by Martin Luther in nearby Wittenberg, was slow to arrive in Berlin. Eventually, though, the wave of reform reached Brandenburg, leaving Elector Joachim II (r 1535–71) no choice but to subscribe to Protestantism. On 1 November 1539 the court celebrated the first Lutheran-style service in the Nikolaikirche in Span-

TIMELINE

1244

Berlin is referenced in a document for the first time in recorded history, although the city's birthday is pegged to the first mention of its sister settlement, Cölln, in 1237.

1307

Berlin and Cölln join forces by merging into a single town to assert their independence from local rulers.

1360

The twin town of Berlin-Cölln joins the Hanseatic League, but never plays a major role in the alliance and quits its membership in 1518.

dau. The event is still celebrated as an official holiday (Reformationstag) in Brandenburg, the German federal state that surrounds Berlin, although not in the city state of Berlin itself.

Berlin prospered for the ensuing decades until drawn into the Thirty Years' War (1618–48), a conflict between Catholics and Protestants that left Europe's soil drenched with the blood of millions. Elector Georg Wilhelm (r 1620–40) tried to maintain a policy of neutrality, only to see his territory repeatedly pillaged and plundered by both sides. By the time the war ended, Berlin lay largely in disarray – broke, ruined and decimated by starvation, murder and disease.

An 8m-long section is all that survives of Berlin's original city wall, built around 1250 from crude boulders and bricks and standing up to 2m tall. See it on Littenstrasse, near Alexanderplatz.

Road to a Kingdom

Stability finally returned during the long reign of Georg Wilhelm's son, Friedrich Wilhelm (r 1640–88). Also known as the Great Elector, he took several steps that helped chart Brandenburg's rise to the status of a European powerhouse. His first order of business was to increase Berlin's safety by turning it into a garrison town encircled by fortifications with 13 bastions. He also levied a new sales tax, using the money to build three new neighbourhoods (Friedrichswerder, Dorotheenstadt and Friedrichstadt) and a canal linking the Spree and Oder Rivers (thereby cementing Berlin's position as a trading hub), as well as the Lustgarten and Unter den Linden.

But the Great Elector's most lasting legacy was replenishing Berlin's population by encouraging the settlement of refugees. In 1671, 50 Jewish families arrived from Vienna, followed by thousands of Protestant Huguenots – many of them highly skilled – who had been expelled from France by Louis XIV in 1685. Between 1680 and 1710, Berlin saw its population nearly triple to 56,000.

The Great Elector's son, Friedrich III, was a man of great ambition, with a penchant for the arts and sciences. Together with his beloved wife, Sophie-Charlotte, he presided over a lively and intellectual court, founding the Academy of Arts in 1696 and the Academy of Sciences in 1700. One year later, he advanced his career by promoting himself to King Friedrich I (elector 1688–1701, king 1701–13) of Prussia, making Berlin a royal residence and the capital of the new state of Brandenburg-Prussia.

The Age of Prussia

All cultural and intellectual life screeched to a halt under Friedrich's son, Friedrich Wilhelm I (r 1713–40), who laid the groundwork for Prussian military might. Soldiers were this king's main obsession and he dedicated much of his life to building an army of 80,000, partly by

1411

German King Sigismund puts Friedrich von Hohenzollern in charge as administrator of Brandenburg, marking the beginning of 500 years of Hohenzollern rule.

1443

Construction of the Berliner Stadtschloss (city palace) on the Spree island begins; it becomes the electors' permanent residence in 1486.

1539

Elector Joachim II celebrates the first Lutheran service and a year later passes a church ordinance making the new religion binding throughout Brandenburg.

1618

Religious conflict and territorial power struggles escalate into the bloody Thirty Years' War, devastating Berlin financially and halving its population to a mere 6000 people.

instituting the draft (highly unpopular even then, and eventually repealed) and persuading his fellow rulers to trade him men for treasure. History quite appropriately knows him as the *Soldatenkönig* (soldier king).

Ironically these soldiers didn't see action until his son and successor Friedrich II (aka Frederick the Great; r 1740–86) came to power. Friedrich fought tooth and nail for two decades to wrest Silesia (in today's Poland) from Austria and Saxony. When not busy on the battlefield, 'Old Fritz', as he was also called, sought greatness through building. His Forum Fridericianum, a grand architectural master plan for Unter den Linden, although never completed, gave Berlin the Staatsoper Unter den Linden (State Opera House); Sankt-Hedwigs-Kathedrale, a former palace now housing the Humboldt Universität (Humboldt University); and other major buildings.

Friedrich also embraced the ideas of the Enlightenment, abolishing torture, guaranteeing religious freedom and introducing legal reforms. With some of the leading thinkers in town (Moses Mendelssohn, Voltaire and Gotthold Ephraim Lessing among them), Berlin blossomed into a great cultural capital that came to be known as 'Athens on the Spree'.

Top Five Prussian Sites

- *Brandenburger Tor (Historic Mitte)*
- *Schloss and Park Sanssouci (Potsdam)*
- *Schloss Charlottenburg (Charlottenburg)*
- *Reichstag (Historic Mitte)*
- *Siegessäule (Tiergarten)*

Napoleon & Reforms

Old Fritz' death sent Prussia into a downward spiral, culminating in a serious trouncing of its army by Napoleon at Jena-Auerstedt in 1806. The French marched triumphantly into Berlin on 27 October and left two years later, their coffers bursting with loot.

The post-Napoleonic period saw Berlin caught up in the reform movement sweeping through Europe. Public servants, academics and merchants now questioned the right of the nobility to rule. Friedrich Wilhelm III (r 1797–1840) instituted a few token reforms (easing guild regulations, abolishing bonded labour and granting Jews civic equality), but meaningful constitutional reform was not forthcoming. Power continued to be concentrated in the Prussian state.

The ensuing period of political stability was paired with an intellectual flourishing in Berlin's cafes and salons. The newly founded Universität zu Berlin (Humboldt Universität) was helmed by the philosopher Johann Gottlieb Fichte and, as it grew in status, attracted other leading thinkers of the day, including Hegel and Ranke. This was also the age of Karl Friedrich Schinkel, whose many projects – from the Neue Wache (New Guardhouse) to the Altes Museum (Old Museum) – still beautify Berlin.

1640

Friedrich Wilhelm, who will go down in history as the Great Elector, comes to power and restores a semblance of normality by building fortifications and infrastructure.

1665

After major fires, a new law requires barns to move outside the city boundaries, thereby creating today's Scheunenviertel (Barn Quarter).

1671

Berlin's first Jewish community forms with just a few families arriving from Vienna at the invitation of the Great Elector. It grows to more than 1000 people by 1700.

1685

Friedrich Wilhelm issues the Edict of Potsdam, allowing French Huguenot religious refugees to settle in Berlin, giving a 10-year tax break and granting them the right to hold services.

Revolution(s)

The Industrial Revolution snuck up on Berliners in the second quarter of the 19th century, with companies like Siemens and Borsig vastly stimulating the city's growth. In 1838 trains began chuffing between Berlin and Potsdam, giving birth to the Prussian railway system and spurring the foundation of more than 1000 factories, including electrical giants AEG and Siemens. In 1840 August Borsig built the world's fastest locomotive, besting even the British in a race.

Tens of thousands of people now streamed into Berlin to work in the factories, swelling the population to more than 400,000 by 1847 and bringing the city's infrastructure close to collapse. A year later, due to social volatility and restricted freedoms, Berlin joined other German cities in a bourgeois democratic revolution. On 18 March two shots rang out during a demonstration, which then escalated into a full-fledged revolution. Barricades went up and a bloody fight ensued, leaving 183 revolutionaries and 18 soldiers dead by the time King Friedrich Wilhelm IV ordered his troops back. The dead revolutionaries are commemorated on Platz des 18 März, immediately west of the Brandenburg Gate. In a complete turnabout, the king put himself at the head of the movement and professed support for liberalism and nationalism.

An elected Prussian national assembly met on 5 May. However, disagreements between delegates from the different factions kept parliament weak and ineffective, making restoration of the monarchy child's play for General von Wrangel, who led 13,000 Prussian soldiers who had remained faithful to the king into the city in November 1848. Ever the opportunist, the king quickly switched sides again, dissolved the parliament and proposed his own constitution while insisting on maintaining supreme power. The revolution was dead. Many of its participants fled into exile.

One of the definitive histories of Prussia, Christopher Clark's *Iron Kingdom: The Rise and Downfall of Prussia* (2006) covers the period from 1600 to 1947 and shows the central role this powerhouse played in shaping modern Europe.

Bismarck & the Birth of an Empire

When Friedrich Wilhelm IV suffered a stroke in 1857, his brother Wilhelm became first regent and then, in 1861, King Wilhelm I (r 1861–88). Unlike his brother, Wilhelm had his finger on the pulse of the times and was not averse to progress. One of his key moves was to appoint Otto von Bismarck as Prussian prime minister in 1862.

Bismarck's glorious ambition was the creation of a unified Germany with Prussia at the helm. An old-guard militarist, he used intricate diplomacy and a series of wars with neighbouring Denmark and Austria to achieve his aims. By 1871 Berlin stood as the proud capital of the German Reich (empire), a bicameral, constitutional monarchy. On 18

1696

Elector Friedrich III founds the Akademie der Künste, Berlin's oldest and most prestigious arts institution.

1701

Brandenburg becomes a kingdom, with Berlin as its capital, when Elector Friedrich III has himself crowned King Friedrich I.

1730

The future king Frederick the Great is caught trying to desert to England along with a friend. Frederick's father orders the friend's execution and makes his son watch.

1740

Frederick the Great, the philosopher king, turns Berlin into 'Athens on the Spree', a centre of the Enlightenment and an architectural showcase.

January the Prussian king was crowned Kaiser at Versailles, with Bismarck as his 'Iron Chancellor'.

The early years of the German empire – a period called *Gründerzeit* (the foundation years) – were marked by major economic growth, fuelled in part by a steady flow of French reparation payments. Hundreds of thousands of people poured into Berlin in search of work in the factories. Housing shortages were solved by building labyrinthine tenements (*Mietskasernen,* literally 'rental barracks'), where entire families subsisted in tiny and poorly ventilated flats without indoor plumbing.

New political parties gave a voice to the proletariat; foremost was the Socialist Workers' Party (SAP), the forerunner of the Sozialdemokratische Partei Deutschlands (SPD; Social Democratic Party of Germany). Founded in 1875, the SAP captured 40% of the Berlin vote just two years later. Bismarck tried to make the party illegal but eventually, under pressure from the growing and increasingly antagonistic socialist movement, he enacted Germany's first modern social reforms, though this went against his true nature. When Wilhelm II (r 1888–1918) came to power, he wanted to extend social reform while Bismarck wanted stricter antisocialist laws. Finally, in March 1890, the Kaiser's scalpel excised his renegade chancellor from the political scene. After that, the legacy of Bismarck's diplomacy unravelled and a wealthy, unified and industrially powerful Germany paddled into the new century.

The green octagonal public pissoirs occasionally seen around Berlin are a legacy of the late 19th century when the municipal sanitation system could not keep up with the exploding population. About two dozen survive, including one on Chamissoplatz in Kreuzberg and another on Senefelderplatz in Prenzlauer Berg. Their nickname is Cafe Achteck (Cafe Octagon).

WWI & Revolution (Again)

The assassination of Archduke Franz Ferdinand, the heir to the Austrian throne, on 28 June 1914, triggered a series of diplomatic decisions that led to WWI, the bloodiest European conflict since the Thirty Years' War. In Berlin and elsewhere, initial euphoria and faith in a quick victory soon gave way to despair as casualties piled up in the battlefield trenches and stomachs grumbled on the home front. When peace came with defeat in 1918, it also ended domestic stability, ushering in a period of turmoil and violence.

On 9 November 1918, Kaiser Wilhelm II abdicated, bringing an inglorious end to the monarchy and 500 years of Hohenzollern rule. Power was transferred to the SPD, the largest party in the Reichstag, and its leader, Friedrich Ebert. Shortly after the Kaiser's exit, prominent SPD member Philipp Scheidemann stepped to a window of the Reichstag to announce the birth of the German Republic. Two hours later, Karl Liebknecht of the Spartakusbund (Spartacist League) proclaimed a socialist republic from a balcony of the royal palace on Unter den Linden. The struggle for power was on.

1806

After defeating Prussia, Napoleon leads his troops on a triumphant march through the Brandenburg Gate, marking the start of a two-year occupation of Berlin.

1830

The Altes Museum opens as the first of five institutions on Museumsinsel (Museum Island). The last (the Pergamonmuseum) opens exactly 100 years later.

1837

The industrial age kicks into high gear with the founding of August Borsig's machine factory, which in 1840 builds the first German locomotive.

1838

Berlin's first train (British built) embarks on its maiden voyage from Berlin to Potsdam, making the city the centre of an expanding rail network throughout Prussia.

Founded by Liebknecht and Rosa Luxemburg, the Spartacist League sought to establish a left-wing, Marxist-style government; by year's end it had merged with other radical groups into the German Communist Party. The SPD's goal, meanwhile, was to establish a parliamentary democracy.

Supporters of the SPD and the Spartacist League took their rivalry to the streets, culminating in the Spartacist Revolt of early January 1919. On the orders of Ebert, government forces quickly quashed the uprising. Liebknecht and Luxemburg were arrested and murdered en route to prison by Freikorps soldiers (right-leaning war volunteers); their bodies were dumped in the Landwehrkanal.

Discover stat after stat on Berlin at the website of the Office of Statistics in Berlin (www.statistik-berlin-brandenburg.de).

The Weimar Republic

In July 1919 the federalist constitution of the fledgling republic – Germany's first serious experiment with democracy – was adopted in the town of Weimar, where the constituent assembly had sought refuge from the chaos of Berlin. It gave women the vote and established basic human rights, but it also gave the chancellor the right to rule by decree – a concession that would later prove critical in Hitler's rise to power.

The so-called Weimar Republic (1920–33) was governed by a coalition of left and centre parties, headed by Friedrich Ebert of the SPD and, later, independent Paul von Hindenburg. The SPD remained Germany's largest party until 1932. The republic, however, pleased neither communists nor monarchists.

Historical Reads

- *Berlin Rising: Biography of a City* (Anthony Read, David Fisher; 1994)
- *Berlin: Portrait of a City Through the Centuries* (Rory MacLean; 2014)
- *Berlin Diary: Journal of a Foreign Correspondent 1934–41* (William Shirer; 1941)
- *The Candy Bombers* (Andrei Cherny; 2006)
- *The Berlin Wall* (Frederick Taylor; 2006)

The Golden Twenties

The giant metropolis of Berlin as we know it today was forged in 1920 from the region's many independent towns and villages (Charlottenburg, Schöneberg, Spandau etc), making Berlin one of the world's largest cities, with around 3.8 million inhabitants.

Otherwise, the 1920s began as anything but golden, marked by the humiliation of a lost war, social and political instability, hyperinflation, hunger and disease. Around 235,000 Berliners were unemployed, and strikes, demonstrations and riots became nearly everyday occurrences. Economic stability gradually returned after a new currency, the *Rentenmark*, was introduced in 1923 and with the Dawes Plan in 1924, which limited the crippling reparation payments imposed on Germany after WWI.

Berliners responded like there was no tomorrow and made their city as much a den of decadence as it was a cauldron of creativity. Cabaret, Dada and jazz flourished. Pleasure pits popped up everywhere, turning the city into a 'sextropolis' of Dionysian dimensions. Bursting with

1848

Berlin is swept up in the popular revolutions for democratic reform and a united Germany, but after a few months the Prussian army restores the old order.

1862

Chief city planner James Hobrecht solves the housing shortage by constructing claustrophobic working-class ghettos of tenement blocks.

1871

Employing an effective strategy of war and diplomacy, Prussian chancellor Otto von Bismarck forges a unified Germany with Prussia at its helm and Berlin as its capital.

1877

Berlin's population reaches the one million mark; this figure almost doubles by 1900.

energy, it became a laboratory for anything new and modern, drawing giants of architecture (Bruno Taut, Martin Wagner, Hans Scharoun and Walter Gropius), fine arts (George Grosz, Max Beckmann and Lovis Corinth) and literature (Bertolt Brecht, Kurt Tucholsky, WH Auden and Christopher Isherwood).

The fun came to an instant end when the US stock market crashed in 1929, plunging the world into economic depression. Within weeks, half a million Berliners were jobless, and riots and demonstrations again ruled the streets. The volatile, increasingly polarised political climate led to clashes between communists and members of a party that had been patiently waiting in the wings – the Nationalsozialistische Deutsche Arbeiterpartei (National Socialist German Workers' Party, NSDAP, or Nazi Party), led by a failed Austrian artist and WWI corporal named Adolf Hitler. Soon jackboots, brown shirts, oppression and fear would dominate daily life in Germany.

Hitler's Rise to Power

The Weimar government's inability to improve conditions during the Depression spurred the popularity of Hitler's NSDAP, which gained 18% of the national vote in the 1930 elections. In the 1932 presidential election, Hitler challenged Hindenburg and won 37% of the second-round vote. A year later, on 30 January 1933, faced with failed economic reforms and persuasive right-wing advisers, Hindenburg appointed Hitler chancellor. That evening, NSDAP celebrated its rise to power with a torchlit procession through the Brandenburg Gate.

As chancellor, Hitler moved quickly to consolidate absolute power and turn the nation's democracy into a one-party dictatorship. The Reichstag fire in March 1933 gave him the opportunity to request temporary emergency powers to arrest communists and liberal opponents. He also pushed through his proposed Enabling Law, allowing him to decree laws and change the constitution without consulting parliament. When Hindenburg died a year later, Hitler fused the offices of president and chancellor to become Führer of the Third Reich.

The Siegessäule (Victory Column) in Tiergarten park has had starring roles in Wim Wenders' movie *Wings of Desire* and U2's 'Stay' music video. It also inspired Paul van Dyk's 1998 trance hit 'For an Angel' and the name of Berlin's leading gay magazine.

Nazi Berlin

The rise of the Nazis had instant, far-reaching consequences for the entire population. Within three months of Hitler's power grab, all non-Nazi parties, organisations and labour unions ceased to exist. Political opponents, intellectuals and artists were rounded up and detained without trial; many went underground or into exile. There was a burgeoning culture of terror and denunciation, and the terrorisation of Jews started to escalate.

1891

Berlin engineer Otto Lilienthal, known as the 'Glider King', makes the world's first successful glider flight, travelling over 25m. Five years later he dies in an air accident.

1902

After two decades of debate and eight years of construction, the first segment of the Berlin U-Bahn network is inaugurated, between Warschauer Strasse and Ernst-Reuter-Platz.

1918

WWI ends on 11 November with Germany's capitulation, following the resignation of Kaiser Wilhelm II and his escape to Holland. The Prussian monarchy is dead.

1919

The Spartacist Revolt, led by Liebknecht, Luxemburg and Pieck, is violently suppressed and ends with the murder of Liebknecht and Luxemburg by right-wing Freikorps troops.

Hitler's brown-shirted Nazi state police, the Sturmabteilung (SA), pursued opponents, arresting, torturing and murdering people in improvised concentration camps, such as the one in the Wasserturm in Prenzlauer Berg. North of Berlin, construction began on Sachsenhausen concentration camp. During the so-called Köpenicker Blutwoche (Bloody Week) in June 1933, around 90 people were murdered. On 10 May, right-wing students burned 'un-German' books on Bebelplatz, prompting countless intellectuals and artists to rush into exile.

Jewish Persecution

Jews were a Nazi target from the start. In April 1933 Joseph Goebbels, *Gauleiter* (district leader) of Berlin and head of the well-oiled Ministry of Propaganda, announced a boycott of Jewish businesses. Soon after, Jews were expelled from public service and banned from many

OLYMPICS UNDER THE SWASTIKA

When the International Olympics Committee awarded the 1936 games to Germany in 1931, the gesture was supposed to welcome the country back into the world community after its defeat in WWI and the tumultuous 1920s. No one could have known that only two years later, the fledgling democracy would be helmed by a dictator with an agenda to take over the world.

As Hitler opened the games on 1 August in Berlin's Olympic Stadium, prisoners were putting the finishing touches on the first large-scale Nazi concentration camp at Sachsenhausen, just north of town. As famous composer Richard Strauss conducted the Olympic hymn during the opening ceremony, fighter squadrons were headed to Spain in support of Franco's dictatorship. Only while the Olympic flame was flickering were political and racial persecution suspended and anti-Semitic signs taken down.

The Olympics were truly a perfect opportunity for the Nazi propaganda machine, which excelled at staging grand public spectacles and rallies, as was so powerfully captured by Leni Riefenstahl in her epic movie *Olympia*. Participants and spectators were impressed by the choreographed pageantry and warm German hospitality. The fact that these were the first Olympics to be broadcast internationally on radio did not fail to impress either.

The games were also a big success from an athletic point of view, with around 4000 participants from 49 countries competing in 129 events and setting numerous records. The biggest star was African-American track-and-fieldster Jesse Owens, who was awarded four gold medals for the 100m sprint, 200m sprint, 4 x 100m relay and long jump, winning the hearts of the German public and putting paid to Nazi belief in the physical superiority of the Aryan race. German Jews, meanwhile, were excluded from participating, with the one token exception being half-Jewish fencer Helene Mayer. She took home a silver medal.

1920

On 1 October Berlin becomes Germany's largest city after seven independent towns, 59 villages and 27 estates are amalgamated into a single administrative unit. The population reaches 3.8 million.

1920s

Berlin evolves into a cultural metropolis, exerting a pull on leading artists, scientists and philosophers of the day, including Einstein, Brecht and Otto Dix.

1921

The world's first highway – called AVUS – opens in the Grunewald after eight years of construction.

1923

Berlin-Tempelhof Airport opens and soon becomes one of Europe's most important airports, along with Croydon in London and Le Bourget in Paris.

professions, trades and industries. The Nuremberg Laws of 1935 deprived 'non-Aryans' of German citizenship and many other rights.

The international community, meanwhile, turned a blind eye to the situation in Germany. Hitler's success at stabilising the shaky economy – largely by pumping public money into employment programs – was widely admired. The 1936 Olympic summer games (p261) in Berlin were a PR triumph, as Hitler launched a charm offensive. Terror and persecution resumed right after the closing ceremony.

For Jews, the horror escalated on 9 November 1938, with the Reichspogromnacht (often called Kristallnacht, or Night of Broken Glass). Using the assassination of a German consular official by a Polish Jew in Paris as a pretext, Nazi thugs desecrated, burned and demolished synagogues and Jewish cemeteries, property and businesses across the country. Jews had begun to emigrate after 1933, but this event set off a stampede.

The fate of those Jews who stayed behind deteriorated after the outbreak of WWII in 1939. At Hitler's request, a conference in January 1942 in Berlin's Wannsee came up with the *Endlösung* (Final Solution): the systematic, bureaucratic and meticulously documented annihilation of European Jews. Sinti and Roma, political opponents, priests, homosexuals and habitual criminals were targeted as well. Of the roughly seven million people who were sent to concentration camps, only 500,000 survived.

Top Five WWII Sites

- *Topographie des Terrors (Historic Mitte)*
- *Sachsenhausen Concentration Camp (Oranienburg)*
- *Holocaust Memorial (Historic Mitte)*
- *Gedenkstätte Deutscher Widerstand (Potsdamer Platz)*
- *Haus der Wannsee-Konferenz (Wannsee)*

WWII & the Battle of Berlin

WWII began on 1 September 1939 with the Nazi attack on Poland. Although France and Britain declared war on Germany two days later, this could not prevent the quick defeat of Poland, Belgium, the Netherlands and France. Other countries, including Denmark and Norway, were also soon brought into the Nazi fold.

In June 1941 Germany broke its nonaggression pact with Stalin by attacking the USSR. Though successful at first, Operation Barbarossa quickly ran into problems, culminating in defeat at Stalingrad (today Volgograd) the following winter, forcing the Germans to retreat.

With the Normandy invasion of June 1944, Allied troops arrived in formidable force on the European mainland, supported by unrelenting air raids on Berlin and most other German cities. The final Battle of Berlin began in mid-April 1945. More than 1.5 million Soviet soldiers barrelled towards the capital from the east, reaching Berlin on 21 April and encircling it on 25 April. Two days later they were in the city centre, fighting running street battles with the remaining troops, many of them boys and elderly men. On 30 April the fighting reached the

1924

Germany's first electric traffic light starts regulating the chaos around Potsdamer Platz.

1929

The Great Depression leaves half a million people unemployed. Thirteen members of the National Socialist German Workers' Party (the Nazi Party) are elected to city parliament.

1933

Hitler is appointed chancellor; the Reichstag burns; construction starts on Sachsenhausen concentration camp; the National Socialist German Workers' Party rules Germany.

1936

The 11th modern Olympic Games, held in Berlin in August, are a PR triumph for Hitler and a showcase of Nazi power. Anti-Jewish propaganda is suspended during the period.

NAZI RESISTANCE

Resistance to Hitler was quashed early by the powerful Nazi machinery of terror, but it never vanished entirely. One of the best known acts of defiance was the 20 July 1944 assassination attempt on the Führer, led by senior army officer Claus Schenk Graf von Stauffenberg. On that fateful day, Stauffenberg brought a briefcase packed with explosives to a meeting of the Nazi high command at the Wolfschanze (Wolf's Lair), Hitler's eastern-front military headquarters. He placed the briefcase under the conference table near Hitler's seat, then excused himself and heard the bomb detonate from a distance. What he didn't know was that Hitler had escaped with minor injuries because the solid oak table had shielded him from the blast.

Stauffenberg and his co-conspirators were quickly identified and shot by firing squad at the army headquarters in the Bendlerblock in Berlin. The rooms where they hatched their plot now house the Gedenkstätte Deutscher Widerstand (p164), an exhibit about German resistance against the Nazis.

government quarter where Hitler was ensconced in his bunker, with his long-time mistress Eva Braun, whom he'd married just a day earlier. Finally accepting the inevitability of defeat, Hitler shot himself that afternoon; his wife swallowed a cyanide pill. As their bodies were burned in the chancellery courtyard, Red Army soldiers raised the Soviet flag above the Reichstag.

Defeat & Aftermath

The Battle of Berlin ended on 2 May with the unconditional surrender of Helmuth Weidling, the commander of the Berlin Defence Area, to General Vasily Chuikov of the Soviet army. Peace was signed at the US military headquarters in Reims (France) and at the Soviet military headquarters in Berlin-Karlshorst, now a German-Soviet history museum (p241). On 8 May 1945, WWII in Europe officially came to an end.

The fighting had taken an enormous toll on Berlin and its people. Entire neighbourhoods lay in smouldering rubble and at least 125,000 Berliners had lost their lives. With around one million women and children evacuated, only 2.8 million people were left in the city in May 1945 (compared to 4.3 million in 1939), two-thirds of them women. It fell to them to start clearing up the 25 million tonnes of rubble, earning them the name *Trümmerfrauen* (rubble women). In fact, many of Berlin's modest hills are actually *Trümmerberge* (rubble mountains), built from wartime debris and reborn as parks and recreational areas. The

1938

On 9 November Nazis set fire to nine of Berlin's 12 synagogues, vandalise Jewish businesses and terrorise Jewish citizens during a night of pogroms called Kristallnacht.

1942

At the so-called Wannsee Conference, leading members of the SS decide on the systematic murder of European Jews, called the 'Final Solution'.

1944

On 20 July senior army officers led by Claus Schenk Graf von Stauffenberg stage an assassination attempt on Hitler. Their failure costs their own and countless other lives.

1945

Soviet troops advance on Berlin in the final days of the war, devastating the city. Hitler commits suicide on 30 April, fighting stops on 2 May and the armistice is signed on 8 May.

best known are the Teufelsberg in the Grunewald and Mont Klamott in the Volkspark Friedrichshain.

Some small triumphs came quickly: U-Bahn service resumed on 14 May 1945, newspaper printing presses began rolling again on 15 May, and the Berliner Philharmoniker orchestra gave its first postwar concert on 26 May.

Occupation

At the Yalta Conference in February 1945, Winston Churchill, Franklin D Roosevelt and Joseph Stalin agreed to carve up Germany and Berlin into four zones of occupation controlled by Britain, the USA, the USSR and France. By July 1945, Stalin, Clement Attlee (who replaced Churchill after a surprise election win) and Roosevelt's successor, Harry S Truman, were at the table in Schloss Cecilienhof in Potsdam to hammer out the details.

Berlin was sliced up into 20 administrative areas. The British sector encompassed Charlottenburg, Tiergarten and Spandau; the French got Wedding and Reinickendorf; and the US was in charge of Zehlendorf, Steglitz, Wilmersdorf, Tempelhof, Kreuzberg and Neukölln. All these districts later formed West Berlin. The Soviets held on to eight districts in the east, including Mitte, Prenzlauer Berg, Friedrichshain, Treptow and Köpenick, which would later become East Berlin. The Soviets also occupied the land surrounding Berlin, leaving West Berlin completely encircled by territories under Soviet control.

Daring Young Men: the Heroism and Triumph of the Berlin Airlift (2011), by Richard Reeves, examines this 'first battle of the Cold War' by telling the stories of the American and British pilots who risked their lives to save their former enemies.

The Big Chill

Friction between the Western Allies and the Soviets quickly emerged. For the Western Allies, a main priority was to help Germany get back on its feet by kick-starting the devastated economy. The Soviets, though, insisted on massive reparations and began brutalising and exploiting their own zone of occupation. Tens of thousands of able-bodied men and POWs ended up in labour camps deep in the Soviet Union. In the Allied zones, meanwhile, democracy was beginning to take root, and Germany elected state parliaments in 1946–47.

The showdown came in June 1948 when the Allies introduced the Deutschmark in their zones. The USSR regarded this as a breach of the Potsdam Agreement, under which the powers had agreed to treat Germany as one economic zone. The Soviets issued their own currency, the Ostmark, and promptly announced a full-scale economic blockade of West Berlin. The Allies responded with the remarkable Berlin Airlift.

1948

After the Western Allies introduce the Deutschmark, the Soviets blockade West Berlin; in response the US and Britain launch the Berlin Airlift, ferrying necessities to the isolated city.

1949

The Bundesrepublik Deutschland (West Germany) and the Deutsche Demokratische Republik (East Germany) are born; Berlin remains under Allied supervision.

1950

GDR leaders raze the remains of the Prussian city palace for ideological reasons, despite worldwide protest.

1950s

Hundreds of thousands of East Germans move to West Berlin and West Germany, depleting the GDR's brain and brawn power.

The Berlin Airlift

The Berlin Airlift was a triumph of determination and a glorious chapter in Berlin's post-WWII history. On 24 June 1948, the Soviets cut off all rail and road traffic into the city to force the Western Allies to give up their sectors and bring the entire city under Soviet control.

For the next 11 months Allied planes flew in food, coal, machinery and other supplies to the now-closed Tempelhof Airport in West Berlin. By the time the Soviets backed down, the Allies had made 278,000 flights, logged a distance equivalent to 250 round trips to the moon and delivered 2.5 million tonnes of cargo. The Luftbrückendenkmal (Berlin Airlift Memorial) honours the effort and those who died carrying it out.

It was a monumental achievement that profoundly changed the relationship between Germany and the Western Allies, who were no longer regarded merely as occupying forces but as *Schutzmächte* (protective powers).

One of many fabulous films by Germany's best-known female director, Margarethe von Trotta, *Rosenstrasse* (2003) is a moving portrayal of a 1943 protest by a group of non-Jewish women trying to save their Jewish husbands from deportation. There's a memorial near the site today.

Two German States

In 1949 the division of Germany – and Berlin – was formalised. The western zones evolved into the Bundesrepublik Deutschland (BRD, Federal Republic of Germany or FRG). An American economic aid package dubbed the Marshall Plan created the basis for West Germany's *Wirtschaftswunder* (economic miracle), which saw the economy grow at an average of 8% per year between 1951 and 1961. The recovery was aided by the immigration of about 2.3 million foreign workers, mainly from Turkey, Yugoslavia and Italy, to Germany, thereby laying the foundation for today's multicultural society.

The Soviet zone, meanwhile, grew into the Deutsche Demokratische Republik (DDR, German Democratic Republic or GDR), making East Berlin its capital and Wilhelm Pieck its first president. From the outset, though, the Sozialistische Einheitspartei Deutschlands (SED, Socialist Unity Party of Germany), led by Walter Ulbricht, dominated economic, judicial and security policy. In order to counter any opposition, the Ministry for State Security, or Stasi, was established in 1950, with its headquarters based in Lichtenberg (now the Stasimuseum). Regime opponents were incarcerated at the super-secret Gedenkstätte Hohenschönhausen (Stasi Prison) nearby.

Economically, East Germany stagnated, in large part because of the Soviets' continued policy of asset stripping and reparation payments. Stalin's death in 1953 raised hopes for reform but only spurred the GDR government to raise production goals even higher. Smouldering discontent erupted in violence on 17 June 1953 when 10% of GDR workers took

1951

Berlin enters the celluloid spotlight with the inaugural Berlin International Film Festival (Berlinale).

1953

The uprising of construction workers on the Stalinallee spreads across the GDR before being crushed by Soviet tanks, leaving several hundred dead and many more injured.

1957

The first Trabant car rolls off the assembly line in East Germany. Production continues until 1990.

1961

On 24 August, just 11 days after the first stone of the Berlin Wall is laid, 24-year-old Günter Litfin is gunned down by border guards while attempting to swim across Humboldt Harbour.

to the streets. Soviet troops quashed the uprising, with scores of deaths and the arrest of about 1200 people.

Top Five Cold War Sites

Gedenkstätte Berliner Mauer (Prenzlauer Berg)

East Side Gallery (Friedrichshain)

Stasi Prison (Lichtenberg)

AlliiertenMuseum Berlin (Dahlem)

Stasimuseum (Mitte)

The Wall Goes Up

Through the 1950s the economic gulf between the two Germanys widened, prompting hundreds of thousands of mostly young and well-educated East Germans to seek a future in the West. Eventually, this exodus strained the troubled GDR economy so much that – with Soviet consent – its government built a wall to keep them in. Construction of the Berlin Wall, the Cold War's most potent symbol, began on the night of 13 August 1961.

This stealthy act left Berliners stunned. Formal protests from the Western Allies, as well as massive demonstrations in West Berlin, were ignored. Tense times followed. In October 1961, US and Soviet tanks faced off at Checkpoint Charlie, pushing to the brink of war.

The appointment of Erich Honecker (1912–94) as leader of East Germany in 1971 opened the way for rapprochement with the West and enhanced international acceptance of the GDR. In September that year the Western Allies and the Soviet Union signed a new Four Power Accord in the Kammergericht (courthouse) in Schöneberg. It guaranteed access to West Berlin from West Germany and eased travel restrictions between East and West Berlin. The accord paved the way for the Basic Treaty, signed a year later, in which the two countries recognised each other's sovereignty and borders and committed to setting up 'permanent missions' in Bonn and East Berlin, respectively.

Life in the Divided City

For 45 years, Berlin was a political exclave in the cross hairs of the Cold War. After the Berlin Wall was built in 1961, the city's halves developed as completely separate entities.

West Berlin

West Berlin could not have survived economically without heavy subsidies from the West German government in the form of tax incentives and bonuses. West Berliners had access to the same aspects of capitalism as all other West Germans, including a wide range of quality consumer goods, the latest technology and imported foods.

Since West Berlin was completely surrounded by East Berlin and East Germany, its residents liked to joke that no matter in which direction you travelled, you were always 'going east'. Still, West Berliners suffered no restrictions on travel and were free to leave and return as they pleased, as well as to choose their holiday destinations. Berlin was

1963

US president John F Kennedy professes his solidarity with the people of Berlin, giving his famous 'Ich bin ein Berliner' speech at the town hall in West Berlin's Schöneberg on 26 June.

1964

A plan to turn Alexanderplatz, East Berlin's central square, into a socialist architectural showcase begins. The square's crowning glory, Fernsehturm (TV Tower), opens in 1969.

1967

The death of Benno Ohnesorg, an unarmed student who is shot by a police officer while demonstrating against the Shah of Persia's visit to West Berlin, draws attention to the student movement.

1971

The four Allies sign the Four Power Accord, which confirms Berlin's independent status. A year later East and West Germany recognise each other's sovereignty in the Basic Treaty.

linked to West Germany by air, train and four transit roads, which were normal autobahns or highways also used by East Germans. Transit travellers were not allowed to leave the main road. Border checks were common and often involved harassment and time-consuming searches.

East Berlin

From the outset, East Germany's economic, judicial and security policy was dominated by a single party, the SED. Among its prime objectives was the moulding of its citizens into loyal members of a new socialist society. Children as young as six years old were folded into a tight network of state-run mass organisations, and in the workplace the unions were in charge of ideological control and conformity. Officially, membership of any of these groups was voluntary, but refusing to join usually led to limits on access to higher education and career choices. It could also incite the suspicion of the much-feared Stasi.

The standard of living in East Berlin was higher than in the rest of East Germany, with the Centrum Warenhaus on Alexanderplatz (today's Galeria Kaufhof) a flagship store. While basic foods (bread, milk, butter, some produce) were cheap and plentiful, fancier foods and high-quality goods were in short supply and could often only be obtained with connections and patience. Queues outside shops were a common sight and many items were only available as so-called *Bückware,* meaning that they were hidden from plain view and required the sales clerk to bend *(bücken)* to retrieve them from beneath the counter. Bartering for goods was also common practice. Western products could only be purchased in government-run retail shops, called *Intershops,* and only by the privileged few who had access to hard currency – the East German mark was not accepted.

After the Wall went up in 1961, East Berliners, along with other East Germans, were only allowed to travel within the GDR and to other Eastern Bloc countries. Most holiday trips were state-subsidised and union-organised. Who was allowed to go where, when and for how long depended on such factors as an individual's productivity and level of social and political engagement.

Women enjoyed greater equality in East Germany than their western counterparts. An extensive government-run childcare system made it easier to combine motherhood and employment, and nearly 90% of all women were employed, many in such 'nontraditional' fields as engineering and construction. However, this gender equality did not necessarily translate into the private sphere, where women remained largely responsible for child-raising and domestic chores. Rising through the ranks at work or in organisations was also rare for women.

To alleviate acute housing shortages, three new satellite cities – Marzahn, Hohenschönhausen and Hellersdorf – consisting of massive prefab housing blocks for 300,000 people were built in the 1970s and '80s on East Berlin's outskirts. Equipped with mod cons like central heating and indoor plumbing, these apartments were much coveted back then.

Australian journalist Anna Funder documents the Stasi, East Germany's vast domestic spy apparatus, by letting both victims and perpetrators tell their stories in her 2004 book *Stasiland*.

1976

The Palace of the Republic, which houses the GDR parliament and an entertainment centre, opens on 23 April, on the site where the royal Hohenzollern palace had been demolished in 1950.

1987

East and West Berlin celebrate the city's 750th birthday separately. On 12 June US President Ronald Reagan stands at the Brandenburg Gate and says 'Mr Gorbachev, tear down this wall!'.

1989

On 9 October East Germany celebrates the 40th anniversary of its founding as demonstrations in favour of reforms reverberate through East Berlin.

1989

On 4 November half a million Berliners in Alexanderplatz demand freedom of speech, press and assembly. The Wall opens on 9 November without a single bullet being fired.

The Wall Comes Down

The first Love Parade, a techno cavalcade that would draw millions of people to Berlin each summer between 1989 and 2006, actually kicked off modestly with just one truck and 150 ravers partying on West Berlin's Kurfürstendamm.

Hearts and minds in Eastern Europe had long been restless for change, but German reunification came as a surprise to the world and ushered in a new and exciting era. The so-called Wende (turning point, ie the fall of communism) came about as a gradual development that ended in a big bang – the opening of the Berlin Wall on 9 November 1989.

The Germany of today, with 16 unified federal states, was hammered out through a volatile political debate and negotiations to end post-WWII occupation zones. This quickly led to a monetary, economic and social union, the abolition of border controls and to the Deutschmark becoming the common currency. On 31 August 1990, the Unification Treaty, in which both East and West pledged to create a unified Germany, was signed in the Kronprinzenpalais on Unter den Linden. Around the same time, representatives of East and West Germany and the four victorious WWII allied powers (the USSR, France, the UK and the US), who had held the right to determine Germany's future since 1945, met in Moscow. Their negotiations resulted in the signing of the Two-Plus-Four Treaty, which ended postwar occupation zones and fully transferred sovereignty to a united Germany. Formal unification became effective on 3 October 1990, now Germany's national holiday. In December 1990 Germany held its first unified post-WWII elections.

In 1991 a small majority (338 to 320) of members in the Bundestag (German parliament) voted in favour of moving the seat of government from Bonn to Berlin and of making Berlin the German capital once again. On 8 September 1994, the last Allied troops stationed in Berlin left the city after a festive ceremony.

The Postunification Years

With reunification, Berlin once again became the seat of government in 1999. Mega-sized construction projects such as Potsdamer Platz and the government quarter eradicated the physical scars of division but did little to improve the city's balance sheet or unemployment statistics. It didn't help that Berlin lost the hefty federal subsidies it had received during the years of division. More than 250,000 manufacturing jobs were lost between 1991 and 2006, most of them through closures of unprofitable factories in East Berlin. Add to that mismanagement, corruption, a banking scandal and excessive government spending and it's no surprise that the city ran up a whopping debt of €60 million.

Elected in 2001, the new governing mayor Klaus Wowereit responded by making across-the-board spending cuts, but with a tax base eroded by high unemployment and ever-growing welfare payments, they did little initially to get Berlin out of the poorhouse. Eventually, though, the

1990

The official reunification of the two Germanys goes into effect on 3 October. The date becomes a national holiday.

1991

Members of the Bundestag (German parliament) vote to reinstate Berlin as Germany's capital and to move the federal government here. Berliners elect the first joint city government.

1994

The last British, French, Russian and American troops withdraw from Berlin, ending nearly half a century of occupation and protection.

1999

On 19 April the German parliament holds its first session in the historic Reichstag building, after complete restoration by Lord Norman Foster.

JEWISH BERLIN

Jews have a long and complex history in Berlin. Friedhof Grosse Hamburger Strasse, Berlin's oldest Jewish cemetery, is the final resting home of Enlightenment philosopher Moses Mendelssohn, who arrived in Berlin in 1743. His progressive thinking and lobbying paved the way for the Emancipation Edict of 1812, which made Jews full citizens of Prussia, with equal rights and duties.

By the end of the 19th century, many of Berlin's Jews, then numbering about 5% of the population, had become thoroughly German in speech and identity. When a wave of Hasidic Jews escaping the pogroms of Eastern Europe arrived around the same time, they found their way to today's Scheunenviertel, which at that time was an immigrant slum with cheap housing.

By 1933 Berlin's Jewish population had grown to around 160,000 and constituted one-third of all Jews living in Germany. The well-known horrors of the Nazi years sent most into exile and left 55,000 dead. Only about 1000 to 2000 Jews are believed to have survived the war years in Berlin, often with the help of their non-Jewish neighbours; their acts of courage are commemorated at the Gedenkstätte Stille Helden (p166). Many memorials throughout the city commemorate the Nazi's victims. The most prominent is, of course, the Holocaust Memorial (p89), near the Brandenburg Gate.

economic restructure away from a manufacturing base and towards the service sector began to bear fruit. Job creation in the capital has outpaced that of Germany in general for almost 12 years. No German city has a greater number of business start-ups. Its export quota has risen steadily, as has its population. The health, transport and green-technology industries are growing in leaps and bounds.

On the cultural front, Berlin exploded into a hive of cultural cool with unbridled nightlife, a vibrant art scene and booming fashion and design industries. In 2006 it became part of Unesco's Creative Cities Network. Some 170,000 people are employed in the cultural sector, which generates an annual turnover of around €13 billion. An especially important subsector is music, with nearly 10% of all related companies, including Universal and MTV, moving their European headquarters to Berlin.

Over the past decade, Berlin has also become the breeding pool for continental Europe's start-up economy, attracting young global tech talent with its multicultural make-up, relative affordability, open-mindedness and high-level of English skills. The city has been the launch pad for such companies as Zalando, SoundCloud, ResearchGate, GoEuro, Foodora and Clue. Almost half of start-ups are founded by neo-Berliners.

2001

Openly gay politician Klaus Wowereit is elected governing mayor of Berlin.

2006

Berlin's first central train station, the Hauptbahnhof, opens on 26 May. Two weeks later Germany kicks off the 2006 FIFA World Cup.

2008

The last flight takes off from Berlin-Tempelhof Airport, which becomes an event space and public park.

2011

Berlin's population passes the 3.5 million mark, growing 1.2%, the most within a single year since reunification in 1990. Most of the growth comes from people moving to Berlin.

In December 2017, 711,000 people living in Berlin (19% of the city's population) were foreigners. There are people from 185 nations, including 19,900 Americans, 13,456 Brits, 3958 Australians and 3515 Canadians. Berlin's Turkish community represents the single largest foreign population with 98,121 people.

Although now stagnating or regressing, Berlin's population was growing steadily in the 2010s, fuelled by a slight increase in the birth rate but mostly by migration from other European countries, asylum seekers and global expats. This development exacerbated an acute housing shortage. Affordable housing in particular remains in short supply as investors, most of them from abroad, snap up precious real estate to build top-flight units or convert existing housing into luxury condominiums.

While Berlin's global community is one of its greatest assets, social and economic integration remain challenges. In 2015 and 2016, more than 70,000 refugees arrived, mostly from war-torn Syria, Iraq and Afghanistan, overwhelming the local bureaucracy and delaying integration efforts. By 2018, the river of newcomers had slowed to a trickle and many private groups have stepped in to boost the government's integration initiatives.

Fortunately, Berlin did not experience as steep a rise of right-wing populism in response to the federal government's asylum policies as other German regions. Even after the city suffered its first terrorist attack in 2016, when an asylum seeker drove a van into a Christmas market killing 12 people, Berliners remained calm.

Pandemic & the Future

Not surprisingly, the Covid-19 pandemic has wreaked significant havoc on Berlin's society and economy. Tourism and the hospitality sector along with the cultural and creative scenes – all crucial building blocks of the city's DNA – have been especially hard hit. The virus also brought Berlin's population growth, which had held steady since 2003, to a halt. This, however, did little to alleviate the chronic shortage of affordable housing. It didn't help that a rent cap law passed in January 2020 by the Berlin parliament was overturned by Germany's constitutional court in April 2021. Indeed, the building of affordable housing was a cornerstone of every single party and candidate running in the September 2021 local and state elections. Traffic, climate change, security, digitalisation and education also ranked high on political agendas.

2015

Chancellor Angela Merkel's offer of temporary asylum to refugees brings well over 70,000 new arrivals to Berlin, mostly from Syria, Iraq and Afghanistan.

2016

A terror attack on the Christmas market on Breitscheidplatz by a Tunisian asylum seeker leaves 12 people dead and 56 injured.

2020

Berlin Brandenburg Airport opens on 31 October after an eight-year delay.

2021

Berlin's rent cap law, passed in January 2020, is deemed unconstitutional by Germany's highest federal court.

City of Architecture

From the Schloss Charlottenburg to the Reichstag, Fernsehturm (TV Tower) to Berliner Philharmonie, the Jewish Museum to the Sony Center – Berlin boasts some mighty fine architecture. It's an eclectic mix, to be sure, shaped by the city's unique history, especially the destruction of WWII and the contrasting urban-planning visions during the years of division. Since reunification, though, Berlin has become a virtual laboratory for the world's elite architects, David Chipperfield, Norman Foster and Daniel Libeskind among them.

Modest Beginnings

Very few buildings from the Middle Ages until the 18th century have survived since much of the historic core around today's Rotes Rathaus was destroyed, first during WWII and then by demolition in the 1960s and '70s. Only two Gothic churches – the red-brick Nikolaikirche (1230)

Above: Museum Nikolaikirche (p122)

BERLIN & ITS WALLS

1250 The first defensive wall is built of boulders and stands 2m high.

14th century The wall is fortified with bricks and raised to a height of 5m.

1648–1734 The medieval wall is replaced by elaborate fortifications.

1734–1866 A customs wall with 18 city gates replaces the bastion.

1961–1989 The Berlin Wall divides the city.

and Marienkirche (1294), both reconstructed – still bear silent witness to the era when Berlin was just a small riverside trading town. The former anchors the Nikolaiviertel, a mock-medieval quarter built on the site of the city's original settlement as East Germany's contribution to Berlin's 750th anniversary celebrations in 1987. It's a hodgepodge of genuine historic buildings like the Knoblauchhaus and replicas of historic buildings such as the Zum Nussbaum inn.

A smidgeon of residential medieval architecture also survives in the outer district of Spandau, both in the Gotisches Haus and the half-timbered houses of the Kolk quarter.

Traces of the Renaissance, which reached Berlin in the early 16th century, are rarer still; notable survivors include the Jagdschloss Grunewald and the Zitadelle Spandau.

Going for Baroque

As the city grew, so did the representational needs of its rulers, especially in the 17th and 18th centuries. In Berlin, this role fell to Great Elector Friedrich Wilhelm, who systematically expanded the city by adding three residential quarters, a fortified town wall and a tree-lined boulevard known as Unter den Linden.

This was the age of baroque, a style merging architecture, sculpture, ornamentation and painting into a single *Gesamtkunstwerk* (complete work of art). In Berlin and northern Germany it retained a formal and precise bent, never quite reaching the exuberance favoured in regions further south.

The Great Elector may have laid the groundwork, but it was only under his son, Elector Friedrich III, that Berlin acquired the stature of an exalted residence, especially after he crowned himself *King* Friedrich I in 1701. Two major baroque buildings survive from his reign, both blueprinted by Johann Arnold Nering: Schloss Charlottenburg, which Johann Friedrich Eosander later expanded into a Versailles-inspired three-wing palace; and the Zeughaus (armoury; today's Deutsches Historisches Museum) on Unter den Linden. The museum's modern annexe, named the IM Pei Bau (IM Pei Building) after its architect, was added in the 1990s. Fronted by a transparent, spiral staircase shaped like a snail shell, it's a harmonious interplay of glass, natural stone and light and an excellent example of Pei's muted postmodernist approach.

Built as a summer palace for King Friedrich I's wife Sophie-Charlotte, Schloss Charlottenburg was originally called Schloss Lietzenburg but was renamed after the popular queen's sudden death in 1705. She is buried in the Mausoleum in the palace gardens.

Meanwhile, back in the early 18th century, two formidable churches were taking shape on Gendarmenmarkt in the heart of the immigrant Huguenot community, who at the time accounted for about 25% of the population. These were the Deutscher Dom (German Church) by Martin Grünberg, and the Französischer Dom (French Church) by Louis Cayart.

No king had a greater impact on Berlin's physical layout than Frederick the Great (Friedrich II). Together with his childhood friend architect Georg Wenzeslaus von Knobelsdorff, he masterminded the Forum

Sankt-Hedwigs-Kathedrale

Fridericianum, a cultural quarter centred on today's Bebelplatz. It was built in a style called 'Frederician rococo', which blends baroque and neoclassical elements. Since the king's war exploits had emptied his coffers, he could only afford to partially realise his vision by building the neoclassical Staatsoper (State Opera House); the Sankt-Hedwigs-Kathedrale (St Hedwig Cathedral), inspired by Rome's Pantheon; the playful Alte Bibliothek (Old Royal Library); and the Humboldt Universität (Humboldt University), originally a palace for the king's brother Heinrich. Knobelsdorff also designed the Neuer Flügel (New Wing) expansion of Schloss Charlottenburg. His crowning achievement, though, was Schloss Sanssouci (Sanssouci Palace) in Potsdam.

After Knobelsdorff's death in 1753, two architects continued in his tradition: Philipp Daniel Boumann, who designed Schloss Bellevue (Bellevue Palace) for Frederick's youngest brother, August Ferdinand; and Carl von Gontard, who added the domed towers to the Deutscher Dom and Französischer Dom on Gendarmenmarkt.

The Schinkel Touch

The architectural style that most shaped Berlin was neoclassicism, thanks in large part to one man: Karl Friedrich Schinkel (1781–1841), arguably Prussia's most prominent architect. Turning away from baroque flourishes, neoclassicism drew upon columns, pediments, domes and other design elements that had been popular throughout antiquity.

Schinkel's earliest commission was the Pomona Temple in Potsdam, completed in 1801 when he was just 19 years old. In Berlin Schinkel assisted with the design of Queen Luise's mausoleum in Schloss Charlottenburg's park in 1810, but didn't truly make his mark until snagging his first major solo commission, the Neue Wache (New Guardhouse,

Top Four Prussian Palaces

Schloss Sanssouci (Potsdam)

Schloss Charlottenburg (Charlottenburg)

Neues Palais (Potsdam)

Schloss Schönhausen (Pankow)

Neue Wache (p97)

1818) on Unter den Linden. Originally an army guardhouse, it is now an antiwar memorial sheltering a haunting sculpture by Käthe Kollwitz.

The nearby Altes Museum (Old Museum) on Museumsinsel (Museum Island), with its colonnaded front, is considered Schinkel's most mature work. Other neoclassical masterpieces include the Schauspielhaus (now the Konzerthaus Berlin) on Gendarmenmarkt and the Neue Pavillon (New Pavilion) in Schlossgarten Charlottenburg. Schinkel's most significant departure from neoclassicism, the turreted Friedrichswerdersche Kirche, was inspired by a Gothic Revival in early-19th-century England. The Tudor-style Schloss Babelsberg in Potsdam is also based on Schinkel's designs.

After Schinkel's death in 1841, several of his disciples kept his legacy alive, notably Friedrich August Stüler, who built the original Neues Museum (New Museum) and the Alte Nationalgalerie (Old National Gallery), both on Museumsinsel, as well as the Matthäuskirche (Church of St Matthew) in today's Kulturforum.

Berlin's architectural growth was notably influenced by advancements in transportation. The first train chugged from Berlin to Potsdam in 1838, the first S-Bahn rumbled along in 1882 and the U-Bahn kicked into service in 1902.

Housing for the Masses

In his 1930 book *Das Steinerne Berlin* (Stony Berlin), Werner Hegemann fittingly refers to Berlin as 'the largest tenement city in the world'. The onset of industrialisation in the middle of the 19th century lured hundreds of thousands to the capital, who dreamed of improving their lot in the factories. Something had to be done to beef up the city's infrastructure and provide cheap housing for the masses, and quick. A plan drawn up in 1862 under chief city planner James Hobrecht called for a city expansion along two circular ring roads bisected by diagonal roads radiating in all directions from the centre – much like the spokes of a wheel. The land in between was divided into large lots and sold to speculators and developers. Building codes were limited to a maximum building height of 22m (equivalent to five storeys) and a minimum courtyard size of 5.34m by 5.34m, just large enough for fire-fighting equipment to operate in.

Such lax regulations led to the uncontrolled spread of sprawling working-class tenements called *Mietskasernen* (literally 'rental barracks') in newly created peripheral districts such as Prenzlauer Berg, Kreuzberg, Wedding and Friedrichshain. Each was designed to squeeze the maximum number of people into the smallest possible space. Entire families crammed into tiny, lightless flats reached via internal staircases that also provided access to shared toilets. Many flats doubled as workshops or sewing studios. Only those in the street-facing front offered light, space and balconies – and they were reserved for the bourgeoisie.

The industrial age saw Berlin's population explode. It more than doubled to 969,050 between 1858 and 1875, doubling again by 1905 and fuelling the need for cheap and plentiful housing.

The Empire Years

The architecture in vogue after the creation of the German Empire in 1871 reflected the representational needs of the united Germany and tended towards the pompous. No new style, as such, emerged as architects essentially recycled earlier ones (eg Romanesque, Renaissance, baroque, sometimes weaving them all together) in an approach called *Historismus* (historicism) or *Wilhelmismus*, after Kaiser Wilhelm I. As a result, many buildings in Berlin look much older than they actually are. Prominent examples include the Reichstag by Paul Wallot and the Berliner Dom (Berlin Cathedral) by Julius Raschdorff, both in neo-Renaissance style. Franz Schwechten's Anhalter Bahnhof and the Kaiser-Wilhelm-Gedächtniskirche (Memorial Church), both in ruins, reflect the neo-Romanesque, while the Bode-Museum by Ernst von Ihne is a neobaroque confection.

While squalid working-class neighbourhoods emerged in the north, east and south of the city centre, western Berlin (Charlottenburg, Wilmersdorf) was developed for the middle and upper classes under none other than the 'Iron Chancellor' Otto von Bismarck himself. He had the Kurfürstendamm widened, lining it and its side streets with attractive townhouses. Those with serious money and status moved even further west, away from the claustrophobic centre. The villa colonies in leafy Grunewald and Dahlem are another Bismarck legacy and still among the ritziest residential areas today.

THE BAUHAUS

The Bauhaus, which turned 100 in 2019, was founded in Weimar by Berlin architect Walter Gropius as a multidisciplinary school that aimed to abolish the distinction between 'fine' and 'applied' arts, and to unite the artistic with daily life. One of its chief mottos was 'form follows function': products were crafted with an eye towards mass production and featured strong, clear lines and little, if any, ornamentation. The movement immediately attracted such heavyweights as Paul Klee, Lyonel Feininger, Wassily Kandinsky, Marcel Breuer and Wilhelm Wagenfeld to its faculty.

After conservative politicians closed the Weimar school in 1925, it found refuge in Dessau before moving to Berlin in 1932 with Ludwig Mies van der Rohe at the helm. Just one year later the Nazis shut down the school for good. Most of its practitioners went into exile. Gropius became director of Harvard's architecture school, while Mies van der Rohe held the same post at the Illinois Institute of Technology in Chicago. Both men were instrumental in developing the Bauhaus' stylistic successor, the so-called International Style.

CANADASTOCK / SHUTTERSTOCK ©

Top: Bode-Museum (p114)
Bottom: Berliner Dom (p120)

Shell-Haus (p278) by architect Emil Fahrenkamp

The Birth of Modernism

While most late-19th-century architects were looking to the past, a few progressive minds managed to make their mark, initially in industrial and commercial design. Sometimes called the 'father of modern architecture', Peter Behrens (1868–1940) taught later modernist luminaries such as Le Corbusier, Walter Gropius and Ludwig Mies van der Rohe. One of his earliest works, the 1909 AEG Turbinenhalle at Huttenstrasse 12-14 in Moabit, is considered an icon of early industrial architecture.

After WWI the 1920s spirit of innovation lured some of the finest avant-garde architects to Berlin, including Bruno and Max Taut, Le Corbusier, Mies van der Rohe, Erich Mendelsohn, Hans Poelzig and Hans Scharoun. In 1924 they formed an architectural collective called Der Ring (The Ring) whose members were united by the desire to break with traditional aesthetics (especially the derivative historicism) and to promote a modern, affordable and socially responsible approach to building. Their theories were put into practice as Berlin entered another housing shortage. Led by chief city planner Martin Wagner, Ring members devised a new form of social housing called *Siedlungen* (housing estates). In contrast to the claustrophobic tenements, it opened up living space and incorporated gardens, schools, shops and other communal areas that facilitated social interaction. Together with Bruno Taut, Wagner himself designed the Hufeisensiedlung (Horseshoe Colony) in Neukölln, which, in 2008, became one of six Berlin housing estates recognised as a Unesco World Heritage Site (p282).

Bauhaus fans fancying a stay in an original, impeccably renovated Bruno Taut residence in the Hufeisensiedlung should check out www.tautes-heim.de.

In nonresidential architecture, expressionism flourished with Erich Mendelsohn as its leading exponent. This organic, sculptural approach is nicely exemplified by the Universum Kino (Universum Cinema; 1926), which is today's Schaubühne theatre, and by the IG-Metall-Haus

Socialist architecture along Karl-Marx-Allee

(1930) at Alte Jakobstrasse 148 in Kreuzberg. Emil Fahrenkamp's 1931 Shell-Haus at Reichspietschufer 60 follows similar design principles. Reminiscent of a giant upright staircase, it was one of Berlin's earliest steel-frame structures, concealed beneath a skin of travertine. Its extravagant silhouette is best appreciated from the southern bank of the Landwehrkanal.

Nazi Monumentalism

Modernist architecture had its legs cut out from under it as soon as Hitler came to power in 1933. The new regime immediately shut down the Bauhaus School (p275), one of the most influential forces in 20th-century building and design. Many of its visionary teachers, including Gropius, Mies van der Rohe, Wagner and Mendelsohn, went into exile in the US.

Back in Berlin, Hitler, who was a big fan of architectural monumentalism, put Albert Speer in charge of turning Berlin into the Welthauptstadt Germania, the future capital of the Reich. Today, only a few buildings offer a hint of what Berlin might have looked like had history taken a different turn. These include the coliseum-like Olympiastadion, Tempelhof Airport and the former air-force ministry that now houses Germany's Federal Finance Ministry.

To envision how Berlin would look if the Nazis had won the war, check out the exhibit Myth of Germania – Vision and Crime in Wedding.

A Tale of Two Cities

Even before the Wall was built in 1961, the clash of ideologies and economic systems between East and West found expression in the architectural arena.

East Berlin

East Germans looked to Moscow, where Stalin favoured a style that was essentially a socialist reinterpretation of good old-fashioned neo-classicism. The most prominent East German architect was Hermann Henselmann, the brains behind the Karl-Marx-Allee (called Stalinallee until 1961) in Friedrichshain. Built between 1952 and 1965, it was East Berlin's showcase 'socialist boulevard' and, with its Moscow-style 'wedding-cake buildings', the epitome of Stalin-era pomposity. It culminates at Alexanderplatz, the historic central square that got a distinctly socialist makeover in the 1960s.

While Alexanderplatz and the Karl-Marx-Allee were prestige projects, they did not solve the cries for affordable modern housing, which reached a crescendo in the early 1970s. The government responded by building three massive satellite cities on the periphery – Marzahn, Hohenschönhausen and Hellersdorf – which leapt off the drawing board in the 1970s and '80s. Like a virtual Legoland for giants, these huge housing developments largely consist of row upon row of rectangular high-rise *Plattenbauten,* buildings made from large, precast concrete slabs. Marzahn alone could accommodate 165,000 people in 62,000 flats. Since they offered such mod cons as private baths and lifts, this type of housing was very popular among East Germans, despite the monotony of the design.

West Berlin

In West Berlin, urban planners sought to eradicate any references to Nazi-style monumentalism and to rebuild the city in a modernist fashion. Their prestige project became the Hansaviertel, a loosely structured leafy neighbourhood of midrise apartment buildings and single-family homes, northwest of Tiergarten. Built from 1954 to 1957, it drew the world's top architects, including Gropius, Oscar Niemeyer, Alvar Aalto and Le Corbusier and was intended to be a model for other residential quarters.

The 1960s saw the birth of a large-scale public building project, the Kulturforum, a museum and concert-hall complex conceptualised by Hans Scharoun. His Berliner Philharmonie, the first building to be completed in 1963, is considered a masterpiece of sculptural modernism. Among the museums, Mies van der Rohe's temple-like Neue Nationalgalerie (New National Gallery) is a standout. A massive glass-and-steel cube, it perches on a raised granite podium and is lidded by a coffered, steel-ribbed roof that seems to defy gravity.

The West also struggled with a housing shortage and built its own versions of mass-scale housing projects, including Gropiusstadt in southern Neukölln and the Märkisches Viertel in Reinickendorf, in northwest Berlin.

The only remaining prewar buildings on Alexanderplatz are the Berolinahaus (1930) and the Alexanderhaus (1932), both by Peter Behrens.

MIES VAN DER ROHE HAUS

Mies van der Rohe's last residential commission before heading into exile in America was the austerely elegant **Villa Lemke** (Haus Lemke; ☎030-9700 0618; www.miesvanderrohehaus.de; Oberseestrasse 60; ⏲11am-5pm Tue-Sun; P; M5) FREE on the Obersee lake. Completed in 1933, its flat roof and reduced outline are enlivened by huge windows, a reddish-brown brick facade and a big terrace that extends the living room. The Bauhaus jewel has been faithfully restored and now hosts several art and architecture exhibits per year.

Combine it with a spin around the petite Obersee or a visit of the infamous Stasi Prison that's just a 15-minute walk away.

Neue Nationalgalerie (p165) by architect Mies Van Der Rohe. Sculpture by Henry Moore.

The Post-Reunification Years

Reunification presented Berlin with both the challenge and the opportunity to redefine itself architecturally. With the Wall and death strip gone, the two city halves had to be physically rejoined across huge gashes of empty space. Critical Reconstruction continued to be the guiding principle under city planning director Hans Stimmann. Architects had to follow a long catalogue of parameters with regard to building heights, facade materials and other criteria. The goal was to rebuild Berlin within its historic forms rather than creating a modern, vertical city.

In the 1920s Adolf Hitler's half-brother Alois was a waiter at Weinhaus Huth, the only building on Potsdamer Platz to survive WWII intact. During the Cold War, it stood forlorn in the middle of the death strip for decades.

Potsdamer Platz

The biggest and grandest of the post-1990 Berlin developments (and, incidentally, an exception to the tenets of Critical Reconstruction), Potsdamer Platz is a modern reinterpretation of the historic square that was Berlin's bustling heart until WWII. From terrain once bisected by the Berlin Wall has sprung an urban quarter laid out along a dense, irregular street grid in keeping with a 'European city'. Led by Renzo Piano, it's a collaboration of an international roster of renowned architects, including Helmut Jahn, Richard Rogers and Rafael Moneo.

Pariser Platz

Pariser Platz in front of the Brandenburg Gate was reconstructed from the ground up. It's a formal, introspective square framed by banks, embassies and the Hotel Adlon. In keeping with Critical Reconstruction, all buildings had to have natural stone facades. The one exception is the glass-fronted Akademie der Künste (Academy of Arts). Its architect,

Paul-Löbe-Haus (p93) and the Marie-Elisabeth-Lüders-Haus (p94)

Günter Behnisch, had to fight tooth and nail for this facade, arguing that the square's only public building should feel open, inviting and transparent. The Adlon, meanwhile, is practically a spitting image of the 1907 original.

Regierungsviertel

The 1991 decision to move the federal government back to Berlin resulted in a flurry of building activity in the empty space between the Reichstag and the Spree River. Designed by Axel Schultes and Charlotte Frank, and arranged in linear east–west fashion, are the Federal Chancellery, the Paul-Löbe-Haus and the Marie-Elisabeth-Lüders-Haus. Together they form the Band des Bundes (Band of Federal Buildings) in a symbolic linking of the formerly divided city halves across the Spree.

Overlooking all these shiny new structures is the Reichstag, home of the Bundestag (German parliament), the glass dome of which is the most visible element of the building's total makeover masterminded by Norman Foster.

The glass-and-steel 'spaceship' on the northern riverbank is Berlin's first-ever central train station, the sparkling Hauptbahnhof, designed by the Hamburg firm of Gerkan, Marg und Partner and completed in 2006. Another eyecatcher is the vast Federal Ministry of Education and Research that has hugged the river south of the train station since 2014.

With its cool, calm facade, the DZ Bank on Pariser Platz seems atypical for its exuberant architect, Frank Gehry. The surprise, though, lurks beyond the foyer leading to a light-flooded atrium anchored by an enormous sci-fi-esque stainless-steel sculpture used as a conference room.

More Architectural Trophies

In Kreuzberg, Daniel Libeskind's deconstructivist Jüdisches Museum (1999) is among the most daring and provocative structures in post-reunification Berlin. With its irregular, zigzagging floor plan and shiny zinc skin pierced by gash-like windows, it is not merely a museum but a powerful metaphor for the troubled history of the Jewish people.

Anyone interested in edgy architectural drawings should swing by the Tchoban Foundation, a private museum in a cool modernist building in Prenzlauer Berg.

Another highlight is David Chipperfield's reconstruction of the Neues Museum (2009) on Museumsinsel. Like a giant jigsaw puzzle, it beautifully blends fragments from the original structure, which was destroyed in WWII, with modern elements. Chipperfield also designed the adjacent James Simon Gallery that opened in 2019 as the central entrance to the museums on Museumsinsel.

The City West has also garnered several high-profile additions including the towering Waldorf Astoria Hotel and its equally soaring neighbour Upper West, a residential and commercial tower. Construction on Zoom, an office-and-retail building with a 150m-long, three-storey glass facade opposite the Astoria/Upper West twin towers, has also been completed.

UNCOMMON ENVIRONS FOR THE COMMON FOLK

Architecturally speaking, Museumsinsel, Schloss Sanssouci and the Hufeisensiedlung in Neukölln could not be more different. Yet all have one thing in common: they are Unesco World Heritage Sites. Along with five other working-class housing estates throughout Berlin, the Hufeisensiedlung was inducted onto this illustrious list in 2008.

Created between 1910 and 1933 by such leading architects of the day as Bruno Taut and Martin Wagner, these icons of modernism are the earliest examples of innovative, streamlined and functional – yet human-scale – mass housing and stand in stark contrast to the slumlike, crowded tenements of the late 19th century. The flats, though modest, were functionally laid out and had kitchens, private baths and balconies that let in light and fresh air.

Hufeisensiedlung, Neukölln (Lowise-Reuter-Ring; U-Bahn: Parchimer Allee) Taut and Wagner dreamed up a three-storey-high horseshoe-shaped colony (1933–35) with 1000 balconied flats wrapping around a central park. From the station follow Fritz-Reuter-Allee north.

Gartenstadt Falkenberg, Köpenick (Akazienhof, Am Falkenberg & Gartenstadtweg; S-Bahn: Grünau) Built by Taut between 1910 and 1913, the oldest of the six Unesco-honoured estates is a cheerful jumble of colourfully painted cottages. Approach from Am Falkenberg.

Siemensstadt, Spandau (Geisslerpfad, Goebelstrasse, Heckerdamm, Jungfernheideweg, Mäckeritzstrasse; U-Bahn: Siemensdamm) This huge development (1929–31) combines Walter Gropius' minimalism, Hugo Häring's organic approach and Hans Scharoun's ship-inspired designs. Best approach is via Jungfernheideweg.

Schillerpark Siedlung, Wedding (Barfussstrasse, Bristolstrasse, Corker Strasse, Dubliner Strasse, Oxforder Strasse, Windsorer Strass; U-Bahn: Rehberge) Inspired by Dutch architecture, this large colony was masterminded by Taut (1924–30) and sports a dynamic red-and-white-brick facade. Best approach is via Barfussstrasse.

Weisse Stadt, Reinickendorf (Aroser Allee and side streets; U-Bahn: Residenzstrasse; bus 120: Weisse Stadt) Masterminded by Martin Wagner, the fanshaped 'White City' (1929–31) gets its name from the white facades of its 1200 apartments. The main artery is Aroser Allee, which is spanned by an iconic bridge building at the intersection with Genfer Strasse.

Wohnstadt Carl Legien, Prenzlauer Berg (streets around Erich-Weinert-Strasse; S-Bahn: Prenzlauer Allee) For this development (1928–30) in Prenzlauer Berg, Taut arranged rows of four-to-five-storey-high houses and garden areas in a semi-open space. Approach via Erich-Weinert-Strasse.

Cube Berlin

Recent Developments & the Future

You'd think that, more than 30 years after reunification, the ballet of cranes would finally have disappeared, but there are still plenty of major projects on the drawing board or under construction.

Construction of the replica of the former Prussian city palace (Berliner Stadtschloss), which began in 2013, was completed in 2020. Called Humboldt Forum, it resembles its historic predecessor only from the outside, with the modern interior housing museums and cultural institutions.

Also completed in 2020 was the striking Cube Berlin overlooking the Spree from its perch in front of the Hauptbahnhof. Designed by the Danish architecture firm 3XN, it is considered one of Europe's 'smartest' office buildings and features a mirrored facade with triangular sections that push inward to create outdoor terraces.

North of the main train station, Berlin's biggest building project is swiftly taking shape. Called Europa-City, the emerging neighbourhood occupies 40 hectares and will have its own S-Bahn station, a bridge across the canal and leafy squares.

The year 2020 also saw the completion of the new headquarters of German publisher Axel Springer on Zimmerstrasse in Mitte. Designed by OMA, the firm helmed by Rem Koolhas, it centres on a 45m-high light-filled atrium with offices set up on cascading terraces. The ground floor lobby is open to the public and a rooftop bar is in the works.

Top Buildings Since 1990

Jüdisches Museum (Daniel Libeskind; Kreuzberg)

Reichstag Dome (Norman Foster; Historic Mitte)

Sony Center (Helmut Jahn; Potsdamer Platz)

Neues Museum (David Chipperfield; Museumsinsel)

Cube Berlin (3XN; Historic Mitte)

Painting & Visual Arts

The arts are fundamental to everything Berlin holds dear, and the sheer scope of creative activity in the city is astounding. Berlin itself provides an iconic setting for a spectrum of visual arts, its unmistakable presence influencing artists and residents just as it does those canny visitors who take the time to dive in.

Early Beginnings

Fine art only began to flourish in Berlin in the late 17th century, when self-crowned King Friedrich I founded the Akademie der Künste (Academy of Arts) in 1696, egged on by court sculptor Andreas Schlüter. Schlüter repaid the favour with outstanding sculptures, including the *Great Elector on Horseback,* now in front of Schloss Charlottenburg, and the haunting masks of dying warriors in the courtyard of today's Deutsches Historisches Museum (German Historical Museum). Artistic accents in painting were set by Frenchman Antoine Pesne, who became Friedrich I's court painter in 1710. His main legacy is his elaborate portraits of the royal family members.

The arts also enjoyed a heyday under Friedrich I's grandson, Friedrich II (Frederick the Great), who became king in 1740. Friedrich drew heavily on the artistic expertise of his friend Georg Wenzeslaus von Knobelsdorff, a student of Pesne, and amassed a sizeable collection of works by French artists such as Jean Antoine Watteau.

The 19th Century

The coppersmith Emanuel Jury, who cast the *Quadriga* sculpture atop the Brandenburg Gate, used his cousin as a model for the Goddess Victoria, pilot of the chariot.

Neoclassicism emerged as a dominant sculptural style in the 19th century. Johann Gottfried Schadow's *Quadriga* – the horse-drawn chariot atop the Brandenburg Gate – epitomises the period. Schadow's student Christian Daniel Rauch had a special knack for representing idealised, classical beauty in a realistic fashion. His most famous work is the 1851 monument of Frederick the Great on horseback on Unter den Linden. More sculpture by Rauch and contemporaries like Johann Gottfried Schadow is displayed in the dreamy Karl Friedrich Schinkel-designed Friedrichswerdersche Kirche (church) in Mitte.

In painting, heart-on-your-sleeve romanticism that drew heavily on emotion and a dreamy idealism dominated the 19th century. A reason for this development was the awakening of a nationalist spirit in Germany, spurred by the Napoleonic Wars. Top dog of the era was Caspar David Friedrich, best known for his moody, allegorical landscapes. Although more famous as an architect, Karl Friedrich Schinkel also created some fanciful canvases. Eduard Gärtner's paintings documenting Berlin's evolving cityscape found special appeal among the middle classes.

A parallel development was the so-called Berliner Biedermeier, a more conservative and painstakingly detailed style that appealed to the emerging Prussian middle class. The name itself is derived from the German word for conventional *(bieder)* and the common surname of Meier; visit the Knoblauchhaus in the Nikolaiviertel for fine examples (though check first as it was closed during the Covid pandemic).

The Alte Nationalgalerie on Museumsinsel and the Neuer Pavillon of Schloss Charlottenburg (also closed during Covid) are both showcases of 19th-century paintings.

Into the 20th Century

Berliner Secession

The Berliner Secession was formed in 1898 by a group of progressively minded artists who rejected the traditional teachings of the arts academies that stifled any new forms of expression. The schism was triggered in 1891, when the established Verein Berliner Künstler (Berlin Artist Association) refused to show paintings by Edvard Munch at its annual salon, and reached its apex in 1898 when the salon jury rejected a landscape painting by Walter Leistikow. Consequently, 65 artists banded together under the leadership of Leistikow and Max Liebermann and seceded from the Verein. Other famous Berliner Secession members included Lovis Corinth, Max Slevogt, Ernst Ludwig Kirchner, Max Beckmann and Käthe Kollwitz.

A student of Christian Daniel Rauch, the sculptor Reinhold Begas developed a neobaroque, theatrical style that met with a fair amount of controversy in his lifetime. Major works include the Neptune fountain near the Fernsehturm (TV Tower), and the Schiller memorial on Gendarmenmarkt.

Expressionism

In 1905 Kirchner, along with Erich Heckel and Karl Schmidt-Rottluff, founded the artists' group Die Brücke (The Bridge) in Dresden: it turned the art world on its head with groundbreaking visions that paved the way for German expressionism. Abstract forms, a flattened perspective and bright, emotional colours characterised this new aesthetic. Die Brücke moved to Berlin in 1911 and disbanded in 1913. The small Brücke-Museum in the Grunewald has a fantastic collection of these influential artists.

Ironically, it was the expressionists who splintered off from the Berliner Secession in 1910 after their work was rejected by the Secession jury. With Max Pechstein at the helm, they formed the Neue Secession. The original Berliner Secession group continued but saw its influence wane, especially after the Nazi power grab in 1933.

The Bauhaus & Art Under the Nazis

The year 1919 saw the founding of the Bauhaus (p275) movement and school in Weimar. It was based on practical anti-elitist principles bringing form and function together, and had a profound effect on all

BERLIN DADA

Dada was an avant-garde art movement formed in Zurich in 1916 in reaction to the brutality of WWI. It spread to Berlin in 1918 with the help of Richard Huelsenbeck, who held the first Dada event in a gallery in February that year and later produced the *First German Dada Manifesto*. Founding members included George Grosz, photomontage inventor John Heartfield and Hannah Höch; Marcel Duchamp, Kurt Schwitters and Hans Arp were among the many others who dabbled in Dada.

Dada artists had an irrational, satirical and often absurdist approach, imbued with a political undercurrent and a tendency to shock and provoke. The First International Dada Fair in 1920, for instance, took place beneath a suspended German officer dummy with a pig's head.

One artist greatly influenced by Dadaism was Otto Dix, who, in the 1920s, produced a series of dark and sombre paintings depicting war scenes – disfigured, dying and decomposing bodies – in graphic detail. Dix and Grosz went on to become key figures of the late 1920s Neue Sachlichkeit (New Objectivity), an offshoot of expressionism distinguished by an unsentimental, practical and objective look at reality.

modern design. Although the school moved to Dessau in 1925 and only came to Berlin in 1932, many of its most influential figures worked in Berlin. The Nazis forced it to close down in 1933. Unfortunately, the Bauhaus Archive, the museum built by Walter Gropius, is closed for renovation.

After the Nazi takeover many artists left the country and others ended up in prison or concentration camps, their works confiscated or destroyed. The art promoted instead was often terrible, favouring straightforward 'Aryan' forms and epic styles. Propaganda artist Mjölnir defined the typical look of the time with block Gothic scripts and idealised figures.

Art-world honchos descend upon Berlin in late April for the annual Gallery Weekend, when you can hop-scotch around 40 galleries, and the Berlin Biennale, a curated forum for contemporary art held over two months in spring or summer in even-numbered years.

Post WWII

After WWII, Berlin's art scene was as fragmented as the city itself. In the east, artists were forced to toe the social realism line, at least until the late 1960s when artists of the so-called Berliner Schule, including Manfred Böttcher and Harald Metzkes, sought to embrace a more interpretative and emotional form of expression inspired by the colours and aesthetic of Beckmann, Matisse, Picasso and other classical modernists. In the '70s, when conflicts of the individual in society became a prominent theme, underground galleries flourished in Prenzlauer Berg and art became a collective endeavour.

In postwar West Berlin, artists eagerly embraced abstract art. Pioneers included Zone 5, which revolved around Hans Thiemann, and surrealists Heinz Trökes and Mac Zimmermann. In the 1960s politics was a primary concern and a new style called 'critical realism' emerged, propagated by artists like Ulrich Baehr, Hans-Jürgen Diehl and Wolfgang Petrick. The 1973 movement, Schule der Neuen Prächtigkeit (School of New Magnificence), had a similar approach. In the late 1970s and early 1980s, expressionism found its way back on to the canvases of Salomé, Helmut Middendorf and Rainer Fetting, a group known as the Junge Wilde (Young Wild Ones). One of the best-known German neoexpressionist painters is Georg Baselitz.

To keep a tab on the contemporary art scene, check out the latest shows at the city's many high-calibre galleries, such as Galerie Eigen+Art or Contemporary Fine Arts, and visit the collections at Hamburger Bahnhof, the Sammlung Boros and the Julia Stoschek Collection.

The Present

Berlin hosts one of the most exciting and dynamic arts scenes in Europe. An estimated 20,000 professional artists make their home here, including many major leaguers. Olafur Eliasson, Thomas Demand, Jonathan Meese, Via Lewandowsky, Isa Genzken, Tino Seghal, Esra Ersen, John Bock and the artist duo Ingar Dragset and Michael Elmgreen all live and work in Berlin, or at least have a second residence here. Chinese dissident artist Ai Weiwei also had a studio in Berlin and a guest professorship at the Universität der Künste. But, disenchanted with life in Germany, he decamped to London in 2019.

Berlin has also emerged as a European street art capital with some major international artists like Blu, JR, Os Gemeos and Shepard Fairey leaving their mark on the city. Local top talent includes Alias and El Bocho. Street art is especially prevalent in eastern Kreuzberg (especially around the U-Bahn station Schlesisches Tor) as well as in Mitte (Haus Schwarzenberg), at the RAW Gelände in Friedrichshain and at the Teufelsberg ex-spy station. In 2016, Urban Nation, the world's first museum dedicated entirely to street art, opened in Berlin's Schöneberg district.

The Literature & Film Scenes

Since its beginnings, Berlin's literary scene has reflected a peculiar blend of provincialism and worldliness, but the city's pioneering role in movie history is undeniable: in 1895 Max Skladanowsky screened early films on a bioscope, in 1912 one of the world's first film studios was established in Potsdam, and since 1951 Berlin has hosted a leading international film festival.

Literature

First Words

Berlin's literary history began during the 18th-century Enlightenment, an epoch dominated by humanistic ideals. A major author from this time was Gotthold Ephraim Lessing, noted for his critical works, fables and tragedies, who wrote the play *Minna von Barnhelm* (1763) in Berlin. During the Romantic period, an outgrowth of the Enlightenment, it was the poets who stood out, including Achim von Arnim, Clemens Brentano, and Heinrich von Kleist, who committed suicide at Wannsee lake in 1811.

In the mid-19th century, realist literature captured the imagination of the newly emerging middle class. Theodor Fontane raised the Berlin society novel to an art form by showing both the aristocracy and the middle class mired in their societal confinements. His 1894 novel, *Effi Briest,* is among his best-known works. Naturalism, a spin-off of realism, painstakingly recreated the milieux of entire social classes. Gerhard Hauptmann's portrayal of social injustice and the harsh life of the working class won him the Nobel Prize for Literature in 1912.

Berlin Cult Novels

Berlin Alexanderplatz (Alfred Döblin, 1929)

Goodbye to Berlin (Christopher Isherwood, 1939)

Alone in Berlin (Hans Fallada, 1947)

Zoo Station, (Christiane F, 1978)

Berlin Blues (Sven Regener, 2001)

Modernism & Modernity

In the 1920s, Berlin became a literary hotbed, drawing writers like Alfred Döblin, whose definitive *Berlin Alexanderplatz* is a stylised meander through the seamy 1920s, and Anglo-American import Christopher Isherwood, whose brilliant semi-autobiographical *Berlin Stories* formed the basis of the musical and film *Cabaret.* During his time in Berlin in the 1930s, Vladimir Nabokov penned *The Gift* about a writer and Russian émigré who fled the Russian Revolution for Berlin.

Other notables include the political satirists Kurt Tucholsky and Erich Kästner. Many artists left Germany after the Nazis came to power, and those who stayed often kept their mouths shut and worked underground, if at all.

In West Berlin, the postwar literary revival was led by *The Tin Drum* (1958), by Nobel Prize–winner Günter Grass, which traces recent German history through the eyes of a child who refuses to grow. In the mid-1970s, a segment of the East Berlin literary scene began to detach itself slowly from the socialist party grip. Christa Wolf is one of the best and most controversial East German writers, while Heiner Müller had the distinction of being unpalatable in both Germanys. His dense, difficult works include *The Man Who Kept Down Wages* and the *Germania* trilogy of plays.

In 1978, the autobiography called *Zoo Station: The Story of Christiane F*, about a teenager who descends into heroin abuse and prostitution in West Berlin, made headlines worldwide and became a movie in 1981.

New Berlin Novel

In the 1990s, a slew of novels dealt with German reunification; many are set in Berlin, including Thomas Brussig's tongue-in-cheek *Heroes Like Us* (1998), Uwe Timm's *Midsummer Night* (1998), Peter Schneider's *Eduard's Homecoming* (1999) and Jana Hensel's *After the Wall: Confessions from an East German Childhood and the Life that Came Next* (2002). The late Nobel Prize–winner Günter Grass contributed *A Wide Field* (1995) to the debate. Also worth reading is Cees Nooteboom's *All Souls Day* (2002).

The lighter side of post-reunification Berlin is represented by Sven Regener, frontman of the Berlin band Element of Crime, whose hugely successful *Berlin Blues* (2001) is a boozy trawl through Kreuzberg nights at the time of the fall of the Wall. The runaway success story, however, was Russian-born author Wladimir Kaminer's *Russendisko* (Russian Disco, 2000), a collection of amusing, stranger-than-fiction vignettes about life in Berlin. Both *Berlin Blues* and *Russendisko* were made into feature films.

For an in-depth study of literature that emerged in Berlin after the fall of the Wall, pick up a copy of *Writing the New Berlin* (2008) by Katharina Gerstenberger.

Another popular German author is Volker Kutscher whose Weimar Republic–era detective novels *Der Nasse Fisch* (2008, English edition: *Babylon Berlin*) and *The Silent Death* (2009) form the basis of the Netflix series *Babylon Berlin*.

Foreign authors also continue to be inspired by Berlin. Ian McEwan's *The Innocent* (1990) and Joseph Kanon's *Leaving Berlin: A Novel* (2015) are both spy stories set in the 1950s. Kanon also wrote *The Good German* (2002), which was made into a motion picture. The *Berlin Noir* trilogy (1989–91), by the late British author Philip Kerr, features a private detective solving crimes in Nazi Germany. Berlin history unfolds in a dreamlike sequence in *Book of Clouds* (2009) by Chloe Aridjis.

Film

Before 1945

The legendary UFA (Universum Film AG), one of the world's first film studios, began shooting in Potsdam, near Berlin, in 1912 and continues to churn out both German and international blockbusters in its modern incarnation as the Filmstudios Babelsberg. The 1920s and early '30s were a boom time for Berlin cinema, with UFA emerging as Germany's flagship dream factory and Marlene Dietrich's bone structure and distinctive voice seducing the world. As early as 1919, Ernst Lubitsch produced historical films and comedies such as *Madame Dubarry,* starring Pola Negri and Emil Jannings; the latter went on to win the Best Actor Award at the very first Academy Awards ceremony in 1927. The same year saw the release of Walter Ruttmann's classic *Berlin: Symphony of a City,* a fascinating silent documentary that captures a day in the life of Berlin in the '20s.

Catch free silent movies with live organ accompaniment on Saturdays at midnight at the famous Babylon cinema in Mitte.

Other 1920s movies were heavily expressionistic, using stark contrast, sharp angles, heavy shadows and other distorting elements. Well-known flicks employing these techniques include *Nosferatu,* a 1922 Dracula adaptation by FW Murnau, and the groundbreaking *Metropolis* (1927) by Fritz Lang. One of the earliest seminal talkies was Josef von Sternberg's *Der Blaue Engel* (1930) starring Dietrich. After 1933, though, filmmakers found their artistic freedom, not to mention funding, increasingly curtailed, and by 1939 practically the entire industry had fled to Hollywood.

Films made during the Nazi period were mostly of the propaganda variety, with brilliant if controversial Berlin-born director Leni Riefenstahl (1902–2003) greatly pushing the genre's creative envelope. Her most famous film, *Triumph of the Will,* documents the 1934 Nuremberg Nazi party rally. *Olympia,* which chronicles the 1936 Berlin Olympic Games, was another seminal work.

After 1945

Like most of the arts, filmmaking has generally been well funded in Berlin since 1945, especially in the West. During the 1970s in particular, large subsidies lured directors back to the city, including such New German Film luminaries as Rainer Werner Fassbinder, Volker Schlöndorf, Wim Wenders and Werner Herzog. It was Wenders who made the highly acclaimed *Wings of Desire* (1987), an angelic love story swooping around the old, bare wasteland of Potsdamer Platz.

Cool places to plug into German movie history are the Museum für Film und Fernsehen at Potsdamer Platz, the Filmmuseum Potsdam and the Filmpark Babelsberg.

Some of the best films about the Nazi era include Wolfgang Staudte's *Die Mörder sind unter uns* (Murderers among Us, 1946); Fassbinder's *Die Ehe der Maria Braun* (The Marriage of Maria Braun, 1979); Margarethe von Trotta's *Rosenstrasse* (2003), and Oliver Hierschbiegel's extraordinary *Der Untergang* (Downfall, 2004), depicting Hitler's final days.

The first round of post-reunification flicks were light-hearted comedy dramas. A standout is the cult classic *Good Bye, Lenin!* (2003), Wolfgang Becker's witty and heart-warming tale of a son trying to recreate the GDR life to save his sick mother. It was Florian von Donnersmarck who first trained the filmic spotlight on the darker side of East Germany, with *The Lives of Others* (2006), an Academy Award–winner that reveals the stranglehold the East German secret police (Stasi) had on ordinary people.

MARLENE DIETRICH

Marlene Dietrich (1901–92) was born Marie Magdalena von Losch into a middle-class Berlin family. After acting school, she first captivated audiences as a hard-living, libertine flapper in 1920s silent movies, but quickly carved a niche as the dangerously seductive femme fatale. The 1930 talkie *Der Blaue Engel* (The Blue Angel) turned her into a Hollywood star and launched a five-year collaboration with director Josef von Sternberg. Her work on Sternberg's movie *Morocco* (1930) led to her only Oscar nomination. Although she never recaptured the successes of her early career, she continued making movies until 1984.

Dietrich built on her image of erotic opulence – dominant and severe but always with a touch of self-irony. She stayed in Hollywood after the Nazi rise to power, though Hitler, not immune to her charms, reportedly promised perks and the red-carpet treatment if she moved back to Germany. She responded with an empty offer to return if she could bring along Sternberg – a Jew and no Nazi favourite. She took US citizenship in 1937 and entertained Allied soldiers on the front.

After the war, Dietrich retreated slowly from the public eye, making occasional appearances in films but mostly cutting records and performing live cabaret. Her final years were spent in Paris, bedridden and accepting few visitors, immortal in spirit as mortality caught up with her. She's buried in **Berlin** (Stubenrauchstrasse 43-45; ⌚8am-6pm; Ⓢ Bundesplatz, Ⓤ Bundesplatz).

TOP FIVE 'UNORTHODOX' FILMING LOCATIONS

Few other internationally successful productions have put Berlin into the spotlight as much as the 2020 Emmy-winning Netflix production *Unorthodox*. Relive moments from the series by visiting these sites.

Musikinstrumenten-Museum (p165) The museum stands in as the music academy where Esty meets her new friends.

Winterfeldtplatz (p177) Esty's mother lives in the eccentric apartment building by Hinrich Baller on this central Schöneberg square.

Strandbad Wannsee (p238) In the seminal 'rebirth' scene, Esty wades into Lake Wannsee fully clothed before taking off her wig and floating in the water.

Jüdischer Friedhof Weissensee Esty's estranged husband Yankey and his brother Moishe go for a walk here.

The Barn (p168) Esty meets Robert for the first time in this cafe in the historic Haus Huth.

Today

These days, 'Germany's Hollywood' is no longer in Munich or Hamburg but in Berlin, with an average of 300 German and international productions and co-productions being filmed on location and at the Filmstudios Babelsberg each year. Well-trained crews, modern studio and postproduction facilities, government subsidies and authentic 'old world' locations regularly attract such Hollywood royalty as Quentin Tarantino (*Inglourious Basterds,* 2009) and George Clooney (*The Monuments Men,* 2014). Other recent big productions include Brian Percival's *The Book Thief* (2013), *The Grand Budapest Hotel* (2014), *The Hunger Games: Mockingjay Part 2* (2015), Tom Hanks' *A Hologram for the King* (2015), the entire fifth season of the TV series *Homeland* (2015) and Steven Spielberg's *Bridge of Spies* (2015).

Aside from the headline-grabbing Berlinale, dozens of other film festivals are held throughout the year, including the Jewish Film Festival, Arab Film Festival and the Too Drunk to Watch punk festival. See www.berliner-filmfestivals.de for the schedule.

Noteworthy recent films about Berlin include *A Coffee in Berlin* (*Oh Boy* in German, 2012), a tragicomedy about a young man struggling to find meaning in life in Berlin in the early 2000s, and *Victoria* (2015), filmed in a single continuous take, about a young Spanish woman who meets three Berlin guys after a night of clubbing and ends up robbing a bank, all in one night. *Axolotl Overkill* (2017), based on the 2010 novel by Helene Hegemann, also takes viewers on a high-paced ride around Berlin's notoriously hedonistic nightlife through the eyes of 16-year-old Mifti. On a more serious note, *Alone in Berlin* (2016), based on Hans Fallada's novel by the same name, deals with an innocent couple that falls victim to the Gestapo.

Internationally successful TV series starring Berlin are *Berlin Station* (2016), a high-tension spy drama, *Babylon Berlin* (2017), a lushly filmed detective story set in Berlin just before the Nazis' power grab and, most famously, the Emmy-winning Netflix series *Unorthodox* (2020), about a young Hasidic woman's escape from Brooklyn and spiritual rebirth in Berlin.

Germany's Music Capital

Just like the city itself, Berlin's music scene is a shape-shifter, fed by the city's appetite for diversity and change. With at least 2000 active bands and dozens of indie labels, Berlin is Germany's undisputed music capital. About 60% of the country's music revenue is generated here, and it's where Universal Music and MTV have their European headquarters.

Beginnings

For centuries, Berlin was largely eclipsed by Vienna, Leipzig and other European cities when it came to music. One notable exception is Carl Maria von Weber's *Der Freischütz* (The Marksman), which premiered in 1821 at today's Konzerthaus on Gendarmenmarkt and is considered the first important German Romantic opera. Weber's music also influenced Berlin-born Felix Mendelssohn-Bartholdy's *A Midsummer Night's Dream* from 1843. The same year, fellow composer Giacomo Meyerbeer became Prussian General Music Director.

The Berliner Philharmoniker was established in 1882 and quickly gained international stature under Hans von Bülow and, after 1923, Wilhelm Furtwängler. After WWII, Herbert von Karajan took over the baton. In East Germany, a key figure was Hanns Eisler, composer of the country's national anthem.

The 1920s

Cabaret may have been born in 1880s Paris, but it became a wild and libidinous grown-up in 1920s Berlin. Jazz was the dominant sound, especially after American performer Josephine Baker's headline-grabbing performances at the Theater des Westens dressed in nothing but a banana skirt. More home-grown cabaret music came in the form of the Berlin *Schlager* – light-hearted songs with titles like 'Mein Papagei frisst keine harten Eier' ('My parakeet doesn't eat hard-boiled eggs'), which teetered on the silly and surreal.

The most successful *Schlager* singing group was the a cappella Comedian Harmonists, a 'boy band' founded in 1927 by Harry Frommermann in the vein of the American group the Revelers. With a baritone, a bass, three tenors and a piano player, they performed

BERLIN TRACKS

1973

Berlin (Lou Reed) Dark song about the tragedy of two star-crossed junkies.

1977

Heroes (David Bowie) Two lovers in the shadow of the 'Wall of Shame'.

1980

Wir stehen auf Berlin (Ideal) Love declaration by the seminal *Neue Deutsche Welle* band.

1991

Zoo Station (U2) Bono embarks on a surreal journey inspired by a Berlin train station.

1995

Born to Die in Berlin (The Ramones) Drug-addled musings revealing Berlin's dark side.

2000

Dickes B (Seeed) Reggae ode to the 'Big B' (ie Berlin).

2007

Kreuzberg (Bloc Party) Looking for true love…

2008

Schwarz zu Blau (Peter Fox) Perfect portrait of Kottbusser Tor grit and grunge.

2013

Where Are We Now? (David Bowie) Melancholic reminiscence of Bowie's time in 1970s Berlin.

perfect vocal harmonies, which sounded like musical instruments. The group disbanded in 1934 because three of its members were Jewish; they subsequently fled Germany. The 1997 movie *The Harmonists* charts the course of the band's origin and success.

Another runaway hit was *The Threepenny Opera,* written by Bertolt Brecht with music by Kurt Weill. It premiered in 1928 with such famous songs as 'Mack the Knife'. Friedrich Hollaender was also a key composer in the cabaret scene, noted for his wit, improvisational talent and clever lyrics. Among his most famous songs is 'Falling in Love Again', sung by Marlene Dietrich in *Der Blaue Engel.* Like so many other talents (including Weill and Brecht), Hollaender left Germany when the Nazis brought down the curtain, and continued his career in Hollywood.

The pulsating 1920s drew numerous classical musicians to Berlin, including Arnold Schönberg and Paul Hindemith, who taught at the Akademie der Künste and the Berliner Hochschule, respectively. Schönberg's atonal compositions found a following here, as did his experimentation with noise and sound effects. Hindemith explored the new medium of radio and taught a seminar on film music.

A memorial plaque marks the house at Hauptstrasse 155 in Schöneberg, where the late David Bowie and his buddy Iggy Pop bunked in the late '70s. The seven-room flat was on the 1st floor; Pop later moved into his own digs across the back courtyard.

Pop, Punk & Rock Before 1990

Since the end of WWII, Berlin has spearheaded many of Germany's popular-music innovations. In West Berlin, Tangerine Dream helped to propagate the psychedelic sound of the late 1960s, while Ton Steine Scherben, led by Rio Reiser, became a seminal German-language rock band in the '70s and early '80s. Around the same time, Kreuzberg's subculture launched the punk movement at SO36 and other famous clubs. Regular visitors included David Bowie and Iggy Pop, who were Berlin flat buddies on Hauptstrasse in Schöneberg in the 1970s. Trying to kick a drug addiction and greatly inspired by Berlin's brooding mood, Bowie partly wrote and recorded his Berlin Trilogy *(Low, Heroes, Lodger)* at the famous Hansa Studios, which he dubbed the 'Hall by the Wall'. Check out Thomas Jerome Seabrook's *Bowie in Berlin: A New Career in a New Town* (2008) for a cool insight into those heady days.

In East Germany, access to Western rock and other popular music was restricted and few Western stars were invited to perform live. The

HANSA STUDIOS: BOWIE'S HALL BY THE WALL

Complete this analogy: London is to Abbey Road as Berlin is to...well? **Hansa Studios** (Map p336; www.meistersaal-berlin.de; Köthener Strasse 38; M41, U Potsdamer Platz, S Potsdamer Platz), of course, that seminal recording studio that has exerted a gravitational pull on international artists since the Cold War. Now used as an event location, the only way to get inside this famous building (and find out why Depeche Mode's Martin Gore stripped down naked for the recording of a love song) is with the highly recommended Berlin Music Tours (p301).

The 'Big Hall by the Wall' was how David Bowie fittingly dubbed its glorious Studio 2, better known as the Meistersaal (Masters' Hall). As you look through arched windows, imagine Bowie looking over the concrete barrier and perhaps waving at the gun-toting guards in their watchtowers. In the late '70s, the Thin White Duke recorded his tortured visions for the seminal album *Heroes* here, after completing *Low,* both part of his Berlin Trilogy. Bowie also produced *The Idiot* and *Lust for Life* with Iggy Pop.

There's a long list of other music legends who have taken advantage of the special sound quality at Hansa Studios, including Nina Hagen, Nick Cave, David Byrne, Einstürzende Neubauten, Die Ärzte, Snow Patrol, Green Day, REM, the Hives and the Pet Shop Boys. Depeche Mode produced three albums here – *Construction Time Again, Some Great Reward* and *Black Celebration* – between 1983 and 1986.

artistic freedom of East German talent was greatly compromised as all lyrics had to be approved and performances were routinely monitored. Nevertheless, a slew of home-grown *Ostrock* (eastern rock) bands emerged. Some major ones like the Puhdys, Karat, Silly and City managed to get around the censors by disguising criticism with seemingly innocuous metaphors, or by deliberately inserting provocative lyrics that they fully expected to be deleted by the censorship board. All built up huge followings on both sides of the Wall.

Many nonconformists were placed under an occupational ban and prohibited from performing. Singer-songwriter Wolf Biermann became a cause célèbre when, in 1976, he was not allowed to return to the GDR from a concert series in the West despite being an avid – albeit regime-critical – socialist.

When other artists rallied to his support, they too were expatriated, including Biermann's stepdaughter Nina Hagen, an East Berlin pop singer who later became a West Berlin punk pioneer. The small but vital East Berlin punk scene produced Sandow and Feeling B, members of whom went on to form the industrial metal band Rammstein in 1994. Although its dark and provocative songs are almost entirely sung in German, it is one of Germany's top musical exports, with fans around the world.

The Berlin-based Barenboim-Said Akademie opened in 2016 and was named after its founders Daniel Barenboim and the American-Palestinian scholar Edward Said. It is an accredited music academy focused on students from the Middle East and North Africa.

Once in West Berlin in 1977, Hagen founded the Nina Hagen Band in Kreuzberg and soon delighted teens (and shocked their parents) with her provocative lyrics, shrieking voice and theatrical performances. One of her famous early songs is *'Auf'm Bahnhof Zoo'*, which is about Zoo station, then an infamous drug hang-out and teenage prostitution strip.

Hagen also helped chart the course for *Neue Deutsche Welle* (German New Wave), a major musical movement in the early 1980s, which produced such West Berlin bands as DAF, Trio, Neonbabies, Ideal and UKW, as well as Rockhaus in East Berlin. The '80s also saw the birth of Die Ärzte, who released their last album, the live recording *Die Nacht der Dämonen*, in 2013. Einstürzende Neubauten pioneered a proto-industrial sound that transformed oil drums, electric drills and chainsaws into musical instruments. Its founder Blixa Bargeld joined the Bad Seeds, helmed by Nick Cave, who spent some heroin-addled time in Berlin in the early 1980s.

Pop, Rock & Hip-Hop After 1990

Since reunification, hundreds of indie, punk, alternative and goth bands have gigged to appreciative Berlin audiences. The still active Die Ärzte, Element of Crime and Einstürzende Neubauten were joined by other successful exports, such as alternative punk rockers Beatsteaks, and the pop-rock band Wir sind Helden, helmed by the charismatic Judith Holofernes, who released her first solo album in 2014. The Beatsteaks made headlines the same year with their seventh studio album.

The Beauty of Transgression: a Berlin Memoir (2011) by US-born artist Danielle de Picciotto (partner of Einstürzende Neubauten bassist Alexander Hacke) beautifully captures the atmosphere and history of Berlin's creative underground from the 1980s to recent times.

Other fine Berlin music originates from a jazz/breaks angle (electrojazz and breakbeats, favouring lush grooves, obscure samples and chilled rhythms). Remix masters Jazzanova are top dogs of the downtempo scene. Their Sonar Kollektiv label also champions similar artists, including Micatone. Reggae-dancehall has been huge in Berlin ever since Seeed was founded in 1998; frontperson Peter Fox's solo album *Stadtaffe* (2008) was one of the best-selling albums in Germany and also won the 2010 Album of the Year Echo Award (the 'German Grammy'). Also commercially successful is Culcha Candela, who have essentially pop-ified the Seeed sound and released their seventh studio album, *Feel Erfolg*, in 2017.

Home-grown rap and hip-hop have a huge following, thanks to Sido, Fler, Bushido and Kool Savas, who cofounded Masters of Rap (MOR) in 1996. Sido, meanwhile, founded the duo Alles ist die Sekte (A.i.d.S.) with his roomie B-Tight in 1998. His graphic lyrics are considered extreme even by hip-hop standards; endorsing the theories of the QAnon conspiracy movement during the Covid-19 pandemic did not generate positive headlines for him either.

Paul Kalkbrenner's 2008 semi-autobiographical *Berlin Calling* was the first mature film about the techno scene in Berlin.

Also hugely successful are Berlin-based Casper and Marteria. K.I.Z., meanwhile, are more of a gangsta rap parody with often ironic lyrics that address the absurdities of society and politics. Other famous Berlin-based artists include eccentric Canadian transplant King Khan, who fuelled the garage rock revival; the country and western band Boss Hoss; the electro-folky singer-songwriter Clara Hill; the indie rock band Gods of Blitz; and the uncategorisable 17 Hippies.

Techno Town

Call it techno, electro, house, minimal – electronic music is the sound of Berlin and its near-mythical club culture has defined the capital's cool factor and put it on the map of global hedonists. The sound may have been born in Detroit but it came of age in Berlin.

The seed was sown in dark and dank cellar club UFO on Köpenicker Strasse in 1988. The 'godfathers' of the Berlin sound, Dr Motte, Westbam and Kid Paul, played their first gigs here, mostly sweat-driven acid house all-night raves. It was Motte who came up with the idea to take the party to the street with a truck, loud beats and a bunch of friends dancing behind it – and the Love Parade was born (it peaked in 1999 with 1.5 million people swarming Berlin's streets).

The Berlin Wall's demise, and the artistic freedom it created, catapulted techno out of the underground. The associated euphoria, sudden access to derelict and abandoned spaces in eastern Berlin and lack of control by the authorities were all defining factors in making Berlin a techno mecca. In 1991 the techno-sonic gang followed UFO founder Dimitri Hegemann to the label Tresor, which launched camouflage-sporting DJ Tanith along with trance pioneer Paul van Dyk. Today Tresor is still a seminal brand representing Jeff Mills, Blake Baxter and Cristian Vogel, among many others.

The 2014 documentary *B-Movie: Lust & Sound in West Berlin 1979–1989*, by Mark Reeder, is a tour de force on the subcultural 1980 music scene, featuring Joy Division, Nick Cave, Die Ärzte, Einstürzende Neubauten and others.

Key label BPitch Control, founded by Ellen Allien in 1999, launched the careers of Modeselektor, Apparat, Sascha Funke and Paul Kalkbrenner. Another heavyweight is the collective Get Physical, which includes Booka Shade, Nôze and the dynamic duo M.A.N.D.Y., who fuse house and electro with minimal and funk to create a highly danceable sound. The charmingly named Shitkatapult, founded in 1997 by Marco Haas (aka T.Raumschmiere), does everything from cutting-edge electronica to tech-rock and mellow ambient. Another mainstay is the deep house duo Tiefschwarz. Other leading Berlin DJs include Berghain residents Ben Klock, Marcel Dettmann, Tama Sumo and Steffi, who are all represented by the Ostgut label.

Foreign artists have also influenced the Berlin scene, including the provocative Canadian songster and performance artist Peaches, UK-Canadian techno innovator Richie Hawtin and Chilean minimal master Ricardo Villalobos.

U-bahn crossing Oberbaum Bridge

PHOTOCREO MICHAL BEDNAREK/SHUTTERSTOCK ©

Survival Guide

Transport

ARRIVING IN BERLIN

Most visitors arrive in Berlin by air. After an eight-year delay, Berlin Brandenburg Airport (BER), about 27km south of the city centre, finally launched its inaugural flight on 31 October 2020.

Lufthansa and many other major European airlines and low-cost carriers operate direct flights to Berlin from throughout Europe. Travel from outside Europe usually involves changing planes in another European city such as Frankfurt or Amsterdam.

Depending on your departure point, travel to Berlin by train or bus is a viable alternative. Flights, cars and tours can be booked online at lonelyplanet.com/bookings.

Berlin Brandenburg Airport (BER)

Berlin Brandenburg Airport (BER; ☎030-609 160 910; https://ber.berlin-airport.de; Schönefelder Allee) has two terminals: the spanking new – and adjacent – Terminal 1 (T1) and Terminal 2 (T2). Only T1 will initially be open.

Note that Terminal 5 (T5), the old Schönefeld airport, was decommissioned in March 2021 due to low passenger numbers .

The tourist office in T1 is open from 9am to 4pm, subject to change.

S-Bahn & Trains

The railway station is below Terminal 1 and is linked by S-Bahn to Terminal 5. You'll need an ABC ticket (€3.80) for any of the following journeys:

FEX Airport Express Travels every half hour between 4am and midnight between the Hauptbahnhof (main train station) and T1/2 in 30 minutes. Also stops at Gesundbrunnen and Ostkreuz.

Regional Trains Regular Deutsche Bahn trains designated RE7 and RB14 make hourly trips from the city centre to T1/T2 (30 minutes).

S-Bahn S-Bahns run along the same tracks but stop more frequently. The S9 leaves every 20 minutes and needs about 45 minutes to/from the city centre. The S9 also heads straight to the trade fair grounds (exit Messe Süd). Alternatively, take the S45 to Südkreuz, change to the S41 and get off at Messe Nord/ICC.

U-Bahn

BER is not directly served by the U-Bahn. The nearest station, Rudow, is about a 20-minute ride on bus X7, X71 or 171 from T1/2. From Rudow, the U7 takes you straight into the city centre. This connection is useful if you're headed for Neukölln or Kreuzberg. You'll need an ABC ticket (€3.80).

Taxi

There are taxi ranks outside T1. Budget about €50 to €60 and an hour of your time for the cab ride to central Berlin.

Car Rental & Car Sharing

Avis, Enterprise, Europcar, Hertz, Sixt and Terstappen are the car rental companies at BER.

Four car-sharing providers have vehicles at the airport: Share Now, Miles, Sixt Share and We Share. Pick up your vehicle in car park P4 at T1/T2.

Berlin Hauptbahnhof

Berlin's **Hauptbahnhof** (Main Train Station; Map p324; www.bahnhof.de; Europaplatz 1; 📶; Ⓢ Hauptbahnhof, Ⓤ Hauptbahnhof) is in the heart of the city, just north of the government district, and has train connections throughout Germany and neighbouring countries. Taxis, trams and buses leave from outside the north exit (Europaplatz). For hotels, the Spree River and the government district, take the south exit

CLIMATE CHANGE & TRAVEL

Every form of transport that relies on carbon-based fuel generates CO_2, the main cause of human-induced climate change. Modern travel is dependent on aeroplanes, which might use less fuel per kilometre per person than most cars but travel much greater distances. The altitude at which aircraft emit gases (including CO_2) and particles also contributes to their climate change impact. Many websites offer 'carbon calculators' that allow people to estimate the carbon emissions generated by their journey and, for those who wish to do so, to offset the impact of the greenhouse gases emitted with contributions to portfolios of climate-friendly initiatives throughout the world. Lonely Planet offsets the carbon footprint of all staff and author travel.

(Washingtonplatz). There's a tourist office near the north exit.

Buy tickets in the Reisezentrum (travel centre) located between tracks 12 and 13 on the first upper level (OG1), online at www.bahn.de, at station vending machines or from the DB Navigator app.

Lockers are located behind the Reisebank currency exchange on level OG1 between platforms 14 and 15.

Public Transport

S-Bahn trains S5 and S7 leave from the top level (OG2) and travel east–west. Both stop at Zoo Station, Alexanderplatz and Ostkreuz (for Friedrichshain). For the trade fair grounds, take the S5 to Messe Nord/ICC.

Since December 2020, the new U-Bahn line U5 has travelled from the Hauptbahnhof below Unter den Linden to Alexanderplatz and on to Friedrichshain.

Trams leave from Europaplatz. The M5 travels to Alexanderplatz via the Scheunenviertel, the M8 serves Alexanderplatz via Rosenthaler Platz, the M10 goes to the Warschauer Strasse (Friedrichshain) via Prenzlauer Berg. Tickets cost €3 (Tariff AB).

Taxi & Ride-Sharing Services

Taxi ranks are located outside Europaplatz. Uber and Free Now pick up and drop off here as well.

Central Bus Station (ZOB)

Travelling to Berlin by coach is easy, affordable and popular. Flixbus (www.flixbus.de) is now the main operator with only Eurolines (www.eurolines.de) left competing with it, for now.

The **Zentraler Omnibusbahnhof** (ZOB, Central Bus Station; ☎030-3010 0175; www.zob-berlin.de; Messedamm 8; SMesse Nord/ICC, UKaiserdamm) is near the trade fairgrounds on the western city edge. Flixbus also stops at around a dozen other points in town, including the BER airport and Alexanderplatz.

Public Transport

The closest U-Bahn station to ZOB is Kaiserdamm, about 300m north and served by the U2 line, which travels to Zoologischer Garten in about eight minutes and to Alexanderplatz in 28 minutes.

The nearest S-Bahn station is Messe Nord/ICC, about 400m southeast of ZOB. It is served by the Ringbahn (circle line) S41/S42 and handy for such districts as Prenzlauer Berg, Friedrichshain and Neukölln.

All journeys require an AB ticket (€3).

Taxi & Ride-Sharing Services

Taxis and ride-share services pick up and drop off at the ZOB main entrance on Masurenallee. Budget about €15 for a taxi to the western city centre around Zoo station and €28 to the eastern city centre around Alexanderplatz.

GETTING AROUND

Walking around Berlin's neighbourhoods (*Kieze* in local parlance) is a joy, but to travel between them you want to use the comprehensive public transport system (or rent a bicycle). It is administered by BVG (www.bvg.de) and consists of the U-Bahn (subway, underground), the S-Bahn (light rail), buses, trams and ferries. U-Bahn and S-Bahn are the most efficient methods of transport. Tickets are valid for all forms of public transportation.

Check the website (also in English) for trip planning and general information. Network maps are posted at stations (usually on platforms), in U-Bahn and S-Bahn carriages, and on trams.

U-Bahn

The U-Bahn is the quickest way of getting around Berlin. Lines (referred to as U1, U2 etc) operate from 4am until about 12.30am and throughout the night on Friday,

Saturday and public holidays (all lines except the U4). From Sunday to Thursday, night buses take over in the interim.

S-Bahn & Regional Trains

S-Bahn trains (S1, S2 etc) don't run as frequently as the U-Bahn, but they make fewer stops and are thus useful for covering longer distances. Trains operate from 4am to 12.30am and all night on Friday, Saturday and public holidays.

Destinations further afield are served by RB and RE trains. You'll need an ABC or **Deutsche Bahn** (☎01806 996 633; www.bahn.de) ticket to use these trains.

Bus

Buses are slow but useful for sightseeing on the cheap (especially routes 100, 200 and 300). They run frequently between 4.30am and 12.30am. Night buses (N1, N5 etc) take over after 12.30am. MetroBuses, designated M19, M41 etc, operate 24/7.

Tram

Trams *(Strassenbahn)* operate almost exclusively in the eastern districts. Those designated M1, M2 etc run 24/7. A useful line is the M1, which links Prenzlauer Berg with Museum Island via Hackescher Markt. The M5, M8 and M10 serve Hauptbahnhof.

Taxi

You can order a **taxi** (☎030-210 101, 030-443 322, 030-210 202; www.taxi-in-berlin.de) by phone or app (eg Free Now, Taxi Berlin, taxi.eu), flag one down or pick one up at a rank. At night, cars often wait outside theatres, clubs and other venues.

Flag fall is €3.90, then it's €2.30 per kilometre up to 7km and €1.65 for each additional kilometre. You can pay with cash, debit or credit card. Tip about 10%.

Short trips up to 2km are charged at a flat €6 provided you flag down a moving taxi and request the *Kurzstrecke* tariff upon getting into the vehicle. If you want to continue past 2km, regular rates apply to the entire trip.

TAXI JOURNEY	SAMPLE FARE
Alexanderplatz to Zoo Station	€20
East Side Gallery to Brandenburger Tor	€18
Jüdisches Museum to Hackescher Markt	€12
Kollwitzplatz to Gendarmenmarkt	€15

TICKETS & PASSES

- The easiest way to obtain tickets is through BVG's ticket app (also in English).
- Paper tickets are available from vending machines at U-Bahn and S-Bahn stations and on trams. They must be validated (stamped) before boarding.
- Due to Covid-19, bus drivers no longer sell tickets, so make sure to obtain one from another source before boarding.
- Getting caught without a valid ticket results in a €60 fine.
- Vending machines in U-Bahn and S-Bahn stations accept cash, debit and credit cards as well as Google and Apple Pay. Tram vending machines only take coins; sometimes exact change is required.
- For most rides you need an AB ticket; tickets are valid for two hours in one direction (no roundtrips).
- A *24-Stunden-Karte* (24-hour ticket) is valid for unlimited rides on all forms of public transport for 24 hours starting from the moment of validation. The *24-Stunden-Karte Kleingruppe* (group 24-hour ticket) is valid for up to five people travelling together.
- The *Kurzstreckenticket* (€2) is good for three stops on the U-Bahn or S-Bahn, or six stops on any bus or tram; no changes allowed.

TICKET TYPE	AB (€)	BC (€)	ABC (€)
Einzelfahrschein (single)	3	3.50	3.80
Ermässigt (reduced single)	1.90	2.40	2.70
24-Stunden-Karte (24-hour ticket)	8.80	9.20	10
24-Stunden-Karte Kleingruppe (group 24-hour ticket)	25.50	26	26.50
Wochenkarte (7-day pass)	36	37	43

HAVE A BLAST ON THE BUS

It's a poorly kept secret that one of Berlin's best bargains is a self-guided city tour aboard bus 100, 200 and 300, whose routes check off nearly every major sight in the city centre for the price of a public transport ticket (tariff AB, €3). You can even get on and off and switch lines within the two hours of the ticket's validity period. If you plan to explore all day, a *24-Stunden-Karte* (24-hour ticket, €8.80) is your ticket to savings.

Bus 100 travels from Zoologischer Garten (Zoo Station) to Alexanderplatz, passing the Gedächtniskirche, the Siegessäule in the Tiergarten, the Reichstag, Brandenburg Gate and Unter den Linden.

Bus 200 also links Bahnhof Zoo and Alexanderplatz but follows a more southerly route via the Kulturforum museums, the Philharmonie and Potsdamer Platz. It then follows Leipziger Strasse east before hooking north to Karl-Liebknecht-Strasse past the Berliner Rathaus.

Bus 300 runs between the Philharmonie and U-/S-Bahn station Warschauer Strasse via Potsdamer Platz, Unter den Linden, Alexanderplatz and the East Side Gallery.

Ride Share & Ride Pooling

Ride-sharing is a cheaper alternative to regular taxis. Uber has a fleet of UberX, Comfort, UberXL, Premium and Green vehicles; all are operated by licensed drivers.

Uber main competitor in Berlin is the local app Free Now, which lets you order either a regular taxi or a licensed private vehicle (called 'Ride'), which is better value. Sometimes a taxi will show up even if you have selected 'Ride', but you only pay the Ride fare.

Lyft does not operate in Berlin.

Ridepooling is offered through the BerlKönig app but it operates only in the eastern city centre (Mitte, Prenzlauer Berg, Friedrichshain, Kreuzberg and Neukölln).

Bicycle & E-Scooters

Bicycles are handy both for in-depth explorations of local neighbourhoods and for getting across town. More than 1100km of bike paths make getting around less intimidating even for riders who are not experienced or confident.

Having said that, always be aware of dangers caused by aggressive or inattentive drivers. Watch out for car doors opening and for cars turning right in front of you at intersections. Getting caught in tram tracks is another potential problem. Helmets are not compulsory but wearing one is a smart idea.

Bicycles may be taken aboard designated carriages on the U-Bahn and S-Bahn (look for the bicycle symbol) as well as on trams and night bus lines N1 to N9. You need a separate *Fahrrad-Ticket* (€2, day ticket €4.90). Taking a bike on regional trains (RE, RB) costs €3.30 per trip or €6 per day.

The websites www.bikemap.net and www.bbbike.de are handy for route planning, while the app Komoot is good for tour planning.

Bicycle Hire

Many hostels and hotels have guest bicycles, often for free or a nominal fee, and rental stations are at practically every corner. These include not only the expected locations (bike shops, gas stations) but also convenience stores, cafes and even clothing boutiques.

Prices start at €8 per day, although the definition of 'day' can mean anything from eight hours to 24 hours. A cash or credit-card deposit and/or photo ID is usually required.

The following companies are recommended. Be sure to book ahead in summer.

Fahrradstation (Map p324; ☎01805 108 000; www.fahrradstation.com; Dorotheenstrasse 30; bike rentals per day/week €15/49; S Friedrichstrasse, U Friedrichstrasse) Large fleet of quality bikes, English-speaking staff and two branches in Mitte. E-bikes available. Book online. Also delivers and picks up bikes (€60) and organises bike tours (€35).

Lila Bike (Map p334; www.berlin-citytours-by-bike.de; Schönhauser Allee 41; first 24hr €8, additional 24hr €5; ⏲10am-8pm Mon-Sat, 1-8pm Sun Apr-Aug, 10am-7pm Mon-Sat, 1.30-7pm Sun Sep-Mar; U Eberswalder Strasse) Small outfit in Prenzlauer Berg with quality bikes and great prices.

Bike-Share Schemes

Berlin has experienced a boom in bike-share schemes with several operators in the market. Bikes can now be found at just about every corner in the central districts (within the Ringbahn, circle line) and sometimes even beyond. All work on an automated self-service system with pick-up and drop-off either at docking stations or dockless anywhere within their business area. Usage

TRAVELLING AT NIGHT

No matter what time it is, there's always a way to get around Berlin on public transport.

- U-Bahn lines run every 15 minutes all night long on Friday, Saturday and public holidays (all but the U4).
- From Sunday to Thursday, night buses (N1, N2 etc) run along the U-Bahn routes between 12.30am and 4am at 30-minute intervals.
- MetroBuses (designated M11, M19 etc) and Metro-Trams (M1, M2 etc) run nightly every 30 minutes between 12.30am and 4.30am.

requires downloading the app to your smartphone and registering there, online, via a hotline or at streetside terminals. Hiring a bike usually involves scanning the QR code to undo the electronic lock. Rates vary by company but are very reasonable. Expect to pay about €0.50 per half hour and no more than €15 per day.

The main providers are Donkey Republic, Nextbike, Lime Bike and Call a Bike.

E-Scooters

Germany officially legalised e-scooters in June 2019 and, although not everybody likes them, it looks like they are here to stay. As with bike-share schemes you need a credit card or PayPal and smartphone to download the app and unlock the scooter. The main providers are Lime, Tier, Circ and Voi, which charge a base rate of €1 plus 20 to 25 cents per minute. And naturally there are some rules:

- Riding is permitted on roads and bike paths, but not on footpaths.
- Only one person per scooter.
- The speed limit is 20km/h.
- Helmets are not compulsory but are recommended.

Car & Motorcycle

Driving in Berlin is more hassle than it's worth, especially since parking is expensive and difficult to find.

All the big internationals maintain branches at the airport, major train stations and throughout town. Book in advance for the best rates. Taking your rental vehicle into an Eastern European country, such as the Czech Republic or Poland, is often a no-no; check in advance if you're planning a side trip from Berlin.

Car-Sharing

If you need a car for a few hours or for short trips, car-sharing is a good alternative to a classic rental. Download the app to sign up and locate the nearest vehicle, unlock it and off you go. You're free to drop off the car in any legal parking spot within the company's service area.

The main providers are Share Now, Sixt Share, We Share and Miles. We Share has only electric vehicles fuelled by green electricity. All charge by the minute except Miles, which charges by kilometre. Miles also has a sizeable fleet of vans. Multi-hour or day packages are also available.

TOURS

Walking Tours

Alternative Berlin Tours (☎0162 819 8264; www.alternativeberlin.com; tours €14-35) Not your run-of-the-mill tour company, this outfit peels back the layers of the city on its six offerings, including an excellent street-art tour (with optional workshop), a nightlife tour and a 'real Berlin' tour. For a Berlin primer, join the daily tip-based 'Free Tour'. The website has all the details and a booking function. All tours in English.

Original Berlin Walks (☎0177 302 9194; www.berlinwalks.de; adult/concession from €20/18) Berlin's longest-running English-language walking-tour company has a general city tour plus a roster of themed tours (eg WWII & The Third Reich, East Berlin, Queer Berlin), as well as a street-art tour, a craft-beer tour and trips out to Sachsenhausen concentration camp and Potsdam. All tours are led by experienced and knowledgeable guides. The website sells tickets and has details on timings and meeting points.

Insider Tour Berlin (☎030-692 3149; www.insidertour.com; adult/concession €19/16) This well-established company offers an insightful general city tour plus themed tours (eg Cold War, Third Reich, Jewish Berlin) and trips to Sachsenhausen concentration camp, Potsdam and Dresden. A guided tour of the Pergamon Museum and the New Museum is also available. Check the website for timings, tickets and meeting points.

New Berlin Tours (www.newberlintours.com; adult/concession from €15/13) Entertaining and informative city spins by the pioneers of the donation-based 'free tour'. Also offers tours to Sachsenhausen concentration camp, a Berlin Wall tour, and an alternative culture and street-art tour, among others. Check the website for timings, tickets and meeting points.

Bicycle Tours

Fat Tire Tours Berlin (Map p328; ☎030-2404 7991; www.fattiretours.com/berlin; Panoramastrasse 1a; adult/concession incl bicycle from €28/26; S Alexanderplatz, U Alexanderplatz) This top-rated outfit runs English-language tours by bike, e-bike and Segway. Options include a classic city spin, a Berlin Wall tour, a Third Reich tour and a trip to Potsdam. Tours leave from the Fernsehturm (TV Tower) main entrance. Reservations advised.

Berlin on Bike (Map p334; ☎030-4373 9999; www.berlinonbike.de; Knaackstrasse 97, Kulturbrauerei, Court 4; tours incl bike adult/concession €29/25, bike rental per 24hr €10-15; ⊙8am-8pm mid-Mar–mid-Nov, 10am-4pm Mon-Fri mid-Nov–mid-Mar; M1, U Eberswalder Strasse) This well-established company has a busy schedule of insightful and fun bike tours led by locals. There are daily English-language city tours (Berlin's Best) and Berlin Wall tours as well as Alternative Berlin and Street Art tours on a more limited schedule. Other tours (eg night tours) are available on request. Check online for timings and tickets.

Bus Tours

Hop-on hop-off sightseeing buses tick off the key sights on two-hour loops with basic taped commentary in multiple languages. Buses depart roughly every 15 or 30 minutes between 10am and 5pm or 6pm daily; tickets are sold on board and cost from €10 to €20 (discounts for children). Traditional tours (where you stay on the bus), combination boat and bus tours as well as trips to Potsdam Spreewald are also available. Look for flyers in hotel lobbies or at tourist offices.

Boat Tours

A lovely way to experience Berlin on a warm day is from the deck of a boat cruising along the city's rivers, canals and lakes. Tours range from one-hour spins around the historic centre to longer trips to Schloss Charlottenburg via the Landwehrkanal.

The main operators:

Stern + Kreis (☎030-536 3600; www.sternundkreis.de; tours from €17; ⊙Mar-Dec)

Reederei Bruno Winkler (☎030-349 9595; www.reedereiwinkler.de; tours €16-27; ⊙Apr–mid-Oct)

Reederei Riedel (☎030-6293 3194; www.reederei-riedel.de; tours from €17; ⊙Mar-Oct)

Speciality Tours

Refugee Voices Tours (☎0157 5221 5445; www.refugeevoicestours.org; ⊙by request) Nearly one million refugees arrived in Germany in 2015, mostly from war-torn Afghanistan, Syria and Iraq. On this two-hour tour, you can learn first-hand from a Syrian refugee about the daily life and dangers that drove him and so many others to flee their homeland and resettle in Berlin. The tour also draws parallels between German and Syrian history. It wraps up with an optional meal at Mandi restaurant (€8).

Berlin Music Tours (☎0172 424 2037; www.musictours-berlin.com; Bowie walk €19; ⊙Bowie walk noon Sat & Sun Apr-Oct, 11.30am Nov-Mar, other tours by request) Berlin's music history – Bowie to U2 and Rammstein, cult clubs to the Love Parade – comes to life during expertly guided bus and walking tours run by this well-respected outfit. There's a regularly scheduled walk in Bowie's footsteps; other options (a multimedia bus tour and U2 and Depeche Mode tours) run by request only. Some get you inside the fabled Hansa Studios. English tours by request (price depends on group size).

Berlinagenten (☎030-4372 0701; www.berlinagenten.com) Get a handle on all facets of Berlin's urban lifestyle with an insider private guide who opens doors to hot and/or secret bars, boutiques, restaurants, clubs, private homes and sights. Dozens of culinary, cultural and lifestyle tours on offer, including the best-selling 'Gastro Rallye' for the ultimate foodie. Prices depend on group size.

Eat the World (☎030-206 229 990; www.eat-the-world.com; tours adult weekday/weekend €29/39, child €20) Experience Berlin's neighbourhoods one bite at a time during these three-hour 'foodseeing' tours that stop at cafes, delis, bakeries, ice-cream parlours and other tasty places. There are tours through nine neighbourhoods, including off-the-tourist-track routes through Friedenau and Wedding.

Directory A–Z

Accessible Travel

Berlin has made major improvements when it comes to the needs of mobility-impaired people, wheelchair users, blind or partially sighted visitors and people with hearing impairments.

➡ The Visit Berlin tourist office has compiled an excellent detailed accessibility online guide at www.visitberlin.de/en/accessible-berlin (also in English).

➡ Access ramps and/or lifts are available in many public buildings, including train stations, museums, concert halls and cinemas. Newer hotels have lifts and rooms with extra-wide doors and spacious bathrooms. For a databank assessing the accessibility of cafes, restaurants, hotels, theatres and other public spaces (in German), check with Mobidat (www.mobidat.de).

➡ Most buses, trains and trams are accessible and many U-Bahn and S-Bahn stations are equipped with ramps or lifts. Many stations also have grooved platforms to assist blind and vision-impaired passengers. Seeing-eye dogs are allowed everywhere. For the hearing-impaired, upcoming station names are electronically displayed. For trip-planning assistance, contact the BVG (☎030-194 49; www.bvg.de), Berlin's public transport company.

➡ For information when travelling on trains, including the S-Bahn, see www.bahn.de/barrierefrei.

➡ **Rollstuhlvermietung** (Wheelchair Rentals; ☎0177 833 5773; www.rollstuhlvermietung.berlin; ⌚24hr) provides 24-hour wheelchair repairs and rentals with delivery service to any location within Berlin.

➡ Download Lonely Planet's free *Accessible Travel* guide from https://shop.lonelyplanet.com/categories/accessible-travel.

Customs Regulations

Goods brought in and out of countries within the EU incur no additional taxes provided duty has been paid somewhere within the EU and the goods are only for personal use. Duty-free shopping is only available if you're leaving the EU.

Discount Cards

Berlin Welcome Card (www.berlin-welcomecard.de; travel in AB zones 48/72 hours €23/33, travel in ABC zones 48/72 hours €28/38, AB/ABC zones 72 hours incl admission

IMPORT RESTRICTIONS

ITEM	DUTY-FREE (ARRIVING FROM OUTSIDE EU)	TAX & DUTY PAID WITHIN EU
alcohol	1L spirits (over 22% per volume, eg gin) *or* 2L sherry or other fortified wine *and* 16L beer *and* 4L wine (17yr minimum age)	10L spirits, 20L sherry or other fortified wine, 110L beer, 60L sparkling wine, no limit on regular wine
tobacco	200 cigarettes or 100 cigarillos or 50 cigars or 250g tobacco or a combination thereof (17yr minimum age)	800 cigarettes or 400 cigarillos or 200 cigars or 1kg tobacco
other goods	up to a value of €300 if arriving by land or €430 if arriving by sea or air (€175 for those under 15yr)	n/a

to Museumsinsel €51/55) Valid for unlimited public transport for one adult and up to three children under 14; up to 50% discount to 200 sights, attractions and tours; available for up to six days. Sold online, at tourist offices, from U-Bahn and S-Bahn ticket vending machines and at BVG sales points.

CityTourCard (www.citytourcard.com; travel in AB zone 48 hours/72 hours/five days €19.90/29.90/42.50, ABC zone €22.90/33.90/46.90) Operates on a similar scheme as the Berlin Welcome Card – it's a bit cheaper, but offers fewer discounts. Available for up to six days online, from tourist offices and U-Bahn and S-Bahn ticket vending machines.

Museumspass Berlin (adult/concession €29/14.50) Buys admission to the permanent exhibits of about 30 museums for three consecutive days, including big draws like the Pergamonmuseum. Sold online, at tourist offices, participating museums and many hotels.

Electricity

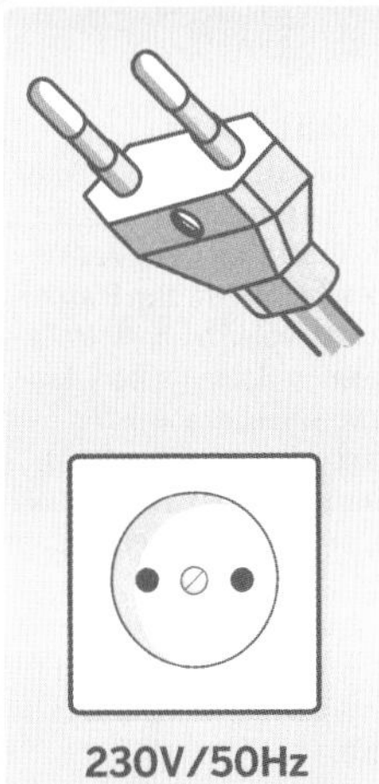

230V/50Hz

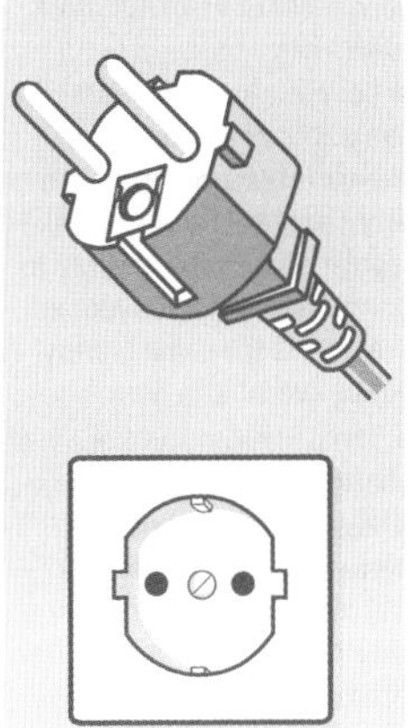

230V/50Hz

PRACTICALITIES

Clothing For women's clothing sizes, a German size 36 equals a size 6 in the US and a size 10 in the UK, then increases in increments of two, making size 38 a US 8 and UK 12, and so on.

Newspapers Widely read local dailies are *Tagesspiegel, Berliner Zeitung, Berliner Morgenpost* and *taz*.

Magazines *Tip* for general events listings, *Siegessäule* is a freebie for the LGBTIQ+ community. *Exberliner* is an expat-geared English-language culture magazine.

Radio & TV Radio 1 (95.8 FM) and Flux FM (00.6 FM) are popular radio channels. For local TV news, tune into RBB station.

Tap Water Tap water is perfectly fine to drink, although most people prefer bottled sparkling or still water.

Weights & Measures Germany uses the metric system.

Emergency

Ambulance	☎112
Fire department	☎112
Germany's country code	☎49
International access code	☎00
Police	☎110

Internet Access

- Almost without exception, free wi-fi access (W-LAN in Germany; pronounced vay-lan) is available at hotels, hostels and flat rentals.
- In some hotels wi-fi may be limited to some rooms and/or public areas; if you need reliable in-room access, be sure to specify at the time of booking.
- Many cafes, bars and even bakeries, supermarkets and boutiques have free wi-fi hotspots, although you usually need to ask for a password.
- Free public wi-fi under the network 'Free Wifi Berlin' is available at 2000 access points throughout the city, including public squares, landmarks like the Brandenburger Tor, train stations, museums, libraries, courthouses and town halls. Check www.berlin.de/en/wifi for more information and locations.
- Public transport network BVG also provides free hot spots at many U-Bahn stations and, if you're lucky, even on trains.

➡ Internet cafes have pretty much gone the way of the dodo; ask at your hotel.

Legal Matters

➡ By law you must possess some form of photographic identification, such as your passport, national identity card or driving licence, although you are not required to carry it with you at all times.

➡ The permissible blood-alcohol limit is 0.05% for drivers and 0.16% for cyclists. Anyone caught exceeding this amount is subject to stiff fines, a confiscated licence or even jail time. Drinking in public is not illegal, but be discreet about it.

➡ The possession, purchase and cultivation of cannabis is illegal. If you're caught, you can be prosecuted but charges are usually dropped if the amount does not exceed 10g. Dealers face much stiffer penalties, as do people caught with any other recreational drugs. Searches upon entering clubs are common.

➡ If arrested, you have the right to make a phone call and are presumed innocent until proven guilty, although you may be held in custody until trial. If you don't know a lawyer, contact your embassy.

Medical Services

➡ High-level health care is available from a *Rettungsstelle* (emergency department) at a *Krankenhaus* (hospital) or from an *Arztpraxis* (doctor's office). Most doctors speak at least some English, especially in the hospitals.

➡ The most central hospital with a 24-hour emergency room is the renowned **Charité Mitte** (Map p324; ☎030-450 50; www.charite.de; emergency room Luisenstrasse 65; ⊙24hr; 🚌147, Ⓤ Oranienburger Tor).

➡ For minor illnesses (headache, bruises, diarrhoea), pharmacists can provide advice, sell over-the-counter medications and make doctors' referrals if further help is needed.

➡ Condoms are widely available in drugstores, pharmacies and supermarkets. Birth control pills require a doctor's prescription but the morning after pill does not and is sold in pharmacies for €16 to €18.

Pharmacies

➡ German chemists (drugstores, *Drogerien*) do not sell any kind of medication, not even aspirin. Even over-the-counter *(rezeptfrei)* medications for minor health concerns, such as a cold or upset stomach, are only available at an *Apotheke* (pharmacy).

➡ For more serious conditions, you will need to produce a *Rezept* (prescription) from a licensed physician. If you take regular medication, be sure to bring a full supply for your entire trip, as the same brand may not be available in Germany.

➡ The names and addresses of pharmacies open after hours (these rotate) are posted in every pharmacy window, or call 011 41 for a recorded message of after-hour and Sunday pharmacies.

Money

See the First Time Berlin chapter (p21) for information on tipping and taxes.

ATMs & Debit Cards

➡ ATMs *(Geldautomat)* are the easiest way to get cash. Most are accessible 24/7 and are linked to international networks such as Cirrus, Plus, Star and Maestro.

➡ ATMs not affiliated with major banks may charge higher transaction fees (€5 or more). ATMs do not recognise PIN numbers with more than four digits.

➡ Most places use the 'chip and pin' system: instead of signing, you enter your PIN. If your card isn't chip-and-pin enabled, you may be able to sign the receipt, but not always – ask first.

➡ Your bank may charge a transaction fee and, if applicable, a currency conversion fee.

Cash

It took the Coronavirus pandemic to change the German habit of relying almost exclusively on cash. Although plastic is now preferred in most places, do carry some cash with you at all times.

Changing Money

Currency exchange offices *(Wechselstuben)* can be found at the airport and major train stations. They usually have better hours and charge lower fees than commercial banks. Some convenient offices:

Reisebank (www.reisebank.de) Zoologischer Garten, Hauptbahnhof, Ostbahnhof and Bahnhof Friedrichstrasse.

Euro-Change (www.euro-change.de) Alexanderplatz station; Europa Center, Friedrichstrasse 80.

Credit Cards

➡ As a side effect of the Coronavirus pandemic, contactless credit card payment has skyrocketed in Germany. Plastic is now accepted by most retailers, hotels, restaurants, bars, taxi drivers, venues and public transport vending machines. There are some cash-only holdouts (mostly small retailers and restaurants).

➡ Visa and MasterCard are more commonly accepted than American Express and Diner's Club.

➡ Some places require a minimum purchase with credit card use.

➡ Cash advances on credit cards via ATMs usually incur steep fees – check with your card issuer.

Opening Hours

The following are typical opening hours, although there are no hard and fast rules. Expect seasonal changes and different hours by location (city centre or the suburbs). There is no closing time for bars and clubs.

Banks 9.30am–6pm Monday–Friday, some to 1pm Saturday

Bars 5pm–1am or later

Boutiques 11am–7pm Monday–Friday, to 6pm Saturday

Cafes 8am–8pm

Clubs 11pm–5am or later

Post Offices 9am–6pm Monday–Friday, to 1pm Saturday

Restaurants 11am–11pm

Shops 10am–8pm Monday–Saturday

Supermarkets 8am–8pm or later

Public Holidays

Shops, banks and public and private offices are closed on the following nationwide *gesetzliche Feiertage* (public holidays):

Neujahrstag (New Year's Day) 1 January

Internationaler Frauentag (International Women's Day) 8 March

Ostern (Easter) March/April; Good Friday, Easter Sunday and Easter Monday

Christi Himmelfahrt (Ascension Day) Forty days after Easter, always on a Thursday

Maifeiertag (Labour Day) 1 May

Pfingsten (Whitsun/Pentecost Sunday and Monday) May/June

Tag der Deutschen Einheit (Day of German Unity) 3 October

Weihnachtstag (Christmas Day) 25 December

Zweiter Weihnachtstag (Boxing Day) 26 December

Responsible Travel

Overtoursim

➡ Travel off-season: avoid the summer months (May–Sep) and Easter, and opt for midweek instead of weekends.

➡ Expand your sightseeing to Berlin's outer districts and discover such gems as a horseshoe-shaped Bauhaus complex, a Renaissance military fortress or a bucolic Chinese garden.

➡ Peruse the bilingual GoLocal magazine produced by the local tourism authority Visit Berlin. (www.visitberlin.de/system/files/document/visitBerlin_Going-Local-Magazin_Vol2_1.11_DS_0.pdf) or download the GoLocal app)

➡ Stay more than a couple of days and take the train to crystal-clear lakes, a romantically ruined monastery, nature preserves or World War II battlefields in the surrounding Brandenburg countryside.

Support Local & Give Back

➡ Frequent organic, sustainable, vegan, vegetarian or zero-waste cafes and restaurants.

➡ Before booking accommodation, check if a property follows sustainable hospitality standards.

➡ Look into volunteering opportunities with Give Something Back to Berlin (https://gsbtb.org)

Leave a Light Footprint

➡ Ditch the plane or car and travel by train or coach instead – Berlin is well-served from throughout Europe.

➡ Berlin has a brilliant public transport system. Use it!

➡ You'll find bike and e-scooter rental schemes throughout the city. Or rent a kayak and explore Berlin by water.

Telephone

Mobile Phones

➡ Mobile phones *(Handys)* work on GSM900/1800.

➡ In 2017, the European Union implemented the 'roam like at home' rules. If your phone is registered in an EU country,

SMOKING REGULATIONS

➡ Except in designated areas, smoking (including e-cigarettes) is not allowed in public buildings, airports, or U-Bahn or S-Bahn train stations.

➡ Smoking is not allowed in restaurants, bars and clubs unless there is a completely separate and enclosed room set aside for smokers. This rule is often ignored.

➡ Owners of single-room bars and pubs smaller than 75 sq metres, who don't serve anything to eat and keep out customers under 18 years of age, may choose to be a *'Raucherbar'*, ie allow smoking. The venue must be clearly designated as such.

➡ *Shisha* bars may operate as long as no alcohol is available and no one under 18 is allowed in.

you don't pay roaming charges when calling, sending SMS, using data or receiving calls or texts while in another EU country (provided your tariff plan includes those services).

- If you don't have a phone registered in an EU country, getting a local SIM card might work out cheaper than using your own network, provided you have an unlocked phone. US and Canadian phones need to be multi-band.
- SIM cards are sold at supermarkets, convenience stores and electronics shops for as little as €5 and can be topped up as needed.
- Calls made from landlines to German mobile phone numbers are charged at higher rates than those to other landlines. Incoming calls on mobile numbers are free.
- Use of a mobile phone while driving is only allowed if you have a hands-free system.

Phone Codes

German phone numbers consist of an area code, starting with 0, and the local number. The area code for Berlin is 030. When dialling a Berlin number from a Berlin-based landline, you don't need to dial the area code. When you're using a landline outside Berlin, or a mobile phone, you must dial it.

German mobile numbers begin with a four-digit prefix such 0151, 0157 or 0173.

Calling Berlin from abroad Dial your country's international access code, then 49 (Germany's country code), then the area code (dropping the initial 0, so just 30) and the local number.

Calling internationally from Berlin Dial 00 (the international access code), then the country code, the area code (without the zero if there is one) and the local number.

Time

Clocks in Germany are set to central European time (GMT/UTC plus one hour). Daylight-savings time kicks in on the last Sunday in March and ends on the last Sunday in October. The 24-hour clock is the norm (eg 6.30pm is 18.30). As daylight-savings time differs across regions, the following times are indicative only:

CITY	NOON IN BERLIN
Cape Town	1pm
Tokyo	8pm
Sydney	9pm
Auckland	11pm
San Francisco	3am
New York	6am
London	11am

Toilets

- German toilets are sit-down affairs; it is customary for men to sit when peeing.
- Free-standing, 24-hour self-cleaning public toilet pods have become quite commonplace. The cost is €0.50 and you have 15 minutes to finish your business. Most are wheelchair-accessible.
- Toilets in malls, clubs, beer gardens etc often have an attendant who expects a tip of around €0.50.

Tourist Information

Visit Berlin (www.visitberlin.de), the Berlin tourist board, operates five walk-in offices, info desks at the airports, and a **call centre** (☎030-2500 2333; ⌚9am-6pm Mon-Fri) whose multilingual staff field general questions and make hotel and ticket bookings.

Berlin Brandenburg Airport (☎030-250 025; Terminal 1, Level 0; ⌚9am-4pm; 🚆Flughafen BER Terminal 1-2, Ⓢ Flughafen BER Terminal 1-2)

Brandenburger Tor (Map p324; ☎030-250 023; Pariser Platz, Brandenburger Tor, south wing; ⌚10am-7pm Apr-Aug, to 6pm Sep-Mar; Ⓢ Brandenburger Tor, Ⓤ Brandenburger Tor)

Hauptbahnhof (Map p324; ☎030-250 025; Hauptbahnhof, Europaplatz entrance, ground fl; ⌚8am-8pm; Ⓢ Hauptbahnhof, 🚆Hauptbahnhof)

Humboldt Forum (opens summer 2021)

Visas

- EU nationals need only their national identity card or passport to enter Germany. If you intend to stay for an extended period, you must register with the authorities (*Bürgeramt*, or Citizens' Office) within two weeks of arrival.
- Citizens of Australia, Canada, Israel, Japan, New Zealand, Switzerland and the US are among those who need only a valid passport (no visa) if entering as tourists for a stay of up to three months within a six-month period.
- Passports must be valid for at least three months beyond the planned departure date.
- Unless you're an EU national or from a nation without visa requirements, you need a Schengen Visa to enter Germany. Visa applications must be filed with the embassy or consulate of the Schengen country that is your primary destination. It is valid for stays of up to 90 days. Legal permanent residency in any Schengen country makes a visa unnecessary, regardless of your nationality.
- For full details and current regulations, see www.auswaertiges-amt.de or check with a German consulate in your country.

Language

German belongs to the West Germanic language family and has around 100 million speakers. It is commonly divided into Low German *(Plattdeutsch)* and High German *(Hochdeutsch)*. Low German is an umbrella term used for the dialects spoken in Northern Germany. High German is the standard form; it's also used in this chapter.

German is easy for English speakers to pronounce because almost all of its sounds are also found in English. If you read our coloured pronunciation guides as if they were English, you should be understood just fine. Note that kh sounds like the 'ch' in 'Bach' or in the Scottish 'loch' (pronounced at the back of the throat), r is also pronounced at the back of the throat, zh is pronounced as the 's' in 'measure', and ü as the 'ee' in 'see' but with rounded lips. The stressed syllables are indicated with italics in our pronunciation guides. The markers (pol) and (inf) indicate polite and informal forms.

BASICS

Hello.	*Guten Tag.*	*goo*·ten tahk
Goodbye.	*Auf Wiedersehen.*	owf *vee*·der·zay·en
Yes./No.	*Ja./Nein.*	yah/nain
Please.	*Bitte.*	*bi*·te
Thank you.	*Danke.*	*dang*·ke
You're welcome.	*Bitte.*	*bi*·te
Excuse me.	*Entschuldigung.*	ent·*shul*·di·gung
Sorry.	*Entschuldigung.*	ent·*shul*·di·gung

WANT MORE?

For in-depth language information and handy phrases, check out Lonely Planet's *German Phrasebook*. You'll find it at **shop.lonelyplanet.com**, or you can buy Lonely Planet's iPhone phrasebooks at the Apple App Store.

How are you?
Wie geht es Ihnen/dir? (pol/inf) — vee gayt es ee·nen/deer

Fine. And you?
Danke, gut. — *dang*·ke goot
Und Ihnen/dir? (pol/inf) — unt ee·nen/deer

What's your name?
Wie ist Ihr Name? (pol) — vee ist eer *nah*·me
Wie heißt du? (inf) — vee haist doo

My name is ...
Mein Name ist ... (pol) — main *nah*·me ist ...
Ich heiße ... (inf) — ikh *hai*·se ...

Do you speak English?
Sprechen Sie Englisch? (pol) — *shpre*·khen zee *eng*·lish
Sprichst du Englisch? (inf) — shprikhst doo *eng*·lish

I don't understand.
Ich verstehe nicht. — ikh fer·*shtay*·e nikht

ACCOMMODATION

guesthouse	*Pension*	pahng·*zyawn*
hotel	*Hotel*	ho·*tel*
inn	*Gasthof*	*gast*·hawf
youth hostel	*Jugend-herberge*	*yoo*·gent·her·ber·ge

Do you have a ... room?	*Haben Sie ein ...?*	*hah*·ben zee ain ...
double	*Doppelzimmer*	*do*·pel·tsi·mer
single	*Einzelzimmer*	*ain*·tsel·tsi·mer

How much is it per ...?	*Wie viel kostet es pro ...?*	vee feel *kos*·tet es praw ...
night	*Nacht*	nakht
person	*Person*	per·*zawn*

Is breakfast included?
Ist das Frühstück inklusive? — ist das *frü*·shtük in·kloo·*zee*·ve

KEY PATTERNS

To get by in German, mix and match these simple patterns with words of your choice:

When's (the next flight)?
Wann ist (der nächste Flug)? — van ist (dair *naykhs*·te flook)

Where's (the station)?
Wo ist (der Bahnhof)? — vaw ist (dair *bahn*·hawf)

Where can I (buy a ticket)?
Wo kann ich (eine Fahrkarte kaufen)? — vaw kan ikh (*ai*·ne *fahr*·kar·te *kow*·fen)

Do you have (a map)?
Haben Sie (eine Karte)? — *hah*·ben zee (*ai*·ne *kar*·te)

Is there (a toilet)?
Gibt es (eine Toilette)? — gipt es (*ai*·ne to·a·*le*·te)

I'd like (a coffee).
Ich möchte (einen Kaffee). — ikh *merkh*·te (*ai*·nen *ka*·fay)

I'd like (to hire a car).
Ich möchte (ein Auto mieten). — ikh *merkh*·te (ain *ow*·to *mee*·ten)

Can I (enter)?
Darf ich (hereinkommen)? — darf ikh (her·*ein*·ko·men)

Could you please (help me)?
Könnten Sie (mir helfen)? — *kern*·ten zee (meer *hel*·fen)

Do I have to (book a seat)?
Muss ich (einen Platz reservieren lassen)? — mus ikh (*ai*·nen plats re·zer·*vee*·ren *la*·sen)

DIRECTIONS

Where's ...?
Wo ist ...? — vaw ist ...

What's the address?
Wie ist die Adresse? — vee ist dee a·*dre*·se

How far is it?
Wie weit ist es? — vee vait ist es

Can you show me (on the map)?
Können Sie es mir (auf der Karte) zeigen? — *ker*·nen zee es meer (owf dair *kar*·te) *tsai*·gen

How can I get there?
Wie kann ich da hinkommen? — vee kan ikh dah *hin*·ko·men

Turn ...	*Biegen Sie ... ab.*	bee·gen zee ... ab
at the corner	*an der Ecke*	an dair *e*·ke
at the traffic lights	*bei der Ampel*	bai dair *am*·pel
left	*links*	lingks
right	*rechts*	rekhts

EATING & DRINKING

I'd like to reserve a table for ...	*Ich möchte einen Tisch für ... reservieren.*	ikh *merkh*·te *ai*·nen tish für ... re·zer·*vee*·ren
(eight) o'clock	*(acht) Uhr*	(akht) oor
(two) people	*(zwei) Personen*	(tsvai) per·*zaw*·nen

I'd like the menu, please.
Ich hätte gern die Speisekarte, bitte. — ikh *he*·te gern dee *shpai*·ze·kar·te *bi*·te

What would you recommend?
Was empfehlen Sie? — vas emp·*fay*·len zee

What's in that dish?
Was ist in diesem Gericht? — vas ist in *dee*·zem ge·*rikht*

I'm a vegetarian.
Ich bin Vegetarier/ Vegetarierin. (m/f) — ikh bin ve·ge·*tah*·ri·er/ ve·ge·*tah*·ri·e·rin

That was delicious.
Das hat hervorragend geschmeckt. — das hat her·*fawr*·rah·gent ge·*shmekt*

Cheers!
Prost! — prawst

Please bring the bill.
Bitte bringen Sie die Rechnung. — *bi*·te *bring*·en zee dee *rekh*·nung

Key Words

bar (pub)	*Kneipe*	*knai*·pe
bottle	*Flasche*	*fla*·she
bowl	*Schüssel*	*shü*·sel
breakfast	*Frühstück*	*frü*·shtük
cold	*kalt*	kalt
cup	*Tasse*	*ta*·se
daily special	*Gericht des Tages*	ge·*rikht* des *tah*·ges
delicatessen	*Feinkost-geschäft*	*fain*·kost·ge·sheft
desserts	*Nachspeisen*	*nahkh*·shpai·zen
dinner	*Abendessen*	*ah*·bent·e·sen
drink list	*Getränke-karte*	ge·*treng*·ke·kar·te
fork	*Gabel*	*gah*·bel
glass	*Glas*	glahs
grocery store	*Lebensmittel-laden*	*lay*·bens·mi·tel·lah·den
hot (warm)	*warm*	warm
knife	*Messer*	*me*·ser
lunch	*Mittagessen*	*mi*·tahk·e·sen

market	*Markt*	markt
plate	*Teller*	*te*·ler
restaurant	*Restaurant*	res·to·*rahng*
set menu	*Menü*	may·*nü*
spicy	*würzig*	*vür*·tsikh
spoon	*Löffel*	*ler*·fel
with/without	*mit/ohne*	mit/*aw*·ne

Meat & Fish

beef	*Rindfleisch*	*rint*·flaish
carp	*Karpfen*	*karp*·fen
fish	*Fisch*	fish
herring	*Hering*	*hay*·ring
lamb	*Lammfleisch*	*lam*·flaish
meat	*Fleisch*	flaish
pork	*Schweinefleisch*	*shvai*·ne·flaish
poultry	*Geflügelfleisch*	ge·*flü*·gel·flaish
salmon	*Lachs*	laks
sausage	*Wurst*	vurst
seafood	*Meeresfrüchte*	*mair*·res·frükh·te
shellfish	*Schaltiere*	*shahl*·tee·re
trout	*Forelle*	fo·*re*·le
veal	*Kalbfleisch*	*kalp*·flaish

Fruit & Vegetables

apple	*Apfel*	*ap*·fel
banana	*Banane*	ba·*nah*·ne
bean	*Bohne*	*baw*·ne
cabbage	*Kraut*	krowt
capsicum	*Paprika*	*pap*·ri·kah
carrot	*Mohrrübe*	*mawr*·rü·be
cucumber	*Gurke*	*gur*·ke
fruit	*Frucht/Obst*	frukht/awpst
grapes	*Weintrauben*	*vain*·trow·ben
lemon	*Zitrone*	tsi·*traw*·ne
lentil	*Linse*	*lin*·ze
lettuce	*Kopfsalat*	*kopf*·za·laht
mushroom	*Pilz*	pilts
nuts	*Nüsse*	*nü*·se
onion	*Zwiebel*	*tsvee*·bel
orange	*Orange*	o·*rahng*·zhe
pea	*Erbse*	*erp*·se
plum	*Pflaume*	*pflow*·me
potato	*Kartoffel*	kar·*to*·fel
spinach	*Spinat*	shpi·*naht*
strawberry	*Erdbeere*	*ert*·bair·re
tomato	*Tomate*	to·*mah*·te
vegetable	*Gemüse*	ge·*mü*·ze
watermelon	*Wasser-melone*	*va*·ser·me·law·ne

Other

bread	*Brot*	brawt
butter	*Butter*	*bu*·ter
cheese	*Käse*	*kay*·ze
egg/eggs	*Ei/Eier*	ai/*ai*·er
honey	*Honig*	*haw*·nikh
jam	*Marmelade*	mar·me·*lah*·de
pasta	*Nudeln*	*noo*·deln
pepper	*Pfeffer*	*pfe*·fer
rice	*Reis*	rais
salt	*Salz*	zalts
soup	*Suppe*	*zu*·pe
sugar	*Zucker*	*tsu*·ker

Drinks

beer	*Bier*	beer
coffee	*Kaffee*	*ka*·fay
juice	*Saft*	zaft
milk	*Milch*	milkh
orange juice	*Orangensaft*	o·*rang*·zhen·zaft
red wine	*Rotwein*	*rawt*·vain
sparkling wine	*Sekt*	zekt
tea	*Tee*	tay
water	*Wasser*	*va*·ser
white wine	*Weißwein*	*vais*·vain

EMERGENCIES

Help!	*Hilfe!*	*hil*·fe
Go away!	*Gehen Sie weg!*	*gay*·en zee vek

SIGNS

Ausgang	Exit
Damen	Women
Eingang	Entrance
Geschlossen	Closed
Herren	Men
Toiletten (WC)	Toilets
Offen	Open
Verboten	Prohibited

Call the police!
Rufen Sie die Polizei! — roo·fen zee dee po·li·*tsai*

Call a doctor!
Rufen Sie einen Arzt! — roo·fen zee *ai*·nen artst

Where are the toilets?
Wo ist die Toilette? — vo ist dee to·a·*le*·te

I'm lost.
Ich habe mich verirrt. — ikh *hah*·be mikh fer·*irt*

I'm sick.
Ich bin krank. — ikh bin krangk

It hurts here.
Es tut hier weh. — es toot heer vay

I'm allergic to ...
Ich bin allergisch gegen ... — ikh bin a·*lair*·gish *gay*·gen ...

SHOPPING & SERVICES

I'd like to buy ...
Ich möchte ... kaufen. — ikh *merkh*·te ... *kow*·fen

I'm just looking.
Ich schaue mich nur um. — ikh *show*·e mikh noor um

Can I look at it?
Können Sie es mir zeigen? — *ker*·nen zee es meer *tsai*·gen

How much is this?
Wie viel kostet das? — vee feel *kos*·tet das

That's too expensive.
Das ist zu teuer. — das ist tsoo *toy*·er

Can you lower the price?
Können Sie mit dem Preis heruntergehen? — *ker*·nen zee mit dem prais he·*run*·ter·gay·en

There's a mistake in the bill.
Da ist ein Fehler in der Rechnung. — dah ist ain *fay*·ler in dair *rekh*·nung

ATM	*Geldautomat*	*gelt*·ow·to·maht
post office	*Postamt*	*post*·amt
tourist office	*Fremden-verkehrsbüro*	*frem*·den·fer·kairs·bü·raw

TIME & DATES

What time is it?
Wie spät ist es? — vee shpayt ist es

It's (10) o'clock.
Es ist (zehn) Uhr. — es ist (tsayn) oor

QUESTION WORDS

What?	*Was?*	vas
When?	*Wann?*	van
Where?	*Wo?*	vaw
Who?	*Wer?*	vair
Why?	*Warum?*	va·*rum*

At what time?
Um wie viel Uhr? — um vee feel oor

At ...
Um ... — um ...

morning	*Morgen*	*mor*·gen
afternoon	*Nachmittag*	*nahkh*·mi·tahk
evening	*Abend*	*ah*·bent

yesterday	*gestern*	*ges*·tern
today	*heute*	*hoy*·te
tomorrow	*morgen*	*mor*·gen

Monday	*Montag*	*mawn*·tahk
Tuesday	*Dienstag*	*deens*·tahk
Wednesday	*Mittwoch*	*mit*·vokh
Thursday	*Donnerstag*	*do*·ners·tahk
Friday	*Freitag*	*frai*·tahk
Saturday	*Samstag*	*zams*·tahk
Sunday	*Sonntag*	*zon*·tahk

January	*Januar*	*yan*·u·ahr
February	*Februar*	*fay*·bru·ahr
March	*März*	merts
April	*April*	a·*pril*
May	*Mai*	mai
June	*Juni*	*yoo*·ni
July	*Juli*	*yoo*·li
August	*August*	ow·*gust*
September	*September*	zep·*tem*·ber
October	*Oktober*	ok·*taw*·ber
November	*November*	no·*vem*·ber
December	*Dezember*	de·*tsem*·ber

TRANSPORT

Public Transport

boat	*Boot*	bawt
bus	*Bus*	bus
metro	*U-Bahn*	*oo*·bahn
plane	*Flugzeug*	*flook*·tsoyk
train	*Zug*	tsook

At what time's the ... bus?	*Wann fährt der ... Bus?*	van fairt dair ... bus
first	*erste*	*ers*·te
last	*letzte*	*lets*·te
next	*nächste*	*naykhs*·te

A ... to (Cologne).	*Eine ... nach (Köln).*	*ai*·ne ... nahkh (kerln)
1st-/2nd-class ticket	*Fahrkarte erster/zweiter Klasse*	*fahr*·kar·te *ers*·ter/*tsvai*·ter *kla*·se
one-way ticket	*einfache Fahrkarte*	*ain*·fa·khe *fahr*·kar·te
return ticket	*Rückfahrkarte*	*rük*·fahr·kar·te

At what time does it arrive?
Wann kommt es an? van komt es an

Is it a direct route?
Ist es eine direkte Verbindung? ist es *ai*·ne di·*rek*·te fer·*bin*·dung

Does it stop at ...?
Hält es in ...? helt es in ...

What station is this?
Welcher Bahnhof ist das? *vel*·kher *bahn*·hawf ist das

What's the next stop?
Welches ist der nächste Halt? *vel*·khes ist dair *naykh*·ste halt

I want to get off here.
Ich möchte hier aussteigen. ikh *merkh*·te heer *ows*·shtai·gen

Please tell me when we get to ....
Könnten Sie mir bitte sagen, wann wir in ... ankommen? *kern*·ten zee meer *bi*·te *zah*·gen van veer in ... *an*·ko·men

Please take me to (this address).
Bitte bringen Sie mich zu (dieser Adresse). *bi*·te *bring*·en zee mikh tsoo (*dee*·zer a·*dre*·se)

platform	*Bahnsteig*	*bahn*·shtaik
ticket office	*Fahrkarten-verkauf*	*fahr*·kar·ten·fer·kowf
timetable	*Fahrplan*	*fahr*·plan

Driving & Cycling

I'd like to hire a ...	*Ich möchte ein ... mieten.*	ikh *merkh*·te ain ... *mee*·ten
4WD	*Allrad-fahrzeug*	*al*·raht·fahr·tsoyk
bicycle	*Fahrrad*	*fahr*·raht
car	*Auto*	*ow*·to
motorbike	*Motorrad*	*maw*·tor·raht

How much is it per ...?	*Wie viel kostet es pro ...?*	vee feel *kos*·tet es praw ...
day	*Tag*	tahk
week	*Woche*	*vo*·khe

bicycle pump	*Fahrradpumpe*	*fahr*·raht·pum·pe
child seat	*Kindersitz*	*kin*·der·zits

NUMBERS

1	*eins*	ains
2	*zwei*	tsvai
3	*drei*	drai
4	*vier*	feer
5	*fünf*	fünf
6	*sechs*	zeks
7	*sieben*	*zee*·ben
8	*acht*	akht
9	*neun*	noyn
10	*zehn*	tsayn
20	*zwanzig*	*tsvan*·tsikh
30	*dreißig*	*drai*·tsikh
40	*vierzig*	*feer*·tsikh
50	*fünfzig*	*fünf*·tsikh
60	*sechzig*	*zekh*·tsikh
70	*siebzig*	*zeep*·tsikh
80	*achtzig*	*akht*·tsikh
90	*neunzig*	*noyn*·tsikh
100	*hundert*	*hun*·dert
1000	*tausend*	*tow*·sent

helmet	*Helm*	helm
petrol	*Benzin*	ben·*tseen*

Does this road go to ...?
Führt diese Straße nach ...? fürt *dee*·ze *shtrah*·se nahkh ...

(How long) Can I park here?
(Wie lange) Kann ich hier parken? (vee *lang*·e) kan ikh heer *par*·ken

Where's a petrol station?
Wo ist eine Tankstelle? vaw ist *ai*·ne *tangk*·shte·le

I need a mechanic.
Ich brauche einen Mechaniker. ikh *brow*·khe *ai*·nen me·*khah*·ni·ker

My car/motorbike has broken down (at ...).
Ich habe (in ...) eine Panne mit meinem Auto/Motorrad. ikh *hah*·be (in ...) *ai*·ne *pa*·ne mit *mai*·nem *ow*·to/*maw*·tor·raht

I've run out of petrol.
Ich habe kein Benzin mehr. ikh *hah*·be kain ben·*tseen* mair

I have a flat tyre.
Ich habe eine Reifenpanne. ikh *hah*·be *ai*·ne *rai*·fen·pa·ne

Are there cycling paths?
Gibt es Fahrradwege? geept es *fahr*·raht·vay·ge

Is there bicycle parking?
Gibt es Fahrrad-Parkplätze? geept es *fahr*·raht·park·ple·tse

GLOSSARY

You may encounter the following terms and abbreviations while in Berlin.

Bahnhof (Bf) – train station

Berg – mountain

Bibliothek – library

BRD – Bundesrepublik Deutschland (abbreviated in English as FRG – Federal Republic of Germany); see also *DDR*

Brücke – bridge

Brunnen – fountain or well

Bundestag – German parliament

CDU – Christliche Demokratische Union (Christian Democratic Union), centre-right party

DDR – Deutsche Demokratische Republik (abbreviated in English as GDR – German Democratic Republic); the name for the former East Germany; see also *BRD*

Denkmal – memorial, monument

Dom – cathedral

ermässigt – reduced (eg admission fee)

Fahrrad – bicycle

Flohmarkt – flea market

Flughafen – airport

FRG – Federal Republic of Germany; see also *BRD*

Gasse – lane or alley

Gästehaus, Gasthaus – guesthouse

GDR – German Democratic Republic (the former East Germany); see also *DDR*

Gedenkstätte – memorial site

Gestapo – Geheime Staatspolizei (Nazi secret police)

Gründerzeit – literally 'foundation time'; early years of German empire, roughly 1871–90

Hafen – harbour, port

Hauptbahnhof (Hbf) – main train station

Hof (Höfe) – courtyard(s)

Imbiss – snack bar, takeaway stand

Insel – island

Kaiser – emperor; derived from 'Caesar'

Kapelle – chapel

Karte – ticket

Kiez(e) – neighbourhood(s)

Kino – cinema

König – king

Konzentrationslager (KZ) – concentration camp

Kristallnacht – literally 'Night of Broken Glass'; Nazi pogrom against Jewish businesses and institutions on 9 November 1938

Kunst – art

Kunsthotels – hotels either designed by artists or liberally furnished with art

Mietskaserne(n) – tenement(s) built around successive courtyards

Ostalgie – fusion of the words Ost and Nostalgie, meaning nostalgia for East Germany

Palais – small palace

Palast – palace

Passage – shopping arcade

Platz – square

Rathaus – town hall

Reich – empire

Reisezentrum – travel centre in train or bus stations

Saal (Säle) – hall(s), large room(s)

Sammlung – collection

S-Bahn – metro/regional rail service with fewer stops than the U-Bahn

Schiff – ship

Schloss – palace

See – lake

SPD – Sozialdemokratische Partei Deutschlands (Social Democratic Party of Germany)

SS – Schutzstaffel; organisation within the Nazi Party that supplied Hitler's bodyguards, as well as concentration camp guards and the Waffen-SS troops in WWII

Stasi – GDR secret police (from Ministerium für Staatssicherheit, or Ministry of State Security)

Strasse (Str) – street

Tageskarte – daily menu; day ticket on public transport

Tor – gate

Trabant – GDR-era car boasting a two-stroke engine

Turm – tower

Trümmerberge – rubble mountains

U-Bahn – rapid transit railway, mostly underground; best choice for metro trips

Ufer – bank

Viertel – quarter, neighbourhood

Wald – forest

Weg – way, path

Weihnachtsmarkt – Christmas market

Wende – 'change' or 'turning point' of 1989, ie the collapse of the GDR and the resulting German reunification

Behind the Scenes

END US YOUR FEEDBACK

/e love to hear from travellers – your comments keep us on our toes and help make our books etter. Our well-travelled team reads every word on what you loved or loathed about this book. though we cannot reply individually to your submissions, we always guarantee that your edback goes straight to the appropriate authors, in time for the next edition. Each person ho sends us information is thanked in the next edition – the most useful submissions are warded with a selection of digital PDF chapters.

Visit **lonelyplanet.com/contact** to submit your updates and suggestions or to ask for help. ur award-winning website also features inspirational travel stories, news and discussions.

Note: We may edit, reproduce and incorporate your comments in Lonely Planet products uch as guidebooks, websites and digital products, so let us know if you don't want your omments reproduced or your name acknowledged. For a copy of our privacy policy visit nelyplanet.com/legal.

RITER THANKS

ndrea Schulte-Peevers

big heartfelt thanks to the following wonderful eople who have plied me tips, insight, information, ideas and encouragement in researching this ook (in no particular order): Henrik Tidefjärd, arbara Woolsey, Kerstin Riedel, Claudia Scheffler, ank Engster, Heiner and Claudia Schuster, Anna übbe, Renate Freiling, Shachar and Dorit Elkanati, ernd Olsson, Friederike Werner and, of course, avid Peevers.

ACKNOWLEDGEMENTS

Cover photograph: Fernsehturm (TV Tower), Alexanderplatz, Sabine Lubenow/AWL Images ©

THIS BOOK

This 12th edition of Lonely Planet's *Berlin* guidebook was researched and written by Andrea Schulte-Peevers. The previous edition was also written by Andrea. This guidebook was produced by the following:

Senior Product Editor Sandie Kestell
Regional Senior Cartographer Mark Griffiths
Product Editors Paul Harding, Kate James
Book Designers Hannah Blackie, Fergal Condon, Aomi Ito
Assisting Editors Sarah Bailey, Michelle Bennett, Bruce Evans, Monique Perrin, Gabrielle Stefanos, Saralinda Turner, Simon Williamson
Cartographer Julie Dodkins
Assisting Cartographers Rachel Imeson, Julie Sheridan
Cover Researcher Brendan Dempsey-Spencer
Thanks to Karen Henderson, Darren O'Connell

Index

See also separate subindexes for:

EATING P317
DRINKING & NIGHTLIFE P319
ENTERTAINMENT P319
SHOPPING P320
SPORTS & ACTIVITIES P320
SLEEPING P320

A

B

C

D

Sights 000
Map Pages **000**
Photo Pages **000**

EATING

Sights 000
Map Pages **000**
Photo Pages **000**

DRINKING & NIGHTLIFE

ENTERTAINMENT

SHOPPING

SPORTS & ACTIVITIES

Sights 000
Map Pages **000**
Photo Pages **000**

SLEEPING

Berlin Maps

Sights

- Beach
- Bird Sanctuary
- Buddhist
- Castle/Palace
- Christian
- Confucian
- Hindu
- Islamic
- Jain
- Jewish
- Monument
- Museum/Gallery/Historic Building
- Ruin
- Shinto
- Sikh
- Taoist
- Winery/Vineyard
- Zoo/Wildlife Sanctuary
- Other Sight

Activities, Courses & Tours

- Bodysurfing
- Diving
- Canoeing/Kayaking
- Course/Tour
- Sento Hot Baths/Onsen
- Skiing
- Snorkelling
- Surfing
- Swimming/Pool
- Walking
- Windsurfing
- Other Activity

Sleeping

- Sleeping
- Camping
- Hut/Shelter

Eating

- Eating

Drinking & Nightlife

- Drinking & Nightlife
- Cafe

Entertainment

- Entertainment

Shopping

- Shopping

Information

- Bank
- Embassy/Consulate
- Hospital/Medical
- Internet
- Police
- Post Office
- Telephone
- Toilet
- Tourist Information
- Other Information

Geographic

- Beach
- Gate
- Hut/Shelter
- Lighthouse
- Lookout
- Mountain/Volcano
- Oasis
- Park
- Pass
- Picnic Area
- Waterfall

Population

- Capital (National)
- Capital (State/Province)
- City/Large Town
- Town/Village

Transport

- Airport
- Border crossing
- Bus
- Cable car/Funicular
- Cycling
- Ferry
- Metro station
- Monorail
- Parking
- Petrol station
- S-Bahn/Subway station
- Taxi
- T-bane/Tunnelbana station
- Train station/Railway
- Tram
- U-Bahn/Underground station
- Other Transport

Routes

- Tollway
- Freeway
- Primary
- Secondary
- Tertiary
- Lane
- Unsealed road
- Road under construction
- Plaza/Mall
- Steps
- Tunnel
- Pedestrian overpass
- Walking Tour
- Walking Tour detour
- Path/Walking Trail

Boundaries

- International
- State/Province
- Disputed
- Regional/Suburb
- Marine Park
- Cliff
- Wall

Hydrography

- River, Creek
- Intermittent River
- Canal
- Water
- Dry/Salt/Intermittent Lake
- Reef

Areas

- Airport/Runway
- Beach/Desert
- Cemetery (Christian)
- Cemetery (Other)
- Glacier
- Mudflat
- Park/Forest
- Sight (Building)
- Sportsground
- Swamp/Mangrove

Note: Not all symbols displayed above appear on the maps in this book

MAP INDEX

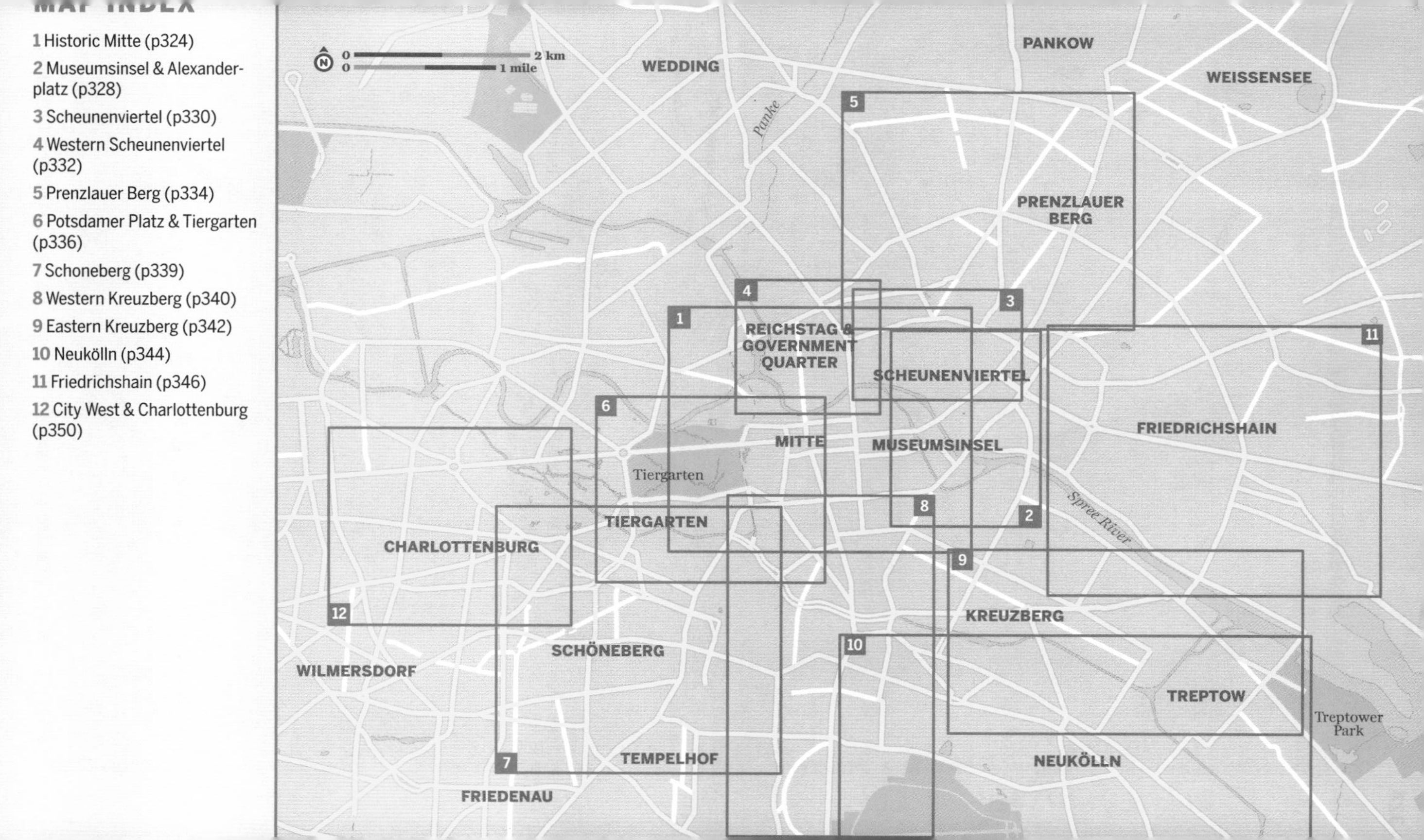

0 2 km
0 1 mile
N
PANKOW
WEISSENSEE
WEDDING
Panke
PRENZLAUER BERG
REICHSTAG & GOVERNMENT QUARTER
SCHEUNENVIERTEL
FRIEDRICHSHAIN
MITTE
MUSEUMSINSEL
Tiergarten
TIERGARTEN
Spree River
CHARLOTTENBURG
KREUZBERG
SCHÖNEBERG
WILMERSDORF
TREPTOW
Treptower Park
TEMPELHOF
NEUKÖLLN
FRIEDENAU
1
2
3
4
5
6
7
8
9
10
11
12

Key on p326

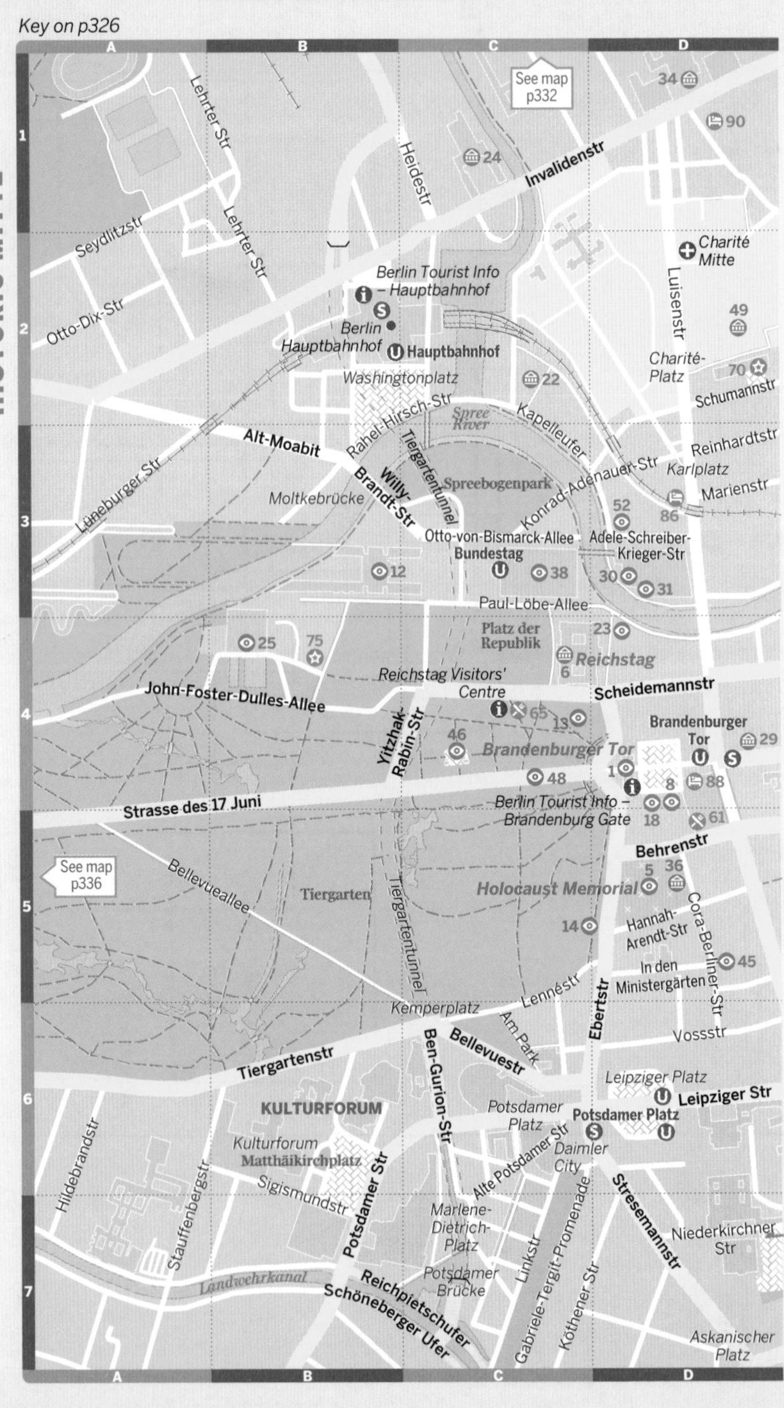

See map p332
See map p336
Lehrter Str
Heidestr
Invalidenstr
Seydlitzstr
Otto-Dix-Str
Berlin Tourist Info – Hauptbahnhof
Berlin Hauptbahnhof
Hauptbahnhof
Washingtonplatz
Rahel-Hirsch-Str
Spree River
Kapelleufer
Alt-Moabit
Lüneburger Str
Moltkebrücke
Willy-Brandt-Str
Tiergartentunnel
Spreebogenpark
Konrad-Adenauer-Str
Otto-von-Bismarck-Allee
Bundestag
Adele-Schreiber-Krieger-Str
Paul-Löbe-Allee
Platz der Republik
Reichstag
Reichstag Visitors' Centre
Scheidemannstr
John-Foster-Dulles-Allee
Yitzhak-Rabin-Str
Brandenburger Tor
Strasse des 17 Juni
Berlin Tourist Info – Brandenburg Gate
Behrenstr
Holocaust Memorial
Bellevueallee
Tiergarten
Hannah-Arendt-Str
Cora-Berliner-Str
In den Ministergärten
Lennéstr
Kemperplatz
Ebertstr
Am Park
Vossstr
Bellevuestr
Ben-Gurion-Str
Tiergartenstr
Leipziger Platz
Leipziger Str
KULTURFORUM
Potsdamer Platz
Kulturforum
Matthäikirchplatz
Alte Potsdamer Str
Daimler City
Hildebrandstr
Sigismundstr
Potsdamer Str
Stauffenbergstr
Marlene-Dietrich-Platz
Linkstr
Gabriele-Tergit-Promenade
Stresemannstr
Niederkirchner Str
Landwehrkanal
Reichpietschufer
Schöneberger Ufer
Potsdamer Brücke
Köthener Str
Askanischer Platz
Charité Mitte
Luisenstr
Charité-Platz
Schumannstr
Reinhardtstr
Karlplatz
Marienstr

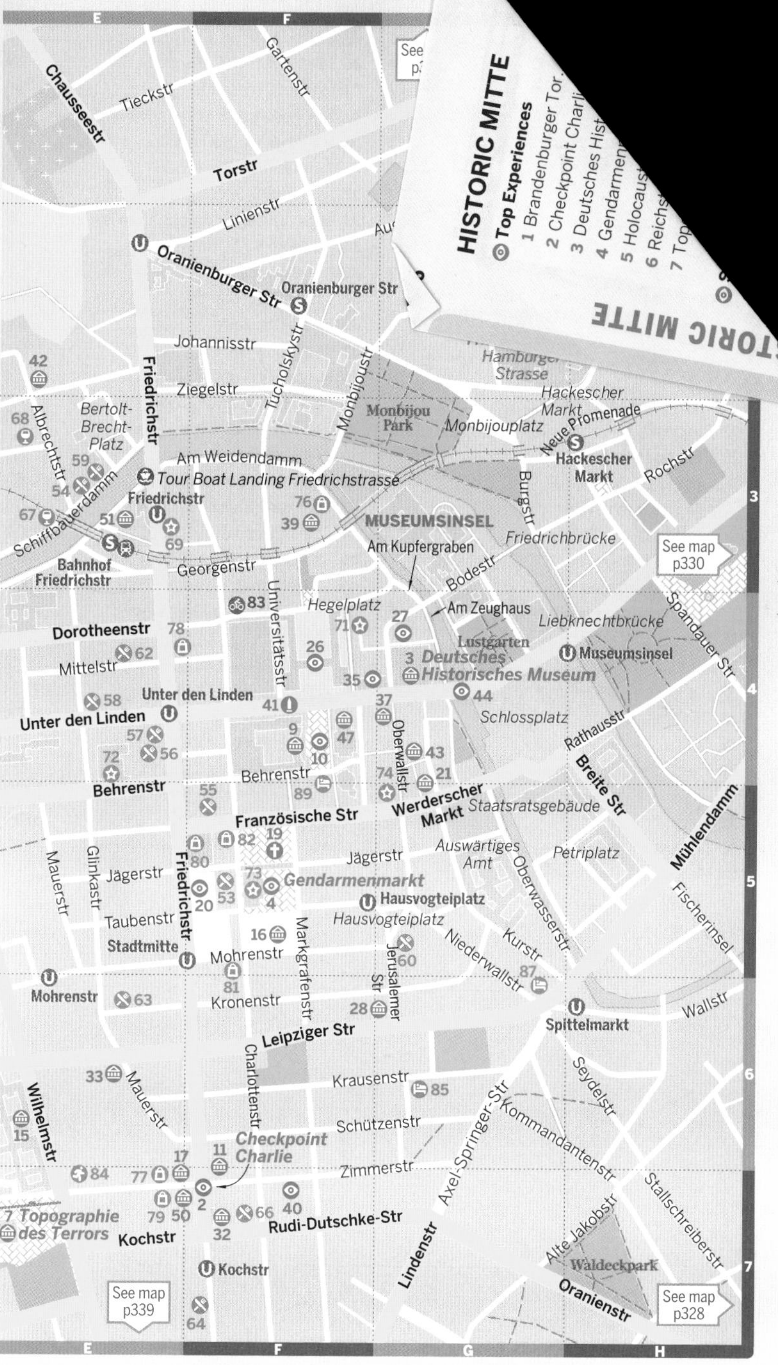

HISTORIC MITTE
Top Experiences
1 Brandenburger Tor
2 Checkpoint Charli
3 Deutsches Hist
4 Gendarmen
5 Holocaust
6 Reichst
7 Top
Chausseestr
Tieckstr
Gartenstr
Torstr
Linienstr
Oranienburger Str
Johannisstr
Tucholskystr
Monbijoustr
Ziegelstr
Friedrichstr
Albrechtstr
Bertolt-Brecht-Platz
Monbijou Park
Monbijouplatz
Hamburger Strasse
Hackescher Markt
Neue Promenade
Rochstr
Am Weidendamm
Tour Boat Landing Friedrichstrasse
Schiffbauerdamm
Bahnhof Friedrichstr
MUSEUMSINSEL
Burgstr
Friedrichbrücke
Am Kupfergraben
Georgenstr
Bodestr
See map p330
Universitätsstr
Hegelplatz
Am Zeughaus
Liebknechtbrücke
Spandauer Str
Dorotheenstr
Lustgarten
Museumsinsel
Mittelstr
3 Deutsches Historisches Museum
Unter den Linden
Schlossplatz
Oberwallstr
Rathausstr
Behrenstr
Breite Str
Werderscher Markt
Staatsratsgebäude
Mühlendamm
Französische Str
Auswärtiges Amt
Petriplatz
Jägerstr
Mauerstr
Glinkastr
Gendarmenmarkt
Oberwasserstr
Fischerinsel
Hausvogteiplatz
Taubenstr
Markgrafenstr
Stadtmitte
Mohrenstr
Jerusalemer Str
Niederwallstr
Kurstr
Kronenstr
Spittelmarkt
Wallstr
Leipziger Str
Charlottenstr
Seydelstr
Krausenstr
Wilhelmstr
Axel-Springer-Str
Kommandantenstr
Schützenstr
Checkpoint Charlie
Zimmerstr
Stallschreiberstr
7 Topographie des Terrors
Kochstr
Rudi-Dutschke-Str
Lindenstr
Alte Jakobstr
Waldeckpark
Oranienstr
See map p339
See map p328

p86

...D4
...e ...F7
...orisches Museum ...G4
...markt ...F5
...t Memorial ...D5
...tag ...C4
...ographie des Terrors ...E7

ights p93

8 Akademie der Künste – Pariser Platz ...D4
9 Alte Bibliothek ...F4
10 Bebelplatz ...F4
11 BlackBox Kalter Krieg ...F6
12 Bundeskanzleramt ...B3
13 Denkmal für die im Nationalsozialismus ermordeten Sinti und Roma Europas ...C4
14 Denkmal für die im Nationalsozialismus verfolgten Homosexuellen ...C5
15 Detlev Rohwedder Building ...E6
16 Deutscher Dom ...F5
17 Die Mauer – asisi Panorama Berlin ...E7
18 DZ Bank ...D4
19 Französischer Dom ...F5
20 Friedrichstadtpassagen ...F5
21 Friedrichswerdersche Kirche ...G4
22 Futurium ...C2
23 Gedenkort Weisse Kreuze ...D4
24 Hamburger Bahnhof – Museum für Gegenwart ...C1
25 Haus der Kulturen der Welt ...B4
26 Humboldt Universität zu Berlin ...F4
27 IM Pei Bau ...G4
28 Julia Stoschek Collection ...G6
29 Madame Tussauds ...D4
30 Marie-Elisabeth-Lüders-Haus ...D3
31 Mauer-Mahnmal im Marie-Elisabeth-Lüders-Haus ...D3
32 Mauermuseum ...F7
33 Museum für Kommunikation Berlin ...E6
34 Museum für Naturkunde ...D1
35 Neue Wache ...F4
36 Ort der Information ...D5
37 Palais Populaire ...G4
38 Paul-Löbe-Haus ...C3
39 Pergamonmuseum. Das Panorama ...F3
40 Peter Fechter Memorial ...F7
41 Reiterdenkmal Friedrich der Grosse ...F4
42 Sammlung Boros ...E2
43 Schinkel Pavillon ...G4
44 Schlossbrücke ...G4
45 Site of Hitler's Bunker ...D5
46 Sowjetisches Ehrenmal Tiergarten ...C4
47 Staatsoper Unter den Linden ...F4
48 Strasse des 17 Juni ...C4
49 Tieranatomisches Theater ...D2
50 Trabi Museum ...E7
51 Tränenpalast ...E3
52 Wall Memorial 'Parlament der Bäume' ...D3

Eating p100

53 Augustiner am Gendarmenmarkt ...F5
54 Berliner Republik ...E3
55 Borchardt ...F5
56 Cookies Cream ...E4
57 Crackers ...E4

Drinking & Nightlife **p103**

Entertainment **p103**

Shopping **p104**

Sports & Activities **p105**

Sleeping **p247**

MUSEUMSINSEL & ALEXANDERPLATZ

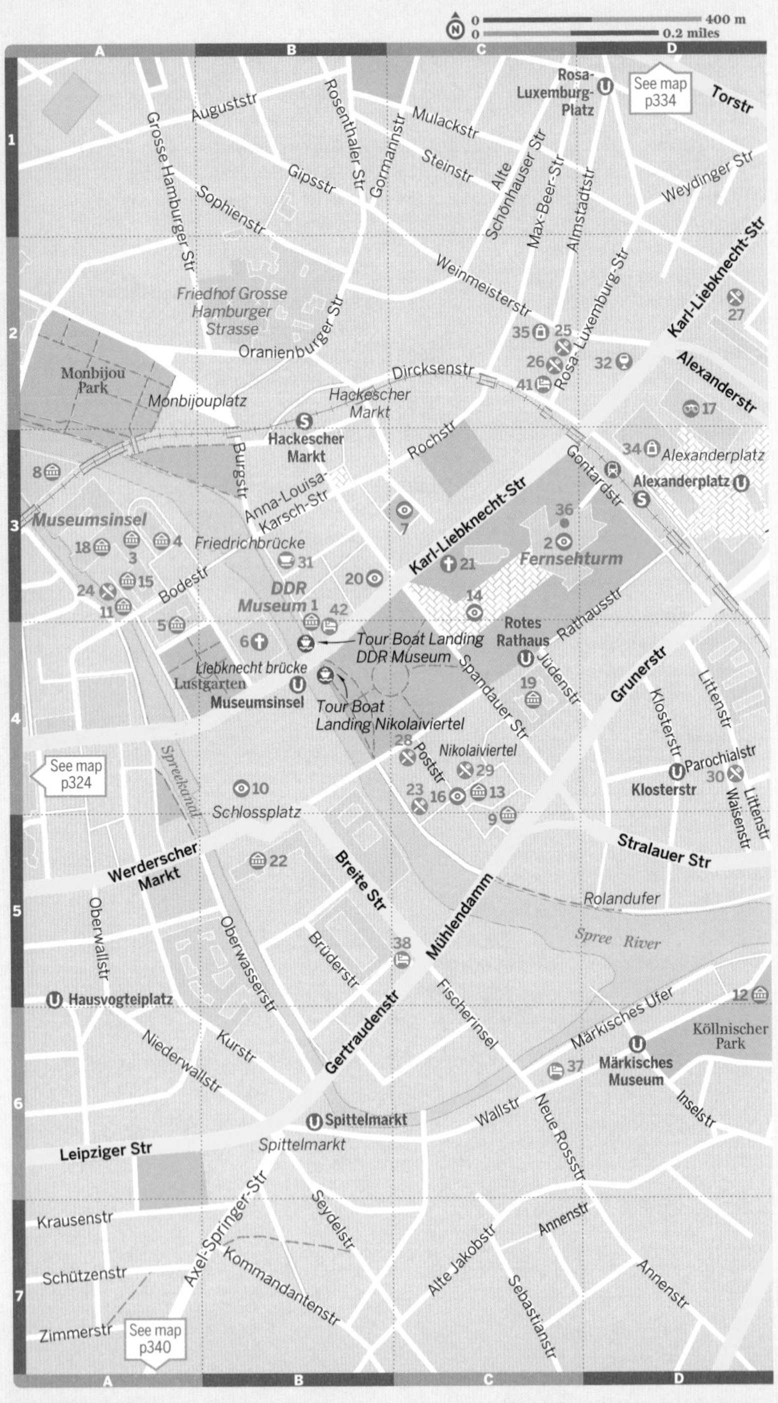

Top Experiences p108

1 DDR Museum B4
2 Fernsehturm C3
3 Museumsinsel A3

Sights p119

4 Alte Nationalgalerie A3
5 Altes Museum A4
6 Berliner Dom B4
7 Block der Frauen C3
8 Bode-Museum A3
9 Hanf Museum Berlin C5
10 Humboldt Forum B4
11 James-Simon-Galerie A3
12 Märkisches Museum D5
13 Museum Nikolaikirche C4
14 Neptunbrunnen C3
15 Neues Museum A3
16 Nikolaiviertel C4
17 Park Inn Panorama Terrasse D2
18 Pergamonmuseum A3
19 Rotes Rathaus C4
20 Sealife Berlin B3
21 St Marienkirche C3
22 Staatsratsgebäude B5

Eating p123

23 Brauhaus Georgbraeu C4
24 Cu29 ....A3
25 Dolores C2
26 Good Bank C2
27 Hofbräuhaus Berlin D2
28 Ngon C4
Sphere ....(see 2)
29 Zum Nussbaum C4
30 Zur Letzten Instanz D4

Drinking & Nightlife p124

31 Allegretto Gran Cafe B3
32 Braufactum Berlin D2

Shopping p125

33 Alexa E4
34 Galeria Kaufhof D3
35 IC! Berlin C2

Sports & Activities p301

36 Fat Tire Tours Berlin C3

Sleeping p247

37 art'otel berlin mitte C6
38 Capri by Fraser C5
39 Hostel One80° E2
40 Hotel Indigo Alexanderplatz E2
41 Motel One Berlin-Hackescher Markt C2
Park Inn by Radisson Berlin Alexanderplatz ....(see 17)
42 Radisson Blu Hotel B4

SCHEUNENVIERTEL
0
400 m
0
0.2 miles
See map p334
Nordbahnhof
Invalidenstr
Weinbergspark
Brunnenstr
Weinbergsweg
Rosenthaler Platz
Senefelderplatz
Teutoburger Platz
Kollwitzstr
Metzer Str
Saarbrücker Str
Schönhauser Allee
Strassburger Str
Choriner Str
Ackerstr
Bergstr
Tieckstr
Gartenstr
Novalisstr
Torstr
Linienstr
Koppenplatz
Tucholskystr
Grosse Hamburger Str
Auguststr
Gipsstr
Sophienstr
Sophie-Gips-Höfe
Rosenthaler Str
Gormannstr
Mulackstr
Steinstr
Alte Schönhauser Str
Max-Beer-Str
Almstadtstr
Rosa-Luxemburg-Platz
Weydinger Str
Karl-Liebknecht-Str
Hirtenstr
Wadzeckstr
Rosa-Luxemburg-Str
Münzstr
Weinmeisterstr
Neue Schönhauser Str
Dircksenstr
Hackesche Höfe
Krausnickstr
Heckmann Höfe
Oranienburger Str
Neue Synagoge
Johannisstr
Ziegelstr

Spree River
Am Weidendamm
Planckstr
Spree River
22
Monbijoustr
49
Monbijou Park
See map p334
Monbijouplatz
Grosse Präsidentenstr
31
Burgstr
Neue Promenade
Hackescher Markt
Rosenstr
Rochstr
Karl-Liebknecht-Str
Dircksenstr
Gontardstr
Bahnhof Alexanderplatz
Alexanderplatz
Alexanderplatz
Alexanderstr
A B C D E F G
5

Top Experiences p128
1 Hackesche Höfe D4
2 Neue Synagoge B4

Sights p129
3 Anne Frank Zentrum D4
4 Friedhof Grosse Hamburger Strasse C4
5 Haus Schwarzenberg D4
6 Heckmann-Höfe B4
Jüdische Mädchenschule .... (see 8)
7 KW Institute for Contemporary Art B3
Monsterkabinett .... (see 3)
Museum Blindenwerkstatt Otto Weidt .... (see 3)
8 Museum Frieder Burda – Salon Berlin B3
9 Sammlung Hoffmann D3
10 Times Art Center Berlin D1

Eating p131
11 Beets & Roots C3
12 Cecconi's G3
13 Clärchens Ballhaus C3
14 Daluma D2
15 District Môt D3
16 Father Carpenter E4
17 Frea B2
18 Katz Orange B1
19 Kopps C2
20 KWA C3
Mogg .... (see 8)
Muret La Barba .... (see 15)
21 Night Kitchen B4
Pauly Saal .... (see 8)
22 Petit Bijou B5
23 Remi F2
24 Rosenthaler Grill und Schlemmerbuffet D2
25 Schwarzwaldstuben B3
26 Store Kitchen G3
27 Tadshikische Teestube B4
28 To the Bone E2

Drinking & Nightlife p134
Amano Bar .... (see 53)
29 Aufsturz B4
30 Buck & Breck C1
Café Bravo .... (see 7)
Cafe Cinema .... (see 5)
31 Coven D5
Eschschloraque Rümschrümp .... (see 3)
32 Mikkeler D2
33 Rosengarten D1
34 Torbar B2

Entertainment p137
35 Babylon F3
36 b-Flat E4
37 Chamäleon D4
Hackesche Höfe Kino .... (see 37)
Kino Central .... (see 3)
38 Sophiensaele D4

Shopping p138
39 1. Absinth Depot Berlin E4
40 Ampelmann Berlin D4
41 Bonbonmacherei B4
42 Do You Read Me?! C3
43 Hundt Hammer Stein E3
44 Kauf Dich Glücklich D3
45 lala Berlin F2
46 Paper & Tea E3
47 Schwarzer Reiter G3
48 Trippen Flagship Store D4

Sports & Activities p31
49 Kinderbad Monbijou C5

Sleeping p248
50 Casa Camper D3
51 Circus Hostel D2
52 Flower's Boardinghouse Mitte E3
53 Hotel Amano D2

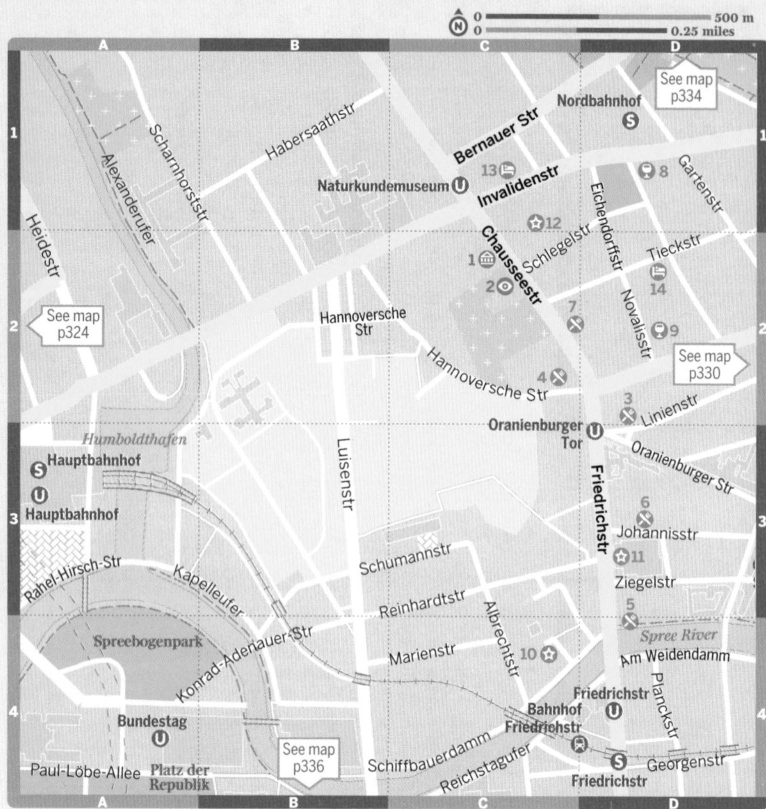

Sights p129
1 Brecht-Weigel Museum ... C2
2 Dorotheenstädtischer Friedhof I ... C2

Eating p131
3 Dada Falafel ... D2
4 Einsunternull ... C2
5 Grill Royal ... D4
6 House of Small Wonder ... D3
7 Rutz ... C2
Zenkichi ... (see 6)

Drinking & Nightlife p134
8 Castle ... D1
9 Melody Nelson ... D2

Entertainment p137
10 Berliner Ensemble ... C4
11 Friedrichstadt-Palast Berlin ... D3
12 Kunstfabrik Schlot ... C1

Sleeping p248
13 Boutique Hotel i31 ... C1
14 Honigmond Boutique Hotel ... D2

PRENZLAUER BERG

Key on p333

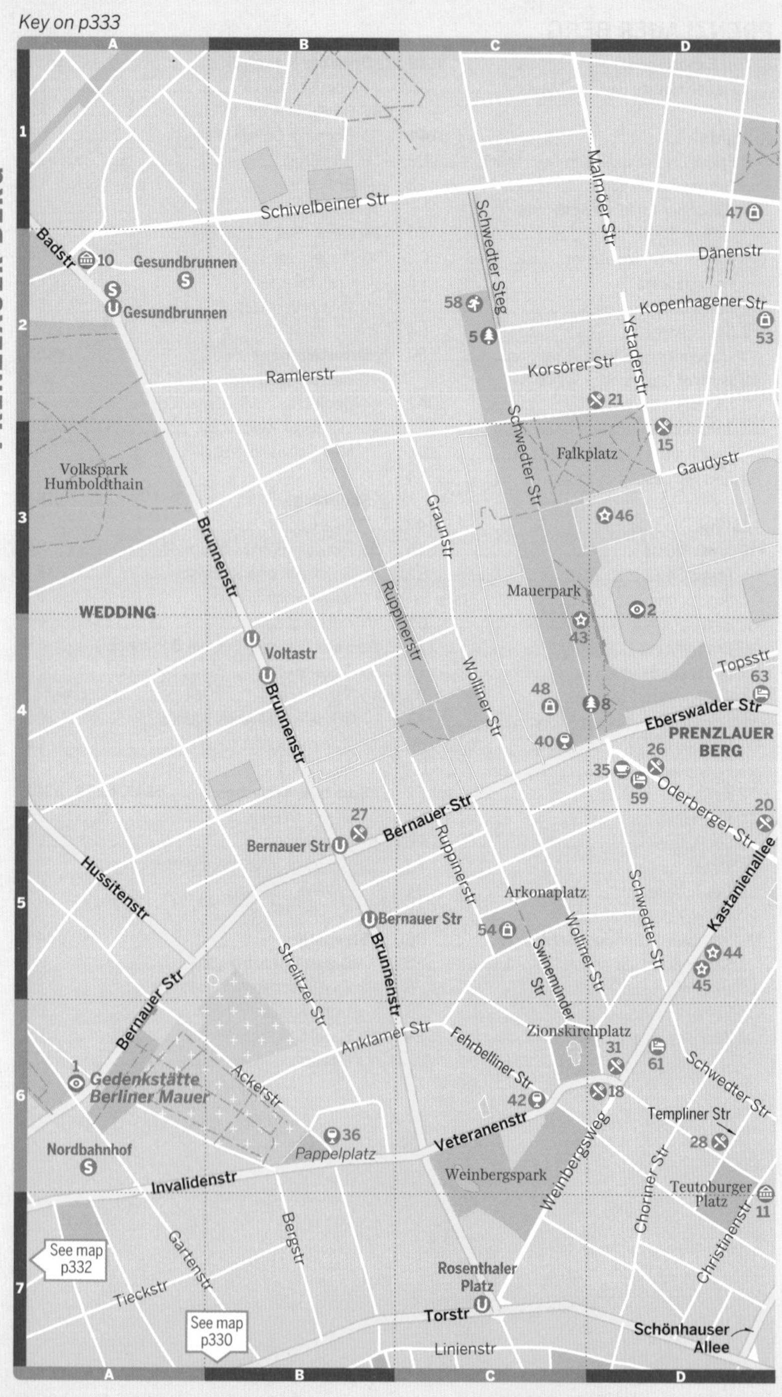
A
B
C
D
1
2
3
4
5
6
7
Schivelbeiner Str
Malmöer Str
Schwedter Steg
47
Dänenstr
Badstr
10
Gesundbrunnen
Gesundbrunnen
58
5
Kopenhagener Str
53
Ystaderstr
Ramlerstr
Korsörer Str
21
15
Schwedter Str
Falkplatz
Gaudystr
Volkspark
Humboldthain
Graunstr
46
Brunnenstr
Ruppinerstr
Mauerpark
2
WEDDING
43
Voltastr
Brunnenstr
Wolliner Str
Topsstr
63
48
8
Eberswalder Str
40
PRENZLAUER
BERG
26
35
59
Oderberger Str
20
27
Bernauer Str
Bernauer Str
Ruppinerstr
Hussitenstr
Kastanienallee
Schwedter Str
Arkonaplatz
Bernauer Str
54
Wolliner Str
Swinemünder Str
Brunnenstr
44
45
Strelitzer Str
Bernauer Str
Anklamer Str
Zionskirchplatz
Fehrbelliner Str
31
61
1
Gedenkstätte
Berliner Mauer
Ackerstr
42
18
Schwedter Str
Templiner Str
36
Veteranenstr
28
Nordbahnhof
Pappelplatz
Weinbergsweg
Invalidenstr
Weinbergspark
Choriner Str
Teutoburger
Platz
11
Bergstr
Gartenstr
Christinenstr
See map
p332
Rosenthaler
Platz
Tieckstr
Torstr
See map
p330
Schönhauser
Allee
Linienstr

PRENZLAUER BERG
0 400 m
0 0.2 miles
Schloss Schönhausen (3.5km)
PANKOW
Wisbyer Str
Prenzlauer Promenade
Paul-Robeson-Str
Kuglerstr
Rodenbergstr
Schivelbeiner Str
Wichertstr
Greifenhagener Str
Stahlheimer Str
Gudvanger Str
Ostseestr
Schönhauser Allee
Erich-Weinert-Str
Gleimstr
Zelter Str
Wichertstr
Prenzlauer Allee
Gaudystr
Wohnstadt Carl Legien
Cantianstr
Schönhauser Allee
Pappelallee
Stargarder Str
Prenzlauer Allee
Gubitzstr
Grellstr
Lettestr
Lychener Str
Helmholtz-platz
Dunckerstr
Senefelderstr
Diesterwegstr
Eberswalder Str
Schliemannstr
PRENZLAUER BERG
Raumerstr
Danziger Str
Ella-Kay-Str
Fröbelplatz
Husemannstr
Sredzkistr
Knaackstr
Ernst-Thälmann-Park
Danziger Str
Chodowieckistr
Jablonskistr
Rykestr
Wörther Str
Christburger Str
Kollwitzplatz
Jüdischer Friedhof Schönhauser Allee
Knaackstr
Marienburger Str
Kollwitzstr
Belforter Str
Immanuelkirchstr
Winsstr
Greifswalder Str
Pasteurstr
Senefelderplatz
Hufelandstr
Metzer Str
Heinrich-Roller-Str
Käthe-Niederkirchner-Str
Bötzowstr
Strassburger Str
See map p346
E
F
G
H
1
2
3
4
5
6
7
39
3
19
14
34
25
22
51
49
12
33
32
41
23
9
57
7
55
56
29
16
13
62
37
50
6
52
17
4
24
30
60
38

Key on p338

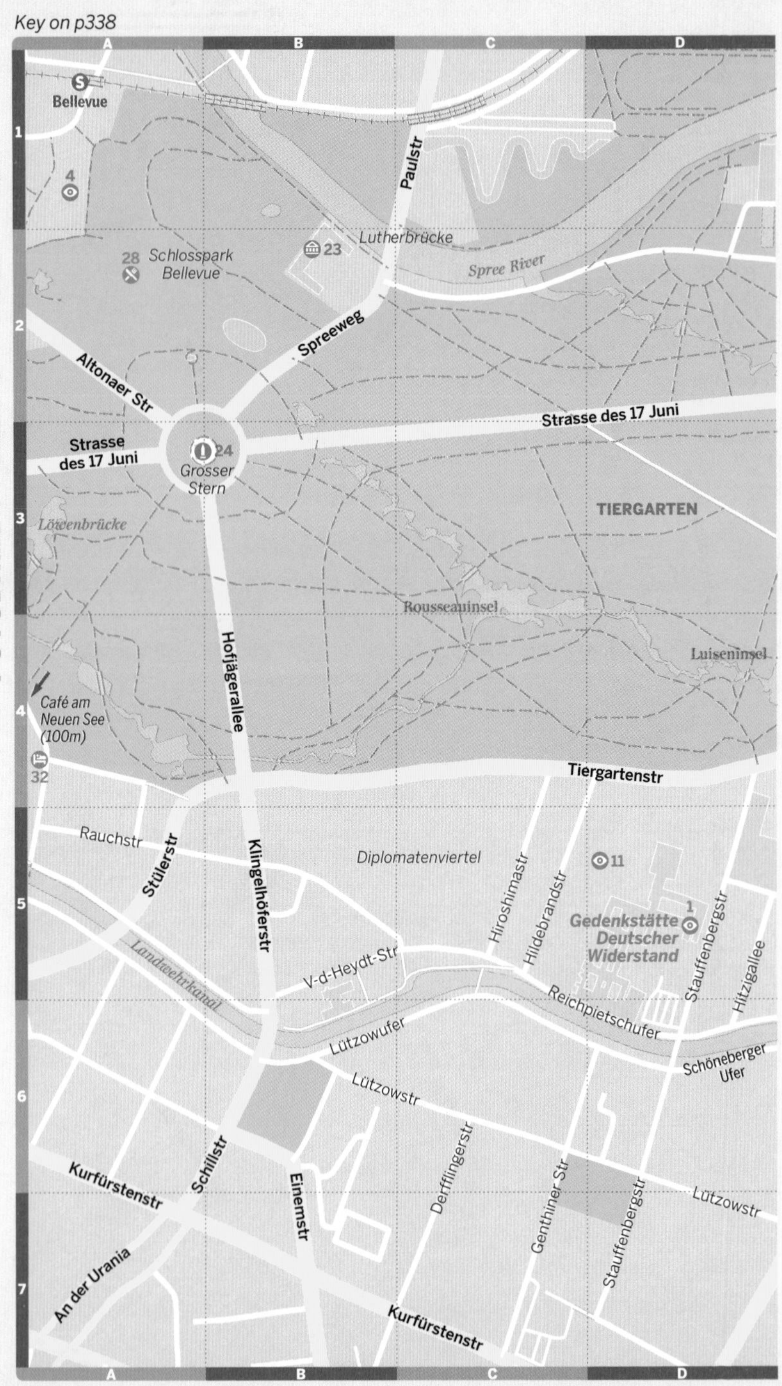

A
B
C
D
1
2
3
4
5
6
7
Bellevue
4
Paulstr
Lutherbrücke
23
28
Schlosspark Bellevue
Spree River
Spreeweg
Altonaer Str
Strasse des 17 Juni
Strasse des 17 Juni
24
Grosser Stern
TIERGARTEN
Löwenbrücke
Rousseauinsel
Luiseninsel
Hofjägerallee
Café am Neuen See (100m)
32
Tiergartenstr
Rauchstr
Stülerstr
Klingelhöferstr
Diplomatenviertel
11
Hiroshimastr
Hildebrandstr
1
Gedenkstätte Deutscher Widerstand
Stauffenbergstr
Hitzigallee
Landwehrkanal
V-d-Heydt-Str
Reichpietschufer
Lützowufer
Schöneberger Ufer
Lützowstr
Derfflingerstr
Genthiner Str
Stauffenbergstr
Lützowstr
Kurfürstenstr
Schillstr
Einemstr
An der Urania
Kurfürstenstr

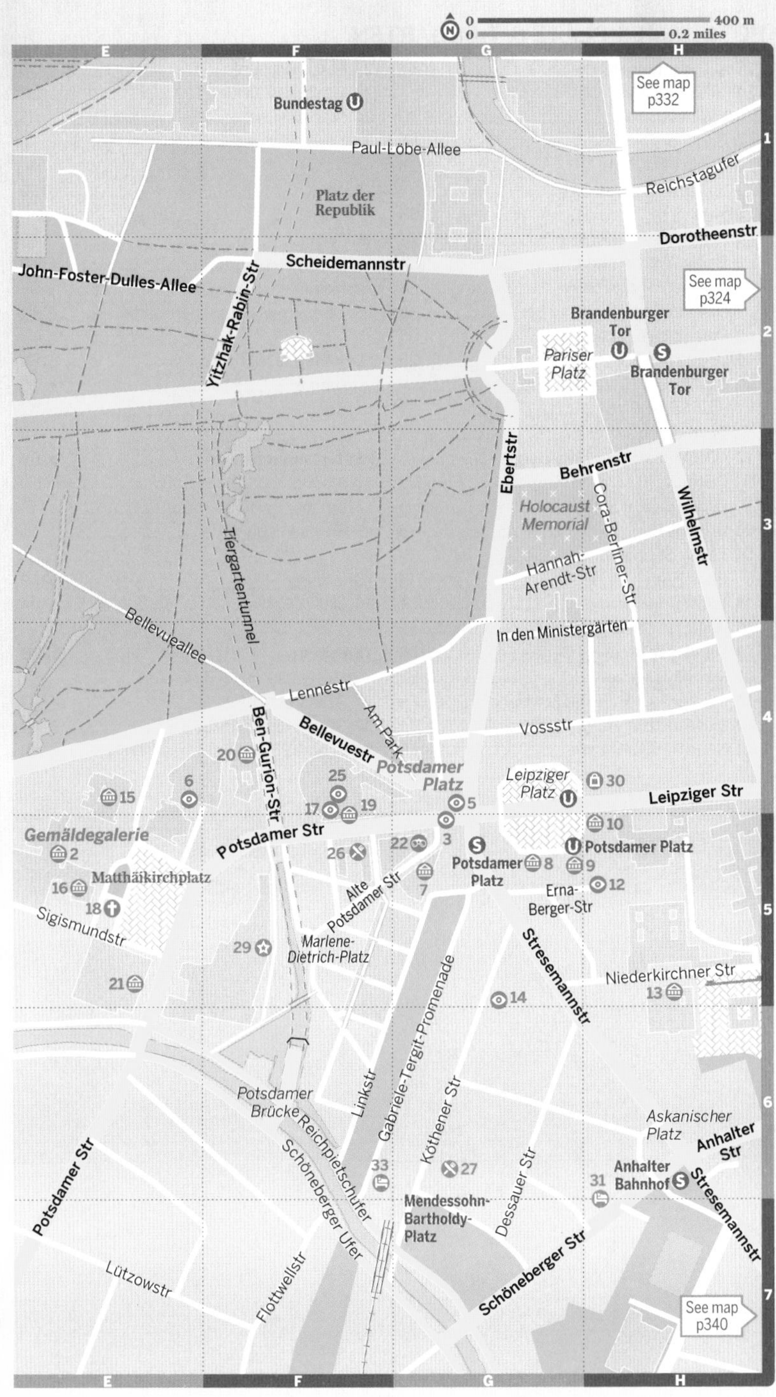

0
400 m
0
0.2 miles
E
F
G
H
1
2
3
4
5
6
7
See map p332
See map p324
See map p340
Bundestag
Paul-Löbe-Allee
Platz der Republik
Reichstagufer
Dorotheenstr
Scheidemannstr
John-Foster-Dulles-Allee
Yitzhak-Rabin-Str
Brandenburger Tor
Pariser Platz
Brandenburger Tor
Ebertstr
Behrenstr
Holocaust Memorial
Cora-Berliner-Str
Wilhelmstr
Hannah-Arendt-Str
Tiergartentunnel
Bellevueallee
In den Ministergärten
Lennéstr
Am Park
Vossstr
Bellevuestr
Ben-Gurion-Str
Potsdamer Platz
Leipziger Platz
Leipziger Str
Gemäldegalerie
Potsdamer Str
Matthäikirchplatz
Sigismundstr
Alte Potsdamer Str
Potsdamer Platz
Potsdamer Platz
Erna-Berger-Str
Marlene-Dietrich-Platz
Stresemannstr
Niederkirchner Str
Gabriele-Tergit-Promenade
Linkstr
Köthener Str
Potsdamer Brücke
Reichpietschufer
Schöneberger Ufer
Askanischer Platz
Anhalter Str
Anhalter Bahnhof
Stresemannstr
Dessauer Str
Mendessohn-Bartholdy-Platz
Potsdamer Str
Lützowstr
Flottwellstr
Schöneberger Str
2
3
5
6
7
8
9
10
12
13
14
15
16
17
18
19
20
21
22
25
26
27
29
30
31
33

POTSDAMER PLATZ & TIERGARTEN

Top Experiences **p157**

1 Gedenkstätte Deutscher Widerstand ... D5
2 Gemäldegalerie ... E5
3 Potsdamer Platz ... G5

Sights **p163**

4 Akademie der Künste ... A1
5 Berlin Wall Segments ... G4
6 Berliner Philharmonie ... E4
7 Daimler Contemporary Berlin ... G5
8 Dalí – Die Ausstellung ... G5
9 Deutsches Spionage Museum ... G5
10 Die Mauer / The Wall Museum am Leipziger Platz ... H5
11 Diplomatenviertel ... D5
12 GDR Watchtower Erna-Berger-Strasse ... H5
Gedenkstätte Stille Helden ... (see 1)
13 Gropius Bau ... H5
14 Hansa Studios ... G5
Haus Huth ... (see 7)
15 Kunstgewerbemuseum ... E4
16 Kupferstichkabinett ... E5
17 Legoland Discovery Centre ... F4
18 Matthäuskirche ... E5
19 Museum für Film und Fernsehen ... F5
20 Musikinstrumenten-Museum ... F4
21 Neue Nationalgalerie ... E5
22 Panoramapunkt ... G5
23 Schloss Bellevue ... B2
24 Siegessäule ... A3
25 Sony Center ... F4

Eating **p166**

Beba ... (see 13)
26 Facil ... F5
Ki-Nova ... (see 19)
27 Mabuhay ... G6
28 Teehaus im Englischen Garten ... A2

Drinking & Nightlife **p168**

Barn ... (see 7)
Stue Bar ... (see 32)

Entertainment **p169**

Arsenal ... (see 19)
Berliner Philharmoniker ... (see 6)
29 Spielbank Berlin ... F5

Shopping **p169**

30 Mall of Berlin ... H4

Sleeping **p250**

31 Mövenpick Hotel Berlin Am Potsdamer Platz ... H7
32 S/O Berlin Das Stue ... A4
33 Scandic Berlin Potsdamer Platz ... F6

Sights p172

1 Alter St Matthäus Kirchhof D3
2 David Bowie Apartment C3
3 Kammergericht C3
4 Kleistpark C3
5 Museum der Unerhörten Dinge C4
6 Rathaus Schöneberg B4
7 Schwules Museum C1
8 Urban Nation Museum C2

Eating p173

9 Bonvivant Cocktail Bistro B3
10 BRLO Brwhouse D2
11 Frühstück 3000 .... C2
12 Irma La Douce C2
13 Jones Ice Cream C3
14 Joseph-Roth-Diele D1
15 Kin Dee C1
16 Malakeh C2
Rocket + Basil .... (see 24)
17 Sticks'n'Sushi D2
18 Taverna Ousia A3
19 Witty's Bioland Imbiss B1

Drinking & Nightlife p176

20 Double Eye C4
21 Green Door C2
22 Hafen B2
23 Heile Welt B2
24 Kumpelnest 3000 .... D1
25 Möve im Felsenkeller C4
26 Sally Bowles B2
27 Stagger Lee B2
Tom's Bar .... (see 22)
Victoria Bar .... (see 12)

Entertainment p177

Wintergarten Varieté .... (see 12)

Shopping p177

Acne Studios .... (see 17)
Flohmarkt am Rathaus Schöneberg .... (see 6)
28 KaDeWe B2
29 Markt am Winterfeldtplatz C2
30 Öz-Gida Supermarkt C4
31 Winterfeldt Schokoladen C3

Sports & Activities p173

32 Sultan Hamam Berlin D3

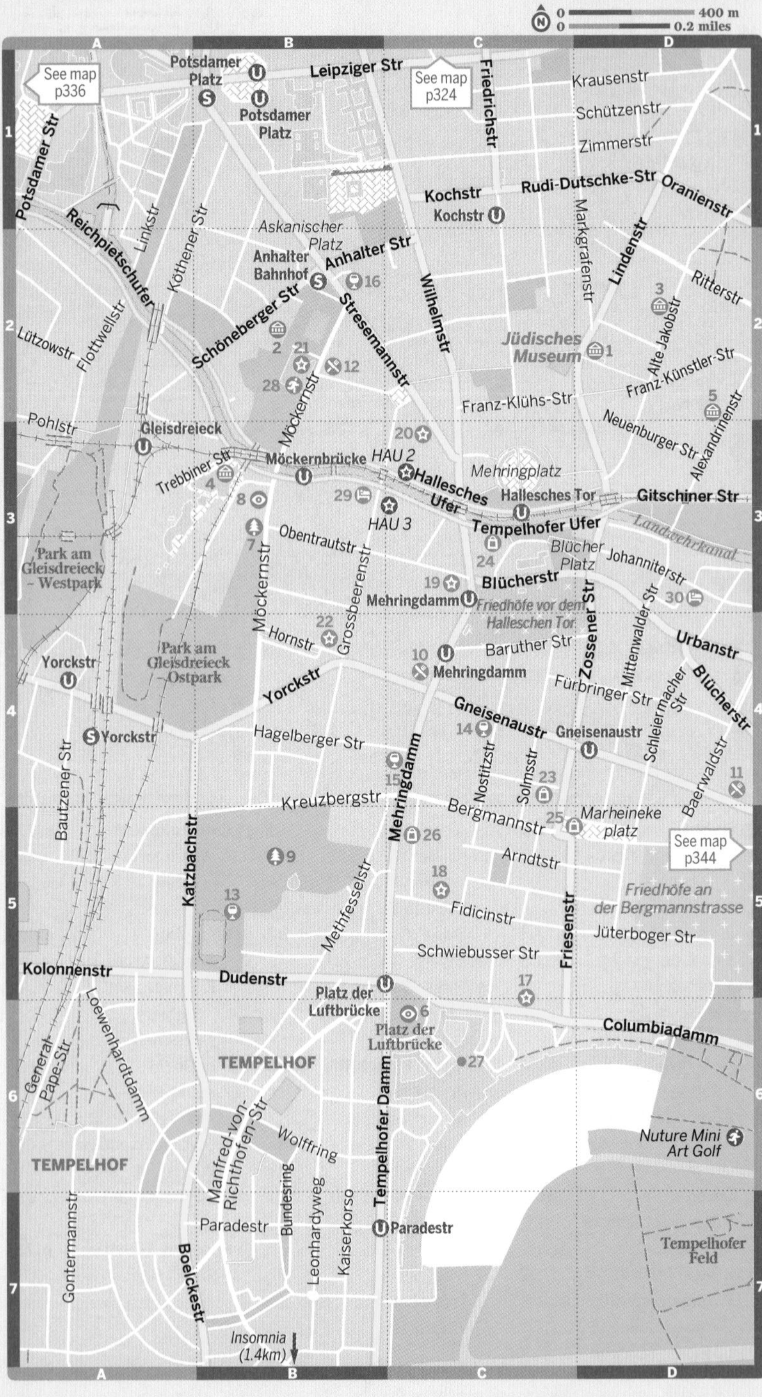

400 m
0.2 miles
See map p336
See map p324
See map p344
Potsdamer Platz
Leipziger Str
Friedrichstr
Krausenstr
Schützenstr
Zimmerstr
Potsdamer Str
Kochstr
Rudi-Dutschke-Str
Oranienstr
Reichpietschufer
Linkstr
Köthener Str
Askanischer Platz
Anhalter Bahnhof
Anhalter Str
Markgrafenstr
Lindenstr
Ritterstr
Schöneberger Str
Stresemannstr
Wilhelmstr
Jüdisches Museum
Alte Jakobstr
Lützowstr
Flottwellstr
Franz-Künstler-Str
Möckernstr
Franz-Klühs-Str
Neuenburger Str
Alexandrinenstr
Pohlstr
Gleisdreieck
Möckernbrücke
HAU 2
Mehringplatz
Trebbiner Str
Hallesches Ufer
Hallesches Tor
Gitschiner Str
HAU 3
Tempelhofer Ufer
Landwehrkanal
Obentrautstr
Blücher Platz
Johanniterstr
Park am Gleisdreieck – Westpark
Blücherstr
Mehringdamm
Friedhöfe vor dem Halleschen Tor
Mittenwalder Str
Hornstr
Grossbeerenstr
Baruther Str
Zossener Str
Urbanstr
Yorckstr
Park am Gleisdreieck – Ostpark
Fürbringer Str
Gneisenaustr
Schleiermacher Str
Hagelberger Str
Nostitzstr
Solmsstr
Baerwaldstr
Bautzener Str
Kreuzbergstr
Bergmannstr
Marheineke platz
Katzbachstr
Arndtstr
Methfesselstr
Fidicinstr
Friedhöfe an der Bergmannstrasse
Friesenstr
Jüterboger Str
Schwiebusser Str
Kolonnenstr
Dudenstr
Platz der Luftbrücke
Columbiadamm
Loewenhardtdamm
General-Pape-Str
TEMPELHOF
Tempelhofer Damm
Manfred-von-Richthofen-Str
Wolffring
Nuture Mini Art Golf
Bundesring
Leonhardyweg
Kaiserkorso
Paradestr
Gontermannstr
Boelckestr
Tempelhofer Feld
Insomnia (1.4km)

WESTERN KREUZBERG

EASTERN KREUZBERG

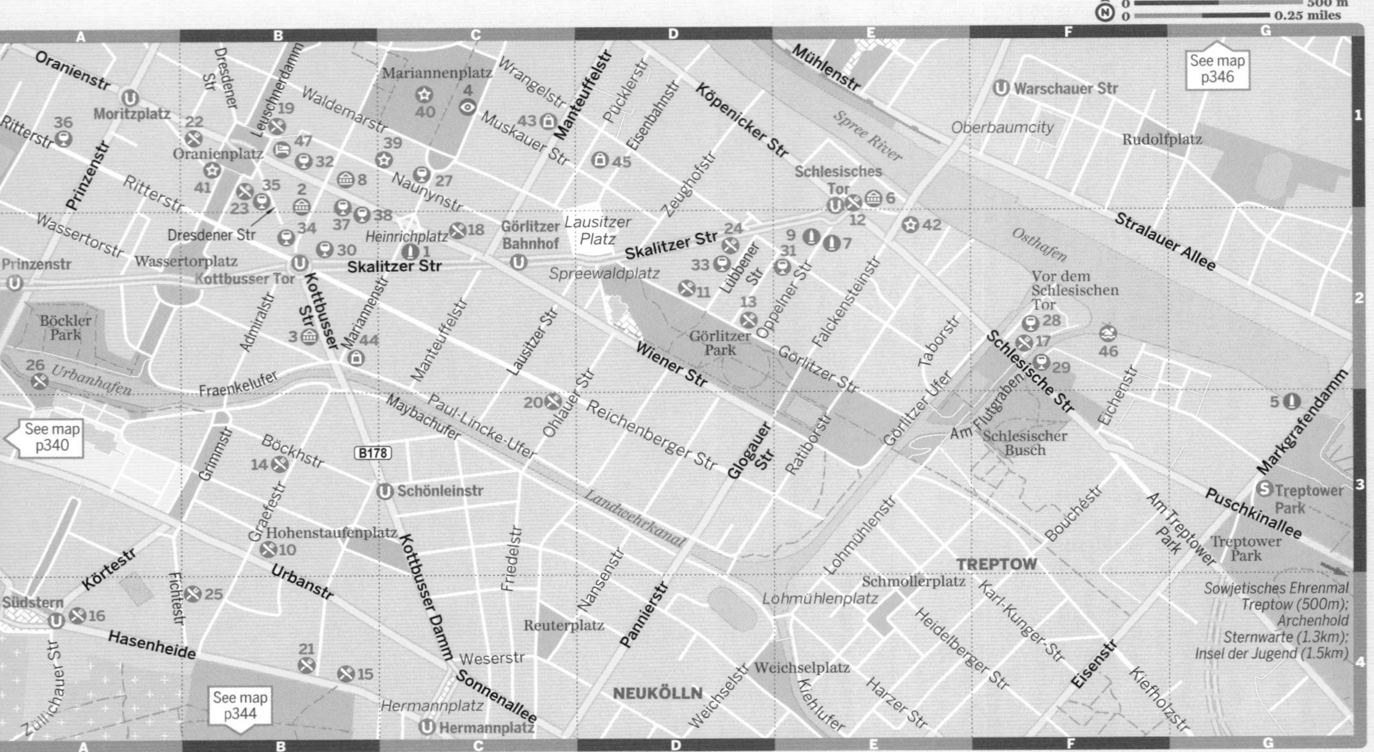

EASTERN KREUZBERG

Sights p184

1 Astronaut Mural ... C2
2 FHXB Friedrichshain-Kreuzberg Museum ... B1
3 Künstlerhaus Bethanien ... B2
4 Kunstquartier Bethanien ... C1
5 Molecule Man ... G3
Pink Man Mural ... (see 42)
6 Ramones Museum ... E1
7 Rounded Heads Mural ... E2
8 Werkbund Archiv- Museum der Dinge ... B1
9 Yellow Man Mural ... E2

Eating p186

10 Albatross Bakery & Cafe ... B3
11 Annelies ... D2
12 Burgermeister ... E1
13 Café Mugrabi ... D2
14 Cocolo Ramen X-Berg ... B3
15 Con Tho ... B4
16 Fes Turkish BBQ ... A4
17 Freischwimmer ... F2
18 Goldies ... C2
19 Henne ... B1
20 Mama Shabz ... C3
21 Masaniello ... B4
22 Max und Moritz ... B1
23 Ora ... B1
Orania.Restaurant ... (see 47)
Sironi ... (see 45)
24 Ta'Cabrón Taquería ... D2
25 Tulus Lotrek ... B4
26 Van Loon ... A2

Drinking & Nightlife p189

27 Apotheken Bar ... C1
28 Birgit & Bier ... F2
29 Club der Visionäre ... F2
30 Fahimi Bar ... B2
GMF ... (see 36)
31 Hopfenreich ... E2
32 Luzia ... B1
33 Madame Claude ... D2
34 Möbel Olfe ... B2
35 Otto Rink ... B1
36 Ritter Butzke ... A1
37 Roses ... B1
38 SO36 ... B2
Würgeengel ... (see 35)

Entertainment p191

39 Ballhaus Naunynstrasse ... C1
40 Freiluftkino Kreuzberg ... C1
41 fsk-Kino ... B1
42 Musik & Frieden ... E2

Shopping p192

43 Folkdays ... C1
44 Hard Wax ... B2
45 Markthalle Neun ... D1
VooStore ... (see 8)

Sports & Activities p193

46 Badeschiff ... F2

Sleeping p250

47 Orania.Berlin ... B1

NEUKÖLLN

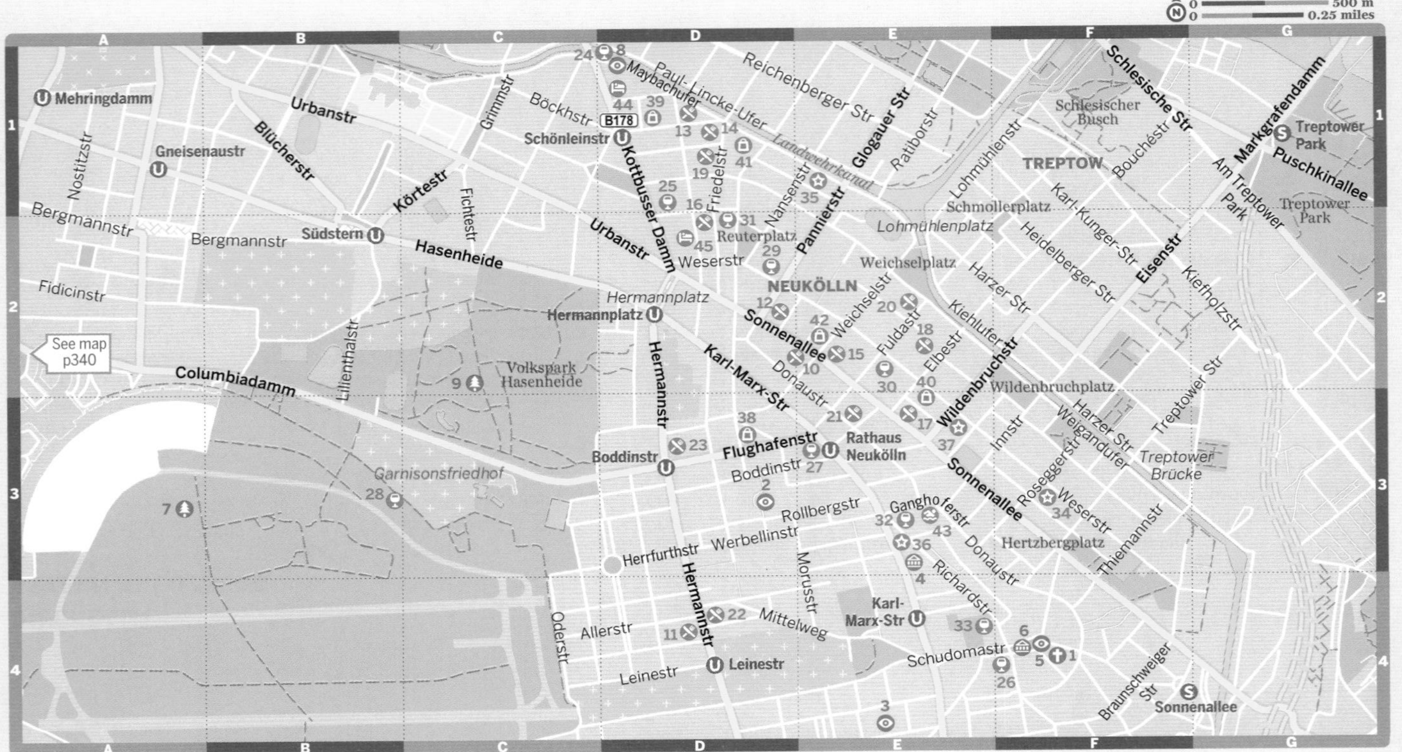
0 500 m
0 0.25 miles
Mehringdamm
Urbanstr
Blücherstr
Gneisenaustr
Nostitzstr
Bergmannstr
Fidicinstr
See map p340
Columbiadamm
Grimmstr
Körtestr
Fichtestr
Südstern
Hasenheide
Lilienthalstr
Volkspark Hasenheide
Garnisonsfriedhof
Böckhstr
B178
Schönleinstr
Maybachufer
Paul-Lincke-Ufer
Landwehrkanal
Reichenberger Str
Glogauer Str
Ratiborstr
Kottbusser Damm
Friedelstr
Nansenstr
Pannierstr
Reuterplatz
Weserstr
Hermannplatz
NEUKÖLLN
Weichselstr
Weichselplatz
Lohmühlenplatz
Sonnenallee
Karl-Marx-Str
Donaustr
Fuldastr
Elbestr
Kiehlufer
Wildenbruchstr
Wildenbruchplatz
Hermannstr
Flughafenstr
Rathaus Neukölln
Boddinstr
Rollbergstr
Werbellinstr
Herrfurthstr
Morusstr
Mittelweg
Allerstr
Leinestr
Oderstr
Ganghoferstr
Richardstr
Karl-Marx-Str
Schudomastr
Braunschweiger Str
Sonnenallee
Hertzbergplatz
Thiemannstr
Roseggerstr
Weigandufer
Harzer Str
Innstr
Treptower Brücke
Treptower Str
Kiefholzstr
Eisenstr
Heidelberger Str
Karl-Kunger-Str
Schmollerplatz
Lohmühlenstr
TREPTOW
Schlesischer Busch
Schlesische Str
Bouchéstr
Markgrafendamm
Treptower Park
Puschkinallee
Am Treptower Park

NEUKÖLLN

Sights **p196**

1 Bethlehemskirche F4
2 Kindl Centre for Contemporary Art D3
3 Körnerpark E4
4 Puppentheater-Museum Berlin E3
5 Rixdorf F4
6 Rixdorfer Schmiede F4
7 Tempelhofer Feld A3
8 Türkischer Markt D1
9 Volkspark Hasenheide C2

Eating **p197**

10 Azzam D2
11 Barra D4
12 Berlin Burger International D2
Brammibal's Donuts .... (see 44)
13 Cafe Jacques D1
14 Chicha D1
15 City Chicken E2
16 Coda D2
17 Damaskus Konditorei E3
18 eins44 .... E2
19 Fräulein Frost D1
20 Knödelwirtschaft E2
21 La Bolognina E3
22 La Stella Nera D4
23 Two Planets D3

Drinking & Nightlife **p199**

24 Ankerklause D1
25 Geist im Glass D1
26 Herr Lindemann F4
27 Klunkerkranich E3
28 Luftgarten B3
29 Thelonius D2
30 TiER E2
31 Truffle Pig D2
32 Velvet Bar E3
33 Zosse E4

Entertainment **p200**

34 Comedy Café Berlin F3
35 Il Kino E1
36 Neuköllner Oper E3
37 Wolf Kino E3

Shopping **p201**

38 Curious Fox D3
39 Kollateralschaden D1
40 Neuzwei E3
41 Nowkoelln Flowmarkt D1
42 Shio Store E2

Sports & Activities **p201**

43 Stadtbad Neukölln E3

Sleeping **p251**

44 Hotel Prens Berlin D1
45 Hüttenpalast D2

Key on p348

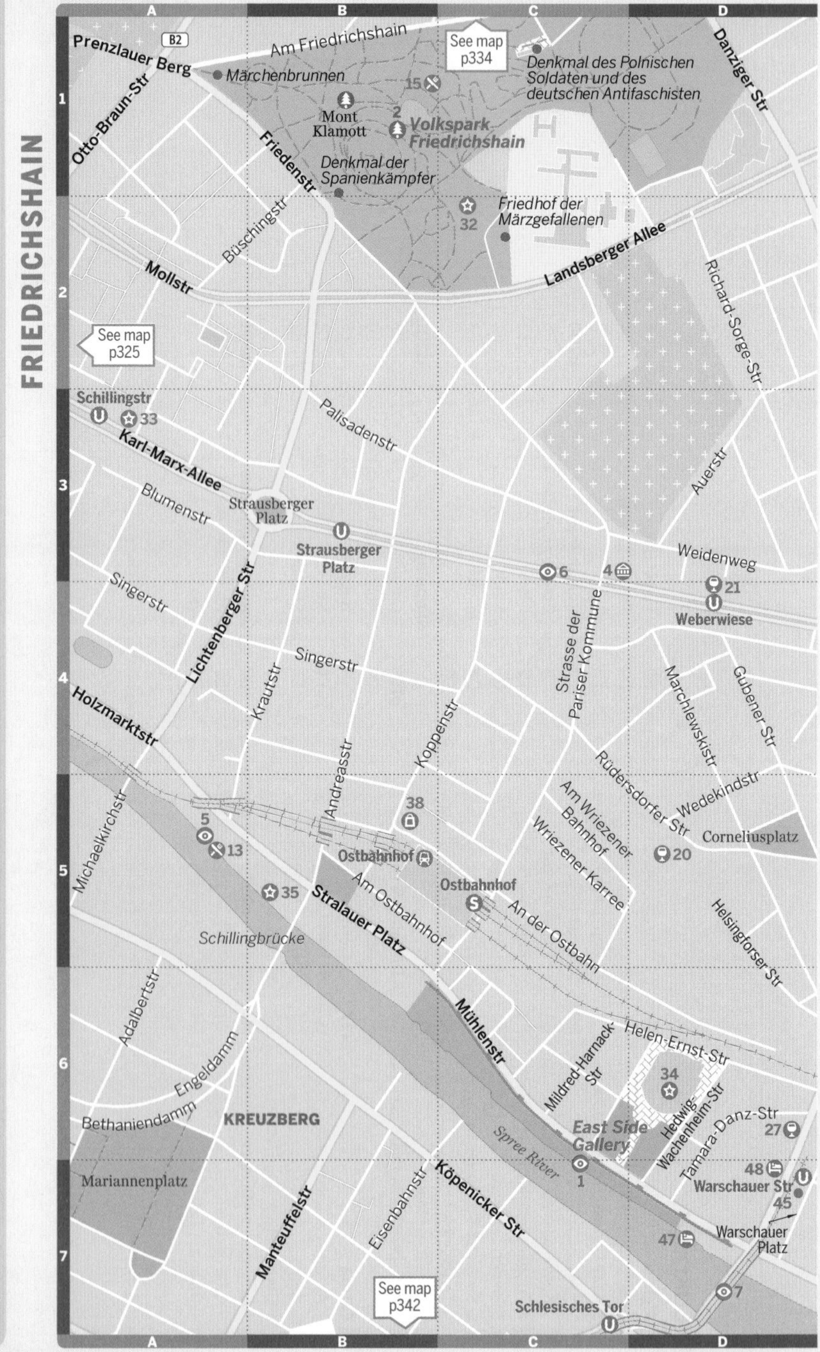

FRIEDRICHSHAIN

A B C D

1 2 3 4 5 6 7

B2
Prenzlauer Berg
Am Friedrichshain
See map p334
Denkmal des Polnischen Soldaten und des deutschen Antifaschisten
Danziger Str
Märchenbrunnen
15
Otto-Braun-Str
Mont Klamott
2
Volkspark Friedrichshain
Friedenstr
Denkmal der Spanienkämpfer
Friedhof der Märzgefallenen
32
Büschingstr
Landsberger Allee
Richard-Sorge-Str
Mollstr
See map p325
Schillingstr
33
Palisadenstr
Karl-Marx-Allee
Auerstr
Blumenstr
Strausberger Platz
Strausberger Platz
Weidenweg
6
4
21
Weberwiese
Singerstr
Lichtenberger Str
Strasse der Pariser Kommune
Singerstr
Holzmarktstr
Krautstr
Marchlewskistr
Gubener Str
Koppenstr
Andreasstr
Rüdersdorfer Str
Am Wriezener Bahnhof
Wedekindstr
Michaelkirchstr
38
5
13
Ostbahnhof
Wriezener Karree
Corneliusplatz
20
Am Ostbahnhof
Ostbahnhof
35
Stralauer Platz
An der Ostbahn
Helsingforser Str
Schillingbrücke
Mühlenstr
Adalbertstr
Helen-Ernst-Str
Mildred-Harnack-Str
34
Engeldamm
Bethaniendamm
KREUZBERG
Spree River
East Side Gallery
Hedwig-Wachenheim-Str
Tamara-Danz-Str
27
1
48
Warschauer Str
45
Mariannenplatz
Manteuffelstr
Eisenbahnstr
Köpenicker Str
47
Warschauer Platz
7
See map p342
Schlesisches Tor

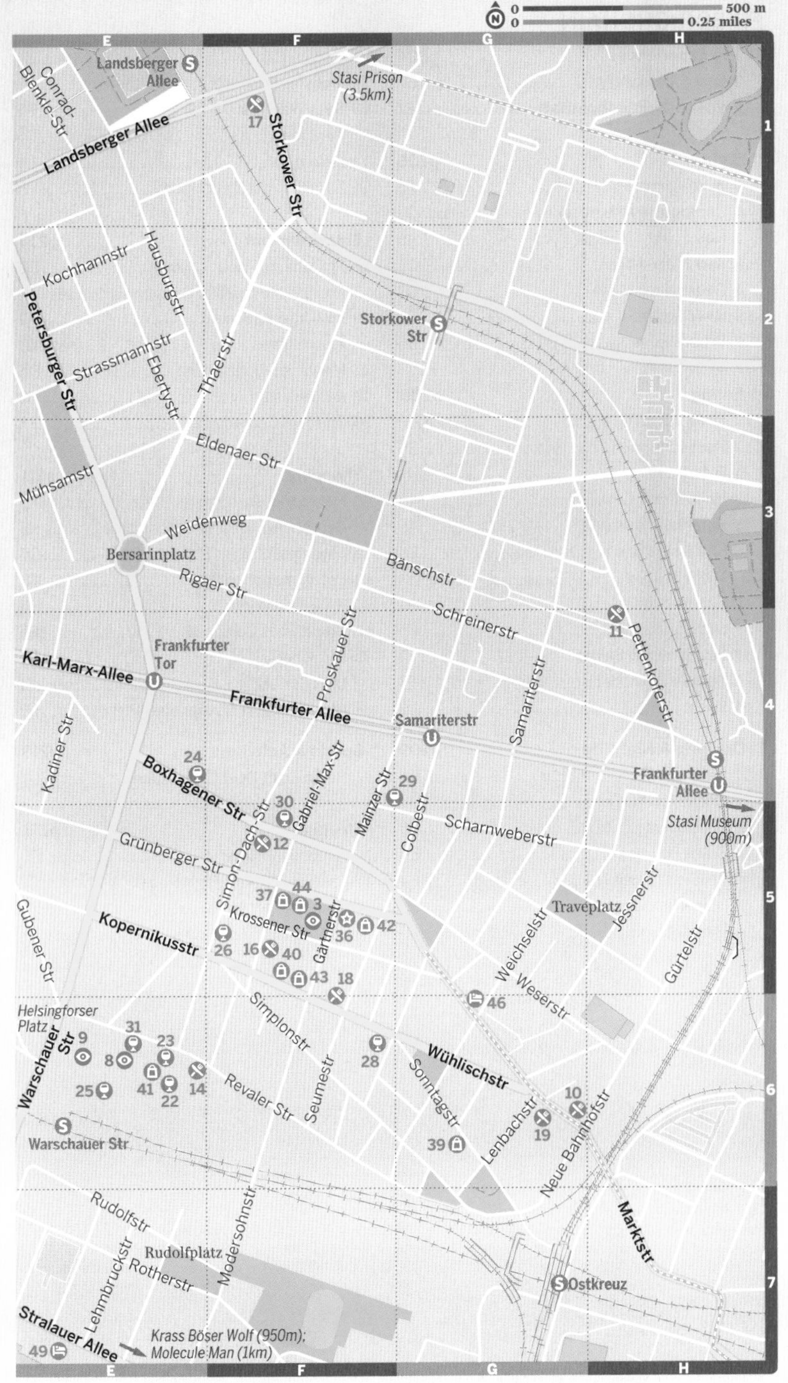
FRIEDRICHSHAIN
0 500 m
0 0.25 miles
E
F
G
H
1
2
3
4
5
6
7
Landsberger Allee
Landsberger Allee
Conrad-Blenkle-Str
Stasi Prison (3.5km)
Storkower Str
17
Kochhannstr
Hausburgstr
Petersburger Str
Strassmannstr
Ebertystr
Thaerstr
Storkower Str
Eldenaer Str
Mühsamstr
Weidenweg
Bersarinplatz
Rigaer Str
Bänschstr
Schreinerstr
Pettenkoferstr
11
Frankfurter Tor
Karl-Marx-Allee
Frankfurter Allee
Proskauer Str
Samariterstr
Samariterstr
Kadiner Str
Boxhagener Str
24
Gabriel-Max-Str
Mainzer Str
29
30
Simon-Dach-Str
Colbestr
Frankfurter Allee
Stasi Museum (900m)
Scharnweberstr
12
Grünberger Str
37
44
3
Krossener Str
Gärtnerstr
36
42
Traveplatz
Jessnerstr
Gubener Str
Kopernikusstr
26
16
40
43
18
Weichselstr
Weserstr
Gürtelstr
46
Simplonstr
Helsingforser Platz
Warschauer Str
9
8
31
23
41
22
14
25
28
Wühlischstr
Sonntagstr
Revaler Str
Seumestr
10
19
Lenbachstr
Neue Bahnhofstr
Warschauer Str
39
Marktstr
Rudolfstr
Modersohnstr
Rudolfplatz
Rotherstr
Lehmbruckstr
Ostkreuz
Stralauer Allee
49
Krass Böser Wolf (950m); Molecule Man (1km)

FRIEDRICHSHAIN

CITY WEST & CHARLOTTENBURG

Key on p349

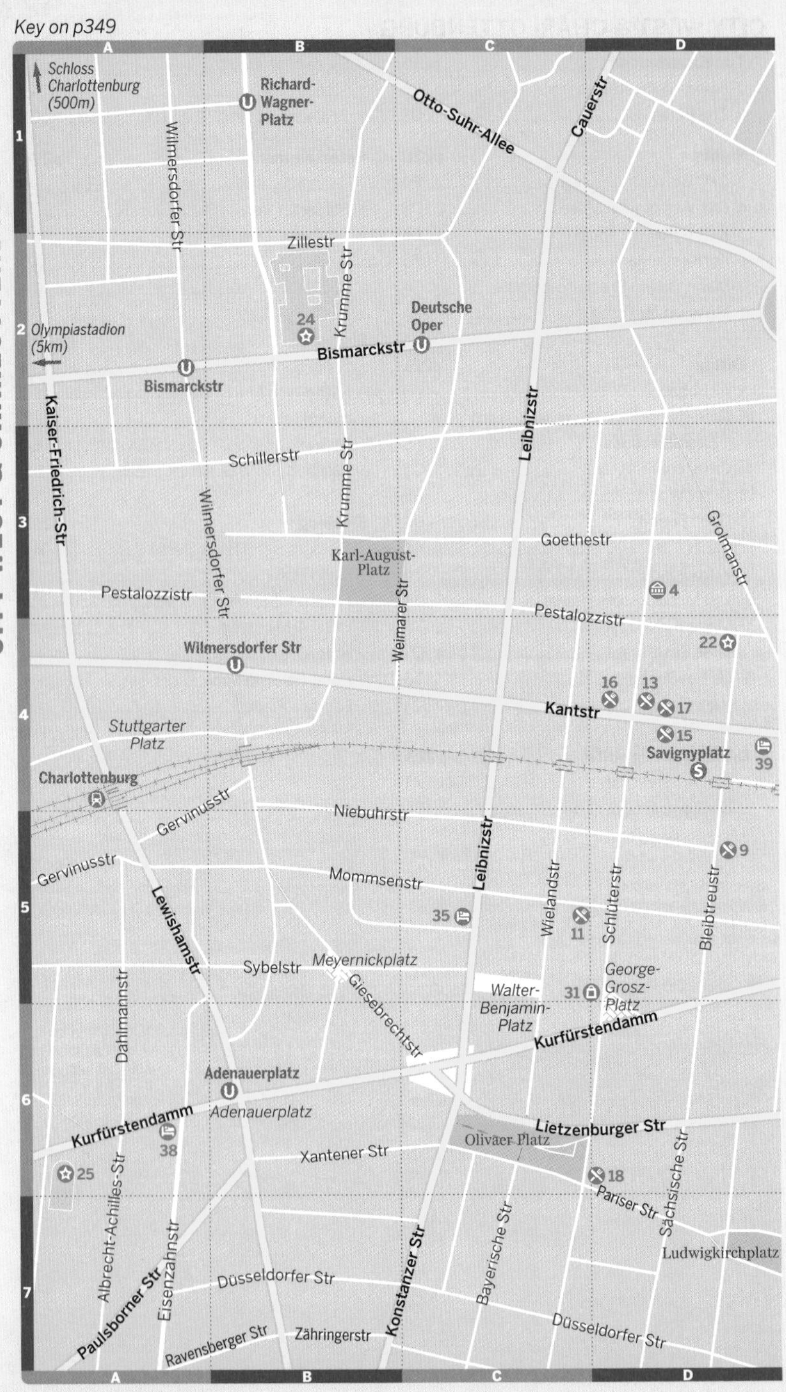

Schloss Charlottenburg (500m)
Richard-Wagner-Platz
Otto-Suhr-Allee
Cauerstr
Wilmersdorfer Str
Zillestr
Krumme Str
24
Deutsche Oper
Olympiastadion (5km)
Bismarckstr
Bismarckstr
Leibnizstr
Kaiser-Friedrich-Str
Schillerstr
Krumme Str
Grolmanstr
Goethestr
Karl-August-Platz
Wilmersdorfer Str
Pestalozzistr
Weimarer Str
4
Pestalozzistr
22
Wilmersdorfer Str
16
13
17
Kantstr
Stuttgarter Platz
15
Savignyplatz
39
Charlottenburg
Gervinusstr
Niebuhrstr
Gervinusstr
Leibnizstr
9
Mommsenstr
Lewishamstr
35
Wielandstr
11
Schlüterstr
Bleibtreustr
Sybelstr
Meyernickplatz
Giesebrechtstr
George-Grosz-Platz
Walter-Benjamin-Platz
31
Dahlmannstr
Kurfürstendamm
Adenauerplatz
Adenauerplatz
Lietzenburger Str
Kurfürstendamm
38
Olivaer Platz
Xantener Str
25
Albrecht-Achilles-Str
18
Pariser Str
Sächsische Str
Eisenzahnstr
Konstanzer Str
Bayerische Str
Ludwigkirchplatz
Paulsborner Str
Düsseldorfer Str
Düsseldorfer Str
Ravensberger Str
Zähringerstr
A
B
C
D
1
2
3
4
5
6
7

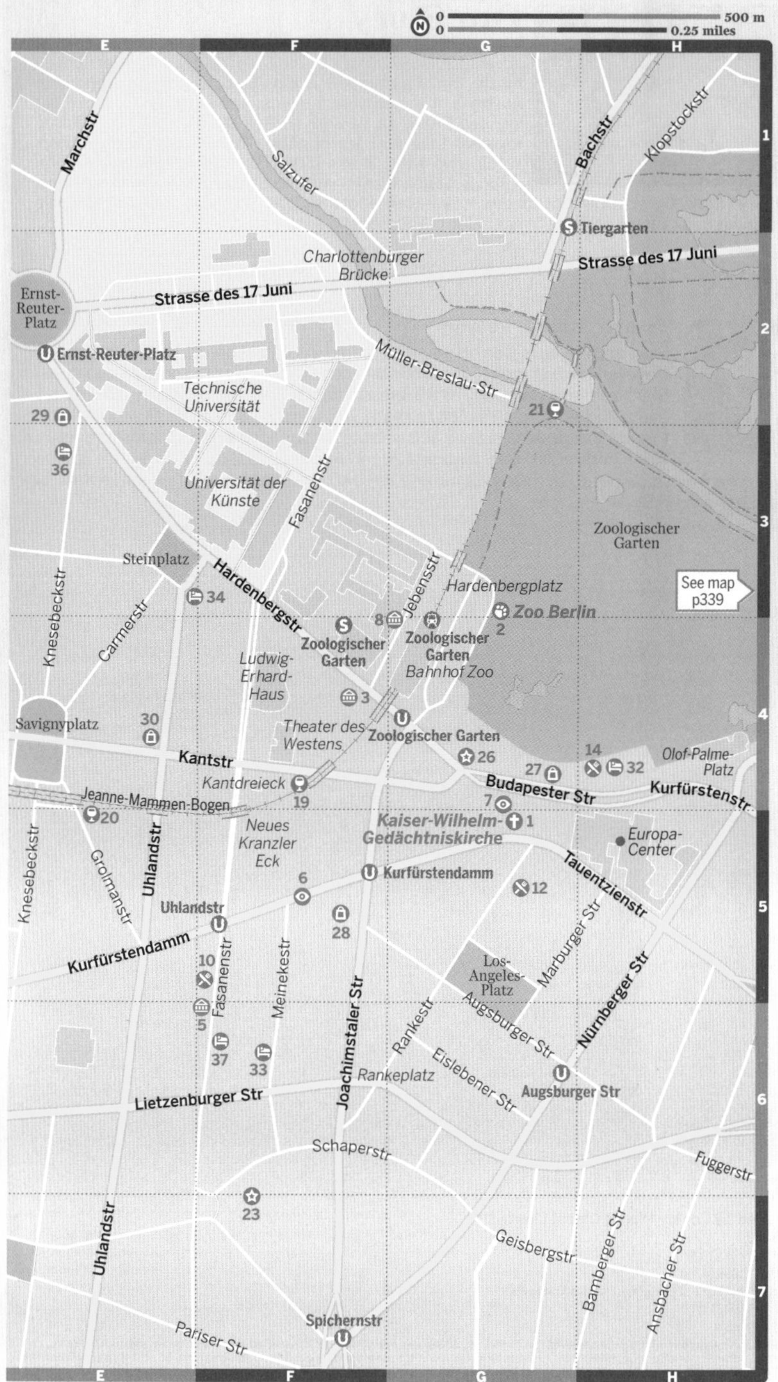

0 500 m
0 0.25 miles
E
F
G
H
1
2
3
4
5
6
7
CITY WEST & CHARLOTTENBURG
Marchstr
Salzufer
Bachstr
Klopstockstr
Tiergarten
Charlottenburger Brücke
Strasse des 17 Juni
Ernst-Reuter-Platz
Ernst-Reuter-Platz
Müller-Breslau-Str
Technische Universität
29
36
21
Universität der Künste
Fasanenstr
Zoologischer Garten
Steinplatz
Hardenbergstr
Jebensstr
Hardenbergplatz
See map p339
34
8
Zoo Berlin
2
Knesebeckstr
Carmerstr
Zoologischer Garten
Zoologischer Garten
Bahnhof Zoo
Ludwig-Erhard-Haus
3
Savignyplatz
30
Theater des Westens
Zoologischer Garten
Kantstr
26
14
Olof-Palme-Platz
27
32
Kantdreieck
19
Budapester Str
Kurfürstenstr
Jeanne-Mammen-Bogen
7
20
Neues Kranzler Eck
Kaiser-Wilhelm-Gedächtniskirche
1
Europa-Center
Knesebeckstr
Grolmanstr
Uhlandstr
6
Kurfürstendamm
Tauentzienstr
12
Uhlandstr
28
Kurfürstendamm
10
Fasanenstr
Meinekestr
Los-Angeles-Platz
Marburger Str
Nürnberger Str
5
Joachimstaler Str
Rankestr
Augsburger Str
37
33
Eislebener Str
Rankeplatz
Augsburger Str
Lietzenburger Str
Schaperstr
Fuggerstr
23
Uhlandstr
Geisbergstr
Bamberger Str
Ansbacher Str
Spichernstr
Pariser Str

Our Story

A beat-up old car, a few dollars in the pocket and a sense of adventure. In 1972 that's all Tony and Maureen Wheeler needed for the trip of a lifetime – across Europe and Asia overland to Australia. It took several months, and at the end – broke but inspired – they sat at their kitchen table writing and stapling together their first travel guide, *Across Asia on the Cheap*. Within a week they'd sold 1500 copies. Lonely Planet was born.

Today, Lonely Planet has offices in the US, Ireland and China, with a network of over 2000 contributors in every corner of the globe. We share Tony's belief that 'a great guidebook should do three things: inform, educate and amuse'.

Our Writer

Andrea Schulte-Peevers

Born and raised in Germany and educated in London and at UCLA, Andrea has travelled the distance to the moon and back in her visits to some 75 countries. She has earned her living as a professional travel writer for over two decades and authored or contributed to nearly 100 Lonely Planet titles as well as writing for newspapers, magazines and websites around the world. She also works as a travel consultant, translator and editor. Andrea's destination expertise is especially strong when it comes to Germany, Dubai and the UAE, Crete and the Caribbean Islands. She makes her home in Berlin.

Published by Lonely Planet Global Limited
CRN 554153
12th edition – Jan 2022
ISBN 978 1 78868 073 8

10 9 8 7 6 5 4 3 2
Printed in China